UNITED STATES HEGEMONY AND THE FOUNDATIONS OF INTERNATIONAL LAW

The foundations of international law have been shaped by successive hegemonic powers throughout history. This book examines whether the current predominance of the United States is leading to foundational change in the international legal system. A range of leading scholars in international law and international relations consider six foundational areas that could be undergoing change, including international community, sovereign equality, the law governing the use of force, and compliance. The authors demonstrate that the effects of US predominance on the foundations of international law are real, but also intensely complex. This complexity is due, in part, to a multitude of actors exercising influential roles. And it is also due to the continued vitality and remaining functionality of the international legal system itself. This system limits the influence of individual States, while stretching and bending in response to the changing geopolitics of our time.

MICHAEL BYERS is Associate Professor of Law at Duke University. His recent publications include *Custom, Power and the Power of Rules* (1999) and (as editor) *The Role of Law in International Politics* (2000).

GEORG NOLTE is Professor of Law at the University of Göttingen. His recent publications include *Eingreifen auf Einladung* (*Intervention upon Invitation*) (1999) and *Beleidigungsschutz in der Freiheitlichen Demokratie* (*Defamation Law in Democratic States*) (1992).

UNITED STATES HEGEMONY AND THE FOUNDATIONS OF INTERNATIONAL LAW

Edited by

MICHAEL BYERS

GEORG NOLTE

PUBLISHED BY THE PRESS SYNDICATE OF THE UNIVERSITY OF CAMBRIDGE
The Pitt Building, Trumpington Street, Cambridge CB2 1RP, United Kingdom

CAMBRIDGE UNIVERSITY PRESS
The Edinburgh Building, Cambridge, CB2 2RU, UK
40 West 20th Street, New York, NY 10011-4211, USA
477 Williamstown Road, Port Melbourne, VIC 3207, Australia
Ruiz de Alarcón 13, 28014 Madrid, Spain
Dock House, The Waterfront, Cape Town 8001, South Africa

http://www.cambridge.org

First published 2003

Printed in the United Kingdom at the University Press, Cambridge

Typeface Adobe Minion 10.5/13.5 pt   *System* LaTeX 2_ε [TB]

A catalogue record for this book is available from the British Library

ISBN 0 521 81949 0 hardback

CONTENTS

v

CONTRIBUTORS

Michael Byers is Associate Professor of Law at Duke University. He is the author of *Custom, Power and the Power of Rules* (Cambridge University Press, 1999), editor of *The Role of Law in International Politics* (Oxford University Press, 2000) and translator of Wilhelm Grewe, *The Epochs of International Law* (Walter de Gruyter, 2000). He is a regular contributor to the *London Review of Books*.

Michel Cosnard is Professor of International Law at the University of Maine (Le Mans, France). He is the author of *La soumission des états aux tribunaux internes: face à la théorie des immunités des états* (Pedone, 1996) and a contributor to Denis Alland (ed.), *Droit international public* (Presses universitaires de France, 2000).

Jost Delbrück is Professor Emeritus and former director of the Walther-Schücking-Institute of International Law, Kiel, Germany, as well as Professor of Law at Indiana University School of Law–Bloomington. He is coeditor of the *German Yearbook of International Law* and of the *Indiana Journal of Global Legal Studies*.

Pierre-Marie Dupuy is Professor of Public International Law at the University of Paris (Panthéon-Assas) and at the European University Institute in Florence. He is the author of more than sixty articles and a number of books, including *Droit international public* (6th edn.) (Précis Dalloz, 2002). He has served as Counsel and Advocate in thirteen cases before the International Court of Justice and, in 2000, delivered the general course on public international law at the Hague Academy of International Law.

Gregory Fox is Visiting Professor at Wayne State University Law School. He is the co-editor (with Brad Roth) of *Democratic Governance and International Law* (Cambridge University Press, 2000), as well as the author of numerous articles. He has held fellowships at the Schell Center for

International Human Rights at Yale Law School and the Max Planck Institute for Comparative Public Law and Public International Law. He has also been legal counsel to the State of Eritrea and counsel in several human rights cases in US courts.

Thomas M. Franck is Murry and Ida Becker Professor of Law Emeritus at New York University School of Law. His most recent work is *Recourse to Force: State Action Against Threats and Armed Attacks* (Cambridge University Press, 2002). Professor Franck is past president of the American Society of International Law and a former Editor-in-Chief of the *American Journal of International Law*. He has also acted as legal advisor or counsel to many governments, and currently serves as a judge ad hoc at the International Court of Justice.

Jochen Abr. Frowein is Director Emeritus of the Max Planck Institute for Comparative Public Law and Public International Law in Heidelberg, and Professor emeritus of Constitutional and Public International Law at the University of Heidelberg. He served as Vice-President of the German Research Foundation in 1977–1980, Vice-President of the European Commission on Human Rights in 1981–1993, and Vice-President of the Max Planck Society in 1999–2002.

Matthias Herdegen is Professor of Public Law and Director of the Institute for International Law at the University of Bonn. He is the author of the most recent editions of textbooks on international law, European law, and international economic law published by C. H. Beck, and coeditor (with George A. Bermann and Peter L. Lindseth) of *Transnational Regulatory Co-operation* (Oxford University Press, 2000).

Rainer Hofmann is Director of the Walther-Schücking-Institute for International Law at Kiel University and President of the Advisory Committee under the Council of Europe Framework Convention for the Protection of National Minorities. He has published extensively on German constitutional law and public international law, in particular on human rights, refugee law and minority rights. He is coeditor of the *German Yearbook of International Law*.

Andrew Hurrell is University Lecturer in International Relations and Fellow of Nuffield College, Oxford. Recent publications include (as co-editor with Ngaire Woods) *Inequality, Globalization and World Politics* (Oxford

University Press, 1999), (with Kai Alderson) *Hedley Bull on International Society* (Macmillan, 2000), and (as co-editor with Rosemary Foot and John Gaddis) *Order and Justice in International Relations* (Oxford University Press, 2003).

Pierre Klein is Professor of International Law and Director of the Centre for International Law at the Université libre de Bruxelles. He is the author of *La responsabilité des organisations internationales dans les ordres juridiques internes et en droit des gens* (Bruylant, 1998), and co-author of *Droit d'ingérence ou obligation de réaction?* (Bruylant, 1992, 2nd edn. 1996) and *Bowett's Law of International Institutions* (Sweet & Maxwell, 5th edn., 2001).

Marcelo Kohen is Professor of International Law at the Graduate Institute of International Studies in Geneva. Author of more than thirty substantial articles and contributions to collective works, his publications include *Possession contestée et souveraineté territoriale* (Presses universitaires de France, 1997), which was awarded the 1997 Paul Guggenheim Prize. His research focuses on the place of the State in international law, on territorial disputes, and on judicial dispute settlement.

Martti Koskenniemi is Professor of International Law at the University of Helsinki, Hauser Global Professor of Law at New York University, and a Member of the UN International Law Commission. His main publications are *From Apology to Utopia. The Structure of International Legal Argument* (Finnish Lawyers' Publishing Co., 1989) and *The Gentle Civilizer of Nations. The Rise and Fall of International Law 1870–1960* (Cambridge University Press, 2002).

Nico Krisch is a Visiting Senior Fellow at the Center for International Studies at New York University School of Law and a Postdoctoral Fellow of the Max Planck Society for the Advancement of Science. He is the author of *Selbstverteidigung und kollektive Sicherheit* (Springer, 2001) and of several articles on the use of force in international affairs.

Edward Kwakwa is Deputy Legal Counsel and Head of the Legal and Constitutional Affairs Section at the World Intellectual Property Organization (WIPO). He holds law degrees from the University of Ghana, Queen's University and Yale University. Before joining WIPO, he practiced with the law firm of O'Melveny and Myers in Washington, DC, and worked with the Commission on Global Governance, the Office of the UN High Commissioner for Refugees and the World Trade Organization.

Vaughan Lowe is Chichele Professor of Public International Law, and a Fellow of All Souls College, Oxford. He was formerly Reader in International Law and a Fellow of Corpus Christi College, Cambridge, and lecturer at the universities of Cardiff and Manchester. He practices as a barrister from Essex Court Chambers, London.

David Malone is President of the International Peace Academy. A career Canadian foreign service officer, he has directed the policy, international organizations and global issues bureaus of the Department of Foreign Affairs and International Trade in Ottawa. While Canadian Ambassador at the United Nations in 1992–1994 he chaired the work of the UN's Special Committee on Peacekeeping Operations. He serves as an Adjunct Professor at New York University School of Law.

Georg Nolte is Professor of Law at the University of Göttingen. He is the author of *Eingreifen auf Einladung* (Intervention upon Invitation) (Springer, 1999). He has published widely on issues of public international law and comparative constitutional law. He is a member for Germany of the Council of Europe's European Commission for Democracy through Law (the "Venice Commission").

Andreas Paulus is Wissenschaftlicher Assistent (Assistant Professor) at the Ludwig Maximilians University in Munich. He is the author of *Die internationale Gemeinschaft im Völkerrecht* (C.H. Beck, 2001) and assistant editor of *The Charter of the United Nations: A Commentary* (Oxford University Press, 2nd. edn., 2002), as well as co-editor of the book review section of the *European Journal of International Law*. He was Counsel for Germany in the *LaGrand* case (Germany v. United States).

Alain Pellet is Professor at the University of Paris X–Nanterre and a Member and former Chair of the UN International Law Commission. He is the author or editor of several books and many articles on public international law, including *Droit international public* (with P. Daillier, 7th edn., 2002) and *La Charte des Nations Unies* (with J.-P. Cot, 2nd. edn., 1991). He has been involved as Counsel in more than twenty cases before the International Court of Justice.

Steven R. Ratner is Albert Sidney Burleson Professor in Law at the University of Texas School of Law. He is the author or co-author of three books, including *Accountability for Human Rights Atrocities in International Law* (Oxford, 1997 and 2001), as well as numerous articles. He is a member of the Board of Editors of the *American Journal of International Law* and has been a Fulbright Senior Scholar.

Catherine Redgwell is Reader in Public International Law and Yamani Fellow at St. Peter's College, Oxford. She has published widely on treaty law, international environmental law, and energy law, including *Intergenerational Trusts and Environmental Protection* (Manchester University Press, 1999) and, with co-editors, *Energy Law in Europe: National, EU and International Law and Institutions* (Oxford University Press, 2001).

Volker Rittberger is Professor of Political Science and International Relations and Director of the Center for International Relations/Peace and Conflict Studies at the University of Tübingen, Germany. His latest publications include *Global Governance and the United Nations System* (editor and contributor) (UN University Press, 2001) and *German Foreign Policy Since Unification – Theories and Case Studies* (editor and contributor) (Manchester University Press, 2001).

Brad R. Roth is Associate Professor of Political Science and Law at Wayne State University. He is author of *Governmental Illegitimacy in International Law* (Oxford University Press, 1999), winner of the American Society of International Law's 1999 Certificate of Merit for "best work in a specialized area," and is co-editor (with Gregory Fox) of *Democratic Governance and International Law* (Cambridge University Press, 2000). He has written extensively on issues of state sovereignty and human rights.

Shirley Scott is Senior Lecturer in International Relations and Coordinator of Postgraduate Coursework Programs in the School of Politics and International Relations at the University of New South Wales. She has published on the international law–world politics nexus in several leading journals of international law, including the *European Journal of International Law*, the *International and Comparative Law Quarterly*, and the *Australian Yearbook of International Law*.

Bruno Simma is Professor of International and European Community Law at the University of Munich as well as a member of the Affiliate Overseas Faculty of the University of Michigan. He was a member of the UN Committee on Economic, Social and Cultural Rights in 1987–1996, and has been a member of the UN International Law Commission since 1997. He is co-author (with Alfred Verdross) of *Universelles Völkerrecht. Theorie* *und Praxis* (Duncker & Humblot, 1984), and editor of *The Charter of the United Nations. A Commentary* (Oxford University Press, 2nd. edn., 2002).

Achilles Skordas is Assistant Professor at the University of Athens, and a member of the Department of Studies of the Greek Parliament. His recent publications include "La Commission spéciale des Nations Unies (UNSCOM)" in *L'effectivité des organisations internationales: Mécanismes de suivi et de contrôle* (A. Sakkoulas/A. Pedone, 2000) and "Epilegomena to a Silence: Nuclear Weapons, Terrorism and the Moment of Concern," *Journal of Conflict and Security Law* (2001).

Peter-Tobias Stoll is Professor at and managing director of the Institute of International Law at the University of Göttingen. He heads the Institute's Department for International Economic Law. He has just completed a book on the World Trade Organization, in German, and is a member of the Research Council of the German United Nations Association.

Daniel Thürer is Professor of Law at the University of Zürich and a member of the International Committee of the Red Cross. He has served as a judge on the Constitutional Court of Liechtenstein and as a member of the Independent Commission of Experts on "Switzerland and the Second World War." He is the author of numerous books and articles on international law, European law, and comparative constitutional law.

Christian Tomuschat is Professor of International and Constitutional Law at Humboldt University, Berlin. He is a former member of both the UN Human Rights Committee under the International Covenant on Civil and Political Rights and the UN International Law Commission. In 1999, he delivered the general course on public international law at the Hague Academy of International Law.

Stephen J. Toope is President and CEO of the Pierre Elliott Trudeau Foundation. He is a Professor (on leave) at the Faculty of Law, McGill University. The author of *Mixed International Arbitration* (Cambridge University Press, 1990), he has written numerous articles for leading journals including the *American Journal of International Law*, the *Columbia Journal of Transnational Law*, and the *Harvard International Law Journal*. His work with Professor Jutta Brunnée was awarded the Francis Deák Prize of the American Society of International Law.

Rüdiger Wolfrum is Director of the Max Planck Institute for Comparative Public Law and Public International Law and Professor of Law at the University of Heidelberg. He is Vice-President of the Max-Planck-Society and, in 1999, was reelected as Judge at the International Tribunal for the Law of the Sea. He is the author and editor of numerous publications on various issues of public international law.

PREFACE

This volume represents the culmination of a two-year project that began with an informal debate in Göttingen in May 2000. The question then, as now, was whether the current predominance of the United States is leading to foundational change in the international legal system – and if so, how.

Our interest in the issue of foundational change and the impact of geopolitics on international law is derived in part from the work of Wilhelm G. Grewe, who, in his *Epochen der Völkerrechtsgeschichte*, argued that successive dominant powers have always contributed decisively to changing the international legal system. And yet Grewe, in an epilogue to the English version of his book, in 1998 suggested that the post-Cold War epoch might be different, in that the development of an "international community" could promote a reshaping of the foundations of the international legal system in a different direction, so as to favor global interests rather than simply the national interests of the United States – the dominant power of our time.

Ten years after the fall of the Berlin Wall, it seemed to us time for a preliminary evaluation of the situation. We identified six areas or concepts for examination: international community, sovereign equality, the law governing the use of force, customary international law, the law of treaties, and compliance. Although hardly exhaustive of the areas and concepts worthy of examination, in our view these six categories provided a broad overview of important foundational aspects that might possibly be undergoing change.

We then identified twelve relatively young scholars from a range of cultural, linguistic, and academic backgrounds to write chapters on each of the six areas or concepts (i.e. two authors to each area/concept). Two of the twelve chapter authors come from developing countries; three are North American; six are European. Two of the twelve are political scientists. It is our hope that this book, by bringing these perspectives and ideas together, will add energy and diversity to debates about the role and character of contemporary international law.

To add yet further diversity of perspective, background, and thinking, we invited eighteen more senior scholars to provide short commentaries on the principal chapters. These commentaries are not intended to be stand-alone pieces; they should be read in conjunction with the principal chapters towards which they are directed. Nor are they intended to plumb the depths of the additional issues they raise. The goal, instead, is simply to expose a healthy complexity of viewpoints and insights, leaving ample room for further analysis and debate.

The project has been highly collaborative in character. Each of the principal chapters was discussed and reworked three times. Early versions were subject to a brainstorming workshop at Duke University in February 2001. We are grateful to a small group of colleagues, including Andrew Hurrell, Robert Keohane, Madeline Morris, and Volker Rittberger, who served as facilitators at that workshop. Their ideas have subsequently shaped not only the individual chapters, but also the project as a whole. We are also grateful to Duke University for funding the workshop, and to Patti Meyer for her skilled assistance with logistics and organization.

After that initial workshop, each of the principal authors reworked their chapter before presenting it again, this time at a conference in Göttingen in October 2001. At the conference, each pair of chapters received three commentaries – early versions of the contributions published in this book – as well as considerable input from the floor. We are grateful to all those who participated, as well as to the Volkswagen Foundation for its generous financial support, the Max Planck Institute for History for the use of its facilities, the support of the International Peace Academy as well as of the University of Göttingen, and the staff of the Institute of International Law at the University of Göttingen, in particular Christiane Becker, for their excellent organization.

Finally, all of the principal chapters and commentaries were reworked one additional time, taking into account all of the various comments and criticisms received. We are thankful for the professionalism and good cheer of the contributors, and the close cooperation that ensued amongst them, as they did their bit to make this a truly collective, collaborative work. We are also thankful for the diligent efforts of, again, Christiane Becker, who co-ordinated the submissions, collated the text, and accomplished a myriad of other essential tasks, of Seyda Dilek Emek, who checked the footnotes, and of Hadley Ross, who proof-read the final text.

It will already be apparent that this project predates the pivotal date of 11 September 2001, but was not completed until summer 2002 – well after the terrorist atrocities in New York and Washington. In late September 2001, we seriously considered rescheduling the Göttingen conference, given that the overall topic, and particularly the issue of the use of force, was at that point not only prominent but also emotionally charged. In the end, and after consulting with all of the contributors, we decided to go ahead. As a result a lively and, at times, difficult debate animated the conference. Ultimately we were glad that the conference went ahead as planned, and are grateful to all those who participated.

We have learned much during the course of this project, not least that a shared desire for understanding transcends cultures, backgrounds, and disciplines. The impact of the United States on the international legal system of the twenty-first century is an issue that academic international lawyers and scholars of international relations cannot and should not avoid. And yet, as with the proverbial nettle, grasping hold of this issue is hardly a comfortable task. Fortunately for us, the task has been made less uncomfortable – and more enlightening – as a result of the support and collaboration of all of the people involved in this project, from both sides of the Atlantic and beyond.

M. B.

G. N.

Introduction

The complexities of foundational change

MICHAEL BYERS

Wilhelm Grewe, in *Epochen der Völkerrechtsgeschichte*, argued that successive hegemons have shaped the foundations of the international legal system.[1] In the sixteenth century, Spain redefined basic concepts of justice and universality so as to justify the conquest of indigenous Americans. In the eighteenth century, France developed the modern concept of borders, and the balance of power, to suit its principally continental strengths. In the nineteenth century, Britain forged new rules on piracy, neutrality, and colonialism – again, to suit its particular interests as the predominant power of the time.

As Shirley Scott points out in her contribution to this volume, Grewe did not claim that the changes wrought to the international legal system as a consequence of hegemony were necessarily planned or directed: "It was not that the dominant power controlled every development within the system during that epoch but that the dominant power was the one against whose ideas regarding the system of international law all others debated."[2] Nor did the changes occur abruptly: they were instead the result of a gradual process, as the international legal system adapted itself to the political realities of a new age.

Robert Keohane, in *After Hegemony*, demonstrated that the influence of dominant powers is considerably more complex than traditional international relations realists assumed, and that international regimes sometimes develop a life of their own that carries them forward after the influence of the hegemon wanes.[3] Keohane and others built on this insight to develop

---

[1] Wilhelm Grewe, *Epochen der Völkerrechtsgeschichte* (Baden-Baden: Nomos, 1984). For a similar view from the discipline of international relations, with regard to the influence of "dominant powers" on the international system as a whole, see Martin Wight, *Power Politics*, ed. Hedley Bull and Carsten Holbraad (London: Royal Institute of International Affairs, 1978), pp. 30–40.

[2] Scott, below, p. 451.

[3] Robert Keohane, *After Hegemony* (Princeton: Princeton University Press, 1984).

regime theory and then institutionalism – sophisticated explanations as to the interaction of power and normative structures in a world of sovereign yet interdependent States.[4] Other international relations scholars, working from much the same intellectual base, later advanced constructivist explanations for the development and perseverance of regimes, institutions, and, more recently, international law.[5] According to these explanations, the development and evolution of shared understandings through communicative processes among technocratic and political elites can give rise, not only to normative structures, but also to associated, deeply felt conceptions of legitimacy, which then contribute significantly to the resilience of the norms.

Grewe's argument, honed during a lifetime of both scholarship and practical experience (as legal adviser to the West German Foreign Ministry and ambassador to the United States and NATO at the height of the Cold War), thus anticipated important aspects of subsequent theories. Dominant powers are indeed able to reshape the foundations of the international legal system. However, this process takes time, the essence of foundations being that they are relatively resistant to change. As a result, foundational change is seldom the consequence of deliberate planning, but is instead the outcome of repeated claims and actions that challenge existing legal limits, and thus prompt shifting patterns of response and debate on the part of other States.

Complicating the picture yet further is the epilogue that Grewe wrote in 1998 to the English version of his book.[6] Here he suggested that the United States might, in the post–Cold War epoch, not be as successful as previous hegemons in reshaping the foundations of international law. The development of an "international community" extending beyond the traditional nation-State meant that community interests could now play a role in the evolution of international law. Grewe concluded that it was too soon to tell which influence would prevail, the influence of the single superpower in

---

[4] See e.g. Robert Keohane, *International Institutions and State Power* (Boulder: Westview, 1989); Oran Young, *International Cooperation* (Ithaca: Cornell University Press, 1989); Volker Rittberger (ed.), *Regime Theory and International Relations* (Oxford: Clarendon Press, 1993).

[5] See e.g. John Ruggie, *Constructing the World Polity* (New York: Routledge, 1998); Alexander Wendt, *Social Theory of International Politics* (Cambridge: Cambridge University Press, 1999); Jutta Brunnée and Stephen Toope, "International Law and Constructivism: Elements of an Interactional Theory of International Law" (2000) 39 *Columbia Journal of Transnational Law* 19.

[6] Wilhelm Grewe, *The Epochs of International Law*, trans. and rev. Michael Byers (Berlin: de Gruyter, 2000).

the development of a legal system suited to its particular interests, or the influence of the international community in the development of a system more favorable to broader needs and concerns.

This volume addresses the issue whether, and how, the current predominance of the United States is leading to foundational change in the international legal system. It contains chapters written by twelve scholars of international law and international relations, who between them address six key areas or concepts that could be undergoing change: international community, sovereign equality, the law governing the use of force, the process through which customary international law is made, the law of treaties, and compliance. An analysis of the current state of each of these areas or concepts, as seen from a long-term perspective, should provide some insight into the possible effects of US predominance on the foundations of international law.

The concept of international community is an obvious place to start. Has the development of this concept restrained the influence of the United States on the international legal system, as Grewe suggested it might? Or has it perhaps facilitated US influence, acting as a tool for the advancement of US interests and values? Most provocatively, is the United States in fact a part of the international community, or does it instead stand somewhat apart?

In the first chapter, Edward Kwakwa argues that the United States, when behaving in a unilateralist or isolationist manner, "acts according to its perceived interests, as does any other State," and that its lack of support for community interests is thus the norm rather than the exception.[7] The difference, Kwakwa explains, is that "the sheer might and superpower status of the United States are such that its actions are bound to have a greater impact on the international community and on the foundations of international law."[8]

The United States does often cooperate with States sharing the same interests and values. Kwakwa draws on some fascinating examples from the World Intellectual Property Organization to demonstrate that United States law-making efforts usually require "the active cooperation of key segments of the rest of the international community; the incredible power of the United States will not be enough to enable it to 'go it alone'..."[9] But does the fact that the United States relies on other States support the

---

[7] Kwakwa, below, p. 26.   [8] Kwakwa, below, p. 26.   [9] Kwakwa, below, p. 26.

concept of international community? Or are these instances of cooperation instead only ad hoc and temporary coalitions of convenience on the part of a purely self-interested superpower?

The true power of the United States, and the limits of the concept of international community, are most readily apparent when it decides *not* to participate in lawmaking. As Kwakwa explains, "the global reach of the United States often makes it an indispensable party in multilateral treaty making."[10] Thus, "while US refusal to join a legal regime does not equate with US rejection of international law, it is arguable that in those instances in which the United States is an indispensable party for the formulation of international law, any unilateralist stance by the United States could be tantamount to the single superpower impeding or opposing the development of that law."[11] In issue areas such as global warming, arms control and international crime, disinterest or active opposition on the part of the United States causes major problems for efforts at multilateral cooperation. Indeed, it is arguable that, under the administration of President George W. Bush, the United States increasingly sees itself as an absolute sovereign whose favored position could be compromised by the concept of international community – and thus by many aspects of international law.

Kwakwa suggests that the "special position of the United States" implies "a distinctive and, by definition, a greater responsibility in the international community... a responsibility arising from the undisputed facts of American dominance in almost all aspects of human endeavour."[12] But would such a position be consistent with the concept of an international community that included the United States? One of the arguments advanced by the United States in opposition to the Rome Statute of the International Criminal Court is that the United States has special responsibilities with regard to international security.[13] In this particular instance, at least, the "special position" of the United States is used to justify its opposition to a quintessentially community-oriented lawmaking exercise: the creation of mechanisms for the prosecution of individuals for crimes under international law.

Perhaps the problem with the Rome Statute is not the fact that it promotes community interests, but rather that it does so through a new supranational institution. As Andreas Paulus explains, the debate about international

---

[10] Kwakwa, below, p. 51.   [11] Kwakwa, below, p. 56.   [12] Kwakwa, below, p. 36.
[13] See, e.g., David J. Scheffer, "The United States and the International Criminal Court" (1999) 93 *American Journal of International Law* 12 at 18.

community has revolved around the tension between the apparent need for international institutions, on the one hand, and the potential problems arising from new forms of governance or government on the other. Faced with this tension, "US perspectives have exerted a decisive influence on the concept of international community, gearing it away from governmental analogies towards the propagation of liberal values in an inter-State setting."[14]

Paulus concludes that "it is unlikely that the international community will be able to develop without regard to these basic US views on what the international community is about and, especially, on what it is not about: the building of truly global governance, let alone government."[15] But if this conclusion is accurate, how does one explain the adoption and coming into force of the Rome Statute, the adoption and coming into force of the Ottawa Landmines Convention, or current lawmaking efforts directed at curbing climate change? The United States initially sought to negotiate exceptions for itself in all three regimes – along the lines of the special treatment accorded the five permanent members of the Security Council in the UN Charter – but these efforts were rebuffed by other States. The influence of the United States on the concept of international community clearly does matter, but perhaps not as much as it may at first seem.

If the concept of international community is changing, what about our understanding of the relationship among the principal actors within that community? Is the concept of sovereign equality perhaps changing as well?

Michel Cosnard certainly does not think that it is. As he explains, the propensity of powerful States to stand aloof from new rules and institutions does not challenge the concept of sovereign equality:

> when a state is not bound by an international obligation, it chooses not to be *above* international law, but *beside* international law. This situation has always been possible because no rule is totally universal, precisely because of the principle of sovereign equality; it has always been the privilege of powerful states to invoke this principle. Since the main regulating principle of sovereign equality is still operative, international law as a system is not as affected as some authors suggest. It is another thing to think that the United States could be above the law, which would mean that when it is legally bound, it could freely choose not to observe its international obligations. This proposition is not legally sustainable, because it purely and simply denies the existence of international law.[16]

---

[14] Paulus, below, p. 89.   [15] Paulus, below, p. 89.   [16] Cosnard, below, pp. 125–6.

Nor, in Cosnard's view, does the existence of unequal rules or other forms of special treatment affect the concept of sovereign equality:

> the mere fact that unequal rules exist is not a symptom in itself of a retreat from the principle of sovereign equality, and certainly not one that results from the appearance of the United States as a single superpower. It would be so only if the United States, and the United States alone, now enjoyed systematic exception or exemption from the law – and not for reasons of diplomatic impossibility or convenience – so that we could consider the emergence of a new principle of inequality in its favor. We could even say that, because there always have been unequal rules in international law, US predominance has no real effect on the principle of sovereign equality.[17]

Cosnard's argument is highly positivist, focusing on consent as an essential aspect of legal obligation and regarding inequalities based on consent as supportive rather than undermining of sovereign equality. But unlike most positivists, he carries the argument further, suggesting that one should ask why consent is so frequently forthcoming. As he explains, when considering possible changes to the concept of sovereign equality, "it is important to focus on the values that are behind the predominance of the United States."[18] It is here that Cosnard's position transcends positivism:

> The limitations on sovereignty are not due to the predominance of the United States, but are rather the consequence of the victory of the values of the Western world. The reasons for the absence of resistance to the United States' will at the political level may be found in an absence of real determination to oppose the values that this will represents. Certainly, the lack of alternative, or of counterweight, might lead to an erosion of exclusivity. But at the present stage, as long as we can find motives for the abstention of other States, we might conclude that it is not a balance of power as such which causes the phenomenon.[19]

The existence of alternative explanations, together with the fact that US influence has not yet led the international system to shift from an oligarchic to monarchical model, reinforce, for Cosnard, his view that the foundations of the international legal system remain largely unchanged. "The difference from the bipolar world is," he explains, "that the opposition is not as Manichean as it could be during the Cold War."[20]

---

[17] Cosnard, below, pp. 121–2.   [18] Cosnard, below, p. 131.
[19] Cosnard, below, pp. 131–2.   [20] Cosnard, below, p. 133.

Importantly, Cosnard concedes that a single superpower could change the foundations of the international legal system, if it deliberately set out to do so. Positivism does not provide an insurmountable bulwark against the truly determined hegemon:

> The unchanged nature of the international legal system is not only due to its ability to contain a superpower. Like any legal system, it could not resist a *coup de force* by a superpower less benevolent than the United States. The United States has never planned to govern the world, with all the duties such a program bears. There is certainly a particularity in the fact that we are now in an era of the *United States'* predominance, and we can be sure that the effects on the international legal system would not be the same were another State predominant. The United States is aware of its power and feels that it is sometimes necessary to show it to the rest of the world; at other times it just wants not to be bothered and isolates itself as only a continent-country can do. This leads to a somehow erratic international policy, with only a few obsessional enemies, too unconstructed to provoke fundamental changes.[21]

This last point again raises the question whether the United States has, in the last two years, become more deliberate with regard to the reshaping of international law. If the United States is now embarked on a conscious effort to alter the foundations of the international legal system, will the concept of sovereign equality eventually change?

Nico Krisch argues that the concept of sovereign equality has, in fact, already changed as a result of US predominance. However, this change has occurred, not only because the United States has sought to modify traditional international law, but because it has moved away from that law and towards an increased use of its own domestic law to govern relations at the international level. Krisch provocatively suggests that the United States is developing into an early form of international government.

Krisch begins by noting that "the concept of sovereign equality has always been a source of irritation for powerful States, and so it is today for the United States as the sole remaining superpower."[22] He explains that the effects of sovereign equality are most significant at the foundational level of lawmaking, since the concept "operates as a regulative ideal for the further development of international law."[23] Sovereign equality makes it "very difficult to deviate from the parties' equality in rights and obligations" when

---

[21] Cosnard, below, p. 134.   [22] Krisch, below, p. 136.   [23] Krisch, below, p. 136.

creating new legal instruments, and thus limits the ability of powerful States to influence the direction of change.[24]

In response to these limitations:

> the United States has chosen to retreat from international law: it has made extensive use of reservations and frequently refused to sign or ratify important new treaties. Instead, it has increasingly relied on institutions in which it enjoys superior status or which do not face the formal restrictions of international law, and it has turned to unilateral means, and notably to its domestic law, as a tool of foreign policy.[25]

In Krisch's view, the "hierarchical superiority" of the United States that has resulted from this shift in focus to alternative instruments and domestic law "is either inconsistent with sovereign equality, or – if one wants to defend hierarchy – sovereign equality has to be abandoned as a principle of international law."[26]

Interestingly enough, Cosnard's and Krisch's seemingly divergent positions are not incompatible with each other. Within the traditional confines of international law, the principle of consent and the concept of sovereign equality could still operate in the usual way. Krisch's point is that, rather than seeking to change that part of the international legal system, the United States has shifted its lawmaking efforts elsewhere. Whether this shift is simply an unconscious response to the priorities of an internally focused, commercially oriented domestic system, or instead reflects a strategic effort to avoid opposition, remains unclear. What is clear is that any analysis of the effects of US predominance on the foundations of the international legal system has to examine areas that, in the past, might not have been regarded as falling within international law. Krisch makes an important contribution here, identifying a new area of complexity and raising yet more difficult questions.

The use of force in international relations has fallen squarely within the domain of international law since the adoption of the UN Charter in 1945. At the same time, the use of force remains a highly politicised area where, in terms of the capacity actually to use force, the United States maintains a substantial lead. It might therefore be assumed that the law governing the use of force is particularly susceptible to change as a result of US predominance.

---

[24] Krisch, below, p. 136.   [25] Krisch, below, p. 136.   [26] Krisch, below, p. 174.

According to Marcelo Kohen, such an assumption would be misplaced:

> There is no doubt as to the American military position: the United States is the most powerful State in the world. Its supremacy is overwhelming. But military power is one thing, its legal use is another. Rousseau stated more than two centuries ago: "The strongest is never strong enough to be always the master, unless he transforms strength into right, and obedience into duty." It remains to be demonstrated that American supremacy has already been transformed into law.[27]

Taking the example of the US response to the events of 11 September 2001, Kohen points out that

> With the nearly unanimous position taken by States after the terrorist at-tacks... the United States had a unique opportunity to revert to the rule of law at the international level. The conditions were largely favorable for the adoption of a bundle of collective measures, including some forcible action undertaken at least with Security Council approval. The US government made considerable progress toward multilateralism in different fields of international cooperation against terrorism, with only one, but none the less remarkable, exception: the use of force. It preferred not to alter its doc-trine of self-defense, in order to maintain its freedom to use force unilaterally whenever it considers it necessary to do so.[28]

Since the 1980s, the United States has repeatedly claimed that the right of self-defense extends to military action against States that harbor or other-wise support terrorists. The terrorist attacks on New York and Washington, and the widespread sympathy for the United States that followed, may have provided an opportunity to transform this claim into a widely accepted modification of customary international law.[29] In Kohen's view, however, recent State practice simply does not provide the widespread, nearly un-equivocal support necessary for a change to a well-established customary rule. And the lack of support for the US legal claim is reinforced, Kohen suggests, by the serious practical ramifications that such a change would have, for instance, by opening the way for "unforeseeable uses of force in a great number of actual or potential situations in future."[30] The claim

---

[27] Kohen, below, p. 229.   [28] Kohen, below, p. 229.
[29] See Michael Byers, "Terrorism, the Use of Force and International Law after 11 September" (2002) 51 *International and Comparative Law Quarterly* 401.
[30] Kohen, below, p. 230.

"amounts to the negation of Article 2(4) of the Charter and the collective security system," with all of the negative consequences that would entail.[31]

Brad Roth also addresses the law governing the use of force, but from a different angle. His focus is "the role of jurists, through their characterizations and assessments of US-led practice and their advocacy of doctrinal stability or change, in bolstering or undermining the capacity of international law to serve as a normative basis for constraining United States unilateralism in a unipolar world."[32] Scholarly discourse is an important element within the international legal system, and certain doctrinal approaches are more supportive of United States hegemony than others. For this reason, Roth considers it important that the various approaches are subject to close scrutiny, and that choices between them are carefully made.

Roth canvasses the different arguments advanced by academic lawyers to justify the 1999 NATO intervention in the former Yugoslavia in order to demonstrate, and then dissect, two approaches to international law that are particularly influential in the United States, namely "policy-oriented jurisprudence" and "moralistic positivism." He then suggests an alternative approach – the "incremental extension" of legal principles and policies "to cover the case at hand" – that he believes would do less damage to the delicate balance underlying this area of international law. As he explains:

> At stake is the viability of any meaningful international law of peace and security. The essence of the project entails generally applicable norms, arrived at through a process of accommodation among notionally equal juridical entities that cannot be expected to agree comprehensively on questions of justice.[33]

And yet, despite his concern to maintain the integrity of a legal system applicable to all States, Roth acknowledges that

> Today, the unrivalled military power of the United States and the ascendancy of its articulated ideals call into question the continued vitality of such a project, as well as its continued justification on moral and policy grounds. The legal principle of sovereign equality, always limited in practical effect, may seem all the less relevant in conditions of unipolarity, where weak States confronting US-led alliances have no powerful supporters to bolster their position. US assertions of prerogative are thus emboldened. In the designation of "rogue states" and in the post-11 September 2001 warning that States not "with us" will be deemed to be "with the terrorists" the rhetoric of US foreign

---

[31] Kohen, below, p. 230.   [32] Roth, below, p. 233.   [33] Roth, below, p. 260.

policy is suggestive of a Schmittian "friend–enemy" distinction at odds with any concession to sovereign equality. To the extent that the international system fails to resist such unilateral (or narrow multilateral) designations of particular States as unentitled to the protections of the peace and security order, it acquiesces in a fundamental shift in the terms of international interaction.[34]

Once again, we return to the question whether the influence of the United States has become sufficiently focused – and unopposed – for changes to the foundations of the international legal system to have become a real possibility. Roth, like Kwakwa, Cosnard, and Kohen, cautions that we should not be quick to provide an affirmative response:

> far too little time has passed in the unipolar era, and far too little practice adduced, to substantiate so sweeping a change in the premises of the international system. It is characteristic of legal orders that the statuses and rights they confer reflect long-term power and interest accommodations. These statuses and rights typically withstand short-term fluctuations in the relative influence of the legal community's actors. Although fundamental changes cannot be ruled out *a priori*, one cannot properly infer from a limited number of episodes the demise of the foundations of the Charter-based order.[35]

Stephen Toope is similarly cautious about the possibility of foundational change in favor of the United States. He argues that, as a result of a deep ambivalence within the United States about that country's role in world affairs, the United States rarely seeks to act as a hegemon, and that even when it does, it is unable to exercise the degree of influence – at least with regard to the formation of customary international law – that one might expect.

It is arguable whether, and to what degree, the United States lacks hegemonic aspirations following the terrorist attacks of 11 September 2001. Be that as it may, it is Toope's understanding of customary international law that is the most interesting and challenging aspect of his chapter. Toope argues that "customary law is now created in part through processes that do not require the unanimous and continuing consent of all States, even those most directly interested in a given norm."[36] This change, he suggests, "implies that the 'persistent objector' rule is falling into desuetude," that in some issue areas at least, "States find themselves bound by customary international norms even when they are clear in their opposition to

---

[34] Roth, below, p. 261.   [35] Roth, below, p. 261.   [36] Toope, below, p. 290.

the norm."[37] And this change, Toope argues, has been buttressed by a re-conception of the role of *opinio juris*, which has taken on a broader, constructivist tinge. Today, the binding quality of customary law is "an expression of the legitimacy of the processes through which it is created and of its power as rhetoric, not a result of fictitious state intention."[38]

The consequence of this change is that the lawmaking influence of the United States has been diminished rather than enhanced. In shaping customary international law, "the United States cannot rely on its raw material power to exert brute force, because such practice will simply fail to partake of a legitimate process of law creation."[39] Instead, it must "*persuade* other States of the need for normative consolidation or change."[40]

Toope's argument links up nicely with the alternative path to legal development identified by Grewe. Toope is arguing that, at least with respect to how customary international law is made and changed, the international community is beginning to gain the upper hand over powerful States. The process of customary international law is, in his view, today rooted in concepts of legitimacy and community that resist superpower manipulation and instead require ongoing discussion and cooperation.

The picture painted by Toope is an attractive one that provides considerable space, not only for less powerful States, but also for a range of nongovernmental organizations, individuals, and other sub-State actors. But it is a picture that should be carefully scrutinized. To what degree might it provide an accurate description of some areas of international law – for example, human rights and environmental protection – but not of others, such as the law governing the use of force and international trade? To what degree might it describe a direction of development that peaked during the late 1990s and has since been realigned by a more interventionist and, in terms of its own obligations, avowedly consensualist United States? To what degree might it actually conceal a deliberate neglect of traditional international law by the United States coupled with a shift to other, less apparent lawmaking forums, as Krisch suggests?

Moreover, Toope's argument may carry hidden risks. A developing antagonism towards some aspects of United States foreign policy – such as its opposition to the Rome Statute, the Landmines Convention and the Kyoto Protocol – suggests that, instead of influencing legal change, the

---

[37] Toope, below, p. 290.   [38] Toope, below, p. 315.
[39] Toope, below, p. 316.   [40] Toope, below, p. 316.

United States could be losing some of its ability to "persuade." Negative perceptions of its opposition to these agreements may also be undermining its efforts to influence legal developments more generally. And this growing loss of influence could, in turn, aggravate antagonism within the United States towards much of international law, creating an environment where suggestions that the United States is bound by new rules that it has consistently opposed are likely to be quite badly received. In this context, does it really make sense to argue for a new approach to customary international law that could turn the single superpower against the international legal system? Or does the traditional consent requirement retain some practical value, by protecting that system against the destructive impulses of powerful States – much as the veto power protects the UN Charter against five powerful countries that would not take lightly being subject to decisions they strongly opposed?

Achilles Skordas agrees with Toope that "the primary rules of customary international law have not undergone any dramatic change as a consequence of the dominant position of the United States in the international system."[41] However, as he goes on to argue:

> Hegemony finds its expression, not in the abrupt transformation of the international legal order, but in the incidental infiltration of concepts, the "flexibilization" of custom, the maximization of the discretionary powers of policy makers and the increased impact of society on *opinio necessitatis*.[42]

These gradual changes are not necessarily the result of US governmental action, but may be caused by the activities of non-State actors, particularly the global media, based in or closely connected with the United States. This transnational society of non-State actors can, among other things, provide the psychological element of an *opinio necessitatis*, which in turn can supplement traditional State practice and *opinio juris*, if and where necessary, so as to assist in the "birth" of a new rule:

> International humanitarian law, human rights law, the democratic principle, a human rights exception to state immunity, and the standard of necessity in the law governing the use of force are all areas in which non-State actors may exert an autonomous, but still complementary, "pull."[43]

Skordas also describes "a progressive movement of the 'interpretative centre of gravity' of customary rules from the dichotomy of 'legal/illegal' toward

---

[41] Skordas, below, p. 317.   [42] Skordas, below, p. 317.   [43] Skordas, below, p. 317.

a more complex balancing of interests and, consequently, a relative indeterminacy of the rules."[44] This balancing of interests is driven by a greater
prominence on the part of "structural principles" – such as the "principles
of humanity" and the "dictates of public conscience" in international humanitarian law, necessity and proportionality in the law governing the use
of force, and, in international human rights law, the right to vote and participate in public life. It results in "norm peripheries": zones of relative
indeterminacy that facilitate "legal communication" while reducing the
normativity of customary international law. As Skordas explains:

> The transition from the "legal/illegal" dichotomy to a more complex bal-
> ancing exercise is driven by certain features of the contemporary interna-
> tional system. During the Cold War, international law needed to maintain
> a minimum order between two hegemonic poles having their own internal
> practical and bureaucratic constraints. It was of utmost importance to avoid
> acts characterized as "illegal" that could cause major friction between the an-
> tagonistic blocs. In the post-Cold War era, the hegemonic structures are looser
> and more complex and, the primacy of the United States notwithstanding,
> are composed of a number of concentric and intersecting spheres (US, EU,
> NATO, G-8, Australia, Japan). International law has become a major integra-
> tive tool for international society and, thus, tends to become more cognitive
> and flexible than in the past. In that respect, different kinds of tensions might
> arise between peace and legality. Moreover, there is very little place for "gaps"
> in the law; every act attributable to a State is capable of being qualified as legal
> or illegal, though it is also necessary to evaluate the gravity and consequences
> of the eventual illegality.[45]

Customary international law is thus undergoing a significant change as
a result of US predominance, though not the kind of change one might
intuitively expect. It is the combination of State and societal power, hegemony broadly defined, coupled with the transition from a bipolar to a
more complex, "uni-multipolar" world (to borrow language from Samuel
Huntington), that is altering customary international law.[46] Most importantly, these changes do not only concern the underlying rules governing
the formation and change of customary international law, but also the very
character itself of this particular kind of international law.

---

[44] Skordas, below, p. 318.   [45] Skordas, below, p. 346.
[46] See Samuel Huntington, "The Lonely Superpower" (1999) 78(2) *Foreign Affairs* 35; and discussion, below, p. 450.

Similar indirect but nevertheless profound changes may be under way in the law of treaties, the other main source of international law. Here, Pierre Klein's analysis leads him to conclude that

> Generally speaking, recent US practice does not reveal a tendency of calling into question the fundamental principles of the law of treaties. In various contexts, US representatives have consistently referred to the accepted rules of the law of treaties, as they are reflected in the 1969 Vienna Convention, in order to assert and support their legal positions in litigation or in negotiation processes.[47]

Although the United States has in recent years demonstrated a "significant tendency" to disregard some aspects of the law of treaties, this does not, Klein argues, mean that it considers fundamental principles such as *pacta sunt servanda* to be obsolete. Moreover, contrary behavior on the part of the United States cannot in itself change international law. As Klein explains, even if the divergent positions of the United States were clearly established, it is difficult to assert that they "could lead to a significant evolution of the law of treaties as accepted by the other States."[48]

However, Klein does suggest that the relevance of treaties themselves, as a source of international obligations, might be "very seriously threatened as a consequence of US predominance in international relations":[49]

> That State's privileged position as a permanent member of the UN Security Council, combined with the strong leadership it often exerts in international affairs, means that it has been able on some occasions, by promoting the adoption of Security Council resolutions binding on all UN member States by virtue of Article 25 of the Charter, to generalize treaty regimes which served its current interests or, to the contrary, to put aside treaty obligations which impeded its actions on specific matters. Such actions have until now been exceptional. However, this scheme may well be repeated every time the balance of power and interests enables the United States to make such use of the Security Council procedures. Power would then enable the United States to exert an overwhelming influence over the formation of international law by making it possible for that State to interfere in the production of international norms through one of the more traditional means, the conclusion of (multilateral) treaties.[50]

---

[47] Klein, below, p. 390.   [48] Klein, below, p. 391.
[49] Klein, below, p. 391.   [50] Klein, below, p. 391.

In other words, instead of changing the law of treaties, the United States might, through the application of political power, be able to shift exercises in law-making to a different, more advantageous forum. A recent example of such a shift is UN Security Council Resolution 1373 of 28 September 2001, whereby the provisions of the 1999 International Convention for the Suppression of the Financing of Terrorism were imposed on all States through the application of Chapter VII of the Charter.

There is thus a clear parallel between Klein's and Krisch's analyses. Krisch also pointed to a shift in lawmaking forum as an important manifestation of the effect of United States predominance on international law. But it is noteworthy that these shifts do not represent a change to the foundations of international law, so much as a move from one to another part of the system.

Catherine Redgwell shares Klein's view that fundamental aspects of the law of treaties have not changed. She finds it difficult to detect any negative effect, on the principle of *pacta sunt servanda*, of the US practice of making reservations, understandings, and declarations to human rights treaties. However, she does point to a number of negative effects on the overall integrity of human rights regimes:

> the United States stance . . . will certainly have reinforced the position of those States which had already made incompatible reservations to the Covenant and other human rights instruments. It will also have undermined further the generality of international human rights, not to mention the multilateral institutional machinery designed to ensure their observance, while strengthening an approach which prioritizes universality of participation over the integrity of the treaty text.[51]

As importantly, Redgwell points out that the US approach to reservations – as well as worries about provoking the active opposition of the United States – may have had the effect of retarding further advancements in international human rights, at least through traditional mechanisms. As she explains:

> This is one area where strong countervailing regional practice – the Strasbourg approach – may be having an impact on US predominance, particularly in the suggestions that the United States should be considered bound to the ICCPR without reliance on incompatible reservations. Yet in terms of the evolution of the law of treaties, the US approach, in its response both to General Comment

---

[51] Redgwell, below, p. 413.

No. 24 and to the work of the International Law Commission on reservations to treaties, has been to buttress the traditional Vienna Convention approach . . . What has been left open is the reporting system under the ICCPR as a mechanism for the open scrutiny of, among other things, the compatibility of US reservations, understandings, and declarations with the ICCPR. Perhaps in order to keep this mechanism working, the Human Rights Committee stopped short of explicitly pronouncing on the issue of severance of the offending reservations. Doing so would have undoubtedly provoked a strong US response and, no doubt, a "constitutional crisis" within the ICCPR as to the proper legal scope of the Committee's jurisdiction and functions.[52]

Redgwell concludes that it is not yet possible to tell whether the US approach represents "due regard for time-tested and authentically American institutions and practices, or merely the arrogance of a superpower that exempts itself from the accommodation of international sensibilities that it demands of other states . . ."[53] And so, here again, we have the suggestion that the United States could be carving out an exceptional set of rules for itself alone, while also seeking to shift exercises in lawmaking to a different, more advantageous forum – in this case United States domestic law.

The example of US reservations, understandings, and declarations to human rights treaties raises another important issue, that of compliance with international law. Shirley Scott considers eight case studies of US noncompliance with international law. The eight instances of noncompliance – the Helms–Burton Act, the *Tuna-Dolphin* and *Shrimp-Turtle* disputes, the nonpayment of UN dues, the *Breard* and *LaGrand* cases, and the use of force against Iraq in December 1998, against terrorist targets in Afghanistan and Sudan in August 1998, and against Yugoslavia during the Kosovo crisis – led to a variety of different outcomes. Sometimes noncompliance actually led to improved compliance; at other times it resulted in the development of new multilateral instruments or the clarification of particular points of law. In yet other instances noncompliance prompted debate on the relevant law but no clarification or the avoidance of clarification altogether, or, in at least one instance, had no effect at all.

Scott is interested in the factors that contributed to these different outcomes, and her conclusions reinforce those reached by others elsewhere in this book:

---

[52] Redgwell, below, pp. 413–14.
[53] Redgwell, below, p. 415, quoting Brad Roth, "Understanding the 'Understanding': Federalism Constraints on Human Rights Implementation" (2001) 47 *Wayne Law Review* 891 at 909.

What is perhaps most noticeable about these outcomes is that, where US non-compliance has been particularly irksome to other States, those States have been able to help shape the impact on international law of those actions/inactions. Although there has been considerable academic discussion regarding US unilateralism, and although the acts of alleged noncompliance (other than the 1998 bombing of Iraq and that of the Federal Republic of Yugoslavia during the Kosovo crisis) were, indeed, undertaken by the United States on its own, other States and international institutions became involved in each case and the impact on international law of US noncompliance has therefore generally been indirect... This would seem to highlight the fact that international law is more than simply a blank slate onto which the most powerful can translate their policy desires. International law is a genuine system with all the complexity and dynamism that one might expect from any other system.[54]

Scott shares Samuel Huntington's view, referred to above, that since the United States is unable to resolve important issues on its own, we are living in a "uni-multipolar" rather than a "uni-polar" world.[55] Moreover, she agrees with Grewe that what is important is not the exercise of raw power as such, but that the dialogue concerning the future shape of the international legal system is "conducted in response to US rhetoric and actions, including those of noncompliance, particularly in relation to the use of force."[56]

Scott emphasises the difficulty of drawing causal connections between US behavior and international law. Sometimes unilateral action on the part of the United States is prompted by the illegal acts of others; sometimes the impact of US actions will only become apparent after several repetitions; sometimes instances of noncompliance will attract different kinds of response, depending on the areas of international law involved. As Scott explains: "Individual acts of alleged noncompliance on the part of the United States are each single moves in a two-way interchange between US rhetoric and actions and those of other actors within or outside the system of international law."[57] Foundational change is, in short, a highly complex phenomenon that does not result from the actions of a single State alone.

Scott also points out that the United States is not the only State that has sometimes failed to fulfil its obligations, and that its compliance rate over

---

[54] Scott, below, pp. 449–50.   [55] Huntington, "The Lonely Superpower," above, note 46, 35.
[56] Scott, below, p. 45.   [57] Scott, below, p. 451.

the last decade has been neither particularly low nor unprecedented. During the Cold War, the United States and other countries clashed repeatedly over issues such as extraterritorial jurisdiction and the unilateral application of military force, much as they do today.

Scott concludes that the outcomes of her case studies are not as unequivocally negative as might have been expected, that her findings highlight how "the modern system of international law is a genuine system in which the oft maligned promise of sovereign equality can, at least some of the time, translate into effective participation in the evolution of legal rules and principles."[58]

Peter-Tobias Stoll confirms, in his concluding chapter, that compliance is both central to the question of the effects of US predominance on the foundations of the international legal system, and highly complex. Unilateral action on the part of the United States can sometimes promote the development of new rules and institutions, or help ensure compliance with existing ones. But such actions can, at the same time, "give rise to questions of compliance and the lawfulness of measures of enforcement."[59]

Stoll points to the creation of the World Trade Organization as an example of the double-edged character of unilateral action:

> The threat of US unilateral action was a significant driving force behind the establishment of the WTO, which widely satisfies US interests and – it should be added – those of other industrialized countries. That said, the WTO dispute settlement system has effectively curbed some unilateral aspirations of the United States, so far.[60]

In other words, by threatening to violate existing law, the United States was able to promote the development of new rules and mechanisms that subsequently limited its ability to act unilaterally. But of course, the United States did not and does not act in a vacuum. As Stoll explains, when considering the international legal system, its development, and the conduct and influence of the United States, it is important to look as well at the role and responsibility of other States:

> In a legal system which relies on its own subjects to make laws and enforce them, size matters, but so do individual engagement and collective action. Resolute action by a small number of States halted the application of the Helms–Burton Act, and, arguably, a powerful move by a larger number of

---

[58] Scott, below, p. 455.   [59] Stoll, below, p. 476.   [60] Stoll, below, p. 476.

States, including the provision of troops and materials, could make collective security work a great deal better and render it more difficult to find an excuse for unilateral action.[61]

Other States, if sufficiently motivated and willing to cooperate, can sometimes block or at least realign the lawmaking efforts of the United States, or succeed in their own lawmaking efforts despite US opposition. Nevertheless, the decision to oppose US policies is rarely an obvious one. As Stoll reaffirms, the values and interests pursued by the United States are by and large shared by a larger group of States, which means that those States will often have to choose between relying on their powerful ally "in spite of its sometimes doubtful methods," or taking up "the burdensome task of actively translating such values and interests into a more rule-oriented and effective international legal order."[62] Consequently, noncompliance by the single superpower may be as much the result of the decision making of other States as it is the result of deliberate unilateralism.

Acquiescence by others in the lawmaking efforts of the United States is clearly an important element in foundational change, one that is promoted by the existence of shared values and interests (as Cosnard also notes) as well as by the use of persuasion and other tools of soft power (as Toope argues). Once again, the effects of US predominance are most likely to be indirect, incremental, and highly dependent on the reactions of other international actors to the initiatives and influence of the single superpower. This complexity is due, in part, to the existence of a multitude of other international actors – the international community – who exercise influential roles. And it is due in part to the continued vitality of the international legal system itself, which retains the capacity to limit the influence of individual States while stretching and bending in response to the changing geopolitics of our time.

Of course, within the limits imposed by the legal system and the international community, the United States may well be seeking – either consciously or unconsciously – to reshape the rules. Evidence of such an effort might be seen in a number of tendencies evident in the approaches taken by the United States, and many US scholars, to foundational aspects of international law. In treaty interpretation, at least in some contexts, greater emphasis would now seem to be placed on the supposed purposes of the treaty, rather than on what the words actually say.[63] In analyses of State

---

[61] Stoll, below, p. 476.   [62] Stoll, below, p. 476.   [63] See Klein, below, pp. 380–1.

practice for the purposes of customary international law, ever more weight would seem to be accorded to physical acts, as compared with statements, whereas resolutions and declarations of the UN General Assembly are now accorded almost no weight at all. And decisions of the International Court of Justice are no longer treated as having much probative value – even though most countries still regard them as authoritative determinations of the existence and content of international rules.

It remains to be seen whether and to what degree these and other diverging tendencies will influence the approaches taken by other countries. And yet, since these tendencies emanate from the single superpower, they will almost necessarily promote discussion, reassessment, and the possibility of realignment elsewhere. They thus constitute the precursor elements of foundational change, rather than manifestations of change itself – in a manner consistent with the view that what we are witnessing today is not the direct, but the indirect, hegemonic reshaping of international law.

But what of the possibility, raised by several contributors to this volume, that instead of seeking general changes the United States is attempting to create new, exceptional rules for itself alone? Similar such rules have been created in the past, albeit on a more limited and superficial basis. In 1984, West Germany abandoned its universally accepted claim to a three-mile territorial sea in the waters off Hamburg and claimed a new, unprecedented limit on the basis of a sixteen-mile box defined by geographical coordinates.[64] The new claim, which was explicitly designed for the limited purpose of preventing oil spills in those busy waters, met with no public protests from other states. This was perhaps because the balance of interests in that situation was different from that which existed more generally – different enough that other countries were prepared to allow for the development of an exception to the general rule.

The same might be said of the position and interests of the single superpower in the post–Cold War period, in which case the development of exceptional rules would depend on the responses of other countries, and other actors, to the exceptional claims. And given the potentially substantial political, military, and economic costs of opposing the United States in any particular lawmaking situation, one might think it likely that acquiescence would occur – at least with regard to those claims that are not substantially contrary to the most important interests of others. But as we have already seen with regard to the Rome Statute, the Landmines Convention

---

[64] See Decree of 12 November 1984, reproduced in (1986) 7 *Law of the Sea Bulletin* 9.

and the Kyoto Protocol, the acquiescence of others in exceptionalist claims should not be presumed. Although power is important in international law, its influence is tempered by the existence of fundamental concepts and principles, such as international community and sovereign equality, which militate against such exceptional treatment. These foundational aspects of the international legal system magnify the power and influence of those actors who operate within the rules, who seek change with rather than against the grain of legal development. And it is for this reason that the stridently unilateralist, avowedly consensualist Bush administration is unlikely to have much impact on the core aspects of the international legal order – at least in the short term.

As for the long term, it is still too soon to tell whether, and how, the foundations of the international legal system will respond to the combined and sometimes competing pressures of a single superpower and a new, increasingly diverse international community. For this reason, amongst others, this book could never be the last word on the effects of US predominance on the foundations of international law.

I

International community

1

The international community, international law, and the United States: three in one, two against one, or one and the same?

EDWARD KWAKWA

When governments, urged along by civil society, come together to create the International Criminal Court, that is the international community at work for the rule of law. When we see an outpouring of international aid to the victims of recent earthquakes in Turkey and Greece – a great deal of it from those having no apparent link with Turkey or Greece except for a sense of common humanity – that is the international community following its humanitarian impulse. When people come together to press governments to relieve the world's poorest countries from crushing debt burdens ... that is the international community throwing its weight behind the cause of development. When the popular conscience, outraged at the carnage caused by land mines, succeeds in banning these deadly weapons, that is the international community at work for collective security. There are many more examples of the international community at work, from peacekeeping to human rights to disarmament and development. At the same time there are important caveats. The idea of the international community is under perfectly legitimate attack because of its own frequent failings.

> Kofi A. Annan, Secretary-General of the United Nations[1]

How does one reconcile the position of the United States as the single superpower with the realities of interdependence and an ever-expanding international legal order that governs relations in the international community?

I am grateful to Chris Borgen for his comments on an earlier draft. The views expressed here are my personal views and are not necessarily shared by WIPO or by the United Nations.
[1] See "Secretary-General Examines 'Meaning of International Community' in Address to DPI/NGO Conference," Press Release SG/SM/7133, PI/1176 (15 Sept. 1999).

To what extent can the United States, acting alone, be a guardian, a dictator, a rule maker and/or a mediator in the international community? What is the significance of the United States' single superpower status vis-à-vis the evolution of the fundamental aspects of the international legal system?

In addressing these and other related questions, this chapter starts with a definition and analysis of the term "international community." It argues for an inclusive definition of the term, in order to embrace various non-State entities that play an important role in international politics. The next two sections explore the position of the United States in the international community and vis-à-vis international law. It is almost taken as a truism that the United States' interests and actions are not always coterminous with those of the wider international community. Indeed, the term American "unilateralism" or "isolationism" is frequently used to refer to US action that is not sanctioned by the "international community." The chapter argues that in being unilateralist or isolationist, the United States acts according to its perceived interests, as does any other State. The difference, however, is that the sheer might and superpower status of the United States are such that its actions are bound to have a greater impact on the international community and on the foundations of international law. Indeed, because of the strength and dominance of the United States in almost all aspects of human endeavor, even the most insignificant changes in US foreign policy can have disproportionate and far-reaching consequences in the international community and for international law. The restraints on the United States during the Cold War period are much reduced today, and thus its influence on international relations and the international legal system is all the more obvious.

That said, this chapter argues that the inexorable trend of globalization and interdependence is such that the national interests of the United States would be better served by multilateralist rather than unilateralist policies, and concludes that the United States now has both an unprecedented opportunity and a pressing need to influence some of the fundamental aspects of the international legal order. In doing so, however, the United States will need the active cooperation of key segments of the rest of the international community; the incredible power of the United States will not be enough to enable it to "go it alone" in international rule making.

This chapter identifies international organizations (governmental as well as nongovernmental) as one of the most obvious forms or manifestations of the international community.[2] In view of the importance of international organizations in the international community and in the formulation of international law, the position of the United States and its participation in international organizations seems to be a useful means by which to ascertain the role of the United States in the international community and in influencing international law. This chapter therefore places particular emphasis on the role of the United States in international organizations.

The "international community"

The phrase "international community" is used in this chapter to refer not only to the community of States, but also to the whole array of other actors whose actions influence the development of international legal rules. This includes intergovernmental organizations, international (and national) nongovernmental organizations (NGOs), transnational corporations and even individuals. I use this expanded definition of the international community for three reasons. First, a wide array of actors participates in the formulation of international law. Second, various experts who have studied and written on the issue agree that the concept of an international community is wider than just States. And third, the rationale for the existence of the international community strongly suggests that the community comprises not only States, but also various non-State entities. These three reasons are explained below.

The term "international community"[3] has found its way into international legal literature and now seems to be used with reckless abandon. Too often, however, the term is unaccompanied by any explanation of its precise

[2] In this regard, it is worth remembering that under traditional international law, there was only one kind of international actor – the State. Under this formulation, the "international community" would be restricted to the community of States in the international system, and there were very few States. At present, however, there are almost 200. The primary means through which these States interact at the multilateral level is international organizations. It is also instructive that several international organizations now have non-State entities as members, and that NGOs also play an active part, indirectly and directly, in the deliberations and policy making of several international organizations. Moreover, international organizations are generally structured such as to require a large degree of cooperation and collaboration among their members. With the ineluctable advance of globalization and interdependence, international organizations have become much more important in the international community.

[3] "International community" is sometimes used in the literature interchangeably with "world community" or "global community." In the 1970s and the 1980s, "global community" was frequently used by Marxists, who tended to look beyond the State at the ways in which classes existed and affected each other worldwide.

form or contents. As Philip Allott explains, the use of the term "international community" "by politicians, diplomats, journalists, and academic specialists is tending to establish within general consciousness a fictitious conceptual entity with effects and characteristics which surpass the practical purposes of those who make use of it."[4]

What does it really mean to refer to the "international community" in an international law and/or international relations context? A starting point is recognition of the obvious truth that any number of plausible definitions of the term "international community" is conceivable.

The reference to "international community" is found in several international legal instruments and documents. At the treaty level, one of the most well-known examples is the 1969 Vienna Convention on the Law of Treaties, which defines *jus cogens* as "a norm accepted and recognized by the international community of States as a whole as a norm from which no derogation is permitted."[5] Clearly, the Convention uses the term "international community" to refer only to States. A more recent treaty that incorporates the term is the Rome Statute of the International Criminal Court, which limits the Court's jurisdiction to "the most serious crimes of concern to the international community as a whole."[6] This seems to be a more inclusive use of the term, insofar as the "international community" is not expressly limited to States.

---

[4] Phillip Allott, "The True Function of Law in the International Community" (1998) 5 *Journal of Global Legal Studies* 391, 411. See also Philip Allott, "The Concept of International Law" in Michael Byers (ed.), *The Role of Law in International Politics* (Oxford: Oxford University Press, 2000), pp. 69–89.

[5] Vienna Convention on the Law of Treaties, UN Doc. A/CONF.39/27 (1969) at article 53, reprinted in (1969) 63 *American Journal of International Law* 875. The United States signed the Vienna Convention on the Law of Treaties on 24 April 1970, but has not yet ratified the Convention. See UN Treaty Database, at http://untreaty.un.org (last visited 8 March 2002). It is generally accepted, however, that certain provisions of the Convention reflect customary international law. A good candidate for this would be Article 18 of the Convention, which provides that "until it shall have made its intention clear not to become a party to the treaty," a State is obliged to refrain from acts which would defeat the object and purpose of that treaty. For an excellent discussion of the legislative history of the Vienna Convention on the Law of Treaties, see generally Richard Kearney and Robert Dalton, "The Treaty on Treaties" (1970) 64 *American Journal of International Law* 495–561.

[6] See the Preamble and Article 5 of the Rome Statute of the International Criminal Court, adopted and opened for signature 17 July 1998, UN Doc. A/Conf. 183/9 (1998); (1998) 37 *International Legal Materials* 999. The position of the US government in relation to the Rome Statute of the International Criminal Court is now well known. See generally David Scheffer, "The United States and the International Criminal Court" (1999) 93 *American Journal of International Law* 12–22.

There are also specific references to the "international community" in the jurisprudence of the International Court of Justice. There is, for example, the ICJ's famous statement in the Barcelona Traction case, confirming the existence of certain legal obligations of States towards "the international community as a whole."[7] The juxtaposition of States with "the international community as a whole," in this context, would seem to suggest a tacit acknowledgment that the "international community" comprises States and an undefined universe of other entities. The ICJ has also invoked the term in several other cases.[8]

The third and most frequent set of references to the "international community" can be found in the resolutions, declarations, and decisions of international organizations, in particular the UN General Assembly and the UN Security Council. For example, in its landmark 1970 Declaration on the Principles of International Law Concerning Friendly Relations and Cooperation among States, an "ambitious codification of contemporary international law [that] has been widely accepted,"[9] the General Assembly stressed that all States "are equal members of the international community."[10] Once again, the reference was to States.

Several other resolutions often invoke the name of the international community, without specifying the entity to which that term refers. In their textual formulation, however, it seems clear that the drafters of those resolutions assumed that the international community did not refer exclusively to States. Indeed, there are several resolutions in which the organizations of the United Nations system and even non-State entities, such as private donors, are expressly referred to as integral parts of the international community. For example, in the context of international assistance for the rehabilitation and reconstruction of Nicaragua, the General Assembly commended

---

[7] Barcelona Traction, Light and Power Company (Belgium v. Spain), Judgment, (1970) ICJ Reports 3.

[8] See e.g. Legal Consequences for States of the Continued Presence of South Africa in Namibia (South-West Africa) Notwithstanding Security Council Resolution 276 (1970), Advisory Opinion, (1971) ICJ Reports 16, 56 (stating that Namibia is entitled to look to the "international community for assistance"); United States Diplomatic and Consular Staff in Tehran, Judgment, (1980) ICJ Reports 43 (appealing to the "international community").

[9] Michael Reisman, "The Resistance in Afghanistan is Engaged in a War of National Liberation" (1987) 81 American Journal of International Law 906, 908.

[10] Declaration on the Principles of International Law Concerning Friendly Relations and Co-operation among States in accordance with the Charter of the United Nations (Declaration on Friendly Relations), 24 October 1970, GA Res. 2625, 25 UN GAOR Supp. (No. 28) at 121, UN Doc. A/8028 (1970).

"the efforts made by the international community, *including the organs and organizations of the United Nations system*, to supplement the action taken by the Government of Nicaragua."[11] Similarly, the same body, in the context of international cooperation on humanitarian assistance in the field of natural disasters, encouraged "Governments in natural-disaster-prone countries to establish, with the support of *the international community, in particular the donors*, national spatial information infrastructures relating to natural disaster preparedness, early warning, response and mitigation."[12] And in its resolution on the implementation of the First UN Decade for the Eradication of Poverty, the UN General Assembly recognizes that "while it is the primary responsibility of *States* to attain social development, the *international community* should support the efforts of the developing countries to eradicate poverty and to ensure basic social protection."[13] It is arguable that the General Assembly adopted the text of this resolution in recognition of the fact that "States" and "the international community" are not one and the same entity.[14]

Finally, it is worth noting that the term "international community" is sometimes used by way of distinguishing it from what it is not rather than designating what it is.[15] Indeed, that seems to be the basis on which some States have at times been referred to as "rogue States," "pariah States," or "States of concern," and other entities as terrorists against which the international community is at war.[16]

---

[11] See GA Res. A/47/169 (22 Dec. 1992) (emphasis added).

[12] See GA Res. A/55/163 (14 Dec. 2000) (emphasis added).

[13] See GA Res. A/55/210 (10 Dec. 2000) (emphasis added).

[14] Similarly, in a resolution adopted in the context of the terrorist attacks on the United States in September 2001, the UN Security Council called on "the international community to redouble their efforts to prevent and suppress terrorist acts": UN Doc. S/RES/1368 (2001), 12 Sept. 2001. It is instructive to note that in the preceding paragraph, the resolution called on "States," not on "the international community."

[15] Under such formulations, "international community" would be distinguished from entities that are deemed to be undesirable in that community. See e.g. Kofi Annan, "Fighting Terrorism on a Global Front," *New York Times*, 21 Sept. 2001, 35 (op-ed, asserting that "The international community is defined not only by what it is for, but by what and whom it is against").

[16] Thomas Henriksen, for example, states that "what has become painfully clear during the 1990s is that a handful of rogue States have rejected the global economic order and international standards for their own belligerent practices." The most dangerous category of such States, he argues, is the "terrorist rogue State." According to Henriksen, this "deadly manifestation in the emerging world order has captured Washington's attention. These nation-States fail to comply with the rules of international law. Their behavior is defiant and belligerent. They promote radical ideologies. They share an anti-Western bias, in general, and an anti-American hatred, in particular. Rogue political systems vary, but their leaders share a common antipathy toward their citizens' participating in the political process. They suppress human and civil

It would serve no policy goal to restrict "international community" to State actors. First, a wide array of non-State actors participate in the formulation of international law. As McDougal and Reisman have pointed out, international law is formulated through a diverse process of communication within the international community:

> The peoples of the world communicate to each other expectations about policy, authority, and control not merely through state or intergovernmental organs, but through reciprocal claims and mutual tolerances in all their interactions. The participants in the relevant process of communication... include not merely the officials of states and intergovernmental organizations but also the representatives of political parties, pressure groups, private associations, and the individual human being *qua* individual with all his or her identifications.[17]

Nongovernmental organizations such as Amnesty International, the International Committee of the Red Cross and other non-State entities are very active members of the international community and influential in the formulation of international legal rules. It is fair to suggest that the Statute for the International Criminal Court and the Ottawa Landmines Convention[18] would not have seen the light of day without the active lobbying of networks of NGOs.[19] Nor can one ignore the role of the global media.[20] Non-State actors are likely to play increasingly important roles in much decision making in the international community and in the formulation of international law, as governments increasingly lose control over the flow of technology, information, and financial transactions across their borders.

---

rights as do diplomatic rogue States, but their international bellicosity is the key variable drawing our attention to them": Thomas Henriksen, "Using Power and Diplomacy to Deal With Rogue States," Hoover Essays in Public Policy No. 94 (February 1999), reprinted at http://www.hoover.stanford.edu/publications/epp/94/94b.html (last visited 8 March 2002).

[17] Myres McDougal and Michael Reisman, "The Prescribing Function: How International Law is Made" (1980) 6 *Yale Studies in World Public Order* 249, reprinted in Myres McDougal and Michael Reisman, *International Law in Contemporary Perspective: The Public Order of the World Community* (New York: Foundation Press, 1981), p. 84.

[18] Convention on the Prohibition of the Use, Stockpiling, Production and Transfer of Anti-Personnel Mines and on their Destruction, concluded at Oslo on 18 September 1997. To quote one author, this convention, "perhaps the most celebrated example of NGO influence, has been hailed as a defining moment in the democratization of international law making." See Stewart Patrick, "America's Retreat from Multilateral Engagement" (2000) 641 *Current History* 434.

[19] See also Michael Reisman, "Redesigning the United Nations" (1997) 1 *Singapore Journal of International and Comparative Law* 17 (arguing that the remarkable advances in human rights and environmental protection were largely a result of lobbying and other efforts by NGOs).

[20] See chapter by Achilles Skordas, below.

In the context of the Internet, as argued below, the Internet Corporation for Assigned Names and Numbers (ICANN), a nongovernmental entity, is playing the lead role in formulating policy relating to the governance of the Internet. And it is noteworthy that the UN Secretary-General has launched a global compact with the business community,[21] and that it was an individual, Ted Turner, who paid the $34 million deficit when the United Nations and the United States reached agreement on the payment of the United States' arrears to the United Nations.[22] In short, while States make the ultimate decisions, one cannot simply ignore the impact of non-State entities on the ultimate decision-making processes of States.

Secondly, several writers agree that the concept of an international community is wider than States. Bruno Simma, for example, opines that the international community is "a community that comprises not only States, but in the last instance all human beings."[23] Christian Tomuschat also argues that "it would be wrong to assume that States as a mere juxtaposition of individual units constitute the international community. Rather, the concept denotes an overarching system which embodies a common interest of all States and, indirectly, of mankind."[24] Hedley Bull seems to have had the concept of the international community in mind when he referred to a "great society of all mankind." His words are instructive: "the ultimate units of the great society of all mankind are not States (or nations, tribes, empires, classes or parties) but individual human beings, which are permanent and indestructible in a sense in which groups are not."[25]

---

[21] The Global Compact was launched by UN Secretary-General Kofi Annan at the 1999 World Economic Forum in Davos, Switzerland, when he challenged the business community to enter into a compact in which they would embrace and help enact a set of core values in the areas of human rights, labor standards, and environmental practices. This challenge has received favorable responses from the international business community. See generally http://www.un.org/News/facts/business.htm (last visited 8 March 2002). For a discussion on the objectives and operation of the Global Compact, see generally John Gerard Ruggie, "global_governance.net: The Global Compact as Learning Network" (2001) 7 *Global Governance* 371–78.

[22] The British Ambassador to the United Nations, Jeremy Greenstock, actually joked that "clearly the UN has recognized Turner as a government." See "UN OKs reduced US dues in accord; Turner donation plays crucial role," *Washington Times*, 23 Dec. 2000, A1.

[23] Bruno Simma, "From Bilateralism to Community Interest" (1994) 250(VI) *Recueil des cours* 215 at 234.

[24] Christian Tomuschat, "Obligations Arising for States Without or Against their Will" (1993) 241(IV) *Recueil des cours* 209, 227.

[25] Hedley Bull, *The Anarchical Society: A Study of Order in World Politics* (London: Macmillan, 1977), p. 22.

These are remarkably prescient words, given the period when they were written.

The third and, perhaps, most compelling reason why the reference to "international community" should not be restricted to States is to be found in the rationale for the existence of such a community. The importance of the concept of an international community lies in the simple truth that it is this community that provides a sociological foundation – a *raison d'être* – for international law. We thus learn from political theory that a viable community rests on a minimum consensus of shared values. In that sense, members of the community generally accept the community's rules because of a shared sense of commonality.[26]

The UN Secretary-General succinctly explains the common values of the international community as follows:

> What binds us into an international community? In the broadest sense there is a shared vision of a better world for all people, as set out, for example, in the United Nations Charter. There is our sense of common vulnerability in the face of climate change and weapons of mass destruction. There is the framework of international law. There is equally our sense of shared opportunity, which is why we build common markets and, yes, institutions – such as the United Nations. Together, we are stronger.[27]

A few examples should help establish what may be seen as a sense of community. In September 2000, the largest-ever gathering of world leaders, including ninety-nine heads of state, three crown princes and forty-seven heads of government, met at the United Nations in New York and adopted a Millennium Declaration, in which they stated expressly their belief that certain fundamental values were essential to international relations in the twenty-first century. The specific values they identified were:

---

[26] See also Simma, "From Bilateralism to Community Interest in International Law," above note 23, at 233 (putting forward a "first, very tentative, definition of 'community interest'" as "a consensus according to which respect for certain fundamental values is not to be left to the free disposition of States individually or *inter se* but is recognized and sanctioned by international law as a matter of concern to all States").

[27] See "Secretary-General Examines 'Meaning of International Community'" above note 1. See also Georges Abi-Saab, "Whither the International Community?" (1998) 9 *European Journal of International Law* 248, 251 (arguing, in the context of the law of cooperation, that it is "based on the awareness among legal subjects of the existence of a common interest or common value which cannot be protected or promoted unilaterally, but only by a common effort. In other words, it is based on a premise or an essential presumption, which is the existence of a community of interests or of values").

freedom, equality, solidarity, tolerance, respect for nature, and shared responsibility.[28] The Global Compact, alluded to earlier, sets out a core set of nine principles in the areas of human rights, labor standards and the environment. These principles have been embraced and are being enacted not only by States and international organizations, but, more importantly, also by private sector and business entities.[29] And in the context of the September 2001 terrorist attacks on the United States, debates around the world made it explicit that the international community shared certain core values that had to be promoted and protected.[30]

The examples cited all point to the existence of certain basic common interests among members of the international society. While the common interests or core values are often identified and discussed in the context of intergovernmental meetings or among State elites, it is undeniable that the core values in question are generally assumed to be equally applicable to non-State entities. It is this commonality that constitutes the foundation stones of an "international community." To be sure, international law is a system of principles and norms governing relations in the international community. Indeed, the very idea of community rests on the implicit assumption that certain issues affect the world as a whole, and therefore they cannot effectively be addressed or tackled unilaterally.[31]

In addition to the changing nature of its participants, the "international community" is also becoming increasingly interdependent – economically, politically, environmentally, and culturally. This increased interdependence has made international cooperation an indispensable tool for the survival of the "international community." As Thomas Franck puts it, there now

---

[28] See GA Res. 55/2 (8 Sept. 2000), reprinted at http://www.un.org/Depts/dhl/resguide/r55all.htm (last visited 8 March 2002).

[29] See generally http://www.unglobalcompact.org/un/gc/unweb.nsf/content/thenine.htm (last visited 8 March 2002).

[30] See e.g. statement by Jeremy Greenstock (United Kingdom) to the Security Council, UN Press Release SC/7143 (12 Sep. 2001) (confirming the conclusion of the European Union that the terrorist acts were "not only against the United States, but against humanity itself and the life and freedom shared by all"); statement by Wang Yingfan (China), *ibid.* (arguing that the attacks "took place in the United States, but represented an open challenge to the international community as a whole"); statement by Alfonso Valdivieso (Colombia), *ibid.* (the attacks "were not only against the United States, but against the entire community of civilized people and their values"); statement by Anund Priyay Neewoor (Mauritius), *ibid.* (the acts were "also aimed at democracy and the free world"); and statement by Jean-David Levitte (France), *ibid.* (taking the view that the terrorist acts "were a challenge to the international community as a whole").

[31] The notions of international public policy or *jus cogens*, as well as obligations *erga omnes*, all presuppose a community of common interests or shared values.

exists a "global community, emerging out of a growing awareness of irrefutable interdependence, its imperatives and exigencies."[32] The increasing globalization and interdependence of the world community is a subject on which much has been written. In large measure, interdependence and globalization, however defined, are processes that are shaped more by markets than by governments. Most relevant in this context is the observation that certain institutions are now shedding their status as intergovernmental organizations and converting into fully private companies.[33]

The place and the role of the United States in the international community

Robert Keohane and Joseph Nye distinguish between "behavioral power" – "the ability to obtain outcomes you want" – and "resource power" – "the possession of the resources that are usually associated with the ability to get the outcomes you want."[34]

---

[32] Thomas M. Franck, *Fairness in International Law and Institutions* (New York: Oxford University Press, 1997), p. 12.

[33] Two of the best-known examples are the International Telecommunications Satellite Organization (INTELSAT) and the International Maritime Satellite Organization (INMARSAT). In July 2001, INTELSAT severed its ties with its 146 member governments and transformed itself into a Bermuda-based holding company. See generally http://www.intelsat.com (last visited 8 March 2002).

INMARSAT also converted, in April 1999, from an international treaty organization to a private company. See generally http://www.inmarsat.org (last visited 8 March 2002). Also significant is what Jan Klabbers refers to as "the straddling of the public/private divide or, in better-sounding terms, the creation of public–private partnerships." He provides the example of the International Organization for Standardization (ISO), which sets standards of considerable influence in the field of environmental regulation, and encompasses the standardization in statutes of a number of States. See Jan Klabbers, "Institutional Ambivalence by Design: Soft Organizations in International Law" (2001) 70 *Nordic Journal of International Law* 403 at 406 (citing Naomi Roht-Arriaza, "Shifting the Point of Regulation: The International Organization for Standardization and Global Law Making on Trade and the Environment" (1995) 22 *Ecology Law Quarterly* 479–539).

[34] Keohane and Nye further divide "behavioral power" into "hard" and "soft" power. Hard power, they contend, is "the ability to get others to do what they otherwise would not do through threat of punishment or promise of reward," and soft power is "the ability to get desired outcomes because others want what you want; it is the ability to achieve desired outcomes through attraction rather than coercion": Robert Keohane and Joseph Nye, *Power and Interdependence*, 3rd edn. (New York, 2001), p. 220. See also Michael Reisman, "Law From the Policy Perspective," in Myres McDougal and Michael Reisman, *International Law Essays: A Supplement to International Law in Contemporary Perspective* (New York: Foundation Press, 1981), p. 8 (defining power simply as "the capacity to influence"), but cf. Reisman, "Redesigning the United Nations," above note 19, at 8 (defining power as "the relative capacities of actors to influence events without regard for lawful arrangements"); Michael Byers, *Custom, Power and the Power of Rules* (Cambridge: Cambridge

There can be little doubt that the United States is, by any measure, the most powerful country in the international community today. As aptly put by Joseph Nye, "not since Rome has one nation loomed so large above the others."[35] The military might of the United States is unchallenged and without rival. The US economy is the largest and most influential in the world. For example, the United States accounts for over 15 percent of total world exports and imports, and is the world's largest exporter of goods and services.[36] In short, US global, economic, technological, military, and diplomatic influence is unparalleled in the international community, among nations as well as global, international, and regional organizations.

There are certain consequences that flow ineluctably from this special position of the United States. It implies, for example, that the United States has a distinctive and, by definition, a greater responsibility in the international community. It is a responsibility arising from the undisputed facts of American dominance in almost all aspects of human endeavor. This point is forcefully made by Phillip Allott:

> the people of the United States bear a very heavy responsibility for the future of humanity – an imperial responsibility. It is the same kind of responsibility that the British exercised, for better and for worse, in the nineteenth century; that Rome exercised in the last century B.C. and the first and fourth centuries A.D.; that Greece exercised at the time of Alexander, in the fourth century B.C. It is a responsibility based on the sheer facts of American military and economic and cultural power, and the extent of American economic and political and military investment in the rest of the world.[37]

The fact that the United States is called upon to act and indeed expected to play a lead role far more than any other State is a reality in the international system.[38]

University Press, 1999), p. 5 (defining power as "the ability, either directly or indirectly, to control or significantly influence how actors – in this case States – behave").

[35] Joseph Nye, *The Paradox of American Power: Why the World's Only Superpower Can't Go It Alone* (New York: Oxford University Press, 2002), p. 1.

[36] See generally *World Trade Annual Report 2001* (Geneva: WTO, 2001). Admittedly, in terms of world trade and impact at the World Trade Organization, it is arguable that the European Union is on an equal footing with the United States. This should, however, be viewed in the light of the fact that the European Union is composed of fifteen distinct economies.

[37] Phillip Allott, "The True Function of Law in the International Community" (1998) 5 *Journal of Global Legal Studies* 391.

[38] See also Henriksen, "Using Power and Diplomacy," above note 16, at 5 ("As the remaining superpower, the United States faces a unique political environment. It is both the world's reigning hegemon and sometime villain. America's economic, military, and technological prowess endows it with what [former] Secretary of State Madeleine K. Albright has termed indispensability.

There is another aspect to the story: the superpower status of the United States in the international community not only creates expectations in the rest of the international community, but also creates perhaps even stronger expectations or perceptions, within the United States, of what should be the role of the single superpower. US National Security Adviser Condoleezza Rice makes the point clearly when she suggests that "Great powers do not just mind their own business," and that the power that a superpower such as the United States wields "is usually accompanied by a sense of entitlement to play a decisive role in international politics."[39]

Another corollary of being the single superpower may very well be a feeling of insecurity or extreme sensitivity to even the most remote sign of external threats, resulting in a foreign policy that seeks to ensure, among other things, absolute security.[40] On the other hand, there are reasons to suggest that peace and prosperity, particularly in a single superpower, could encourage a sense of complacency or preoccupation with internal domestic affairs, and thus make the average American forget that they are a part of a larger international community.[41]

Whatever the political upheaval or humanitarian crisis, other States expect the United States to solve the world's problems and to dispense good deeds. Those expectations arise from the fact that America has often come to the rescue in the past and that the United States is not a traditional nation").

[39] Condoleezza Rice, "Promoting the National Interest," (2000) 79 *Foreign Affairs* 45 at 49. Rice has also opined that "there are times when the US isn't going to be in a position of agreement with everybody else, and given our particular role in the world, we have an obligation to do what we think is right." See Massimo Calabresi, "Condi Rice: The Charm of Face Time," *Time*, 10 Sept. 2001, 48.

[40] We are told that an important Pentagon planning document stated in 1992: "Our first objective is to prevent the re-emergence of a new rival . . . that poses a threat on the order of that posed formerly by the Soviet Union . . . Our strategy must now refocus on precluding the emergence of any potential future global competitor." See John Mearsheimer, "The Future of the American Pacifier" (2001) 80(5) *Foreign Affairs* 46.

[41] John Ikenberry highlights the issue when he points out in a recent study that "in a world of unipolar power Americans need to know very little about what other governments or peoples think, but foreigners must worry increasingly about the vagaries of congressional campaigns and the idiosyncratic prejudices of congressional committee chairmen." G. John Ikenberry, "Getting Hegemony Right" (2001) 63 *The National Interest* 17 at 19.

The phenomenon of one State dominating the international system is not without precedent. Nor is US isolationism, unilateralism or even multilateralism necessarily a phenomenon only of the post–Cold War world. As Paul Johnson eloquently reminds us, "there is nothing unique, as many Americans seem to suppose, in the desire of a society with a strong cultural identity to minimize its foreign contacts. On the contrary, isolationism in this sense has been the norm whenever geography has made it feasible." Johnson lists examples including ancient Egypt ("which, protected by deserts, tried to pursue an isolationist policy for 3,000 years with unparalleled success"), Japan ("a more modern example of a hermit State" which "used its surrounding seas to pursue a policy of total isolation"), China ("isolationist for thousands of years,

What is the record of the United States in respect of intergovernmental organizations? It is instructive that a large majority of the American public seems to favor an active American involvement in the international community and in the United Nations in particular.[42] The more significant fact, however, is that while over 80 percent of the United States public want to strengthen the United Nations, American policy makers think that only 14 percent of the public favor such action.[43] This naturally raises questions as to whether official United States positions vis-à-vis the international community and international law are necessarily a reflection of the preferences of the American people.

In the particular context of the United Nations, let us consider the following statistics for a minute:

• US citizens hold more UN Secretariat jobs than the citizens of any other member State, as well as the top posts at the United Nations Children's Fund (UNICEF), the World Bank (IBRD), the World Food Program (WFP) and the Universal Postal Union (UPU);
• the United Nations is headquartered in the United States city of New York, and the United States government has signed a headquarters agreement with the United Nations to that effect. In addition, the United States is a member of every specialized agency of the United Nations (including, after an eighteen-year absence, the United Nations Educational, Scientific and Cultural Organization – UNESCO) and other significant intergovernmental organizations;
• of the $318 million in procurements approved by the UN Secretariat in New York in 1998, American companies alone received 31 percent of the business, or $98.8 million.[44]

These and other related statistics seem to point to the obvious: that the United States is heavily involved in international community activity, and that the United States benefits significantly from such activity. There are,

albeit an empire at the same time") and Britain (which "has been habitually isolationist even during the centuries when it was acquiring a quarter of the world"). Paul Johnson, "The Myth of American Isolationism: Reinterpreting the Past" (1995) 77(3) *Foreign Affairs* 159 at 160.
[42] See "Setting the Record Straight: What do Americans Really Think of the UN?" at http://www.un.org/News/facts/think.htm (last visited 8 March 2002) published by DPI/1963/Rev. 2 June 1999.
[43] *Ibid.*
[44] See "Setting the Record Straight: Facts about the United Nations," at http://www.un.org/News/facts/setting.htm (last visited 8 March 2002) published by DPI/1753/Rev. 17 June 1999.

in addition, other statistics that refute the criticisms of inefficiency and waste that are sometimes leveled at the United Nations by United States government officials.[45] For example, consider the following:

- The budget for the United Nations' core functions – the Secretariat's operations in New York, Geneva, Nairobi, and Vienna and the five regional commissions – is $1.25 billion a year. This is about 4 percent of New York City's annual budget;
- the total expenditure of the entire UN system – including the United Nations' funds, programs and specialized agencies – was just over $10 billion in 1997. This is roughly half of the annual revenue of a United States corporation such as Dow Chemical, which earned over $20 billion in 1997; and
- the total cost of all UN peacekeeping operations in 1998 was some $907 million – the equivalent of less than 0.5 percent of the US military budget, and less than 0.2 percent of global military spending.[46]

These statistics speak volumes. On the one hand, they suggest that the United Nations does not spend (or "waste") anywhere near as much money as is often claimed by the US government. On the other hand, they could also suggest that the United Nations is so inexpensive that the United States can easily afford to be involved in UN activity, regardless of whether the United States cares about the UN.

There are reasons to suggest that the United States tends to be much more supportive of organizations whose membership comprises like-minded market democracies than of more heterogeneous or universal bodies. Examples of the former are the Organization for Economic Cooperation and Development (OECD) and the North Atlantic Treaty Organization (NATO), and examples of the latter are the United Nations and some of its

---

[45] US and other government officials often allege that the UN is a bloated bureaucracy that wastes taxpayers' money. For a discussion of various arguments used by US government officials to support withholding of US payments to the United Nations, see generally Richard Nelson, "International Law and US Withholding of Payments to International Organizations" (1986) 80 *American Journal of International Law* 973–83; Elisabeth Zoller, "The Corporate Will of the United Nations and the Rights of the Minority" (1987) 81 *American Journal of International Law* 610–34; President, "Statement on Signing Consolidated Appropriations Legislation for Fiscal Year 2000" (1999) 35 *Weekly Compilation of Presidential Documents* 2458; and Sean Murphy, "Contemporary Practice of the United States Relating to International Law: States and International Organizations" (2000) 94 *American Journal of International Law* 348–50.

[46] "Setting the Record Straight: United Nations," above note 44.

specialized agencies. The United States similarly places greater importance on organizations that reflect its dominance, whether through a formal system of weighted voting, as in the World Bank and the International Monetary Fund (IMF), or through a system where it has veto power, as in the UN Security Council.[47] This is manifested, for example, in the fact that the United States has been eager to reduce its contribution of 25 percent of the UN regular budget, notwithstanding the fact that it pays the equivalent of $1.11 per American, compared with, say San Marino, whose contribution to the UN regular budget, while less than a fraction of 1 percent, amounts to $4.26 per citizen of San Marino.

The saga involving the United States' payment of its arrears (dues) and annual contributions to the United Nations is a good example of the impact of the single superpower's financial contributions on international community activity. In 1999, the United States Congress adopted legislation authorizing the payment of certain arrears to international organizations over a three-year period. This payment was, however, made subject to the fulfillment of certain conditions, one of which was action by the UN General Assembly to reduce the regular budget ceiling assessment (for the United States) from 25 percent to 22 percent, and the United States' assessed share of peacekeeping operations from 31 percent to 25 percent. Although the United States refusal to pay its arrears may have been based on political grounds, that action had the effect of redrawing the scales of assessments for contributions by member States to the United Nations,[48] and presumably affected the Organization's ability to engage in international community activities of various kinds.

The position of the United States on the UN Commission on Human Rights (UNCHR) provides an example of the value the single superpower attaches to certain international bodies. In April 2001, the United States was surprisingly voted off the UNCHR.[49] The loss of a seat on the commission

---

[47] While most observers would readily argue that the UN General Assembly represents the community of States, being the only truly legitimate, in the sense of representative, body that decides through a majoritarian process of discussion and largely nonbinding votes or consensus, this view has not always found favor with the United States.

[48] See "Scale of Assessments for the Apportionment of the Expenses of the United Nations," GA Res. A/Res/55/5B-F (23 Dec. 2000).

[49] This was the first time since 1947 (the creation of the commission) that the United States had been voted off the commission. The vote, which was conducted by secret ballot, means that the United States will not be represented on the commission from 1 Jan. 2002 to 31 Dec. 2004. See *The Economist* at http://www.economist.com/library/focus/displaystory.cfm (last visited

was not without effect. It meant that the United States was unable to sponsor any resolution within the commission, such as a resolution condemning Cuba for human rights violations. Even if the United States could find another country to act as the main sponsor of such a resolution, the fact remained that the United States was unable to vote on it.

A single superpower that placed little or no value in multilateral institutions probably would have ignored the vote removing it from the UNCHR. Quite clearly, however, there are those in the United States who see value in having the United States remain engaged in the international community. There is no other way to explain the fact that the United States House of Representatives voted to withhold $244 million in dues unless the United States was restored to the UNCHR, as well as the statement by United States Secretary of State Colin Powell that "one thing I can guarantee is that [the United States] will be back [on the UNCHR] next year"[50] – which indeed it was. Whatever one thinks about the UNCHR, there is no denying that it has effectively enunciated important statements of principle and sensitized public opinion by establishing commissions of inquiry or appointing special rapporteurs to investigate gross human rights violations.[51] The

8 March 2002). It is significant that among the various reasons given for the loss of the seat were the fact that the United States had not, at the time, confirmed who would be its permanent representative at the United Nations, and the fact that it had recently shown increased disdain for multilateralism, for example, by rejecting the Kyoto Protocol and the Anti-Ballistic Missile Treaty.

Also significant is the fact that on the same day, and in the same room in which the United States was voted off the UNCHR, the United States lost its seat on the UN International Narcotics Control Board, which it had helped found in 1964, and which had been co-chaired for several years by Herbert S. Okun, a senior American diplomat.

[50] For reactions to the United States' loss of its seat on the UNCHR, see generally Marc Lacey, "House Warns UN of Pocketbook Revenge," New York Times, 11 May 2001, 8. See also David Sanger, "House Threatens to Hold Back UN Dues for Loss of Seat," New York Times, 9 May 2001, 1.

[51] For example, the UNCHR has repeatedly adopted annual resolutions condemning Myanmar's human rights practices, and appointed a Special Rapporteur on the Situation of Human Rights in Myanmar (then Burma) in 1992, whose mandate has been extended since then. See Situation of Human Rights in Myanmar, Commission on Human Rights Res. 1999/17, UN ESCOR, 52nd mtg; UN Doc.E/CN.4/ RES/1999/17 (1999), available at http://www.unhchr.ch/Huridocda (last visited 8 March 2002). In 2001, a new Special Rapporteur was appointed to succeed the incumbent. See UN Press Release (6 Feb. 2001).

At its 2001 Session, the commission strongly condemned human rights abuses in Afghanistan, Burundi, Iran, and Iraq, expressed grave concern at human rights abuses in Cuba, Democratic Republic of Congo, Sierra Leone and Sudan, and strongly censured Russia for its actions in Chechnya. See UNCHR Report of the Fifty-Seventh Session (19 March–27 April 2001), E/CN.4/2001/167E/2001/23 (1 Oct. 2001). These resolutions have had the effect of highlighting

determination of the single superpower to remain engaged with the commission, while possibly a face-saving measure, nevertheless shows, contrary
to popular wisdom, the importance that United States policy makers attach
to certain multilateral institutions.

It would seem that what the United States perceives as its vital interests
inevitably determines the degree of US involvement in any community
activity. US government pronouncements are replete with examples that
demonstrate that the United States often acts to protect its own specific
interests, rather than those of the international community as a whole.
A good example was provided when the administration of President Bill
Clinton adopted, in the context of multilateral peace operations, a policy
position stating that the United States would participate in UN actions only
if its own interests were involved. This is the import of Presidential Decision
Directive 25 of 4 May 1994. In the directive, the United States government
set criteria for United States involvement that placed a clear premium on
United States interests: "If US participation in a peace operation were to
interfere with our basic military strategy... we would place our national
interest uppermost. The United States will maintain the capability to act
unilaterally or in coalitions when our most significant interests and those
of our friends and allies are at stake. Multilateral peace operations must,
therefore, be placed in proper perspective among the instruments of US
foreign policy."[52]

the plight of victims of human rights abuses, encouraging condemnation and rebuke from large
segments of the international community, and thus putting the governments concerned under
pressure to modify their human rights policies. In effect, even bodies that ostensibly are not
known for their effectiveness or efficiency may well have an impact with their decisions.

[52] See Bureau of International Organizations Affairs, US Dept. of State, Pub. No. 10161, repr.
in (1994) 33 *International Legal Materials* 795, 801–02 (summarizing classified Presidential
Decision Directive (No. 25) on Reforming Multilateral Peacekeeping Operations, 4 May 1994).
    A most extreme form of US policy in respect of the United Nations was explained to the
Members of the UN Security Council by Senator Jesse Helms, then chair of the US Senate
Foreign Relations Committee. According to this view, the United States, as the single largest
investor in the United Nations, has "not only a right, but a responsibility, to insist on specific
reforms in exchange for [its] investment," in view of the fact that most Americans see the
United Nations "as just one part of America's diplomatic arsenal," and that "a United Nations
that seeks to impose its presumed authority on the American people without their consent begs
for confrontation and... eventual US withdrawal." It bears repeating that the rest of the US
government did not necessarily share this view. Indeed, the then Secretary of State, Madeleine
Albright, made it clear that "only the President and the Executive Branch can speak for the United
States. Today, on behalf of the President, let me say that the Administration, and I believe most
Americans, see our role in the world, and our relationship to this organization, quite differently
than does Senator Helms." See "Senator Helms Addresses UN Security Council" (2000) 94

The election of executive heads of multilateral organizations is one area in which the role played by the United States easily lends credence to the belief that the system of international governance advances the interests of the most powerful State in the international community. Consider for a moment: in 1996, the United States was able single-handedly to block the reappointment of Boutros Boutros Ghali as Secretary-General of the United Nations. Indeed, fourteen of the Security Council's fifteen members had voted in favor of his reappointment.[53] A similar power was exercised in 2000 when the United States effectively vetoed the candidacy of Germany's first choice to head the IMF, and in 2002 when it engineered the removal of the head of the Organization for the Prohibition of Chemical Weapons.[54] And even in institutions such as the WTO, where decision making ostensibly takes place on a consensus basis, the United States wields considerably more influence than other members of the WTO.[55]

The result of US predominance in the selection of executive heads of intergovernmental organizations has been a sense of disempowerment among other members of the international community, and the initiation of studies in response to several calls for a more expedient, fair, and transparent process for such appointments.[56]

It seems natural that any State should seek to shape international law and relations in ways that support its national interests and reflect the philosophical beliefs of that State. Thus in 1999 China vetoed the extension of the mandate of a UN force in the former Yugoslav Republic of Macedonia, not on the basis of disagreement as to the need for such a force, but for the

---

American Journal of International Law 350–54. These clashing sentiments again raise the issue of how one determines the preferences of the American people – and the constitutional issue of competence for foreign policy setting in the United States.

[53] See Sydney Bailey and Sam Daws, *The Procedure of the UN Security Council*, 3rd edn. (Oxford: Oxford University Press, 1998), p. 329.

[54] See Michael Elliott, "There's Got to Be a Better Way," *Newsweek*, 13 March 2000, 4; Marlise Simmons, "U. S. Forces Out Head of Chemical Arms Agency," *New York Times*, 23 April 2002, 4.

[55] At the WTO, trade laws are agreed upon less as a result of democratic voting than through a process of bargaining, negotiations, and reciprocal concessions. In effect, the WTO members exchange economic opportunities. By definition, then, the single superpower, having the most powerful economy, will derive a disproportionate advantage over other members in the formulation of trade law and policy. For a discussion on setting the rules for regulating the international economy and the role of the more powerful economies, see generally Edward Kwakwa, "Regulating the International Economy: What Role for the State?" in Michael Byers (ed.), *The Role of Law in International Politics* (Oxford: Oxford University Press, 2000), pp. 227–46.

[56] The IMF, the World Bank and the WTO have each started the process of reviewing their institutions' appointment methods; and the member States of WIPO recently adopted a new set of Policies and Practices for the Nomination and Appointment of Directors General.

simple reason that Macedonia had established a relationship with Taiwan. And in 1995, President Jacques Chirac of France announced that France would unilaterally test nuclear warheads in the Pacific Ocean. On both occasions, while some members of the international community protested, the protests were not as loud or as sustained as they might have been if the US government had carried out the actions. The reason may, again, lie in the fact that the single superpower status of the United States implies that actions by the US government carry greater weight and have deeper effects on the foundations of international law than similar actions by other governments. If that is the case, then it would seem to be that it is not unilateralism per se, but *American* unilateralism that has the most profound impact on the international community and the foundations of international law.

History and contemporary international relations are replete with examples of powerful States seeking to influence the international community in such a way as to promote their own values or perceived interests. John Gerard Ruggie admits as much when he suggests that "The most that can be said about a hegemonic power is that it will seek to construct an international order in *some* form, presumably along lines that are compatible with its own international objectives and domestic structures."[57] Louis Henkin makes a similar point by reminding us that international law seeks to promote "State commitment to its *national interest*, as the State sees it. State autonomy and impermeability imply the right of a State (not of others) to determine its national interest; to further that interest, not the interests of other States; to promote its own values as it determines them, not the values of other States or values determined by other States. A State's national interest and values, as it sees them, may (or may not) include altruistic consideration for other States, or concern for the welfare of some or all of its inhabitants."[58]

The United States government does nothing wrong or exceptional in seeking to do what it has always done, what any other single superpower would do, and what is generally admitted by scholars and observers to be common practice. States *do* act in their own national interests. The more important issue, however, is how the vital or national interests of States, or in this case, of the single superpower, are defined. Defining US interests

---

[57] John Gerard Ruggie, "Multilateralism: The Anatomy of an Institution," in John Gerard Ruggie (ed.), *Multilateralism Matters: The Theory and Praxis of an Institutional Form* (New York: Columbia University Press, 1993), p. 25.
[58] Louis Henkin, *International Law: Politics and Values* (Dordrecht: Kluwer, 1995), p. 101.

can be particularly thorny in some contexts. Robert Keohane and Joseph Nye, for example, admit that "The ambiguity of the national interest raises serious problems for the top political leaders of governments... National interests will be defined differently on different issues, at different times, and by different governmental units."[59] This observation, made in the context of any State, has particular resonance in the case of the single superpower.

United States foreign policy, Condoleezza Rice suggests, should "proceed from the firm ground of the national interest, not from the interest of an illusory international community."[60] This statement sends very mixed signals to the international community. First, it assumes that there is an identifiable or undisputed US national interest. Second, it assumes, erroneously, in my view, that the "international community" is "illusory" or nonexistent. Third, and perhaps most troubling, is its assumption that the national interests of a single superpower are necessarily at variance with, or in conflict with, the interests of the rest of the international community.

Former President Clinton's National Security Adviser had somewhat different views. Indeed, Anthony Lake was clearly of the opinion that the US national interest at any one time was a function of the interests of the wider international community.[61]

There are dozens of issues – from the Asian financial crisis to the plight of the world's least developed countries – where the United States' national interests may not easily be separable from those of the "international community." For example, US Secretary of State Colin Powell has rightly admitted that Africa's AIDS epidemic is a national security issue for the United States.[62] Similarly, despite the superpower status of the United States, it

---

[59] Keohane and Nye, *Power and Interdependence*, above note 34, at 30.
[60] Rice, "Promoting the National Interest," above note 39, at 62.
[61] In his own words:

> Those obsessed with saving America's sovereignty from the clutches of international institutions are missing the fundamental point about the new world. America's sovereignty is being lost. To some degree, it is lost to the UN and other international bodies. But to a far greater degree, America's sovereignty is being lost to the forces of globalization. The unilateralists can try to build all the walls and barriers they want. They can insist that America act alone or not at all. But many of the threats we face today, such as currency crises, international crime, drug flows, terrorism, AIDS, and pollution, cannot be defeated single-handedly or shut out at the border. Turning our backs will not turn back the clock. It will only leave us more vulnerable. (Anthony Lake, *Six Nightmares* [Boston, MA: Little, Brown & Co., 2000], p. 283.)

[62] See Jeffrey Sachs, "The Best Possible Investment in Africa," *New York Times*, 10 Feb. 2001, p. 15.

can hardly be denied that the fortunes of US workers and businesses are inextricably tied to, in addition to being the driving force for, the overall performance of the world economy. Former President Bill Clinton clearly stated in his 1993 Inaugural Address that "There is no longer division between what is foreign and what is domestic – the world economy, the world environment, the world AIDS crisis, the world arms race – they affect us all."[63]

In the context of its analysis of the IMF in 2000, the Meltzer Commission reminded us that, in 1945, the United States espoused an unprecedented definition of a nation's interest by defining its position in terms of the peace and prosperity of the global community. In the commission's words, today, "Global economic growth, political stability and the alleviation of poverty in the developing world are in the national interest of the United States."[64] This implies that the United States has a compelling interest in ensuring that relevant multilateral institutions are efficient and are able to address issues of concern to the international community as a whole. Even small-scale conflicts can sometimes have an impact on American strategic interests, as demonstrated by the conflict in Kosovo, which took place in the backyard of NATO, perhaps the most important strategic alliance to which the United States belongs.

An effective implementation of US policy in pursuit of US interests (however broadly or narrowly they may be conceived) requires cooperation from other members of the international community. It would, for example, be stating the obvious to suggest that a global organization such as the United Nations remains an indispensable instrument for the advancement of important US foreign policy objectives. Thus, the United States is currently trying to build international support for a tribunal to prosecute Iraqi President Saddam Hussein for war crimes and crimes against humanity; in the UN Security Council, the United States has recently led an effort to justify the use of force in "restoring democracy," as in Haiti, in tackling ethnic cleansing, as in Kosovo, or in disarming warlords, as in Somalia. More

---

[63] Bill Clinton, First Inaugural Address (21 Jan. 1993), reprinted at http://www.bartley.com/124/pres64.html (last visited 8 March 2002).

[64] See the Meltzer Commission Report, at http://lists.essential.org/pipermail/stop-imf/2000q1/000080.html (last visited 8 March 2002). The Meltzer Commission was established by the US Congress in 1998 to consider the future roles of seven international financial institutions, namely: International Monetary Fund, World Bank Group, Inter-American Development Bank, Asian Development Bank, African Development Bank, World Trade Organization, and Bank for International Settlements.

recently, following the terrorist attacks on 11 September 2001 on New York, Washington and Pennsylvania, the US government went out of its way to ensure that any retaliatory action was taken within the context of as broad a global coalition as possible.[65] And in the context of global finance, the US government admits itself that the international financial institutions "are among the most effective and cost-efficient means available to advance US policy priorities worldwide."[66] This is a clear recognition that any global financial stability promoted by multilateral institutions serves to enhance US prosperity.

The international community remains a critically important instrument for the advancement of US national interests and foreign policy objectives.[67] As discussed below, the United States also remains a critically important State, in several respects, in the international community's formulation of international law.

The place and the role of the United States in international law

The ascent of a sole superpower has clearly affected the distribution of capabilities or responsibilities among members of the international community. In effect, the growing inequalities in the international community serve to enhance the role of the more powerful. This is the sense in which the United States has the greatest opportunity, but also the most pressing need, to influence the development of international law more heavily than it did in the past.

There are aspects of the international community endeavor whose rules the United States has played an active part in crafting, but it has subsequently refused to sign on to the final product, especially when the majority of States adopt positions that the United States does not perceive to be in its interests. A recent example is the US refusal to ratify the Rome Statute of the International Criminal Court, citing, among others, its military reach and

---

[65] There is every reason to suggest that the terrorist attacks of September 2001 initially had the effect of making the United States more constructively involved internationally. The US government's renewed policy of cooperative engagement after the terrorist attacks was a striking departure from its earlier policies of unilateralism.

[66] See US Department of the Treasury Response to Report of the International Financial Institutions Advisory Commission, 2, reprinted at http://www.treas.gov/press/releases/docs/response.pdf.

[67] On the subject of international law and the US national interest, see generally Michael Byers, "International Law and the American National Interest" (2000) 1 *Chicago Journal of International Law* 257–61.

the global deployment of US troops as a reason why it was concerned about some of the statute's provisions.[68] This US practice of actively participating in treaty making but declining to ratify at the end has been compared to the title character in the Hollywood film *The Runaway Bride*, in which Julia Roberts always led her partners to the altar after negotiating elaborate prenuptial agreements, only to rescind her decision during the final wedding ceremonies.[69]

There are also instances in which the United States has been actively involved in international law making, but subsequently sought, in applying that law, to subordinate it to domestic US law. To cite only one example, when the US Congress enacted domestic legislation to implement the Uruguay Round Final Act setting up the World Trade Organization, it made sure to provide that no provision of the WTO agreements, nor the application of any such provision to any person or circumstance, that is inconsistent with any United States law shall have effect. The legislation also precluded private parties from using the WTO agreements as a basis for challenging any federal, state or local action in a United States court.[70] In this regard, it is instructive to recall Harold Koh's argument that norm internationalization – the process by which States incorporate or internalize international law domestically – is a critical factor in ascertaining why States obey international law.[71] In the case of the United States, its unique system of federalism, in particular the intricacies of the relationship between the federal government and the state governments, as well as the separation of powers enshrined in the United States Constitution, not to mention the generally complicated relationship between treaty law and United States domestic law, arguably introduce certain important factors or impediments to multilateral cooperation that do not exist in other countries. These factors

---

[68] See David Scheffer, "The United States and the International Criminal Court" (1999) 93 *American Journal of International Law* 12 (arguing that "No other country, not even our closest military allies, has anywhere near as many troops and military assets deployed globally as does the United States"). *Ibid.*, 18.

[69] See Patrick, "America's Retreat," above note 18, at 430 (quoting American University Law Professor Kenneth Anderson).

[70] See Section 102, Uruguay Round Agreements Act (1994).

[71] See Harold Koh, "Why do Nations Obey International Law?" (1997) 10 *Yale Law Journal* 2599, 2646. See also Harold Koh, "Bringing International Law Home" (1998) 35 *Houston Law Review* 623–81 (in the context of how nations internalize or domesticate international law, discussing why nations obey, as opposed to merely comply with, international law).

may be relevant in assessing the degree of importance that the single super-power attaches to international law.[72]

The United States has not always had its way in lawmaking, and there is evidence to suggest that a mere refusal by the United States to participate in a legal regime does not automatically spell the death knell of that regime. For example, the 1982 UN Convention on the Law of the Sea, which the United States refused to sign and has failed to accede to, entered into force in 1994 and now has 138 parties. The 1992 Convention on Biological Diversity was signed but has not been ratified by the United States. Nevertheless, it has gained an almost universal membership of 183 States party as of March 2002. And the 1997 Ottawa Landmines Convention, which the United States refused to sign and has not acceded to, currently has 122 States party, including all the traditional economic and military allies of the United States. In November 1999, during the Seattle Ministerial Conference of the WTO, the United States government proposed sanctions on countries that failed to meet new labor and environmental standards. This proposal was immediately rejected not only by the developing countries, but also by the United States' closest trading partners. These examples, at a minimum, suggest that there are limits to the indispensability of the United States in international lawmaking.

But in several other respects, the United States has more or less had its way in international lawmaking, as the examples below demonstrate.

One of the most worn-out phrases in the last few years is the reference to the knowledge-based economy. According to a widely held view, knowledge, which is defined to include information technology, is the newest and most important factor of production in the global economy.[73] If this

---

[72] For example, under a time-honored principle of US foreign relations law, treaties, and statutes are equal in status, and their order of priority is determined by the later in time rule. This rule, the separation of powers doctrine and the impact of the US system of federalism on the international legal obligations of the United States are the subject of extensive discussion in the literature. See, e.g., Harry Blackmun, "The Supreme Court and the Law of Nations" (1994) 104 *Yale Law Journal* 39–49; special issue by various authors on "The United States Constitution in its Third Century: Foreign Affairs" (1989) 83 *American Journal of International Law* 713–900; Frederic Kirgis, "International Agreements and United States Law" (*American Society of International Law Insight*, May 1997), repr. at http://www.asil.org/insights/insigh10.htm (last visited 8 March 2002); John Jackson, "Status of Treaties in Domestic Legal Systems: A Policy Analysis" (1992) 86 *American Journal of International Law* 310–40.

[73] See, e.g., World Bank, *World Development Report 1998/99: Knowledge for Development* (New York: Oxford University Press, 1999). Keohane and Nye, among others, predicted that in this

view holds true, then it has important implications for the contours of our inquiry. For example, the technological supremacy of the United States has had the effect of projecting the power of US nongovernmental organizations in lawmaking in the field of electronic commerce, particularly as it relates to the Internet. In 1998, the Internet Corporation for Assigned Names and Numbers (ICANN) was formed in response to a suggestion by the United States government that the private sector create such a body to assume responsibility for certain administrative and technical aspects of the Domain Name system, the Internet address space allocation and root server system management functions.[74] As stated in its Articles of Incorporation, ICANN is a nonprofit public interest corporation organized under the California Nonprofit Public Benefit Corporation Law.[75] In that sense, ICANN is simply a US entity and not an intergovernmental organization with global representation.[76]

In its relatively short period of existence, however, ICANN has had a significant impact in the area of the governance of the Internet Domain Name system. Among other initiatives, it has introduced seven new generic Top Level Domains (gTLDs) into the Domain Name system.[77] More significantly, ICANN adopted a proposal by the World Intellectual Property Organization (WIPO), an intergovernmental organization with

century, "information technology, broadly defined, is likely to be the most important power source." Robert Keohane and Joseph Nye, "Power and Interdependence in the Information Age" (1998) 77(5) *Foreign Affairs* 81, at 87. See also Nye, *The Paradox of American Power*, above note 35, pp. 41–76 (describing the impact of the information revolution on the nature of governments and sovereignty, the role of non-State actors and the conduct of American foreign policy).

[74] In June 1998, the National Telecommunications and Information Administration (NTIA), an agency of the United States Department of Commerce, issued a "White Paper" that called for the creation of a new, private, not-for-profit corporation that would be responsible for coordinating certain domain name system functions for the benefit of the Internet as a whole. The creation of ICANN was a result of the process that followed the publication of the White Paper. See http://www.ntia.doc.gov/ntiahome/domainname/6_5_98dns.htm (last visited 8 March 2002).

[75] ICANN's Articles of Incorporation, at http://www.icann.org/general/articles/htm (last visited 8 March 2002).

[76] In response to criticism of its legitimacy, ICANN held a worldwide online vote in 2000 aimed at obtaining a large, globally diverse membership. As a result of that vote, five new members were elected to the ICANN Board of Directors from each of five geographic regions: Africa, Asia/Australasia/Pacific, Europe, Latin America/Caribbean, and North America. See http://www.members.icann.org (last visited 8 March 2002).

[77] At its meeting in November 2000, ICANN selected the following new gTLDs: .aero, .biz, .coop, .info, .museum, .name and .pro. See http://www.icann.org/minutes.prelim-report-16nov00.htm# Second Annual Meeting (last visited 8 March 2002).

179 member States, to establish the Uniform Domain Name Dispute Resolution Policy (UDRP).[78] This has resulted in the implementation of a successful administrative system for resolving domain name disputes involving trademarks as well as a system of best practices for domain name registration authorities, designed to avoid such disputes.[79] The UDRP is now used worldwide and has, in effect, set clear standards for the resolution of intellectual property disputes in cyberspace. It seems fair to conclude that the initiatives that ICANN has undertaken to date follow the US view of what the substantive policy should be in respect of the Internet. Clearly, the global reach and technological supremacy of the United States has not only made that country an indispensable actor in several areas of international law, but has also made some United States-based nongovernmental entities indispensable players in certain aspects of international legal regulation.[80]

It can hardly be denied that the global reach of the United States often makes it an indispensable party in multilateral treaty making. A recent event at WIPO provides a case in point. In December 2000, the member States of WIPO met in a diplomatic conference aimed at adopting a treaty on the protection of audiovisual performers – actors, singers, and musicians – in a digital age. Although the delegates reached provisional agreement on nineteen of the twenty articles which were to make up the proposed treaty, they were unable to adopt a treaty at the end of the conference, for a simple

---

[78] As explained in the Report of the Second WIPO Internet Domain Name Process, however, the UDRP "does not seek to regulate the whole universe of the interface between trademarks and domain names, but only to implement the lowest common denominator of internationally agreed and accepted principles concerning the abuse of trademarks. The exercise was less about legislation than about the efficient application of existing law in a multijurisdictional and cross-territorial space." Moreover, the Second WIPO Internet Domain Name Process involves more difficult and as yet unanswered questions that have far-reaching implications for the manner in which the international community creates law in this completely new area. See WIPO, *The Recognition of Rights and the Use of Names in the Internet Domain Name System: Report of the Second WIPO Internet Domain Name Process* (3 Sept. 2001), para. 66, reprinted at http://wipo2.wipo.int (last visited 8 March 2002).

[79] In its first year of operation alone, the UDRP of WIPO received some 2,000 cases, including submissions from such celebrities as Julia Roberts, Bruce Springsteen, Venus and Serena Williams, Isabelle Adjani and Madonna, as well as major corporations such as Microsoft, General Electric and Nokia. See http://arbiter.wipo.int/domainsbackground/index.html (last visited 8 March 2002).

[80] For a more general discussion of the changing playing field in rule making in the intellectual property arena, see Edward Kwakwa, "Some Comments on Rule Making at the World Intellectual Property Organization" (2002) 12 *Duke Journal of Comparative and International Law* 179–95.

reason: there was fundamental disagreement between the United States and the European Union over how performers' rights are transferred to producers, who then export the works for commercial use. The United States insisted on ensuring the international recognition of its domestic system, under which performers automatically sign over their rights to producers, but receive payments for their work negotiated by trade unions. The majority of the States represented at the conference did not lose sight of the fact that, with the possible exception of India, the United States happens, thanks to Hollywood, to be the world's largest producer of films. The United States was therefore accused of trying indirectly to enforce US law abroad.[81] The fact remains, however, that the States involved recognized and accepted the obvious truth – that they could not adopt a treaty on the protection of audiovisual performers if the single superpower was not on board, given the pervasive nature and dominance of the US audiovisual industry.

Similarly, in 1989 the member States of WIPO adopted a Treaty on Intellectual Property in Respect of Integrated Circuits. As it turns out, that Treaty never entered into force. It has been rendered inoperable because the United States (which owns more than 50 percent of the world's semiconductor industry associated with integrated circuits) refused to sign the final text, which did not reflect its position.[82]

These examples are all taken from a single organization, WIPO. However, they cover a wide spectrum of subjects in terms of law creation. They also reinforce the perception that the international community cannot do without the United States in certain areas of international law.[83] The position of the United States vis-à-vis law creation through treaty making is

---

[81] See generally Frances Williams, "Dispute Hits Performing Rights Deal," *Financial Times*, 22 Dec. 2000.

[82] It is significant that although the Treaty on Intellectual Property in Respect of Integrated Circuits never entered into force, it is cited and incorporated by reference in such major treaties as the Marrakesh Agreement Establishing the World Trade Organization. See, e.g., Art. I (3) of the Agreement on Trade-Related Aspects of Intellectual Property Rights, reprinted in WTO, *The Results of the Uruguay Round of Multilateral Trade Negotiations* (Geneva: WTO, 1995) 366.

[83] There are also certain instances in which the economic might of the United States has enabled it to engage in indirect lawmaking. A good example of this is the use of Section 301 to pressure developing countries such as Brazil into accepting the TRIPS Agreement. For a general discussion of Section 301 and its application to developing and other countries, see Lynne Puckett and William Reynolds, "Rules, Sanctions and Enforcement Under Section 301: At Odds with the WTO?" (1996) 90 *American Journal of International Law* 675–89; Matthew Schaefer, "Section 301 and the World Trade Organization: A Largely Peaceful Coexistence to Date" (1998) 1 *Journal of International Economic Law* 156–60.

the subject of more extensive analysis in other chapters in this book.[84] For purposes of our topic, however, it suffices to observe the following: in the last couple of years alone, the United States government has distanced itself from much of the international community in respect of various attempts at lawmaking. In January 2001, it announced that it would not send the treaty establishing an International Criminal Court to the Senate for ratification; in March 2001, it abrogated agreements on global warming regulations as defined in the 1997 Kyoto Protocol; in May 2001, it threatened to repudiate the 1972 Anti-Ballistic Missile Treaty, and later did so; and in July 2001, it rejected a draft protocol that would have added enforcement mechanisms to the 1972 Biological Weapons Convention. This prompted the *Economist* magazine to inquire in one of its editorials: "Has George Bush ever met a treaty that he liked?"[85]

Richard Haass, the US State Department's Director of Policy Planning, refers to the US government's attitude as "à la carte multilateralism."[86] According to this view, the United States government will look at each agreement and decide on a case-by-case basis which treaties clearly promote the national interest and will therefore be adopted by the United States. Of course, "à la carte multilateralism" is at the heart of the foreign policy planning and strategy of most States: I can hardly think of a State that would adopt a treaty that did not meet or promote its national interest. The difference, once again, is that "à la carte multilateralism" by the single superpower means a lot more in international law and in the international community than "à la carte multilateralism" on the part of, say, tiny San Marino.

The fact that most of the evidence seems to be consistent with what Richard Haass terms "à la carte multilateralism" should hardly comfort those who deem a strengthening of international law and international organizations to be essential for the international community. Indeed, as aptly pointed out by Volker Rittberger, "we should be clear that 'à la carte multilateralism' is really not multilateralism at all, if this idea involves a generalized commitment to international cooperation and international institutions based on diffuse reciprocity."[87]

[84] See chapters by Catherine Redgwell and Pierre Klein, below.
[85] See *The Economist*, 28 July 2002, 47.
[86] See Thom Shanker,"White House Says the US is Not a Loner, Just Choosy," *New York Times*, 31 July 2001, 1.
[87] See Rittberger, below, p. 110.

Also worrying is the fact that what constitutes the US "national interest" will always be a dynamic, shifting pole rather than a fixed and determinate constant. It will inevitably change from time to time, and from government to government. In that situation, "à la carte multilateralism" by the single superpower could have potentially hazardous effects on the formulation or ascertaining of international law and its impact on the international community.

Refusal by the United States to ratify international treaties or to join legal regimes that are accepted by a wide segment of the international community should not be construed to mean a rejection of the international community by the United States. Indeed, US refusal to participate in a legal regime is a sovereign right that should be distinguished from the question of US compliance with its treaty obligations. Adherence to a legal regime and compliance with obligations under that regime are separate and distinct acts. The point remains, nevertheless, that to the extent that treaty bodies and other international organizations extend participation rights only to member States, the United States thereby loses the opportunity to help shape those international regimes that it rejects. For example, it is now conventional wisdom that the United States will not ratify the Statute of the International Criminal Court in the near future. It is noteworthy, however, that the United States participated fully in the negotiating process and, as a result, managed to obtain the inclusion of certain provisions that were deemed vital to US national interests. The reasonable conclusion seems to be that the extent to which the United States can affect certain international community activity outcomes is a function of the extent to which the United States is involved in the community activity.

Similarly, for as long as the United States abstains from ratification of the nuclear test ban treaty, any American efforts to discourage additional countries from developing nuclear weapons are taken less seriously by the rest of the international community. The refusal to ratify also seriously hampers US efforts, in the wake of the September 2001 terrorist attacks, to strengthen the verification safeguards needed to ensure the peaceful use of nuclear capabilities. And US refusal to join the Convention on the Rights of the Child can only slow efforts by the international community to protect human rights in that area.

To be sure, the benefits of United States multilateralism for the United States itself, and for the international community as a whole, are hardly recondite. As argued by Michael Byers, isolationist or unilateralist policies can only have a detrimental effect upon the long-term national interest of the United States.[88] A turn toward isolationism will, in all likelihood, adversely affect the United States' reputation and leadership role in the international community. US multilateralism, on the other hand, may be an effective means of persuading other States to participate in activities that ultimately serve US interests. Above all, the global nature of transnational challenges, and the mutual interests of the United States and the rest of the international community not only suggest, but also dictate, the need for active US participation in international community activity and lawmaking.

Michael Reisman makes the point with particular clarity when he states, in the context of designing and managing the future of the State, that:

> Even the security of the remaining Superpower cannot be accomplished alone. In terms of military matériel, the United States may have been the only country that could have fought the Gulf War on its own. But it could not *afford* to do it on its own ... And when other national security issues, such as preventing the diffusion of nuclear, chemical and biological weapons to state and non-State entities, are augmented by other concerns, such as stemming the transnational migration of disease, protecting the environment, and assuring access to external markets, national subordination to international arrangements is seen as ineluctable.[89]

By weakening multilateral organizations the United States makes itself more vulnerable to the risks and dangers posed by a more globalized post–Cold War world. Our analysis has shown that the United States' superpower status does not make it immune from events or activities in the international community, however the common values and interests of that community, or even of the United States alone, are defined. Admittedly, the common interests of the international community will not always be easily identifiable.

---

[88] Byers, "International Law and the American National Interest," above note 67, at 260.

[89] Michael Reisman, "Designing and Managing the Future of the State," (1997) 8 *European Journal of International Law*, 409–10. Joseph Nye has convincingly argued in his most recent book that the world's only superpower *must* adopt a more cooperative and multilateral engagement with the rest of the international community. See generally Nye, *The Paradox of American Power*, above note 35. For other recent critiques of US unilateralism, see e.g. Peter Malanczuk, "The International Criminal Court and Landmines: What are the Consequences of Leaving the US Behind?" (2000) 11 *European Journal of International Law* 77; Pierre-Marie Dupuy, "The Place and Role of Unilateralism in Contemporary International law," *ibid.*, 19; Bernard Jansen, *ibid.*

For views to the contrary, see e.g. Jesse Helms, "American Sovereignty and the UN" (2000/01) 62 *The National Interest* 31–4; Rice, "Promoting the National Interest," above note 39; and David Rivkin Jr. and Lee Casey, "The Rocky Shoals of International Law" (2000/01) 62 *The National Interest* 35–45.

But they will be more easily identified and be better served if as many members of the international community as possible participate in promoting them. In that regard, the participation of the single superpower could be crucial. Indeed, while US refusal to join a legal regime does not equate with US rejection of international law, it is arguable that in those instances in which the United States is an indispensable party for the formulation of international law, any unilateralist stance by the United States could be tantamount to the single superpower impeding or opposing the development of that law.

Conclusion

The need for a more effective system of creating and applying international law in this period of single superpowerdom is more urgent than it was during the Cold War. The single superpower status of the United States poses a paradox: the international community cannot do without the United States in most areas of international community activity and in most areas of international lawmaking. At the same time, the United States needs the international community in order to promote its own national interests and foreign policy objectives. In other words, the United States needs the international community and international law as much as the international community and international law need the United States. The challenge to international law and international relations scholars is to ascertain and clarify continuously how best this paradox can be resolved.

It seems reasonable to conclude that, although the international community, international law, and the United States are not one and the same, neither are they two against one, as is often assumed. There are several instances in which the United States has demonstrated that it is one on its own, but that is a far cry from being one against the other two.

When the interests of the United States coincide with those of the wider international community, international law will more easily be made and a greater level of compliance will result. At other times, the interests of the United States will be at variance with those of a significant segment of the international community. In those instances, the chances for the creation and application of effective international law will often, but not always, be greatly diminished.

2

The influence of the United States on the concept of the "international community"

ANDREAS PAULUS

> But do the nations constitute a community? . . . The history of International Law is, largely, the history of the formation of this community, so far as it may be said to have been formed – the building up of common opinions upon common practices and the writings of commonly accepted commentators.
>
> Woodrow Wilson, later president of the United States[1]

> Foreign policy in a Republican administration will most certainly be internationalist . . . But it will also proceed from the firm ground of the national interest, not from the interests of an illusory international community.
>
> Condoleezza Rice, now US National Security Advisor[2]

> Every nation in every region now has a decision to make. Either you are with us, or you are with the terrorists . . .
> This is not, however, just America's fight. And what is at stake is not just America's freedom. This is the world's fight. This is civilization's fight. This is the fight of all who believe in progress and pluralism, tolerance and freedom.
>
> George W. Bush, president of the United States[3]

In the age of globalization, the "international community" appears omnipresent: it acts and intervenes, as in the case of Kosovo, it helps the victims of natural disasters, is called upon to redouble its efforts to prevent

[1] "Notes for a Classroom Lecture," 8 March 1892, in Arthur S. Link (ed.), *The Papers of Woodrow Wilson*, VII (Princeton: Princeton University Press, 1969), p. 455.
[2] Condoleezza Rice, "Promoting the National Interest" (2000) 79 *Foreign Affairs*, 45–62.
[3] George W. Bush, "Address to the Nation by the President of the United States," 147 *Congressional Record* H5737, 5859, 5861 (daily edn. 20 Sept. 2001).

and suppress terrorist acts, as after the attacks against the United States on September 11,[4] or seems helpless and inactive in spite of its best intentions, as in Congo or Sudan. Resolutions of international organizations and NGO conferences alike use the term in an almost inflationary way. It is not only one of the favorites of UN Secretary-General Kofi Annan,[5] but is also invoked by statespersons around the world. Pierre Klein has found the term in no less than seventy documents connected with NATO's intervention in the Kosovo conflict.[6] It is perhaps no coincidence that the popularity of the concept has grown along with the awareness of the consequences of globalization. Whereas the latter stands for the sometimes harsh economic realities of an age which seems no longer to allow for the territorial protection of local habits and mores, the "international community" connotes the emergence of a new global home, a worldwide village of human commonality emphasizing interpersonal bonds more than territorial borders. And yet, it may also be used for the exclusion of others; rogue States, terrorists,[7] and even antiglobalization activists seem not to be part of it.

The frequent use of the concept, however, is not matched by any clarity of content.[8] For instance, when announcing NATO's decision to attack the Federal Republic of Yugoslavia despite the absence of an authorizing UN Security Council resolution, NATO's Secretary-General, Javier Solana, explained:

> This military action is intended to support the political aims of the international community . . . Our objective is to prevent more human suffering and more repression and violence against the civilian population of Kosovo.[9]

From that perspective, NATO did not need backing from the world organization to protect the political and humanitarian goals of the international

---

[4] See UN Doc. S/RES/1368 (2001), 12 Sept. 2001, operative para. 4.

[5] Kofi A. Annan, "The Meaning of International Community," Address to the 52nd DPI/NGO Conference, 15 Sept. 1999, UN Press Release SG/SM/7133, PI/1176, 2. See also Annan, "Fighting Terrorism on a Global Front," New York Times, 21 Sept. 2001, A 35.

[6] Pierre Klein, "Les Problèmes soulevés par la référence à la 'communauté internationale' comme facteur de légitimité," in Olivier Corten and Barbara Delcourt (eds.), Droit, légitimation et politique extérieure: l'Europe et la guerre du Kosovo (Brussels: Bruylant 2000), p. 262.

[7] Cf. Annan, "Fighting Terrorism on a Global Front," above note 5.

[8] For a particularly acerbic critique of the incoherence of the use of the term during the Kosovo crisis, see Klein, "Les Problèmes soulevés," above note 6, 265–81.

[9] Press Statement by Javier Solana, Secretary-General of NATO, 23 March 1999, in Marc Weller (ed.), International Documents and Analysis 1 (Cambridge: Documents & Analysis Publishing, 1999), p. 495.

community. It was India's permanent representative at the United Nations, Kamlesh Sharma, who challenged that assumption:

> Those who continue to attack the Federal Republic of Yugoslavia profess to do so on behalf of the international community and on pressing humanitarian grounds. They say that they are acting in the name of humanity. Very few members of the international community have spoken in this debate, but even among those who have, NATO would have noted that China, Russia and India have all opposed the violence that it has unleashed. The international community can hardly be said to have endorsed their actions when already representatives of half of humanity have said that they do not agree with what they have done.[10]

Sharma was thereby not only charging NATO with hypocrisy, but insisting on the need of representative pronouncements in order to claim the support of the "international community." Note also that the criterion of representation was not the number of State governments supporting this or that action, but the number of people they represent.

The importance of this debate is not limited to the dictates of the day or the necessity of justifying a contested unilateral intervention. It expresses a much deeper schism which permeates the use and understanding of the concept of "international community." Even if none of the representatives cited in the previous few paragraphs are American, the debate is nonetheless telling concerning the differences of understanding between the United States as the sole superpower and other members of the international community.

Before we trace the usage of the concept and the US influence on it, we should first answer the question why it is that such a nebulous term has covered such broad ground. What distinguishes a "community" from a "society"? As a more extensive inquiry has shown,[11] the usage is far from uniform. Nevertheless, one may say – with the necessary caution – that a community adds a normative element, a minimum of subjective cohesion to the social bond between its members. Whereas "society" emphasizes

---

[10] Security Council, Fifty-fourth Year, 3989th mtg., 24 March 1999, UN Doc. S/PV 3989 (1999), 16; cf. Vera Gowlland-Debbas, "The Limits of Unilateral Enforcement of Community Objectives in the Framework of UN Peace Maintenance," (2000) 11 *European Journal of International Law* 361 at 376–7.

[11] Andreas L. Paulus, *Die internationale Gemeinschaft im Völkerrecht* (Munich: Beck, 2001), pp. 9 *et seq.*, 439 *et seq.*

factual interconnections and interrelations, "community" looks to values, beliefs, and subjective feelings of commonality. The differentiation between "society" and "community" thus echoes the German sociologist Ferdinand Tönnies' distinction in his groundbreaking book *Gemeinschaft und Gesellschaft*.[12] But despite the inclusiveness of the term, even a universal community knows an outside, an environment against which it defines and delineates its identity.[13] Hence the debate on "rogue States" and an alleged "axis of evil" comprising Iran, Iraq, and North Korea,[14] all of which are outside the alleged consensus.

The use of the concept of the "international community" is of particular relevance to an analysis of the background understandings of the contemporary world in general, and to international law more specifically. It also reveals differing positions on many international problems. This chapter will analyse both the US position on the usage of the "international community" concept in some of the pertinent legal documents and the influence of US doctrine and practice on the use of the concept by others.

The concept of "international community" in United States scholarship

Every concept of international law is based on an understanding of the social structure to which international law applies. Accordingly, every theory of international law involves, explicitly or implicitly, a concept of international community or society. At the same time, those "background understandings" are mostly not of an exclusively legal character. They refer both to a perception of the international political environment and to an ethical or normative understanding of the purpose of international law. Thus, legal, political, and ethical understandings are closely intertwined.

Of course, it will not be possible to trace the development of the concept of community in this brief chapter. But there is enough space to sketch out the debate as it relates to the international sphere, with a special emphasis on US perspectives. I shall develop four different approaches to the

---

[12] Ferdinand Tönnies, *Gemeinschaft und Gesellschaft: Grundbegriffe der reinen Soziologie*, 8th edn. (Leipzig: Buske, 1935).

[13] Bruno Simma and Andreas L. Paulus, "The 'International Community': Facing the Challenge of Globalization," (1998) 9 *European Journal of International Law* 266, at 268.

[14] George W. Bush, State of the Union Address by the President of the United States, 148 *Congressional Record* H83, 98, 99 (daily edn. 29 Jan. 2002).

concept of international community which have been heavily influenced by US scholars – or, rather, scholars working in the United States – coming not only from a background in international law, but also international relations or ethics. A *traditional* conception corresponds to much of the Realist literature in the first half of the twentieth century. An *institutionalized* understanding not only represents the ideals of the 1960s, but also expresses the current understanding of most States and many academics. A *liberal* interpretation is largely consonant with US self-understanding and doctrinal views frequently expressed by US writers. Finally, I will add a *postmodern* understanding of international community – or rather its absence.

None of those concepts is exclusively American. And none of them is a monolith which knows not of internal differences and even contradictions, sometimes even in the writings of a single scholar at different historical junctures. It is thus not my intention simply to juxtapose an "American" view with that of the "rest of the world." This would not only amount to a denial of one of the greatest American virtues, namely the diversity of perspectives and the culture of open discussion and debate. It would also underestimate the American influence on the rest of the world, both in terms of power and ideology. The discussion between Javier Solana and Kamlesh Sharma on the Kosovo intervention, the one European, the other Indian, is a case in point. Nevertheless, the discussion on the meaning and impact of community reveals a considerable American bias whose influence over the concept can hardly be underestimated. The US influence on the term also perfectly demonstrates that country's double role in the international system, as both a hegemonic power providing for public goods and shared values, and as the sole superpower able and willing to act unilaterally in its own interests.[15]

The point of departure: a realist understanding of the international legal community

The distinction drawn by Ferdinand Tönnies between *Gesellschaft* (society) on the one hand and *Gemeinschaft* (community) on the other, is very

---

[15] See Bruce Cronin, "The Paradox of Hegemony: America's Ambiguous Relationship with the United Nations" (2001) 7 *European Journal of International Relations*, 103, at 104 *et passim*, and the statement by Rice, "Promoting the National Interest", above note 2 and accompanying text. See also Robert O. Keohane, *After Hegemony: Cooperation and Discord in the World Political Economy* (Princeton: Princeton University Press, 1986).

popular in international legal writing.[16] The German sociologist of the late nineteenth and early twentieth century understood *Gemeinschaft* as referring to an organic unity with natural bonds between its members, whereas *Gesellschaft* was artificially created. *Gemeinschaft* is an aim in itself; *Gesellschaft* serves the individual purposes of its members. Community is prior to its members; society is subordinate to their interests. Tönnies characterized modernity as a move from community to society. Transferred to the international level, this led to an understanding of international relations as a society of States fighting for survival.[17]

Similarly, for American political realists and neorealists such as Hans Morgenthau and Kenneth Waltz, the State is the basic unit and power the main instrument of international relations.[18] From this perspective, the use of the term "international community" serves nothing but the rhetorical purpose of masking the pursuit of power. Although institutionalists such as Robert Keohane emphasize the benefits of inter-State cooperation and common institutions, they share with realists the background assumption of the analytical priority of the State as the basic unit of international relations, if only for analytical purposes.[19]

---

[16] Compare Marcel M. T. A. Brus, *Third Party Dispute Settlement in an Interdependent World* (Dordrecht, Boston, London: Nijhoff 1995), pp. 89, 108; René-Jean Dupuy, *La Communauté internationale entre le mythe et l'histoire* (Paris: Economica 1986), p. 15; Louis Henkin, *International Law: Politics and Values* (Dordrecht: Nijhoff 1995), at 7, 106, 298 n. 11; Hermann Mosler, "The International Society as a Legal Community," (1974) 140 *Recueil des cours* 1 at 27–30, 70; Bruno Simma, "From Bilateralism to Community Interest in International Law," (1994) 250 *Recueil des cours* 217 at 245; Christian Tomuschat, "Obligations Arising for States without or against Their Will," (1993) 241 *Recueil des cours* 195 at 222–36; Tomuschat, "International Law: Ensuring the Survival of Mankind on the Eve of a New Century. General Course on Public International Law," (1999) 281 *Recueil des cours* 9 at 72–88.

[17] Ferdinand Tönnies, *Wege zu dauerndem Frieden?* (Leipzig: C.L. Hirschfeld, 1926), p. 34 *et passim*.

[18] See only Hans J. Morgenthau, *Politics Among Nations: The Struggle for Power and Peace*, 5th rev. edn. (New York: Alfred A. Knopf 1977), pp. 4–12; Kenneth N. Waltz, *Theory of International Politics* (Reading, MA: Addison-Wesley 1977), pp. 88–99. See also Robert O. Keohane, "Theory of World Politics: Structural Realism and Beyond," in Robert Keohane (ed.), *Neorealism and Its Critics* (New York: Columbia University Press, 1986), pp. 164–5.

[19] Arthur Stein, "Coordination and Collaboration: Regimes in an Anarchic World," in Stephen Krasner (ed.), *International Regimes* (Ithaca, London: Princeton University Press, 1983), 115, at 140; cf. Andrew Hurrell, "International Society and the Study of Regimes: A Reflective Approach", in Volker Rittberger (ed.), *Regime Theory and International Relations* (Oxford: Clarendon Press 1993), 49, pp. 55–6. For a critique of the rationalism of much of IR theory, see Daniel Warner, "The Nuclear Weapons Decision by the International Court of Justice: Locating the raison behind raison d'état," (1998) 27 *Millennium* 299 at 323.

Even if international relations is a discipline dominated by American writers,[20] this view was not limited to researchers from – or who had emigrated from Europe to[21] – the United States. On the contrary, it is, with some variations, representative for the whole discipline at least in the West, be it French, as in the case of Raymond Aron,[22] or British, as in the cases of Edward Hallett Carr and Hedley Bull.[23] However, in American writings of the neorealist school, there is a particular emphasis on, even predominance of, hard factors such as military strength and economic capacity, whereas scholars teaching in Europe, such as Bull or Aron, have preferred more holistic approaches.

The influence of a realist analysis on the understanding of "international community" is obvious. If States are serving their individual interest, the space for a true community in Tönnies' sense is minimal. In the words of Gene Lyons and Michael Mastanduno:

> realists are skeptical of the notion of international community and hold that international intervention can still best be understood in terms of the power and interests of particular nation-states, especially great powers, acting individually or collectively. Those states may cloak their interests in the language of the common good and may claim to be acting in the name of the international community, but ultimately they are driven by calculations of national interest rather than by the appeal of community values.[24]

As "community" does not adequately describe the international reality, it merely constitutes a phenomenon of the "Überbau," of the philosophical (and propagandist) super-structure, as Karl Marx would have put it. On

---

[20] But see Knud Erik Jørgensen, "Continental IR Theory: The Best Kept Secret", (2000) 6 *European Journal of International Relations* 9.

[21] Jørgensen, *ibid.*, at 13, claims that "Morgenthau's realist thinking was... based on typical Continental political thought." Indeed, it would be incorrect to call realist thinking an American project, as it inherits such European figures as Thucydides, Machiavelli, and Hobbes. American political realism was, in fact, largely founded by fugitives from Germany, such as Morgenthau, Niebuhr and Wolfers. Jørgensen concludes: "Much criticism of state-centric realism is probably, in reality, American critique of Continental conceptions of the state." *Ibid.*, at 15.

[22] Raymond Aron, *Paix et Guerre entre les nations* (Paris: Calmann-Lévy, 1962).

[23] Hedley Bull, *The Anarchical Society: A Study of Order in World Politics* (London: Macmillan 1977).

[24] Gene M. Lyons and Michael Mastanduno, "International Intervention, State Sovereignty, and the Future of International Society," in Gene Lyons and Michael Mastanduno (eds.), *Beyond Westphalia? State Sovereignty and Intervention* (Baltimore, London: Johns Hopkins University Press, 1995), p. 13. Similarly Rice, "Promoting the National Interest," above note 2.

the one hand, it invites abuse for the purposes of propaganda. On the other, it calls for strong leadership backed by power not from "above," from the system, so to speak, but from the strongest component of the system. In other words, it calls for leadership by the strongest power, providing both the necessary "hardware" and the values of the community.

The concept of a "community" by superpower leadership is very popular in US international relations theory, as much after the Cold War as before. For example, in Robert Keohane's writing[25] the European reader recognizes a nostalgia for the happy days of undisputed American hegemony. Such a view can be used in the post–Cold War world to justify American hegemony with reference to its achievements for world peace and stability.[26] In that sense, institutions are useful for the stabilization of benign hegemony rather than for its substitution. They are tools for the realization of the individual values of the participants, not for the realization of a collective good. After the end of the Cold War, even a leading institutionalist such as Joseph Nye believes in the virtues of American leadership[27] rather than in new institutional designs for a new world order.

The realist view of the limits of international community also restricts the possibility of international law. Louis Henkin emphasizes that "state values" of traditional international law prevail over "community values" such as human rights or sustainable development.[28] Still, after the end of the Cold War, he also sees the possibility of change on the horizon.[29] When dealing with the legitimacy of international law shortly before the end of the Cold War,[30] Thomas Franck presented a weak version of the concept of a "legal community" and maintained that nothing but the existence of law turns

[25] Keohane, *After Hegemony*, above note 15, at 243–7.
[26] See also Lea Brilmayer, *American Hegemony: Political Morality in a One-Superpower World* (New Haven, London: Yale University Press, 1994), pp. 169–72; John Gerard Ruggie, *Winning the Peace* (New York: Columbia University Press, 1996), 48–49. For a more skeptical British view see Susan Strange, *States and Markets* 2nd edn. (London, Washington, DC: Pinter, 1994), pp. 237–42; cf. also Robert G. Gilpin, *The Political Economy of International Relations* (Princeton: Princeton University Press, 1987), p. 345.
[27] Joseph Nye, *Bound to Lead: The Changing Nature of American Power* (New York: Basic Books, 1990). See also Brilmayer, *American Hegemony*, above note 26; Ruggie, *Winning the Peace*, above note 26. But see Joseph Nye, *The Paradox of American Power: Why the World's Only Superpower Can't Go It Alone* (New York: Oxford University Press, 2002).
[28] Henkin, *International Law*, above note 16, pp. 109 *et seq.*
[29] *Ibid.*, pp. 2, 279.
[30] Thomas Franck, *The Power of Legitimacy Among Nations* (New York, Oxford: Oxford University Press, 1990).

international society into something resembling a "rulebook community" in the Dworkinian sense.[31] He thus emphasized the formal legitimacy of international law over its material justice and fairness. The international law described by Henkin and Franck consequently remains underdeveloped, providing only for some minimal rules and not for common principles. Ultimately, only more or less isolated instances of rules render international society a community. This raises the question whether a community constructed only on rules can be viable. The stronger international law grows, however, the better the prospect for the development of this (mere) legal community into a true community of mankind.

This carefully circumscribed view of the role of international law in the Cold War world was by no means limited to US writers, however.[32] Just the opposite: it seems that, finally, non-Americans had learnt to eschew Wilsonian idealism and had come around to a realistic view of international community and the role of law within it. For a short period before the end of the Cold War, a more or less common "Western" analysis had taken hold. The discussion on the nature and future of American hegemony remained in the background.

Community concepts in the age of globalization

Globalization seems to diminish the role of the State and to open up international society for new actors, both benign and malign. Economic actors seem increasingly able to circumvent State regulation, which leads to a regulatory "race to the bottom" between States. As representatives of "international civil society", nongovernmental organizations claim a place at the table. But less benign forces also do not need to be connected to States: crime and terrorism have also globalized, leaving States scrambling to find ways to counter that elusive threat.[33] The terrorist attacks of

---

[31] *Ibid.*, at 202. On the distinction between a "rulebook community" and a "community of principle" see Ronald Dworkin, *Law's Empire* (Cambridge, MA: Harvard University Press, 1986), pp. 208–11.

[32] See, e.g., Aron, *Paix et Guerre*, above note 22, and Bull, *Anarchical Society*, above note 23. This does not mean of course that there were no significant differences between these writers.

[33] Compare some of the most recent conventions adopted by the UN General Assembly: International Convention for the Suppression of Terrorist Bombings of 12 Jan. 1998, UN Doc. A/RES/52/164, 15 Dec. 1997, Annex, UNTS No. 37517, entered into force 23 May 2001; International Convention for the Suppression of the Financing of Terrorism, *opened for signature* 10 Jan. 2000, UN Doc. A/RES/54/109, 6 Dec. 1999, Annex, entered into force 10 April 2002;

11 September 2001 were of a magnitude and viciousness comparable only to inter-State armed conflict. And despite the close relationship between the al-Qaida network and the Taliban de facto government, it seems that the latter depended on the former at least as much as vice versa. Accordingly, the UN Security Council qualified the terrorist attacks against New York and Washington as threats to international peace and security, implicitly equating them with "armed attacks" in the sense of Article 51 of the Charter of the United Nations.[34] And "domestic" terrorist groups too may be linked with transnational crime, as recent allegations of contacts between the Irish Republican Army and the Colombian drug cartels have shown.

Richard Falk[35] sees the State squeezed between globalization from above (business) and below (NGOs). Susan Strange said farewell to classical political realism and spoke of the retreat of the State.[36] Sociologists emphasize the importance of modern communications media for the proximity in time and space on Planet Earth. For some (for instance Anthony Giddens[37]), this leads to little more than political interdependence between States; for others (Niklas Luhmann[38]), it signifies the definitive shift from territorial

United Nations Convention against Transnational Organized Crime, New York, *opened for signature* 12 Dec. 2000, UN Doc. A/55/383 (2000), 15 Nov. 2000, not yet in force, and UN Doc. S/RES/1368 (2001) of 12 Sept. 2001, and 1373 of 28 Sept. 2001, adopted in the aftermath of the terrorist attacks of 11 September 2001 against the United States, and SC res. 1269 (1999), 19 Oct. 1999.

[34] See SC Res. 1368, above note 33, preambular para. 3, operative para. 1, and SC Res. 1373, above note 33, preambular para. 4, operative para. 3 and 4. For critical remarks on this qualification, see Antonio Cassese, "Terrorism is also Disrupting Some Crucial Legal Categories of International Law" (2001) 12 *European Journal of International Law* 993 at 995–8; Jonathan I. Charney, "The Use of Force Against Terrorism and International Law" (2001) 95 *American Journal of International Law*, 835 at 836; Pierre-Marie Dupuy, "The Law after the Destruction of the Towers"; Giorgio Gaja, "In What Sense was There an 'Armed Attack'?"; Alain Pellet, "No, This is not War!" all available at http://www.ejil.org (last visited 10 Jan. 2002); but see Thomas Franck, "Terrorism and the Right to Self-Defense," (2001) 95 *American Journal of International Law*, 839 at 840.

[35] Richard Falk, "The Nuclear Weapons Advisory Opinion and the New Jurisprudence of Global Civil Society" (1997) 7 *Transnational Law and Contemporary Problems* 333 at 335. See also Christine Chinkin, "Human Rights and the Politics of Representation: Is There a Role For International Law?" in Michael Byers (ed.), *The Role of Law in International Politics: Essays in International Relations and International Law* (Oxford: Oxford University Press, 2000), p. 131.

[36] Susan Strange, *The Retreat of the State: The Diffusion of Power in the World Economy* (Cambridge: Cambridge University Press, 1996), pp. xv, 4, 13–14.

[37] Anthony Giddens, *The Consequences of Modernity* (Stanford: Stanford University Press, 1990), pp. 70–71.

[38] Niklas Luhmann, *Die Gesellschaft der Gesellschaft* (Frankfurt am Main: Suhrkamp, 1997), pp. 158–160.

borders to functional boundaries between different issue areas. From the perspective of an individualist ethics, globalization questions State values. Common interests of humankind, such as human rights, the protection of the environment, or nuclear nonproliferation, are increasingly salient. Radical liberals such as Thomas Pogge and Charles Beitz transfer Rawlsian ethics from the domestic to the international sphere and demand the effective protection and implementation of basic human rights and social justice for all human beings regardless of inter-state borders.[39]

Nevertheless, all agree that the State is here to stay, being the central institution in which political decisions can be legitimized by democratic means and where both security and social services can be provided. Still, the diminishment in regulatory power of the State and increase in challenges facing the whole of humanity – poverty, global warming, human rights, terrorism – create a demand for new structures and decision-making processes on the international plane. Thus, the slogan "Governance Without Government" has gained popularity among political scholars and practitioners alike[40] – but it constitutes the description of a problem rather than of a solution. Thus, on the one hand, global issues would seem to demand global institutions. On the other, the lack of trust in institutional responses generates a healthy skepticism towards great regulatory designs. It is on these lines that the current debate on international community takes place – and it is here where American approaches differ markedly from those of the rest of the world.

The institutionalist response to globalization

Inspired by republican and communitarian sources, many writers aim at the development of a true international community or society on the basis of a new societal consciousness encompassing the whole of humanity.[41] Discourse ethics and democracy theory emphasize the need to embed global

---

[39] Charles R. Beitz, *Political Theory and International Relations* (Princeton: Princeton University Press, 1979); Thomas W. Pogge, *Realizing Rawls* (Ithaca, London: Cornell University Press, 1989), pp. 242 *et seq.*; Fernando R. Tesón, "The Kantian Theory of International Law" (1992) 92 *Columbia Law Review* 53 at 84, 97.

[40] See, e.g., the contributions to Ernst-Otto Czempiel and James N. Rosenau (eds.), *Governance Without Government: Order and Change in World Politics: A Theory of Change and Continuity* (Cambridge: Cambridge University Press, 1990).

[41] See, e.g., Philip Allott, *Eunomia: New Order for a New World* (Oxford: Oxford University Press, 1989); Dupuy, *La Communauté internationale*, above note 16.

democracy in institutional designs,[42] and international legal scholars have followed suit. Long before 1989, Wolfgang Friedmann established the distinction between the "classical" law of coexistence and the "modern" law of cooperation.[43] Some contemporary scholars, especially in the German constitutional tradition, have taken up that distinction and developed concepts of a much narrower, and much more institutionalized, international community. International law accordingly moves – or should move – "from bilateralism to community interest" (Bruno Simma),[44] is about to establish "world interior politics" (Jost Delbrück),[45] or shall ensure "the survival of mankind on the eve of a new century" (Christian Tomuschat).[46] Instances of this "new order" in contemporary international law can be seen in *jus cogens*, obligations *erga omnes*, the concept of the common heritage of mankind,[47] the "constitutionalization" of the UN Security System[48] and of the WTO trade system[49] and, of course, the establishment of the International Criminal Court.[50]

That globalization leads to the quest for a new global "super-law" is not by itself surprising. Those who believe in a parallelism between legal norms and institutions – what Georges Abi-Saab has called the "law or

---

[42] Jürgen Habermas, *Die Einbeziehung des Anderen* (Frankfurt/Main: Suhrkamp, 1996), pp. 133, 672; David Held, *Democracy and the Global Order* (Stanford: Stanford University Press, 1995).

[43] Wolfgang Friedmann, *The Changing Structure of International Law* (London: Stevens & Sons, 1964); see also Wilfried C. Jenks, *A Common Law of Mankind* (London: Stevens & Sons, 1958); David Mitrany, *A Working Peace System* (Chicago: Quadrangel Books, 1966).

[44] Bruno Simma, "From Bilateralism to Community Interest in International Law" (1994) 250 *Recueil des cours* 217.

[45] Jost Delbrück, "Globalization of Law, Politics, and Markets – Implications for Domestic Law – A European Perspective" (1993/4) 1 *Indiana J. of Global Legal Studies* 9.

[46] Tomuschat, "Obligations Arising for States", above note 16.

[47] Dupuy, "La Communauté internationale," above note 16, at 159–168.

[48] Bardo Fassbender, *UN Security Council Reform and the Right to Veto: A Constitutional Perspective* (Den Haag/London/Boston: Kluwer Law International, 1998), 114; Jochen Abr. Frowein, "Reactions by Not Directly Affected States to Breaches of Public International Law," (1994) 248 *Recueil des cours* 345, at 355–6; Simma, "From Bilateralism to Community Interest," above note 44, at 258–62, paras. 25–26 (but see – considerably more skeptical – Simma, "Comments on Global Governance, the United Nations, and the Place of Law" (1998) 9 *Finnish Yearbook of International Law* 61 at 65); Tomuschat, "Obligations Arising for States," above note 16, at 216–40.

[49] Ernst-Ulrich Petersmann, "How to Reform the UN System? Constitutionalism, International Law, and International Organizations" (1997) 10 *Leiden Journal of International Law* 421.

[50] Rome Statute of the International Criminal Court, 17 July 1998, UN Doc. A/CONF:183/9* (1998), (1998) 37 *International Legal Materials* 999, entry into force 1 July 2002, as of 1 January 2003, 87 ratifications/accessions (UN Treaty Website, http://untreaty.un.org). The Preamble speaks several times of the "most serious crimes of concern to the international community as a whole."

fundamental hypothesis of 'legal physics' "[51] – now demand the establishment of global institutions to implement laws for the regulation of
globalization. What is notable, however, is the almost complete absence
of American writers sharing that view. Of course, there are wholehearted
American supporters of the International Criminal Court and of all the
other just-mentioned examples of "community law." Indeed, the American
attitude toward international institutions is cyclical rather than displaying
a persistent pattern of rejection, at least as long as the institutions remain
faithful to their original blueprints, which are often inspired by American
ideas or the US government.[52] Following the end of the Cold War, some
Americans are – or have been – in no less a jubilant mood than their
European counterparts. But the American skepticism towards governmental institutions of any kind – and even more so of an international kind –
seems not to allow for new institutional blueprints. The famous "new world
order" of George Bush Sr.[53] was probably misinterpreted when he was understood to have called for a new global order led by the United Nations.[54]

---

[51] Georges Abi-Saab, "Whither the International Community?" (1998) 9 *European Journal of International Law* 248 at 256.

[52] For a summary of the relationship of the United States towards international institution build-ing, combined with a passionate plea for a mutual reengagement, see Edward C. Luck, *Mixed Messages. American Politics and International Organization 1919–1999* (Washington, DC: Brook-ings Institution Press, 1999); see also Stewart Patrick, "Multilateralism and Its Discontents: The Causes and Consequences of US Ambivalence," in Stewart Patrick and Shepard Forman (eds.), *Multilateralism and US Foreign Policy: Ambivalent Engagement* (Boulder, London: Lynne Rienner, 2001), p. 1. For the Wilsonian origins of institutional globalism, see Thomas J. Knock, *To End All Wars. Woodrow Wilson and the Quest for a New World Order* (New York: Oxford Uni-versity Press, 1992). Knock distinguishes between the "progressive" internationalism of Wilson and his supporters on the left and a "conservative" internationalism of Republicans such as President William H. Taft and Judge Elihu Root of the Permanent Court of International Jus-tice, *ibid.*, at 48 *et seq. et passim*. For the determining American influence in the creation of the United Nations (and its greater realism as compared with the League), see Townsend Hoopes and Douglas Brinkley, *FDR and the Creation of the UN* (New Haven: Yale University Press, 1997); Ruth B. Russell and Jeannette E. Muther, *A History of the United Nations Charter* (Washington, DC: Brookings Institution, 1958). See also "The UN Charter as History," (1995) 89 *American Society of International Law Proc.*, at 45–61, with contributions by Paul Kennedy, Oscar Schachter, and Louis B. Sohn.

[53] See statements of 11 Sept. 1990, 29 Jan. and 13 April 1991 in (1990) 2 *Public Papers of the Presidents of the United States: George Bush* 1219; (1991) 1 *Public Papers of the Presidents of the United States: George Bush* 79, 366; "Address Before a Joint Session of the Congress on the Cessation of the Persian Gulf Conflict, March 3, 1991," (1991) 27 *Weekly Compilation of Presidential Documents* 259.

[54] For an example of the disappointment concerning the lack of such a new order see Georges Abi-Saab, "A 'New World Order'? Some Preliminary Reflections," (1994) 7 *Hague Yearbook of International Law* 87.

Even if institutional work in American international relations literature abounds,[55] most US authors do not question the analytical priority of the State over the international community and privilege the analysis of State sovereignty over the search for universal "communitarian" interests.[56] The existence of regimes in specific issue areas is considered the exception calling for an explanation, not vice versa. Thus, regime theory tends to regard regimes as a sort of rule-governed island in the sea of inter-State power struggles.[57]

Most of the American enthusiasm for globalization – and even more so the disillusionment which followed – is nurtured, not by an effort to institutionalize and legalize international relations, but by another impulse: the advent of the global liberal age.

The (neo) liberal response to globalization

As has already been mentioned, globalization has also curbed the belief in the benefit of governmental institutions, be they national or global. Liberals and neoliberals demand a reconstruction of international law on an interindividual basis. Whereas more moderate representatives of liberal ethics, such as John Rawls[58] or Terry Nardin,[59] justified classical international law as

---

[55] This is especially valid for the so-called "regime theory." See Stephen D. Krasner (ed.), *International Regimes* (Ithaca, London: Princeton University Press, 1984); Andreas Hasenclever, Peter Mayer, and Volker Rittberger, *Theories of International Regimes* (Cambridge: Cambridge University Press, 1997).

[56] For instance, Stephen Krasner, one of the leading regime theorists, argues that international institutions have never become "embedded," that is, are unable to dictate behaviour and endure over time. He explicitly rejects any thesis of an international socialization which is behind the idea of an international community; see Stephen Krasner, *Sovereignty: Organized Hypocrisy* (Princeton: Princeton University Press, 1999), pp. 226 *et seq.* But see, e.g., James N. Rosenau, *Turbulence in World Politics: A Theory of Change and Continuity* (Princeton: Princeton University Press, 1990), for a more pluralist US view; Hasenclever, Mayer, and Rittberger, *Theories of International Regimes*, above note 55, for a presentation of alternative views of regimes, including a strong cognitivism which questions rationalist assumptions: *ibid.*, pp. 154 *et seq.*

[57] Joseph Weiler and Andreas L. Paulus, "The Structure of Change in International Law or Is There a Hierarchy of Norms in International Law?" (1997) 8 *European Journal of International Law* 545, at 557.

[58] John Rawls, *A Theory of Justice* (Cambridge, MA: Harvard University Press, 1971), pp. 377 *et seq.*; Rawls, "The Law of Peoples," in Stephen Shute and Susan Hurley (eds.), *On Human Rights: The Oxford Amnesty Lectures* (New York: Basic Books, 1993), p. 41; Rawls, *The Law of Peoples with The Idea of Public Reason Revisited* (Cambridge, MA, London: Harvard University Press, 1999), pp. 3–128.

[59] Terry Nardin, *Law, Morality, and the Relations of States* (Princeton: Princeton University Press, 1983), pp. 183 *et seq.*

allowing for multiple, diverse societies, more radical philosophers challenge the almost exclusive focus of Rawls' earlier work on national societies and demand the establishment of a "world social order" fulfilling the promises of human rights and Rawls' difference principle at the international level.[60] At the same time, radical liberals attack traditional legal limits on unilateral intervention for the protection of human rights.[61] However, they do not include blueprints for the establishment of an institutional mechanism of distribution.

Whereas radical Rawlsians thus "globalize" the tasks of the nation-state, Rawls himself introduces a fateful distinction into the foundations of international law: that between "liberal" and "non-liberal" States, with "authoritarian" but not "totalitarian" States in the middle.[62] International law seems only to be possible in the interrelationship of liberal and, maybe, authoritarian States. For the rest, there can only be very limited relations of classical international law. Here we find the liberal justification for the outlawing of certain States as "rogue States" or "States of concern." What international law loses in terms of universality, it gains in ideological cohesion and therefore effectiveness. In the realm of liberal States, arguments of multiculturalism and ethical exceptionalism will not be tolerated. In both variants of Rawlsian ethics, however, one notes the widespread lack of an institutional design. Though this absence may be acceptable in ethics, it might not suffice in international law.

Thomas Franck has translated the ideas of the liberal moral philosophers into legal concepts. The change in his writings after the end of the Cold War is not least remarkable because it contrasts so nicely with his earlier work. Whereas Franck formerly emphasized formality over substance, legitimacy over fairness,[63] he now enthusiastically approves the advent of a new liberal and democratic era:

> The infant entitlement [to democracy] is sufficiently widely understood to be almost universally celebrated. It is welcomed from Malagache to Mongolia, in the streets, the universities, and the legislatures, not only for its promise of a new global political culture supported by common rules and communitarian

---

[60] See Beitz, *Political Theory*, above note 39, pp. 8–9, 128; Pogge, *Realizing Rawls*, above note 39, p. 244 *et seq.*; but see Rawls, *Theory of Justice*, above note 58, p. 457.
[61] Beitz, *Political Theory*, p. 90; Tesón, "Kantian Theory", above note 39, at 68, 84.
[62] Rawls, *Law of Peoples*, above note 58, p. 44 *et seq.*, 55 *et seq.*
[63] See above note 30 and accompanying text.

implementing institutions, but also because it opens up the stagnant politics, economies, and culture of states to development.[64]

In his vision, the international community, the interstatal community and other communities are not mutually exclusive, but overlapping:

> International law has matured into a complete legal system covering all aspects of relations among states, and also, more recently, aspects of relations between states and their federated units, between states and persons, between persons of several states, between states and multinational corporations, and between international organizations and their state members.[65]

In this post-1989 view, the international community is no longer (solely) constructed on formal legitimacy, but on material fairness, with "shared moral imperatives and values."[66] At last, international law governs a "community of principles," not only a rulebook community.[67] However, Franck's new emphasis on fairness instead of mere (procedural) legitimacy post-1989 cannot explain why the power-constraining function of formal processes is deemed less relevant now than it was just a few years ago. The new value system comes with no new institutions; democracy is based on the parallel wills of people, on its "universal celebration." But if democracy makes itself, what is law needed for? Why an entitlement to democracy if there is no institution to implement it?

The New Haven School had already shifted the emphasis from formal norms emanating from States to a process of decision making oriented toward human dignity. The Yale scholars thereby tried both to gain a more realistic picture of international relations and to maintain the normative character of the legal process. By renouncing the binding character of rules, however, they also gave up the guidance of international law beyond the more arbitrary application of vague principles. They diminished the possibility of finding a pragmatic consensus between different value systems based on means, not ends. In addition, their optimism regarding the identity of the values of at least the "Western" participants in the international legal process sometimes resembled more a fiction than reality – McDougal,

---

[64] Thomas Franck, *Fairness in International Law and Institutions* (Oxford: Clarendon Press, 1995), p. 138. Originally in Thomas Franck, "The Emerging Right of Democratic Governance" (1992) 86 *American Journal of International Law* 46 at 90.
[65] Franck, *Fairness*, above note 64, p. 6.   [66] *Ibid.*, pp. 10–11.
[67] Ibid., p. 203. Cf. above note 31 and accompanying text.

Lasswell and Reisman themselves spoke of a postulation.[68] As in liberal ethics, their focus is a single world community of individuals, not States:

> A relevant jurisprudence will recognize that the whole of mankind does today constitute a community, in the sense of interdetermination and interdependence, and will extend its focus of inquiry to include this largest community, embracing the whole earth–space arena. It will observe that this largest earth–space community process operates through many different lesser communities – from local, through regional and national, to global... The important actors in community process, at all levels, will be seen to be individual human beings, but it will be noted that individuals identify and affiliate with, and make demands on behalf of, many different groups...[69]

However, the recognition of the existence of a world social process does not result in a global institutional design. On the contrary: Reisman emphasizes his hostility toward global bureaucracies lacking "the resources and the incentives necessary to fulfill the essential value demands that individuals make on their political communities."[70] This position translates into a justification of unilateral – mostly American – intervention, be it in Kosovo or Haiti, for the postulated universal value of human dignity, without institutional checks and balances.

Yale scholars and radical liberals unite on this point. In the words of a leading liberal proponent of humanitarian intervention, Fernando Tesón:

> current international law is wrongly conceptualized in terms of prerogatives of rulers... we should move toward a theory of international law that has the individual, not the state, as its subject and basic moral unit.[71]

Thus, in a liberal community of individuals, the shield of State sovereignty is removed when the State fails to protect the rights of its citizens:

> Because protection of human rights is the justification of having states in the first place, only governments that represent the people (in the sense of

---

[68] Myres S. McDougal, Harold Lasswell, and W. Michael Reisman, "Theories about International Law: Prologue to a Configurative Jurisprudence," in McDougal and Reisman (eds.), *International Law Essays* (New York, Mineola: Foundation Press, 1981), 43, p. 58. See also McDougal, "The World Constitutive Process of Authoritative Decision", *ibid.*, p. 201.

[69] McDougal, Lasswell and Reisman, "Theories," above note 68, p. 54.

[70] W. Michael Reisman, "Designing and Managing the Future of the State" (1997) 8 *European Journal of International Law* 409 at 412.

[71] Tesón, "Kantian Theory," above note 39, at 96.

having their consent and respecting their rights) are entitled to the protection afforded by international law.[72]

Combined with a certain disdain for the UN security system,[73] this leads to the justification of unilateral intervention for the protection of human rights – an argument which is, with that degree of emphasis, rarely heard elsewhere.

Whereas Tesón and – to a lesser degree – the New Haven scholars emphasize global liberal values at the expense of State sovereignty, Anne-Marie Slaughter enthusiastically embraces globalization for disaggregating the State into its various functional components (legislative, executive, and judicial branches), at least among "liberal" States.[74] Radicalizing Philip Jessup's transnational law approach, Slaughter emphasizes international interagency cooperation without however providing for adequate democratic control, at least at the international level. Apparently, the existence of similar (but not identical) Western values among "liberal States" is supposed to guarantee fair outcomes. Global forum shopping develops from a vice into a virtue; institutions do not any more represent a parochial national community, but fulfill service functions for transnational individuals. Classical international law is only supposed to govern relations with nonliberal States.

This model has not remained without critique, both in the United States and elsewhere.[75] As with the other approaches cursorily treated here, one can of course find, with this writer as with Franck or Reisman, much more cautiously crafted statements. However, the features mentioned exemplify, much better than less radical models, the specific incidence of the US approach to the characteristics of the international community:

---

[72] Fernando Tesón, *Humanitarian Intervention: An Inquiry into Law and Morality*, 2nd edn. (New York: Transnational Publishers, 1997), p. 98.

[73] *Ibid.*, pp. 157–62.

[74] Anne-Marie Slaughter, "International Law in a World of Liberal States" (1995) 6 *European Journal of International Law* 503.

[75] See, e.g., Philip Alston, "The Myopia of the Handmaidens: International Lawyers and Globalization" (1997) 8 *European Journal of International Law* 435 at 439–40; Andrew Hurrell and Ngaire Woods, "Globalisation and Inequality" (1995) 24 *Millennium* 447 at 453–4; Outi Korhonen, "Liberalism and International Law: A Centre Projecting a Periphery" (1996) 65 *Nordic Journal of International Law* 481 at 481–4, 501–03; Harold H. Koh, "Why Do Nations Obey International Law" (1997) 106 *Yale Law Journal* 2599 at 2650; Susan Marks, "The End of History? Reflections on Some International Legal Theses" (1997) 8 *European Journal of International Law* 449; Andreas L. Paulus, "Law and Politics in the Age of Globalization" (2000) 11 *European Journal of International Law* 465 at 469.

- the enthusiasm about the universalization of democratic and liberal values after the end of communism;
- the significance, if any, of institutions as an intervening, not as an independent, variable;[76]
- the informality of legal processes, ultimately resulting in the lack of distinction between "is" and "ought"; and, not least,
- the distinction between "liberal" and "non-liberal" law, resulting in an apparent disregard for the remaining pluralism in the multifaceted international community.

But, of course, these views are not the only "American" views of community. In fact, the fiercest challenge to the liberal view also comes from the United States.

The postmodern critique of community

In a *postmodern* understanding, community is not possible without exclusion and suppression of "the other." The exclusion of others is as much the part of a community concept as is their inclusion.[77] Thus, "community" may be used as an ideological construct for the maintenance of structures of power, excluding the "other," the marginal, the different. Postmodernists criticize both the social-democratic enthusiasm for new international bureaucracies and the neoliberal reliance on liberal values.

The liberal concept of community is rejected because it does not take account of the multiplicity of ethical approaches and marginalizes those opposed to the dominant liberal model, as visible in the distinction between "liberal" and "non-liberal" States, the latter enjoying a diminished status.[78] In the last resort, liberal models of the international community stabilize – voluntarily or involuntarily – American hegemony. The reliance on the market hides the political nature of this choice, though it ultimately fails to shield neoliberalism from critique. The postmodern critique of institutionalism is no less acerbic than the neoliberal one: "it is time to let go of the myth of a progressive history that moves from institutional

---

[76] See Stephen Krasner, "Structural causes and regime consequences: regimes as intervening variables," in Krasner, *International Regimes*, above note 19, pp. 1–21; Kennedy, "Regimes and the limits of realism: regimes as autonomous variables" *ibid.*, pp. 355–68.

[77] For a recent expression of this view, see Annan, "Fighting Terrorism on a Global Front" above note 5.

[78] David Kennedy, "The Disciplines of International Law and Policy" (2000) 12 *Leiden Journal of International Law* 9 at 123.

fragmentation to unity."[79] The vision of unity shares the vice of the ideal of a liberal community: it excludes and marginalizes the outsider. In addition, an international institutionalism cannot cure the lack of legitimacy of its universalist model.

In the eyes of postmodernists, international community is nothing but a fantasy to justify individual disciplinary projects, a "reification"[80] of a theoretical construct. David Kennedy speaks of the "fantasy that there is something called an 'international community' which, in a disembodied way, has 'agreed' to some things and foregone agreement on others." He further elaborates:

> When people say "the international community"... it is both a way of referring to a particular group of people – perhaps the few hundred people active on a particular issue in the governmental bureaus of significant states – and a way of suggesting that this "community" is more than the sum of their efforts.[81]

Instead, he proposes to regard

> international law not as a set of rules or institutions, but as a group of professional disciplines in which people pursue projects in various quite different institutional, political, and national settings.[82]

Kennedy demands to break the silences of traditional international law, to revolt against the acceptance of the background conditions of international society by international law, "serenely treating the everyday divisions of wealth and poverty, the background norms for trade in arms and military conflict as part of the global donnée."[83] Instead, international lawyers should understand globalization as a chance to embrace diversity and to

---

[79] Martti Koskenniemi, "Repetition as Reform: Georges Abi-Saab Cours Général de droit international public," (1998) 9 European Journal of International Law 405 at 411.

[80] For the meaning of this term see Anthony Carty, "Critical International Law: Recent Trends in the Theory of International Law," (1991) 2 EJIL 66 at 67.

[81] Kennedy, "Disciplines of International Law," above note 78, at 83–4.

[82] Ibid., at 83.

[83] David Kennedy, "The Nuclear Weapons case," in Laurence Boisson de Chazournes and Philippe Sands (eds.), International Law, the International Court of Justice and Nuclear Weapons, 462 (Cambridge: Cambridge University Press, 1999), p. 472. Similarly Kennedy, "Disciplines of International Law," above note 78, at 125.

judge the global political order "by the distribution it effects among such groups."[84]

The alternative postmodern community consists of an embrace of cultural difference and a politicization of the "private," economic realm:

> Perhaps we will develop an internationalism based on a global politics of identity, a shifting sand of cultural claims and contestations among constructed and overlapping identities about the distribution of resources and the conditions of social life.[85]

Beyond the respect for and legitimacy of the otherness of the other, this political project is not accompanied by a particular vision of community. The postmodern onslaught on international law as a means to contain conflict and implement shared values is not matched by any proposal for improvement. Indeed, one might argue that the impossibility of a normative vision of community does not lead to more tolerance or respect for the other, but rather to unfettered political realism.[86]

Is postmodernism distinctly American? Of course not. Even if postmodernism found its way into legal theory via the United States, its philosophical roots lie in France.[87] Despite considerable differences among postmodernists, one could cite European scholars such as Martti Koskenniemi or Australian feminists such as Hilary Charlesworth and Christine Chinkin just as well as David Kennedy. Nevertheless, there is another commonality besides the fact that most postmodernists have studied or taught at Harvard. Postmodernists share with American liberals and even neoliberals the reticence towards institutions and the focus on individual choice, and with American realists the aversion to ideological constructs which mask the pursuit of power. With these two features, postmodernism appears closer to its American counterparts than it may itself acknowledge.

---

[84] *Ibid.*, at 112.   [85] *Ibid.*, at 133.

[86] Compare Jürgen Habermas, *Der philosophische Diskurs der Moderne* (Frankfurt: Suhrkamp, 1985), pp. 11–12 *et passim*. Similarly Chris Brown, *International Relations Theory: New Normative Approaches* (New York: Columbia University Press, 1992), pp. 218, 237. For a more extensive treatment see Andreas L. Paulus, "International Law After Postmodernity" (2001) 14 *Leiden Journal of International Law* 727, 727–55.

[87] Compare Bruno Simma, "Editorial" (1992) 3 *European Journal of International Law* 215; Weiler and Paulus, "Structure of Change in International Law," above note 57, at 548–51.

United States perspectives on the "international community" in positive international law

Thus it seems that there is a distinct American contribution to the understanding of international community in scholarly writing. But what about international law as such? Ultimately, only an analysis of positive international law can show whether adequate images of the international legal community are provided by the institutionalist reliance on a constitutionalization of the international system, or by the neoliberal delegitimization of the state.

In what follows, I briefly consider two examples of community approaches in international law and examine the official position of the United States with regard to them. This focus is not meant to imply, however, that the US government is able to monopolize the role of American society in international affairs. Increasingly, nongovernmental organizations, transnational commerce, and even individuals take their own stand and, very often, contradict the influence of the US government. The International Criminal Court may only be the most visible instance of the developing influence of non-State actors on international relations, within the United States and elsewhere.[88]

The United Nations security system: from collective security to the "franchising" of State intervention

As is well known, the original Charter idea that the Security Council should have the monopoly in the international use of force was only a modest success. Although the Charter not only established the power of the Security Council to decide on sanctions binding on UN members, but also provided – in the form of the special agreements under Article 43 and the Military Staff Committee in Article 47 – for an institutional framework for UN-led military interventions, this regime never materialized. Instead, the

---

[88] One needs only to look at the websites of leading supporters of the ICC to get an impression of the large influence of the American "civil society"; see, e.g., the Coalition for an International Criminal Court at http://www.iccnow.org (last visited 4 Jan. 2002); or the Washington Working Group on the International Criminal Court at http://www.wfa.org/issues/wicc/wicc.html (last visited 4 Jan. 2002). For an insider's critique of NGO influence, see Kenneth Anderson, "The Ottawa Convention Banning Land Mines, the Role of International Non-governmental Organizations and the Idea of International Civil Society" (2000) 11 *European Journal of International Law* 91.

United Nations called upon individual States to implement its decisions in conformity with Article 48, as in the case of the Korean War,[89] or sent peacekeeping forces with the consent of the parties, the so-called "Chapter-VI-and-a-half."[90] Of course, this development was not primarily due to US reluctance to accept global institutional solutions, but was mainly dictated by the Cold War and the lack of willingness of States to enter into special agreements under Article 43.

Nevertheless, in the conflict arising from the Iraqi occupation of Kuwait, the United States decided in favor of a recourse to Security Council prerogatives in line with the original purposes of Chapter VII of the Charter. But, the "new world order" announced by President George Bush Sr.[91] did not, in the United States view, result in a strengthening of the organizational capabilities of the United Nations to control the exercise of Security Council mandates by its members. Resolution 678 did not reinvigorate Articles 43 or 47 of the Charter, but authorized "Member States cooperating with the Government of Kuwait... to use all necessary means to uphold and implement" the Security Council resolutions.[92] The subsequent dispute whether this authorization falls under multilateral intervention under Article 42 or collective self-defence under Article 51 has become one of the classics of UN law.[93] It is not at all surprising to find the United States on the side of those who regard the Security Council resolutions as an authorization of collective self-defence,[94] and not as a collective enforcement action of the

---

[89] On Korea, see, e.g., Michael Bothe, "Commentary on Peace-Keeping," in Bruno Simma *et al.* (eds.) *The Charter of the United Nations: A Commentary*, 2nd ed. (Oxford, New York: Oxford University Press, 2002) MN 3; Rosalyn Higgins, *United Nations Peacekeeping 1946–67* (London: Oxford University Press, 1970), pp. 153 *et seq.*

[90] See: Bothe, "Commentary", above note 89, MN 5 *et seq.*

[91] For references see above note 53.

[92] UN SC Resolution 678 (1990), 29 Nov. 1990, UN SCOR, 45th year, 2963rd mtg., UN Doc. S/INF/46, at 27, para. 2.

[93] For a brief discussion and further literature, see Jochen Abr. Frowein and Nico Krisch, Commentary on Art. 42, in Simma, *Charter*, above note 89, MN 22–23; see also the contributions to the *American Journal of International Law* Agora, "The Gulf Crisis in International and Foreign Relations Law" (1991) 85 *American Journal of International Law*, 63–74, 506–35; Oscar Schachter, "United Nations Law in the Gulf Conflict," (1991) 85 *American Journal of International Law* 452 at 459–65, but see also his remarks at 471–2 on the limits of self-defense.

[94] Schachter, "Gulf Conflict," above note 93, at 459–60. In its joint resolution authorizing the use of force, the US Congress used both justifications – the inherent right to (collective) self-defense and authorization by SC resolution 678 (1990) of 29 Nov. 1990; see Authorization for Use of Military Force Against Iraq Resolution, (1991) 30 *International Legal Materials* 296 at 297, US Public Law 102–1 of Jan. 14, 1991, 22nd Congress, 105 Stat. 3–4.

Security Council to be implemented by member States. Again, in the US view, collective authorization by the Security Council may be useful, but is not required.

The United Nations has, with the support of the United States, subsequently developed the so-called "franchise system,"[95] according to which the United Nations authorizes, in order to intervene in a State, the use of force by member States. This is not the place for a critical assessment of that practice.[96] Suffice it to say that such a "franchise" remains in most cases the only possibility of strong military response by the United Nations, but is also open to abuse – as exemplified by the French "Opération turquoise," which may have contributed more to protecting the Rwandan genocidaires than it did to establishing peace. The problem has again come to the fore in the Kosovo intervention. As already mentioned, both NATO and the opponents of its bombing campaign claimed to stand for the interests of the international community. In NATO's view, it was enforcing community values only because a minority was preventing the United Nations from acting. For the opponents, the unilateral use of force for the protection of human rights is an abuse of community values if and to the extent that it is not authorized by the Security Council. Again, it was the United States that insisted that the Security Council had legitimized the NATO action, even if the Security Council had reserved further measures to itself.[97]

---

[95] A term apparently coined by Thomas Franck, "The United Nations as Guarantor of International Peace and Security: Past, Present, Future," in Christian Tomuschat (ed.), *The United Nations at Age Fifty: A Legal Perspective* (The Hague: Kluwer Law International, 1995), pp. 25–38, p. 31.

[96] For a comprehensive treatment see Danesh Sarooshi, *The United Nations and the Development of Collective Security: The Delegation by the UN Security Council of its Chapter VII Powers* (Oxford: Oxford University Press, 1999), pp. 142 *et seq.*

[97] For a rejection of that view see Georg Nolte, "Kosovo und Konstitutionalisierung: zur humanitären Intervention der NATO-Staaten" (1999) 59 *Zeitschrift für allgemeines öffentliches Recht und Völkerrecht* 941 at 944; Bruno Simma, "NATO, the UN and the Use of Force: Legal Aspects," (1999) 10 *European Journal of International Law* 1 at 12; but see Ruth Wedgwood, "NATO's Campaign in Yugoslavia" (1999) 93 *American Journal of International Law* 828, at 829–32; see also the texts of S/RES/1199 (1998), 23 Sept. 1998, UN Doc. S/RES/1199 (1998) and S/RES/1203 (1993), 24 Oct. 1998, UN Doc. S/RES/1203 (1998), which are difficult to reconcile with such an interpretation. For the related discussion whether SC Res. 1244 (1999), 10 June 1999, UN Doc. S/RES/1244 (1999), has retroactively authorized the NATO campaign, see L. Henkin, "Kosovo and the Law of 'Humanitarian Intervention'" (1999) 93 *American Journal of International Law* 824 at 827 ("ratification" of NATO action); against him, convincingly, Vera Gowlland-Debbas, "The Limits of Unilateral Enforcement of Community Objectives in the Framework of UN Peace Maintenance" (2000) 11 EJIL 361 at 374–6.

Likewise, it would be naive to expect a change in the US position toward multilateral involvement in international affairs as a consequence of the horrendous terrorist attacks committed against and, even more importantly, within the United States on 11 September 2001. By securing Security Council approval for tough measures against international terrorism[98] – without defining this phenomenon, however – the United States has voluntarily received international backing for its decision to exercise self-defense. As significant as the long list of obligations for States under Resolution 1373 (2001) may be, ranging from the freezing of terrorist assets to the denial of safe haven for terrorists,[99] the most startling element is the abdication of Security Council responsibility for taking "the measures necessary to maintain international peace and security" (Article 51 of the UN Charter) in favor of a confirmation of "the inherent right of individual or collective self-defence," that is, the provision of indirect support for the unilateral use of force by the United States against the terrorist bases in Afghanistan and, eventually, elsewhere.[100] Accordingly, the United States reported to the Security Council that it had initiated its attack against the Taliban regime and the al-Qaida network "in the exercise of its inherent right of individual and collective self-defence."[101]

Thus, the current US administration does not object to seeking and receiving the support of international institutions as such. It regards multilateral support as a useful tool for the pursuit of its national interests. In the words of Condoleezza Rice, now National Security Advisor:

> multilateral agreements and institutions should not be ends in themselves. United States interests are served by having strong alliances and can be promoted within the UN and other multilateral organizations, as well as through well-crafted international agreements.[102]

That means that support for international institutions is subject to the United States national interests, not vice versa. American national interests

---

98 See UN Doc. S/RES/1368 (2001) 12 Sept. 2001; and UN Doc. S/RES/ 1363 (2001), 28 Sept. 2001.

99 *Ibid.*, operative para. 1 (c) and 2 (c).

100 See SC Res. 1368, above note 98, preambular para. 3, SC Res. 1373, above note 98, preambular para. 4. Cf. the voices cited above note 34.

101 Letter dated 7 Oct. 2001 from the Permanent Representative of the United States of America to the United Nations addressed to the President of the Security Council, UN Doc. S/2001/946, 7 Oct. 2001.

102 Rice, "Promoting the National Interest", above note 2.

come first, and predate any international involvement. American interests are not shaped by any institutionalized pursuit of community interests. Andrew Moravcsik is probably right when he argues that a combination of geopolitical power, democratic domestic institutions, ideological conservatism, and political decentralization leads to an antimultilateralist bias in United States policies.[103]

From obligations erga omnes and international crimes of State to international crimes of individuals

In three different areas, the "international community" as such plays a role in contemporary international law. Article 53 of the Vienna Convention on the Law of Treaties defines a "peremptory norm of general international law" (*jus cogens*) as "a norm accepted and recognized by the international community of States as a whole as a norm from which no derogation is permitted..."[104] In its *Barcelona Traction* judgment, the International Court of Justice opined that "an essential distinction should be drawn between the *obligations of a State towards the international community as a whole*, and those arising vis-à-vis another State in the field of diplomatic protection."[105] The International Law Commission (ILC), during the first reading of the draft articles on State responsibility, created the term "international crime of States," which was defined as "an international obligation so essential for the protection of fundamental interests of the international community that its breach is recognized as a crime by that community as a whole."[106] Obligations *erga omnes* and international crimes increasingly merge.[107] Although the concept of "international crimes" did

---

[103] Andrew Moravcsik, "Why Is US Human Rights Policy So Unilateralist?" in Patrick and Forman, *Multilateralism and US Foreign Policy*, above note 52, p. 347.
[104] UNTS 1155, p. 331.
[105] *Barcelona Traction, Light and Power Company, Limited*, (1970) ICJ Reports 3 at 32, para. 33 (emphasis added).
[106] *ILC Yearbook 1996*, II/2, p. 60.
[107] In the Draft articles adopted on second reading, the Commission uses the concept of *jus cogens* for establishing particular consequences for the violation of certain obligations (Art. 40, 41) and the concept of "obligations owed towards the international community as a whole" for allowing any State to invoke the responsibility of another State (Art. 48). See the Commentary, above note 108, para. 77, at 281–82, subpara. 7 before Art. 40: "First, serious breaches of obligations arising under peremptory norms of general international law can attract additional consequences, not only for the responsible State but for all other States. Secondly, all States are entitled to invoke responsibility for breaches of obligations to the international community as a whole."

not survive the second reading, the articles as finally adopted created a regime for "serious breaches of obligations under peremptory norms of general international law"[108] and confirmed the existence of obligations toward the international community as a whole by providing for rights of States other than a (directly) injured State.[109]

The United States has signed, but not ratified, the Vienna Convention.[110] The US position on the concept of "international crime of State" is negative. Whereas the ILC draft adopted on first reading in 1996 was informed by a coalition between Special Rapporteur Ago, and socialist and Third World representatives, the version originally adopted by the Drafting Committee on second reading in 2000 seemed to be inspired by the willingness both to legitimize, and to set limits to, the policy of unilateral "third party" sanctions for the protection of human rights and other "community interests."[111] Nevertheless, the attempt to link that policy with a defense of the supreme values of the "international community" has not met with the approval of the United States, which is also hostile to the codification of strict limits on unilateral sanctions.[112] Along with this objection goes an (intentional?) misunderstanding of the concept of "international crimes" as a system of "criminal responsibility."[113] As a result, the ILC, when finally adopting the

---

[108] Draft articles on Responsibility of States for internationally wrongful acts, in "Report of the International Law Commission on the work of its fifty-third session" GAOR, 56th Sess., Supp. No. 10, UN Doc. A/56/10 (2001), p. 43, para. 76, Art. 40, 41, at pp. 53, 54. See also UN Doc. GA Res. 56/38, 12 Dec. 2001, taking note of the articles.

[109] Art. 48, *ibid.*, at 56.

[110] Multilateral Treaties deposited with the Secretary-General, Status as at 31 Dec. 2000, UN Doc. ST/LEG/SER.E/19 (2001), Part 2, Ch. XXIII 1. See also http://untreaty.un.org

[111] International Law Commission, 52nd session, State responsibility, Draft articles provisionally adopted by the Drafting Committee on second reading, Art. 49, UN Doc. A/CN.4/L.600, 11 Aug. 2000; also in: International Law Commission, Report on the work of its fifty-second session, UN GAOR, 55th sess., Supp. No. 10, UN Doc. A/55/10 (2000), Appendix after para. 405.

[112] See US Comments on ILC Draft Articles on State Responsibility, 1 March 2001, partly reproduced in Sean D. Murphy (ed.), "Contemporary Practice of the United States Relating to International Law" (2001) 95 *American Journal of International Law*, 626–28; Statement by the United States on State responsibility made in the Sixth Committee of the 55th UN General Assembly during the debate on agenda item 159 at the 18th mtg., 27 Oct. 2000 (on the 2nd draft of the Drafting Committee, above, n. 108); United States: "Comments on the Draft Articles on State Responsibility [adopted on first reading]," (1997) 37 *International Legal Materials* 468: "The United States strongly opposes the inclusion of distinctions between delicts and so-called 'state crimes,' for which there is no support under customary international law and which undermine the effectiveness of the state responsibility regime as a whole."

[113] US Comments 1997, above note 112, 475.

draft articles on second reading in 2001, refrained from its initial willingness to codify third-party countermeasures, opting instead for a mere saving clause.[114]

In arguing against the codification of "international crimes of State," the United States referred to individual responsibility for the commission of international crimes within the framework of humanitarian law, thereby following the individual approach of liberal international law theory:

> it is one thing to recognize the responsibility of individuals and quite another to establish a criminal regime punishing states for such violations. Practically, two regimes of responsibility – one for individuals and one for states – could help insulate the individual criminal from international sanction.[115]

When it comes to the prosecution of individual crimes, the United States is, however, only rarely prepared to subscribe to an international institutional machinery, especially if this means subjecting its own citizens to international scrutiny. The United States clearly prefers ad hoc tribunals established by the Security Council under Chapter VII and Article 29 of the UN Charter, as in the case of the International Criminal Tribunal for the Former Yugoslavia. And that particular tribunal's mere claim of jurisdiction over US and NATO forces in the Kosovo intervention raised more than eyebrows at Washington, even though an indictment was not issued.[116] The United States is hardly a supporter of the permanent International Criminal Court, despite its reluctant signature of the ICC Statute in December 2000. It is only willing to participate if it would not be compelled to surrender its own nationals, especially its military personnel. Thus, David Scheffer, former US Ambassador-at-Large, argued that due to the particular exposure of a superpower to political controversies, a partial exemption of US military personnel from ICC jurisdiction was necessary.[117] As long as there is no such agreement between the court and the United States, the US government – especially the

---

[114] Art. 54, in ILC Report 2001, at 58.   [115] US Comments 1997, above note 112, at 476.

[116] See "Final Report to the Prosecutor by the Committee Established to Review the NATO Bombing Campaign Against the Federal Republic of Yugoslavia," (2000) 39 *International Legal Materials* 1257.

[117] David J. Scheffer, "The United States and the Criminal Court," (1999) 93 *American Journal of International Law* 12 at 12, 18. For a critical evaluation, see Peter Malanczuk, "The International Criminal Court and Landmines: What Are the Consequences of Leaving the United States Behind?" (2000) 11 EJIL 77 at 80–84.

Senate – has no interest in ratifying the Statute.[118] Most recently, President Bush has signed into law the American Servicemembers' Protection Act (ASPA), which blocks any cooperation with the International Criminal Court and even allows the president actively to pursue the liberation of American soldiers under ICC jurisdiction.[119]

Two features of this position are particularly remarkable. First, according to US law, the extradition of US nationals to other countries is in principle not excluded, especially in cases where those nationals are considered "hostes humani generis".[120] However, the United States refuses to surrender its own citizens to international institutions. Second, the Security Council may demand, with binding force, the extradition of a country's own nationals. But when an International Criminal Court providing all guarantees of due process does the same thing, this is deemed unacceptable.

The troubling implication is that military exposure renders problematic the observance of international criminal law standards and the jurisdiction of an international tribunal – an argument apparently not valid for other States whose soldiers are subject to the jurisdiction of the existing UN criminal tribunals.[121]

Proposals to surrender the perpetrators of the 11 September 2001 atrocities to an international tribunal along the lines of the Yugoslav and Rwanda tribunals[122] are well intentioned but unrealistic. Under the principle of territorial jurisdiction, the United States is perfectly entitled to bring alleged terrorists to justice before its national courts and try them under domestic law. However, the supporters of the idea of an international tribunal claim that such a tribunal would benefit from improved legitimacy because of its broader political and legal base. Still, as much as a special tribunal of this kind might further the international legitimacy of eventual

---

[118] See statement of President William J. Clinton authorizing the United States to sign the Treaty on the International Criminal Court, reprinted in Murphy, "Contemporary Practice of the United States," above note 112 at 387, 399. The United States went so far as to "unsign" the Statute in May 2002. See Communication of the United States Government to the UN Secretary-General, 6 May 2000, available at http://untreaty.un.org.

[119] American Servicemembers' Protection Act, Pub L. No. 107–206, §§2001–2015, 116 Stat. 820 (2002), 22 USCA §§7421–7433 (West Supp. 2002); see also Sean Murphy, "Contemporary Practice of the United States Relating to International Law," (2002) 96 AJIL 956 at 975–7.

[120] Compare *Demjanjuk v. Petrovsky*, 776 F 2d 571, 582, 6th Cir. 1985, 79 ILR 535, 545–46.

[121] See: Malanczuk, "The ICC and Landmines," above note 117, at 82.

[122] George Robertson, *Guardian*, 14 Sept. 2001, 22; Anne-Marie Slaughter, "Terrorism and Justice" *Financial Times*, 12 Oct. 2001, 23; Douglass Cassel, "Try bin Laden – but where?" *Chicago Daily Law*, 11 Oct. 2001, 6.

convictions, any acquittals are unlikely to be accepted by US policy makers and voters. Thus, it is not surprising that the United States prosecutes alleged terrorists before its own courts and, eventually, separate Military Commissions.[123]

To summarize the US position: State responsibility and individual responsibility must be strictly separated. States are only responsible in a civil law sense – there is no concept of State criminality, not even of serious violations of essential obligations toward the international community. Individuals are responsible individually, but only before national jurisdictions if and to the extent those jurisdictions are as liberal and democratic as the United States. The preference for individual responsibility conforms to a liberal understanding of the international community and general US individualism. The hostility towards international institutions exercising penal jurisdiction is the almost perfect expression of the anti-institutionalist bias. Hence the US position against collective and in favor of individual criminal responsibility, as well as its reluctance to accept an institutional machinery to enforce the latter, perfectly reflects the American position on the limits of the concept of an "international community."

Conclusion: The concept of "international community" from the United States perspective

By its very terminology, the concept of "international community" transfers the notion of community to the international sphere: Just as domestic societies have developed into collectivities sharing common values and projects, in the age of globalization, the international sphere seems to be developing slowly into a realm of shared purposes and values, if only with regard to the exclusion of terrorist and other groups challenging both the traditional State system and the most basic principles of human commonality and reciprocal respect. However, there seems to be no agreement as to how far this commonality goes and whether it should translate into common institutions.

---

[123] See, e.g., US v Lindh, 212 F. Supp. 2d 541 (E.D. Va. 2002); Presidential Military Order on the Detention, Treatment, and Trial of Certain Non-Citizens in the War Against Terrorism, 13 Nov. 2001, (2002) 41 *International Legal Materials* 252.

Even if there is, of course, no coherent and one-dimensional "United States" approach to this question, the distinctive features of American ideology at the beginning of the twenty-first century point in three directions:

1. a reluctance with regard to an all-encompassing institutionalization of the international realm, combined with an insistence on national prerogatives;
2. a reliance on the universality of democracy, human rights and the market economy as basic conditions for international welfare and as minimal conditions for the legitimacy of governments, protecting them from foreign intervention; and
3. the realist insistence on the relevance of (national) power and capabilities compared to the lack of resources at the international level, and the insistence on super-power prerogatives.

Not all American concepts of community share all three characteristics. Postmodernists, for instance, might accept parts of proposition 1 and 3 but not proposition 2, liberals could subscribe to propositions 1 and 2, but not all of them to 3, realists might embrace propositions 1 and 3 but not necessarily 2, and so forth.

Still, as the practical examples show, recent United States foreign policy has remained more or less true to these background positions: It has consistently turned down any attempt to install a UN monopoly on the use of force or to construct permanent institutions – even in cases where it was behind the change of philosophy, as in the case of the International Criminal Court. It has claimed legitimacy for the unilateral use of force in cases where the target state has not met the basic conditions of respect for democracy and human rights or has supported or "harbored" terrorists who committed acts of a magnitude equal to an armed attack. It has relied on the development of its own technological capabilities rather than on international treaties and institutions in security matters, as in the case of the construction of the (National) Missile Defense system or in the debates over the Biological Weapons Convention.[124] Following its

---

[124] Convention on the Prohibition of the Development, Production and Stockpiling of Bacteriological (Biological) and Toxin Weapons and on their Destruction, signed 10 Apr. 1972, entry into force 26 Mar. 1975, UNTS 1015, p. 163. Recently, the Bush administration has refused to

more recent rejections of international treaties and institutions, some have even claimed that it is the United States, rather than Iraq or North Korea, which should be called "the ultimate rogue nation."[125] But this is clearly an overstatement, or worse. The international solidarity with the United States displayed after the terrorist attacks of 11 September 2001, along with the increased willingness of the United States to seek international support and legitimacy for its response, may have dispelled the most far-reaching criticisms of United States hegemony, at least for the time being. An increasing awareness of global interdependence and of the need for US involvement in international affairs may be one of the more positive side effects of the new threats on the horizon, from the scourge of terrorism to the threat of biological weapons.

But one should be careful not to overstate the novelty of the current situation either. As long as its national interest and the perceived community interest are identical, the United States has never been opposed to receiving international support. Indeed, the presidential logic of "either you are with us or with the terrorists"[126] demonstrates that the current administration intends to continue to regard international issues through the prism of the US national interest. As Condoleezza Rice has put it:

> Many in the United States are... uncomfortable with the notions of power politics, great powers, and power balances... The "national interest" is replaced with "humanitarian interests" or the interests of "the international community... To be sure, there is nothing wrong with doing something that benefits all humanity, but that is, in a sense, a second-order effect. America's pursuit of the national interest will create conditions that promote freedom, markets, and peace. Its pursuit of national interests after World War II led to a more prosperous and democratic world. This can happen again.[127]

agree to an optional protocol to this convention establishing an inspection system in spite of the anthrax attacks against members of the US Senate and other public figures. The US alternative proposal instead relies on traditional international criminal law concepts and after the fact investigation of suspicious outbreaks or allegations of biological weapons use. See Statement by the President, "Strengthening the International Regime against Biological Weapons," 1 Nov. 2001, available at http://www.whitehouse.gov (last visited 10 Jan. 2002). See also Judith Miller, "US Publicly Accusing 5 Countries of Violating Germ-Weapons Treaty," *New York Times*, 19 Nov. 2001, 1. For US criticism, see Editorial, "An Enforceable Ban on Bioterror," *New York Times*, 3 Nov. 2001, 22.

[125] Noam Chomsky, *Rogue States: The Rule of Force in World Affairs* (Cambridge, MA: South End Press, 2000).
[126] See above note 3 and accompanying text.
[127] Rice, "Promoting the national interest," above note 2.

Thus, the international community is welcome if, and to the extent that, it propagates US values.

Of course, there is no necessary opposition between US and global values. As this chapter has shown, US perspectives have exerted a decisive influence on the concept of international community, gearing it away from governmental analogies towards the propagation of liberal values in an inter-State setting. It is unlikely that the international community will be able to develop without regard to these basic US views on what the international community is about and, especially, on what it is not about: the building of truly global governance, let alone government. In the words of Senator Jesse Helms, former chairman of the Senate Foreign Relations Committee:

> The demands of the United States have not changed much since Henry Cabot Lodge laid out his conditions for joining the League of Nations 80 years ago: Americans want to ensure that the United States of America remains the sole judge of its own internal affairs, that the United Nations is not allowed to restrict the individual rights of United States citizens, and that the United States retains sole authority over the deployment of United States forces around the world.[128]

Still, if there was any good in the terrorist attacks of 11 September or their aftermath, it is the recognition that the egregious violation of the most basic human right and supreme value – human life – by non-State actors affects the whole human community, not only a particular State, religion, or civilization. When the American people needed support from the rest of the "international community," they received it in abundance, from their allies, the United Nations, and even from States which are each other's enemies, such as India and Pakistan. Clearly, the international community was with the Americans and not with the terrorists, though this should not be interpreted as a blank cheque for every single action which the US government deems appropriate in its response to terrorism. In the long

---

[128] Address before the Security Council, *New York Times*, 21 Jan. 2000, available at http:// foreign.senate.gov/minority/2000/pr012000.cfm (last visited 10 Jan. 2002), also complaining of a "lack of gratitude" on the part of the United Nations towards the United States. For a recent account of the "League fight" between the Senate and President Wilson over the ratification of the League of Nations Covenant alluded to by Helms, see John M. Cooper, *Breaking the Heart of the World. Woodrow Wilson and the Fight for the League of Nations* (Cambridge: Cambridge University Press, 2001) and above note 52; for an account from the perspective of his opponents see William C. Widenor, *Henry Cabot Lodge and the Search for an American Foreign Policy* (Berkeley: University of California Press, 1980), pp. 300–48.

run, one may hope that it is this experience of support in need, and not the disenchantment with this or that individual decision, that will remain in the hearts and minds of Americans, as with the rest of the world, and thereby contribute to something which also lies at the heart of the community concept: the realization that we share more than that which divides us. And this should be valid not only in the "Western" world, but for all of humanity.

3

Comments on chapters 1 and 2

Martti Koskenniemi

Reflecting upon the nature of the Roman Empire in the fifth decade before Christ, Cicero stated what was to be a key point in the classical heritage. There was but one right law – just as there was one right reason. "[A]ll nations at all times will be bound by this eternal and unchangeable law." The political implication was clear: reason being law, all people sharing reason, they also share the law – "and those who have these things in common must be considered members of the same state."[1] This membership was what differentiated human beings from animals and made them resemble gods. The way to Empire, too, was firmly set: "Do we not see that the best people are given the right to rule by nature herself, with the greatest benefit to the weak?"[2] Rome is law, law is reason, reason is universal: Rome is universal.

But community is in the eye of the beholder and synthetic thought is just as able to find it anywhere as the tools of analysis convince us that it "really" is nowhere. As Andreas Paulus points out, the idea of a legal system implies the presence of a legal community. Correspondingly, "poststructuralist" deconstruction reduces every community into a series of polar opposites between any number of its elements. Hence the paradoxical fact that nationalism and internationalism, statehood and the universal community, appear to be bound together in a dialectical unity that Jonathan Rée has labelled "internationality."[3] This is what made the first professional international lawyers in the late nineteenth century conceive of their

[1] Cicero, *On the Commonwealth and On the Laws*, ed. James E. G. Zetzel (Cambridge: Cambridge University Press, 1999), p. 113.
[2] *Ibid.*, pp. 71, 73.
[3] Jonathan Rée, "Cosmopolitanism and the Experience of Nationality," in Pheng Cheah and Bruce Robbins (eds.), *Cosmopolitics. Thinking and Feeling beyond the Nation* (Minneapolis: University of Minnesota Press, 1998), p. 80.

nationalism as perfectly compatible with their cosmopolitanism and enabled their followers to understand the (European) state form as the great
globalizing force.[4] Whether or not this conception reflects a basic existential
tension – the desire to live in community with others and separate from
them, for instance – it has not been well integrated into a tradition of international legal thinking that still poses itself the question of the priority
of one over the other. Let me postulate once and for all: like the principles
of individualism and altruism, identity and community, the State and the
international are not only opposite but depend on each other, drawing their
life blood from the combination of mutual desire and revulsion that marks
their tormented relationship.

One of the ways in which that relationship manifests itself is expressed
in *the hegemonic argument* that is so striking in Cicero's discourse, the
argument through which the particular tries to fulfil the space of that which
is universal, the special to represent that which is general.[5] In Andreas
Paulus' chapter it is represented by Javier Solana's claim that the action
by the North Atlantic Treaty Organization in Kosovo in 1999 was action
by the "international community" – a claim immediately challenged by
India's permanent representative in the UN Security Council and by much
subsequent academic commentary.[6] A parallel controversy underlies the
examination in this volume of the nature of American leadership – which
Edward Kwakwa discussed benevolently in terms of an *expectation* thrown
upon the United States by its overwhelming power. Yet the absence of a
theory of hegemony left many of the positions without real traction with
regard to the larger structural problem of United States predominance and
completely overlooked the ambivalent, neurotic, and often hypocritical
politics of hegemony from which *Europeans* often articulate their criticisms
of the American Empire.

Europe's own history – and particularly its Christian universalism – is
of course replete with examples of the hegemonic argument. The Crusades

---

[4] Martti Koskenniemi, *The Gentle Civilizer of Nations. The Rise and Fall of International law
1870–1960* (Cambridge: Cambridge University Press, 2002), pp. 63–7.

[5] This understanding comes from Gramsci as influentially propagated in Ernesto Laclau and
Chantal Mouffe, *Hegemony and Socialist Strategy*, 2nd edn. (London: Verso, 2001).

[6] Cf. e.g. Pierre Klein, "Les problèmes soulevés par la référence à la 'communauté internationale'
comme facteur de légitimité," in Olivier Corten and Barbara Delcourt (eds.), *Droit, légitimation
et politique extérieure: L'Europe et la guerre du Kosovo* (Brussels: Bruylant, 2000), pp. 261–97; and
Michel Feher, *Powerless by Design. The Age of the International Community* (Durham, NC: Duke
University Press, 2000).

may originally have been motivated by the need to protect Church property and the realm of the empire. Sometime between 1095 and 1099, however, the additional (but limited) objective of the reoccupation of the Tomb of Christ had turned to colonial conquest of heretic lands.[7] Four centuries later, the validity of the claim by the crown of Castile that its rights over the land discovered by Columbus were legally founded on the 1492 bulls by Pope Alexander VI "seems to have been unquestioned."[8] In the sixteenth century the monarchy finally adopted the view earlier propagated by the Dominican theologian Bartolomé de Las Casas that the Indians, too, were in possession of a soul and governed by God's universal law. As Tony Anghie has noted, that conclusion also provided a welcome defense for Spanish trade and proselytising as well as a language of rectitude through which the Indians would henceforth be disciplined.[9] Las Casas was no less a colonialist than Hernando Cortés, and the two represent the opposition between the principle of love and the principle of economic interest that has permanently affected our understanding of empire.[10]

This ambivalence was in evidence also as the French nation enacted in 1789 the *Declaration des droits de l'homme et du citoyen* and, in doing so, claimed to be speaking not only for the French but for humankind. Universalism was an ineradicable aspect of political Enlightenment, but it also provided the basis for the French self-image during the wars of the twentieth century as the champion of what is universal (and good) against what was particular (and dangerous). The antagonism between *civilisation* and *Kultur* gave expression to ideas about cosmopolitanism or "world citizenship" that followed on from Cicero and Kant and have in the twentieth century enabled members of privileged classes – including those habitually residing around Second Avenue, between 43rd and 49th streets New York – to imagine their mores as unbounded, universal.[11]

---

[7] Cf. Jean Flori, *La guerre sainte. La formation de l'idée de croisade dans l'Occident chrétien* (Paris: Aubier, 2001) esp. pp. 345–8.

[8] Julius Gobel, *The Struggle for the Falkland Islands. A Study in Legal and Diplomatic History* (New Haven: Yale University Press, 1927) p. 49.

[9] Cf. Antony Anghie, "Francisco de Vitoria and the Colonial Origins of International Law" (1996) 5 *Social and Legal Studies* 321–36.

[10] Tzvetan Todorov, *The Conquest of America. The Question of the Other*, trans. Richard Howard (New York: Harper, 1984), pp. 168–82.

[11] For a brief, sympathetic intellectual history, cf. Martha Nussbaum, "Kant and Cosmopolitanism," in James Bohmann and Matthias Lutz-Bachmann (eds.), *Perpetual Peace. Essays on Kant's Cosmopolitan Ideal* (Cambridge, MA: MIT Press, 1997), pp. 25–57.

Universalism provided a firm justification for the assimilationist technique of French colonialism. But all European powers saw themselves as representing an international community when they carried out the *mission civilisatrice*. Soon after it was established in 1873, the Institut de droit international began to lobby for a conference on African affairs to prevent colonial conflict from undermining this mission. They noticed little of its ambivalence when, after the 1885 Berlin West African Conference, they joined one of their number, the Baltic-Russian professor Frederic Martens, who thanked King Léopold of the Belgians in gracious terms: "It is without a doubt thanks to the generosity and the political genius of King Léopold that the Congo State will have a regime in full conformity with the requirements of European culture."[12]

Colonialism illustrates the functioning of the logic of hegemony behind an argument about the international community. So does communist emancipation. Now the working class sought to establish itself as the universal class: the particular became an objective representative of what was universal. No wonder the Soviet Union was always split between advancing proletarian internationalism and Russian self-interest. Or think about globalization. Now it is Western ways of life – the Coke bottle, the Nike logo – that claim to represent something universal, the laws of economic and technological progress, modernity. To describe all this, we no longer speak of natural law, as Grotius did. From Vattel, we have learned the critique of the rationalist utopia of the *Civitas maxima*. The shared sense of the inevitability – perhaps inevitable beneficiality – of globalization is not difficult to redescribe in terms of the internalization of the hegemonic pursuits of the institutions of the market and of liberal democracy. Yet no sense of impending doom need accompany such recountings. Globalization is politically ambivalent and strategies of resistance are embedded in the cultural hybrids that it produces within and beyond the West.[13]

---

[12] Frédéric de Martens, "La Conférence du Congo à Berlin et la politique coloniale des états modernes" (1886) XVIII *Revue de droit international et de législation comparée*, 268. For the text of the enthusiastic address to King Léopold adopted by the Institut on 7 September 1885, cf. (1885–1886) 8 *Annuaire de l'Institut de droit international* 17–19. Cf. further, Koskenniemi, *Gentle Civilizer*, above note 4, pp. 155–66.

[13] On strategies of appropriation and resistance through the innovative use of artefacts of globalising popular culture, cf. e.g. Rosemary J. Coombe, *The Cultural Life of Intellectual Properties* (Durham, NC: Duke University Press, 1998). For a discussion of the pros and cons of hybridity, cf. Pheng Cheah, "Rethinking Cosmopolitical Freedom in Transnationalism" in Cheah and Robbins, *Cosmopolitics*, above note 3, pp. 292–303.

The language and critique of hegemony have been conventionally associated with the political "realist" view on international relations laid down
in a representative way by E. H. Carr:

> Just as pleas for "national solidarity" in domestic politics always come from
> a dominant group which can use this solidarity to strengthen its control over
> the nation as a whole, so pleas for international solidarity and world union
> come from those dominant nations which may hope to exercise control over
> a unified world... "International order" and "international solidarity" will
> always be slogans of those who feel strong enough to impose them on others.[14]

Now I think this is right and nothing that Andreas Paulus or Edward Kwakwa
have said undermines this. On the contrary, they take it for granted. The
logic of hegemony is an intrinsic part of modern politics:[15] the attempt
by *me* to represent *my* interests and *my* values as universal, *my* rule as
community. Like most truisms, however, it is not very informative. Surely
the question should be, "So what if 'community' means rule by those who
are able to articulate their interests as universal ones, provided that produces
an acceptable result?" If it works, don't fix it. There are two variants of this.

One is the *idealist* position that the hegemon is acceptable because it is
wise or its values are good. In this case, hegemony would in fact buttress
community against identity politics, nationalism, racism, different kinds of
negative particularism. The "institutional" and "liberal" concepts of community discussed by Paulus come under this view. Many Americans see US
hegemony in this light – and the fact that they do does not prove the argument wrong. The hard question, however, is how to convince those who
disagree and insist that what may appear as (mere) factual subordination in
fact takes the normative colour of domination. Here the intrinsic tendency
of the liberal mind to think of its own preferences as universal preferences –
for example, because of their "reasonableness" – is of little assistance. If it
is right, then deviating positions are unreasonable by definition, and States
that represent them become *outlaw States*.[16] Bomb them!

This result is often avoided by recourse to universalist language that
diplomacy produces to veil material disagreement: we may agree that there

---

[14] E. H. Carr, *The Twenty Years' Crisis 1919–1939* (2nd edn., London: Macmillan, 1946), p. 86.
[15] That is to say, a politics after the division of society into mutually exclusive, antagonistic camps
such as free men / slaves, ancien régime / people. Cf. Laclau and Mouffe, *Hegemony*, above note 5,
pp. 150–52.
[16] John Rawls, *The Law of Peoples: with the Idea of Public Reason Revisited* (Cambridge, MA:
Harvard University Press, 1999), p. 90.

must be *jus cogens*, or norms that are accepted "by the international community as a whole" but completely disagree about what might count as such. It is not necessary to think of such facade agreement as mere ideological obfuscation. It both defers disagreement and unblocks the avenue of pragmatic progress, singling out universality as a kind of a regulative ideal while allowing political adjustment and compromise in the matter at hand. It is a *procedural* strategy of community (or "society"), a formalist technique to enable disagreeing agents to live together.[17] It works as long as the hegemon is content to look on benevolently; but its weakness becomes evident as soon as the hegemon throws in the towel: the ICC, the *Breard* case, Kyoto protocol, human rights treaties, biological weapons, ABM...

As Paulus pointed out, even *realists* often accept the less demanding argument that a hegemony is good inasmuch as it prevents the *bellum omnium*. If survival depends on the presence of a hegemon, then shut up and obey! Many of us remember the collapse of the League of Nations and think about the position of the "P-5" and the Security Council in this way. Is it possible to accept the hegemonic exception, but to prevent it from turning into a tyrant? After a bad night even the enlightened monarch may have his servants whipped.

This to me is the problem with Kwakwa's approach. The world needs the United States – but the United States also needs the world, in order to fulfill its own interests. Under such circumstances, Kwakwa's strategy would be to try to convince the United States that this is so. Perhaps "we" (who?) may thereby be able to bind its hands: killing the Empire with kindness.

But I wonder about this image of the United Nations, or of Europe, or the rest of the world, as beggars of security at the door of the White House. The theory of hegemonic cooperation casts the rest as weaklings. There is something to be said about self-sufficiency, in favor of J. S. Mill's argument against external intervention. Perhaps real community cannot be brought in from the outside.[18] In John Updike's early novel *The Coup* there is a scene where an American relief worker – who had "marched for civil rights through college" – lands in a United States Air Force C-130 carrier somewhere in the Sahel to bring grain to a starving population. There is a brief encounter with an educated Saheli Prince, Ellelou. Then, the Tuareg rise

---

[17] Cf. e.g. Terry Nardin, *Law, Morality and the Relations of States* (Princeton: Princeton University Press, 1983).

[18] For a discussion, cf. Michael Walzer, *Just and Unjust Wars. A Moral Argument with Historical Illustrations*, 2nd edn. (New York: Harper, 1992), pp. 87–91.

against the American. They set the sacks of relief food on fire, put him on top of the pyre, and celebrate, firmly convinced that the State Department had anyway prepared him for a martyr's death.[19]

Neither the idealist–formalist nor the realist defense of community is convincing to someone like Frantz Fanon, arguing that all Western wealth and power is a result of centuries of oppression. "Europe must pay," he wrote in the 1960s, and the horror of 11 September is not enough to make the non-Western world forget. Fanon spoke of revolution in the South in terms of finally "reintroducing mankind into the world."[20] Again, hegemonic discourse portrays that which is particular, namely the struggle against colonialism, as that which is in fact universal. And again, the fact that it does so is not itself proof of its moral rectitude. That assessment must hinge on political choices, evaluation of the acceptability of the types of (international) community that hegemonic policies hope to inaugurate.

This is where we might be blocked by relativism. Is it possible to assess notions of community from a perspective that might transcend the immediate objectives of hegemonic actors? Fanon himself stated that in the colonial struggle "there is no truthful behavior; and the good is simply what is evil for 'them'."[21] The colonial slave will enslave his former master. The anticolonial struggle reverses the hegemonic relationship, but oppression remains.

Paulus correctly observes that community is defined by reference to the Other. And Kwakwa quotes Kofi Annan: "the international community is defined not only by what it is for but by what and whom it is against." Both restate Carl Schmitt's well-known theory of politics as having to do with the friend–enemy opposition. For Schmitt, the particular danger of humanitarian universalism lies in its implicit definition of the Other as the existential enemy, as not a member of humanity at all. Consequently, no measures against him would seem excessive.[22] "Whoever invokes humanity wants to cheat," Schmitt also wrote, pointing to the core of the hegemonic struggle that is waged over what notions such as "humanity," "international community," *jus cogens*, or "obligations owed to the international community

---

[19] John Updike, *The Coup* (Harmondsworth: Penguin, 1956), pp. 38–42.

[20] Frantz Fanon, *The Wretched of the Earth*, trans. Constance Farrington (New York: Grove Press, 1963), p. 106.

[21] *Ibid.*, p. 50.

[22] Carl Schmitt, *The Concept of the Political*, trans. Georg Schwab, intr. Tracy Strong (Cambridge, MA: MIT Press, 1996 [1934]), pp. 45–54, and Schmitt, *Die Wendung zum diskriminierenden Kriegsbegriff*, 2nd edn. (Berlin: Duncker & Humblot, 1988), pp. 37–54.

as a whole" *mean*: whose policy will they include, and whose policy will they condemn? The language of fighting against Evil,[23] first used by President Bush at an unguarded moment, like the language of the crusade, intensifies the hegemonic struggle and thereby, perversely, projects Osama bin Laden as the great liberator, as the last symbol of the antihegemonic struggle.

In such a situation, complete exclusion is met by complete exclusion; the structure of domination repeats itself in an apparently endless cycle of reversals of hegemonic positions. Can the cycle be broken?

Clearly, the language of community, albeit always a language of hegemony, need not be a language of complete exclusion. After all, Cicero and the Stoic cosmopolitans never thought of foreigners as fundamentally alien or hostile.[24] The question is how to maintain the ideal of universality in the conditions of hegemonic struggle. How does one create space between Empire and identity politics (or perhaps these are ultimately the same)?

As we have admired America's achievements in the past, we have often been surprised at what it has been *unable to achieve*, at its errors and its ignorance – which are perfectly comparable to our own errors and ignorance. The time of conspiracy theories is over. There is neither an overall "plan" nor overarching wisdom located in the United States, or elsewhere. Edward Kwakwa is right to point out that, however the international community is seen, it cannot be reduced to the decision-making activity of the some 200 formal governments out there. But instead of making room for only a few nongovernmental decision makers, I am tempted by the larger vision of Hardt and Negri that the world is in transit toward what they, borrowing from Michel Foucault, call a biopolitical Empire, an Empire that has no capital, that is ruled from no one spot but that is equally binding on Washington and Karachi, and all of us. In this image, there are no interests that arise from States – only interest-positions that are dictated by an impersonal, globally effective economic and cultural logic. This is a structural Empire which is no less powerful as a result of not being ruled by formal decision-making from anywhere.[25]

This image of the Empire almost inevitably gives the notion of international community a new lease of life. Its great merit is that it would allow, indeed encourage, various counterhegemonic strategies in regard to

---

[23] Cf. Jarna Petman, "Fighting the Evil with International Economic Sanctions," (1999) 10 *Finnish Yearbook of International Law* 209–230.

[24] Nussbaum, "Kant and Cosmopolitanism," above note 11, 33–35.

[25] Michael Hardt and Antonio Negri, *Empire* (Cambridge, MA: Harvard University Press, 2000).

particular aspects of the Empire. There would be no single frontier – and no simple exclusion or inclusion – but countless small struggles: poverty, land mines, the International Criminal Court, human rights; struggles in regard to the policies of the World Trade Organization, the Washington consensus, environmental degradation. Each of such struggles creates a different constellation of actors and interests. None of them is the "final battle." Nonetheless, it is easy to describe the small struggles as aspects, or partial articulations, of new or emergent ideas about "international community." Hardt and Negri write of the counterimperial "multitude." Others might refer to separate activities within the civil society or by social movements that create what Ernesto Laclau has called "chains of equivalence" within which these actions articulate themselves as aspects of larger battles that sometimes claim to occupy the notion of "international community."[26]

The logic of imperial administration is, as Andreas Paulus points out, against formal institutions. But instead of supporting the homogeneous *national* power of the United States, it now works through military, financial and cultural structures that have become independent of political goal-setting and institutional control.[27] The implied notion of "international community" refers to abstract values such as "democracy," the "market," or "good governance" that bear no relationship to the constitutive exclusions through which these bureaucracies reproduce themselves outside the marginalized spheres of official international politics. This is why what unites counterimperial struggles today is the emphasis given to institutions and formal procedures: rights, mechanisms of accountability and distribution. This is no surprise. For formal law and formal rights are about binding those in positions of power, about mistrust of informal "values," about openness and inclusion, and about rejecting the complacent assumption – sometimes made by Paulus and Kwakwa, too – that authority is an effect of power.

International law may be understood as an anti-imperial strategy through its articulation of the perspective of a truer "international community." The

---

[26] Cf. Ernesto Laclau, "Subject of Politics, Politics of Subject," in *Emancipation(s)* (London: Verso, 1996), pp. 57–60, and "Constructing Universality," in Judith Butler, Ernesto Laclau, and Slavoj Žižek (eds.), *Contingency, Hegemony, Universality. Contemporary Dialogues on the Left* (London: Verso, 2000), pp. 301–4.

[27] This is what Hardt and Negri mean when they characterize the imperial power as "biopolitical." Such activities have become constitutive aspects, and not simple effects, of its "life," *Empire*, above note 25, pp. 343–50.

"truth" of this community would lie in the fact that it is not received from a positive substance, principle, value, or political program. Though it embodies different substantive claims, these claims are united in terms of a *negative* and *formal* datum – their shared antagonism to the Empire, their lack of some aspect of their identity (lack of rights, lack of resources, lack of self-determination etc.) that they experience as caused by the Empire. The "international community" implied here would consist of a "chain of equivalences" that link claims or identities by their not having been realized. Its universalism would not be a substance but a "placeholder for an absence," or a "horizon" that cannot be detached from the particular claims in which it appears. "Women's human rights" is a typical formal claim of this paradoxical type: both particular in referring to "women" and universal in referring to "human rights."[28] Its emancipatory potential lies in part in its critique of some social arrangement as preventing the particular identity from being "full" in some regard, while doing this in terms of what is universal – "human rights." In part it results from the understanding that every substance (a notion of "woman") is premised and every community (a particular regime of "human rights") is founded on an exclusion and that it must be a part of an acceptable community's self-definition that it negotiates that exclusion: "the only democratic society is one which permanently shows the contingency of its own foundation."[29]

This kind of "international community" receives its identity from the horizon of universality that is part of its self-definition. Not being the handmaid of some hegemonic substance or other, its constitutive forms are everything the Empire is not: transparent, rule-oriented and inclusive. This involves the familiar ideals of equality, rule of law and due process, but also a broad commitment to what could be called situated cosmopolitanism: seeing international law also as a continuation of the traditions of hospitality (in the sense of the "Third Definitive Article" of Kant's *Perpetual Peace*) that encourage and support continuous exchange and translation beyond the boundaries of political communities. Both particular and universal, local and cosmopolitan, we might be able to see therein some of Cicero's cosmopolitan patriotism – but without the imperial consequences of his

---

[28] Judith Butler, "Restaging the Universal," in Butler, Laclau, and Žižek, *Contingency*, above note 26, pp. 39–40.

[29] Laclau, "Identity and Hegemony: the Role of Universality in the Constitution of Political Logics," in Butler, Laclau, and Žižek, *Contingency*, above note 26, p. 86.

language. This is a fragile utopia; but perhaps it can remain anti-imperial only by so being.

Steven Ratner

In this short reply to the papers prepared by Edward Kwakwa and Andreas Paulus, I hope to challenge some of the basic assumptions made by the two authors. These papers, like those of many contributors to this volume, tend to totalize and homogenize the American perspective about the notion of international community. Consequently, they conclude that America's relationship to that community is defined by a special set of conditions, unique among all global actors. I begin this comment by questioning their initial assumption about a single American viewpoint. In my view, each community within the United States has diverse views that defy each explanation. Later I will question the conclusion that flows from that incorrect assumption.

Before beginning, I would point out that, although it would be laudable if global actors endorsed the broad view of the international community that Edward Kwakwa espouses, the term itself really should be used very sparingly. David Kennedy is thus right in identifying the term as a subterfuge.[30] In fact, the various actors of the global legal and political processes act with one voice or react with one view on exceedingly few issues. One does not need to be a critical legal scholar to accept this position.

The diversity of American academia

Andreas Paulus ably reviews the various schools of American academic approaches to the international community and attempts to find four unifying themes, which he then asserts drive American foreign policy. But academics in the United States are very much divided on all the criteria in the section of Paulus' paper on "The (neo)liberal response to globalization." Though he claims to accept both the diversity of American academia and the sharing by Americans and non-Americans of many academic perspectives, he tries

---

[30] David Kennedy, "The Disciplines of International Law and Policy" (1999) 12 *Leiden Journal of International Law* 9 at 83–84.

too hard to find common ground among the US approaches, something uniquely American about them.[31]

As an initial matter, American legal scholars are not all or even predominantly members of the New Haven School – though it must be added that that approach is diverse enough to include scholars such as Richard Falk, Henry Richardson, Rosalyn Higgins, and Shigeru Oda among its disciples.[32] American legal scholars, whether in the New Haven School or not, do not reject the distinction between the "is" and the "ought." Many are very concerned about the so-called "relative normativity"[33] of international law, as Brad Roth's paper amply demonstrates. Even those, like myself, who are not in particular agreement with Prosper Weil's fears, do not reject the category of hard law, but simply point out that some norms are softer than others, and that norms can change over time. Many Europeans have written favorably about soft law, so it is hardly an object of uniquely American attraction.[34]

This is not to say that there are no distinctions between the European and American academies. For one, legal realism and legal process approaches have a far greater influence within the American academy than they do within Europe. In addition, as a result of the pedagogy of US law schools, US-based scholars generally seem to have a greater recognition of the intimate connection between law and politics. But those scholars most insistent on that link – those in international law's critical legal studies movement – are mostly non-Americans.[35] And more fundamentally, as Paulus recognizes,

---

[31] Indeed, even to speak of American academia is difficult. Many international legal scholars teaching at American law schools are not US citizens or permanent resident aliens. And many international lawyers of US nationality teach abroad. It is unclear whether the authors of the papers mean to include only US citizens teaching at US law schools. If so, they assume a great deal about how citizenship affects approaches to international law.

[32] For an excellent description, see Siegfried Wiessner and Andrew R. Willard, "Policy-Oriented Jurisprudence and Human Rights Abuses in Internal Conflict: Toward a World Public Order of Human Dignity" (1999) 93 *American Journal of International Law* 316.

[33] Prosper Weil, "Vers une normativité relative en droit international?" (1982) *Revue générale de droit international public* 5.

[34] See, e.g., Hartmut Hillgenberg, "A Fresh Look at Soft Law" (1999) 10 *European Journal of International Law*, 499; Francesco Francioni, "International 'Soft Law': A Contemporary Assessment," in Vaughan Lowe and Malgosia Fitzmaurice (eds.), *Fifty Years of the International Court of Justice: Essays in Honour of Sir Robert Jennings* (Cambridge: Cambridge University Press, 1996), p. 167; Christine Chinkin, "The Challenge of Soft Law: Development and Change in International Law" (1989) 38 *International and Comparative Law Quarterly* 850.

[35] See, e.g., Martti Koskenniemi (ed.), "Special Issue: New Approaches to International Law" (1996) 65 *Nordic Journal of International Law* 569–95.

the American academy is highly diverse (and constantly open to new ideas), and the handful of American scholars asked to contribute to this volume are hardly representative of that diversity.

Second, most American legal scholars are not, as Paulus implies, liberals in the sense of those authors who downplay the role of states in international affairs in favor of subnational actors engaging in transnational relationships. While important for making linkages between international law and international relations theory (although other strands of IR theory have been equally integrated into international law thinking), the liberal approach does not, as Jose Alvarez's recent work demonstrates,[36] represent a dominant American view.

Third, and relatedly, those scholars who see democracy as an ideal do not favor its imposition or its replacement of fundamental human rights as the touchstone of a world public order. Liberal democracy is not, by the way, some uniquely American idea, as Kofi Annan's June 2001 Cyril Foster Lecture at Oxford shows.[37]

Fourth, *pace* Paulus, US scholars do not regard international institutions as marginal, let alone irrelevant actors. Most American international lawyers take them quite seriously. As even the most superficial perusal of the plethora of US international law journals makes clear, American academics routinely write about the importance of the Security Council and General Assembly, the European Union, the Organization of American States, the World Trade Organization, the International Monetary Fund, the World Bank, the UN and regional human rights bodies, and myriad other institutions. Some scholars wish to delegate more authority to international institutions; others are more skeptical, but most seem to want to improve both their legitimacy and their effectiveness.

Academia and governmental policy

Beyond these divergences within American academia, there is little correlation between academic visions of international law and United States foreign policy attitudes. Republicans are divided between realists like Henry Kissinger and idealists who think the United States should be spreading

---

[36] Jose E. Alvarez, "Do Liberal States Behave Better? A Critique of Slaughter's Liberal Theory" (2001) 12 *European Journal of International Law* 183.
[37] Kofi Annan, "Why Democracy is an International Issue," Cyril Foster Lecture, University of Oxford, 19 June 2001.

Christianity around the globe. Democrats are more united in principle, but usually end up compromising in practice because their views are not politically tenable with the public. The description of the American ideology in the conclusion of Paulus' essay sounds as European as it does American in most respects.

Equally important, American policy makers are not significantly influenced by the debates among international lawyers. They are not generally readers of theoretical literature, and certainly not theoretical literature in international *law*. Indeed, it is safe to say that the European governments listen to their academic international lawyers – whether through their membership (or leadership) of intergovernmental delegations or their retention as counsel in international judicial proceedings – far more than does the US government.

An American outlook?

The authors' flawed assumptions of unity at home leads to a questionable conclusion about the uniqueness of the US position toward the international community. If we turn to the particular issues discussed in the two papers on which the United States is said to have played some special role vis-à-vis the international community, we can ask if there is really an American outlook. With respect to Kosovo, most Americans supported NATO's war against Serbia (as did most West Europeans); academics were, however, clearly divided, and those divisions reflected views of international lawyers everywhere. Indeed, the most eloquent advocates of what has become the conventional wisdom among most international lawyers – that the war was unlawful but justified (a position with which the author incidentally disagrees) – have been European.[38] Regarding the International Criminal Court, where I do think that the United States government should move toward the position of others, is it really a uniquely American opposition, or is it a view shared by other powerful states, such as China and Russia, that will not, despite their signature, ratify the ICC Statute? Granted, there is a public attitude in the United States that is suspicious

---

[38] See, e.g., Bruno Simma, "NATO, the UN and the Use of Legal Force: Legal Aspects" (1999) 10 EJIL 1; Antonio Cassese, "Ex iniuria ius oritur: Are We Moving towards International Legitimation of Forcible Humanitarian Countermeasures in the World Community?" (1999) 10 EJIL 23.

COMMENTS ON CHAPTERS 1 AND 2

about involvement in international alliances that might involve compromising US interests;[39] but foreign policymakers are generally more subtle and
far-sighted, as attested to by US involvement in numerous areas of international cooperation and its willingness to compromise on most international
regimes (e.g., key trade issues, aspects of the Law of the Sea Convention, and
others).

Redefining the problematic

In a sense, then, the only American perspective that I would present here
is the need to question the assumption among the papers – and the editors
of this volume – that there is such a thing as an American perspective
vis-à-vis the international community. I thus propose that we redefine the
problematic presented in these papers as follows.

There is, indeed, a dilemma or paradox regarding the American relationship with other power clusters on the planet, but it is not quite the somewhat
uncomplicated symbiotic relationship that Kwakwa's paper describes. It
should instead be viewed as follows: On the one hand, the dominant voices
in non-United States governments, civil society, and academia who speak
about American responsibility to the international community look at it
in terms of *liability* – almost akin to state responsibility: the power of the
United States makes it liable for the injustices of the world, either because
(1) the United States is said to have some role in creating them, or (2) it
has some power to remedy them. On the other hand, these same advocates
do not in fact want the United States to take a predominant role in fixing
the problem, or, if they do, they expect the United States to subordinate its
wishes to, or redefine them as, everyone else's.

On the first point, concerning responsibility, whatever the divisions
among Americans on their relationship to the so-called international community, most American citizens and governmental leaders do not see
their dominance as creating responsibilities based on either of the above
rationales. Rather, they see US power as creating opportunities for action
when acts abroad affect American interests. And what constitutes American

[39] See Robert Skidelsky, "Imbalance of Power" (2002) 2 *Foreign Policy* at 46, 50 ("Americans do
not think naturally in terms of alliance politics. They either want to be uninvolved or masters
of the situation . . . [They] like to think that their own country is the uniquely godly power in
a world of fallen angels and that their plans and their ways of thinking are genuinely good for
everyone").

interests changes over time. The intervention in Somalia in 1992 to ensure delivery of humanitarian supplies shows an American interest quite generous in its scope. The blockage of the Kyoto Protocol shows the opposite.

On the second point, namely the subordination of US policy, a suggestion that the United States should simply reject its interests in favor of those of other states, or redefine them to be the same as others' wishes, is simply too much to ask of any power. Although Kwakwa's piece is quite careful in this regard, others in the book seem to suggest that the United States should join all legal regimes accepted by a large majority of States. Does that mean that the United States must agree to nuclear disarmament? Does it mean that the United States – along with Germany, the United Kingdom, and Japan – should have agreed to the seabed mining regime of the original 1982 United Nations Convention on the Law of the Sea merely because most other states signed it? Does it mean that those three states, along with many other Western states, were wrong to oppose certain aspects of the New International Economic Order, simply because many or most governments in the developing world favored (or said they favored) it?[40]

I am not, of course, suggesting that the United States is free to violate international law; the issue here concerns when, during the prescription of international law, it should join an emerging consensus or oppose it. In that respect, America's relationship with the international community is somewhat complex, as Kwakwa recognizes. The question for those of us committed to an international order based on legal norms and not just power then becomes when and how the United States can say no.

The effect of American superpower status on relations with other actors

Assuming that there is some kind of international community, can we describe a unique set of relationships between its most powerful member and the others? The editors of this volume seem to assume that the answer is yes, and most other contributors seek to critique that relationship and prescribe a better one.

I would suggest instead that there is little to be gained by singling out the US position. It changes with political administrations; and it is not often

---

[40] Even the Southern states were divided on the question of the quantum of compensation in the event of an expropriation. See *Texaco Overseas Petroleum Co. v. Libyan Arab Republic*, (International Arbitration Tribunal 1978), 17 *International Legal Materials* 1, paras. 85–89.

unique but supported by other states. It seems that the last three or so years of rather blatant American unilateral acts regarding a number of major treaties and regimes – the Landmines Convention, the Comprehensive Test Ban Treaty, the ICC Statute, and the Kyoto Protocol – have overly influenced the thinking of some scholars on this question. In other words, I remain unconvinced that the sole superpower status of the United States creates some unique relationship that changes the foundations of international law. Instead, when the power, interests, values, and views of international law held by the full panoply of actors in the international system are considered, it becomes clear that these actors exhibit similar ambiguities and tensions in their relationships with the international community.

For example, to take two medium-sized powers, would India and Pakistan let the United Nations decide the future of Kashmir? Would Greece and Turkey allow other actors to determine the fate of Cyprus? Or would Morocco vis-à-vis Western Sahara? Did France stop nuclear testing when the International Court of Justice told it to do so in 1973?[41] What were the EU negotiations in Nice in 2000 or the ongoing constitutional convention all about? Or consider Russia's views about Chechnya or the Montreal Ozone Protocol, or Brazil's about the rainforest, or Japan's or Norway's about whaling, or Australia's position on asylum seekers. Each of these states – goaded by domestic nonstate actors, whether the general public, businesses, or NGOs – defines its own interest on these issues, at variance with the expectations of most other states, and seeks to use international law to advance those interests. The question is whether the United States simply does this more persistently than those states because it has more global interests than they do, or whether it is engaged in a fundamentally different exercise. Kwakwa points in his paper to objections to *American* unilateralism. But we need to scrutinize whether that unilateralism is so different from the unilateralism that other states like to use from time to time.

Instead, we should disaggregate the issues in these two papers – and perhaps the volume as a whole – and shift our discussions to the substantive issues about which the United States disagrees with other states. We should not see this as a debate that is always framed in terms of America versus the rest. Obviously, international law has to be authoritative and controlling.

---

[41] See *Nuclear Test Cases (Australia v. France, New Zealand v. France)* (Interim Protections) (1973) ICJ Reports 99.

And for each subject area, whether trade, the environment, human rights, or arms control, the constellation of states necessary to achieve this goal is different. For some issues, the United States need not be included; for others, it may well be better if it is not; and for others, it may be indispensable. If US participation is needed for lawmaking and law application on an issue, other states will need to explain their position to the United States – its government and nongovernmental actors. And, of course, the United States must do the same to other states if their support is needed. This is the stuff of normal interstate relations and negotiations in our international system; it is not something that can be described as part of a unique dynamic between the United States and the international community.

Volker Rittberger

Edward Kwakwa and Andreas Paulus have written chapters which are well-argued, insightful and nuanced, and hence provide us with an excellent point of departure for this book. What is more, they have done so in an "efficient" way, as it were, for while *both* chapters address conceptual and factual issues, their foci are different: Kwakwa's chapter places its emphasis on tracing the complex relationship between the United States as the sole remaining superpower and the international community particularly as represented by global international organizations such as the United Nations; in contrast, Paulus' chapter highlights the variety of understandings of the concept of the international community that inform legal scholarship in the United States and also affect (although unevenly) the US government's attitude vis-à-vis the international community. In this way, the latter chapter tends to further develop and explore more deeply the themes that the former has broached.

    Kwakwa's chapter breaks down into two parts. The first part addresses the issue of how best to define the concept of "international community." This is certainly a worthwhile effort, since, as both authors point out, the high degree of popularity that this notion currently enjoys among scholars and practitioners alike is not matched by a similar degree of conceptual clarity – a mismatch, which, of course, should not be taken for a paradox: one is probably right in suspecting that this very vagueness is part of the reason why so many actors and observers feel attracted to this concept and the promises it holds for them. Acknowledging that there is no such thing as *the* adequate definition of "international community," Kwakwa advocates what he calls an "inclusive" definition, according to which the community is not composed exclusively of states but encompasses "the whole array of other actors whose actions influence the development of international legal rules," including intergovernmental organizations, NGOs, transnational corporations and even individuals.[42]

While this conclusion has a certain appeal, particularly from the point of view of "cosmopolitan democracy" as advanced by David Held,[43] I am less convinced by the way it is reached by Kwakwa. One of his arguments for an inclusive understanding of the term "international community" is based on its usage in international legal instruments and documents. It seems to me, however, that the textual evidence that is cited in the chapter is much more ambiguous than the author admits and therefore not as strong as it should be to back up his argument. It is true that Kwakwa also points to some substantive reasons for not restricting the membership of the international community to states: on some occasions non-State actors have had an indisputable influence on the formulation of international law,[44] and the shared values that contemporary international law is based upon are applicable not only to states but to other kinds of actors as well.[45] However, to develop the full potential of these arguments, it seems necessary to be more explicit about the criteria that govern the decision to consider a given actor (or entity) as a part of the legal community in question. For example, is it sufficient for such an actor occasionally to have an influence on the process of lawmaking, or should we not require a more firmly established claim to participation for it to be legitimately counted among the members of the community in question? Is the inclusive "international community" perhaps not too asymmetrical to support the proposed usage? How do we answer the skeptical supposition that non-State actors are part of the international community only when States – the "real" members and gatekeepers of the international community – decide that the participation and support of non-State actors are helpful in achieving their own purposes? Moreover, how are we to conceive of the formation of the collective will of this inclusively defined international community? And last but not least, who are the legitimately empowered agents of this community?

---

[42] Kwakwa, above, p. 27.
[43] Cf. David Held, *Democracy and the Global Order. From the Modern State to Cosmopolitan Governance* (Cambridge: Polity Press, 1995).
[44] Kwakwa, above, p. 31.   [45] Kwakwa, above, p. 33.

Unless we find adequate answers to these questions, an inclusive definition of "international community," instead of a narrow one confining itself
to States and, perhaps, intergovernmental organizations, may provide a
politically convenient mystification of hegemonic rule instead of shedding
light on the still to be determined state of normative integration in today's
world.

In the second part of his chapter, Kwakwa addresses the relationship between the United States and the international community and makes it clear
that simple formulas such as "unilateralism" or "multilateralism" do not
take us very far. The picture that emerges is a much more complicated and
ambiguous one. As the author concludes, "the international community,
international law and the United States are not one and the same, neither
are they two against one, as is often assumed. There are several instances
in which the United States has demonstrated that it is one on its own, but
that is a far cry from being one against the other two."[46] The United States
is not "against" the international community or international law, because,
as a general stance, this would clearly not serve its interests well. If simple
formulas are off the mark, however, perhaps a slightly less simple one such
as Richard Haass' "à la carte multilateralism" sheds much more light on the
US approach to the international community and its aspirations. It is my
impression that most of the evidence Kwakwa presents is consistent with
this notion, and this is hardly good news for those who regard a strengthening of international law and international institutions as essential for world
progress. For we should be clear that "à la carte multilateralism" is really
not multilateralism at all, if this idea involves a generalized commitment to
international cooperation and international institutions based on diffuse
reciprocity.[47] In this context, Kwakwa's remark that "the international community remains a critically important *instrument* for the advancement of
US national interests and foreign policy objectives"[48] is particularly telling
because it sets the United States apart from other industrially developed
nations which tend toward embracing what I call "principled multilateralism" as, for example, Germany has continued to do even after unification.[49]

---

[46] Kwakwa, above, p. 56.
[47] Cf. John Gerard Ruggie, "Multilateralism: The Anatomy of an Institution," in John Gerard
Ruggie (ed.), *Multilateralism Matters. The Theory and Praxis of an Institutional Form* (New
York: Columbia University Press, 1993), 3–47.
[48] Kwakwa, above, p. 47 (emphasis added).
[49] Cf. Volker Rittberger (ed.), *German Foreign Policy Since Unification: Theories and Case Studies*
(Manchester: Manchester University Press, 2001).

Kwakwa helpfully reminds us that US behavior vis-à-vis the international community is not unique, as sometimes appears. This applies in both a diachronic and a synchronic sense. Diachronically, there are precedents of other countries leaning towards a more or less pronounced "unilateralism." Synchronically, what is special is less what the United States *does*: after all, Kwakwa suggests, every state conducts its foreign policy with a view to furthering its national interests; what is special is *who* does it or rather *what kind of state* does it. For, since the United States is by far the most powerful member of the international community, its actions – be they legal or nonlegal, cooperative or noncooperative – are necessarily different in that they are much more consequential than formally similar ones carried out by lesser actors. Similarly, both the expectations of other states and the expectations of the United States itself are in large measure derivable from the special position of the United States in the international system. Note, however, that "who" and "what kind of state" can mean different things in this context: by using these expressions one can refer to a *structural position*, in this case the position of a hegemon; or one can refer to a state's *identity* which is not fully reducible to, and may even be largely independent of, this position. Kwakwa opts for the first understanding, which is basically a neorealist one.[50] But this may not suffice, for it may make a difference that this hegemon is also a *liberal* state, as authors as different as Gilpin and Ruggie have pointed out.[51] Liberal hegemons may exhibit a preference for more benign forms of leadership, whereas dominant states whose domestic political system is autocratic or authoritarian may tend to act as coercive or exploitative hegemons. (This said, a liberal hegemon in decline or under attack may also be tempted to find benevolence too costly and, therefore, adopt behaviors which make it less distinguishable from non-liberal hegemons.)

Paulus' chapter is also in two parts. In the first part, he gives a concise and illuminating overview of scholarly conceptions of the international community and, hence, the foundations of international law, as found in US legal discussion: a realist conception that denies the existence of a real community at the international level, perceiving instead a society of selfish, power-seeking States; an institutionalist conception that calls for institutions of

[50] The seminal neorealist work is Kenneth N. Waltz, *Theory of International Politics* (New York: Random House, 1979).

[51] Cf. Ruggie, "Multilateralism," above note 48; and Robert Gilpin, *War and Change in World Politics* (Cambridge: Cambridge University Press, 1981).

global governance to match the ongoing process of globalization of both activities and problems; a liberal conception that envisages a cosmopolitan world community defined by democracy, markets, and individualism, and that is skeptical of a major role for international institutions; and finally a postmodern conception that debunks the discourse on international community as an ideology suppressing and marginalizing different identities and serving powerful interests and that thus, ironically, comes close to many traditional realist tenets. Paulus' point is that these schools of thought are not equally strong in the scholarly international law community of the United States and also not equally reflected in the attitude and behavior of the United States government toward international law and the international community (which he sets out to demonstrate in the second part of his paper): in both spheres, liberal and to a lesser extent realist views are dominant, whereas institutionalist views, as developed especially by scholars "in the German constitutional tradition,"[52] are clearly in the minority and of lesser weight.

As a political scientist, I am struck by the close parallels that appear to exist between this legal debate and the controversies that are familiar to me in my own field of international relations. On reflection, this is, of course, not surprising at all, given that the sociology of international law, which the debate is basically about, must, as Paulus points out, make reference to ethical ideas and social conditions that are external to the realm of law. Not being an expert on the philosophy of international law, I shall confine my remarks to this salient interface between international law and international relations theory. On a general level, Paulus' reconstruction of this legal debate has once more demonstrated to me that there is great potential for fruitful co-operation between international law and international relations – two disciplines that long had very little to say to one another and often seemed to pursue their agendas in mutual lack of interest and ignorance.[53] In a more specific vein, I would like to conclude by offering three comments or observations with respect to the debate as reconstructed by Andreas Paulus.

First, it is striking that one of the most influential schools in international relations theory in recent years, constructivism, is apparently not

[52] Paulus, above, p. 68.
[53] But see now Judith L. Goldstein, Miles Kahler, Robert O. Keohane, and Anne-Marie Slaughter (eds.), Legalization and World Politics (Special Issue of International Organization) (Cambridge, MA: MIT Press, 2001).

represented in this debate – except perhaps in its extreme form of post-modernist criticism rather than acknowledging Alexander Wendt's *Social Theory of International Politics*.[54] Is this because constructivism has little to offer to international lawyers or is it because it has, in a sense, too much to offer in that international law *is* about social constructions and the debate is only about whether realist, liberal or institutionalist descriptions of these constructions and intersubjective meanings are the most appropriate?

Second, I wonder whether the discussion of the liberal position on the international community[55] might have benefited from distinguishing more clearly welfare (or egalitarian) liberalism à la Rawls[56] from market liberalism (or libertarianism) à la Nozick or Gauthier.[57] For it would seem that the first version of liberalism is much less hostile to powerful and even redistributive institutions than the latter. This holds true even in the international realm, when we look at the work of Beitz and Pogge,[58] who advocate a globalization of the "difference principle," and not merely at that of Rawls himself, whose normative vision of the international order is much more conservative and institutionally thin and, consequently, has disappointed many of his followers.[59]

Third, I wonder whether the minority status of institutionalism in the United States legal debate is in part an artefact of an implausibly narrow conception of "institutionalism." Of course, this may be due to my disciplinary affiliation. In international relations theory, at any rate, institutionalism does not enjoy a minority status and is not about "a new global 'super-law'"[60] or about world government, as the prominent place of regime theory within this agenda clearly demonstrates. International regimes are issue-specific international institutions, which are neither necessarily global in reach nor accompanied by extensive, highly bureaucratized international

[54] Alexander Wendt, *Social Theory of International Politics* (Cambridge: Cambridge University Press, 1999).

[55] Paulus, above, pp. 70–75.

[56] John Rawls, *A Theory of Justice* (Cambridge, MA: Harvard University Press, 1971).

[57] Robert Nozick, *Anarchy, State and Utopia* (New York: Basic Books, 1974); David Gauthier, *Morals by Agreement* (Oxford: Clarendon Press, 1986).

[58] Charles R. Beitz, *Political Theory and International Relations* (Princeton, NJ: Princeton University Press, 1979); Thomas W. Pogge, *Realizing Rawls* (Ithaca, NY: Cornell University Press, 1989).

[59] John Rawls, "The Law of the Peoples," in Stephen Shute and Susan Hurley (eds.), *On Human Rights. The Oxford Amnesty Lectures 1993* (New York: Basic Books, 1993), pp. 41–82; John Rawls, *The Law of Peoples. With "The Idea of Public Reason Revisited"* (Cambridge, MA: Harvard University Press, 1999).

[60] Paulus, above, p. 68.

administrations. Moreover, regimes grow not in accordance with a global master plan but rather, depending on "local" conditions of supply and demand, in a patchwork pattern. This does not mean that they are not fit for playing a major part in a complex, multi-layered system of global governance. (In my contribution to the recent Festschrift for Dieter Senghaas, I have tried to elaborate on this idea.[61]) Obviously, institutionalists who focus on these kinds of international institutions are *not* a marginalized minority within the US academic discourse on international relations, nor are they realists by another name, as Paulus seems to suggest when discussing Keohane's work. Rather, institutionalism is a rich source of theorizing about the institutionalization of international relations comprising two variants, a rationalist and a sociological one, which both compete with, and complement, one another.[62] Moreover, institutionalism as espoused by international relations scholars has not been ignored by their colleagues in the law schools, as a recent article by Slaughter and others in the *American Journal of International Law* has persuasively demonstrated.[63] In fact, institutionalism offers a theoretically well-developed basis for further fruitful cooperation between the disciplines of international law and international relations.

[61] Volker Rittberger "Globalisierung und der Wandel der Staatenwelt: Die Welt regieren ohne Weltstaat," in Ulrich Menzel (ed.), *Vom Ewigen Frieden und vom Wohlstand der Nationen* (Frankfurt a.M.: Suhrkamp, 2000), pp. 188–218.

[62] Cf. Robert O. Keohane, "International Institutions. Two Approaches" (1988) 32 *International Studies Quarterly* 379–96, as well as Andreas Hasenclever, Peter Mayer, and Volker Rittberger, *Theories of International Regimes* (Cambridge: Cambridge University Press, 1997).

[63] Anne-Marie Slaughter, Andrew S. Tulumello, and Stepan Wood, "International Law and International Relations Theory: A New Generation of Interdisciplinary Scholarship" (1998) 92 *American Journal of International Law* 367–97.

II

Sovereign equality

4

Sovereign equality – "the *Wimbledon* sails on"

MICHEL COSNARD

The disappearance of the USSR is one of the most important changes in a world governed by international law because, for the first time since the international legal system came into existence, one country, the United States, is the only superpower, an *"hyperpuissance"* in the words of former French Foreign Minister Hubert Vedrine. Actually, the United States was already an *"hyperpuissance,"* but was more or less challenged by the USSR. The most significant change is that, since 1992, no State has seemed powerful enough to resist the United States' policy. This situation has not been seen since the Roman Empire, and it may be feared that the United States could take advantage of its predominance to rule the world according to its own and sole will. It cannot be denied that the whole international system has been drastically disrupted. This change will certainly produce changes in the substance of some rules, and maybe in some mechanisms of international law. However, it is questionable whether it will provoke fundamental alterations in the international legal system, especially as concerns the basic principle on which the international legal order rests, namely sovereign equality.

One of the particularities of the international legal system is that it has to deal constantly with the principle of equality, whereas domestic systems do not. This is why any substantial change in the equilibrium may endanger the whole system; it is also why it may be difficult to circumscribe exactly the scope of this chapter vis-à-vis the other chapters of this book. I have therefore chosen not to focus on the subject of inequality in lawmaking, although the major expression of this principle is the entitlement to participate in the formation of international law and take on international obligations. Nor will I examine in detail the situation of the United States as the most powerful State militarily,[1] or other aspects of substantive sovereignty which are discussed elsewhere.

This chapter aims to answer the general question of this book: what are the effects of the United States' recent predominance on the foundations of international law? My task is to observe whether the advent of this predominance may affect the concept of sovereign equality in international law, irrespective of whatever US foreign policy can be and of any idealistic conception of what sovereign equality should be. My approach is a simple one: I explore the roots of a phenomenon, that is, a possible erosion of state sovereignty or equality, and not its manifestations. If sovereign equality has never been an absolute principle, as can easily be demonstrated,[2] then the unequal nature of international law is not due to the United States' predominance as a sole superpower. This is why it is necessary to begin this study with an analysis of the concept of sovereign equality as a main foundation of international law. But it is also obvious that the last ten years have seen infringements of certain aspects of state sovereignty or equality, and that the United States has been tempted, as any powerful country would be, to impose its views on the rest of the world. A study of the way sovereign rights are exercised may reveal such an erosion, though I do not believe that it has any influence on the survival of the concept as a principal factor in the functioning of the international legal system.

United States predominance and the concept of sovereign equality

Sovereign equality is often examined as what it is not or what it ideally should be, rather than as what it is and always has been. One element of explanation could be that the principle of sovereign equality contains its own contradictions and sources of tension. It puts two concepts together – sovereignty and equality – which both tend towards the absolute and which are supposed to temper each other. The principle of sovereign equality is not a substantive principle, but rather an abstract concept, used to explain how international law functions. It is thus necessary to study what sovereignty

---

[1] Though it renders our task more difficult to accomplish, since the most significant limit on the exercise of a State's sovereignty is the regulation of the use of force in international relations.

[2] R. P. Anand, "Sovereign Equality of States in International Law" (1986) 197 *Recueil des cours* 9–228; and the contribution of Nico Krisch in this volume.

means as a principle of international law, and how the international legal order deals with the principle of equality.

The concept of sovereignty as a legal principle

The study of sovereignty is a static one, in that it focuses attention on the State's status taken individually, without taking into account the ties with other countries that this State, whatever it is, may have. The analysis of sovereignty does not aim to describe the extent of one State's power, but to explain why a subject of international law is legally empowered. As Jean Combacau said, "la souveraineté n'est pas la puissance suprême mais la suprématie de la puissance."[3] Power is not "suprême," because its exercise is limited by international law. But a State is sovereign because it is independent from any other State: it is only bound by international law, as the expression of the legal order of the international community of States.[4] Sovereignty is a legal quality of power, recognized by international law as belonging to *every* State, and it is this which clearly distinguishes state sovereignty as a legal institution from international sovereignty as a mere fact. It is irrelevant what a State can or cannot do from a practical point of view. The stress is on the liberty to be bound or not bound by legal rules, and to assume the legal consequences of any breach of these commitments. This conception places the elaboration and opposability of legal obligations on the one hand, and liability on the other hand, at the heart of the international legal system. It is an abstract perception of the notion of sovereignty that aims at describing the legal mechanisms but not the content of legal rights and duties, which do not matter. If one supports this conception of state sovereignty, then it is inconceivable that any change in the factual situation could affect the foundations of the international legal system, or its functioning.

If we were to adhere to a more substantial definition of sovereignty, more closely connected with the extent of a State's power, we could think that the advent of a single superpower might alter the content of state sovereignty. But we must first assume that, if one observes a relative lack of sovereignty, it is largely – as we will see below – a matter of the exercise of sovereign

---

[3] "Pas une puissance, une liberté: la souveraineté internationale de l'État" (1993) 67 *Pouvoirs* 47–58, 50. Our translation: "Sovereignty is not supreme power but the supremacy of power."
[4] H. Kelsen, "Théorie du droit international public" (1953) 84 *Recueil des cours* 1–203, at 79–85.

rights by other States. Secondly, such a conclusion could be drawn only if we idealize the system as it was in the past. States were not "more equally sovereign" before than they are now. There have always been infringements on other States' sovereignty, or, more exactly, on other States' rights. If we set aside the situation of "rogue States," which will be analyzed later on, the only State which would be less sovereign today than yesterday would be Russia, since it has lost part of its influence on the content of international law. For the others, the situation in terms of the extent of their powers is not that different from what it was in the context of a bipolar world, the only difference lying in the geographical extent of the phenomenon. The interventions during the Hungarian crisis or the Suez crisis in 1956, the Czechoslovak crisis in 1968, or more recently in Grenada in 1983, illustrate sufficiently that States' sovereignties were no more the expression of total freedom then than they are now. "Limited sovereignty" was a theory in the East, and almost a fact in the West. Nonetheless, theoretically, and from a juridical point of view, there is no reason to analyze the situation differently now. We must establish a principle of coherence when apprehending a study of an assumed change in the international legal system: the tools of the analysis must be the same when approaching the past, the present or the potential future. If we stick to a single theory, whatever it may be, we must conclude that the predominance of the United States may have induced a change of degree in sovereignty – if one thinks sovereignty can be divided – but not a change of nature. Sovereignties may be affected, but not sovereignty. Furthermore, we must consider that US predominance affects the equal character of "material sovereignty" more than it does the concept of sovereignty itself, because this quantitative approach results in a sort of equation according to which some States are less sovereign than the United States (or that the United States is more sovereign than they are). Although we may regret that the situation is not better than we might have hoped it would be after the 1990s, it is not necessarily worse.

The principle of sovereign equality

It is hard to define the exact scope and nature of the principle of sovereign equality. Most writers begin by stressing the "equal" dimension of sovereign equality, and generally agree to emphasize its mainly formal nature. Many examples of inequalities can be brought to light in order to demonstrate that, in spite of the assertion of the principle, it does not represent the reality of international relations, nor of the international legal system. This emphasis on equality, however, widens the exact scope of the principle of "sovereign equality," which is not tantamount to the principle of "equality." The first is only one facet of the second, which is a general principle, directed at governing every aspect of international relations.[5] The international legal system as laid down by European countries in past centuries contemplates the principle of equality between States as a pacifying response to power-hungry sovereigns. It is a concession between peers, a goal to be achieved, but not a reality as such in the legal world, and it would be hazardous to assert that it was ever meant to be so. This does not mean that it is ineffective: it inspires most of the solutions to problems appearing in international relations, including the settlement of disputes.[6] But in any case, equality would be a principle governing the substance of the rules of law. There is nothing here to be surprised at: all legal systems set out the principle of equality, but treat differently persons or situations which are different in nature; every legal system contains rules perpetuating actual inequalities, and the international legal system is no exception.

The principle of sovereign equality appeared as a necessary consequence of the coexistence of several sovereign States. Equality is the only answer to the problem of regulating relations between States which are sovereign: first, sovereignty is attributed as a legal quality to each State individually; the principle of equality then derives from the existence of many sovereigns. So, equality is a corollary of sovereignty and not of statehood,[7] nor of the equality of the real power of States. It is simply a principle of organization of the international community, which does not imply an equality between subjects of international law: it is an equality before the rule, not within the rule.[8] Thus, the mere fact that unequal rules exist is not a symptom in itself of a retreat from the principle of sovereign equality, and certainly not one that results from the appearance of the United States as a single superpower. It would be so only if the United States, and the United States

---

[5] M. Virally, "Panorama du droit international contemporain" (1983) 183 *Recueil des cours*, 9–382, at 84–5.

[6] It is particularly true if we contemplate the application of the principle of consent to the settlement of disputes, especially to issues of jurisdiction, where it applies equally to every State, whatever its power may be.

[7] P. Reuter, "Principes de droit international public" (1961) 103 *Recueil des cours* 425–656, at 510–12.

[8] "Il ne s'agit évidemment pas d'une égalité dans le droit, mais d'une égalité devant le droit," Kelsen, "Théorie du droit international public," above note 4, 104–5.

alone, now enjoyed systematic exception or exemption from the law – and not for reasons of diplomatic impossibility or convenience – so that we could consider the emergence of a new principle of inequality in its favor. We could even say that, because there always have been unequal rules in international law, United States predominance has no real effect on the principle of sovereign equality.

When we look more closely at applications of the principle of sovereign equality, or at expressions of the so-called principle of inequality, it becomes necessary to distinguish between institutional law and relational law.[9]

The most important field where unequal rules can be observed is the institutional one. The main particularity of the international legal system is that inequalities are laid down mostly in procedural law, rarely in substantive law. The most typical example is the right of veto in the United Nations Security Council, which the United States shares with four other States; it was accorded in 1945 for the mere reason that no peace could be foreseen without the agreement of the most powerful States, from a military and strategic point of view, on the analysis of a situation which might endanger international peace, and on the means of restoring that peace.[10] This right was therefore agreed in order to create a sort of legal condominium in the field of international security – and only on this topic – and not to enshrine the predominance of just one State. Even within the Security Council, which is often stigmatized as the echo chamber of the United States at the international level, formally the other permanent members may oppose the United States' will.[11] Even if it is sometimes difficult for them to do so, for political or diplomatic reasons, the legal system as such does not ratify the actual situation, and preserves the right of veto of the other four permanent members. The right of veto is in fact twofold: on the one hand, it preserves the faculty of each of the five permanent members not to have decisions imposed by the UN; on the other, it legally allows these States to oppose the will of one.[12] It is important to bear in mind that the Security Council is a political body, not a lawmaking one. Although its

---

[9] We here transcribe the major distinction drawn by René-Jean Dupuy; see "Communauté internationale et disparités de développement" (1979) 165 *Recueil des cours* 9–231.

[10] M. Virally, *L'organisation mondiale* (Paris: Armand Colin, 1972), pp. 102–4.

[11] It is worth noticing that no resolution was barred by a United States veto until 1970. P. Tavernier, "Article 27," in J.-P. Cot and A. Pellet (eds.), *La Charte des nations unies* (Paris: Economica-Bruylant, 1985), pp. 499–518, pp. 512–15.

[12] This constraining dimension of the veto on the United States is evidenced by its taking of actions without reference to the Security Council, the legality of which is then discussed; see the contribution of Marcelo Kohen, below.

decisions are binding, they are simply meant to implement international law so as to preserve the peace. Other illustrations we might find, in international economic organizations such as the IMF, for example, share the same specifications. It must be added that all these unequal international rules appeared before the United States became the only superpower, and, significantly, they are granted to the same States now as they were originally. It might then be concluded that the fact that the United States is now predominant does not affect unequal rules, given that they already existed. On the contrary, most of the procedural rules set down recently tend toward equality, as in the World Trade Organization or the International Criminal Court, or continue to benefit States other than the United States, as in the New York Agreement of 29 July 1994 concerning the implementation of the United Nations Convention on the Law of the Sea.[13]

When we analyze the relational dimension of international law, we have to make a distinction between bilateral and multilateral relations. We could easily find many examples, either in bilateral treaties, or outside a strict legal framework, of where the United States takes advantage of its predominance in bilateral relations, and then undermines the principle of sovereign equality. But this is not due to the hegemonic position of the United States; it is the consequence of a favorable balance of power in an inter-State relationship that does not modify the foundations of international law. If power plays a role in the context of bilateral relations, it is mainly because there are no international rules to govern them. For example, in the investment field, if bilateral treaties are unequal, and if the United States may impose its conditions on the other contracting party, it is because there are no international rules protecting that country, only permissive rules. This lack of regulation could be partly due to the prior opposition of the United States,[14] but this is a matter of multilateral relations, not bilateral ones. This deficiency affects bilateral relations other than those with the United States. These relations are governed by international law or by rules set down by the parties, but the United States is unable to impose any rules governing relations to which

---

[13] See for example T. Treves, "Réflexions sur quelques conséquences de l'entrée en vigueur de la Convention des Nations unies sur le droit de la mer" (1994) *Annuaire Français de Droit International* 849–63, and J.-P. Quéneudec, "Le 'nouveau' droit de la mer est arrivé" (1994) *Revue Générale de Droit International Public* 865–70.

[14] Sometimes, States other than the United States can abort the elaboration of an international regulation, as was the case with France for the Multilateral Agreement on Investment; see Société Française de Droit International, *Un accord multilatéral sur l'investissement: d'un forum de négociation à l'autre?* (Paris: Pedone, 1999), and P. Juillard, "À propos du décès de l'AMI," (1998) *Annuaire Français de Droit International* 595–612.

it is not a party. It may sometimes interfere, but does so at its own risk, this kind of unilateral intervention being subject to international law, even though – as we will see below – that law might have changed as a result of globalization.

Yet it is impossible to limit the study of the effects of the United States' predominance to an account of bilateral relations. Within the framework of the present book, we are tempted to focus on the United States' external relations. But though the United States is a major actor in international relations, international law is not centered on it; it is therefore important to examine whether other legal relations, those in which the United States is not involved, are also regulated by it. If so, one could conclude that the United State is becoming a kind of international government.[15] The question of the effects of the predominance of the United States at a multilateral level is addressed elsewhere in this book.[16] We will just quickly observe that, even in this area, the foundations of international law are virtually unchanged, because the behavior of other States remains the same. Indeed, because an international rule not involving the participation of a superpower – whether it is alone or shares its hegemonic position – would be next to meaningless, negotiators always seek a compromise which would appeal to the United States. But though the United States now appears to be the sole arbitrator of these negotiations, the situation does not turn the negotiating process upside down. The United States is legally powerless if it wants to oblige others to engage in new obligations and the result of the negotiations is unsatisfactory to the other States, or if despite the concessions the United States does not ratify the treaty. Other States are still formally free to express their consent, no differently than they were before. It is true that because the United States is powerful – and not because it is the most powerful country – it could, and still can, prevent the elaboration of rules which limit its power. The explanation for this phenomenon is, once again, very classic: a powerful State may consider that it has no interest in submitting to binding regulations. The United States is now the only State able to be a persistent objector, because it is the only country that can resist external pressure.[17] It

---

[15] See the chapter by Nico Krisch, below.

[16] See the contributions of Pierre Klein, Catherine Redgwell, Stephen Toope, Achilles Skordas.

[17] See Pierre-Marie Dupuy, "À propos de l'opposabilité de la coutume générale: enquête brève sur l' 'objecteur persistant'," in Michel Virally (ed.), *Le droit international au service de la paix, de la justice et du développement: Mélanges Michel Virally* (Paris: Pedone, 1991), 257–72. For a contrary view, see Stephen Toope, this volume.

is clear that formal bilateral reciprocity is insufficient to prevent the discrep-
ancies of power from operating. The means of pressure from a less powerful
country are not dissuasive, unless a significant number of countries presents
a united front, as in the European Union. This issue, where States merge
to oppose a new, more powerful entity, will be considered below; but it is
worth underlining that it may happen that the United States has no choice
but to take part in a multilateral effort to create new norms. Depending on
the subject matter, it sometimes has to join the rest of the world, because it
would be unsustainable for it to be excluded from, for example, the World
Trade Organization.[18] Of course, it can be said that the United States, like
other States, defends its own interests in entering into multilateral relations.
Entering into an international agreement is never legally imposed on any
State. Each country is free to accept new obligations, and does so when it
can foresee an advantage in a situation where other States are likewise engaged. The limitation of its own sovereignty is counterbalanced somewhat
by the limitation of others' freedoms. Actually, the exercise of sovereignty
has always been limited: the whole international legal order exists because
there are such limitations. Any obligation is by nature a restriction, not on
sovereignty, but on the exercise of it. As was held in the famous case of
the SS *Wimbledon*: "No doubt any convention creating an obligation of this
kind places a restriction upon *the exercise* of the sovereign rights of the
State, in the sense that it requires them to be exercised in a certain way.
But the right of entering into international engagements is an attribute
of State sovereignty."[19] In such a system, there can be no infringement of
sovereignty, only of the exercise of it. Consequently, any infringement of
sovereignty, understood as an encroachment on the freedom to enter – or
not enter – into an international obligation, is always a fact, outside the
international legal order.

Therefore, when a State is not bound by an international obligation,
it chooses not to be *above* international law, but *beside* international law.
This situation has always been possible because no rule is totally universal,
precisely because of the principle of sovereign equality; it has always been
the privilege of powerful States to invoke this principle. Since the main

[18] See T. Flory, "Chronique de droit international économique" (1994) *Annuaire Français de Droit International* 708–16 at 711–12.

[19] SS *Wimbledon* (*United Kingdom, France, Italy, Japan v. Germany*) 1923, PCIJ (Ser. A), No 1, 28, emphasis added.

regulating principle of sovereign equality is still operative, international law as a system is not as affected as some authors suggest. It is another thing to think that the United States could be above the law, which would mean that when it is legally bound, it could freely choose not to observe its international obligations. This proposition is not legally sustainable, because it purely and simply denies the existence of international law.

The United States and the exercise of sovereign rights

If sovereign equality, as a legal concept, remains untouched by the factual circumstance of the end of the bipolar world, because it is by definition indifferent to the real power of States, changes are nonetheless observable in the way in which States exercise their sovereignty. However, it is questionable whether observable restrictions on sovereignty, that is on the ability of a State to decide or to behave freely, are rooted in a change in the balance of power on the international scene. This is why we must first scrutinize the limitations on the exercise of sovereignty, and then turn to the reasons for such limitations.

Limitations on the exercise of sovereign rights

The first aspect of the United States' predominance resides in the fact that it has more opportunities to exercise its sovereign rights, a fact which is meaningless with regard to the legal equality of States. The predominance of the United States would only truly jeopardize sovereign equality if the United States could unilaterally impose rules limiting the sovereignty of other States, so that they would have no choice other than to decide or behave accordingly. Moreover, there would only be an effect on the foundations of international law if the United States could impose its will on the whole community of States, and not just on some of them. In other words, it is important to distinguish the exercise of sovereign rights by the United States when it tries to lessen the sovereignty of some States, from those occasions when it aims to change the substance of the law.

It would be unrealistic not to consider the situation of "rogue States." On the one hand, they are not totally free to exercise their sovereignty. On the other hand, most of the time it is not a worldwide impossibility, but rather one that only affects their relations with a few States, for motives of international policy. It is difficult to say that the designation of "rogue State" violates a sovereign right to entertain relations with other States, because such a right does not exist in customary international law. The demonizing speeches scarcely go beyond the rhetorical and political sphere. Their practical effects must be distinguished from their legal effects.

It is thus important to examine the situation of the target State and, first of all, to agree on a definition of "rogue State." The first element of the definition is of course the qualification made by the United States: a State is a rogue State because the United States so decides.[20] But while this may be sufficient for US international policy, it is necessary, to be a qualification valid at the international level, that a majority of States, representative of the whole international community, acquiesce. The United States is well aware of this requirement, and acknowledges that the measures it intends to take will be more effective if accepted and supported by others. The Helms–Burton Act is a very good illustration of this point.[21] The US Congress adopted legislation to prevent companies engaged in international trade from dealing with any kind of Cuban assets which were formerly American-owned property, at the same time that it asked the president to propose and obtain from the Security Council a binding international embargo against Cuba:[22] this power is intended to be used not only as such, for example to impose restrictions on economic operators abroad, but also as a diplomatic means to influence the content of international obligations. In a way, this example emphasizes the United States' consciousness of the limits of its unilateral power and of its relative inability objectively to determine which States deserve to take part in international relations, and which do not. In this context, it is also worth noting that the D'Amato–Kennedy Act is partially rooted in the undesired effects of the prohibition made in 1995 on American investments in Iran, that is, the conclusion of oil exploration and exploitation contracts by European companies, mainly because American companies were forbidden to do so.[23] Therefore, there are two kinds of sanctions: those adopted unilaterally by the United States, because other

---

[20] See R. S. Litwak, *Rogue States and US Foreign Policy* (Washington, DC: Woodrow Wilson Center Press, 2000).

[21] M. Cosnard, "Les lois Helms–Burton et d'Amato–Kennedy, interdiction de commercer avec d'investir dans certains pays" (1996) *Annuaire Français de Droit International* 33–61.

[22] Section 101 (2).

[23] B. Stern, "Vers la mondialisation juridique? Les lois Helms-Burton et d'Amato-Kennedy" (1996) *Revue Générale de Droit International Public* 979–1003.

States either do not follow, or are free to withdraw from the sanctions at any time, and those which are binding because they are adopted through a Security Council resolution.

The only example of imposing real limitations on the sovereignty of a State would be the situation of Iraq since sanctions have been imposed on it. In a controversial decision rendered on 15 July 1999, the French Cour de Cassation, though it seemed to endorse the proposition that international sanctions deprived Iraq of its right to invoke its immunity from execution, spoke only of "limitations apportées à la souveraineté de l'État irakien."[24] The problem raised before the Court was not the right to enjoy immunity from execution, but to invoke it, which meant that Iraq would not be entitled to an essential attribute of state sovereignty. It must be stressed that, even in a case where the issue concerned such an essential prerogative of sovereignty, the judges spoke in terms of a limitation on its exercise, and not of restrictions on Iraqi sovereignty itself. But the example of Iraq is not as topical as it may appear, when seeking to understand the notion of "rogue State." At the time the sanctions were adopted, the international community agreed to them, and the resolutions were adopted in a consensual, if not unanimous, context, with the acquiescence of all the permanent members of the Security Council. It is not the imposition of sanctions that is the result of United States influence – rather than its power – but the continuation of them, despite the criticism that this attitude generates.[25] The United States' veto power in the Security Council authorized it to oppose the lifting of the sanctions against Iraq. This situation is thus not totally novel from a juridical perspective: this possibility of transforming the United States' external policy into a binding obligation was accorded to it in 1945. It is not the result of any kind of political surrender by the other States, due to any recognition of the legitimacy of an alleged American will to govern the world. The fortunes of the sanctions adopted by the Security Council against Libya show that any of the permanent members – here both United States and United Kingdom – can oppose their removal on discretionary grounds, without having legally to justify its opposition.[26]

---

[24] Dumez GTM c. État irakien et autres (2000) *Journal de droit international* 2000, 45–55 at 45. Our translation: "limitations placed on the sovereignty of the Iraqi State."

[25] R. Mehdi (ed.), *Les Nations Unies et les sanctions: quelle efficacité?* (Paris: Pedone, 2000), esp. R. Ben Achour, pp. 91–108.

[26] M. Cosnard, "Observations à propos de l'arrêt rendu par la Haute Cour de justice écossaise dans l'affaire de Lockerbie" (2000) *Annuaire Français de Droit International* 643–53.

The unilateral actions of the United States may also be directed at changing existing international law. When exercising its sovereign rights, the
United States may be tempted to impose its point of view on other States,
to use its power as an international legislator. Sometimes it succeeds, but
not necessarily because of its predominance, that is, not because it is more
powerful, but because the substantial rules it proposes fit the situation and
receive the agreement of other international actors (see below). But these
attempts also allow other States to invoke the principle of sovereign equality
to oppose the United States' endeavors. The examples of the Helms–Burton
Act and D'Amato–Kennedy Act prove, on the one hand, that the United
States may have a will to govern other States' behavior, but, on the other
hand, that the principle of sovereign equality prevents it from doing so.
The enacting of these statutes, especially the first one, and the reactions
to them, is particularly interesting for the purposes of our study, because
one of the reasons advanced by Congress for adopting the Helms–Burton
Act was that, after the fall of the Soviet Union, Cuba was weaker than ever
and lacked external support.[27] We might then interpret this act as a direct
consequence of the emergence of the United States as a single superpower.
It also has to be remembered that both these endeavors were failures, which
proves that being a superpower is not sufficient to create or impose rules
on other States when they are not ready or willing to accept them because
they infringe a substantive aspect of their sovereignty.[28] It is one thing to
examine on a political level the attempt by the United States to regulate all
trade with Cuba and all investments in Iran and Libya, but it is important
not to forget the legal outcome: every unilateral act of the United States is
a proposition of regulation, subject to the acceptance of other States – in
this case, it might become a rule through the traditional processes of rule-
making in international law, or through a judicial decision, which could
lead to a declaration of the non-liability of the United States in international law. Therefore, the equal sovereignty of other States is challenged, but
not necessarily reduced. The reaction of the United States to the events of
11 September 2001 and its legality can be analyzed from the same perspective. The legality of the use of force against Afghanistan is seriously

---

[27] Findings, section 2 (1).

[28] The position adopted by the European Union was decisive, as well as its complaint before the
WTO. The imbalance between powers must then be put into perspective according to the areas
observed, and the institutional system in which the United States has been engaged is of meaningful significance in its foreign policy.

challenged.[29] The main question is whether this use of force will lead to substantial modifications in international law. The only way to answer this question is by scrutinizing the reactions: the support – or the opposition – offered by the community of all States.[30] The legality of United States unilateralism is either dependent on the general mechanisms of international law, or there is no more international law.

On another and more general level, the examples of limitations on the exercise of sovereign rights that can be found, mainly in the economic field, cannot be analyzed as infringements on sovereign *equality*. If it can be said that most States are no longer sovereign in economic matters, this reflects a trend affecting every State. The United States is not in an exceptional position with regard to these new rules. The most prominent so-called limitation on sovereignty is the restriction of state immunity to *de jure gestionis* acts.[31] But insofar as this restriction is justified by the assumption that a State should not be entitled to sovereign immunity when it does not act as a sovereign, it would be self-contradictory to assert that the functional conception of state immunity is a limitation on sovereignty. Anyhow, the United States was not an originator of this phenomenon,[32] even if it now seeks unilaterally to extend the scope of exceptions to immunity to cases involving violations of human rights. Moreover, the restrictive theory of state immunity applies *equally* to all States. Since reciprocity governs the evolution of the state immunity rules – quoting Gamal Moursi Badr, immunity is a two-way street[33] – every State, including the United States, grants immunity to other States to the exact same extent that it will claim immunity for itself. The content of the famous Tate Letter is a perfect illustration of this assumption: it suggested that the United States courts should not allow immunity to other States with respect to commercial or economic activities, partly because the executive branch did not claim such

---

[29] See Kohen, below.

[30] L. Condorelli, "Les attentats du 11 septembre et leurs suites: où va le droit international" (2001) *Revue Générale de Droit International Public* 829–48.

[31] M. Cosnard, *La soumission des états aux tribunaux internes face à la théorie des immunités des états* (Paris: Pedone, 1996).

[32] It was only in 1976 that the United States joined the restrictive theory, by adopting the Foreign Sovereign Immunities Act. Since 1945, the US courts had followed the Executive's suggestions, according to the leading decision of the Supreme Court in *Republic of Mexico v. Hoffman* (324 US 31).

[33] Gamal Moursi Badr, *State Immunity: An Analytical and Prognostic View* (The Hague: M. Nijhoff, 1984), p. 99.

immunity when it was subjected to foreign judicial proceedings involving contract or torts. Therefore, if infringements on sovereignty are still alleged to be rooted in the predominance of the United States, one must also concede that it is as much affected by those infringements as other States.

Thus, the sovereignty of some States may be diminished, but not the principle of sovereign equality. The situation of some States must be reevaluated within the system of international responsibility and of unilateral sanctions, which has always been unequal. Nonetheless, if States consent to be "less" sovereign, it is not because they give way to the United States' strength. If the question of the power of the United States arises more critically now, it may be because this power looks irrepressible. It should then be asked why States are willing, more or less spontaneously, to conform to the positions taken by the United States.

The reasons for the limitations on the exercise of sovereign rights

The advent of the United States as the single superpower is neither the result of a sudden gain in power, nor of a kind of "coup d'état." It was caused by the dissolution of the only other power that could credibly oppose the United States. This dissolution was in turn due to the adherence of the populations of the East to the economic and democratic standards of the West, which took place after a serious erosion – in fact if not in discourse – of the Third World's protest against the "Western international order." Therefore, as far as sovereign equality is concerned, it is important to focus on the values which are behind the predominance of the United States, that is, it is important to try to understand why they are now predominant. It is not only because the United States is powerful – it has been so since World War I – but also because there is no country offering an ideological alternative. The limitations on sovereignty are not due to the predominance of the United States, but are rather the consequence of the victory of the values of the Western world.[34] The reasons for the absence of resistance to the United States' will at the political level may be found in an absence of real determination to oppose the values that this will represents. Certainly, the lack of alternative, or of counterweight, might lead to an erosion of exclusivity. But at the present stage, as long as we can find motives for the abstention of other States, we might conclude that it is not a balance of

---

[34] See generally E. Loquin and C. Kessedjian (eds.), *La mondialisation du droit* (Paris: Litec, 2000).

power as such which causes the phenomenon. The same conclusion can be drawn in the economic arena, maybe more accurately: there is a general withdrawal of States from engagement in economic affairs.

It may also appear that States are no longer free, as is proclaimed by international law, to choose their constitutional system, as a consequence of economic pressure together with the globalization of values. The principle of self-determination is severely challenged by the practice of conditionality adopted by international organizations and States. The IMF and the World Bank often require structural changes in exchange for granting loans or other financing. Following the same policy, many States provide financial assistance only if the beneficiary makes substantial improvements in democratization and human rights protection.[35] This trend is common to all Western countries. It is of course paradoxical, not to say cynical, to analyze the implementation of human rights and the establishment of genuine democracy as limitations on sovereignty. But once again, the United States' predominance has nothing to do with this evolution, if indeed we are witnessing a real change in international law.[36] We can observe that the United States is sometimes at ease with dictatorships, and does not systematically seek to impose democratic government. When it does so, it is often as a sequel to the Cold War, as in the case of Cuba, with the adoption of the "program" of setting up a democratic government in Title II of the Helms–Burton Act.

One might see the invisible hand of the United States behind these general changes. This explanation is not totally satisfactory, however, because it is always difficult to perceive the purposes of attitudes taken by States, especially when they are said to be giving up their sovereignty. The fact that the phenomenon affects all States shows that the United States is not the only country at the origin of the movement, though it does heavily participate in, and sometimes initiate, change. The predominance of the United States ensures that it plays a major role in the definition of the substance of the rules. These rules are usually established by national judges, because they concern relations between individuals or between individuals and States. Since Western countries are more powerful economically, they have more opportunities to generate and impose new rules of law, especially since their

---

[35] For example, the new Title XXI of the European Union Treaty, adopted in Nice 11 Dec. 2001.
[36] J.-Y. Morin, "L'État de droit: émergence d'un principe du droit international" (1995) 254 *Recueil des cours* 9–462; M. Delmas-Marty, *Trois défis pour un droit mondial* (Paris: Seuil, 1998).

private international rules relative to jurisdiction favor their own judges.[37] This inequality in terms of participation in the lawmaking process is, once again, not totally novel, and is shared with other States. The example of the implementation of the restrictive theory of state immunity is highly illustrative here.[38]

Among the values underpinning the international community at the beginning of the twenty-first century, there is one in particular which ensures that with regard to its basic principle of sovereign equality the international legal system is not endangered. This value is the acceptance of the system for the international settlement of disputes. The United States accepts international judges, especially in the system established in the WTO. The United States' predominance finds its limits in the principle of international responsibility: if one can identify infringements of sovereign equality, the question whether they are violations of the international rules which prohibit such behavior will be juridically discussed.[39] Were this not possible, these infringements would be the expression of an evolution of the main principle on which the international legal order is based.

As a temporary conclusion, it seems that some observers are victims of a utopian vision, which was born of the end of the Cold War and sees the advent of a world adhering to approximately the same values. There was, then, a hope that the balance of power would become blurred or even vanish. It may be this illusion of a better world that accounts for some of the theories about a so-called dilution of sovereign equality. The predominance of the United States has not changed the international legal system from "anarchy" (i.e. a system in which every subject is equal) to "monarchy" (a system where one is superior to all others). In reality, the world was an "oligarchy" (a system where a few were superior to the others). In many areas, it has not changed much: the adherence to new values is not uniform, and counterweights are beginning to appear as a result of not all countries sharing the same conception of economic liberalization. The difference from the bipolar world is that the opposition is not as Manichean as it could be during the Cold War. That said, containing the United States' power in a world submitted to economic laws may be just as effective.

---

[37] See P. Lagarde, "Le principe de proximité dans le droit international privé contemporain" (1996) 196 *Recueil des cours* 3–238.
[38] M. Cosnard, "La soumission des États," above note 31, esp. 16–25.
[39] See the contributions of Shirley Scott and Peter-Tobias Stoll, below.

The unchanged nature of the international legal system is not only due to its ability to contain a superpower. Like any legal system, it could not resist a *coup de force* by a superpower less benevolent than the United States. The United States has never planned to govern the world, with all the duties such a program bears. There is certainly a particularity in the fact that we are now in an era of the *United States'* predominance, and we can be sure that the effects on the international legal system would not be the same were another State predominant. The United States is aware of its power and feels that it is sometimes necessary to show it to the rest of the world; at other times it just wants not to be bothered and isolates itself as only a continent-country can do. This leads to a somewhat erratic international policy, with only a few obsessional enemies, too unconstructed to provoke fundamental changes.

Since 11 September 2001, we have entered a period of great legal uncertainties, as always when faced with a major international crisis. The fact that it was the United States which suffered, for the first time in centuries, a territorial attack, and that it was the target of terrorists, might be of great significance for the content of the legal consequences. Without any ambition to foresee what new international situation will arise in the near future, it is possible at least to draw the conclusion that we no longer live in an exclusively inter-State world. This in itself is not a new insight, but what is new is that threatening power on a large scale is no longer a State monopoly. It is difficult to apprehend these criminal acts within the traditional international legal order. If the division of the world into two camps based on ideological conceptions has vanished, it may soon be replaced by an opposition rooted in differing social conceptions.[40]

For the moment, the principle of sovereign equality remains as it always was. The *Wimbledon* sails on.

---

[40] See CEDIN, *L'émergence de la société civile internationale, vers la privatisation du droit international?*, forthcoming. A review is published in (2001) 3 *International Law FORUM du droit international* 145–6.

5

More equal than the rest? Hierarchy, equality and US predominance in international law

NICO KRISCH

Sovereign equality is one of the great utopias of international law, but also one of its great deceptions. Just like the equality of individuals, the principle of sovereign equality of States embodies a far-reaching promise – a promise to abolish all unjustified privileges based on power, religion, wealth, or historical accident, a promise to transcend the blatant injustices of the international system. This utopian aspiration has always been one of the most appealing aspects of international law, has contrasted it to the blunt realities of international politics, and has helped raise the hope that international law can serve as a "gentle civilizer" of nations.[1] But its contrast to the reality of power made sovereign equality also seem empty and unreal, and made international lawyers often appear – as they did to Kant – as "sorry comforters."[2] Torn between aspiration and reality, sovereign equality came to occupy an uneasy place: although international law has embodied the aspiration of sovereign equality since the sixteenth century, it consistently interprets it in a very restrictive way. When it comes to concrete rules, sovereign equality has for the most part been reduced to a few norms ensuring some degree of formal equality – mainly the requirement of consent for lawmaking, and freedom from other States' jurisdiction. As a result, international law imposes few restraints on situations of predominance and hegemony; it provides only limited protection against the exercise of unequal power, and disappoints those who had hoped for a more transformative power on the part of sovereign equality.

---

[1] See Martti Koskenniemi, *The Gentle Civilizer of Nations* (Cambridge, New York: Cambridge University Press, 2002).

[2] Immanuel Kant, "Perpetual Peace," in *Kant's Political Writings*, ed. Hans Reiss, 2nd edn. (Cambridge, New York: Cambridge University Press, 1990), pp. 93–130, p. 103.

Nonetheless, the concept of sovereign equality has always been a source of irritation for powerful States, and so it is today for the United States as the sole remaining superpower. Even the few rules ensuring formal equality seem to conflict with its demands on the international legal system, and accordingly the United States has put strong pressure on them. But sovereign equality is irritating to the powerful in a far more basic way as well: still striving for the utopian goal and including an aspiration for not only formal but also substantive equality, the concept operates as a regulative ideal for the further development of international law. As a result, when creating new legal instruments, it is very difficult to deviate from the parties' equality in rights and obligations. Law creation is governed by a far more substantive conception of equality than is expressed in concrete rules, and the impact of this substantive conception is growing with the increasingly universal and institutionalized character of international law.

Sovereign equality thus maintains its place between reality and utopia and, against this background, powerful States have difficulty in transforming their factual power into legal superiority, which leaves them discontented with international law as a tool of foreign policy. While they sometimes succeed in having their superior position recognized in new treaties, they often see their demands rejected, and thus turn to other instruments. This is especially true for the United States: while it had some success in weakening the rules of formal sovereign equality and in gaining superior status in instruments such as the UN Charter and the Non-Proliferation Treaty, its wishes have often been resisted and most new instruments deviate at least in part from US preferences. As a result, the United States has chosen to retreat from international law: it has made extensive use of reservations and frequently refused to sign or ratify important new treaties. Instead, it has increasingly relied on institutions in which it enjoys superior status or which do not face the formal restrictions of international law, and it has turned to unilateral means, and notably to its domestic law, as a tool of foreign policy. As I shall argue, the combination of these different tools adds up to a far-reaching hierarchical system which enables the United States to subordinate other States to law it has itself created – which enables the United States, in effect, to govern other States. In this light, the concept of sovereign equality, though not necessarily formally violated, loses most of its meaning.

In this chapter, I trace the different mutual influences of sovereign equality and United States predominance. I first seek to clarify the normative concept of sovereign equality and highlight its double structure as formal rule and substantive aspiration, as torn between reality and utopia. I then try to show how even its formal rules have come under pressure from United States policy in recent years, before turning to the operation of the substantive ideal of equality and the increasing resistance it offers to the transformation of factual power into legal rules. In the same section, I also try to highlight the degree to which the substantive ideal of equality has had to bow to the demands of power, and why the United States has nevertheless found international law an often unsatisfactory tool of foreign policy. I then describe the tools the United States has come to use instead, and the hierarchical system it has set up to achieve its aims, which add up to the assumption of functions of a world government. I conclude with a reflection on the role of the concept of sovereign equality in this hierarchical system.

Sovereign equality and factual inequality

International affairs have always been characterized by extreme inequalities. For most of history they have been dominated by very few States, and their modern history is, in an important part, that of the "rise and fall of the great powers."[3] Similarly, the history of international law can be divided into epochs according to the respective dominant powers:[4] these powers have shaped international law to a far larger degree than most other States combined could ever hope to do themselves. How else could it be if today almost half the States have fewer than five million inhabitants and one state in six fewer than 500,000 – while the five most populous States account for roughly half of the world's population? In these conditions, the claim to equality among States can either reflect an entirely unrealistic ideal or mean something very different from what equality usually means. In international law, it does both: sovereign equality is a far-reaching promise with a largely indeterminate content, while on a concrete level it embodies few, very formal rules that ensure only minimal protection against factual inequalities.

---

[3] Paul M. Kennedy, *The Rise and Fall of the Great Powers* (New York: Random House, 1987).
[4] Wilhelm G. Grewe, *The Epochs of International Law*, trans. and rev. Michael Byers (Berlin, New York: de Gruyter, 2000).

The double structure of sovereign equality

When the concept of sovereign equality was established in international law, it was far more coherent and meaningful than it is today. It evolved in Europe with the decline of the authority of the Holy Roman Empire and the disintegration of Christendom, when independent States emerged from their subjection to an overarching ruler and could not deny each other the equal sovereignty they all had desired.[5] In later centuries, writers, most notably Pufendorf and Vattel, increasingly took up the concept of equality.[6] At this time, though, international law consisted to a large degree of rules of natural law which, due to that concept of equality, could only be construed as equally applicable to all. As a result, equality in the seventeenth and eighteenth centuries, while far from achieving factual equality among States, meant not only equality before the law but also equality in the law – equality in rights and obligations, at least as far as these were derived from natural law. This is most famously expressed in Vattel's dictum that "ce qui est permis à l'une [nation] est aussi permis à l'autre."[7]

However, the scope of sovereign equality shrank with the rise of positivism, as rules were no longer regarded as per se applicable to all but as emanating from the consent of every single State. On this background, it seemed sufficient that States had the equal capacity to enter into new rules while the rules themselves could embody a high level of inequality, especially when created by way of treaty. Thus, in the nineteenth century, most writers saw sovereign equality reduced to the requirement of the consent of States

---

[5] Cf. Pieter H. Kooijmans, *The Doctrine of the Legal Equality of States* (Leyden: A. W. Sythoff, 1964), at 52–57; R. P. Anand, "Sovereign Equality of States in International Law," (1986) 197 *Recueil des cours* at 52–3; Julius Goebel, *The Equality of States* (New York: Columbia University Press, 1923), traces the concept further back, while Edwin D. W. Dickinson, *The Equality of States in International Law* (Cambridge, MA: Harvard University Press, 1920), pp. 68 *et seq.*, sees it emerging only after Grotius. On the history of the principle, see also Bardo Fassbender, "Article 2(1)," in Bruno Simma *et al.* (eds.), *The Charter of the United Nations*, 2nd edn. (Oxford, New York: Oxford University Press, 2002).

[6] Samuel Freiherr von Pufendorf, *De iure naturae et gentium*, Book VIII, Ch. 4, at para. 21, in James Brown Scott (ed.), *Classics of International Law* (Oxford: Clarendon Press; London: H. Milford, 1934); Emer de Vattel, "Le droit des gens," Préliminaires, at para. 21, in James Brown Scott (ed.), *Classics of International Law* (Washington: Carnegie Institution of Washington, 1916). See in detail Kooijmans, *Doctrine*, above note 5, 71 *et seq.*

[7] Vattel, "Droit des gens," above note 6, Préliminaires, at para. 21.

to new obligations, and to the principle of *superiorem non recognoscere*, the freedom from formal subjection to another State.[8] As was pointed out by writers at the time, these specific rules could well have been derived in the absence of any requirement of equality,[9] and some drew the conclusion that sovereign equality had become an empty shell that should be abandoned altogether.[10] Indeed, the concept had acquired an entirely formal content and did not even protect against inequalities as blatant as those under the Concert of Europe[11] – such inequalities were regarded as merely political and outside the law.[12] This distinction between law and politics was maintained through the twentieth century, and even such privileges as were enshrined in the UN Charter for the permanent members of the Security Council were regarded as consistent with sovereign equality since they had been consented to by UN member States.

   Despite this far-reaching reduction of the concrete content of sovereign equality, despite its "redundancy" and "fallacies,"[13] the concept was not, however, abandoned. Many States, especially less powerful ones, stuck to the notion because it embodied a utopian aspiration that transcended the grim realities of the concrete rules. As Anand puts it, "the smaller States and many publicists doggedly clung on to the idealistic though unrealistic principle not only because habits die hard, but also in the hope that some day it may be realized in practice."[14] And for powerful States, the principle was important as a legitimizing resource for the entire structure of international

---

[8] See Lassa Oppenheim, *International Law*, 3rd edn. (London, New York: Longman, Green, 1920), I, 196–7.

[9] Philip J. Baker, "The Doctrine of Legal Equality of States" (1923–4) 4 *British Year Book of International Law* 12; James L. Brierly and Humphrey Waldock (eds.), *The Law of Nations*, 6th edn. (New York: Oxford University Press, 1963), 131–2.

[10] E.g., Thomas J. Lawrence, *Essays on Some Disputed Questions in International Law* (Cambridge: Deighton, Bell and Co., 1884), 213.

[11] See, e.g., Thomas J. Lawrence, *The Principles of International Law*, 6th edn., (Boston: D.C. Heath, 1915), p. 276; John Westlake, *Chapters on the Principles of International Law* (Cambridge: Cambridge University Press, 1894), p. 92. See also the historical survey in Heinrich Triepel, *Die Hegemonie: ein Buch von führenden Staaten*, 2nd edn. (Stuttgart: Kohlhammer, 1943), pp. 204–08.

[12] Cf., e.g., Lassa Oppenheim, *International Law* (London, New York: Longman, 1905), I, pp. 162–64; Georg Dahm, Jost Delbrück and Rüdiger Wolfrum, *Völkerrecht*, 2nd edn. (Berlin, New York: de Gruyter, 1989), I/1, pp. 238–39; see Benedict Kingsbury, "Sovereignty and Inequality," (1998) 9 *European Journal of International Law* at 609–10.

[13] Baker, "Legal Equality," above note 9, at 18.

[14] Anand, "Sovereign Equality," above note 5, at 190.

law. Thus, while Japan failed to secure a reference to the principle in the Covenant of the League of Nations, its inclusion in the UN Charter was never in doubt,[15] and it received much attention after 1945. Many States worked hard to give the concept of sovereign equality a more fitting, more substantial meaning, but no agreement could be reached on anything more than the traditional content. Consensual statements remained sufficiently vague to allow all sides a favorable interpretation: at the 1945 San Francisco conference, it was pointed out that States "are juridically equal,"[16] and the 1970 Friendly Relations Declaration spelled out that "they have equal rights and duties."[17] The promise of sovereign equality was kept alive but indeterminate. As such, it came to serve as a regulative ideal for the creation of new rules, and deviations from equality, as in the UN Charter, the Bretton Woods institutions or the Non-Proliferation Treaty, are difficult to achieve and require at least some justification. Sovereign equality has thus acquired a double meaning: a highly indeterminate, promising principle, and a quite restrictive, concrete set of rules.[18]

The endurance of sovereign equality in a highly unequal system

The double structure of sovereign equality made it possible to maintain the concept (and its utopian appeal) despite the extreme factual inequalities of the international system – any stronger reading of the concept on the concrete normative level would have clashed too obviously with the realities of power. This restrictive interpretation alone, however, would not have sufficed to cope with all the factual inequalities: two additional factors were in play. First, in order not to create excessively obvious contradictions between facts and norms, international law refrained from regulating certain highly political areas. In particular, it largely refrained from regulating the use of force: while international lawyers had long pondered over theories of the just war, they never produced a coherent set of norms

---

[15] On the discussions at San Francisco, see Fassbender, "Article 2(1)," above note 5.

[16] UNCIO VI, p. 457, Doc. 944, 1/1/34(1).

[17] General Assembly Resolution 2625 (XXV) of 24 Oct. 1970. On attempts at further definition since 1945, see also Fassbender, "Article 2(1)," above note 5.

[18] This duality is not only a result of diverging interpretations, as exemplified in Martti Koskenniemi, *From Apology to Utopia: The Structure of International Legal Argument* (Helsinki: Lakimiesliiton Kustannus, 1989). The dual structure of sovereign equality is important to all participants, for reasons of both realism and legitimation.

in this area and later gave up the task entirely.[19] War was beyond the law, and so equality in the law could not impose restraints upon the ambitions of the powerful to use force. In most important areas, the customary rules were sufficiently weak to be observed by all, or sufficiently indeterminate to be interpreted and applied according to the powerful's needs.[20] International law's abstention from stricter regulation of these areas thus alleviated the difficulties equality could have created for those with superior might.

Second, the most egregious cases of inequality were simply excluded from the purview of international law, and thus also from the purview of the principle of sovereign equality. Sovereignty was accorded only to those States within the family of nations, that is the Western, Christian States; international law was European law. The relationship with actors outside this area was outside the law: in the nineteenth century, many of them were regarded as "uncivilized" and therefore not as members of that family – as a result, they did not enjoy protection against intervention by the colonial powers.[21] The restriction on membership in the international community made it far easier to maintain at least some notion of equality *within* the community; those who were members were relatively equal anyway. The inclusion of other entities would have required even further weakening, and perhaps even an outright abandoning of the notion of sovereign equality.

Formal equality under pressure

Sovereign equality therefore has a peculiar normative structure and is an inherently unstable concept, always torn between idealist aspirations and realist concessions. At its most palpable level – the level of concrete rules – it has never imposed significant constraints on the exercise of predominant power, but has accommodated the most overt forms of hegemony. Thus it would seem that sovereign equality would not pose problems for the

---

[19] For the development of the doctrine, see Joachim Elbe, "The Evolution of the Concept of the Just War in International Law" (1939) 33 *American Journal of International Law* 665–88.
[20] See Brierly, *Law of Nations*, above note 9, p. 74.
[21] See, e.g., Antony Anghie, "Finding the Peripheries: Sovereignty and Colonialism in Nineteenth-century International Law" (1999) 40 *Harvard International Law Journal* 1–80; Gerry Simpson, "Two Liberalisms" (2001) 12 *European Journal of International Law* 537–71 at 544–9.

United States' exercise of superior power. However, rather than rejecting the principle outright, the United States has simply come to regard the traditional elements of sovereign equality as outdated – and sought to revise them in a "modern" fashion.

Equality, consent, and the return of natural law

The most important ingredient of sovereign equality has long been the power of States to participate in the creation of their legal obligations and not to be subject to rules to which they have not agreed.[22] The long-prevailing doctrine of the sources of international law reflected this in its emphasis on consent with respect to both treaty law and custom. The preeminent role of consent, however, has been questioned for quite some time, and weakened yet further by the recent tendency of the United States and other Western States to refer to arguments reminiscent of natural law.

The most striking example of this approach involves the Kosovo intervention of 1999. The United States justified the use of force by NATO mainly by reference to the "humanitarian catastrophe" in Kosovo, and thereby asserted a right deriving from noble values rather than any process of law creation. Moreover, NATO States claimed to act in the interest and on behalf of the "international community" – a community with a shape so unclear and interests so ill-defined that little restraint is imposed on action in its name.[23]

The recourse to arguments similar to natural law is, of course, not new. It did not entirely disappear even in the most positivist times, and in the United States has taken a prominent place, for example, in the approach of the New Haven School. But since the end of the ideological divide with the Soviet Union, such arguments have become easier to use, and traces of them have resurfaced not only in the Kosovo intervention, but also in other instances – for example, in the extension of individual criminal

---

[22] See Oppenheim, *International Law*, above note 8, at 196–7.

[23] On the justifications advanced by NATO member States, see Nico Krisch, "Unilateral Enforcement of the Collective Will: Kosovo, Iraq, and the Security Council" (1999) 3 *Max Planck Yearbook of United Nations Law* 59–103 at 81–3. On the nonexistence of a right to humanitarian intervention in international law prior to Kosovo, see Sean D. Murphy, *Humanitarian Intervention* (Philadelphia: University of Pennsylvania Press, 1996). For a more recent account, see Simon Chesterman, *Just War or Just Peace? Humanitarian Intervention and International Law* (Oxford, New York: Oxford University Press, 2001).

responsibility to internal conflicts by the International Criminal Tribunal for the Former Yugoslavia, which had been strongly supported by the United States.[24] Similar arguments have played a role in the extension of the scope of application of the Alien Tort Claims Act to violations of international law committed abroad: in its *Filartiga v. Peña-Irala* opinion, a federal appeals court held that such an extension was justified because "the torturer has become – like the pirate and slave trader before him – *hostis humani generis*, an enemy of all mankind."[25] In 1998, a federal district court used the same language to justify the restriction of sovereign immunity for States deemed to be sponsors of terrorism, pursuant to a recent legislative amendment to the same effect.[26] It is here that the close relationship between natural law arguments and arguments based on the values or interests of the "international community" becomes most apparent. The latter have played a significant role in all the instances cited above, and to some degree they form the rhetorical frame for the reintroduction of natural law into the international legal order.[27]

If the tendency described proved durable, it could entail severe modifications of the traditional concept of sovereign equality. It would abolish the requirement of consent for the creation of legal obligations which has, for a considerable time, been the main instrument for ensuring at least some formal equality. And it would replace consent as the principal element of law creation by the recognition of rules through reason, or by deriving them from some imagined community interest. This would allow for wide discretion, and discretion will usually favor those with the power to use it[28] – if

---

[24] See: ICTY, *Tadic (Jurisdiction)*, Judgment of 2 Oct. 1995, (1996) 35 *International Legal Materials* 32 at 68, para. 119 ("What is inhumane, and consequently proscribed, in international wars, cannot but be inhumane and inadmissible in civil strife"). For the United States position, see the statement of the United States representative in the Security Council, UN Doc. S/PV. 3217, 25 May 1993, 14–15.

[25] *Filartiga v. Peña-Irala*, 630 F.2d 876, 890 (2d Cir. 1980). See also Jeffrey M. Blum and Ralph G. Steinhardt, "Federal Jurisdiction over International Human Rights Claims: The Alien Tort Claims Act after *Filartiga v. Peña-Irala*" (1981) 22 *Harvard International Law Journal* 53–113 at 60–62.

[26] *Flatow v. Islamic Republic of Iran*, 999 F. Supp. 1, 23 (D.D.C. 1998). See also the US Anti-Terrorism and Effective Death Penalty Act of 1996, Public Law 104–132, Section 221, 24 April 1996, partly reproduced in (1997) 36 *International Legal Materials* 759–60.

[27] For an analysis of the concept of the international community, see Andreas L. Paulus, *Die internationale Gemeinschaft im Völkerrecht* (Munich: C. H. Beck, 2001); and *ibid.*, "The Influence of the United States on the concept of the 'International Community,' " this volume.

[28] For the flexibilization of customary law under US pressure and the effects of the resulting discretion, see also Achilles Skordas, "Hegemonic Custom?" this volume.

the United States is unable to control the General Assembly, it can at least claim to know what the "international community" desires. This reliance on indeterminate concepts rather than on formal procedures is nothing new: already in 1932, Carl Schmitt noted a similar tendency on the part of the United States with respect to the concept of war in the Kellogg-Briand Pact, and concluded that it was "one of the most important phenomena in the legal and intellectual life of humanity as a whole that he who has real power, is also able to define concepts and words. *Caesar dominus et supra grammaticam.*"[29]

Par in parem non habet imperium: *the erosion of state immunity*

The second traditional element of sovereign equality is the principle that States are not subject to other States' jurisdiction. While this was sometimes understood as excluding any judgment by one State on the legality of the behavior of another, the common approach was always more limited and, in the last century, the scope of acts for which States enjoy immunity has again been significantly restricted. As a result, doctrine at the end of the twentieth century held that the principle mainly prohibited the formal exercise of jurisdiction with respect to other States' acts *jure imperii*.[30]

Even in this limited version, however, the principle has come under severe pressure from the United States and other, mainly Western, States. In 1996, as part of its efforts to counter terrorism, the United States began denying immunity from jurisdiction to States deemed "sponsors of terrorism," with the effect that these States can now be sued before US courts for acts of torture, extrajudicial killings, and acts of terrorism.[31] Since then, a significant number of proceedings have been instituted; some of them have resulted in awards of hundreds of millions of dollars against States such as Cuba and Iran. The execution of these judgments has, however, remained difficult,

---

[29] Carl Schmitt, "USA und die völkerrechtlichen Formen des modernen Imperialismus," paper presented at Königsberg, 1932 (copy on file with the author), 141.

[30] Cf. Ian Brownlie, *Principles of Public International Law*, 5th edn. (Oxford: Clarendon Press, 1998), pp. 328–35.

[31] See, e.g., S. Jason Baletsa, "The Cost of Closure: a Reexamination of the Theory and Practice of the 1966 Amendments to the Foreign Sovereign Immunities Act" (2000) 148 *University of Pennsylvania Law Review* 1247–1301; Lee M. Caplan, "The Constitution and Jurisdiction Over Foreign States: the 1996 Amendment to the Foreign Sovereign Immunities Act in Perspective," (2001) 41 *Virginia Journal of International Law* 369–426.

and the US Congress has accordingly taken new steps with a view to restricting the immunity of state assets, too. But the executive branch has until now sought to counter this by the exercise of its waiver authority, and execution has not yet occurred.[32] Immunities have come under pressure in other countries as well, in particular in the United Kingdom with the Pinochet extradition decisions, but also in France in proceedings against Muammar al-Qadhafi,[33] and in Belgium with the indictments of the Foreign Minister of the Democratic Republic of the Congo and of the Prime Minister of Israel. This development might have been slowed down by the decision of the International Court of Justice in the *Arrest Warrant* case,[34] but in many Western States immunities are still regarded as a prime obstacle to the effective implementation of human rights, and tendencies to curtail them are strong.

This development, crucial as it may be for adequate responses to egregious violations of international law, tends to undermine not only the diplomatic intercourse of States but also the second main element of formal sovereignty, that of *par in parem non habet imperium*. It enables States to subject others to their jurisdiction in order to determine the legality of their acts, and thus allows them to take a formally superior position. While this possibility is, in theory, open to every State with respect to every other, only States with sufficient actual power will in fact be able to exercise it.

Groups, conditions, and the restriction of membership in the international community

The restriction of state immunity points to a further trend – that of a restriction in the membership of the international community. As was noted

---

[32] See Sean D. Murphy, "United States Practice in International Law" (1999) 93 *American Journal of International Law* 181–6; (2000) 94 *American Journal of International Law* 117–24; (2001) 95 *American Journal of International Law* 134–9.

[33] See Frederic L. Kirgis, "French Court Proceedings against Muammar Qadhafi," *American Society of International Law Insight*, Oct. 2000, available at http://www.asil.org/insights/insigh56.htm. Immunity has eventually been upheld by the Cour de Cassation, see Salvatore Zappalà, "Do Heads of State in Office Enjoy Immunity from Jurisdiction for International Crimes? The *Ghaddafi* Case Before the French Cour de Cassation," (2001) 12 *European Journal of International Law* 595–612.

[34] International Court of Justice, *Case Concerning the Arrest Warrant of 11 April 2000 (Democratic Republic of the Congo v. Belgium)*, Judgment, 14 Feb. 2002, available at http://www.icj-cij.org/icjwww/idocket/iCOBE/iCOBEframe.htm (last visited 2 March 2002).

above, membership has been a central element in the concept of sovereign equality: for a long time, the denial of full membership in the "family of nations" prevented the application of sovereign equality to many States. This allowed for their extreme subordination while making it possible to maintain the principle of sovereign equality within the "family." In the twentieth century, membership expanded significantly through the process of decolonialization, but current tendencies seem to be reversing this process to some degree. The designation of "rogue States" reveals the ideological underpinning of these tendencies: for more than a decade, the United States has consistently designated some States as rogues and accordingly relegated them from civilized, peace-loving international society. This group mainly comprised Iran, Iraq, Libya, North Korea, and Cuba, which the United States sought to contain and to "transform... into constructive members of the international community," or to make "rejoin the family of nations."[35] With the formation of the "Coalition against Terrorism" and the targeting of Afghanistan after the attacks of 11 September 2001, the distinction between the true international community and outlaw States has only been exacerbated, both through the threat and use of force and the designation of Iraq, Iran, and North Korea as an "axis of evil."[36] While the consequences attached to such exclusion remained mostly political (though no less grave), they turned palpably legal with the restriction of state immunity described above. Since this restriction applies to those States designated as "sponsors of terrorism" by the US State Department, it affects mostly those States which fall into the category of rogue States – with the result that they now enjoy second-class status not only politically, but also legally. Moreover, as interests and values of the "international community" become decisive for the formulation of new and the modification of existing norms, the exclusion of these States from this community has the effect of excluding them from processes of lawmaking as well.

The rogue State concept has been confined to a small number of States, as have its successors, the notion of "States of concern" and the more radical

---

[35] Cf. Robert S. Litwak, *Rogue States and US Foreign Policy* (Washington, DC: Woodrow Wilson Center Press, 2000). For important policy statements in this respect, see Anthony Lake, "Confronting Backlash States" (1994) 73 *Foreign Affairs* 45–55; Madeleine Albright, "Preserving Principle and Safeguarding Stability: United States Policy Toward Iraq," address of 26 March 1997, reproduced in Litwak, *Rogue States*, pp. 263–65, at p. 264.

[36] For the latter, see "United States President's State of the Union Address of 29 January 2002," *New York Times*, 30 Jan. 2002, 22.

"axis of evil." Another tendency applies to a far larger group of States: that of privileging democratic States and governments. This tendency manifests itself mainly in regional organizations such as the Organization of American States and the Council of Europe, and has now spread to other continents, most notably Africa: governments that have come to power through unconstitutional means are, to different degrees, barred from participating in the work of these organizations. This is coupled with a change in the practice of recognition: in the recognition of new States and governments, strong emphasis is now placed on democratic credentials.[37] These changes in state practice correspond to significant new strands in theory. In the 1990s, various US scholars sought to redefine international law as a law of individuals, a liberal international law, in which only States with sufficiently liberal structures deserve protection against intervention or the right to participate in international lawmaking.[38] Such a redefinition might lead to a return to a world divided into zones, with the most civilized in the centre, the half- and non-civilized at the peripheries, and a corresponding gradation of rights.[39]

The scope of equality: loosening the restrictions on the use of force

Sovereign equality in international law, as has been pointed out above, has long been acceptable to great powers because of the limited reach of the international legal order – and in particular because it did not place severe

---

[37] See Brad R. Roth, *Governmental Illegitimacy in International Law* (Oxford, New York: Oxford University Press, 2000), pp. 365–412; Sean D. Murphy, "Democratic Legitimacy and the Recognition of States and Governments," in Gregory H. Fox and Brad R. Roth (eds.), *Democratic Governance and International Law* (Cambridge, New York: Cambridge University Press, 2000), pp. 123–54; Stephen J. Schnably, "Constitutionalism and Democratic Government in the Inter-American System," *ibid.*, pp. 155–98. See also Gregory H. Fox and Brad R. Roth, "Introduction: the Spread of Liberal Democracy and its Implications for International Law," *ibid.*, pp. 1–22, pp. 8–10.

[38] See W. Michael Reisman, "Sovereignty and Human Rights in Contemporary International Law" (1990) 84 *American Journal of International Law* 866–76; Fernando R. Tesón, "The Kantian Theory of International Law," (1992) 92 *Columbia Law Review* 53–102. In the work of Anne-Marie Slaughter, the normative claims are weaker; see Anne-Marie Slaughter, "International Law in a World of Liberal States" (1995) 6 *European Journal of International Law* 503–38; and the comments of José E. Alvarez, "Do Liberal States Behave Better? A Critique of Slaughter's Liberal Theory" (2001) 12 *European Journal of International Law* 183–246, at 189; Simpson, "Two Liberalisms," above note 21, at 562, 566–7.

[39] See Kingsbury, "Sovereignty and Inequality," above note 12, at 621–2; Simpson, "Two Liberalisms," above note 21, at 556–70.

restrictions on the use of force and thus allowed for the exercise of superior power through the most effective tool available in international affairs. This has changed significantly in the twentieth century: since the end of World War I the regulation of the use of force has become one of the primary aims of international law, and, especially since the adoption of the UN Charter, the unilateral use of force has been outlawed for most practical purposes apart from self-defense.

Such a strict limitation on admissible means in international politics affects, of course, especially those States that can expect to use force success-fully, and thus the militarily most powerful. Accordingly, the United States has always been uneasy with the strict rules on the use of force, and has sought to limit their application in several ways. Already in 1919, it success-fully insisted upon an affirmation of the Monroe Doctrine in the Covenant of the League of Nations[40] and, when it concluded the Kellogg–Briand Pact in 1928, it made a reservation for self-defense that was so broadly worded that it could have undermined significantly the prohibition on war enacted by the treaty. Its core claim – the power to define itself when a situation called for self-defense – was soon dismissed, most notably by the Nuremberg War Crimes Tribunal with respect to Germany. But despite this, it has reappeared in US foreign policy on different occasions since.[41]

Even more significantly, the United States has been one of the few States to press for broad exceptions to the prohibition on the use of force. It has interpreted the right to self-defense so as to encompass the protection of nationals abroad, anticipatory self-defense, responses to terrorism and humanitarian intervention.[42] The latter two in particular have come to the fore most recently and, with the widespread approval of its military action against Afghanistan, the United States seems to have broadened the range of admissible uses of force yet further.[43] Moreover, since the 1990s the United States has claimed a right to use force to implement resolutions of the UN Security Council that evidently did not contain authorizations of such action.[44] All these attempts add up to a serious challenge to the

---

[40] See Art. 21 of the Covenant of the League of Nations.
[41] See Oscar Schachter, "Self-Defense and the Rule of Law" (1989) 83 *American Journal of International Law* at 260–3.
[42] See Christine Gray, *International Law and the Use of Force* (Oxford, New York: Oxford University Press, 2000), 22–3, 84–119; Marcelo Kohen, "The Use of Force by the United States after the End of the Cold War and Its Impact on International Law," this volume.
[43] Cf. Michael Byers, "Terrorism, the Use of Force and International Law after 11 September" (2002) 51 *International and Comparative Law Quarterly* 401.
[44] See Krisch, "Unilateral Enforcement," above note 23.

strict limits on the use of force. If successful, they would not only threaten international peace and security, but also open up far greater opportunities for the United States than for any other State. The United States military enjoys superiority over any other State (and the Western alliance, NATO, over any other alliance) and could accordingly make use of broader rights in ways that other States, for both political and military reasons, could not. The United States can also use its position in the Security Council to prohibit other States from using force, as it has done several times in the 1990s: especially in the conflicts in Bosnia-Herzegovina and between Eritrea and Ethiopia, the Security Council severely curtailed the right to self-defense of the States involved.[45] Asserting one's own broad rights to self-defense while denying these to others amounts to a highly unequal distribution of rights, and of possibilities, in one of the politically most sensitive areas.

Change is not necessarily bad, and even a concept as important as sovereign equality should not enjoy sanctity if other, conflicting objectives are more compelling. The attempts by the United States to promote change might even be desirable, especially with a view to making international law more responsive to concerns about human rights violations and the position of the individual. Nonetheless it is striking that the United States (and, in part, its Western allies) is striving for these changes precisely at the moment when it has gained a virtually unchallenged position in international affairs. The United States, having seen the other superpower disappear, now seeks to discard the legal equality of sovereigns and reinstate concepts (such as restricted membership and broad rights to use force) that were so characteristic of the international legal order of 150 years ago. Indeed, this past order would seem to have been considerably more amenable to hegemonic aspirations than the international law of today.

Sovereign equality in contemporary international law: the double challenge

Sovereign equality possesses an inherently unstable character, oscillating between promise and reality. For most of the history of international law, the balance between both could be struck by relying on the classical, formal elements discussed above, which neither entirely neglected the utopian

---

[45] See Nico Krisch, *Selbstverteidigung und kollektive Sicherheit* (Berlin, Heidelberg, New York: Springer-Verlag, 2001), pp. 96–9, 117–33.

promise of "real" equality nor lost sight of the factual constraints of the international system. This balance has, however, become increasingly unstable in recent decades, as international law has changed. The classical concept of sovereign equality appears increasingly inadequate on both counts: the formal rules can no longer claim to redeem the promise, or to satisfy the wishes of the powerful. Sovereign equality is torn in two directions, leaving both sides discontented with the state of international law.

The constitutionalization of international law and the pull toward greater equality

Over the course of the twentieth century, international law moved rapidly toward a greater similarity with domestic legal systems: it abandoned its primarily customary character in favor of more clear-cut treaty rules, it established a great number of institutions to develop and implement its norms, and international treaties have taken on a more universalistic character. International law now forms a relatively precise, universal order with significant institutional support. This new character, however, leaves formal sovereign equality, as it has traditionally been understood, appearing as an increasingly inadequate interpretation of the broader egalitarian promise.

The universal character. Classical international law consisted mainly of rather vague universal customary rules and an important number of bilateral treaties. In this system, the concept of formal sovereign equality could secure at least a reasonable degree of equality in international law, even without embodying equality in rights and obligations. Customary law applied equally to everyone,[46] and treaties, which were mostly bilateral, resembled contracts rather than laws and thus did not lay claim to equal application – or only to a lesser degree, since in bilateral exchange relationship obligations are usually unequal in form, and substantial inequality is far more difficult to measure. Only the most extreme examples of unequal treaties were subject to sustained, though legally unsuccessful, criticism.[47]

---

[46] For the effect of equality on the development of customary rules, see Michael Byers, *Custom, Power, and the Power of Rules* (Cambridge: Cambridge University Press, 1999), pp. 88–105. On the limited role of power in this process, see also Stephen Toope, "Powerful But Unpersuasive? The Role of the United States of America in the Evolution of Customary International Law," this volume.

[47] See, e.g., Lucius Caflisch, "Unequal Treaties" (1992) 35 *German Yearbook of International Law* 52–80. See also Alfred Verdross, "Forbidden Treaties in International Law" (1937) 31 AJIL 571–7.

In an order characterized by multilateral, often almost universal, treaties, however, inequalities pose far greater problems. By their very nature, such treaties create abstract norms (*traités-lois*) and are susceptible of equal application to every State, so inequalities are obvious and require justification: they are too manifest a deviation from the utopian ideal to be simply ignored. As a result, unequal rights and obligations in multilateral treaties arouse strong criticism and are extremely difficult to achieve. Such privileges as those enshrined in the UN Charter for the permanent members of the Security Council and in the Non-Proliferation Treaty for the nuclear-weapon-States are anomalies, and it has proved impossible for the United States to extend them, for example, into the Statute of the ICC. During the negotiations leading to the Rome Statute, the US claim that special responsibilities required special rules was widely rejected.[48] The pull toward equal application of *traités-lois* is also reflected in the increasingly suspicious reactions to reservations. In their most typical fields of application, such as human rights treaties, the scope of admissible reservations has been restricted severely, and the United States' heavy reliance on reservations has met with widespread criticism.[49] In most cases, certainly, reservations remain admissible, as does the right to abstain from treaties. Even the latter, however, seems now to require some justification if it deviates from the stance of the great majority of States, as the reactions of many States to US abstention from the ICC Statute, the Ottawa Landmines Convention and the Kyoto Protocol have demonstrated. As in domestic legal systems, equality of rights and obligations has become an important demand; and freedom of contract plays an ever-decreasing role when it comes to law-like treaties.

The institutionalization. In classical international law, norms were created directly by States, and as such were implemented and their implementation supervised. In such a system, a formally equal footing at the basic level of law

---

[48] For these US claims, see David Scheffer, "The United States and the Criminal Court" (1999) 93 AJIL 12–22. On this and the reactions of other States, see Peter Malanczuk, "The International Criminal Court and Landmines: What are the Consequences of Leaving the United States Behind?" (2000) 11 EJIL 77–90; Georg Nolte, "Unilateralism, Multilateralism, and US Foreign Policy: The Case of the International Criminal Court," in David Malone and Yuen Foong Khong (eds.), *Unilateralism and US Foreign Policy: International Perspectives* (Boulder: Lynne Rienner Publishers, 2003).

[49] See Catherine Redgwell, "United States Reservations to Human Rights Treaties: All for One or None for All?" this volume. See also Elena A. Baylis, "General Comment 24: Confronting the Problem of Reservations to Human Rights Treaties" (1999) 17 *Berkeley Journal of International Law* 277–329.

creation might have seemed sufficient to fulfill at least the most elementary demands of the promise of equality: even though the factual influence on lawmaking and implementation differed, at least formally the appearance of equality could be upheld. It is doubtful, however, whether formal equality in law creation can fulfil the same function in a system that has transferred the creation, implementation, and enforcement of the law to international institutions. The fact that States have consented equally to the creation of an institution does not secure the appearance of basic equality if the institution itself embodies inequality – thus the fact that all members have consented to the UN Charter does not remove concerns about inequality in the Security Council. Similarly, a domestic setting governed by bilateral contracts that reflect the power inequalities of their parties would pose fewer problems than the institutionalization of the same inequalities in, say, a parliament – factual inequality is easier to maintain than, for example, different voting rights according to wealth or income. Likewise, in international law the stronger institutional structure demands an extension of equality into the institutions; deviations from this principle, as in the UN Security Council, are mostly seen as illegitimate and are very difficult to achieve, even though they often simply transform the factual distribution of power into the legal system.

The structure of law thus tends to resist inequality, and this resistance increases with the strength of the legal order – the more international law moves from contracts to law and from primary to secondary rules and institutions, the more the resistance grows. The more international law becomes constitutionalized, the more it pulls toward equality; and the classical, formal elements of sovereign equality are increasingly unable to cope with this challenge. Until recently, it has been possible to accommodate the pressures arising from factual inequality within the range of possible interpretations of the ideal of equality, but this is no longer the case. Instead, some degree of equality "in the law," of equality of rights and obligations, is necessary if in the future the concrete rules of international law are to reflect the utopian promise of sovereign equality in a minimally adequate way.

The expansion of international law, its politicization, and the pull toward inequality

While the strengthening of the international legal order thus demands stronger rules on equality, the same phenomenon, somewhat paradoxically,

also leads to stronger demands for inequality. The rules of sovereign equality were compatible with the needs of powerful States because of some very
specific factors, among them restrictions on membership in the international community and the limited reach of the international legal order.
Both changed in the twentieth century and, as we have seen, the United
States has sought to reverse this trend by reintroducing distinctions among
members and reducing the scope of the prohibition on the use of force. But
in principle, the expansion of the international legal order both in terms
of membership and of areas covered has been successful: international law
now applies to almost all conceivable States and regulates most areas of
international affairs. In former times, many rules of international law were
concerned with primarily "nonpolitical" issues, such as diplomatic relations and technical cooperation; they now extend to all of the most highly
politicized areas of international relations. International law has created
comprehensive rules for economic affairs, environmental protection, arms
control, and peace and security. Moreover, its rules have become increasingly precise and are defined and enforced by various institutions; deviation
has thus become more costly. In sum, international politics have to an important degree become "legalized."[50]

The legalization of inequality. The greater reach and strength of international law, however, reduces the possibilities for keeping inequalities
"outside the law," which, for centuries, had been the strategy for mitigating the effects of sovereign equality on the exercise of superior power.
Powerful States therefore try to introduce inequalities into international
law – the expansion and institutionalization of international law leads to
a need for a legalization of inequality.[51] This is precisely what the United
States sought during the last century. For example, it successfully pressed
for the recognition of its Monroe Doctrine in the Covenant of the League of
Nations, secured a privileged position in the United Nations and differentiated voting rights in international financial institutions, and successfully
invoked special responsibilities on the part of the nuclear powers in order to
secure privileges in the Non-Proliferation Treaty. It has pursued a very active
policy of reservations to multilateral treaties, resulting in a differentiated set

---

[50] See the special issue on "Legalization and World Politics" (2000) 54(3) *International
Organization.*
[51] See already Joseph Markus, *Grandes puissances, petites nations et le problème de l'organisation
internationale* (Neuchâtel: Edition de la Baconnière, 1947), esp. at 109–12. See also Fassbender,
"Art. 2(1)," above note 5.

of obligations. And in the 1990s, it pressed for the recognition of a special status in the Statute of the ICC and the Landmines Convention.[52] In these latter cases, however, other States were not prepared either to grant the Security Council the desired role in the operation of the court or to accede to US wishes for an exception for its operations in Korea from the purview of the Ottawa Convention. The increasingly universal, law-like character of international legal instruments has resisted the insertion of inequalities.[53]

The inequality of legalization. In many cases, the United States has reacted to such resistance by abstaining from the respective instruments. Where it could not secure the legalization of inequality, it opted for unequal legalization – other States became subject to new rules, while the United States did not. Abstention from international treaties is, of course, no new phenomenon for the United States: the roots of United States abstention can be seen in the late-eighteenth-century desire to avoid "entangling alliances." However, the tendency has been especially marked since the United States' rise to power in the twentieth century. After World War II, the United States has become party to only 63 percent of the treaties deposited with the UN Secretary-General that have been ratified by more than half of all States. In contrast, other States are, on average, party to 76 percent of these treaties, and the other members of the G-7 to 93 percent of them. In the 1990s, this divergence became even more accentuated, with the United States refusing to ratify many treaties which are regarded as cornerstones of the development of international law, in particular the Comprehensive Test Ban Treaty, the Kyoto Protocol, the ICC Statute, the Landmines Convention, the Convention on Biological Diversity and the amended Convention on the Law of the Sea. The superpower, uneasy with the success of international law, has chosen to opt out of it to a significant degree.[54] Its practice with

---

[52] See, in general, Nico Krisch, "Weak as a Constraint, Strong as a Tool: The Place of International Law in US Foreign Policy," in David Malone and Yuen Foong Khong (eds.), *International Perspectives on US Unilateralism* (Boulder, London: Lynne Rienner Publishers, 2002). On the ICC, see above note 48; on the United States position on the land mine treaty, see Malanczuk, "Leaving the United States Behind," above note 48, at 85.

[53] See Pierre Klein, "The Effects of United States Predominance on the Elaboration of Treaty Regimes and on the Evolution of the Law of Treaties," this volume. For similar processes of resistance in customary law, see Toope, "Powerful but Unpersuasive," above note 46.

[54] See, in greater detail, Krisch, "Place of International Law," above note 52. On the United States retreat from multilateralism and its causes in general, see Stewart Patrick, "Multilateralism and Its Discontents: The Causes and Consequences of US Ambivalence," in Stewart Patrick and Shepard Forman (eds.), *Multilateralism and US Foreign Policy* (Boulder, London: Lynne Rienner Publishers, 2001), pp. 1–44.

regard to reservations only serves to underline this: through reservations, the United States can ensure that it is bound by international instruments to a lesser degree than other States, and while its strong use of this instrument has met with criticism even by close allies, the United States insists on its continuation, with the Senate even urging the president to reject in treaty negotiations any provision excluding reservations.[55] This seems to confirm the prediction that "no great power and even less an imperial power will bind itself to a set of strict norms and concepts that someone else could use against it,"[56] and reflects more generally the observation that powerful States will evade institutions based on equality and seek to make decisions outside their framework.[57]

Opting out, though, does not solve the problem entirely. It removes the necessity of bowing to international law's demands for greater equality, but does not provide a new instrument for bringing superior power to bear – law is not only a constraint on power, but also a tool for its exercise. As Rousseau observed, "[the] strongest man is never strong enough to be master all the time, unless he transforms force into right and obedience into duty."[58] Moreover, in the contemporary world, law has become almost indispensable: transboundary interactions have become so common that negotiations in every instance would be far too costly and, in many areas, the involvement of private actors renders stable expectations a paramount concern.[59] Finally, international transactions now often extend into the domestic legal sphere – and thus do not only concern the State as a unitary entity. All these reasons render it virtually impossible to renounce law as an instrument of foreign policy. And indeed, United States foreign policy relies heavily on law, but it is domestic rather than international law that is preferred. As I try to show in the next section, the United States uses its domestic law along with such international law as sufficiently reflects its superior position. This results in a strong hierarchical subordination of

---

[55] See *Treaties and International Agreements: The Role of the United States Senate – a Study Prepared for the Committee on Foreign Relations* (Washington: Congressional Research Service, Library of Congress, 2001), pp. 274–6.

[56] Schmitt, "USA und die völkerrechtlichen Formen," above note 29, at 127.

[57] For such an observation with regard to the League of Nations, see Herbert W. Briggs, "Power Politics and International Organization" (1945) 39 AJIL 664–79 at 670.

[58] Jean-Jacques Rousseau, *The Social Contract*, trans. and int. Maurice W. Cranston (Baltimore: Penguin Books, 1968), I, Ch. 3, 52.

[59] See, e.g., Frederic M. Abbott, "NAFTA and the Legalization of World Politics: a Case Study" (2000) 54 *International Organization* 519–47.

other States by means of law and, finally, an (admittedly still weak) form of international government.

The quest for hierarchy: the subjection of international law

Hierarchy through international legal instruments

Despite all resistance, international law has given in to United States demands for inequality to a significant degree, and it is hardly surprising that the United States shows a particular sympathy for instruments reflecting such inequality. In addition, the United States relies heavily on informal means of lawmaking and enforcement, as this very informality allows it to disregard many of the constraints otherwise imposed by sovereign equality. Whether formally or informally, though, the United States has found numerous ways to place itself *above* the law – to control the content of the law without becoming subject to it.

The United Nations Security Council. The prime example of a privileged position in international law is the UN Security Council. The United States has increasingly made use of the Council in the last decade, which has provoked serious charges that it serves as a tool of United States foreign policy rather than as a truly international organ.[60] In the course of this development, the Security Council has significantly broadened its powers: not only has it, as initially conceived, taken forceful measures to stop inter-State war, it has also extended the reach of its mandatory measures to internal conflicts and humanitarian emergencies. Moreover, it has established itself as a law-enforcement organ in matters of peace and security,[61] and even engaged in far-reaching exercises in lawmaking. It has, in particular, broadened the scope of economic sanctions so as to include the long-term regulation of matters relating to security, as most recently with the far-reaching quasi-legislative measures on the financing of terrorism, the criminalization of terrorist acts, and the tightening of border controls.[62] Moreover, the Security Council has enacted binding measures for the

---

[60] See, e.g., the discussion in David D. Caron, "The Legitimacy of the Collective Authority of the Security Council" (1993) 87 AJIL 552–88 at 562–5.

[61] Cf. Vera Gowlland-Debbas, "Security Council Enforcement Action and Issues of State Responsibility" (1994) 43 *International and Comparative Law Quarterly* at 61–90.

[62] UN Doc. S/RES/1373 (2001) of 28 Sept. 2001.

settlement of disputes, for example through the demarcation of the border between Iraq and Kuwait. And it has created several important institutions, such as the UN Compensation Commission for Iraq, the criminal tribunals for the former Yugoslavia and Rwanda, and the territorial administrations in Kosovo and East Timor.[63] The criminal tribunals are a particularly good example of the United States' privileged use of the Security Council as opposed to conventional forms of international lawmaking: the United States pressed for the establishment of these *ad hoc* tribunals by the Security Council, but rejected proposals to found the International Criminal Tribunal for the former Yugoslavia (ICTY) on a conventional basis or through the General Assembly and, eventually, to establish the International Criminal Court by way of treaty. It was prepared to accept the latter court only if its own citizens were protected from prosecution, in large part by providing the Security Council with a strong role in the Court's work.

The World Bank and the International Monetary Fund. In the Bretton Woods institutions, the United States enjoys privileged voting rights because of the amount of its contributions, and these institutions, too, have enjoyed special regard by the United States, far more than, for example, the United Nations Conference on Trade and Development (UNCTAD). During the 1990s, they have increasingly served to develop numerous conditions for countries in need of loans. The World Bank has begun to focus on "good governance," and by this means has more than ever influenced the internal structure of developing countries. States seeking funding by the World Bank must now in general prove progress in the establishment of liberal-democratic institutions.[64] Likewise, the IMF has started to pay greater attention to the internal structure of receiving countries and has required far-reaching structural transformations of their domestic institutions, most notably after the Asian financial crisis.[65] Western (and in

---

[63] See Jochen A. Frowein and Nico Krisch, "Introduction to Chapter VII," in Bruno Simma *et al.* (eds.), *The Charter of the United Nations*, 2nd edn. (Oxford, New York: Oxford University Press, 2002).

[64] See Michelle Miller-Adams, *The World Bank: New Agendas in a Changing World* (London, New York: Routledge, 1999), pp. 100–33.

[65] See, e.g., Eva Riesenhuber, *The International Monetary Fund under Constraint* (The Hague, Boston: Kluwer Law International, 2001), pp. 36–59; Kimberley A. Elliott and Gary C. Hufbauer, "Ambivalent Multilateralism and the Emerging Backlash: The WTO and IMF," in Patrick and Forman, *Multilateralism and US Foreign Policy*, above note 54, pp. 377–413, pp. 382–6.

particular US) dominance in these institutions makes it possible to use them as a convenient substitute for unilateral aid; the (limited) loss in autonomy in the formulation of policy is usually outweighed by the comparatively greater legitimacy and effectiveness of action provided by the multilateral framework. Through these institutions, Western States exercise informal but far-reaching lawmaking authority which sometimes resembles that which existed under the Mandate system of the League of Nations.[66]

Exclusive rule-making and informal networks. In yet another case of quasi-hierarchical rule-making, specific influence has not been conferred by a legal instrument, but is the result of the exclusion from decision making of the States targeted by the decisions. The Organization for Economic Cooperation and Development (OECD) is the most prominent case in point. It unites the thirty economically most advanced countries, but does not restrict its activities to this group of States. Instead, it establishes standards that, though not legally binding, are to be observed by third States if they desire access to OECD markets or other privileges. For example, during the 1990s the OECD negotiated a Multilateral Agreement on Investment (MAI) without the participation of developing States, although the main purpose of the instrument presumably was to harmonize rules for foreign investment in precisely those countries.[67] Although this effort failed, in part due to protests against the exclusionary character of the decision-making procedure, many other, politically less charged, efforts succeeded. For example, the OECD has set up the Financial Action Task Force on Money Laundering (FATF), which has developed an impressive body of rules through its forty recommendations of 1990, as revised in 1996.[68] Though formulated only by OECD members, the FATF recommendations purport

---

[66] Antony Anghie, "Time Present and Time Past: Globalization, International Financial Institutions, and the Third World" (2000) 32 *New York University Journal of International Law and Politics* 243–90 at 246. See also David P. Fidler, "A Kinder, Gentler System of Capitulations? International Law, Structural Adjustment Policies, and the Standard of Liberal, Globalized Civilization" (2000) 35 *Texas International Law Journal* 387–413 at 398–408.

[67] See the revealing explanation of the choice of the OECD instead of the WTO as a forum of negotiations by Stephen J. Canner, "The Multilateral Agreement on Investment" (1998) 31 *Cornell International Law Journal* 657–81 at 665–6. See also Edward Kwakwa, "Regulating the International Economy: What Role for the State?" in Michael Byers (ed.), *The Role of Law in International Politics* (Oxford, New York: Oxford University Press, 2000), pp. 227–46, pp. 234–6.

[68] See http://www1.oecd.org/fatf/40Recs_en.htm (last visited 25 Sept. 2001).

to apply worldwide and, accordingly, the FATF monitors their observance by third States. In 2001, for example, seventeen non-OECD countries or territories were listed as "noncooperative," and the FATF recommended countermeasures against three of them.[69] Due to the impact of the recommendations, third States have even set up specific mechanisms to implement the FATF measures. For example, Caribbean States have created the Caribbean Financial Action Task Force, the primary purpose of which is to "endorse and implement the FATF Forty Recommendations"; an Asia/Pacific Group on Money Laundering as well as an Eastern and Southern Africa Anti-Money Laundering Group have been established for the same purpose.[70] The OECD has thus, albeit in a legally nonbinding way, instituted a highly sophisticated and institutionalized framework for coping with money laundering – a framework designed for third States.[71] But the phenomenon of informal regulation of third States' affairs is not restricted to the OECD: in other fora as well, informal networks have been established to deal with global problems. Some of them, for example the Basel Committee on Banking Supervision, are deliberately restricted to the world's most powerful States. Others are less exclusive, but, as one of their most ardent defenders admits, their informality and flexibility nevertheless "privileges the expertise and superior resources of United States government institutions in many ways."[72] In the absence of legally binding force, standards set in such an informal way are not subject to the restrictions sovereign equality places on the development of international law,[73] and they are accordingly far superior as a tool of hierarchy.

---

[69] See http://www1.oecd.org/fatf/pdf/NCCT2001_en.pdf (last visited 25 Sept. 2001). The use of the term "countermeasure" by the FATF even implies the violation of legal obligations by the non-member States.

[70] On these groups, see http://www1.oecd.org/fatf/Members_en.htm (last visited 25 Sept. 2001).

[71] See Beth Simmons, "International Efforts against Money Laundering," in Dinah Shelton (ed.), *Commitment and Compliance* (Oxford, New York: Oxford University Press, 2000), pp. 244–63, pp. 255–60. I am grateful to Noelle Wright-Young, Junior Fellow, Center for International Studies, New York University School of Law, for insights on this issue.

[72] Anne-Marie Slaughter, "Governing the Global Economy through Government Networks" in Byers, *Role of Law in International Politics*, above note 67, pp. 177–205, p. 205.

[73] See also the remark of Slaughter, "Governing the Global Economy," at 199 ("government networks can be seen as a way of avoiding the universality of international organizations and the cumbersome formality of their procedures that is typically designed to ensure some measure of equality of participation").

Hierarchy through United States domestic law

International legal instruments, even if they embody special privileges for the United States, always require some kind of compromise with others, be they the other members of the Security Council, other holders of heavily weighted votes in the financial institutions, or the other members of the OECD. This need for compromise ensures greater international legitimacy but also leads to greater restrictions than exist for purely unilateral action. In many areas, the United States has sought to evade these strictures by relying instead on tools provided by its own domestic law, which often produce effects similar to those of binding international norms.

Certification mechanisms. Certification mechanisms have become a common tool for the United States to define rules for other States and monitor their observance, and now exist for areas as diverse as abortion, arms control, environmental protection, human rights, narcotics, and terrorism.[74] Usually the United States Congress defines some substantive standard and charges the president with providing reports on whether the standard has been met. Accordingly, the administration produces extensive and detailed annual reports, which often lead (automatically or not) to the adoption of sanctions. In many of the areas mentioned, for example human rights, the standards set for the most part follow the lines of international law.[75] In others, in particular narcotics, the norms initially established significantly exceeded by far the international rules existing at the time, and many States, especially in Latin America, have felt compelled to adapt their laws accordingly. Later on, some of these rules were adopted in the framework of multilateral organizations.[76] A recent and very striking case of a combination of existing and newly created standards is the Africa Growth and Opportunity Act of 2000, in which aid to developing countries is linked to a number of conditions, including the establishment of a market economy, political pluralism and the adoption of measures against corruption. These conditions add up to a comprehensive set of prescriptions for all countries that depend on development aid, and the United States president is required

---

[74] See Mark A. Chinen, "Presidential Certifications in US Foreign Policy Legislation" (1999) 31 *New York University Journal of International Law and Politics* 217–306.

[75] Sarah H. Cleveland, "Norm Internalization and US Economic Sanctions" (2001) 26 *Yale Journal of International Law* 1–102 at 70–3.

[76] See Monica Serrano, "The Certification Process in Latin America," in Malone and Yuen, *International Perspectives on US Unilateralism*, above note 48.

to sit in judgment every year on whether they have obeyed the rules.[77] In any case, the extensive use of the certification mechanism provides a tool for the United States to create law for other States and to monitor its obser-vance, while the United States itself remains unbound and unmonitored. It thereby provides a convenient substitute for treaties and their monitoring bodies, as can best be observed in the area of human rights where the United States has been termed a "trendsetter in unilateralism."[78] The United States is particularly reluctant to subscribe to new international human rights obligations and accept international supervision,[79] but is proactive when it comes to domestic tools for the enforcement of human rights abroad. The annual country report on human rights now covers 195 countries and territories, carefully lists human rights violations around the world and serves as the basis for financial aid, trade privileges, and the imposition of sanctions.[80] Most States in the world can hardly afford to ignore it.

Unilateral sanctions. The certification practice of the United States gains further strength through its combination with unilateral sanctions. Such sanctions have been an integral part of US foreign policy for several decades, and have always provoked significant criticism, most notably, of course, when applied with extraterritorial effect.[81] In many cases, these sanctions seek to enforce international rules. For example, Section 301 of the Trade Act provides for mandatory countermeasures against violations of inter-national trade agreements by other States.[82] And sanctions against Libya

---

[77] See Kwakwa, "Regulating the International Economy," above note 67, at 236; J. M. Migai Akech, "The African Growth and Opportunity Act: Implications for Kenya's Trade and Development" (2001) 33 *New York University Journal of International Law and Politics* 651–702 at 663–70.

[78] Katarina Tomaševski, *Responding to Human Rights Violations* (Cambridge, MA: Martinus Nijhoff Publishers, 2000), pp. 75 *et seq.*

[79] See Rosemary Foot, "Credibility at Stake: Domestic Supremacy in America's Human Rights Policy," in Malone and Yuen, *International Perspectives on US Unilateralism*, above note 48; Andrew Moravcsik, "Why is US Human Rights Policy So Unilateralist?" in Patrick and Forman, *Multilateralism and US Foreign Policy*, above note 54, pp. 345–76.

[80] For the 2000 report, see http://www.state.gov/g/drl/rls/hrrpt/2000 (last visited 25 Sept. 2001).

[81] On the sanctions practice, see in general Michael P. Malloy, *United States Economic Sanctions: Theory and Practice* (The Hague, Boston: Kluwer Law International, 2001). On some of the more prominent examples of extraterritorial sanctions, see Vaughan Lowe, "United States Ex-traterritorial Jurisdiction: The Helms–Burton and D'Amato Acts" (1997) 46 *International and Comparative Law Quarterly* 378–90; Brigitte Stern, "Vers la mondialisation juridique? Les lois Helms–Burton et D'Amato–Kennedy" (1996) 100 *Revue Générale de Droit International Public* 979–1003.

[82] See A. Lynne Puckett and William L. Reynolds, "Rules, Sanctions and Enforcement under Section 301: At Odds with the WTO?" (1996) 90 AJIL 675–89 at 677.

were justified in part as enforcing Security Council sanctions against that country.[83] However, in some cases the rules enforced had a doubtful standing in international law, as for example the supposed prohibition on trafficking in property formerly expropriated by Cuba.[84] Sanctions designed to protect the environment have often relied on a United States assessment of their necessity rather than an international norm.[85] Unilateral sanctions are thus a tool for the enforcement of law as defined or interpreted by the United States; international law does not necessarily play a role.[86]

US courts as international courts. In addition to the United States using its legislative and executive branches for the definition and enforcement of law against other States, US courts have become important fora for suits of an international nature. Since the revitalization of the Alien Tort Claims Act in 1980, certain groups of private persons can bring claims against others for the violation of international law, and the Torture Victim Protection Act of 1991 has further strengthened this tool. Various successful suits have been brought under these provisions, in part against such important international figures as the daughter of former Philippine president Ferdinand Marcos, and the Bosnian Serb leader Radovan Karadzič.[87] Until recently, however, the rules on foreign sovereign immunity barred many claims against States and thus made it impossible to use American courts to deal with the main actors in (and thus also the main violators of) international law. As has been pointed out above, though, this has changed significantly since the mid-1990s: immunity no longer fully protects States deemed "sponsors of terrorism," and the US Congress has taken steps to restrict immunity even further.[88]

---

[83] See Section 3(b) of the D'Amato Act of 1996, (1996) 35 *International Legal Materials* at 1275. For the weak basis of this justification, see Stern, "Les lois Helms-Burton," above note 81, at 996.

[84] See Stern, "Les lois Helms–Burton," at 995; Lowe, "United States Extraterritorial Jurisdiction," above note 81, at 383–4.

[85] For an account of these sanctions, see Elizabeth R. DeSombre, "Environmental Sanctions in US Foreign Policy," in P. G. Harris (ed.), *The Environment, International Relations, and US Foreign Policy* (Washington: Georgetown University Press, 2001), pp. 197–216.

[86] In areas governed by the GATT, however, restrictions might now require a basis in international law; see, e.g., Michael J. Trebilcock and Robert Howse, *The Regulation of International Trade*, 2nd edn. (New York: Routledge, 1999), pp. 428–32, on environmental trade measures.

[87] See Beth Stephens and Michael Ratner, *International Human Rights Litigation in US Courts* (Irvington-on-Hudson: Transnational Publishers, 1996); Marc Rosen, "The Alien Tort Claims Act and the Foreign Sovereign Immunities Act" (1998) 6 *Cardozo Journal of International and Comparative Law* 461–517.

[88] See "Par in parem non habet imperium: the erosion of state immunity," above.

The use of domestic courts for cases concerning violations of international law abroad highlights the way in which international law matters for the United States. From the US perspective, law is an important device for the regulation of international society – as long as it is not applied to itself. Thus, while the Alien Tort Claims Act applies in a virtually unrestricted manner to foreigners, neither the United States nor its employees can be sued under it.[89] International treaties are usually declared to be "non-self-executing," with the result that they cannot be invoked before US domestic courts unless enacted through implementing legislation. And customary law, though generally conceived to be part of American law,[90] is increasingly denied this status in scholarly writing.[91] Even in US courts, international law is thus applied in a highly asymmetrical way – by the United States, but not against it.

Indirect governance. Indirect means of norm-creation and governance are probably even more important, though less formalized than the mechanisms just discussed. They are most evident in the operation of markets: due to the dominant position of the US economy in world markets, US rules often exceed their formal confines and begin to function as global rules.[92] Thus, in a study of thirteen areas of economic regulation, Braithwaite and Drahos have identified the United States as the most or one of the most influential state actors in each of these areas, and it has emerged as by far the most influential actor overall.[93] This is not only because of the exercise of raw political pressure, but more often because of the superior expertise of US agencies, the availability of model norms in US domestic law, and the market dominance of US corporations, especially in the early phases of emerging fields. All these factors favor the modeling of internationally applicable rules on US domestic law, and modeling is, as has been noted, "the

---

[89] The United States enjoys sovereign immunity against such claims unless it is specifically waived, *Sanchez-Espinosa v. Reagan*, 770 F.2d 202 (1985), at 207. Its employees benefit from a specific exception; see Sean D. Murphy, "United States Practice in International Law" (1999) 93 AJIL at 894. See also Stephens and Ratner, *International Human Rights Litigation*, above note 87, pp. 104–8.

[90] See Louis Henkin, "International Law as Law in the United States" (1984) 82 *Michigan Law Review* 1555 at 1561–7.

[91] See Curtis A. Bradley and Jack L. Goldsmith, "Customary International Law as Federal Common Law: A Critique of the Modern Position" (1997) 110 *Harvard Law Review* 815–76.

[92] See, e.g., Beth A. Simmons, "The International Politics of Harmonization: The Case of Capital Market Regulation" (2001) 55 *International Organization* 589–620; Kwakwa, "Regulating the International Economy," above note 67, at 232–40.

[93] John Braithwaite and Peter Drahos, *Global Business Regulation* (Cambridge, New York: Cambridge University Press, 2000), pp. 475–7.

key mechanism of globalization that lays the foundation of global norms."[94] Through this mechanism, the United States is particularly influential with respect to technical standards, as, for example, in the fields of corporation and securities law or air safety, through global reliance on the standards of the United States Security and Exchange Commission (SEC) and the Federal Aviation Administration (FAA).[95] Another case in point is the regulation of the Internet.[96] Originating in the United States, the Internet has developed mainly under US law and thus reflects American regulatory efforts – or, rather, their absence. Moreover, the organization of the Internet takes place through organizations operating under United States law. In the early days of the medium, domain names were assigned by a single person, and later on by private organizations under contract with US government agencies. In 1998, a dispute arose over the future governance of the Internet, with the European Union urging the adoption of an international framework. The United States decided instead to pursue a domestic solution, and ICANN, the Internet Corporation for Assigned Names and Numbers, was created as a private organization under Californian law. Accordingly, Internet organization continues to operate in the shadow of United States jurisdiction, which may have far-reaching implications for the possibility of direct regulation, for matters of competition and for issues of fundamental rights. Through dominance of the markets, US law is spread globally. If and when compromises are necessary, they usually involve only the United States' closest allies in western Europe.

The supremacy of the US Constitution

As illustrated by these examples, the United States has now established hierarchical structures in many areas of the law, some of them subjecting other States to US regulation in a highly formalized way. The United States claim to supremacy over the law on a global scale does, however, reach even further, as evidenced by a common practice in treaty ratification. For

---

[94] *Ibid.*, p. 491, also pp. 578–601.

[95] *Ibid.*, pp. 157–8, 457–60; for further examples taken from the regulation of capital markets, see Simmons, "Capital Market Regulation," above note 92, at 601–15.

[96] See Franc C. Mayer, "Europe and the Internet: The Old World and the New Medium" (2000) 11 EJIL 149–69. See also Edward Kwakwa, "The International Community, International Law and the United States: Three in One, Two Against One, or One and the Same?" this volume.

the most part, the United States accepts new treaties only if they merely mirror US domestic law.[97] It has, for example, made declarations to this effect with respect to certain crucial provisions of the Covenant on Civil and Political Rights[98] and the Convention against Torture,[99] and the extent of the reservations to the Covenant has led the UN Human Rights Committee to state that it "believes that, taken together, [the reservations, declarations, and understandings] intended to ensure that the United States has accepted what is already law of the United States."[100] The United States has achieved a similar result in the negotiations on the recently ratified International Labor Organization (ILO) Convention on the elimination of the worst forms of child labor,[101] has largely exported its drug control laws to Latin America,[102] and refuses to accept any treaty on small arms that would require changes in its domestic law concerning the possession of guns.[103] Other striking examples are the recent OECD and inter-American conventions against corruption, which are modeled on the US Foreign Corrupt Practices Act and were strongly supported by the United States, in large part, it would seem, because of its wish to spread its own law globally.[104]

One can hardly avoid the impression that, in the US view, international law is subject to US governmental powers and, specifically, to the US constitution.[105] This claim has been most actively defended by the former chairman of the Senate Foreign Relations Committee, Jesse Helms,[106] who has even succeeded in introducing a standard condition into Senate resolutions on treaties, stating that nothing in the respective treaty "requires or authorizes legislation or other action by the United States of America that is prohibited by the Constitution of the United States as interpreted

---

[97] See also Klein, "Effects of United States Predominance," above note 53.

[98] See http://untreaty.un.org/ENGLISH/bible/englishinternetbible/partI/chapterIV/treaty5.asp, United States reservations (3) and (5) (last visited 28 Sept. 2001).

[99] *Ibid.*, United States reservation (1) (last visited 28 Sept. 2001).

[100] UN Doc. CCPR/C/79/Add.50 (1995). See also Redgwell, "All for One or None for All?" above note 49.

[101] See *Treaties and Other International Agreements*, above note 55, pp. 289–90.

[102] See Serrano, "Certification Process in Latin America," above note 76.

[103] See Barbara Crossette, "Effort by UN to Cut Traffic in Arms Meets a US Rebuff," *The New York Times*, 10 July 2001, 8.

[104] See Alejandro Posadas, "Combating Corruption Under International Law" (1999) 10 *Duke Journal of Comparative and International Law* 345–414 at 376–94.

[105] See also Foot, "Credibility at Stake," above note 79.

[106] "No treaty or law can ever supersede the one document that all Americans hold sacred: The US Constitution," Address to the UN Security Council, 20 Jan. 2001, at http://www.senate.gov/~helms/FedGov/UNSpeech/unspeech.html (last visited 28 Sept. 2001).

by the United States."[107] Such a condition had been formulated first with respect to the Genocide Convention in 1986, was in varying forms used for a number of treaties in the first half of the 1990s, and has since 1997 become a routine formula. Although it is not usually included in the instruments of ratification themselves, the president sends special notes to this effect to the depositary.[108] This procedure is chosen with a view to avoiding the impression of a reservation which, in the opinion of United States senators, could allow other parties to invoke it on a reciprocal basis as a means of limiting their own obligations:[109] while the United States subjects international law to its constitution, other States are not allowed to subject it to theirs.

This approach certainly reflects the strong role the Constitution plays in United States politics and society in general, but it also corresponds to an increasing emphasis on popular sovereignty in constitutional theory[110] – an emphasis whose absolute character can only surprise Europeans, who have just come to recognize that supranational integration might well be necessary if popular sovereignty is to be made effective in a globalized world.[111] The extent of US power in international affairs, however, easily leads to the conclusion that unbounded national sovereignty can be kept alive, at least for the United States, though probably not for others.

The United States as a world government?

How should one conceptualize all these different strands of hierarchy? Are they single instances of the inevitable privileges of a powerful State, or do they amount to more? Do they combine to make the United States a world government? Already in 1948, Hans Morgenthau argued that the design of the United Nations, instead of setting up a system of true collective security, embodied a world government by the permanent members.[112] But

---

[107] See *Treaties and Other International Agreements*, above note 55, p. 131.

[108] See, for example, the note on the Convention against Torture, at http://untreaty.un.org/ENGLISH/bible/englishinternetbible/partI/chapterIV/treaty12.asp, note 11 (last visited 28 Sept. 2001).

[109] See *Treaties and Other International Agreements*, above note 55, pp. 131–6.

[110] See, e.g., Jeremy A. Rabkin, *Why Sovereignty Matters* (Washington: AEI Press, 1998); Paul B. Stephan, "International Governance and American Democracy" (2000) 1 *Chicago Journal of International Law* 237–56. For a useful critique, see Peter J. Spiro, "The New Sovereigntists" (2000) 79 *Foreign Affairs* 9–15.

[111] See Andrew Moravcsik, "Conservative Idealism and International Institutions" (2000) 1 *Chicago Journal of International Law* 291–314.

[112] Hans J. Morgenthau, *Politics Among Nations* (New York: Knopf, 1948), pp. 379–81.

the Security Council, while exercising far more functions today, still operates in a limited area, and several of its permanent members have seen their influence in international politics diminish. In the case of the United States, though, the privileged position is not restricted to the Security Council, but extends widely into other areas of international law and politics.

Power, institutions and the notion of government

Whether the position of the United States is indeed akin to that of a government depends, of course, on the criteria chosen to define the latter. In the international sphere, no equivalent to the modern Western model of government exists – power is not monopolized, nor are there central institutions formally designated to exercise most public functions. But the modern idea of government is closely connected with the particular vision of an all-encompassing, omnipotent State as it has evolved in Europe since the sixteenth century; and even Western political theory has more recently turned to less unitary conceptions, as reflected, for example, in the emergence of the notion of "governance."[113] In any event, the notion of government seems not as closely tied to the idea of the modern State as is often assumed:[114] different forms of government existed in societies prior to the rise of the modern State, and they were often characterized by far more complex structures and networks of power-wielding entities. Thus, for example, in the Holy Roman Empire, the emperor exercised authority over an unstable territory through difficult interactions with both the pope and local rulers, and he was hardly able to make decisions unilaterally or depart radically from traditions and customs. Still he was considered as governing (as *gubernator*), though certainly not in the later sense of exercising exclusive, sovereign authority in a clearly defined territory.[115] Similarly, in traditional, "primitive" societies governmental powers were often exercised without a centralized political structure, but through webs of interaction

---

[113] See, e.g., Jon Pierre (ed.), *Debating Governance* (Oxford, New York: Oxford University Press, 2000), and the discussion below, "Government or governance?"

[114] See Andrew Vincent, *Theories of the State* (Oxford, New York: Blackwell, 1987), p. 10; Lawrence Krader, *Formation of the State* (Englewood Cliffs: Prentice-Hall, 1968), p. 104.

[115] In the Holy Roman Empire, the stucture of government is said to have been characterized by its "openness": see Grewe, *The Epochs of International Law*, above note 4, at 91–3. This was exemplified in the early empire by the limits on Charlemagne's authority: cf. Dieter Hägermann, *Karl der Große: Herrscher des Abendlandes* (Berlin, Munich: Propyläen, 2000).

among heads of families and tribes and other actors, with dispute settlement through adjudication or arbitration.[116] In many cases, kings were
virtually powerless and dependent on other actors and groups; sometimes,
hierarchical structures were developed only for certain functions but not
for others.[117] In any event, various degrees of centralization and hierarchy existed and still exist in traditional societies, and most of them can be
classified as governmental structures.[118] This suggests that in the international order, too, government should be a function of the degree of existing
hierarchy rather than of the degree of conformity with the modern Western
model of state organization.

For a government to exist, however, the exercise of superior power does
not suffice:[119] in a domestic setting, such power can be exercised by important private actors as well, or even by criminal groups. Moreover, it does not
seem necessary, as is most often domestically the case, that the government
be explicitly designated as such by some formal Act in accordance with legal
rules. Especially in situations of revolution, transition or unrest, new governments emerge without a complete formal basis, and in traditional societies governmental powers are often exercised on the basis of custom. Thus,
government requires more than the mere exercise of power, but less than a
complete institutional basis. I therefore suggest that, in order to qualify as
government, a powerful actor needs to exercise some control over important institutions and to exercise some functions that are typically associated with an established government – both raw power and an institutional
basis of some sort must be present. Still, it is difficult to determine when
power becomes government, especially in the international order, where,
as in traditional societies, structures of hierarchy are not highly formalized and different, interlocking patterns of authority coexist. But whether
or not formalized, what seems decisive is the actual exercise of governmental functions such as rule making, rule enforcement and adjudication

---

[116] See, e.g., Norbert Rouland, *Legal Anthropology* (Stanford: Stanford University Press, 1994), at
153–69.

[117] See, e.g., the description of the Crow, the Kpelle, and the Shilluk, in Krader, *Formation of
the State*, above note 114, pp. 29–42; and the analysis in Henry J. M. Claessen, "The Balance
of Power in the Primitive State," in S. Lee Seaton and Henri J. M. Claessen (eds.), *Political
Anthropology* (The Hague: Mouton, 1979), pp. 183–97.

[118] See Krader, *Formation of the State*, above note 114, p. 104.

[119] But see Lea Brilmayer, *American Hegemony* (New Haven: Yale University Press, 1994), pp. 18–24;
and Triepel, *Die Hegemonie*, above note 11, pp. 139–46, who only sees a gradual difference
between influence, hegemony, and government over another State.

or arbitration. And the more this exercise is effective and accepted by members of society, and the more it finds institutional support and is embedded in formal structures, the more a powerful actor will appear as a government.[120]

The United States and its exercise of governmental functions

Accordingly, there is no unequivocal answer to the question whether the United States qualifies as a world government, though many factors point to a positive response. Not only does the United States possess far superior power in the international system, it has also established a network of international and domestic institutions in support of the exercise of its power. This stabilizes its predominant position, and increasingly resembles the exercise of formal governmental functions: the United States, often assisted by its Western allies, legislates (through, for example, the Security Council, the OECD, or its domestic law in connection with the certification practice), performs executive functions (through the Security Council, unilateral sanctions or the unilateral use of force) and adjudicates (through its own courts as international courts).[121] Moreover, like domestic governments, the United States is not bound by the same rules as most other States – it persistently refuses to subject itself to important international instruments, especially those involving enforcement mechanisms. It remains unbound, while its subjects face ever further-reaching constraints.[122] The asymmetry underlying this approach has become especially obvious in the US strategy toward the ICC Statute: without intention to ratify the statute, the United States signed it at the last minute in order to be able to influence the further development of the court.[123] Similarly, without being a party

---

[120] Applied to the international order, this analysis corresponds to some degree with the concept of a "legalized hegemony," as presented by Triepel, *Die Hegemonie*, above note 11, pp. 202–6; and Markus, *Problème de l'organisation internationale*, above note 51, pp. 47–55. Both authors, however, place less weight on the institutional element in their assessments of hegemonic relationships.

[121] See the elements of hierarchy discussed in "The quest for hierarchy: the subjection of international law," above.

[122] See "The expansion of international law, its politicization, and the pull toward inequality," above. See also James C. Hathaway, "America, Defender of Democratic Legitimacy?" (2000) 11 EJIL 121–34 at 132–3.

[123] See the statement of United States President Clinton upon the signature of the statute: "With signature . . . we will be in a position to influence the evolution of the court. Without signature, we will not," *New York Times*, 1 Jan. 2001, 6.

to the Convention on Biological Diversity and thus enjoying only observer status, the United States, as part of the so-called Miami Group, succeeded in heavily influencing the negotiations on the Biosafety Protocol.[124] In this, the United States resembles the sovereign in Hobbes' first conception of the social contract: while all other members of society become parties to the contract and give up their rights, the sovereign stands apart, remains unbound and governs.[125]

Finally, the United States does not simply claim this privileged position for its own sake, but for the international community as a whole – it assumes a public position. This is most evident in the use of multilateral fora, such as the UN Security Council. But it is also reflected in unilateral action. For example, in the most far-reaching cases of the unilateral use of force at the end of the 1990s – those against Iraq and Yugoslavia – the United States claimed to enforce a collective will as expressed in resolutions of the Security Council; it acted in the name of "humanity."[126] Similarly, in the Afghanistan intervention, while relying on self-defense as the legal basis, the United States stressed that it was reacting to an attack not only against itself but also against the "heart and soul of the civilized world" – and that "the world" had come together to repel this attack, that the "collective will of the world" supported the American operation.[127] Moreover, the United States justified extraterritorial sanctions against Libya as enforcing UN resolutions,[128] and when both extending the scope of application of the Alien Tort Claims Act and restricting the sovereign immunity of States, its courts have claimed to be acting against torturers and terrorists as "enemies of all mankind."[129] Similarly, the United States demanded privileges in the ICC Statute explicitly not for selfish reasons, but because of the "special responsibilities" the United States and its military incur toward the whole

---

[124] See Robert Falkner, "Regulating Biotech Trade: the Cartagena Protocol on Biosafety" (2000) 76 *International Affairs* 299–313.

[125] Cf. Thomas Hobbes, *De Cive*, ed. Howard Warrender (Oxford: Clarendon Press, 1983), pp. 88–90 (Ch. V, nos. VII–XII).

[126] See Krisch, "Unilateral Enforcement of the Collective Will," at 64–86; Nigel D. White, "The Legality of Bombing in the Name of Humanity" (2000) 5 *Journal of Conflict and Security Law* 27–43 at 29–30.

[127] Statements of the United States President, 7 and 11 Oct. 2001, available at http://www.whitehouse.gov/news/releases/2001/10/20011007-8.html, http://www.whitehouse.gov/news/releases/2001/12/100dayreport.html (last visited 14 Jan. 2002).

[128] See Section 3(b) of the D'Amato Act of 1996, (1996) 35 *International Legal Materials* at 1275.

[129] See above notes 25, 26.

world.[130] This corresponds to the deeply rooted desire to make the world "safe for democracy" – a missionary vision that necessarily relies on a perception of a global common good. And though this Wilsonian concept of foreign policy certainly has come under pressure in recent times from proponents of a foreign policy guided by the "national interest," even the most fervent proponents of such a policy argue that "American values are universal values" and that the American national interest is defined "by a desire to foster the spread of freedom, prosperity and peace."[131] Even from this perspective, US foreign policy serves, though in a more indirect way, a global public interest.

The United States is thus exercising public functions, claims to do so in the public interest, and acts to an important degree like a government. Certainly, this government function is subject to severe restrictions and does not reach as far as it would in many domestic settings; in the international sphere, cooperation is still more important than the imposition and enforcement of rules. But this might be a difference in degree, not in kind.[132]

Government or governance?

Given the restrictions on the exercise of governmental functions by the United States, however, one might argue that, instead of talking of "government," one should speak of structures of "governance." This would reflect the insight of recent years that the concept of government, understood as the State's formal regulation of society and the economy, backed by the threat of coercion, is increasingly inadequate to capture the actual structures of authority and power. Governance, in contrast, refers in a more general way to a range of different ways of "steering" society, of reaching certain goals, either by public or private actors, and thus reacts to the transformed role of the State in an age of deregulation, globalization, and greater societal complexity.[133] In the international arena, such a shift in terminology seems even more warranted, given the absence of a formal government and the enduring complex and multicentered structure of world politics. Indeed,

---

[130] See Scheffer, "The United States and the Criminal Court," above note 48, at 12.
[131] Condoleezza Rice, "Promoting the National Interest" (2000) 79 *Foreign Affairs* at 49, 62.
[132] See also Brilmayer, *American Hegemony*, above note 119, at 21.
[133] See, e.g., Jon Pierre, "Introduction: Understanding Governance," in Pierre, *Debating Governance*, above note 113, pp. 1–10, pp. 3–6.

theorists of international relations have been among the first to grapple with the challenge of "governance without government."[134]

This development, in general, deserves praise as it shifts attention away from formal institutions that have lost their centrality, and allows us to concentrate on the structures of power and authority that are actually at work in society. However, the notion of governance often conceals the agent behind such structures and depersonalizes the exercise of power – it focuses on the process by which a certain goal is achieved rather than on the role of a certain actor or institution. It therefore appears useful to retain the category of government beside that of governance, in order to designate centrally responsible and powerful actors within society.

As has been shown above, the United States is an actor of precisely this kind. Classifying it as "government" also seems warranted because the United States, more than other actors, resists the complexities of governance in international affairs: the United States is particularly uneasy with the relatively unstructured distribution of power and its often uncontrollable outcomes, and seeks to replace it with stronger enforcement capabilities of its own. In other words, it seeks to replace the multicentered governance structure of international politics with a far more predictable and centralized system of government. For the United States, international networks and institutions not only seem frequently to pursue the wrong goals, they are also too weak to be relied upon. This has, for example, been the argument against stronger institutional implementation of both the Chemical Weapons and the Biological Weapons Conventions, and in particular in the latter case, the United States preferred its own intelligence and enforcement mechanisms to international ones.[135] Moreover, the United States, more than other States, defends the State-centric structure of international negotiations, for example resisting attempts to integrate more non-State actors, such as nongovernmental organizations.[136] In several respects the United States thus seeks to uphold the traditional, government-based

---

[134] See James N. Rosenau and Ernst-Otto Czempiel (eds.), *Governance Without Government: Order and Change in World Politics* (Cambridge: Cambridge University Press, 1992).

[135] See Amy Smithson, "The Chemical Weapons Convention," in Patrick and Forman, *Multilateralism and US Foreign Policy*, above note 54, 247–65; Elizabeth Olson, "US Calls for Global Action to Counter Germ Weapons," *New York Times*, 20 Nov. 2001, 5.

[136] See Kenneth Anderson, "The Ottawa Convention Banning Landmines, the Role of International Non-Governmental Organizations and the Idea of International Civil Society" (2000) 11 EJIL 91–120.

order in the face of tendencies toward a more elusive system of governance, and in this order it appears as the sole State that can, to a significant degree, still be called sovereign. This said, and despite the caveats above, the United States still operates in a fashion similar to a world government.

Sovereign equality in the face of hierarchy

The predominant position of the United States puts sovereign equality under significant pressure. As has been shown, it affects not only the traditional, formal elements of the legal concept of sovereign equality, but also keeps the United States to a large degree outside the universal legal order created in recent decades, either through US insistence on exceptional treatment, or through its abstention from treaties that otherwise find almost universal support – wherever possible, the United States seeks to evade international law's pull toward equality. Finally, the United States has established hierarchies in many areas of the international system, and often its action amounts to the exercise of quasi-governmental functions.

But in the face of such hierarchies, what is left of sovereign equality? One could respond in the same way as nineteenth-century international lawyers, such as Lawrence or Westlake,[137] responded to the predominance of the Concert of Europe: hierarchies pose few problems as long as the traditional elements of sovereign equality – consent to lawmaking and state immunity – are preserved. Where hierarchies are based on international treaties, such as the UN Charter, the other parties have agreed to them. And where they are not, the rules set by the United States are not binding on third States – compliance with them is voluntary, and only States that want United States money need to observe them; it is their choice.[138]

Given the much greater extent of legalization and institutionalization of international affairs today, this nineteenth-century response would be grossly inadequate. In a legalized world, such a formalist view would hardly reflect the more substantial, utopian promise that was part of sovereign equality's appeal over centuries. Such a view would even be quite cynical: States could even agree to crown a king of the world and, just because of this agreement, we would still claim that all of them, the king included,

---

[137] See above note 11.
[138] For a similar approach, see Michel Cosnard, "Sovereign Equality – 'The *Wimbledon* sails on,'" this volume.

were equal. International law would then end up with that Orwellian commandment on its wall:

All States are equal. But some States are more equal than others.[139]

In order to avoid this embarrassment, we have to strike out one of the sentences: the hierarchical superiority of the United States is either inconsistent with sovereign equality, or – if one wants to defend hierarchy – sovereign equality has to be abandoned as a principle of international law. The latter option is not wholly inconceivable, since the exercise of governmental functions by one State, or a group of States, in the international arena might have many positive effects. In a situation of anarchy, a hegemonic power can provide some degree of order and stability and enforce the rules necessary for coexistence and cooperation.[140] Thus, one might even want to accept the exercise of governmental functions by a particular State, and perhaps especially by a "benevolent" superpower such as the United States. But then one should no longer claim that this State is equal, but instead defend its position on the grounds of a political theory based on inequality.[141]

However, at a time when international institutions are flourishing and international affairs are increasingly subject to multilateral regulation, the situation of anarchy, as presumed in this latter argument, exists to an ever lesser degree. Moreover, it would seem contradictory if the United States, in order to justify its superior role, could rely on an anarchy which is maintained by its own refusal to create stronger international bodies. And if order does not require hegemonic power, neither does justice: the mere fact that some goals that appear desirable under a substantive conception of justice might be achieved faster and more easily within a hegemonic order does not justify the existence of such an order instead of a multilateral system based on equality. As long as conceptions of justice and morality include some emphasis on process and do not rely entirely on substantive considerations,

---

[139] See George Orwell, *Animal Farm* (New York: Harcourt, Brace, 1946), p. 112.
[140] Cf. Robert Gilpin, *War and Change in World Politics* (Cambridge: Cambridge University Press, 1981), p. 34; Robert O. Keohane, *After Hegemony* (Princeton University Press, 1984), pp. 31–46. See also Triepel, *Die Hegemonie*, above note 11, pp. 136–8, who relies mainly on the "integrative effect" of a leading power.
[141] This is the approach taken by Brilmayer, *American Hegemony*, above note 119. For a similar approach with respect to the Concert of Europe, see Westlake, *Chapters on the Principles of International Law*, above note 11, pp. 100–1.

the more inclusive, participatory character of multilateral institutions should, in principle, outweigh the substantive gains of unilateral action.[142]

This conclusion might not appeal to those who have no doubts about the universal validity of their substantive conceptions of justice, and who can, as a result, see little value in procedural restrictions. Against this background, every means might seem justified as long as it serves a cherished end. Sovereign equality might then seem to be simply an outdated obstacle, and an American, or Western, world government a desirable alternative. History, though, should remind Western States that for centuries their ideas of what was good for the rest of the world turned out to be mistaken. Moreover, respect for the equality of others has long been one of the central tenets of their own, liberal conceptions of society, and this respect should find at least some reflection in the international sphere as well. Seen in this light, reaffirming equality is both prudent and necessary.

---

[142] This does not mean, of course, that sovereign equality as it stands now could not undergo change, for example, toward a greater equality of individuals.

6

Comments on chapters 4 and 5

Pierre-Marie Dupuy

The chapters written by Nico Krisch and Michel Cosnard both seem excellent to me. They are rich, and at the same time raise a fundamental problem facing all internationalists today: to what extent the international system (using the term here for the international *legal* system, not the world configuration of power relationships) can accommodate the US aspiration to possession of a special legal status, in some sense replicating in the legal system the advantages its now unequaled power confers in the context of world politics.

It is of course rather uncomfortable to be raising such a point immediately after a dreadful trial for Americans in relation to which we all spontaneously have a feeling of truly fraternal solidarity. The destruction of the Twin Towers on the morning of 11 September 2001 was a sort of Pearl Harbor in Manhattan: indeed in a sense it goes much further, since it was the territory of the United States itself that was attacked. An implicit, widespread feeling that the American sanctuary was invulnerable was common to its leaders and its population; it vanished in a single morning, when the "New World" took a brutal blow from the old. Whatever be their power, the United States now paradoxically shares with its allies, as with its adversaries, the sense of precariousness. Is this a lesson in humility?

Taking inspiration, no doubt implicitly, from Holy Writ, the US president recently stated that whoever is not with the United States is against it! One can understand such statements in the emotional context in which they were made, and no one is dreaming here of disputing the need for a Holy Alliance of all States against transnational terrorism. Yet it is hardly necessary for

Translated by Iain L. Fraser.

the least criticism or questioning of the continued legality of certain acts by the United States to be immediately interpreted, even by some of its intellectuals, as a mark of disavowal, not to say betrayal.

The remarks that follow, like those of the authors I am commenting on, should therefore not be taken as the expression of historical ingratitude or lack of solidarity in this time of trial, but as the thoughts of international lawyers who are not forgetful of their real friendship for the United States, nor of the obligation on all subjects of international law to respect the legal rules common to them, on pain of calling into question the very validity of the legal order to which they are subject.

The question of the compatibility of US conduct with respect to the principle of sovereign equality has nothing polemical nor academic about it. It is the outcome of observation of American practice.[1] If it is worth raising, that is because one sees the multiplicity of cases where the United States has in recent years had recourse to unilateral actions, including unilateral recourse to armed force, stepped up its claim to extraterritorial jurisdiction, and persistently refused to adopt a number of international agreements directed at tackling problems of global concern such as protecting the climate, eliminating antipersonnel mines, combating the spread of chemical weapons, safeguarding biological diversity, respecting the precautionary principle in relation to genetically modified (GM) crops, or prosecuting crimes against humanity before an International Criminal Court.[2]

Since I essentially share the conclusions of the two authors, I shall content myself with a few brief remarks relating, first to the legal status of the principle of sovereign equality, then to the observations the conduct of the United States may inspire in relation to this principle.

First, to say that State sovereignty is endowed with identity in the sense that it is formally identical for all is to reaffirm the most solidly rooted principle in the history of classical international law, a principle that may be traced back to the treaties of Westphalia. The principle of the sovereign equality of States constitutes a basic axiom which may be stated in the terms chosen by Article 2 of the UN Charter[3] but might equally well be

---

[1] See also "Unilateralism in International Law: A United States-European Symposium" (2000) 11 (1 & 2) *European Journal of International Law.*

[2] See "Symposium: The International Criminal Court: The United States v. the Rest?" (1999) 10(1) EJIL.

[3] Article 2(1): "The organization is founded on the principle of the sovereign equality of all its members."

put as follows, drawing inspiration from other declarations: "all States are born free and equal before the law." In a legal system without organic hierarchy founded on the principle of the primacy of sovereign will, it is plainly consubstantial with the system for its norms to apply in the same fashion to all of its primary subjects, namely States.

The principle has, to be sure, been the object of very serious criticism, particularly in the 1960s, from authors keen to promote the rights of developing countries. It was essentially accused of being fictitious in nature.[4] In fact Nico Krisch has rightly insisted on the gap that exists between the formal equality of States in legal terms and their inequality in real power. At the point when they achieved political independence the countries emerging from decolonization were suddenly able to measure how poorly the principle of sovereign equality masked their economic inequality with the powerful.

De facto, the principle of sovereign equality is a fiction. But this is not the sense in which the word is understood in ordinary language. It is a *legal* fiction. But the term legal fiction is used, at least in the terminology of countries in the Latin tradition, to designate that well-known instrument of all legal systems which the great French private lawyer Henri Capitant called "a procedure of legal technique consisting in supposing a fact or situation other than it actually is in order to deduce legal consequences."[5]

One ought not, then, at least from the viewpoint of the science and practice of law, which is primarily a formal universe, to dwell on the existing distortion between the legal assertion of the equality of States and the actual reality of their profound inequality. That would mean betraying the very object of recourse to the legal technique: to establish that what is de facto false should become de jure true. This is done in order to deduce consequences essential to legal intercourse among the subjects of a particular legal order.

International law, like other kinds of law, has long had recourse to the technique of legal fiction. Thus, the Permanent Court of International Justice's judgment in the *Lotus* case tells us, for instance, "the principle

---

[4] See, in particular, M. Bedjaoui, *Pour un nouvel ordre économique international* (Paris: UNESCO, 1979), p. 295.

[5] "Vocabulaire juridique, Vème présomption," cited by P. Foriers, "Présomptions et fictions," in Ch. Perelman and P. Foriers (eds.), *Les présomptions et les fictions en droit* (Bruxelles: Travaux du centre national de recherches de logique, 1974), p. 8.

of freedom of the seas has the consequence that a ship on the high seas is treated as the territory of the State whose flag it flies…"[6]

But in all systems of law, whether international or domestic, some fictions, as institutional constructions, play a more important role than others, indeed, an essential role, that is quite simply a condition for the viability of the whole legal system to which they apply. This is true, in domestic law, of the axiom that "none is held to be ignorant of the law." Since this axiom is set out at the very beginning of the French Civil Code, it cannot be questioned without *ipso facto* attacking the possibility of invoking all the code's articles vis-à-vis all potential addressees.

One could, then, say of such legal fictions, in order to distinguish them from those serving to establish non-fundamental norms, that they have a "constituent" nature in the legal system in the service of which they are stated. It is, I believe, in just this way that the principle of sovereign equality of States has to be understood. It is a *constituent fiction* that requires acceptance if the whole edifice of the international legal system is not to be called into question. This does not of course necessarily imply forbidding all exceptions to applying the principle. It is perfectly acceptable for certain adjustments to be made to it, such as the weighting of votes within the bodies of an international organization, with a privileged institution like the veto on the UN Security Council[7] perhaps constituting the limiting case. But these mitigations have been established on the basis of written, negotiated, assented agreements. They were not imposed at the sole behest of power, nor by the unreflected exercise of restraint.

The principle of sovereign equality means not only that all States are equally subject to the same general obligations laid down within the international legal system. It is also intended to express the fact that States, all States, whatever their material position, ought to be given identical legal treatment by that system. Sovereign equality can thus be seen as the corollary of sovereignty. It is from it that the rules follow which, by limiting the exercise of power by each, protect respect for that of others. It expresses the fact that the existence of the international legal system is founded upon the reciprocal conditioning of its subjects.

---

[6] PCIJ, Series A no. 10, p. 25; see J. Salmon, "Le procédé de la fiction en droit international public," in Perelman and Foriers, *Les présomptions et les fictions en droit*, above note 6, pp. 114–43.

[7] Privileges do, however, have the outstanding feature that they have to be deserved in order to be guaranteed to be able to keep them without a negative counterpart.

In any case, even though they were its first critics during the 1960s, the developing countries soon became aware of the principle of sovereign equality's essentially protective function vis-à-vis their sovereignty. Moreover, it was on this basis that they were able to voice their aspirations to an actual equalization of conditions, and a "right to development," something that might not be so welcome today. It is at any rate the principle of sovereign equality that enables legal relationships to some extent to escape power relationships; it is what enables Equatorial Guinea or Honduras to deal on an equal footing with China or the United Kingdom. Sovereign equality among States is not (or not only) "fictional" in the sense of ordinary language, that is, deceptive, unreal, fallacious, or illusory. On the contrary, it constitutes a *legal institution* on which the subjects to which it applies can rely in order to compensate for or deny in the formal universe of law the reality of their economic, strategic, political, health, cultural, and, in short, social disparities.

Conversely, the sovereign equality of States opposes over-systematic usage of double standards in law or a duality of legal systems applied to States according to their degree of development. It allows the affirmation of minimum standards required of all States, particularly in the area of human rights protection. Neither Trinidad and Tobago nor Haiti, nor Sudan or Sierra Leone could use the precariousness of their economic situation or their political instability to justify serious infringements of the fundamental human rights. As regards due diligence in dealing with foreigners or protecting their property, one can find many illustrations of it in practice. *Dura lex, sed lex*, said the Romans. The law may be hard, but it is the same for all, otherwise it would no longer be law. This is also true of international law.

Finally, there is presumably no need to dwell too long on the fact that it is on the basis of the principle of sovereign equality that such fundamental principles as those of the ban on interference in another State's affairs or non-intervention are established. Each, from the strongest to the weakest, has a right to respect for the general and exclusive nature of their territorial sovereignty. This is as true of the United States as it is of Ghana, the Republic of San Marino, or Russia.

One must not, however, ever forget that the legal universe is, in every sense of the term, a universe of conventions. Each agrees to respect the rules of the game, but without forgetting that it is a game, even if a very necessary one. For one of the players to leave the table claiming there is no longer any need to respect the rules means that the whole game is broken off, for everyone.

How, then, can one call in question, even if implicitly, that is, through one's conduct, such a fundamental principle as sovereign equality without risking the edifice of the whole international system?

Second, does the international practice of the United States threaten the principle of sovereign equality?

I shall be briefer on this point, considering the wealth of illustrations of American practice that lead one to raise this question, as furnished by Michel Cosnard and by Nico Krisch. Several disturbing phenomena attract one's attention, including the frequency of recourse to unilateral action or the persistent refusal to cooperate in projects to which the quasi totality of the rest of the planet has nonetheless indicated its assent.

Without there being any need here to go in detail into the examples of unilateralism cited by these two authors, they all do seem to me to be relevant. I shall merely briefly mention one initial manifestation by this "loose cannon" felt in Europe to be particularly shocking. This is the American pretension to extraterritorial application of national law, especially when associated with the application of more or less deliberately coercive sanctions. In this respect, whatever one might be able to say about their nature, the Helms–Burton and D'Amato acts, even more than the conduct of the United States Supreme Court in the Alvarez Machin case, display the conviction shared by the majority of American congressmen that it would be legitimate actually to subject third parties to the extraterritorial consequences of United States law.[8] Even though one must note the relative failure of these pretensions in practice, it is manifest that they are incompatible with the principle of sovereign equality, since sovereignty is characterized specifically by the exclusivity of a sovereign State's normative powers in its own territory. One should, of course, draw a distinction on the basis of the old *Lotus* case law between the normative powers of national laws and the power to enforce them, with the second being clearly prohibited, since as the Permanent Court of International Justice said, "the primary limitation imposed by international law upon the State is to rule out – save where a

---

[8] See A. Lowenfeld, "Congress and Cuba: the Helms-Burton Act" (1996) 90 *American Journal of International Law* 419–34; B. Clagett, "The Cuban Liberty and Democratic Solidarity Act, Continued, a Reply to Professor Lowenfeld" (1996) 90 *American Journal of International Law* 641–44; B. Stern, "Vers la mondialisation juridique? Les lois Helms–Burton et d'Amato–Kennedy" (1996) 4 *Revue générale de droit international public*, 979–1003.

contrary permissive rule exists – every exercise of its power on the territory of another State." This is not the place for a detailed analysis of these two laws, which has been done elsewhere, but their wrongful nature in the eyes of international law is so obvious that it is not even, at least in private, disputed by the State Department.

Recourse to unilateralism, albeit collective, can be found in many recent manifestations of recourse to force by the United States. It hardly constitutes primordial anti-Americanism to note that the attacks the United States has repeatedly unleashed, particularly by air, against targets located in Iraq, Sudan, and Afghanistan well before the events of autumn 2001, have no serious legal basis, just as one cannot in the name of a distorted conception of humanitarian intervention justify the continuing Anglo-American bombardments of Iraq by appealing to Security Council resolutions that say something quite different.[9]

Another feature impelling one to note the distance the United States takes from the principle of sovereign equality now concerns its practice in relation to treaties. A State is perfectly entitled not to ratify an international agreement it does not see as suiting its interests, or those of the international community as it sees them. By contrast, no State is legally justified in endeavoring, while negotiations on the application of an adopted convention are continuing among the signatory States, to change its content while remaining a third party in relation to it. This strategy, initiated successfully by the United States in relation to the UN Convention on the Law of the Sea, has been subsequently encountered on several occasions, notably, in particularly eloquent fashion, in relation to the Rome Statute of the International Criminal Court.[10]

In more general terms, over and above the undeniable right of the United States not to ratify this or that agreement, one cannot fail to be concerned at its attitude towards such texts as the Kyoto Protocol on climate protection, while it remains by far the world's foremost contributor to greenhouse-gas emissions. Here we come up against the question as to the exact limits of the duty of cooperation laid down in Article 1 of the UN Charter.[11]

---

[9] L. Condorelli, "A propos de l'attaque américaine contre l'Irak du 26 juin 1993: lettre d'un professeur désemparé aux lecteurs du JEDI" (1994) 5 EJIL 134.

[10] See P. Malanczuk, "The International Criminal Court and Land Mines: What are the Consequences of Leaving the United States Behind?" (2000) 11 *European Journal of International Law* 77–90.

[11] See P.-M. Dupuy, "The Place and Role of Unilateralism in Contemporary International Law, Unilateralism in International Law: A United States-European Symposium" (2000) 11 (1 & 2)

Finally, concerns may also be raised by the systematic instrumentalization of recourse not just to such notions as the "international community" but also to the institution that most directly represents it, namely the United Nations itself. Excluded from solving the Bosnian conflict and from the decision to have recourse to force in Kosovo, by contrast convened immediately after the 11 September attacks, the United Nations Security Council henceforth will have to rely first and foremost on the role allotted to it by the single superpower.

Yet one must not in this connection isolate the United States from the other permanent members of the Council. The interpretation made after 11 September of the right of self-defense, called "inherent" in the English version and "natural" in the French version of Article 51 of the Charter, raises a number of questions regarding the interpretation of the current status of this right. The five permanent members of the Security Council and some of their more powerful allies, particularly Western ones, endorse the interpretation that, in its customary version, self-defense can essentially be exercised outside the framework of application defined by Article 51, that is, outside the direct control of the Security Council itself.[12]

We can thus see a sort of new division of labor emerging: to the United States, flanked by the, one must say, residual if not symbolic assistance of its faithful vassals, goes legitimacy in the recourse to force; to the United Nations, then, the hard job of seeking to keep the peace by sending multinational forces.

It is here, then, no doubt, that the American paradox appears. Clearly wishing to exercise leadership of the planet, now organized on the basis of the standards of "good governance" drawn from its experience of democracy alone, which is regarded as in principle superior to that of others, the United States claims simultaneously to subject other States to respect for international law while freeing itself as far as at all possible from the constraints that same law imposes on it. This attitude, in addition to being contradictory, could prove particularly dangerous in a legal system where recourse to a judge and review of the legality of conduct by an impartial third party remain the exception.

EJIL, to be compared to M. Reisman, "Unilateral Action and the Transformations of the World Constitutive Process" (2000) 11(1) *European Journal of International Law* 3–18.

[12] See O. Corten and F. Dubuisson, "Opération 'Liberté immuable': une extension abusive du concept de légitime défense" (2002) 1 *Revue générale de droit international public*.

Before the WTO Appellate Body,[13] or the International Court of Justice in the recent *LaGrand* case,[14] the United States has without particular precaution been called on to respect the rule of law. This is certainly proof that in law the United States enjoys no privilege of power allowing it to be an exception on superpower grounds.

Yet in the majority of other situations, including at the United Nations, the political bodies of which, starting with the Security Council, seem dominated by that all-powerfulness, one does not find the same call for egalitarian respect for international legality. Still more, the other permanent members seem today to be letting themselves be taken over by the idea that recourse to force can very well come about outside the framework laid down by the rules of collective security.

Even if, in agreement with Hans Kelsen, one accepts the idea that analysis by legal scholars must in principle remain descriptive rather than prescriptive, it becomes necessary, faced with the spread of such a lax conception of legality, to denounce it.

However, hope comes at least as much from forces within the United States as from the friendly exhortations its allies might still have the vigor to make. For instance, it is in the United States itself that legal actions have been brought before domestic courts to call on the government to respect the Geneva Conventions in relation to the al-Qaida prisoners. It is from within American opinion too that some of the most virulent criticisms of an ultraliberal conception of globalization have come.

Agreeing at least on this point with President George W. Bush, one may indeed consider it legitimate to talk of the United States as "this great nation." International law and the international legal system constructed after a world war heroically won against absolutism and the imperial ambitions of the Axis powers owe much to the generosity in action and the inspiration of the United States. The same virtues allow the hope that it will once again choose to strengthen the legal system it has helped to build, instead of opting to weaken it.

It is in the final analysis the genuine respect that this great nation inspires that encourages one to ask it quite simply to show more respect for the law, and for the sovereign equality of other States.

---

[13] See, e. g., "United States – Tax treatment for 'foreign sales corporations' recourse to article 21.5 of the DSU by the European Communities," WT/DS108/AB/RW, 14 Jan. 2002.

[14] LaGrand case (Federal Republic of Germany v. United States of America), Judgment of 27 June 2001, available at http://www.icj-cij.org.

Matthias Herdegen

I congratulate both authors for their fine chapters and for complementing each other in a very serendipitous way. Nico Krisch very persuasively states the case for equality in formal terms as a structural and desirable element of the international community, and quite forcefully evokes the actual threats to sovereign equality posed by US predominance. By contrast, Michel Cosnard emphasizes equality as an emanation of State sovereignty. And this approach seems to be far more amenable to making allowances for existing inequalities in terms of economic and political power. From a realist perspective, such allowances seem to be a vital element for a functioning international order. I would go further and suggest that even the sources of international law respond to these pre-existing inequalities and asymmetries in the international community more strongly than indicated by both our authors.

When we talk about United States predominance we should consider that in many instances the United States operates in strategic alliance with its European and other North Atlantic partners. Therefore, the perspective of many third countries often suggests a North Atlantic predominance.

In the normative context, the United States' predominance operates in close relation with indeterminate rules and the process of necessary concretization of these rules. And this interrelation determines to what extent a predominant power can act as a predominant interpreter of normative standards. When evaluating and qualifying the use of force or extraterritorial legislation by the United States, it seems to be pertinent to analyse the confines of arguable, or plausible interpretations of international law before diagnosing a breach of international rules or even a rupture of the foundations of the international legal system. It certainly matters whether unilateral action can be based at least on an arguable or plausible construction of international law. The state of international law doctrine determines whether such constructions live up to the standard of plausibility.

Predominance may catalyse new developments in international law, if and only if assisted by two additional factors. First, it must be assisted by circumstances of the specific case that carry sufficient momentum to have an impact on collective perceptions. And second, it must be assisted by a sufficiently broad segment of international legal doctrine as to allow us to hold a specific action to be at least plausibly justified in terms of international law.

Thus, action by the United States, especially if seconded by other States, may catalyse the transformation of strongly challenged minority views into perfectly sustainable perceptions. In this context it may suffice to refer to the rather miraculous transformation which, in Germany, the mainstream academic doctrine on the supposed illegality of humanitarian intervention underwent in the aftermath of the NATO strikes against Yugoslavia.

From this perspective, our discourse is also about the impact of the United States and North Atlantic predominance on legal and especially academic doctrine, and on academic doctrine's facility for flexible adjustment. If assisted by plausible legal opinion, North Atlantic predominance more easily translates into legal terms in the construction of treaties than in the area of custom. The reason for this is obvious. Dynamics in the interpretation of treaties are not conditional on a sufficiently broad support in the community of States in the same way as the emergence of new customary rules. The strong interrelation between the structural principles of the UN Charter and customary rules enhances the legal impact of political and economic predominance. New dynamism in the construction of the UN Charter quite dramatically undermines and erodes the role of consent as one of the foundations of international law, which in turn reinforces the impact of inequalities on the sources of public international law.

North Atlantic predominance operates in an interplay with structural transformations of international law. This transformation profoundly affects sovereign equality as a guiding principle of international law. In the last decade, the State as a *genotype* has been gradually superseded by the concrete expression of statehood, that is to say the *phenotype*, as a point of reference for the application of many rules. In consequence, the territorial integrity of States, non-intervention and possibly even certain facets of State immunity have lost their sacrosanctity and their previously absolute standing. These formally unbending rules are now amenable to balancing processes. Even the liberty of States to choose their own political system, strongly emphasized by the International Court of Justice in the *Nicaragua* case, no longer stands up to scrutiny. The old structure of sovereign equality resting upon a rather well-defined architecture of broad protective principles and narrowly tailored exceptions has entirely melted down. The new receptiveness of international law to balancing processes has eroded traditional sovereignty and in consequence sovereign equality. New, sometimes grey, areas allowing the unilateral enforcement of national interests and international values have emerged. It is one of the great challenges of legal doctrine closely to monitor this process so as to maintain clear and operable contours for the purposes of this balancing.

We can observe a kind of substantive constitutionalization, similar to developments in domestic law. But unlike in domestic contexts, this process has not been flanked by the construction of judicial mechanisms for the authoritative concretization of controversial rules. All these evolutions facilitate the assertion of political predominance in legal terms. One could go on and cite other instances, like the genesis of democratic credentials or the rise of good governance as emerging normative or semi-normative standards in treaties.

To sum up, the effect of the predominance of the United States – again I would like to add: North Atlantic predominance – on the principle of sovereign equality must be seen in the light of the gradual erosion of this principle and the profound transformation of international law. States now act in a system that is more responsive to normative values which trump the traditional attributes of state sovereignty. The legitimate concern of weaker States does not call for an old-fashioned insistence on equality in formal terms, but rather for a stronger emphasis on substantive and procedural fairness and on a strengthening of judicial mechanisms for conflict resolution. After all, the pull toward strong juridification of political choices must present a sufficient amount of incentives for the predominant actor or predominant actors to limit their power by consent. Thus, a balanced reciprocity of costs and benefits, as well as the responsiveness of international law to existing asymmetries, may shed a somewhat milder light on the predominance of the United States.

Gregory H. Fox

Michel Cosnard and Nico Krisch begin their insightful and provocative chapters by deconstructing the notion of "sovereign equality." Four distinct meanings emerge from their discussions. The first involves the formal and general capacity of States to participate in norm creation. Cosnard finds this to be the essence of sovereign equality and concludes that the United States' predominance in international affairs has not altered the equal distribution of this capacity among all states. Krisch essentially agrees, but finds such "equality before the law" highly abstract and therefore largely irrelevant to the actual condition of most states as legal actors.

The second meaning involves a State's relation to particular legal regimes. United States efforts to secure special standing in some treaty systems and to withhold participation in others fall into this category. Cosnard argues that a State's decision to participate in a treaty regime where the United States has secured a special status is itself an exercise of sovereign discretion and does not compromise that State's equality. Krisch, in stark contrast, focuses on a host of legal arrangements, many beyond multilateral treaties, which in the aggregate suggest to him a fundamental shift in States' capacity to express consent equally. This traditional sovereign prerogative is restricted, in his view, both by United States efforts to erode consent as a basis for new norms and the aggressive imposition of United States law on unwilling national legal systems and treaty partners.

The third meaning involves a State's relation to substantive international rules. While Cosnard disagrees with substantive views of sovereign equality, he focuses on the values underlying substantive norms advocated by the United States and argues that the lack of any coherent opposition to those values explains, and may even mitigate, inequalities in law-making procedures. Any arguable substantive inequalities, in his view, are "the consequence of the victory of the values of the Western world."[15] Krisch will have none of this, dismissing procedural short-cuts even to laudable norms: "as long as conceptions of justice and morality include some emphasis on process and do not rely entirely on substantive considerations, the more inclusive, participatory character of multilateral institutions should, in principle, outweigh the substantive gains of unilateral action."[16]

Fourth is the effect of States' political and economic power on their participation in lawmaking processes. Norm creation and enforcement in this context are seen as responding to economies of scale: powerful States can more easily affect any given normative regime because they are such a pervasive presence in every other regime, and can therefore count on always having a political or economic chip to play in a given negotiation. Both authors agree that this factor now overwhelmingly favors the United States. Krisch, however, combines this factor with others in asking whether the United States has taken on the attributes of a world government.

The authors recognize that each of these factors is present in most discussions of sovereign equality, and I wholly agree with their decision not to reject any out of hand but rather to ask how each is affected by United

---

[15] Michel Cosnard, this volume, p. 131.   [16] Nico Krisch, this volume, pp. 174–5.

States predominance. But one cannot help being tempted by each author's case for which of the factors most usefully expresses the essence of sovereign equality. Cosnard is more the formalist, and his claim that United States actions have not changed States' equal capacity to propose, consider, support, reject, or modify norms in any meaningful sense seems correct. On the other hand, Krisch is persuasive in arguing that when the sum total of substantive inequalities (the first and second categories above) is combined with the unquestionably universalist aspirations of contemporary international law, one finds a legal system that is highly asymmetrical in many of its routine functions. Both views are compelling. Yet Cosnard's is vulnerable to the point that a purely formalist approach would find no meaningful changes in sovereign equality since the principle was proclaimed as a general matter in the 1945 UN Charter. There would be no significance, for example, in the dramatic infusion of life into the self-determination principle by the 1960 Declaration on the Granting of Independence to Colonial Countries; in the enhancement of the non-intervention principle by such events as the Definition of Aggression, the Friendly Relations Declaration and the *Nicaragua* case; in the development of the "optional blank slate" treaty doctrine for newly independent States; in the remarkable extension of state responsibility law beyond denial of justice claims by aliens; and in the erosion (though to a degree that is still controversial) of the Hull Formulation requiring full compensation for expropriated alien property.

Few would disagree that these and similar developments have fundamentally altered the legal relations between weaker and more powerful states. Moreover, they have done so in areas in which the realities of power imbalances have been most keenly felt by smaller States. These are doctrines of international law where inequalities may debilitate fundamental attributes of state sovereignty: a robust anti-intervention norm, for example, works to equalize the standing of small and large States by ensuring that weaker States enjoy the attribute of territorial integrity. The same is true for the optional blank slate doctrine: newly independent States achieved the same capacity to choose their treaty commitments as their former colonial masters. Since the capacity to enter into foreign relations is an element of statehood – a principle that surely includes the capacity to choose in *which* foreign relations one engages – the nexus to sovereignty is again evident. A righting of imbalances in these areas thus affects more than peripheral, discretionary functions; these substantive innovations gave weaker States a greater freedom of action in the areas where powerful States had most effectively used international law to their advantage. Of course, the bulk of Krisch's chapter is filled with examples showing an opposite tendency toward inequality in areas also touching on essential sovereign functions. Here one finds an appeal in Cosnard's formalism, which can dismiss these developments as irrelevant to equality before the law. But one should resist, I think, such a result-oriented jurisprudence.

Yet to agree with Krisch's substantive conception does not necessarily compel one to accept his conclusion that rules congruent with American power function principally to enhance and reinforce that power. Acts identified by the authors as symptoms of American hegemony are not self-evidently zero sum in their effect; that is, subordination of other States' prerogatives is not the necessary consequence of rules that enhance US interests. In economic terms, Pareto optimality is also possible. A relatively benign form of this argument would point out that most norms advanced by the United States in the post–Cold War era are not structured as exemptions designed to account for American exceptionalism (as in the case of its reaction to the ICC), but as traditionally reciprocal rules with costs and benefits accruing to each affected state. If this is true, one must look beyond obvious benefits to the United States in order to understand the systemic consequences of the rules. A more robust version of the argument would assert that at least some of these norms can function to *lessen* asymmetries among states, though that result may be obscured by these norms' resonance with Cold–War era political debates, as well as by the more cynically motivated (and widely condemned) exceptionalist claims. In either case, it is useful to examine one area in which Krisch identifies substantive inequalities but where other factors may actually militate toward less inequality than is suggested.

Robert Jackson and Carl Rosenberg draw an important distinction between the "juridical" and "empirical" State.[17] The juridical State is the legal concept under examination in the two chapters: the fictional entity endowed by international law with rights, responsibilities, and personality. The empirical State is the de facto authority of a national government to impose order and regulate conduct within its territory. Many have observed the widespread absence of empirical statehood in developing countries, due in no small part to the lack of connection between the juridical entity and a

---

[17] Robert H. Jackson and Carl G. Rosenberg, "Why Africa's Weak States Persist: the Empirical and the Juridical in Statehood" (1982) 35 *World Politics* 1, 2.

historically coherent community bound together by common traditions. The two qualities are usually viewed as wholly separate, exemplified by the lack of empirical statehood in Somalia since 1991 having no evident effect on its legal continuity. But Krisch's view of sovereign equality as a substantive matter suggests that the two conceptions of statehood are intimately connected in the State's functional relation to international law. A weak empirical State is unlikely to be a robust participant in the creation of international law, for its attributes – a weak legal infrastructure, a government lacking legitimacy in the eyes of its citizens, an inability to enforce law throughout much of its territory, and so on – mean that it will bring little in the way of carrots or sticks to international negotiations. For similar reasons, the weak empirical State will have great difficulty implementing the highly complex international regulatory norms in areas such as trade, environmental protection, investment protection, intellectual property rights, human rights, and judicial cooperation.[18] In Krisch's substantive view, a State that is barely a presence in the creation and implementation of international law lacks important attributes of sovereign equality. Yet this *juridical* deficiency derives in no small part from the *empirical* deficiencies of weak and illegitimate governing structures.

This important connection relates to the United States because many of the normative projects the United States initiates, joins, or funds are explicitly designed to enhance attributes of empirical statehood in the developing world. At the center of these efforts is the promotion of democratic governance, which, in the US view, necessarily undergirds a regime's legitimacy and effectiveness. Krisch describes the "privileging [of] democratic states and governments" as one point of pressure on formal sovereign equality.[19] The United States has certainly encouraged democratic transitions with incentives of recognition, foreign aid, bilateral cooperation, and ease of membership in international organizations.

---

[18] Many other factors are at work here to be sure, such as lack of resources, colonial and Cold War legacies, etc. But many writers view the essentially ahistorical nature of national boundaries in the developing world as a profound and fundamental disability. As Denham and Lombardi write, "the national identity of Southern peoples was not appreciably affected by the enclosure and consolidation represented by Westphalia and traditional ethnic identifications remained to inhibit the impact and potency of state sovereignty." Mark E. Denham and Mark Owen Lombardi, "Perspectives on Third-World Sovereignty: Problems with(out) Borders," in Mark E. Denham and Mark Owen Lombardi (eds.), *Perspectives on Third World Sovereignty: The Postmodern Paradox* (Basingstoke: Macmillan, 1996), p. 7.

[19] Krisch, this volume, p. 147.

But does this privilege the United States? The United States is hardly alone in aggressively promoting democracy as the preferred form of governance. In Europe, for example, the European Court of Human Rights has described democracy as "without doubt a fundamental feature of the European public order";[20] membership in the European Union is restricted to democratic states;[21] all EU treaties with non-member states contain clauses making continuation of constitutional democracy a material condition of the agreement;[22] and members of the Organization for Security and Cooperation in Europe (OSCE) pledged in the Moscow Document not to recognize the results of coups against democratically elected regimes.[23] Beyond Europe, the Organization of American States (OAS), the new African Union, MERCOSUR and the Commonwealth also have institutionalized prodemocratic policies.

Perhaps more importantly, while it is not self-evident that a steady series of democratic transitions (the consequences of a *successful* United States policy in this area) would ultimately enhance the sovereign status of the United States, newly democratic States will have addressed issues at the core of weak empirical statehood. Their standing as creators and consumers of international norms will thereby be enhanced. In the overall scheme of sovereign equality, therefore, the marginal benefits to the *United States* of democratization over time are uncertain, while the marginal benefits to the *States affected* are substantial. One might argue that in a community of mostly democratic States, the United States is more likely to be regarded as *primus inter pares*. But again focusing on the equal application of norms, this is not necessarily the case. Many of the post-Communist states of eastern and central Europe, for example, have sided squarely with their fellow Europeans in human rights and environmental disputes with the United States.

Both Cosnard and Krisch acknowledge the strain of utopianism that runs through discussions of sovereign equality – the belief that a principle of juridical equality can somehow be reified in a world of dramatic military,

[20] *Case of the United Communist Party of Turkey v. Turkey*, No. 133/1996/752/951, para. 45 (30 Jan. 1998).

[21] Treaty on European Union, Title I(F), (1992) 31 *International Legal Materials* 247, 256.

[22] "On the Inclusion of Respect for Democratic Principles and Human Rights in Agreements between the Community and Third Countries" COM(95) 215 (1995).

[23] CSCE, "Document of the Moscow Meeting on the Human Dimension, Emphasizing Respect for Human Rights, Pluralistic Democracy, the Rule of Law, and Procedures for Fact-Finding" (1991) 30 *International Legal Materials* 1670.

economic, and political imbalances. But both also believe this aspiration has served as a spur to legal reform movements that, at least in the period 1945–90, were effective in reducing inequalities on a variety of substantive fronts. It is, of course, the view of sovereign equality as substantive that made such innovations possible. At the moment, innovations appear to be lagging behind aspirations to a much greater degree than at any point since 1945, though, as noted, reciprocal norms operate quite differently from exceptionalist claims in this regard. But retaining a substantive view leaves open the possibility that events in the future may again begin progress toward the goals of Article 2(1).

III

Use of force

7

The use of force by the United States after the end of the Cold War, and its impact on international law

MARCELO G. KOHEN

The rules relating to the prohibition on the use of force, including its exceptions, are at the core of the international legal order that emerged after the greatest human-made disaster of all times: World War II. In that legal order, peace is perceived as the main value to be protected and the prohibition on the use of force embodied in Article 2(4) of the UN Charter knows only one exception: the right of self-defense as set out in Article 51. Recourse to force in international relations is meant to be the prerogative of the Security Council. In 1945, the motto was "peace through collective security."

What happened in this field between 1945 and 1989 is well known. It is also well known that hopes for a new peaceful international order after the collapse of communism were soon disappointed. The resort to force in international relations is even more prevalent today than it was just one decade ago. It is for this reason legitimate to inquire whether international law has undergone change in this important sphere. Since the United States has become the only superpower, since its military supremacy is overwhelming, since ultimately the United States has been one of the States that has resorted to force the most in the last decade, one is also justified in focusing on both its practice and the legal arguments it invokes, as well as the reactions of other countries to its actions and claims.

The purpose of this chapter is to analyze the impact of the American interpretation of, and practice relating to, the rules governing the use of force in international relations since the end of the Cold War. In order to do so, this chapter will identify the different legal categories in which the use of force by the United States could be encapsulated. It will focus, however, on self-defense, since that has been the main argument advanced by different American administrations to justify the resort to force, most notably in situations generally not seen to be covered by self-defense. Special emphasis will be put on the terrorist attacks of 11 September 2001 and the reaction thereto. For the question is not only whether terrorist attacks open the way to self-defense, but also whether an armed conflict, within the meaning of international law, exists between the State and the terrorist organisations, with all the implications that follow for both the *jus ad bellum* and *jus in bello*.

Although President George Bush Sr. heralded the arrival of a new international order as a consequence of the international community's reaction to Iraq's attempted annexation of Kuwait,[1] the analysis here will begin with Operation "Just Cause" in Panama in December 1989, rather than with Operation "Desert Storm" which took place one year later. The United States invasion of Panama was the first US military operation after the fall of the Berlin wall – it took place less than two months after that event.

The new international realities led Presidents Bush and Clinton, as well as top officials such as General Colin Powell, to elaborate new military doctrines relative to the use of force. The relationship between these doctrines and international law will be analyzed in the first section of this chapter. And in order to ascertain whether there has been a change in the rules concerning the use of force, or at least a change in their interpretation, it will be necessary to consider not only the US arguments and practice, but also – more importantly – the attitude of the international community to them.

American doctrines on the use of force

Each American administration elaborates what is called its "military doctrine." In the last two decades, the Reagan, Bush Sr., Powell, and Clinton doctrines were advanced. If one regards these different doctrines from a legal perspective, one may note on the one hand, that apart from the Reagan doctrine on "collective self-defense," they do not deal with international law at all. The Reagan doctrine was an attempt to enlarge the legal notion of self-defense, in order to embrace the covert military activities of the

---

[1] Curiously enough, he did so on 11 September 1990, exactly eleven years before the terrorist attacks against the United States, in a speech at a joint session of Congress (*Public Papers of the Presidents of the United States: George Bush*, 1990 (Washington, DC: USGPO, 1991) II, 1218, at 1219).

United States in support of anti-communist rebels. On the other hand, the Bush, Powell, and Clinton doctrines were comprehensive explanations of overall United States policy regarding the use of force, irrespective of the matter of legality. However, this does not preclude consideration of these doctrines from a legal perspective.

The Reagan doctrine on "collective self-defense" fell rapidly into disrepute with the arrival in office of Mikhail Gorbachev in the Soviet Union. Its main foundation was the struggle against communist expansionism. In terms of content, the Reagan doctrine espoused the legitimacy of American military support for insurgencies against governments dependent on the Soviet Union.[2] It received a blatant rejection by the ICJ in the *Nicaragua* case[3] and was then abandoned.

In his remarks at West Point Military Academy on 5 January 1993, President Bush Sr. depicted the main features of his military doctrine, elaborated during the interventions in Panama, Iraq and Somalia:

> At times, real leadership requires a willingness to use military force. And force can be a useful backdrop to diplomacy, a complement to it, or, if need be, a temporary alternative ... Military force is never a tool to be used lightly or universally. In some circumstances it may be essential, in others counterproductive ... we cannot always decide in advance which interests will require our using military force to protect them. The relative importance of an interest is not a guide: military force may not be the best way of safeguarding some vital interest, while using force might be the best way to protect an interest that qualifies as important but less vital ... Using military force makes sense as a policy where the stakes warrant, where and when force can be effective, where no other policies are likely to prove effective, where its application can be limited in scope and time, and where the potential benefits justify the potential costs and sacrifice. Once we are satisfied that force makes sense, we must act with the maximum possible support. The United States can and

---

[2] To quote the definition given by President Reagan himself: "we must not break faith with those who are risking their lives – on every continent, from Afghanistan to Nicaragua – to defy Soviet-supported aggression and secure rights which have been ours from birth ... Support for freedom fighters is self-defense": Address Before a Joint Session of the Congress on the State of the Union, 6 February 1985. *Public Papers of the Presidents of the United States: Ronald Reagan*, 1985 (Washington, DC: USGPO, 1985) I, 135. For an attempt at legal justification of the Reagan Doctrine, see Jeane J. Kirkpatrick and Allan Gerson, "The Reagan Doctrine, Human Rights and International Law," *Right v. Might. International Law and the Use of Force* (New York: Council on Foreign Relations, 1991), pp. 19–36.

[3] *Case concerning Military and Paramilitary Activities in and against Nicaragua (Nicaragua v. United States of America)*, (1986) ICJ Reports 109–10, para. 209, 132–3, paras. 262 and 263.

should lead, but we will want to act in concert, where possible involving the United Nations or other multinational grouping... A desire for international support must not become a prerequisite for acting, though. Sometimes a great power has to act alone.[4]

Colin Powell's doctrine on the use of force is merely a development of the Bush doctrine, or rather its adjustment on matters of when, where and how to intervene. The former Chairman of the Joint Chiefs of Staff and now Secretary of State formulated the following points: "do not embark on high risk operations that have a less than overwhelming chance of success; do not start something without a clear idea of how to end it; do not use force incrementally or gradually."[5]

In turn, according to some military experts,[6] the Clinton doctrine was essentially inspired and influenced by the Powell doctrine. President Clinton described three different categories of national interests with correspondingly different guidelines for the use of force: (1) vital interests, such as defense of US territory, citizens, allies, and economic well-being, that call for doing whatever it takes to defend them, including the unilateral and decisive use of military power; (2) important, but non-vital interests, that call for limited and conditional use of military force, depending on conditions including likely success, costs, and risks commensurate with the interests at stake, and the failure of other means used to achieve the objectives; (3) humanitarian interests, for which the United States government tends to rule out combat power and limits use of military forces to situations in which they can provide unique capabilities or respond to urgent, otherwise unattainable needs of those in distress. In these cases, the risks to United States troops are supposed to be minimal.[7]

---

[4] *Public Papers of the Presidents of the United States. George Bush, 1992–93* (Washington, DC: USGPO, 1993), pp. 2228 at 2230–31.

[5] Remarks at the National Press Club, September 28, 1993, reprinted in Stephen Dagget and Nina Serafino, "The Use of Force: Key Contemporary Documents," Report 94-805F (Washington, DC: Congressional Research Service, 1994), 34. See Charles Stevenson, "The Evolving Clinton Doctrine on the Use of Force" (1996) 22 *Armed Forces and Society* 511.

[6] Stevenson, "Clinton Doctrine," above note 5, at 514–16.

[7] William J. Clinton, *A National Security Strategy and Enlargement* (Washington, DC: The White House, 1995), pp. 12–13, quoted in Stevenson, "Clinton Doctrine," above note 5, 518–19. The report went on to consider several critical questions to be raised prior to the commitment of military forces: "Have we considered non-military means that offer a reasonable chance of success? Is there a clearly defined, achievable mission? What is the environment of risk we are entering? What is needed to achieve our goals? What are the potential costs – both human and

Since the terrorist attacks of 11 September 2001, the administration of George W. Bush has been reviewing some aspects of the previous military doctrines, such as those which emphasize that no American lives are to be lost in conflict (one could term it a "zero dead" doctrine); or standing policies which place time limits on military involvement. The policy with respect to Afghanistan and the threats against the so-called "rogue States" – notably against Iraq – show that we are probably witnessing the emergence of a Bush Jr. doctrine, according to which there are no limits to the use of force if American security reasons so require.[8]

Since these doctrines do not contradict one another, they can for our purposes be analyzed together. While military humanitarian intervention is particular to the Clinton doctrine, all three doctrines share the following characteristics:

1. The use of force is considered an instrument of foreign policy.
2. Enforcing respect of international law in cases of grave violations is not per se a reason to use force.
3. The use of force by the United States is not necessarily conditioned by respect for international law.
4. The exhaustion of non-military means before resorting to force, although desirable, is not a precondition.
5. Interest and success are the main considerations when resorting to force.
6. Unilateral use of force (that is to say, without UN endorsement or support from other countries) is not precluded.

Set out in this way, little – if any – insight can be derived from these doctrines which would shed light on the formulation or interpretation of the rules of international law relative to the use of force. These policy statements are nevertheless an essential starting point to understanding the instances in which the United States uses force and how the US government tries to explain its actions from a legal point of view. They primarily demonstrate that law comes after the fact, rather than serving as a basis for the decision to resort to force.

financial – of the engagement? Do we have reasonable assurance of support from the American people and their elected representatives? Do we have timelines and milestones that will reveal the extent of success or failure, and, in either case, do we have an exit strategy?" *ibid.*

[8] See Michael J. Glennon, "Preempting Terrorism. The Case for Anticipatory Self-Defense," *The Weekly Standard*, 28 Feb. 2002, available at http://www.weeklystandard.com.

Is there a new American interpretation and practice concerning the use of force?

There has always been a tension between the US position on the use of force and the postulates of Articles 2(4) and 51 of the Charter. No one denies that, with the collapse of the Soviet Union, US involvement in the recourse to the use of force is decisive in the international relations of today. This reflects the facts that: (1) the US government possesses more freedom to use force than before; (2) the US government is able to impose its military supremacy with greater ease than before; and (3) the US government can influence collective decisions to use force with greater ease than before. These are of course political considerations. The question of concern to us is whether post–Cold War American practice is from a legal perspective new, or simply tantamount to "new wine in old bottles." In order to answer this question, it is necessary to compare old and new legal justifications advanced by the United States. In this respect, five major categories of recourse to the use of force since the end of the Cold War can be identified: self-defense, armed reprisals, military intervention by invitation, Security Council authorizations of the use of force, and armed humanitarian intervention.

Among these five categories, probably only the fourth deserves to be called a novelty. The others are mere reformulations, employing new arguments, of categories already used in the past.

Self-defense

Over the last twelve years, the United States has qualified numerous controversial situations as an "armed attack," leading to the invocation of a purported right of self-defense, be it individual or collective.

Individual self-defense

The invasion of Panama in December 1989 was justified on the basis of General Manuel Noriega's threats and attacks upon Americans in Panama, creating "an imminent danger" to the 35,000 American citizens living there. The objectives of the United States were described as follows: (1) to protect American lives; (2) to assist the lawful and democratically elected government in Panama in fulfilling its international obligations; (3) to seize and arrest General Noriega, an indicted drug trafficker; and (4) to defend the integrity of US rights under the Panama Canal treaties.[9] It was added, as supporting the argument of self-defense, that "the illegitimate" Panamanian National Assembly declared that the Republic of Panama was in a "state of war with the United States," that an American serviceman was killed, another wounded, a third arrested and brutally beaten and his wife threatened with sexual abuse, and finally that Noriega's alleged drug trafficking activities constituted acts of aggression.[10]

The UN General Assembly condemned the invasion and demanded the withdrawal of American forces.[11] The Security Council failed to adopt a resolution to the same effect because of American, British, and French vetoes.[12] The Organization of American States (OAS) General Assembly voted 20 to 1 to condemn the invasion.[13]

On 26 June 1993, the United States launched an aerial attack against the Iraqi Intelligence Headquarters in Baghdad, in response to an alleged failed plot to assassinate former President Bush during a visit to Kuwait more than two months earlier. The legal justification was self-defense, since, according to Madeleine Albright, then US permanent representative at the United Nations, "every member [of the Security Council] would regard an assassination attempt against its former Head of State as an attack against itself, and would react."[14] Some members of the Security Council endorsed the American qualification (the United Kingdom, Russia, Hungary, Japan) or showed "understanding" (France) for the American action, whereas the Non-Aligned Movement and China insisted on the obligation to use force only in conformity with the Charter of the United Nations.[15]

Self-defense was invoked again on 20 August 1998 to justify missile attacks against Osama bin Laden's training camps in Afghanistan and a Sudanese pharmaceutical plant, in response to the bombings of the United States embassies in Nairobi and Dar Es Salaam on 7 August 1998.[16] The missile attacks were not even placed on the agenda of the Security Council. Again, some States showed approval or "understanding" for the attacks

---

[9] See "Contemporary Practice of the United States" (1990) 84 AJIL 545.
[10] *Ibid.* See also the letter dated 20 Dec. 1989 from the Permanent Representative of the United States of America to the UN addressed to the President of the Security Council, Doc. S/21035.
[11] A/Res. 44/240 of 29 December 1989.   [12] (1989) 43 *Yearbook of the United Nations* 175.
[13] Resolution CP/RES.534 adopted on 22 December 1989.
[14] United Nations, S/PV.3245, 27 June 1993, at 3.   [15] *Ibid., passim.*
[16] See the letter from the United States representative dated 20 Aug. 1998: United Nations, S/1998/780.

(the United Kingdom, Germany, Japan, Spain, France) whereas others protested, including the Non-Aligned Movement, the League of Arab States, China, and Russia.

It would not be difficult to show that all these arguments fall far short of the conditions required for self-defense in conformity with Article 51.[17] To say the least, it is only with great difficulty that these situations could fulfill the requirements set out by the International Court of Justice in the *Nicaragua* case as regards self-defense. Our task, however, is to assess their impact on the application or interpretation of Article 51 rather than to scrutinize the legality of these actions. In order to reach a conclusion, it is therefore necessary to examine the attitude of the rest of the international community.[18]

When the cases depicted above are compared with those situations in which the United States invoked self-defense when resorting to force during the Cold War, no major differences emerge, either in theory or in practice. The invasion of Grenada in 1983 and the bombing of Libya in 1986 were also justified on the basis of self-defense.

The terrorist acts of 11 September 2001: a turning point?

Almost immediately after the acts of terrorism of 11 September 2001, the American administration began to speak of "war." The magnitude of the action, the number of victims, the way in which it was carried out and its deep impact on world public opinion could lead to the conclusion that this horrendous act should not simply be categorized as another "terrorist attack." President George W. Bush considered that they "were more than acts of terror. They were acts of war."[19] Secretary of State Colin Powell supported this view, explaining that "the American people had a clear understanding that this is a war. That's the way they see it. You can't see it any other way, *whether legally that is correct or not* . . . and we've got to respond as if it is a war."[20] The legal and political strategy of the United States has been to place in the same category "those nations, organizations or

---

[17] For these conditions, see Georges Abi-Saab, "Cours général de droit international public" (1987) 207 *Recueil des cours*, 368–79.

[18] See below, pp. 221–6.

[19] Remarks by the President in Photo Opportunity with the National Security Team, 12 Sept. 2001, in http://www.whitehouse.gov/news/releases/2001/09/20010912-4.html.

[20] Emphasis added. Interview by ABC News, 12 Sept. 2001 (available at http://www.state.gov/secretary/rm/2001/index.cfm?docid=4864).

persons [who] planned, authorized, committed or aided the terrorist attacks that occurred on September 11, 2001, or harbored such organizations or persons."[21]

There is a complete coherence between the United States interpretation of these acts and its previous practice. As we have seen above, there is nothing new in the United States considering terrorist action as armed attacks and thereby opening the way for self-defense.[22] What has changed, as we shall see below, is the magnitude of the riposte and the attitude of other States vis-à-vis this American position.

This qualification raises the question of the applicability of the rules of international law related to the use of force, in other words, whether these terrorist acts can be considered as constituting uses of force in international relations, that is, "armed attacks" in the sense of Article 51 of the UN Charter, or acts of aggression. Many scenarios can be envisaged. If a State is directly or indirectly implicated in the acts, they would indisputably be acts of aggression. But this point raises another, more difficult question: whether the fact of solely harboring terrorists in its territory makes a State responsible for indirect aggression.

The Definition of Aggression embodied in Resolution 3314 (XXIX) does not cover the harboring of terrorists.[23] And the analysis of the International Court of Justice in the *Nicaragua* case supports the view that simple harboring does not constitute agression.[24] The Court, however, did not address this particular issue in depth. During the Cold War, States belonging to

---

[21] "Authorization for Use of Military Force," Joint Resolution of the Senate and the House of Representatives, 107th Congress, 1st Session SJ RES.23, 17 Sept. 2001 (available at http://www.thomas.loc.gov), as well as declarations by the Executive.

[22] For example, after the Israeli bombing of the headquarters of the Palestine Liberation Organization (PLO) in Tunis in 1985, the American representative to the Security Council declared: "we recognize and strongly support the principle that a State subjected to continuing terrorist attacks may respond with appropriate use of force to defend itself against further attacks. This is an aspect of the inherent right of self-defense recognized in the United Nations Charter. We support this principle regardless of attacker, and regardless of victim. It is the collective responsibility of sovereign States to see that terrorism enjoys no sanctuary, no safe haven, and that those who practice it have no immunity from the responses their acts warrant" (intervention of Mr. Walters, S/PV.2615, 4 October 1985, at 112).

[23] Article 3(g) refers to sending of armed bands, groups, irregulars or mercenaries, which carry out acts of armed force against another State, or to the "substantial involvement" of a State in these acts.

[24] (1986) ICJ Reports, 118–20, paras. 228–30. For an analysis, see Oscar Schachter, "The Lawful Use of Force by a State against Terrorists in another Country" (1989) 19 *Israel Yearbook of Human Rights* 209 at 216–17.

different systems furnished arms and financial or logistic support to rebels who in some cases used terrorist methods. Paradoxically, the US Central Intelligence Agency (CIA) armed, trained, and supported Osama bin Laden's group in its fight against the pro-Soviet regime in Afghanistan.

There is a need to take the analysis further than did the ICJ. A distinction can certainly be made as to the degree of assistance furnished by a State to terrorist organizations. One cannot exclude, for instance, that some form of logistic support is to be included in one of the forms of aggression depicted by Resolution 3314 (XXIX), to the extent that it constitutes a "substantial involvement." Thus, logistic assistance in order to accomplish or facilitate terrorist acts might constitute a form of participation therein.

Accordingly, there is a legal analysis the American government could have followed. Washington could have demonstrated that the Taliban regime, which effectively controlled the major part of Afghanistan and was able to engage the international responsibility of that country, did more than simply harbor Osama bin Laden's network. The close and evident links existing between bin Laden and the Taliban were such that it should not be difficult to establish that the former had become a de facto organ of the State.[25] Still another possibility would have been to engage the responsibility of Afghanistan by considering that the Taliban regime, being aware of the activities of the al-Qaida network, especially after the bombing of the American embassies in Nairobi and Dar Es Salaam, failed to prevent further acts of terrorism by it.[26] Instead of following this course of action, the American government decided, for political reasons, to focus its rhetoric upon a "war against terrorism and those harboring terrorists."

The question remains whether non-State actors, such as terrorist organizations, can be responsible for armed attacks in the sense of the *jus ad bellum*. Nearly fifteen years ago, Oscar Schachter gave the following example, referring to terrorist actions as possible "armed attacks":

> Article 51 does not qualify "armed attack." On its face, it may apply to attacks from any source and therefore allow a State to respond with force to attacks by non-State bands wherever they may be. However, this conclusion

---

[25] Cf. this situation with that, although not identical, of the Ayatollah Khomeini in the *Hostages* case (1980) ICJ Reports 3 at 29–30, para. 59, and 33–5, paras. 71–5. Formally, the Ayatollah Khomeini was not an organ of the State, but the religious leader of the country. As such, the Court considered him, without further elaboration, as an organ of the Iranian State.

[26] For the attribution of terrorist acts to States in general, see Luigi Condorelli, "The Imputability to States of Acts of International Terrorism" (1999) 19 *Israel Yearbook on Human Rights* 232.

seems too simplistic in a world in which territorial sovereignty of States is a dominant principle. Consider whether terrorist attacks by the West German "Red Army Front" against American installations or nationals in Italy would allow the United States or Italy to attack the "Front" in Germany, and seize or kill its suspected terrorists without the explicit consent of the Federal Republic of Germany. To say that "armed attack" in Article 51 applies to any attack, regardless of the source, does not meet this issue.[27]

Of course, one could argue that we are facing a new kind of violence after 11 September 2001. Hence, the existing rules should be adapted, or at least read, in a way that takes into account this new reality. The point, however, is that neither the arguments advanced nor the ways in which it is proposed to fight terrorism with the use of force are new. For example, Israel in 1982 with regard to Lebanon and in 1985 with regard to Tunisia, argued that the harboring of terrorists justified its use of force in self-defense. In both cases, the Security Council did not share this view, and in the latter case explicitly condemned the use of force by Israel.[28] In the 1990s, Turkey also followed this line of argument to justify its use of force in northern Iraq against the Kurds.

Enlarging the concept of aggression so as to include the harboring of terrorists confuses different internationally wrongful acts and opens the door to increased unilateral uses of force, and thus escalation. Although reprehensible and unlawful, harboring terrorists cannot be likened to aggression, which constitutes the most grave of all the uses of force in international relations. It would be the equivalent, in the field of criminal law, of placing in the same category a killer and the person who gives him or her shelter. Harboring terrorist groups acting abroad clearly constitutes a threat to international peace and security, which in turn can justify forcible action as decided upon by the Security Council under Chapter VII of the Charter.

The first question that emerges is why non-State terrorist acts ought to be considered as a particular case of armed attack or even aggression. Is it their violence, their targets, their aims, the number of casualties, or the level of destruction that provides the answer? Putting aside some semantic

---

[27] Oscar Schachter, "The Lawful Use of Force by a State against Terrorists in Another Country" (1989) 19 *Israel Yearbook of Human Rights* 209 at 216.

[28] See Resolutions 501 (1982) and 573 (1985), the former adopted on 25 Feb. 1982 by 13 votes to none, with 2 abstentions (Poland and USSR), the latter on 4 Oct. 1985 14–0, with the abstention of the United States.

distinctions,[29] violence can be the common element shared by terrorist acts and traditional military actions engaged in by one State against another. Is it still valid to consider that, if the same action is committed by a State, the characterization of it as aggression offers no doubt, whereas if it is committed by terrorists this characterization does not stand?

Operation "Enduring Freedom" was conducted under the banner of self-defense. This term of art is employed differently in domestic and international law. In the former, it is a cause of justification in criminal law for individuals having resort to violence. In the latter, it is used essentially as an exception to the prohibition of the use of force by a State (or, as preferred by the International Law Commission and the majority of authors, a "circumstance precluding wrongfulness"). There are, however, other circumstances in which self-defense is used in relation to some situations which international agents may face. For example, agreements or resolutions regarding peacekeeping forces usually establish that these forces or their personnel will not use force except in self-defense.[30]

Usually, there is no need to use the category of "self-defense" when dealing with the repression of terrorism. In different countries in which State agents (police or armed forces) have killed terrorists who have hijacked aircraft, they did so because this was the only way to obtain the release of the hostages. These acts were not qualified as acts of self-defense in the sense of the *jus ad bellum*, irrespective of whether the terrorists came from abroad. They were justified on the basis of domestic law without any need for a reference to self-defense. These were simply cases of the legitimate use of violence by the entity having the monopoly over it within its territory: the State.

Interestingly, both the United Kingdom and France accompanied their ratification of Additional Protocol I to the Geneva Conventions of 12 August 1949 by an interpretative declaration of Articles 1(4) and 96(3), according to which "the term 'armed conflict' of itself and in its context denotes a

---

[29] The English language does not distinguish, as some other languages (such as French) do, between "attaque" and "attentat."

[30] For example, UNIFIL, Report of the Secretary-General on the implementation of Security Council Resolution 425 (1978) of 19 March 1978, 4(d): "The Force will be provided with weapons of a defensive character. It will not use force except in self-defense. Self-defense would include resistance to attempts by forceful means to prevent it from discharging its duties under the mandate of the Security Council" (UN doc. S/12611).

situation of a kind which is not constituted by the commission of ordinary crimes including acts of terrorism whether concerted or in isolation."[31]

Even assuming that terrorist action could be considered an "armed attack" in the sense of Article 51, the situation emerging from the 11 September 2001 terrorist acts did not fall within the ambit of self-defense. The main idea of self-defense, which was summarized by the celebrated Webster formula, implies that the attack is under way and that the aim is to repel it. Once the attack is over, the legal justifications for the use of force must be different. It is not a matter of time, as some authors believe, pretending that self-defense actions can occur many months later, as was the case with the action against Iraq after its invasion of Kuwait more than six months earlier.[32] Putting aside the fact that Chapter VII of the Charter rather than self-defense legally covered the "Gulf War," this idea fails to distinguish between instant and continuing situations. Iraqi aggression was still ongoing in January 1991, since the territory of Kuwait was under military occupation. The terrorist acts of 11 September 2001 are finished. It would be forcing the legal reasoning too much to pretend that they are part of a war declared by the terrorists and that we are therefore facing an ongoing armed conflict. Furthermore, the goals advanced in order to justify the use of force – the prevention of further terrorist attacks, the destruction of the al-Qaida network, the bringing of its members to trial – fall outside the purpose of self-defense. This is not to say that force may not be necessary to achieve these objectives, or that these objectives are not justified, rather that a legal justification other than self-defense is required.

Still, can Security Council Resolutions 1368 and 1373 (2001) be considered as a recognition that the United States was in a situation of self-defense? This certainly was the perception prevailing within political spheres. However, the fact of "recognizing the inherent right of individual or collective self-defense in accordance with the Charter" neither adds nor subtracts anything. The only coherent interpretation of this sentence that is compatible with the Charter is simply that if one or more States were involved in the terrorist attacks and persisted in this action, the victim State could act in self-defense. Of course, this is not the American government's interpretation.

---

[31] Ratification by the United Kingdom on 28 Jan. 1998, by France on 11 April 2001. Texts available at http://www.cicr.org.

[32] This is the view developed by Yoram Dinstein, *War, Aggression and Self-defence*, 3rd edn. (Cambridge: Cambridge University Press, 2001), pp. 212–13.

This vague reference in the preamble of the resolution is a compromise between different interpretations. The American one, although endorsed by NATO, the EU, the States parties to the Rio Treaty and many others, is but one interpretation, and one which does not enjoy universal acceptance, as we will see below.

Collective self-defense

The United States also persists in a broad interpretation of collective self-defense, even after the Security Council has taken action to address threats to peace, breaches of the peace or acts of aggression. This was the case during the crisis provoked by the Iraqi invasion of Kuwait, when the US government considered, before the adoption of the Resolution 678 (1990), that it was free to use force by virtue of a right of collective self-defense emanating from the original Iraqi attack, even in the absence of Security Council authorization. A careful reading of the wording of the relevant Security Council resolutions shows that other members of this organ did not share the American view, especially since the Kuwait crisis can be considered the first case, following the end of the Cold War, in which the Security Council played its role by taking measures to maintain and restore international peace and security.[33]

United States practice on self-defense: an appraisal

The American interpretation of self-defense during the decade following the end of the Cold War rested on the same foundations as before. It has simply been broadened to include cases of drug trafficking and plots to assassinate former heads of State within the concept of "armed attacks" against the United States.

It emerges as a consequence of our analysis that one is not justified in pursuing extraterritorial repression of terrorist groups under the heading of self-defense. For what is principally at stake with the argument of self-defense is whether the victim State can claim the right to act forcibly against terrorist groups no matter where they are and irrespective of any consent from the State whose territory becomes the battlefield. The consequences of allowing self-defense in these situations would be a "new war without borders."

---

[33] The resolutions were worded in such a way as to include both a reference to self-defense in their preambles and action under Chapter VII in the operative parts.

Moreover, it is important to emphasize the conditions for self-defense that the United States has claimed have been fulfilled in the cases arising since the end of the Cold War. With the exception of Operation "Just Cause" in Panama, the requirement of proportionality was always raised. Other conditions asserted were necessity, previous warnings, attempts to achieve the goals through diplomatic means, and the objective of preventing repetition. This practice confirms that necessity and proportionality are requirements that must be met before invoking self-defense. The other conditions referred to can be subsumed within the requirements of necessity and proportionality. Indeed, a reference to previous attempts to solve the problem through diplomatic means amounts to recognition that force is an option of last resort, that peaceful means have been unsuccessfully exhausted. However, the objective of preventing further attacks raises the question of whether proportionality must be measured in relation to the gravity of the attack and the goal of stopping and repelling the aggressor or, on the contrary, whether it can go so far as to include the notion of prevention. As is well known, the notion of preventive self-defense is controversial and, in any case, contrary to the wording of Article 51. There is no consensus in international society acknowledging such an extension of self-defense.[34]

Military intervention by invitation[35]

Within this category of justification one can discern an evolution in the practice of the United States over the last decade. The change began with the aerial action against rebel forces in the Philippines in December 1989, at the request of the legitimate government of Corazon Aquino.[36] It was followed by the deployment of the United States Army in Saudi Arabia following the annexation of Kuwait by Iraq. Both cases involved clear and authentic invitations emanating from the governments of the countries

---

[34] In the *Nicaragua* case, the ICJ carefully avoided pronouncing upon this sensitive topic. See (1986) ICJ Reports 103, para. 194.

[35] On this point, see generally Georg Nolte, *Eingreifen auf Einladung. Zur völkerrechtlichen Zulässigkeit des Einsatzes fremder Truppen im internen Konflikt auf Einladung der Regierung* (Berlin: Springer, 1999).

[36] It is noteworthy that one of the arguments developed by the US government to justify the Panama invasion was a "consultation" with the elected president, Guillermo Endara. However, the US government did not pretend that its action was motivated by an "invitation" issued by him.

concerned, in contrast with American, Soviet or French practice during the Cold War.

Latin America has been the preferred theatre of operations for American interventions, in most cases without any kind of "invitation" at all. The 1994 intervention in Haiti signaled a new approach in this field. Instead of unilateral action, either under cover of a regional endorsement without Security Council authorization as required by Article 53 of the UN Charter (as was the case with the Dominican Republic in 1965), or without such regional endorsement (Guatemala in 1954), the procedure followed was in full conformity with the UN and OAS Charters. First, economic sanctions were adopted, followed by a United States-led peacekeeping operation authorized by Security Council Resolution 940 (1994).

Today, there is some criticism of American military involvement in "Plan Colombia," which is designed to combat the drug industry, put an end to the civil war and develop the economy and democracy of Colombia. From a legal perspective, nothing need be said about this American participation, as it is in response to a request from the Colombian government. The criticisms raised are instead a function of political considerations: the plan, which principally involves a military strategy to tackle illicit drug cultivation and trafficking through substantial assistance to the Colombian armed forces and police, escalates the existing armed conflict and human rights crisis.[37]

After the defeat of the Taliban, the United States has continued to conduct its military activities in Afghanistan, with at least the initial toleration of the new regime. One could therefore speculate whether Operation "Enduring Freedom" has a legal justification in the consent of the government of the State concerned.[38] Yet one cannot call the operation an

---

[37] The Colombian army personnel trained by US special forces have been implicated by action or omission in serious human rights violations, including the massacre of civilians; and military equipment provided to the Colombian armed forces has reportedly been used in the commission of human rights violations against civilians. See Amnesty International's Position on Plan Colombia, June 2000. Available at http://www.amnesty-usa.org/news/2000/colombia07072000.html.

[38] See Article 20 of the ILC Draft Articles on State responsibility, which considers consent to be one of the circumstances precluding wrongfulness. Paragraph 6 of the ILC Commentary on Article 26 of the same Draft Articles states: "in applying some peremptory norms the consent of a particular State may be relevant. For example, a State may validly consent to a foreign military presence on its territory for a lawful purpose." "Commentaries to the Draft Articles on Responsibility of States for Internationally Wrongful Acts adopted by the International Law Commission at its Fifty-third session (2001)," in *Report of the International Law Commission on the work of its Fifty-third session, Official Records of the General Assembly, Fifty-sixth session, Supplement No. 10* (A/56/10), ch.IV.E.2.

"intervention by invitation," since there was no request from the Afghan government. Moreover, the very existence of that government is largely though not exclusively tributary to the American action against the Taliban. From a political perspective, nobody regrets the fall of the odious regime led by Mullah Omar. From a legal perspective, however, it is difficult to accept that military intervention is permissible on the basis that any new government resulting from the intervention retroactively endorses it. This was the excuse used by the Soviet Union legally to justify its invasions of Hungary, Czechoslovakia, and Afghanistan. Certainly, the circumstances today are different, since the new provisional Afghan government is the product of an arrangement between the representatives of almost all components of Afghan society, an arrangement arrived at under UN auspices. At any rate, the American administration did not modify its original argument of self-defense, by shifting to a reliance on consent given by Afghanistan.

To sum up, and putting aside the case of Afghanistan, it can be said that since the end of the Cold War there has been no change in international law regarding intervention by invitation, but that there has been a change in the American attitude in favor of increased compliance with these rules.

Security Council practice under Chapter VII

The major changes since the fall of the Berlin Wall concerning the use of force relate to Security Council practice. The capacity of the Security Council to confer general authorizations to use force has been the object of huge doctrinal controversies, starting with the resolutions adopted with respect to the Kuwait crisis.

Authorizations to use "all necessary means"

Resolution 665 (1990) was the first resolution to authorize member States to use such measures "as may be necessary under the authority of the Security Council" to halt maritime shipping so as to ensure compliance with the economic embargo previously imposed on Iraq by the Council. The second, Resolution 678 (1990), authorized States collaborating with Kuwait "to use all necessary means" to uphold and implement the Security Council resolutions mandating Iraq's withdrawal and the restoration of the legitimate Kuwaiti government.

This kind of action is not exactly what Chapter VII of the Charter envisaged. What took place was not a mandatory action, but rather an authorization. This meant that the decision to resort to force belonged to the member States. Military forces were not put at the disposal of the Council, but instead acted on their own. Neither command nor control of the operation was vested in the United Nations. The Military Staff Committee did not act as envisaged by the Charter. The Secretary-General played no role, to the point where he said that this was not a "United Nations war."[39] For all these reasons, some scholars have argued that the Security Council acted *ultra vires*.[40] However, it is beyond any doubt that all the permanent members, and indeed most other States, considered that it was within the Council's powers to act in such a way. Moreover, there was an antecedent to Resolutions 665 and 678 (1990): in Resolution 221 (1966), the Council authorized the United Kingdom to use force in order to render effective the embargo against Southern Rhodesia.[41] Subsequent practice also confirmed the interpretation of the Charter according to which the Council is empowered to follow such a course of action. Resolution 794 (1992) on Somalia followed exactly the same procedure, as did Resolution 816 (1993) on Bosnia and Herzegovina.

Nonetheless, an important distinction arises when one compares Resolution 678 (1990) with the other resolutions referred to above. The former simply authorised the use of "all necessary means," without mentioning any authority or control vested in the Security Council with respect to such actions. The contrary is true for the latter resolutions.

---

[39] Un Entretien avec M. Perez de Cuellar: "Cette guerre n'est pas celle des Nations Unies, mais elle est légale," *Le Monde*, 9 Feb. 1991.

[40] See Burns H. Weston, "Security Council Resolution 678 and Persian Gulf Decision Making: Precarious Legitimacy" (1991) 85 *American Journal of International Law* 516; Ma. Paz Andrés Saénz de Santa María, "Réplica: Cuestiones de legalidad en las acciones armadas contra Irak," (1991) 43 *Revista Española De Derecho Internacional* 116; Danesh Sarooshi, *The United Nations and the Development of Collective Security. The Delegation by the UN Security Council of its Chapter VII Powers* (Oxford: Clarendon Press, 1999), p. 179.

[41] See Vera Gowlland-Debbas, *Collective Responses to Illegal Acts in International Law. United Nations Actions in the Question of Southern Rhodesia* (Dordrecht, M. Nijhoff, 1990). Resolution 83 (1950), adopted during the Korean war, simply *recommended* "the Members of the United Nations to furnish such assistance to the Republic of Korea as may be necessary to repel the armed attack and to restore international peace and security in the area." Moreover, this recommendation was not the product of a convergence of views amongst the members of the Security Council: the USSR was absent from the voting, two other States did not participate (Egypt, India) and another one voted against (Yugoslavia). Thus, only with difficulty can it be considered a precedent.

It was stated during the military intervention in Afghanistan that Resolution 1373 (2001) arguably provided a mandate to use force and, moreover, one of an almost unlimited character.[42] The argument is based on the fact that in the said resolution the Security Council decided, among a number of provisions concerning the freezing of terrorist assets, that all States "shall take the necessary steps to prevent the commission of terrorist acts." It must be noticed that Resolution 1373 (2001), adopted under Chapter VII, did not provide a general authorization to resort to force in order to achieve its goals, as was the case in previous practice. In its ordinary meaning, the decision that States "shall take the necessary steps to prevent the commission of terrorist acts" implies that they have to take action within their borders in the field of security in order to impede such acts. The context, that is to say, the other measures addressed to the States by the same resolution, also shows that this is the only legally valid interpretation of that paragraph. The fact that the States have not interpreted it in a way authorizing the use of force, confirms this interpretation. In particular, the United States did not invoke it to justify its use of force, though concern for the reciprocal opportunities available to other States may also have been a factor here.

The practice of Security Council authorizations to member States to use force is today too well established to be contested. However, the question remains open whether such authorizations must be subordinated to the authority or control of the Security Council. If one follows the rationale of Chapter VII, the answer should be positive.

This practice of general authorizations suits the United States well. It allows it a high degree of flexibility, it imposes no strict control of the operations by the United Nations and ensures American leadership, since US forces are the most significant in these types of interventions.

Indefinite, implied and *ex post facto* purported Security Council authorizations

In addition to the practice just described, three other arguments have been advanced to justify the use of force by States under a hypothetical Security Council umbrella. The United States and the United Kingdom have argued that the authorization given by Resolution 678 (1990) applies to

---

[42] Michael Byers, "Unleashing Force" (2001) 57(12) *The World Today* 20–22. For a more nuanced version of the argument, see Michael Byers, "Terrorism, the Use of Force and International Law after 11 September" (2002) 51 *International & Comparative Law Quarterly* 401 at 401–3.

the further requirements imposed by the Security Council upon Iraq. This is the ground invoked to justify the "Desert Fox," "Northern Watch," and "Southern Watch" operations, implementing the "no fly zones" in northern and southern Iraq.[43] Such an extensive interpretation of Resolution 678 – which one might term an "indefinite authorization" – is in contradiction with Resolution 687 (1991), which declared a cease-fire after Iraqi acceptance of the said resolution, put an end to the use of force authorized by Resolution 678, and established a new "regime" for Iraq's postwar situation, one which still endures.

The other two arguments have been advanced with respect to more recent experiences, and notably with regard to the Kosovo crisis. According to these arguments, the Security Council can implicitly or retroactively authorize the use of force by a State or a group of States.

The theory of an implied Security Council authorization was "implicitly" advanced by NATO States when, at the beginning of Operation "Allied Force," they sought to justify the bombings on the basis that the Security Council had qualified the situation as a "threat to the peace," and on the basis that Yugoslavia had not complied with previous Security Council resolutions. This position is incompatible, not only with the wording of the Charter, but also with the object and purpose of the collective security system that the Charter enshrines. It is evident that it is for the Security Council to decide whether previous measures adopted by it "have proven to be inadequate" and further forcible action is necessary (Article 42).[44] Moreover, in the case of Kosovo, the Security Council reserved for itself the possibility of adopting other measures.[45]

More recently, it has been argued that, by not adopting the draft resolution, presented by Russia, India, and Ukraine, which condemned the

---

[43] See Jules Lobel and Michael Ratner, "Bypassing the Security Council: Ambiguous Authorizations to Use Force, Ceasefires and the Iraqi Inspection Regime" (1999) 93 *American Journal of International Law* 1, 124–54.

[44] For a convincing and in-depth analysis of this question, see Olivier Corten and François Dubuisson, "L'hypothèse d'une règle émergente fondant une intervention militaire sur une autorisation implicite du Conseil de sécurité" (2000) 104 *Revue Générale de Droit International Public* 873–910.

[45] Resolution 1160 (UN-Doc.: S/RES/1160 (1998)): The SC "Emphasizes that failure to make constructive progress toward the peaceful resolution of the situation in Kosovo will lead to the consideration of additional measures"; Resolution 1199 (UN Doc. S/RES/1199 (1998)): The SC "Decides, should the concrete measures demanded ... not be taken, to consider further action and additional measures to maintain or restore peace and stability in the region."

NATO bombings, the Council implicitly recognized their legality. Again, this interpretation not only flies in the face of the wording and spirit of the Charter, but is also in contradiction with previous practice, when the Security Council did not condemn Soviet or American interventions in Czechoslovakia, Afghanistan, Nicaragua, or Panama, among others. Simply put, the Security Council neither condemned nor authorized the NATO bombings.

The *ex post facto* authorization doctrine has not officially been advanced by the United States or any other government. For the moment, it is merely a doctrinal posture.[46] Logically, *ex post facto* Security Council *authorization* is not possible. The powers conferred by the Charter imply that the prerogative to use force is linked with the existence of an ongoing situation which threatens the peace, is a breach of the peace, or is an act of aggression. The decision to take "action by air, sea, or land forces" has as its purpose to "maintain or restore international peace and security," as Article 42 clearly provides. Moreover, the legality of a particular recourse to the use of force must be determined at the moment it occurs. The Security Council neither performs judicial functions – although it can ascertain the legal qualifications of some acts when fulfilling its functions – nor possesses the capability to preclude the wrongfulness of a previous State action. Its political power to decide to use force is not tantamount to a power to decide retroactively whether force was rightly or wrongly used. The theory of *ex post facto* authorization thus contradicts the rationale of the collective security system.

In any case, none of the three theories of indefinite, implied, or *ex post facto* authorization has met with the support of the international community. The first of the theories has been defended only by the United States and the United Kingdom and met with vigorous objections from the other permanent members of the Security Council, the Non-Aligned Movement and many other States. The weakness of the second theory is acknowledged even by the legal advisers of the interested governments themselves (see below). As such, it does not warrant much consideration from a legal perspective. As for the third theory, a more detailed analysis with regard to

---

[46] See Luigi Condorelli, "La risoluzione 1244 (1999) del Consiglio di Sicurezza e l'intervento NATO contro la Repubblica Federal di Iugoslavia," in N. Ronziti (ed.), *NATO, Conflitto in Kosovo e Costituzione Italiana* (Milan: Giuffrè, 2000), pp. 31–41; Giovanni Distefano, "Le Conseil de sécurité et la validation des traités conclus par la menace ou l'emploi de la force," in Ch.-A. Morand (ed.), *La crise des Balkans de 1999* (Brussels: Bruylant, Paris: LGDJ, 2000), pp. 167–92.

Kosovo can be found elsewhere and thus it will not be further elaborated upon here.[47]

Another position, quite astonishing from a legal perspective, was adopted by the European Council in its extraordinary meeting of 21 September 2001, with regard to the then possible future US military reaction to the terrorist attacks. Is the European Council, in stating that "on the basis of Security Council Resolution 1368, a riposte by the United States is legitimate,"[48] giving to this resolution an interpretation that would authorize or acknowledge the right of the United States to resort to force? If the answer is yes, as it seems to be, different problems arise. Does the Resolution acknowledge that the United States is in a situation of self-defense? Does it authorize the use of force from the characterization of the terrorist attacks as threats to international peace and security? Does this "license" stem from references both to self-defense and to the threat to peace and security? None of these possibilities is supported by legal analysis. The resolution does not recognize that the United States is in a situation of self-defense: it merely recognizes the inherent right of self-defense in general, and furthermore, as limited "in accordance with the Charter." As for the mere acknowledgment that there is a threat to international peace and security, as we have already explained, it is up to the Security Council to adopt the measures that it considers appropriate for dealing with the threat.

The European Council's statement could also suppose that, in these kind of circumstances, some form of intervention by the Security Council would be required, something that the US government would not appreciate. Moreover, a careful consideration of the wording of the declaration leaves open the possibility that the European Council did not make a legal statement, but merely a political one: it considered that an American riposte would be "legitimate," which is something quite different from "legal."[49] For it is obvious that the European Council's extraordinary summit wanted to send two messages at the same time: support for an American forcible action on the one hand, and the pretense that this action was not unilateral,

---

[47] Marcelo G. Kohen, "L'emploi de la force et la crise du Kosovo: vers un nouveau désordre juridique international" (1999) 32 *Revue Belge de Droit International* 122, at 132 and 141–42.

[48] Conclusions and Plan of Action of the Extraordinary European Council Meeting on 21 Sept. 2001, SN 140/01 (available at http://www.europa.eu.int).

[49] For an analysis of the distinction between legality and legitimacy, see Norberto Bobbio, "Sur le principe de légitimité" (2000) 31 *Droits* 147–55.

but had a legal and collective basis. The shadow of the unilateral NATO military action in Kosovo in 1999 still weighed heavily on most European capitals, hence their desire to show that this time things were different, because there would be a Security Council endorsement.

Humanitarian intervention

Much has been written about the existence of a right of humanitarian intervention to deter genocide or other grave and massive violations of human rights. This is not the place to embark on a detailed discussion of this important issue. One may note, however, that the deep differences of opinion among the members of international society concerning the existence of such a right are enough to demonstrate its non-existence in international law. Apart from the negative attitude of two of the five permanent members of the Security Council, the opposition of Third World countries should also be considered. The Ministerial Declaration produced by the Meeting of Foreign Ministers of the Group of 77 held in New York on 24 September 1999, in which 132 States were represented, states that "They rejected the so-called right of humanitarian intervention, which has no basis in the UN Charter or in international law."[50]

Similarly, the Fourth Report of the Foreign Affairs Committee of the UK House of Commons published on 23 May 2000, while recognizing the morality of the NATO action, affirmed its dubious legality: "Our conclusion is that Operation Allied Force was contrary to the specific terms of what might be termed the basic law of the international community – the UN Charter, although this might have been avoided if the Allies had attempted to use the Uniting for Peace procedures... We conclude that, at the very least, the doctrine of humanitarian intervention has a tenuous basis in current international customary law, and that this renders NATO action legally questionable."[51]

Putting aside all legal considerations and focusing instead on ethical considerations, it must be said that the supporters of humanitarian intervention are vested with the *onus probandi* in order to demonstrate that force is the best available tool to safeguard human rights in situations such as Kosovo.

---

[50] Para. 69. Text available at http://www.g77.org/Docs/Decl1999.html.

[51] Paras. 123 and 132. Text available at http://www.publications.parliament.uk/pa/cm199900/cmselect/cmfaff/28/2802.htm.

The results of the NATO experience cannot be seen as encouraging.[52] Assume there was a circumstance in which force was the best approach for stopping such violations and that no action would be taken by the Council because of an actual or potential veto. One can query whether the best way to deal with that resort to force would not be the recognition, by the State or States involved, that they were violating the obligation prohibiting the use of force, but that there nonetheless existed strong moral or political justifications. These justifications could act as a mitigating circumstance, not to preclude wrongfulness, but with regard to the consequences arising from that act with regard to State responsibility.[53]

Armed reprisals

Curiously, some of the forcible actions undertaken by the United States that it seeks to justify as self-defense would be better candidates for forcible countermeasures.[54] The reason why the American government has not resorted to such an argument is simple: today it is common knowledge that forcible countermeasures are prohibited.[55]

Quite surprisingly, during the NATO bombings of Yugoslavia, some distinguished scholars began to speak of "forcible humanitarian countermeasures."[56] The rationale of both countermeasures and humanitarian action militates against such a theory. By definition, the purpose of

[52] See Kohen, "L'emploi de la force," above note 47, at 137–40.

[53] See Michael Byers and Simon Chesterman, "Changing the Rules about Rules? Unilateral Humanitarian Intervention and the Future of International Law," in J. F. Holzgrefe and Robert Keohane (eds.), *Humanitarian Intervention: Principles, Institutions and Change* (Cambridge: Cambridge University Press, forthcoming).

[54] See W. M. Reisman, "Self-defense or Reprisals? The Raid on Baghdad: Some Reflections on Its Lawfulness and Implications" (1994) 5 EJIL 120 at 125. As a matter of course, Reisman considers that there is a trend towards the acceptance of forceful countermeasures.

[55] See the Friendly Relations Declaration of 1970 embodied in GA Resolution 2625(XXV), the *Nicaragua* Judgment of 27 June 1986, (1986) ICJ Reports 127, para. 249, the Advisory Opinion on the *Legality of the Threat or Use of Nuclear Weapons,* (1996) ICJ Reports 246, para. 46 and Article 50 §1(a) of the ILC Draft Articles on State responsibility, above note 38. Moreover, in a study prepared by Julia W. Willis, Deputy Assistant Legal Adviser for European Affairs at the Department of State, about the US position and practice in regard to acts of reprisals, the conclusion was that "the United States has taken the categorical position that reprisals involving the use of force are illegal under international law." "Contemporary Practice of the United States" (1979) 73 AJIL 491.

[56] See Antonio Cassese, "*Ex iniuria ius oritur*: Are We Moving towards International Legitimation of Forcible Humanitarian Countermeasures in the World Community?" (1999) 10 EJIL 23. Afterwards, he recanted his views: "A Follow-Up: Forcible Humanitarian Countermeasures

humanitarian action is the protection of human beings, victims of violations of their basic rights. There must therefore be a necessity to intervene
in order to stop such violations. But countermeasures are not subordinated
to the idea of necessity. In many cases, their goal could be, not to stop an
ongoing wrongful act, but to obtain reparation once the wrongful act is ter-
minated. To speak about "forcible humanitarian countermeasures" would
mean that States could use force in such situations, even if force is not (or
is no longer) able to put an end to the violations of human rights. The
practical dangers of this theory and the rather punitive character of these
"forcible humanitarian countermeasures" need not be stressed.

The attitude of the international community

The first striking fact concerning the attitude of the international community towards recent American uses of force is that almost no attempts have
been made in the Security Council or the General Assembly to condemn
them in circumstances where the violation of Article 2(4) has been blatant,
or at least appeared *prima facie* to be so. This attitude is in stark contrast
with earlier identical experiences before 1990, such as Grenada, Libya, or
Panama. In those cases, the Security Council was prevented from adopting a resolution because of the right of veto, but the General Assembly
clearly condemned the American use of force and its consequences.[57] This
change of attitude cannot, however, lead to the conclusion that the international community has endorsed the American position. The main reason for the change is not the fact that any attempt before the Security
Council is doomed to failure because of the right of veto, though the
influence of this fact should not be dismissed absolutely. The point is
that during the Cold War there were also many occasions on which
force was used by various States (all the permanent members of the
Security Council, as well as many other States) without any condemnation by the United Nations.[58] This fact did not lead States – or authors – to

and Opinio Necessitatis" (1999) 10 EJIL 791. See also his *International Law* (Oxford: Oxford
University Press, 2001), p. 298.

[57] See respectively GA Resolutions 38/7 of 2 Nov. 1983, 41/38 of 20 Nov. 1986 and 44/240 of
29 Dec. 1989.

[58] These examples can be found in A. Mark Weisburd, *Use of Force. The Practice of States Since
World War II* (University Park, PA: Pennsylvania State University Press, 1997), where a short
analysis of all cases of use of force since 1945 is presented.

believe in a change of attitude with regard to the prohibition of the use of force.

More recently, a supportive attitude on the part of the international community towards the US understanding of the use of force against terrorism could, at first glance, be discerned.

The question then arises as whether it is true that the international community has recognised the *legality* of the US armed action in Afghanistan. With the exception of Iran, Iraq, Vietnam, Cuba, North Korea, and of course the Taliban regime of Afghanistan, no States condemned this use of force as being contrary to the obligations emanating from the Charter and general international law. But a general overview is an insufficient basis for reaching a conclusion so serious and important as affirming that the rules relating to the prohibition of the use of force have changed. Although there was considerable political support for the American action, from a legal point of view there was also considerable ambiguity.

A perusal of the statements made by States and international organizations shows different views. The day following the terrorist attack, the Belgian Foreign Affairs Minister declared that there was no "war."[59] Only the Secretary-General of NATO, Lord Robertson, spoke of "aggression."[60] On the contrary, UN[61] and OAS resolutions,[62] as well as the first declarations of the European Union[63] and the North Atlantic Council,[64] the statements of the Euro-Atlantic Partnership Council[65] and the NATO–Russia Permanent Joint Council,[66] referred only to "terrorist attacks," "barbaric acts" or "acts of violence."

The first realignment to the United States position was made by the Statement of the North Atlantic Council of 12 September 2001, in which it "agreed that if it is determined that this attack was directed from abroad against the United States, it shall be regarded as an action covered by Article 5 of the Washington Treaty," consequently justifying collective self-defense.[67] Later on, the European Council went even further. States

---

[59] *Le Soir*, Brussels, 13 Sept. 2001.
[60] Statement by Lord Robertson, Secretary-General of NATO (PR/CP (2001)121), 11 Sept. 2001.
[61] UN Doc. S/RES/1368 (2001) and 1373 (2001), GA Resolution 56/1 (6 Sept. 2001).
[62] Statements by the Secretary-General César Gaviria and the General Assembly gathered in Lima, 11 Sept. 2001 (OAS Press Release E-002/01).
[63] Brussels, 12 Sept. 2001(available at http://www.europa.eu.int).
[64] Brussels (PR/CP (2001)122) 11 Sept. 2001.
[65] Press Release PR/CP (2001) 123, 12 Sept. 2001.   [66] Press Release, 13 Sept. 2001.
[67] Press Release PR/CP (2001)124.

parties to the Rio Treaty (the Inter-American Treaty of Reciprocal Assistance of 1947) followed closely on American heels, in what constitutes
the clearest support for the American legal justification.[68] Thus, it is a remarkable new phenomenon that NATO, the European Union and the Rio
Treaty States came round to the American perception of self-defense against
terrorism.

Although condemnation of the terrorist attacks was nearly unanimous,
the NATO, EU and Latin American attitudes were not followed in all the
other regions of the world. South Africa merely recognized "the right of
the United States government to track down the culprits and bring them
to justice,"[69] and Namibia called for restraint.[70] Even States supporting the
United States were cautious as to the actions justified by the fight against
terrorism. The Costa Rican ambassador to the United Nations, Bernd
Niehaus, stressed that "the war against terrorism does not justify the use of
totalitarian methods."[71]

Contrary to what was presented by the media as an endorsement of the
Anglo-American use of force, UN Secretary-General Kofi Annan confined
himself to issuing a reminder on what the position of those States was, in
an excellent example of the use of cautious diplomatic terms.[72]

Similarly, Security Council members preferred moderate terms rather
than clear support for the legal justification. The permanent representatives of the United States and the United Kingdom informed the Security
Council that the military action was taken in self-defense and directed at
terrorists and those who harbored them, that every effort was being made to

---

[68] The Committee designated by the 24th Meeting of Consultation of Ministers of Foreign Affairs
adopted a resolution entitled "Support for the Measures of Individual and Collective Self-
defense established in Resolution RC.24/RE.1/01," in which it "resolves: 1. That the measures
being applied by the United States of America and other states in the exercise of their inherent
right of individual and collective self-defense have the full support of the states parties to the
Rio Treaty." OEA/Ser.F/II.24, CS/TIAR/RES.1/01. No similar text expressing such unequivocal
support was adopted at the universal level.

[69] Statement of the South African Government on Developments Surrounding Terrorist Actions
in the USA, 19 Sept. 2001 available at www.go.za.

[70] Declaration of Foreign Minister Gurirab, 14 Sept. 2001, available at www.grnnet.gov.na.

[71] Statement at the General Assembly, 1st October 2001, available at www.un.org/News.

[72] "Immediately after the 11 Sept. attacks on the United States, the Security Council expressed
its determination to combat by all means threats to international peace and security caused by
terrorist acts. The Council also reaffirmed the inherent right of individual or collective self-
defense in accordance with the Charter of the United Nations. *The States concerned have set their
current military action in Afghanistan in that context.*" New York, 8 Oct. 2001, On the situation
in Afghanistan, available at http://www.un.org/News/ossg/latestsm.htm (emphasis added).

avoid civilian casualties, and that the action was in no way a strike against the people of Afghanistan, Islam or the Muslim world. According to the statement of the President of the Security Council, "The members of the Council were appreciative of the presentation made by the United States and the United Kingdom."[73]

It is difficult to interpret these vague formulas as indicating acquiescence in the *legal* justification invoked by the States resorting to force in that situation. In order to prove acquiescence, there must be a "consistent and undeviating attitude," a "clear," "definite," and "unequivocal" course of action, showing "clearly and consistently evinced acceptance," to use the wording of the ICJ on different occasions.[74]

One could expect to obtain clear-cut statements in order to show that a rule in general, and especially one of the importance of that related to the use of force in particular, has changed. Instead, what we had were, with the important exceptions mentioned above, in reality vague statements from a legal perspective. What they really represent is a desire on the one hand, not to bother the United States at this difficult time, and on the other, an embarrassed desire to find legal support for its action. They illustrate the dilemma that many countries found themselves in, of wanting to support the United States whilst at the same time showing that "this time" the action fell within a legal framework.

Traditionally, the United Kingdom and Israel share much the same legal approach as the United States on the use of force. However, the three States do not take exactly the same stance on every issue. Surely, it is Israel that adopts the broadest interpretation of the legal uses of force in international law. The radical innovation in this field is that, with the Kosovo crisis, and furthermore after the terrorist attacks of 11 September 2001, some American allies generally reluctant to adopt expansive interpretations of the legal uses of force (e.g. France) ended up bowing to the American position.

We are not discussing here whether force had to be used against those responsible for the terrorist attacks of 11 September. Instead, at issue here is our conception of international law. Can such a fundamental norm as

---

[73] Press Statement on Terrorist Threats by Security Council President, AFG/152, SC/7167, 8 Oct. 2001.

[74] *Temple of Preah Vihear*, Merits, (1962) ICJ Reports 30; *North Sea Continental Shelf*, Judgment, (1969) ICJ Reports 25, para. 28 and 26, para. 30; *Certain Phosphate Lands in Nauru (Nauru v. Australia)*, Preliminary Objections, Judgment, (1992) ICJ Reports 247, para. 13.

the prohibition of the use of force be modified by this kind of practice? Are we "only" witnessing not the modification of an existing rule, but just its "new" interpretation?

Would international practice be less exigent when dealing with *interpretation* rather than the *creation, modification,* or *termination* of rules? One could be tempted to state quite the opposite: if States are "just" interpreting existing rules, they are recognizing that they remain bound by them. Then, the procedure set out in Articles 31 and 32 of the Vienna Convention on the Law of Treaties, which has by now been universally accepted, must be followed in order to determine their significance and scope. Is it nevertheless an "authentic" interpretation? In order to affirm that it is so, it should be demonstrated that a large and representative majority of States agreed with the American and British interpretation. The deliberate ambiguity of most of the statements – and particularly the more important ones coming from the Security Council – proves instead that the international community is far from having accepted an "evolving" interpretation of the rules prohibiting the use of force.

Moreover, in order to invoke an evolving interpretation or change in the rules, it would be necessary to show the same reaction in other, similar situations. For the time being, if one compares the reactions in other cases of terrorism, this is not the case. Only the US government supported the Israeli view according to which it can enter the Palestinian Authority areas and use force. Nor did the Indian government invoke such a right to pursue terrorists in Pakistan, responsible for the bombing of the Parliament in New Delhi. If the will of the international community is to review the existing rules regarding the use of force against terrorists, then one can expect that the same attitude will be taken in other, similar situations. If it is not the case, then one has to conclude that what we are witnessing here is not a change in the rule or in its interpretation, but rather a political attitude on the part of the majority of States supporting in one case only the political aims of one State.

The reasons for States not to condemn actual or potential American illegal uses of force are multiple and not necessarily founded on legal considerations.

Even in cases where there is a lack of condemnation by the whole international community (with the understandable exception of the State victim of the use of force itself), it could be difficult to assert that this situation is tantamount to a change in existing rules or a change in their interpretation. States can decide not to pursue a subject responsible for breaches of international law: this fact does not mean, however, that they believe that the wrongdoer behaved in a correct manner. Even less, that its illegal conduct led to a change in the existing rules. Moreover, in the situation emerging after 11 September 2001, the American pressure put on other States to be supportive was such that it would be hard to understand their statements, or lack thereof, as constituting acquiescence in the United States interpretation of law. In a situation such as this, it was particularly difficult for States to openly defy the American forcible unilateral reaction.

Concluding remarks

If there is one point on which all scholars will probably agree, irrespective of their attitude towards the legality or not of the American use of force in different parts of the world, it is that the collective security system enshrined by the UN Charter stands in a deep crisis.

The last decade of the twentieth century began with an extraordinarily wide Security Council authorization to resort to force and ended with a massive unilateral use of force without any Security Council authorization at all. In both cases, the principal actors were exactly the same. The first decade of the new millennium also began with a large military operation, in response to the most horrific terrorist attack, outside the framework of the collective security system set up by the Charter. And again, the principal actors remained the same.

We are facing here what Antonio Remiro Brotóns called a *"coup de communauté internationale"* on the occasion of the NATO bombing of Yugoslavia during the Kosovo crisis.[75] Again, the United States, together with a number of other States, resorts to force outside the system of collective security enshrined in the Charter. A comparison can indeed be made between the present situation of crisis at the core of the international legal order born in 1945 and the situation of a coup d'état within domestic societies. The latter term signifies a means of acceding to power through unconstitutional means. The "coup de communauté internationale" shows the single superpower forcibly acting as a policeman in international

---

[75] "Un Nuevo Orden contra el Derecho Internacional: el caso de Kosovo" (2001) 4 *Revista Jurídica de la Universidad Autónoma de Madrid* 89 at 92.

relations, without consideration for the powers vested in the Security Council.

One can wonder why the United States, with a unique opportunity to obtain an almost completely blank cheque from the Security Council, decided to act alone. The answer must be simple: the US government wishes to have complete discretion with regard to the use of force, without any authorization, limit, control or – even less – management by the Security Council.

From the legal point of view, the most important development concerning the use of force since the end of the Cold War is undoubtedly the implementation of a new collective security regime under Chapter VII, based on the authorization provided to member States to use force to achieve the goals established by the Security Council. When it wished to do so, the US government succeeded in imposing this practice, which faces no objection today, provided – of course – that the Security Council is able to adopt a resolution based on Chapter VII stipulating in a clear manner this course of action.

Broad interpretations of Article 51 of the Charter have also been advanced, but enlarging the scope of self-defense is tantamount to curtailing – to a corresponding degree – both the scope of Article 2(4) and the powers of the Security Council. The US interpretation of self-defense leads ultimately to the consecration of the supremacy of power over law. It implies a sort of flashback to the state of nature, in the Hobbesian sense.[76] One should recall what the Nuremberg International Military Tribunal stated half a century ago: "whether action taken under the claim of self-defense was in fact aggressive or defensive must ultimately be subject to investigation and adjudication if international law is ever to be enforced."[77] A perusal of the practice shows that these interpretations defy the ordinary meaning of the related norms and are contrary to their object and purpose; they have failed to be generally accepted and remain unilateral, in spite of some ad hoc circumstantial and "interested" instances.

---

[76] On this point, see Marcelo G. Kohen, "The Notion of State Survival in International Law," in Laurence Boisson de Chazournes and Philippe Sands (eds.), *International Law, the International Court of Justice and Nuclear Weapons* (Cambridge: Cambridge University Press, 1999), pp. 293–314. For an analysis of the use of force on grounds of necessity, see Sarah Heathcote, "Necessity in International law" (PhD thesis, University of Geneva, forthcoming).

[77] *Judgment of the International Military Tribunal for the Trial of German Major War Criminals, Nuremberg, 30 Sept. and 1 Oct. 1949* (London, HMSO, 1946), 30.

Article 2(4) of the Charter has presumably been "killed" many times since 1945.[78] Despite all the violations, it is nevertheless still alive. One reason for this was advanced by the ICJ in the celebrated paragraph 186 of its judgment on the merits in the *Nicaragua* Case.[79] Another, probably stronger, reason is the fact that the prohibition on the use of force embodied in the Charter is still considered by the international community as the highest achievement in international law after the catastrophe of 1939–45. The ideas of the Enlightenment which advocate the substitution of force with reason have not been supplanted, notwithstanding postmodernist attempts.[80]

To produce a change in the content of peremptory norms of international law is not an easy task. In order for such a change to occur, one needs more than a simple absence of criticism with regard to some violations of the relevant rule. As stated by Article 53 of the Vienna Convention on the Law of Treaties: "A peremptory norm of general international law is a norm accepted and recognized by the international community of States as a whole as a norm from which *no derogation is permitted* and which *can be modified only by a subsequent norm of general international law having the same character.*"[81] At this stage, it is difficult to deny the *jus cogens* character of the rule embodied in Article 2(4), with its exception recognized in Article 51. Taking into account the serious differences of opinion in the international community, it is also difficult to assert that a new peremptory rule recognizing armed humanitarian intervention, forcible countermeasures, an enlargement of the notion of self-defense, or any new exception to the general prohibition of the threat or the use of force in international relations has emerged.

With the exception of the use of force by its closest allies,[82] the United States has always been reluctant to accept the use of force by other States, and not only by the Soviet Union, its adversary during the Cold War. One must recall United States ambassador Adlai Stevenson's warning after the failure

---

[78] Cf. Thomas M. Franck, "Who killed Article 2(4)?" (1970) 64 AJIL 809; and Louis Henkin, "The Reports of the Death of Article 2(4) Are Greatly Exaggerated" (1971) 65 AJIL 544.

[79] "If a State acts in a way prima facie incompatible with a recognized rule, but defends its conduct by appealing to exceptions or justifications contained within the rule itself, then whether or not the State's conduct is in fact justifiable on that basis, the significance of that attitude is to confirm rather than to weaken the rule," (1986) ICJ Reports 98.

[80] As example: Edward N. Luttwak, "Give War a Chance" (1999) 78 *Foreign Affairs* 36.

[81] Emphasis added.

[82] With, in turn, probably the main and remarkable exception of the use of force by the United Kingdom and France during the Suez crisis in 1956.

of the Security Council, due to the Soviet veto, to condemn India for its takeover of the Portuguese enclaves in December 1961: "We have witnessed tonight an effort to rewrite the Charter, to sanction the use of force in international relations when it suits one's own purposes."[83] Two decades later, following Argentina's resort to force to recover the Falklands/Malvinas islands in April 1982, Charles Lichenstein, the US deputy ambassador to the United Nations, stated in the Council that "the use of force to solve problems is deeply regrettable."[84] One could be tempted to consider that the United States advises the rest of the world: "do what I say, but not what I do."

There is no doubt as to the American military position: the United States is the most powerful State in the world. Its supremacy is overwhelming. But military power is one thing, its legal use is another. Rousseau stated more than two centuries ago: "The strongest is never strong enough to be always the master, unless he transforms strength into right, and obedience into duty."[85] It remains to be demonstrated that American supremacy has already been transformed into law.

With the nearly unanimous position taken by States after the terrorist attacks of 11 September 2001, the United States had a unique opportunity to revert to the rule of law at the international level. The conditions were largely favorable for the adoption of a bundle of collective measures, including some forcible action undertaken at least with Security Council approval. The US government made considerable progress toward multilateralism in different fields of international cooperation against terrorism, with only one, but none the less remarkable, exception: the use of force. It preferred not to alter its doctrine of self-defense, in order to maintain its freedom to use force unilaterally whenever it considers it necessary to do so.

James Rubin, a close adviser to former Secretary of State Madeleine Albright, has revealed that before the NATO bombing of Yugoslavia in

---

[83] UNSC Official Records, S/PV.987, 18 Dec. 1961, 27.   [84] UN Doc. S/PV.2350 at 31.

[85] Explaining that force does not create rights, he went on to deconstruct the idea of the "right of the strongest": "Suppose for a moment that this so-called 'right' exists. I maintain that the sole result is a mass of inexplicable nonsense. For, if force creates right, the effect changes with the cause: every force that is greater than the first succeeds to its right. As soon as it is possible to disobey with impunity, disobedience is legitimate; and, the strongest being always in the right, the only thing that matters is to act so as become the strongest. But what kind of right is that which perishes when force fails? If we must obey perforce, there is no need to obey because we ought; and if we are not forced to obey, we are under no obligation to do so." Jean-Jacques Rousseau, *The Social Contract* (1762), ch. III: "The Right of the Strongest."

1999, there had been a series of strained telephone calls between Albright and UK Foreign Secretary Robin Cook, in which he cited problems "with our lawyers" over using force in the absence of UN endorsement. The American Secretary of State adopted a pure Brechtian[86] approach to such "problems": "Get new lawyers," she suggested.[87] Surely, it is easier to change lawyers than the law which States have such difficulty in forging to govern their relations.

There is no need not to respect international law in order to combat terrorism effectively. International law already provides the necessary legal tools for fighting this scourge, or for improving these tools, as exemplified by the adoption of Resolution 1373 (2001). On the contrary, the rule of law, as one of the most important values of civilization, must not only be defended against terrorism, it must also be applied and preserved in the struggle against it.[88] It would be enough to compare the results of legal or illegal methods used against terrorism in domestic societies to conclude that there is no alternative if we wish to preserve human rights and values.

The analysis of recent practice and the alignment of the NATO, EU and Rio Treaty countries behind the United States' broad conception of self-defense show that the search for legal justifications for what is clearly a departure from international law cannot avoid contradiction. It also opens the way for unforeseeable uses of force in a great number of actual or potential situations in future. It amounts to the negation of Article 2(4) of the Charter and the collective security system.

The time has come to think about the results and consequences of the culture of force prevailing in international relations after the end of the Cold War. Many cases of the last decade show that force does not solve problems, but generally exacerbates them. Moreover, as Juan B. Alberdi,

---

[86] In his poem "Die Lösung," Bertolt Brecht related: "Nach dem Aufstand des 17. Juni liess der Sekretär des Schriftstellerverbands in der Stalinallee Flugblätter verteilen, auf denen zu lesen war, dass das Volk das Vertrauen der Regierung verscherzt habe und es nur durch doppelte Arbeit zurückerobern könne. Wäre es da nicht doch einfacher, die Regierung löste das Volk auf und wählte ein anderes?" *Die Gedichte* (Frankfurt-am-Main: Suhrkamp, 2000), p. 296.

[87] James P. Rubin, "Countdown to a Very Personal War," *Financial Times*, 29 Sept. 2000.

[88] As Secretary-General Kofi Annan reaffirmed in his address to the General Assembly: "the attack of 11 September was an attack on the rule of law – that is, on the very principle that enables nations and individuals to live together in peace, by following agreed rules and settling their disputes through agreed procedures. So let us respond by reaffirming the rule of law, on the international as well as the national levels" (UN Press Release SG/SM/7965, 24 Sept. 2001, 2).

a prominent Argentine jurist of the nineteenth century, wrote after the devastating experience of the War of Paraguay in 1870: "War is a way of administering justice in which each party is at the same time the victim, the prosecutor, the witness, the judge and the criminal."[89]

---

[89] Juan B. Alberdi, *El crímen de la guerra* (Buenos Aires: H. Concejo Deliberante, 1934), p. 50.

8

Bending the law, breaking it, or developing it? The United States and the humanitarian use of force in the post–Cold War era

BRAD R. ROTH

With the global geopolitical and ideological balance of the Cold War era fast receding into distant memory, new issues arise for the continued vitality of international legal constraints on the use of force. The lack of a global competitor to the United States in the security realm, and of a global alternative to liberal internationalism in the ideological realm, has changed perceptions of the role of the peace and security system, especially among Western States, nongovernmental organizations (NGOs), and intellectuals – and particularly with respect to internal armed conflict. The perceived need to accommodate rival conceptions of public order has given way, in many quarters, to a perceived opportunity to harness the unchallenged military power of the United States and its allies to the pursuit of a predominant conception of justice. This development constitutes a potential challenge to the foundations of the international legal system and, above all, to the principle of equal applicability of legal constraints to all States, absent Security Council action. Scholars of that system, it follows, have an onus to position themselves in relation to this development.

This chapter, unlike others in this volume, will focus directly on scholarly discourse. The discussion below will not seek to establish whether the United States, by its practice and influence, has effectuated a change in international law to permit armed humanitarian intervention in the internal affairs of States, for the United States has not sought – indeed, it has expressly avoided seeking – such a change in norms applicable to all members of the international community. Nor will the chapter seek to establish whether the international system has acknowledged a special exemption for the United States from established non-intervention norms, since the conferral of such a special legal status, even on the sole remaining super-power or on the alliances that it leads, would be highly improbable. Rather, the chapter addresses the role of jurists, through their characterizations and assessments of US-led practice and their advocacy of doctrinal stability or change, in bolstering or undermining the capacity of international law to serve as a normative basis for constraining United States unilateralism in a unipolar world.

The issue of humanitarian intervention has created a crisis for legal schol-ars and advocates committed to holding US foreign policy accountable to the strictures of the international peace and security order. The keenly felt need to resolve the tension between those strictures and the perceived demands of humanitarianism has occasioned recourse to dubious jurispru-dential devices. These devices, even though often invoked without ulterior motive, tend effectively to license systematic US (and allied) disregard of legal restraints on the use of force, with troubling long-range consequences.

At the core of the difficulty is the complexity of the relationship between international legality and substantive justice. The legal restraints that hu-manitarians so frequently find inconvenient stem primarily, not from the legacy of the Cold War, but from the more durable and useful tendency of the international system to reflect and respect a plurality of views on fun-damental questions of political order. The international legal order is by nature an accommodation among peoples who persistently disagree about justice. The recent diminution of fundamental differences among partici-pants in the international system, while very real, can all too easily be ex-aggerated in the service of methodological approaches that either assume away fundamental differences or else delegitimate them.

Scholarly reaction to the US-led Kosovo military campaign, undertaken by the North Atlantic Treaty Organization (NATO) in 1999 against the Federal Republic of Yugoslavia (FRY) without United Nations Security Council authorization, illustrates the problematic tendencies. Although the incompatibility of the action with any sound positivistic reading of inter-national law is typically (though not always) acknowledged, the propriety of the action has nonetheless been widely (though by no means universally) affirmed. These affirmations have fallen principally into two diametrically opposed jurisprudential categories. Though so different, both categories entail modes of justification that, taken to their logical conclusions, fatally undermine either the legal substance or the political influence, respectively, of the international law of peace and security. Neither approach successfully preserves international law as a basis for criticizing – let alone restraining – future exercises of military power by the United States and its allies that may be undertaken in the name of purportedly humanitarian goals.

The central debate pits adherents of "policy-oriented jurisprudence," who deny the separation of law from the moral purposes of actors with whom they identify, against those whom I shall call "moralistic positivists," who insist on that separation, but who consciously choose moral over legal duties. The former would reinterpret international law to license humanitarian intervention quite broadly, whereas the latter would, having interpreted international law to preclude humanitarian intervention, advocate violating international law on an ad hoc basis in the service of the greater good.[1]

What both approaches centrally share is disregard for the need to accommodate those who disagree with the dominant view of what count as morally compelling causes. Although this disregard is expressed in the name of international law itself, with reference to human rights norms, it nonetheless (however paradoxically) undermines the foundations of the international legal order.

A preferable third approach is to try to derive substantive criteria and authorization procedures for humanitarian intervention from a common ground of principle in the international system – not a superimposed or idealized common ground, but a common ground demonstrably immanent in the developing historical reality. These criteria and procedures would provide a basis for circumventing manifest abuse of the Security Council veto, but not for circumventing the reality of moral dissidence in the international community. The resulting criteria would inevitably be far too limited, and the resulting procedures far too cumbersome, for many advocates of humanitarian intervention, but they would have the merit of denying open-ended legal or political licenses to the great powers, which have been known throughout history to invoke humanitarianism in pursuit of dubious ends.

---

[1] These conflicting tendencies reproduce, in significant respects, the classic debate between Lon Fuller and H. L. A. Hart over the appropriateness of prosecuting, in postwar West Germany, a Gestapo informant whose actions, when committed, had comported with the applicable positive enactments of the Third Reich. Fuller, understanding law as a purposive process, considered the prosecution consistent with legality, whereas Hart, regarding law as a system of rules, deemed the prosecution unlawful, yet justifiable on grounds of moral exigency. Hart, "Positivism and the Separation of Law and Morals" (1958) 71 *Harvard Law Review* 593 at 615–21; Fuller, "Positivism and Fidelity to Law – A Reply to Professor Hart" (1958) 71 *Harvard Law Review* 630 at 648–61.

Unipolarity and the premises of the Charter peace and security system

The international law of peace and security, as established in the UN Charter and the interpretive practices of States and intergovernmental organizations, embodies not simply a set of rules consented to by the effective leaderships of sovereign States, but also a set of principles and policies premised on a collective moral and political vision that has developed continuously over the history of the Charter system. To assert this is not to deny, but rather to explain, the significance – and even, in many instances, the rigidity – of the rules governing the use of force. These rules designedly preclude unilateral efforts to pursue a particular conception of justice within States at the expense of peace among States.[2]

Having developed over a period in which the international system encompassed widely divergent conceptions of internal political order, the Charter system manifests a commitment to pluralism as a principled basis for peaceful and respectful international relations. That pluralism draws upon aspects of liberal political thought, but it is not in all respects a liberal pluralism.[3] Appeals to higher principle that mistake Charter pluralism for a liberal conception of international justice produce a skewed account of the values and priorities of the international system.

The relationship of Charter pluralism to liberalism can be summarized in three points. First, the Charter follows modern international law generally in imagining, in the style of liberal social contract theory, international

---

[2] As Thomas Franck has put it, "when contemplating military intervention, the United Nations (UN) usually has preferred not to differentiate between just and unjust reasons to intervene. Instead, the nations have favored treating all states as autonomous entities entitled to be left alone, and doing so on grounds of maintaining international peace and order, rather than advancing justice." Franck, "Is Justice Relevant to the International Legal System?" (1989) 64 *Notre Dame Law Journal* 645 at 655.

Franck drew from such observations, and more generally from the system's designation of States rather than individuals as the primary units of analysis, the conclusion that justice is "not among the indicators of legitimacy in the international system," *ibid.*, 662. This conclusion is (or at least was in 1989) correct insofar as the liberal conception, or any particular substantive conception, of justice is concerned; it is misleading to the extent that it implies a straightforwardly amoral order.

[3] Gerry Simpson has recently elaborated a contrast between "Charter liberalism," the pluralist vision associated with the Charter, and the "antipluralist liberalism" of a set of leading US-based international law scholars (i.e., Thomas Franck, Anne-Marie Slaughter, W. Michael Reisman and Fernando Tesón). Simpson, "Two Liberalisms" (2001) 12 EJIL 537. His exposition, while generally astute, overstates liberalism's proclivity to accommodate competing sets of political values, and therefore identifies Charter pluralism too closely with liberalism.

society as arising out of a hypothesized state of nature, with the units of
that society being regarded as juridically equal and at perfect liberty unless
and until bound by their own consent. Second, and importantly, although
the units of the system are States rather than individuals, States are presumed
to be the manifestations of the self-determination of the populations (*qua*
political communities, or "peoples") that they territorially encompass;[4]
state actors, in turn, derive their international authority not from their own
power and will, but from a presumption that they serve as agents of the collectivities they purport to represent. But third, and even more importantly,
notwithstanding the Charter's exhortations regarding "human rights and
fundamental freedoms," the aforementioned presumptions are not necessarily rebuttable in accordance with liberal political principles. Internal
processes are typically accorded deference, even where those processes may
offend liberal principles.[5]

The Charter's pluralism is superficially liberal in that it is tolerant, but
its tolerance exceeds the bounds of any cognizably liberal pluralism. In
brief, the dominant strain of contemporary liberalism is tolerant of errant
conceptions of the proper objects of human striving ("the good"), but not
of the implementation of errant conceptions of justice ("the right").[6] An
alternative within liberalism is to tolerate injustice, but only within freely
formed associations that maintain an unhindered opportunity for their

---

[4] See *Declaration on Principles of International Law Concerning Friendly Relations and Cooperation among States in Accordance with the Charter of the United Nations* (hereafter *Friendly Relations Declaration*), GA Res. 2625 (XXV) (1970) (adopted without a vote), affirming as an imperative the "territorial integrity [and] political unity of sovereign and independent States conducting themselves in compliance with the principle of equal rights and self-determination of peoples . . . and thus possessed of a government representing the whole people belonging to the territory without distinction as to race, creed or colour."

[5] For an in-depth study of the circumstances under which holders of territorial control have and have not been accorded standing to assert rights, incur obligations and authorize acts on behalf of political units in the international system, see Brad R. Roth, *Governmental Illegitimacy in International Law* (Oxford: Oxford University Press, 1999).

[6] See John Rawls, *A Theory of Justice* (Cambridge, MA: Harvard University Press, 1971), pp. 447–8. Rawls' recent work on political morality in international relations, *The Law of Peoples* (Cambridge, MA: Harvard University Press, 1999), adopts a broader pluralism than extrapola-
tion from his earlier, domestic-oriented work might have suggested (though still not co-extensive with the pluralism of the UN Charter), and as such has been criticized by some liberals as a de-
parture from fundamental liberal principles. See, e.g., Fernando Tesón, "The Rawlsian Theory of International Law" (1995) 9 *Ethics and International Affairs* 79 at 98 (complaining that Rawls' later work "embraced a more relativistic, context-based conception of justice and political morality, in which rights and liberties no longer had a foundation in higher principles or liberal views of human nature . . .").

associates to exit.[7] The Charter's pluralism has no such limits. Although it excludes certain deviant governing arrangements – Axis-era fascism from the start, and "alien, colonial, and racist" regimes later on[8] – it otherwise represents an accommodation among radically differing conceptions of justice. It combines overlapping consensus with *modus vivendi,* a least-common-denominator morality with a prudential policy of compromise.[9]

Prior to the post-1989 advent of unipolarity in the international system, the moral and political vision underlying the international law of peace and security enjoyed widespread support in the international community, even as the rules themselves were breached with some frequency. Large majorities in the UN General Assembly and other intergovernmental organizations could be counted on to condemn armed invasions and other interferences in the internal affairs of states.[10] Even the perpetrators typically defended their actions in ways that expressly or tacitly reaffirmed the validity of the rules;[11] the occasional departures from such norm-affirming rhetoric, such as the superpowers' articulations of the Brezhnev and Reagan "Doctrines," met with strong collective censure in international fora, and did not persist.[12]

---

[7] Excellent on this point is Chandran Kukathas, "Are There Any Cultural Rights?" in Will Kymlicka (ed.), *The Rights of Minority Cultures* (Oxford: Oxford University Press, 1995), p. 228.

[8] See *Friendly Relations Declaration,* above note 4 ("subjection of peoples to alien subjugation, domination and exploitation . . . is contrary to the Charter"); *Declaration on the Inadmissibility of Intervention and Interference in the Internal Affairs of States,* GA Res. 36/103 (1981) (120-22-6) ("non-intervention norms shall not prejudice in any manner the right to self-determination, freedom and independence of peoples under colonial domination, foreign occupation or racist regimes").

[9] The contrast between "overlapping consensus" and "*modus vivendi*" derives from John Rawls, *Political Liberalism* (New York: Columbia University Press, 1993), pp. 144–50.

[10] UN General Assembly responses to interventions by Western, socialist, and non-aligned States include: GA Res. 44/240 (1989) (75-20-40) (characterizing the US invasion of Panama as "a flagrant violation of international law"); GA Res. ES-6/2 (1980) (104-18-18) (emergency session resolution demanding an immediate, unconditional, and total Soviet withdrawal from Afghanistan); GA Res. 2793 (XXVI) (1971) (104-11-10) (responding to Indian intervention in East Pakistan by calling "upon the governments of India and Pakistan to take forthwith all measures for an immediate cease-fire and withdrawal of their armed forces on the territory of the other to their own side of the India–Pakistan borders").

[11] Perhaps the most instructive example is the elaborate Soviet effort to characterize its 1956 invasion of Hungary as a result of invitation by the legitimate government. See J. A. Szikszoy, *The Legal Aspects of the Hungarian Question* (Ambilly-Annemasse: Imprimerie Les Presses de Savoie, 1963) (meticulously rebutting the Soviet contention).

[12] Tellingly, the United States did not advance Reagan Doctrine principles in defending the *Nicaragua* case before the International Court of Justice. The court nonetheless reached beyond the pleadings to address arguments "advanced solely in a political context," admonishing

Underlying this normative stability (and the paradox of its coexistence with political instability) were two characteristic premises that dominated Cold War thinking about internal armed conflict. The first was the geopolitical premise that external intervention, irrespective of its announced intentions and the direness of conditions on the ground, was presumptively predatory. The essential grounds for this premise predated and survive the Cold War, but the structure of that confrontation reinforced them. The technology of all-out warfare having rendered direct clashes between the superpowers all but unthinkable, superpower competition had been deflected to the periphery, taking the form of a struggle between the First and Second Worlds for influence in the Third. By the late 1950s, the two rival blocs had nominally committed themselves to peaceful coexistence, while a third, Non-Aligned bloc of mostly poorer and weaker States had emerged, seeking to make real the promises of territorial integrity, political independence, and sovereign equality to which the stronger States, shopping for allegiance, paid lip service.

In this context, transgression of non-intervention norms was viewed simultaneously as East–West escalation and Northern encroachment upon the South (even if actually committed by regional actors), and was in no event perceived as motivated by noble purposes.[13] Moreover, since intervention on one side would almost inevitably draw counter-intervention, it could be expected to exacerbate rather than ameliorate internal conflicts, in the process further empowering and emboldening rather than suppressing human rights abusers. Intervention by either of the rival blocs thus routinely excited the opposition, not only of the other and of the Non-Aligned, but also of intergovernmental and nongovernmental bodies concerned with peace, order, and humanitarianism.

The second relevant premise concerned the essential nature of internal conflict. Internal armed conflict was widely perceived, not as an anomaly or as evidence of "state failure," but as a legitimate way for questions of public

---

against any principle of "ideological intervention." *Military and Paramilitary Activities (Nicaragua v. United States)*, Merits, (1986) ICJ Reports 14, 134–5, paras. 266–8 (27 June 1986).

[13] The international reaction to the 1978–79 Vietnamese invasion of Pol Pot's Democratic Kampuchea is the most striking illustration of the strength of this presumption. See GA Res. 34/22 (1979) (91-21-29) (demanding an "immediate withdrawal" of Vietnamese forces). A similar reaction greeted the 1983 ouster of thuggish and locally despised putschists in Grenada by armed forces of the United States with the participation of the Organization of Eastern Caribbean States. See GA Res. 38/7 (1983) (108-9-27) (denouncing the invasion as a "flagrant violation of international law").

order to be worked out within States. Internal wars typically succeeded in presenting themselves as struggles between ideologically motivated factions for standing to speak for the undivided population, rather than as ethnonationalist bloodletting or as the simple thuggery of armed gangs.[14] After all, during this period, most governments in the world traced their origins more or less directly to a coup d'état, insurrection, or decisive civil war. The image of civil war implicit in international discourse was that of, in effect, a trial by ordeal, in which a winning faction – absent unlawful assistance from a foreign power – demonstrated its worthiness to represent a given political community by achieving and maintaining effective control, that is to say, the acquiescence of the bulk of the populace in that faction's project of public order.[15]

This premise represented, not a repudiation of the moralistic principle of popular sovereignty, but rather an application of that very principle in the absence of shared assumptions about its substantive and procedural requisites. The conventional wisdom held that empirical investigation to ascertain public opinion in a foreign state was most often impracticable, that "popular will" itself was a complex and normatively loaded concept, and that any imposition from abroad of procedures calculated to measure popular will was presumptuous at best, and a usurpation at worst.[16]

This wisdom was reinforced by the very nature of the Cold War, which presented itself to the world as not merely a clash of powers, but a clash of universal creeds. Liberal democracy and revolutionary socialism represented two complete and opposing conceptions of public order struggling for adherence within all nations. Moreover, the intensity of the struggle allowed for the paradoxical rationalization, on both sides, of dictatorial, repressive, and even terroristic means to "democratic" ends. Expressions of principled outrage at such means could easily be dismissed as – and indeed, frequently amounted to – partisan propaganda.

---

[14] There is no doubt that the latter frequently masqueraded as the former, often for the sake of procuring weapons and other assistance from the rival blocs. Somali dictator Mohammed Siad Barre and Angolan rebel leader Jonas Savimbi are two notorious examples of leaders who shifted ideological affectations, as convenient, to enlist foreign support for essentially nonideological agendas. For a skeptical approach to the supposed contrast between Cold War-era and subsequent internal conflicts, see Stathis N. Kalyvas, "'New' and 'Old' Civil Wars: A Valid Distinction?" (2001) 54 *World Politics* 99.

[15] See generally Roth, *Governmental Illegitimacy in International Law*, 136–49, 160–71, 253–364 (detailing the history of that era's practice and pronouncements on civil wars, recognition contests, and political participation).

[16] *Ibid.*

As a matter of both policy and principle, then, the perceived international interest in internal conflict in the Cold War era was more (a) that foreign powers not obtain undue advantage; and (b) that the winner be determined by authentically internal means; than (c) that the armed conflict be halted; or even (d) that human rights abuses be curtailed. This order of priorities reflected, at least in part, both direct and indirect effects of the global geopolitical and ideological confrontation.

The 1990s brought the end of both the geopolitical and the ideological standoff. First, the United States emerged as the sole superpower. As a result, non-humanitarian motivations for US intervention were diminished (though not necessarily eliminated). Moreover, any US-led interventions would be far less likely to occasion counter-intervention by a rival power, and thus far less likely to result in an escalation of internal conflict.

Second, liberal-democratic values, even if not achieving unquestioned international acceptance,[17] no longer faced a competing set of values pretending to universal applicability.[18] This development not only reduced the extent of international dissidence on matters of internal order, but also altered the reigning paradigm of internal conflict. The prior image had been of factions struggling to apply competing conceptions of public order to governance of the undivided whole, with the opposing regular and irregular armed forces as the primary targets and with the ruthlessness of the fighting mitigated, at least to some degree, by competition for the hearts and minds of broad sectors of the population. The new images – reflecting to some extent a change in perception alone, and to some extent a change in reality – were of, on the one hand, unlimited violence aimed at civilian populations directly, inspired by narrowly parochial, ethno-nationalist ideologies reminiscent of the long-repudiated Axis-era fascism (for example, in Rwanda and parts of the former Yugoslavia), and of, on the

---

[17] See Thomas M. Franck, "The Emerging Right to Democratic Governance" (1992) 86 AJIL 46 (the seminal work heralding a shift in international legal norms toward a "democratic entitlement"); Gregory H. Fox and Brad R. Roth (eds.), *Democratic Governance and International Law* (Cambridge: Cambridge University Press, 2000) (compendium of conflicting assessments of whether and to what extent such a shift has taken place).

[18] To be sure, the radical Islamist fringe currently represents such a set of values to the extent that it exhorts universal conversion to Islam and *jihad* against infidels. In general, however, mainstream Islamism, especially as advocated by state actors, demands recognition of Islamic exceptionalism rather than seeking a transformation in the ordering principles of non-Muslim countries or regions. Furthermore, even within countries with large Muslim populations, its political claims typically are not asserted in the name of the latent will of the non-Muslim population.

other hand, efforts by wholly unprincipled armed gangs to usurp control of economic activity and natural resources (for example, in Liberia, Somalia, and Sierra Leone).

These shifts in the geostrategic situation and the paradigm of internal conflict were reflected in the actions of the international community. The Security Council, no longer subject to structurally overdetermined deadlock in cases involving internal affairs, began to characterize even unambiguously domestic humanitarian crises as threats to international peace and security, signaling at least a potential for the authorization, under Charter Articles 41 and 42, of coercive measures. In a few such cases – Somalia, Haiti, Rwanda, and Albania – the Security Council proceeded to authorize the use of force.[19] Even more tellingly, the Security Council provided unambiguous *post hoc* endorsements to unauthorized armed interventions by the Nigerian-led Economic Community of West African States (ECOWAS) in Liberia and Sierra Leone.[20] Moreover, the international community acquiesced in the United States and allied intervention to secure a *de facto* Kurdish autonomous entity in northern Iraq, an intervention nominally predicated on a Security Council resolution that did no more than insist that Iraq allow immediate access by international humanitarian organizations to victims of internal war and repression.[21]

Nonetheless, the extent of the change in the international community's stance toward internal conflict must not be exaggerated. States have, both individually and collectively, been highly reluctant to generalize from the cases that have so far presented themselves. Security Council resolutions have repeatedly sought (if less and less persuasively) to portray the situations leading to the authorization of intrusive measures as *sui generis*,[22] and there has been no move in UN bodies toward an express modification of the use-of-force rules to allow for humanitarian intervention without Security Council authorization. Moreover, changed perspectives are far more evident

---

[19] SC Res. 794 (1992), Res. 814 (1993) (Somalia); SC Res. 929 (1994) (Rwanda); SC Res. 940 (Haiti); SC Res. 1101 (1997) (Albania).

[20] UN Doc. S/22133 (1991) (Security Council statement commending ECOWAS efforts "to restore peace and normalcy in Liberia"); SC Res. 788 (1992) (imposing an arms embargo against Liberian factions resisting ECOWAS); SC Res. 1132 (1997) (imposing an arms embargo against the Sierra Leonean *de facto* government in support of ECOWAS military efforts to restore the elected government).

[21] SC Res. 688 (1991).

[22] See, e.g., SC Res. 940 (1994), (characterizing the authorization of force in Haiti as "an exceptional response" to the "extraordinary nature" and "unique character of the present situation").

among the wealthier and more powerful States (and, of course, among journalists, intellectuals, and NGOs based in those countries); in contrast, the 133 member States of the G-77 have strongly reaffirmed – at least as a general matter – their adherence to the earlier vision of the international peace and security order.[23]

The end of bipolarity in the military and ideological realms has not altered the essential premises to which most of the world's state actors adhere, and thus has not led to a dramatic revision of a legal order established by consent. Yet the dominance of the United States in the military realm and the pre-eminence of liberal-democratic principles in the ideological realm have caused many statespersons, activists, and scholars in the West – and above all in the United States, with its strong traditions of both unilateral action and universalist justification – to question the legitimacy of that order's continued constraints on humanitarian intervention. Constituencies once wedded to those constraints as a matter of both policy and morality now increasingly seek to circumvent them, and look to international law scholars for aid and comfort. And increasingly, international law scholars have obliged, though in sharply differing ways.

Bending the law: policy-oriented jurisprudence

Since the sources of international law, as traditionally conceived, furnish relatively few resources for those who would uphold the legality of the Kosovo action, it is not surprising that the most significant efforts to vindicate

---

[23] Group of 77 South Summit Declaration (April 2000), available at http://www.g77.org/Docs/ Declaration_G77Summit.htm. Among the provisions:

> 49. ... We reaffirm that every State has the inalienable right to choose political, economic, social and cultural systems of its own, without interference in any form by other States ...
> 54. We stress the need to maintain a clear distinction between humanitarian assistance and other activities of the United Nations. We reject the so-called right of humanitarian intervention, which has no legal basis in the United Nations Charter or in the general principles of international law ... Furthermore, we stress that humanitarian assistance should be conducted in full respect of the sovereignty, territorial integrity, and political independence of host countries, and should be initiated in response to a request or with the approval of these States.

> See also para. 48 ("rejecting [all] forms of coercive economic measures, including unilateral sanctions against developing countries, without mentioning any exception for countermeasures against human rights violators").

the action should rely on an alternative methodology. This methodology, known as "policy-oriented jurisprudence," derives from the copious work of the so-called New Haven School – foremostly, the writings of Myres McDougal, Harold Lasswell, and W. Michael Reisman.[24] It is hard to characterize in brief the principles of this jurisprudential trend without being accused of caricaturing them, and any effort to make broad generalizations about the usefulness of the New Haven approach is beyond the scope of this essay. Nonetheless, the elements of this approach that commend it to the project of justifying what otherwise appear as violations of settled norms can easily be identified.

In a recent effort to summarize and defend the principles of policy-oriented jurisprudence, Siegfried Wiessner and Andrew Willard portray law not as "a body of rules," on the one hand, nor as mere "processes of power," on the other, but rather as "an ongoing process of authoritative and controlling decision" through which "members of a community seek to clarify and secure their common interest."[25] In recognition of law's character as a purposive process, policy-oriented jurisprudence has both descriptive and prescriptive components; this jurisprudence is said to provide not only "methods for tracking the development of law," but also "criteria for appraising its contribution to clarifying and securing the common interest, and procedures for improving its performance in any community."[26] Because law "is only a means to an end, not an end in itself," legality is identified with progress in "founding and maintaining *minimum public order* ... [and] advancing toward an *optimum public order*,"[27] both of which are specified in accordance with a set of underlying values said to be broadly shared in the community.

The approach thus combines elements of positivism, realism, and naturalism, as power and morals share the stage with established expectations and authorized procedures. Although this combination is appealing at a high level of abstraction – since positivism, realism, and naturalism each

<hr />

[24] See, e.g., Myres S. McDougal, Harold D. Lasswell and W. Michael Reisman, "Theories About International Law: Prologue to a Configurative Jurisprudence" (1968) 8 *Virginia Journal of International Law* 189; McDougal, Lasswell and Reisman, "The World Constitutive Process of Authoritative Decision" (1967) 19 *Journal of Legal Education* 253.

[25] Siegfried Wiessner and Andrew R. Willard, "Policy-Oriented Jurisprudence and Human Rights Abuses in Internal Conflict: Toward a World Public Order of Human Dignity" (1999) 93 AJIL 316 at 319–20.

[26] *Ibid.*, 321.   [27] *Ibid.*, 324 (emphasis in original).

seem to disclose part, but only part, of the essence of legality – it is not so clear how the pieces fit together to produce determinate conclusions about concrete problems.

First, concessions to realism, in overcoming the inflexibility of established sources of law, may tend to elevate short-run efficacy into both the necessary and sufficient condition of normativity. The expansion of the list of supposed "participants" in international lawmaking, while putatively reflecting the contemporary weight of non-State actors in world affairs, introduces extraordinary room for apologistic sleights of hand. The world social and decision processes, as Wiessner and Willard describe them, include an indeterminate set of actors, to whose words and deeds lawmaking authority is imputed. "Besides the traditional nation-state," these actors may, depending on the circumstances, "include intergovernmental organizations, non-self-governing territories, autonomous regions, and indigenous and other peoples, as well as private entities such as multinational corporations, media, nongovernmental organizations, private armies, gangs, and individuals."[28] Moreover, the juridical significance accorded the acts and opinions of any of these actors is variable: "the authority of institutional arrangements . . . is context-dependent, [and] is never known, with specificity, in advance of a particular problem. The authority and potential authority of each arrangement . . . must always be determined empirically in a given context."[29] Absent a formally structured account of their supposed juridical authority, these various actors can be invoked or ignored, as convenience dictates, by those who have the power to create facts in disregard of the long-term accommodations that positive norms represent.[30]

Second, concessions to naturalism may tend to neglect the contested nature of justice. To speak of law as a purposive project is to beg the question of *whose* purposes drive the project. Any community, let alone the global community, is beset by disagreement about underlying values – if not about

---

[28] *Ibid.*, 323.   [29] *Ibid.*, 324.

[30] As James C. Hathaway has noted, unilateralists can use this method to rationalize departures from a State-based *opinio juris* in either direction. "On the one hand, where unilateral intervention [is] called for by the media and other non-state actors, . . . powerful states enjoy the right to interpret and act upon the prescriptions of this 'constitutive process.' On the other hand, if that same unofficial network suggests the need to rid the world of landmines that kill and maim thousands of innocent civilians every year, . . . powerful states ('those with the wherewithal' to act) remain the final arbiters of the result of the diffuse lawmaking conversation." Hathaway, "America, Defender of Democratic Legitimacy?" (2000) 11 EJIL 121 at 130.

their validity, at least about their order of priority. Where controversial outcomes are claimed to derive from uncontroversial normative premises, this is usually a sign, not that controversy results from faulty reasoning or bad faith, but that the shared premises contain hidden ambiguities. Appeals to authoritative goals such as "minimum public order," employed to attribute to arid formalism the failure of established sources of law to support the proposed outcome, tend to obscure the real limits of consensus and the corresponding need for accommodation.

Third, the combination of strands of realism and naturalism in one jurisprudential package yields a dangerous temptation: realism and natural-ism can achieve unity in the identification of the interests of the hegemonic power with the universal interest.[31] As Martti Koskenniemi has pointed out, law, if reduced to "social facts and moral ideas," becomes nothing but "a servile instrument for power (of what works) to realize its objectives (of what should work)"; "any conception of law as fixed 'rules' seems irrel-evant to the extent that it is not backed by sanction and counterproductive inasmuch as it limits the choices available to those who have the means to enforce them."[32]

That the policy-oriented approach lends itself systematically to justifica-tions for unilateral uses of force can be seen in the multicontextual writings of one of its accredited founders, W. Michael Reisman.[33] The following statement is strikingly illustrative of the groundwork for the positions that he has staked out over time:

> Positivist jurisprudence, which lends itself to decision-making by many of
> the levels of a bureaucracy, identifies lawfulness in terms of compliance with
> rules. The decision-maker at the pinnacle, in contrast, does not think in terms
> of compliance with rules, but in terms of making decisions that optimize the

---

[31] Edward Hallett Carr long ago illuminated the mischievous tendency for the great powers' publi-cists to identify those powers' partisan interests as the interests of the international community. Carr, *The Twenty Years' Crisis, 1919–1939: An Introduction to the Study of International Relations* (New York: Harper & Row Publications, Inc., 1964 [1939]), pp. 41–62.

[32] Martti Koskenniemi, "Carl Schmitt, Hans Morgenthau, and the Image of Law in International Relations," in Michael Byers (ed.), *The Role of Law in International Politics* (Oxford: Oxford University Press, 2000), p. 17, pp. 32, 33, and 29, respectively.

[33] See, e.g., W. Michael Reisman, "Unilateral Actions and the Transformations of the World Consti-tutive Process: The Special Problem of Humanitarian Intervention" (2000) 11 EJIL 3; Reisman, "Kosovo's Antinomies" (1999) 93 AJIL 860 (justifying the NATO bombing of Serbia); Reisman, "Sovereignty and Human Rights in Contemporary International Law" (1990) 84 AJIL 866 (justifying the US invasion of Panama); Reisman, "Coercion and Self-Determination: Constru-ing Charter Article 2(4)" (1984) 78 AJIL 642 (justifying the US invasion of Grenada).

many policies that may be expressed in rules, but which are presented for decision in situations that are anything but routine; if they were routine, they would have been adequately dealt with by bureaucrats at lower levels of the behemoth. From the perspective of the jurist who is deploying a positivist jurisprudential frame, the decision-maker is acting unilaterally and unlawfully. Using a different and quite possibly more appropriate jurisprudential lens could lead to the opposite conclusion.[34]

A more subversive conceptualization of international legality can scarcely be imagined.[35] It is reminiscent of Jean Bodin's conception of sovereignty, in which the prince may unilaterally determine that the covenants limiting his discretion "cease to satisfy the claims of justice"[36] – a conception summed up in Carl Schmitt's famous phrase, "Sovereign is he who decides on the exception."[37] The UN system, of course, designates the bearer of a global power to decide on the exception: the Security Council. Reisman's statement (which he intends as applying to *external* affairs) speaks volumes about his understanding of the role of the United States and its allies in the international legal system.

With respect to the Kosovo action itself, Reisman, continuing the analogy to domestic law, invokes the maxim that "the Constitution is not a suicide pact."[38] The maxim itself is fair enough, but applicable only where adherence to the rule in question jeopardizes the very institutional framework that provides the basis for the rule.

[34] Reisman, "Unilateral Actions," above note 33, 5 n. 2.
[35] I cannot resist invoking here a reference to Richard Nixon's famous words about the legality of the domestic-espionage activities of his Plumbers unit: "When the President does it, that means it is not illegal." Michael Schudson, *Watergate in American Memory* (New York: Basic Books, 1992), p. 191. Perhaps more to the point, the Iran–Contra defendants viewed constitutional limitations in just the way that Reisman's statement suggests. Their apologists tellingly lamented the prosecutions as the "criminalization of policy differences," implying that the question of whether or not to observe the Constitution presented a mere policy choice; see David Johnston, "Bush Pardons 6 in Iran Affair, Aborting a Weinberger Trial; Prosecutor Assails a 'Cover-Up,'" *New York Times*, 25 Dec. 1992, 1, available at http://www.nytimes.com/books/97/06/29/reviews/iran-pardon.html.
[36] Jean Bodin, *Six Books of the Commonwealth* [1576], trans. M. J. Tooley (Oxford: Basil Blackwell, 1955), p. 30 (bk. I, ch. 8).
[37] Carl Schmitt, *Political Theology: Four Chapters on the Concept of Sovereignty* [1922], trans. George Schwab (Cambridge, MA: MIT Press, 1985), p. 5.
[38] Reisman, "Kosovo's Antinomies," above note 33, at 860–1. James Hathaway has already commented adversely on Reisman's use of this oft-cited metaphor (which appears in at least two US Supreme Court opinions), on the ground that its authors sought to limit individual rights in the interest of the general welfare, rather than to expand rights of unilateral action at the expense of a binding collective commitment. Hathaway, "Defender of Democratic Legitimacy," above note 30, at 127–8 & nn. 24–5.

In the present case, the suicide pact analogy is inapt. The FRY's sub-jugation of the Kosovar Albanians and the violent suppression of their independence movement, however offensive to collectively held values and however much denounced by the authoritative organs of the international system, did not augur the destruction of the international peace and security order. Nor has Reisman made the case that Kosovo represented narrowly exceptional circumstances of a kind not anticipated when the rules were drawn up and repeatedly reaffirmed, anticipation of which would mani-festly have occasioned a legal exemption; Reisman's quarrel is with the very fact that Charter law reflects a deliberate choice to favor (at least presump-tively) territorial integrity over other values. Nor was the Security Council "paralyzed," as Reisman puts it – any more than it is paralyzed when the United States vetoes resolutions imposing terms on itself or its allies; Chapter VII procedures establish a default position of inaction that is, by design, difficult to overcome.[39] Moreover, the appropriate remedy for paralysis would have been the convening of a special meeting of the General Assembly under the "Uniting for Peace" procedure,[40] an option that was eschewed – perhaps because of fear of how the restoration of that device might threaten US interests in other contexts, such as the Israeli–Palestinian conflict.

Reisman seeks to harmonize the Kosovo action with Article 2(4) (re-stricting the use of force against the territorial integrity and political in-dependence of States) by radically reinterpreting the latter. In his view, Article 2(4) has been modified by what he terms the "contraction" of Article 2(7) (restricting external intervention in matters essentially within the domestic jurisdiction of States). This contraction, "by effectively elim-inating for serious human rights violations the defense of domestic juris-diction, removed from the sphere of 'political independence' of a State the right to violate in grave fashion and with impunity the human rights of its inhabitants." A change in one part of the Charter must, Reisman contends, occasion "appropriate adjustments in other parts."[41]

---

[39] As Reisman bluntly puts it, "Why was action undertaken without Security Council authoriza-tion? Because the authorization could not be secured." Reisman, "Kosovo's Antinomies", above note 33, at 861. Imagine such an explanation for taking unconstitutional action domestically.

[40] GA Res. 377 (A) (1950) ("where the Security Council, because of lack of unanimity of the perma-nent members, fails to exercise its primary responsibility for the maintenance of international peace and security, . . . the General Assembly shall [if requested by the Security Council on the vote of any seven members, or by a majority of the Members of the United Nations] consider the matter immediately with a view to making appropriate recommendations to Members for collective measures . . .").

[41] Reisman, "Kosovo's Antinomies," above note 33, at 861.

Yet Reisman ultimately attributes the Security Council's failure to do as he sees fit precisely to "profound, possibly unbridgeable, divides between the permanent members" on "the international control of the essential techniques by which governments manage and control their people internally."[42] Thus, the modification of non-intervention norms that Reisman posits is aspirational; in reality, the system's failure to authorize intervention resulted not from an anomaly, but from the legal need to accommodate differences of opinion. Nor are the two recalcitrant permanent members of the Security Council isolated in their non-conforming views on "the international control of the essential techniques by which governments manage and control their people internally."[43] Reisman's "reinterpretation" of the Charter repudiates not merely the rules as written, but their underlying purpose as well: international peace based on accommodation (though not necessarily limitless accommodation) of differences about internal standards of justice.

There is, of course, considerable appeal to Reisman's position on human rights-oriented intervention in the abstract, and perhaps even greater appeal to its application in the concrete circumstances of the Kosovo action. The flaw in Reisman's abstract position, however, is significant: although States are generally agreed (or, almost as importantly, pay lip service to the proposition) that violations of treaty-based and customary international law rights of individuals and groups are not "essentially within the domestic jurisdiction," but rather are proper concerns of the international community as a whole, States are not generally agreed that the invocation of human rights concerns obliterates the considerations of non-intervention. Article 2(7) – and a fortiori Article 2(4) – continues to apply to the implementation of human rights obligations. The fact that States have bound themselves to certain international legal standards (without, it should be noted, accepting any explicit regime of penalties for non-compliance) need not logically entail that States have accepted to be externally compelled to comply with their obligations. These are two separate juridical steps. There is no contradiction in embracing the former while excluding the latter; indeed, Bodin's conception of sovereignty, noted earlier, suggests just this combination.[44] Moreover, the stricture against the unilateral use of

---

[42] Ibid., 862.   [43] See Group-77 South Summit Declaration, above note 23.

[44] See Bodin, Six Books of the Commonwealth, above note 36. According to the authoritative interpretation of Article 2(7) contained in the UN General Assembly's 1970 Friendly Relations Declaration, "Every State has an inalienable right to choose its political, economic, social, and cultural systems, without interference in any form by another State," and "[n]o State or group

force across borders, reflected in Article 2(4), has a special status in the global order; indeed, the International Court of Justice has characterized that stricture as a peremptory norm (*jus cogens*) from which no derogation is permitted.[45]

To be sure, the recent practice of the international system has manifested a considerable diminution of sovereign prerogatives. But there is (as yet) no general principle of the sort that Reisman posits – namely, the exemption of armed redress for "serious" human rights violations from the category of "use of force against political independence." Even more gravely, the community-wide acceptance of the most basic human rights standards does not necessarily entail acceptance of the proposition that reasons of state may never justify "serious" violations (notwithstanding the treaty language limiting derogation); there remains considerable vitality to the view that if the stakes are high enough, few means are too terrible to contemplate.[46] There is little reason to believe that States – or peoples – widely accept that outsiders will have the last word on the means that they might employ to protect what they regard as vital interests. Even putting aside the anxiety about predatory intervention under humanitarian cover, there is considerable appeal in the international community for the licensing of humanitarian intervention only in cases where the Security Council, with its vast range of ideological and cultural perspectives, can come to an agreement on the equities. In other words, the system's failure forcibly to counter injustice is not, in itself, evidence that its rules frustrate its actual purposes.

Policy-oriented jurisprudence is ill-disposed to accept such a conclusion. Unfortunately, the alternative it poses provides little basis for the limitation of great-power impositions that invoke humanitarian concern. At its worst,

---

of States has the right to intervene, directly or indirectly, for any reason whatever, in the internal or external affairs of any other State." *Friendly Relations Declaration*, above note 4. Despite the increasing emphasis on human rights norms, General Assembly reiterations of the non-intervention norm continue, without any indication that the inviolability of the latter norm is, as a general matter, conditioned on compliance with the former. This is not to deny that in some particularly egregious instances of human rights non-compliance, the international community has implicitly adopted such conditionality.

45 *Military and Paramilitary Activities in and against Nicaragua (Nicaragua v. United States)*, (1986) ICJ Reports 14, para. 190.

46 The "*non liquet*" holding of the International Court of Justice Advisory Opinion on *Legality of the Threat or Use of Nuclear Weapons* (1996) ICJ Reports 226 (8 July 1996), paras. 95–97, refusing to rule out the legality of the use of nuclear weapons in the face of dire threats, constitutes a tacit admission of this general point.

the policy-oriented approach equates law with justice as interpreted by the strong.

Breaking the law: moralistic positivism

Policy-oriented jurisprudence, while neither a uniquely American pheno-menon[47] nor uniquely the device of apologists for US foreign policy,[48] remains a controversial mode of legal analysis, especially among those who seek to maintain a critical perspective on US actions. Its leading method-ological competitor, positivism, regards international law as a set of rules derivable (more or less objectively) from accepted sources of law. While the point is not entirely beyond cavil, positivists are generally agreed that the Kosovo intervention cannot be reconciled with the strictures of the United Nations Charter.

For those positivists who are in moral and political sympathy with the Kosovo action, this legal conclusion poses a dilemma of the precise sort that policy-oriented jurisprudence tends to obviate. Positivists regard ac-knowledgment of such dilemmas as a healthy recognition that the universe lacks a moral order that renders all virtues mutually reinforcing; life poses situations in which even the right moral choice may have a moral cost.[49] In morally exigent circumstances, positivists would prefer to admit breaking the law in an isolated case, rather than to bend legality to the moral needs of the moment, thereby concealing the conflict of values and undermining law's restraining function.

Some positivists further hold the related, but not directly deducible, view that even where the violation of existing law is morally justified, it does not necessarily follow that the law ought to be reformed prospectively to accommodate future actions of a similar sort.[50] Although manifestations

---

[47] See Rosalyn Higgins, *Problems and Process: International Law and How We Use It* (New York: Oxford University Press, 1994).

[48] Note, for example, the wide-ranging work of Richard Falk.

[49] See Hart, "Positivism and the Separation of Law and Morals," above note 1, at 619–20.

[50] It is worth noting that the common-law defenses of necessity and excuse are both incompatible with this position. The necessity defense entails assertion of the kind of legal exception being resisted here. As one court has put it:

> In some sense, the necessity defense allows us to act as individual legislatures, amending a particular criminal provision or crafting a one-time exception to it, subject to court review, when a real legislature would formally do the same under those circumstances. For example, by allowing prisoners who escape a burning jail to claim the justification

of support in the international community for the violation of an existing norm present opportunities for jurists to recharacterize the violative act as a step toward the development of an exception to the norm – opportunities that effectively turn international lawyers into lobbyists for changes in the practice and *opinio juris* of States and intergovernmental organizations – many jurists have declined such opportunities with respect to the Kosovo action, even while avowing the moral and political rectitude of the violation. Their concern is that a legal exception to the non-intervention norm, once created with a given humanitarian action in mind, would inevitably swallow the rule, creating an open-ended license for the unilateral use of force.[51] Oscar Schachter articulated this concern as follows in 1991:

> Even in the absence of... prior [Security Council] approval, a State or group of States using force to put an end to atrocities when the necessity is evident and the humanitarian intention is clear is likely to have its action pardoned. But, I believe it highly undesirable to have a new rule allowing humanitarian intervention, for that could provide a pretext for abusive intervention. It would be better to acquiesce in a violation that is considered necessary and desirable in the particular circumstances than to adopt a principle that would open a wide gap in the barrier against unilateral use of force.[52]

The concern is a valid one, but Schachter's advice fails to satisfy it. Although collective acquiescence in a violation does not alone vitiate the violated norm as a general matter, the specific "acquiescence" hypothesized here – manifesting a moral and political judgment that the violation is "necessary and desirable" – cannot help but open a "gap in the barrier." To reject the effort to establish a carefully delimited exception, even while affirming the necessity and desirability of the violation, exposes the whole of the non-intervention norm to discredit.

---

of necessity, we assume the lawmaker, confronting this problem, would have allowed for an exception to the law proscribing prison escapes. (*United States v. Schoon*, 955 F.2d 1238, 1241 [9th Cir. 1992]).

The excuse defense, conversely, while sheltering the actor from blame on ground of diminished agency, concedes that the act is unjustifiable and ought not to have been done. See Joshua Dressler, "Exegesis of the Law of Duress: Justifying the Excuse and Searching for its Proper Limits" (1989) 62 *Southern Californian Law Review* 1331 at 1349 n. 124.

[51] For an elaborate exposition of this stance, see Peter Hilpold, "Humanitarian Intervention: Is There a Need for a Legal Reappraisal?" (2001) 12 EJIL 437.

[52] Oscar Schachter, *International Law in Theory and Practice* (Boston: M. Nijhoff Publications, 1991), p. 126. For a Kosovo-occasioned assessment of Schachter's statement, see Louis Henkin, "Kosovo and the Law of Humanitarian Intervention" (1999) 93 AJIL 824.

In the history of the contemporary peace and security order, the non-intervention norm has, it is true, successfully withstood widespread international acquiescence in the outcomes of purportedly "humanitarian" interventions. That acquiescence, however, has rarely been tantamount to moral or political approval of the interventions themselves, let alone to acknowledgment of armed intervention as an instrument of humanitarianism. In most cases where morally and politically desirable consequences followed from intervention, the international community perceived these consequences to have resulted from an accidental confluence of the intervenor's interests with those of the population of the target state. These happy accidents appeared insufficiently systematic to justify reform of the non-intervention norm (just as the episodes were not so frequent or so similar in their essential characteristics as to give rise to patterns of acquiescence sufficient to indicate the emergence of a customary exception). It therefore made sense to advocate maintenance of the strict rule of non-intervention even while conferring an imprimatur on the fruits of the illegal act (for example, recognition of the state of Bangladesh after the 1971 Indian invasion of East Pakistan, or of the government of the Central African Republic after the 1979 French removal of "Emperor" Bokassa).[53]

Acceptance of a violation of the non-intervention norm as itself necessary and desirable has far different implications, especially in circumstances where the essential characteristics of both the intervenor and the target situation in question can be expected to recur with some regularity. It is one thing to affirm that it is morally and prudentially right to disobey a just and prudent rule that has failed to take into account the characteristics of the situation at hand. It is quite another thing to affirm that it will be morally and prudentially right in the future (given that the essence of normativity lies in the like treatment of like cases) to disobey a rule that is recommended, on moral and prudential grounds, to be retained notwithstanding expectation of the recurrence of such characteristics. The latter affirmation is inconsistent with the practical requisites of normativity in the international system.

---

[53] See, e.g., GA Res. 2793 (XXVI) (1971) (104-11-10) (calling "upon the Governments of India and Pakistan to take forthwith all measures for an immediate cease-fire and withdrawal of their armed forces on the territory of the other to their own side of the India–Pakistan borders," thereby indirectly repudiating the Indian intervention that resulted in the establishment of Bangladesh).

The "barrier against unilateral use of force," such as it is, does not, as Schachter's advice implies, derive from the mere existence of a restrictive legal doctrine. Strictures on the use of force – relying, as they do, not on a centralized system of sanctions but on the moral and political dispositions of constituencies in a position to restrain exercises of military power – cannot endure without being widely regarded as an integral part of a morally and prudentially compelling scheme. To insist on a set of strictures in legal doctrine while simultaneously admitting that they will, under predictable conditions, be morally or prudentially unsustainable in practice is to concede that the strictures are utopian – that is, that their obligatory character is subject to conditions precedent and yet to be realized. Since the charge of utopianism has perpetually dogged efforts to establish the obligatory character of the international law of peace and security, it is imperative to avoid inadvertently bolstering such a charge.

The problem has particular salience in the political context of the US penchant for unilateralism. A long-time observer of US practice cannot help but find irony in Thomas Franck's description of the United States/NATO position on Kosovo:

> Neither the United States Department of State nor NATO seriously attempted to justify the war in international legal terms. They clearly did not want their actions to legitimate a reversion to the pre-Charter era when states or regional organizations could claim an uncircumscribed right of unilateral recourse to military force.[54]

Given that the allied European powers are not serial violators of use-of-force norms, it is plausible that they intended, by avoiding a statement of general principle, to restrict the precedential implications of the action. But the most plausible motivation attributable to US policy makers, given past practice, is just the opposite: *to keep a free hand*. Rather than elaborating an exception that would affirm a commitment to non-intervention in all but the narrowly specified circumstances, the United States remains silent as to the scope of the implied license. By making no effort to place the action under a generally applicable normative standard, whether in the nature of *lex lata* or *lex ferenda*, the initiators of the Kosovo action effectively assert for themselves the privilege (in the literal sense of *privi-lege*) of disregarding

---

[54] Thomas Franck, "Lessons of Kosovo" (1999) 93 AJIL 857 at 859.

acknowledged strictures of international law when (i.e., whenever) they think that they are in the right. Any concern for limitation of license is directed, not at promising restraint in future actions that the United States (and any allies of the moment) might want to take in some unilaterally designated just cause, but at precluding the use of the precedent by non-approved powers.

The United States agenda here is effectively camouflaged by its com-patibility with the rhetorical approach recommended by bearers of the opposite intention. Thus, Bruno Simma seeks, in just the same manner as the State Department, to characterize Kosovo as an isolated case in which "overwhelming humanitarian necessity" justifies an *ad hoc* disregard of legal strictures:

> the decisive point is that we should not change the rule simply to follow our humanitarian impulses; we should not set new standards only to do the right thing in a single case. The legal issues presented by the Kosovo crisis are particularly impressive proof that hard cases make bad law.[55]

But the fact that Simma renders this judgment in a distinctly non-American context is crucial. Simma describes the Bundestag debate of mid-October 1998 on German participation in NATO airstrikes as follows:

> the international legal issues involved were discussed at great length and in considerable depth. The respect for UN Charter law demonstrated through-out the debates was remarkable. . . . it was stressed by all voices in favour of such participation . . . that German agreement . . . was not to be regarded as a "green light" for similar NATO interventions in general.[56]

In Germany (at least on Simma's account), the political legitimacy of the restraining role of the international law of peace and security is not in question.

In the United States, the opposite is true: disrespect for that body of law is longstanding and bipartisan, an artifact of the US role in the Cold War. So, for example, even congressional opponents of US policy in Nicaragua in the mid-1980s only rarely invoked the decision of the International Court of Justice in *Nicaragua v. United States*; to do so was largely perceived in mainstream political circles as a sign of unworthiness to participate in a

---

[55] Bruno Simma, "NATO, the UN, and the Use of Force: Legal Aspects" (1999) 10 EJIL at 14.
[56] *Ibid.*, 12–13.

serious and responsible discussion of US foreign policy. The dominant position among mainstream foreign policy commentators in the United States during the Cold War was that the international law addressed to the use of force had been designed for a better world than then existed.[57] This remained the conventional wisdom even after human rights became an established (and, by 1982, bipartisan) part of the mainstream foreign policy discourse; instructively, direct invocation of moral considerations (including human rights, which were then seen more in moral and domestic-law terms than in international-law terms) was more respectable than invocations of international law.

The end of the Cold War and the new receptiveness of the Security Council to US security initiatives, starting with the 1990 response to the Iraqi invasion of Kuwait, created an opening to inject considerations of international law into US foreign policy discourse on the use of force. Yet it is still only a modest opening. In this context, Simma's suggestion promises to have virtually the opposite effect to that in the German context: far from highlighting the gravity of the dilemma and discouraging future departures from legality, the suggestion that properly construed international law stands in the way of, and therefore must give way to, morally exigent measures threatens again to associate the international law of peace and security as a whole with fuzzy-headed utopianism. The problem is compounded by a refusal to advocate reform of the law to accommodate action of the sort deemed necessary on this occasion; the implication is that not only existing doctrine, but the whole project of legal limitation of all actors on an equal basis, is risible.

Given the historical frequency of violations and the notorious lack of effective sanctions, international law's status as law – at least in the area of peace and security – has long hinged on a felt need to rationalize violative actions in terms of generally accepted legal categories. Hypocrisy thus plays an indispensable role as, so the saying goes, "the tribute that vice pays to virtue." In the words of Hedley Bull, "where a violation takes place[,] the offending state usually goes out of its way to demonstrate that it considers

---

[57] For a noteworthy elaboration of that view, see Jeane Kirkpatrick and Allan Gerson, "The Reagan Doctrine," in Louis Henkin (ed.), *Right v. Might: International Law and the Use of Force*, 2nd edn. (New York: Council on Foreign Relations, 1991), p. 19. Although the Reagan policies were highly controversial on numerous grounds, even opponents tended to accept, at least tacitly, Kirkpatrick and Gerson's proposition that the international law of peace and security was an inadequate guide to US responsibilities in a dangerous world.

itself (and other states) bound by the rule in question."[58] That this is frequently accomplished by factual and analytic distortions merely reaffirms
that States perceive that they cannot afford to portray their present and
future conduct as unfettered by considerations of generally applicable legal
standards. Not only is there, as Bull notes, near-universal "acceptance of the
need to provide an explanation,"[59] but there is also acceptance of common
doctrinal reference points for the evaluation of such explanations.

Individual citizens may, for reasons of conscience, violate the civil or
criminal law in morally compelling circumstances without compromising
the foundations of legality in their societies. The same cannot be said of the
most powerful States in international society, any more than it can be said in
respect of violations of public law by the executive in the domestic context.
An affirmation of the moral and political rectitude of the Kosovo action,
without advocacy of a corresponding modification in the legal doctrine
governing such actions, has the effect of eroding the sociological foundation of use-of-force norms: those with the power to do what is "necessary
and desirable" need no longer provide a legal explanation. This approach
therefore does as great a long-run disservice to the international law of
peace and security as does "policy-oriented jurisprudence."

Humanitarian intervention and the progressive development of the law

Does it follow from the rejection of "policy-oriented" and "moralistic positivist" approaches that there is no room for a jurisprudential defense of
interventions such as the Kosovo action? The answer turns on whether
the intervention can be reconciled with the purposes that animate the international legal order – not the purposes hypothesized or confabulated
by those operating from a particular vantage point or conception of just
political order, but the shared purposes of a wide range of actors whose
frames of reference are not limited to stable, liberal-democratic societies.
In this light, Kosovo is a close case, and space does not permit elaboration
of the many legitimate considerations on both sides. What is advocated
here is a mode of argumentation on the question, rather than a particular
answer.

[58] Hedley Bull, *The Anarchical Society* (New York: Oxford University Press, 1977), p. 138.
[59] *Ibid.*

The international legal order is neither a blueprint for the global advancement of liberal-democratic values nor an amoral alliance of ruling apparatuses with a common bond of mutual advantage. The UN Charter, the Friendly Relations Declaration and an impressive array of other authoritative pronouncements reflect an orientation toward peace based on accommodation among "peoples," or political communities, who share some basic moral premises but can be expected to differ widely in their detailed interpretations of those premises. Peoples have the inalienable right of self-determination, and States, whether or not organized in accordance with liberal-democratic principles, are presumed to represent the expression of the self-determination of all those who live permanently within their boundaries.

The presumption linking state sovereignty to popular self-determination is strong, but not altogether irrebuttable. "Alien, colonial, and racist domination" (illegal conquests and occupations, colonialism, and *apartheid*) and certain spectacularly bad governments (Uganda under Amin, the Central African Republic under Bokassa, Nicaragua under Somoza, Haiti under Cedras, Congo-Kinshasa under Mobutu, Sierra Leone under Koroma) and ruling arrangements (East Pakistan under Islamabad, Iraqi Kurdistan under Baghdad) have explicitly or implicitly lost the protection of the international peace and security order because they violated broadly held premises about acceptable governance and popular sovereignty. Governance is an inherently teleological concept: no culture or ideology classifies as governance the maintenance of effective control at gunpoint by thugs who abuse the population at will and perform no function that any significant part of the populace regards or could regard as beneficial. Similarly, while governments have traditionally found a myriad of dubious devices for representing themselves as manifestations of popular will – and States as manifestations of the self-determination of all those living within their boundaries – there are circumstances in which no respected system of thought furnishes the intellectual basis for such a finding.

For a decade, the vast majority of Kosovars were treated as enemy aliens in their own land. Consequently, the armed rebellion against the territorial integrity of the FRY can scarcely be seen as having been anything but provoked. Yet the worst of the FRY's pre-intervention abuses were occasioned by the rebellion itself (putting aside the fact that the truly massive abuses occurred *after* the foreign intervention commenced), and the rebellion was arguably calculated less to achieve liberation by force of its own arms than to draw foreign intervention by bringing down on the population a merciless wave of Serb retribution. The international system can ill afford to reward such insurgent strategies – for their human costs no less than for the threat they pose to existing structures of power – though it also can ill afford to admit that the state sovereignty it was designed to protect altogether lacks moral underpinnings.

Situations such as Kosovo present a fundamental dilemma for the international system because they are not as exceptional as the international community would like to represent; too sweeping a precedent threatens a widespread unraveling. Yet manifest ethnic oppression – and particularly "ethnic cleansing" – strikes at the core values that States have collectively espoused.

If one is genuinely looking to resolve the issue in light of the shared purposes of the international community, it is to the above considerations that the arguments should be addressed. The Kosovo operation is essentially continuous with a series of other unauthorized but widely supported forcible interventions in the past decade (the interventions of the Western allies in northern Iraq and of ECOWAS in Liberia and Sierra Leone). The groundwork exists for advancing the thesis of an emerging exception, provided that the exception be drawn narrowly, in a manner mindful of the full range of considerations and the principled differences that continue to exist in the international system.[60]

An immediate difficulty in this regard is that Russia and China, though they did not block the characterization of the events in Kosovo as a threat to international peace and security or the demands that the FRY cease and desist from its norm-offending actions in that territory,[61] strongly objected to the NATO action.[62] The blatant circumvention of the dissenting views of permanent members of the Security Council is highly problematic in and of itself. One can justifiably question, though, whether the peace and security scheme – consistent with its current claim to legitimacy rather than with

---

[60] UN Secretary-General Kofi Annan likewise submits that there is a "developing international norm in favour of intervention to protect civilians from wholesale slaughter," while cautioning that "intervention must be based on legitimate and universal principles if it is to enjoy the sustained support of the world's peoples." "Secretary-General Presents His Annual Report to General Assembly," UN Press Release Doc. SG/SM/7136, GA/9596 (20 Sept. 1999).

[61] See SC Res. 1160, 1199, 1203 (1998) (all invoking Chapter VII powers in addressing the Kosovo situation).

[62] See UN Press Release Doc. SC/6659 (26 March 1999) (Russia, China, and Namibia support draft Security Council resolution, defeated 3–12–0, characterizing NATO's "unilateral use of force" as "a flagrant violation of the United Nations Charter" and "demanding an immediate cessation").

the temporal circumstances by which it happens to have arisen – envisages the veto-possessing permanent members as holders of a privilege, to be deployed in their own interests, or as empowered representatives of principled but otherwise under-represented viewpoints. Given the special concerns of Russia over Chechnya and China over Tibet and Taiwan, circumvention might be justified as a means of overcoming recalcitrant wills rather than dissenting opinions.

Any such justification, however, must be put to the test of the opinion of the community of States. The "Uniting for Peace" procedure provides a mechanism for such a test. The refusal to invoke it – where, as here, there was sufficient time for such a special meeting of the General Assembly to be convened on the topic – is surely a strike against the effort to reconcile the NATO action with the demands of international normativity. Even had the protagonists been determined to go forward with the intervention despite the presence of substantial opposition in such a forum, thereby provoking an overt crisis in the legal order, the onus to make the case to the General Assembly would have forced those proposing an exception to the non-intervention norm to draw the exception narrowly so as to minimize opposition. Such an overt crisis – a clash between two conflicting standards of legal constraint – would have been far preferable to the creeping desuetude of substantive and procedural norms that the actual events potentially augur.

Despite the failure of the NATO powers to engage the "Uniting for Peace" procedure as an alternative means of obtaining authorization for the Kosovo action, it remains open to legal scholars to construe the event, in the context of other recent practice, as falling within a narrow, controverted but plausibly emerging, exception to the non-intervention norm (notwithstanding the sweeping, acontextual rhetoric of the G-77 that purports to exclude such an exception). Doing so would have the effect of affirming – and lobbying for – the continued applicability of legal considerations even to dire humanitarian circumstances, rather than abandoning that field to empowered moralism.

Conclusion

Hard cases, it is frequently said, make bad law. It may be more accurate to say that hard cases expose the tensions and ambiguities underlying seemingly straightforward legal standards, and force jurists to come to grips with the principles and policies embodied in those standards.

Policy-oriented jurisprudence purports to do this, but its method does not provide reassurance that the effort is faithful to the complex accommodations among competing interests and competing conceptions of justice that international law represents. Rather, the method seems all too easily to provide jurisprudential cover for empowered actors to exceed the bounds of consensus and compromise. Convenient principles and policies are imputed to the international community on the basis of evidence for which no standards of admissibility and weight have been fixed.

The alternative that I have dubbed "moralistic positivism," however, does not even rise to the normative challenge. In advocating the armed pursuit of a particular conception of international justice, it seeks neither to respect, to reinterpret, nor to reform existing legal limitations on such pursuits. In avoiding a bad legal precedent, it creates a worse political precedent.

The third way to address hard cases is to ascertain the extent to which principles and policies favoring an exception to an apparent rule are embedded in the established source material for the drawing of legal conclusions, and to advocate, if necessary and appropriate, an incremental extension of those principles and policies to cover the case at hand (along with any future case sharing its essential characteristics). Even where this approach acknowledges that the law is being broken on this occasion for a good cause, it manifests a regard for the subordination of empowered will to generally applicable principle, and places before the lawmaking community the question of whether the law's animating purposes justify acts of the sort undertaken.

At stake is the viability of any meaningful international law of peace and security. The essence of the project entails generally applicable norms, arrived at through a process of accommodation among notionally equal juridical entities that cannot be expected to agree comprehensively on questions of justice.

Today, the unrivaled military power of the United States and the ascendancy of its articulated ideals call into question the continued vitality of such a project, as well as its continued justification on moral and policy grounds. The legal principle of sovereign equality, always limited in practical effect, may seem all the less relevant in conditions of unipolarity, where weak states confronting US-led alliances have no powerful supporters to bolster their position. US assertions of prerogative are thus emboldened. In the designation of "rogue States" and in the post-11 September 2001 warning that states not "with us" will be deemed to be "with the terrorists," the rhetoric of US foreign policy is suggestive of a Schmittian "friend–enemy" distinction at odds with any concession to sovereign equality. To the extent that the international system fails to resist such unilateral (or narrow multilateral) designations of particular States as unentitled to the protections of the peace and security order, it acquiesces in a fundamental shift in the terms of international interaction.

Indeed, some might see in recent developments the incipient demise of sovereign equality as the organizing principle of the international order. The increased ability and willingness of the United States (alone and in such alliances and coalitions as pertain from time to time) to use force, without recourse to established procedures and without the felt need to give legal explanations responsive to established doctrines, might be taken as evidence (along with the recent US rebuffs to the land mine and criminal court conventions) of the emergence of a different kind of peace and security order – one in which the United States participates in, but is not subject to, international legal institutions. The failure of most States, in response to the Kosovo intervention, to demand either conformity to Charter procedures or an explanation in accordance with Charter norms might be interpreted as acquiescence in such a development.

Suffice it to say that far too little time has passed in the unipolar era, and far too little practice adduced, to substantiate so sweeping a change in the premises of the international system. It is characteristic of legal orders that the statuses and rights they confer reflect long-term power and interest accommodations. These statuses and rights typically withstand short-term fluctuations in the relative influence of the legal community's actors. Although fundamental changes cannot be ruled out *a priori*, one cannot properly infer from a limited number of episodes the demise of the foundations of the Charter-based order.

Moreover, legal scholars, of all commentators, should be the last to resign themselves to such a conclusion – not only because it is the unique task of jurists to analyze international affairs in light of the legal order putatively in place, but because in accepting such a radical suggestion, jurists might provide crucial encouragement to lawless policy-making activity, and thereby contribute to the order's fall into desuetude. Rather, as this essay has maintained throughout, juridical scholarship should, to the extent possible, contribute to the preservation and strengthening of the legal order by resisting conclusions that undermine its practical or moral relevance.

Determined scholarly resistance to the demise of the Charter-based order presupposes, of course, a commitment to upholding sovereign equality and requiring broad-based consensus as a condition of its derogation. The moral and policy justifications of that order are thus properly in issue. It is natural for those who associate themselves with the conceptions of justice espoused by the United States and its closest allies to ask: why defer to an accommodation made with people who are wrong about justice, and who are not strong enough to prevent or to retaliate against actions taken in the service of justice, or to invoke the precedent for their own dubious purposes?

One answer is that in the long term, international peace cannot be predicated on the privilege of the momentarily strong to pursue forcibly their unilateral determinations of what is just in any given instance. Wagers on the continued weakness of others – and especially on the continued irrelevance of their disposition to cooperate on security issues – are bad long-term bets. As the aftermath of the 11 September 2001 catastrophe has demonstrated, the security of even the great powers requires active collaboration from unlikely quarters, collaboration that cannot always be purchased or coerced.

Another answer is that the practical demands of justice are often fairly contestable and sometimes conflicting: the principle of self-determination of distinct political communities includes, for prudential and perhaps even moral reasons, the right of those communities to be wrong about justice, even in ugly ways, albeit not limitlessly.[63] Outside impositions – affected, as they predictably are, by self-interest and arrogance – cannot be lightly presumed to be salutary. Even at their best, interventions occur in places (for example, in Kosovo, not Sudan, Congo or Rwanda) and in ways (for example, by aerial bombardment of economic infrastructure rather than ground-troop confrontation of *génocidaires*) that reflect political rather than moral priorities; at worst, the interests that are sufficient to motivate the external investment distort humanitarianism beyond recognition. Moreover, assessments of justice from great distances are notoriously unreliable; the news media of global reach (which are heavily dominated by US-based outlets)

---

[63] See, for example, Michael Walzer, "The Moral Standing of States: A Response to Four Critics" (1980) 9 *Philosophy & Public Affairs* 209 (arguing on moral grounds for a presumption against intervention, even where the foreign order at issue is an unjust one).

cannot be counted on to characterize the crises in question in a manner free of sophomoric oversimplification and partisan manipulation.

Instead of asking the typically American question, "What should *we* be allowed to do to further justice abroad?" – to which the answer might well be, "Everything we can" – one might do better to pose, as does much of the rest of the world, the question, "What should powerful foreign states be allowed to do in *our* troubled country in the name of furthering justice?" The answer is likely to be different.

9

Comments on chapters 7 and 8

Thomas Franck

In this comment, I deal first with the chapter written by Brad Roth, before responding to the general argument raised by Marcelo Kohen.

I agree with some of Roth's conclusions, if not always his tone and nuance. I do think that he is basically right about policy-oriented jurisprudence as advocated by the New Haven School, but two elements of the New Haven thesis seem to me to be irrefutable in this context, or at least to have been unrefuted either by legal logic or by recent events in Kosovo and elsewhere. Since disclosure is the name of the game I wish to disclose that I am not now and have never been a Yalie. I am surprised to find that I am a moral positivist, but then, this is reminiscent of the man who was surprised to find that he had been speaking prose all his life. The jurisprudential problem to which the New Haven School addresses itself is the international equivalent of the *United States v. Holmes* case or its British equivalent, in which passengers in an overloaded lifeboat were thrown overboard by crew members in order to prevent its sinking in stormy seas. What the New Haven School contributes to the disposition of the murder charge that was actually brought against the survivors of this incident is a rational search for a way in which the law might seek to avoid self-destructive *reductio ad absurdum*. The New Haven approach tackles this rescue of the law by seeking to interpret it flexibly, to circumvent results that are patently absurd. In the context of *United States v. Holmes*, the lifeboat case, the New Haven School would contend that to punish the survivor as having committed ordinary premeditated murder would not advance the intent of the law of murder.

Relating this to the Kosovo crisis, New Haven lawyers might argue that the intent of the UN Charter would be frustrated rather than advanced by treating NATO's intervention as a straightforward case of aggression under a literal interpretation of Article 2(4) and Article 51. They might add that, if the result of applying the law in accordance with strict positivism means that States capable of effecting rescue must stand aside while Kosovars (or 800,000 Tutsis or 200,000 Bosnians) are slaughtered and that such pacificity is legally incumbent on all States, then surely the law and institutions it serves are unlikely to survive for long the inevitable tide of popular revulsion.

That, it seems, suggests the need for some attempt by lawyers to help rescue the law. Roth, with much logic, suggests that in such circumstances the lawyer should redefine the law to create narrow exceptions that will save it from *reductio ad absurdum*. This of course was not the approach taken by the United States Supreme Court in *United States v. Holmes*. The court refused to carve out any exception for murder even when committed in circumstances of demonstrable extreme necessity. Some legal systems have indeed done just that, have codified exceptions when survivors can eat the cabin boy, but the United States and British legal systems, while finding defendants guilty of murder, consider the circumstances not to be exculpatory in law but relevant only to clemency in mitigation. So there are two different approaches: one is to define exculpatory exceptions; the other is to have an absolute prohibition with no exceptions, but then to have a theory of mitigation that operates after the fact.

I want to examine the implications of those two approaches to criminal law and see what their relevance is to international law in a case like Kosovo.

The penalty actually imposed on the defendants in *United States v. Holmes* was minimal. What the system sought to achieve was justice in the circumstances but to do so without creating specific exceptions to the law, exceptions which, it was feared, would open the doors to abuse. The reason for this approach, using ad hoc mitigation rather than principled exception, was fear of the slippery slope.

The United States courts, which operate in a much more highly developed legal system than is to be found internationally, were wary of creating an exception which any person finding themselves in straitened circumstances might apply too quickly as justification for selfish actions against others. This is all the more persuasive as a reason for not trying to develop a consistent international legal principle by which to permit humanitarian intervention. Such a principle is not difficult to formulate. For example, one might posit a rule borrowed from the criminal law of several States, that an illegal act should not be deemed illegal if it was committed to prevent the occurrence of a greater illegality. Vaughan Lowe has formulated what I think is the best and certainly a much more sophisticated set of possible exceptions that might be used to exculpate the use of force in a humanitarian intervention where the Security Council is blocked by the veto. Such principles have the advantage of seeming to justify the NATO action in Kosovo. Unfortunately, however, it would also leave each State free to interpret for itself whether circumstances, anywhere, had reached the level of a potential illegality greater than the illegality that would ensue from unilateral intervention. The world is simply not ready to adopt such a principle, whatever its theoretical merits.

It is primarily for that reason, not because, as Roth suggests, the United States wanted to keep a free hand for itself, that the United States chose not to follow the Belgian or Dutch examples by arguing that the Kosovo action was lawful humanitarian intervention. Whether to go down that path of exculpation was vigorously argued within the State Department.

The Department's choice was vindicated, I think, by the debates in the 1999 UN General Assembly. It soon became apparent that very few countries were ready to accept the Secretary-General's and the British Foreign Minister's invitation to try to formulate exculpatory general principles.

This does not mean that the international legal system is unable to apply a rational jurisprudential distinction between the NATO intervention in Kosovo, at one end of the legitimacy spectrum, and the Warsaw Pact's invasion of Czechoslovakia, at the other. Rather it means that the system prefers to keep in the hands of the political organs the delicate process of assessing the degree of a State's unlawfulness in engaging in an intervention. Or to put it in another way: the system prefers its response to depend primarily on extenuating facts rather than on legal exceptions to legal rules.

There is no inherent reason for such an allocation of functions, but there are practical reasons. These bespeak a certain modesty about the capacity of lawyers to draft narrow exceptions to rules that depend for legitimacy on their uniform application. Such modesty is especially appropriate when legal exceptions, if drafted and adopted, would be applied not by neutral judges but unilaterally by an intervening party. So it makes sense to leave decisions about mitigation to a sort of jury of peers – the Security Council and the General Assembly – acting in response to specific crises, rather than to codified law, especially a law applied not by judges but by the parties themselves. The politicians of the global system – the Security Council and the General Assembly – have demonstrated considerable wisdom in responding to arguments in mitigation of an unlawful use of force. They have done so case by case, either by defeating proposed resolutions of censure or even by ignoring attempts to lodge a complaint. This is true with respect to India's invasion of Goa, France's invasion of the Central African Empire, Tanzania's invasion of Uganda, Turkey's incursions into Iraq, Iranian incursions into Afghanistan, allied operations to protect Iraqi Kurds, west Africa's ECOWAS interventions in Liberia and Sierra Leone, and, of course, NATO's action against the Federal Republic of Yugoslavia. Each case was judged, not by automatic application of an invariable rule, but on the merits as perceived by the UN membership. Perhaps that jury has not always been wise, but it has usually avoided the law's *reductio ad absurdum*.

Hans Kelsen observed that the law requires a process that can convincingly categorize the use of force either as a delict or as a sanction. This distinction can be made either in a court of law or, lacking a judicial remedy, by any other legitimate expression of the sense of justice of the affected community. In the instance of NATO's action in Kosovo, the circumstances in which it occurred were explained in great detail to the political body representative of the community of States. The Security Council is not a perfect mirror of that community's values and modalities, yet the fact that it voted overwhelmingly not to condemn NATO's intervention is of procedural significance.

At some future time, but surely not yet, the world may feel confident enough about taking its stand on the slippery slope to agree to define precisely the circumstances in which humanitarian intervention would no longer be considered a violation of Article 2(4). To try now for such a redefinition without having previously legalized a process for applying it, is to invite a countervailing circling of the wagons in defense of an absolute non-intervention principle. Such a defense will brook neither a rule of exculpation nor a rule of mitigation, even in circumstances of demonstrable and extreme necessity. No matter how theoretically meritorious, the fight for a sensible exception to Article 2(4) cannot be won in present circumstances. It should therefore not be started, not even for the most theoretically compelling reasons and admirable purposes.

Turning to Marcelo Kohen's chapter, is the United States' use of military force against the Taliban and al-Qaida in Afghanistan lawful under the United Nations Charter? In a recent editorial comment in the *American*

Journal of International Law,[1] I responded as follows to six propositions assayed by some of the participants at the Göttingen conference to demonstrate the alleged illegality of United States recourse to force.

(1) It violates the Article 2(4) of the Charter prohibition against use of force except when authorized by the Security Council under Chapter VII.

(2) Self-defense is impermissible after an attack has ended; that is, after 11 September 2001.

(3) Self-defense may be exercised only against an attack by a State. Al-Qaida is not the government of a State.

(4) Self-defense may be exercised only against an actual attacker. The Taliban are not the attacker.

(5) Self-defense may be exercised only "until the Security Council has taken measures necessary to maintain international peace and security." Since the Council took such measures in Resolution 1373 of 28 September 2001, the right of self-defense has been superseded.

(6) The right of self-defense arises only upon proof that it is being directed against the actual attacker. The United States has failed to provide this proof.

The action violates Article 2(4) of the Charter

It does not.

While Charter Article 2(4) prohibits the unilateral use of force, the prohibition must be read in the context of Article 51, which recognizes "the inherent right of individual or collective self-defense if an armed attack occurs against a Member of the United Nations." This provision was included in the Charter because the drafters feared that the system of standby collective security forces envisaged in Article 43, to be deployed by the Security Council, might not come into being and that, accordingly, States would have to continue to rely on their "inherent right" of self-defense. That concern was well founded. Article 43 languished and no standby force was ever created, let alone deployed against any of the approximately two hundred armed attacks that have taken place since 1945, leaving States' security in their own hands and that of willing allies.

---

[1] Thomas M. Franck, "Terrorism and the Right of Self-Defense" (2001) 95(3) *American Journal of International Law* 839. The editorial comment is reproduced here, as the second part of Professor Franck's commentary, with the permission of the American Society of International Law.

This interpretation accords with Charter practice. A unanimous resolution, passed the day after the attack on the United States, put the Security Council on record as "recognizing the inherent right of individual or collective self-defense in accordance with the Charter," while condemning "in the strongest terms the horrifying terrorist attacks which took place on 11 September 2001."[2]

The resolution recognizes a right to respond in self-defense, but it does not – and legally cannot – authorize its exercise since that right is "inherent" in the victim. Under Article 51, self-defense is a right exercisable at the sole discretion of an attacked State, not a license to be granted by decision of the Security Council. How could it be otherwise? Were States prohibited from defending themselves until after the Council had agreed, assuredly there would not now be many States left in the United Nations Organization.

It is true that the International Court of Justice has ruled that the claim of a right to use force in self-defense must be supported by credible evidence of an armed attack and of the attacker's identity.[3] However, while the production of such evidence is essential to sustaining the right, that emphatically is not a condition precedent to its exercise. This does not leave the field open for bogus self-defenders. Were a State to attack another while falsely claiming to be acting in self-defense, that would constitute an "armed attack" under Article 51 or "aggression" under Article 39, giving both the victim and the United Nations the right to respond with appropriate levels of individual or collective force (see item 6, below).

Self-defense is impermissible after an attack ends

There is nothing in either the *travaux préparatoires* or the text of the Charter to justify this claim, which also defies logic. The assertion that self-defense requires "immediate" action comes from a misunderstanding of the *Caroline* decision, which deals only with anticipatory self-defense. In any event, Osama bin Laden has specifically promised to continue attacks on the United States.

---

[2] SC Res. 1368 (11 Sept. 2001) (emphasis omitted). UN resolutions are available online at http://www.un.org.
[3] *Military and Paramilitary Activities in and Against Nicaragua (Nicaragua v. United States)*, Merits, 1986 ICJ Reports 14, 119–21, 127, paras. 230–4, 248–9.

Self-defense is only exercisable against state acts

Al-Qaida is not a State. Nonetheless, the actions taken against the United States on 11 September 2001 were classified by Security Council Resolution 1368 as "a threat to international peace and security." That signifies a decision to take "measures . . . in accordance with Articles 41 and 42, to maintain or restore international peace and security." Such measures under Article 39 of Chapter VII were, in fact, taken sixteen days later.[4] It is inconceivable that actions the Security Council deems itself competent to take against a non-State actor under Articles 41 and 42 in accordance with Article 39 should be impermissible when taken against the same actor under Article 51 in exercise of a State's "inherent" right of self-defense. If the Security Council can act against al-Qaida, so can an attacked State.

This intuition is supported by the language of Article 51, which, in authorizing a victim State to act in self-defense, does not limit this "inherent" right to attacks by another State. Rather, the right is expressly accorded in response to "an armed attack" and not to any particular kind of attacker. That, evidently, is why Resolution 1368 reiterates the right of self-defense by a State specifically against "terrorist attacks" (para. 3). The Security Council clearly identifies "international terrorism . . . as a threat to international peace and security" against which "individual or collective self-defense" may be exercised.

Self-defense is only exercisable against an attacker

The 11 September 2001 attack was not launched by the Taliban. Does this make US action against that faction illegal?

The question is an important one that has long exercised international lawyers. In 1944, at Dumbarton Oaks, China included the following element in the definition of aggression it proposed to the conference preparing the draft Charter articles later presented to the San Francisco Conference: "Provision of support to armed groups, formed within [a State's] territory, which have invaded the territory of another State; or refusal, notwithstanding the request of the invaded State, to take in its own territory all the measures in its power to deprive such groups of all assistance or protection."[5]

---

[4] SC Res. 1373 (28 Sept. 2001).
[5] "Tentative Chinese Proposals for a General International Organization (23 August 1944)," *Foreign Relations of the United States*, 1 (1944), pp. 718, 725.

China's proposal was not adopted. More recently, the draft articles on State responsibility prepared by the International Law Commission make it clear that a State is responsible for the consequences of permitting its territory to be used to injure another State.[6] Security Council Resolution 1368 makes even clearer, in the context of condemning the 11 September 2001 attack on the United States, the responsibility for terrorism of "sponsors of these terrorist attacks" including those "supporting or harboring the perpetrators" (para. 3). The Taliban clearly fit that designation.

The right of self-defense is superseded after the Security Council invokes collective measures

Article 51 provides that the right of self-defense may be exercised by any State subject to an armed attack "until the Security Council has taken measures necessary to maintain international peace and security." In Resolution 1368 the Security Council recognized the applicability of this right in the context of the 11 September 2001 attack. However, on 28 September 2001, it invoked Chapter VII to require States to impose mandatory controls on the financing of terrorist groups, and to prohibit States from "providing any form of support" to terrorists. Does the imposition of these measures under Chapter VII supersede the attacked State's right to use force in self-defense?

It does not. After the Iraqi invasion of Kuwait, the Security Council, as in the instant case, affirmed the inherent right to use force in individual or collective self-defense.[7] When, almost four months later, it authorized UN members "to use all necessary means" to repel the Iraqi forces,[8] that resolution reaffirmed the Security Council's earlier affirmation of the victim's right to act in self-defense, clearly implying that Chapter VII measures taken under Security Council authority could supplement and coexist with the "inherent" right of a State and its allies to defend against an armed attack (Art. 51). This serves to give Article 51 the sensible interpretation that a victim of an armed attack retains its autonomous right of self-defense at least until further collective measures authorised by the Council have had the effect of restoring international peace and security.

---

[6] International Law Commission, "State Responsibility: Titles and Texts of the Draft Articles on Responsibility of States for Internationally Wrongful Acts Adopted by the Drafting Committee on Second Reading, General Principles," pt. 1, Arts. 9, 11, 21, and pt. 2, Arts. 40, 49, 52, UN Doc. A/CN.4/L.602/Revs.1, 2 (2001).

[7] SC Res. 661, preamble (6 Aug. 1990).   [8] SC Res. 678, para. 2 (29 Nov. 1990).

The same pattern of authorization was followed more explicitly by the Security Council in invoking mandatory measures under Chapter VII on 28 September 2001. This time, the resolution specifically reaffirmed "the inherent right of individual or collective self-defence as recognized by the Charter of the United Nations as reiterated in Resolution 1368 (2001)."[9] That the Council, in invoking collective measures, should ensure that these not be construed as rescinding the "inherent" right of self-defense is hardly surprising, since these new measures mandated on 28 September 2001, useful as they might be, clearly were not intended by themselves to deal decisively with the threat to international peace and security posed by al-Qaida and its Taliban defenders.

It is a *reductio ad absurdum* of the Charter to construe it to require an attacked State automatically to cease taking whatever armed measures are lawfully available to it whenever the Security Council passes a resolution invoking economic and legal steps in support of those measures.

The United States has not provided proof

Resolution 1368, in "recognizing" the right of the United States and its allies to use force against what was deemed, clearly, to be an "armed attack" within the meaning of Article 51, and also in recognizing that those who "harbor... the perpetrators, organizers and sponsors of these acts" are accountable for them, did not specify either the attacker or those who harbored them. In the absence of such clear identification of the perpetrator and sponsor, what authority is there for the exercise of Article 51's "inherent" right of self-defense? Resolution 1373, too, fails to identify the wrongdoer. It applies mandatory economic, fiscal, and diplomatic sanctions against "persons" – defined as "those who finance, plan, facilitate or commit terrorist acts" – without defining which groups are included in the category. Some critics therefore assert that neither resolution specifically authorizes action against either al-Qaida or the Taliban.

This critique conflates two related, but separate, challenges. One is directed to the lack of factual evidence of al-Qaida's and the Taliban's culpability. The other argues that, in law, the right to use force in self-defense arises only after the evidentiary test has been met by proof accepted as adequate by the appropriate institutions of the international system.

[9] SC Res. 1373, above note 4, preamble.

Critics point out that the North Atlantic Council, the governing body of NATO, on 12 September 2001 authorized invocation of Article 5 of its charter – which states that an armed attack on one member shall be regarded as an armed attack on all – subject to the evidentiary caveat, "if it is determined that this attack was directed from abroad against the United States."[10] Even if this condition correctly interprets the intent of NATO's 12 September 2001 decision, it is apparent that the evidentiary test has been satisfied. On 1 October 2001, NATO Secretary-General Lord Robertson reported that the United States had presented to the North Atlantic Council "compelling" and "conclusive" evidence that the attacks were the work of al-Qaida, protected by the Taliban, and that invocation of Article 5 was therefore "confirmed."[11] Only at this point did the US military response, supported by the NATO allies, begin to be implemented.

Does this imply that the Security Council must similarly vote its acceptance of US evidence? There is not a scintilla of evidence to this effect in either the *travaux* or the text of Charter Article 51. Rather, the "inherent right" being preserved in Article 51 is clearly that of a victim State and its allies, exercising their own sole judgment in determining whether an attack has occurred and where it originated. Security Council Resolutions 1368 and 1373, while deliberately expanding the definition of what constitutes an attack and an attacker, in no way tried to take this discretion away from the victim State.

This reading of Article 51 does not mean that the question of evidence is irrelevant in law. It does mean, however, that the right of a State to defend itself against attack is not subordinated in law to a prior requirement to demonstrate to the satisfaction of the Security Council that it is acting against the party guilty of the attack. The law does have an evidentiary requirement, but it arises after, not before, the right of self-defense is exercised. Thus, if a State claiming to be implementing its inherent right of self-defense were to attack an innocent party, the remedy would be the same as for any other aggression in violation of Article 2(4). The innocent party would have the right of self-defense under Article 51, which is exercisable at its sole volition. It could also appeal to the Council to institute collective measures against its attacker under Chapter VII.

---

[10] NATO Press Release (2001) 124, Statement by the North Atlantic Council (12 Sept. 2001). NATO press releases and speeches are available online at http://www.nato.int.

[11] Statement by NATO Secretary-General, Lord Robertson, Brussels, Belgium (2 Oct. 2001).

Any other reading of Article 51 would base the right of self-defense not on a victim State's "inherent" powers of self-preservation, but upon its ability, in the days following an attack, to convince the fifteen members of the Security Council that it has indeed correctly identified its attacker. As a matter of strategic practice, any attacked State is very likely to make an intense effort to demonstrate the culpability of its adversary, limited only by inhibitions regarding the operational effect of sharing intelligence methods. As a matter of law, however, there is no requirement whatever that a State receive the blessing of the Security Council before responding to an armed attack. Were this not so, how many States would deliberately agree to subordinate their security to the Council's assessment of the probity of the evidence on which they based their defensive strategy of self-preservation?

Jochen Abr. Frowein

I fully agree with Marcelo Kohen that the United States has argued self-defense in many cases where it could not be argued in any way: Panama, Grenada, the bombing of Libya after the Berlin incident. However, this should not prevent us from discussing in detail the differences between those instances and what happened on 11 September, so as to determine whether we are in a self-defense situation.

Let me first say that in this respect dimension plays a role. If thousands of people are killed within one hour in the center of one of the member States of the United Nations it is very clear that this is something completely different from the situations mentioned above. The International Court of Justice in the *Nicaragua* case, when discussing the sending of armed bands, raised the dimension issue by putting forward a qualification: "if such an operation, because of its scale and effects, would have been classified as an armed attack...had it been carried out by regular armed forces."[12]

Nobody can argue that the events of 11 September would not be called an armed attack if it could be proved that a State was behind them. Of course, we are not yet clear in this respect. The possibility is not excluded that one day we will find out that there was more State involvement, but we

---

[12] *Nicaragua Case*, Merits, (1986) ICJ Reports 14 at 103.

cannot take this as evident at the moment. What is clear is that the people responsible were based in the territory of Afghanistan.

The Security Council did not say that what should be done or could be done or was in fact done was covered by self-defense. But after it formally quoted the right to self-defense in two resolutions, it is impossible to argue that it did not see self-defense as relevant in this specific situation. Of course, the Security Council did not have to deal with details, nor indeed with proportionality issues. But I think it is very important and legally relevant that the Security Council cited the right to self-defense.

In this respect I clearly separate my position from that taken by Kohen. It is not sufficient to say that the Security Council reserved its position as to whether self-defense could play a role. By including it in the two resolutions, the Security Council recognized that self-defense plays a role in that context. This does not, of course, terminate the issue. What is the situation concerning self-defense in the case of a terrorist threat coming from a specific territory without clear proof that the territorial State is directly involved?

The international community has recognized several times that States have a formal obligation to prevent any terrorist threats arising from their territory. It is clear that the Taliban government of Afghanistan failed to fulfill this important obligation. Does that give the United States the right to act in self-defense against the country? I have argued before that, where a terrorist threat of such a dimension exists and the State refuses to deal with it, and where there is a real threat to the territory of the acting State, a good argument could be made for the use of self-defense against the territory of the first State. I would hope that when all the facts are clear we will see that the response of the United States is covered by that rule.

Let me now make a few remarks concerning authorization by the Security Council. Such an authorization could have been the solution after 11 September, though of course it was not sought by the United States. As in many previous cases, the United States preferred unilateral action. Legally speaking, it is not easy to criticize that preference because, if my general approach is correct, this avenue was open to the United States.

However, authorization by the Security Council has become a very important phenomenon. The United States and Britain have dealt a severe blow to the functioning international community in the United Nations system by unilaterally interpreting Security Council resolutions as justifying the use of force when it is clear from the wording and from the discussion in the Security Council that the other members did not wish to include such a justification. I am referring here to the no-fly zones, and particularly to the use of force against Iraq after the adoption of several resolutions concerning weapons inspections.

There was one very particular case where several of the members of the Security Council confirmed during the debate that the resolution would not provide the right to use force unilaterally. Immediately after the resolution had been adopted, the president of the United States, at that time Bill Clinton, went on record as saying that the resolution did not terminate the right of the United States to use armed force unilaterally on the basis of the old resolutions. In this respect I am in agreement with the criticism contained in Kohen's chapter.

Let me also make a comment concerning *ex post facto* authorization by the Security Council. I admit that it is impossible to argue that *ex post facto* authorization can play the same role as authorization provided before force is used. However, I do believe that *ex post facto* authorization by the Security Council is not at all legally irrelevant. No member of the Security Council, and probably not the UN as an organization, could after such a resolution argue that the use of force was unlawful. Several of the cases we have witnessed are really quite telling. What the Security Council did in these cases was finally to come to the conclusion that the use of armed force did not require its formal authorization. If that is the outcome, this is of great legal relevance for any analysis of the situation.

Let me finally make a short remark concerning the humanitarian intervention issue with which Thomas Franck has dealt with in depth. We are in a dilemma here which we are unable to resolve. The Secretary-General of the United Nations, Kofi Annan, has well described this dilemma in his interventions concerning the situation in Rwanda. Could one really argue that international law does not permit a unilateral armed intervention that is limited to the bombing of a bridge which separates two parts of a country when it is clear that the bombing will prevent the slaughter of human beings on one side? I think it is difficult not to come to the conclusion that under such circumstances one could claim a sort of extreme necessity. However, there are very few cases which are as clear as this one, hence the dilemma. I argued at the time that the Kosovo intervention could be justified as an emergency measure under specific conditions, while criticizing some of the targeting involved. I still believe that the principle of intervention to avoid genocidal action in itself can be defended.

Daniel Thürer

When I first read the title of this symposium, an earlier exchange on this issue sprang to my mind. Some years ago, Pierre Pescatore, a famous former judge at the Court of Justice of the European Communities, gave me a book written by Heinrich Triepel in the 1930s entitled *Die Hegemonie*. Pescatore advised me to read it, noting that "it might already be or soon become relevant again in the rapidly changing law of the international community." I now ask myself whether the book's thesis has indeed become relevant again with the emergence of US predominance in international law after the end of the Cold War.

Another beautifully written book also came to mind: *L'empire et les nouveaux barbares – Rupture Nord–Sud* by Jean-Christophe Rufin, a French writer and doctor.[13] Rufin starts with the observation that the fall of the Soviet Empire as "the enemy on which we counted in the Western World for forty-five years to terrorise us plunged our democracies into a deep melancholy." He recalls the image of Cato who looked over the ruins of Carthage knowing that Rome, having lost its longstanding adversary, had to rethink its way in "the face of the void." Rufin concludes his book with images of "three futures."

The first future, represented by the emperor-philosopher Marcus Aurelius, is the world of the "Limes," the large fortification running through Germany separating the Roman Empire from the outside world. According to this vision, the universal principles of law, justice, and freedom should be cultivated within the "Limes" and the outside world of the barbarians kept at a distance by means of arms. Aurelius' vision of the world was a "pact" between (internal) justice and (external) security. Justice, liberty, and prosperity were to be protected by way of isolation in a divided world.

The second future is represented by Kléber, General of the Armies of the French Revolution and First Consul in Egypt, for whom nothing was distant, who felt the same proximity everywhere, who saw no limits between

---

[13] Jean-Christophe Rufin, *L'empire et les nouveaux barbares – Rupture Nord–Sud* (Paris 1991), pp. 225 ff.

territories and peoples and who was an universalist accepting the idea of a "democratic imperialism." For Kléber there was no conquest without fraternity, no security without justice. He would have rejected the vision of a "Limes" between north and south. He would have extended democracy to the south, and he would have gone south. Kléber was assassinated in Cairo.

The third future is represented by Roman von Ungern, a former tsarist officer who, defeated by the Red Army, took up a lonely fight against the Bolsheviks. His aim was to conquer Moscow, which for him symbolized a cold machine of economic power. Moscow, like ancient Rome and Constantinople, would fall before the vigor of heroic fighters for freedom. Roman von Ungern died, abandoned, on the Mongolian steppes.

I would like to limit my observations on the chapters written by Brad Roth and Marcelo Kohen to three points that are central to our theme: humanitarian intervention, self-defense (the case of Afghanistan) and the applicability of humanitarian law in both situations.

Humanitarian intervention

I agree with Brad Roth, who rejects the positivist, formalist view that so-called humanitarian interventions should be considered illegal simply because this justification for the use of force is not mentioned in the text of the UN Charter. I share his view concerning what he calls "moralistic positivism" because I think that the international legal order, as it has evolved and "matured" to date, offers ways to avoid appeals to extra-legal, moral conceptions against positive law. Solutions to the dilemma of choosing between formal legality and substantive justice may be found *within* the international legal order, when it is understood as an all-embracing, comprehensive, structured legal system.

I further agree with Roth that the dilemma of the legality of so-called humanitarian intervention should be dealt with methodologically, that is by interpreting the Charter in a teleological way. The starting point of our interpretation is that the Charter provisions concerning the system of collective security should be followed according to their clear meaning. As Roth correctly observes, the provisions reflect and represent a plurality of views on fundamental questions of political order and justice that must be taken into consideration. There are, however, fundamental principles and values underlying the system, the violation of which cannot be tolerated, and there must be means to prevent the Security Council veto from being manifestly abused.

I share Roth's opinion that it should not be left to the judgment of the "strong" to define within their sphere of responsibility whether a humanitarian intervention is justified. The temptation would be irresistible to allow the power politics of the pre-Charter era to return to modern international law under the cloak of morality. Rather, substantive criteria and authorization procedures should be elaborated in order to permit humanitarian interventions in exceptional circumstances. These should be followed up in a principled way by organs of the international community as trustees of its common interest.

I wonder whether the basic values that I mentioned might not be defined, *inter alia*, with reference to international crimes as listed in the statutes of the ad hoc tribunals for the former Yugoslavia and Rwanda and the International Criminal Court. We may also want to consider the following question. When we talk about the basic values underlying the system of international law, and about the implicit structural ambiguities and tensions, would it not be natural to take a "constitutional" approach to interpretation? A constitutional lawyer would be quite familiar with the concept of "implicit" law as well as with methods of weighing up the "stakes" (values and interests) involved and the means contemplated for their implementation. It seems to me that Roth supports this idea in the "third approach" mentioned in his analysis. I would like, generally, to introduce into our discussion "constitutionalism" as a concept and method for understanding and interpreting the purposes and structure of international law as a whole.[14]

Self-defense

Many difficult problems arise in this context: were the terrorist attacks of 11 September acts of "use of force" as prohibited by Article 2(4) of the UN Charter or simply acts of violence falling within the ambit of the domestic law of the United States? In other words was international law at all applicable in this situation?

Assuming that the attacks fall within the Charter's ambit, other problems arise. I discussed them with a journalist, one of those "outsiders" who pose

---

[14] For more details, see my article "Der Kosovo-Konflikt im Lichte des Völkerrechts: Von drei – echten und scheinbaren – Dilemmata" (2000) 38 *Archiv des Völkerrechts* 1.

better questions than those experts who have become prisoners of their own way of thinking. The journalist wondered why it was not up to the Security Council, acting under Chapter VII, to determine whether force should be used. I replied that the Security Council was indeed entrusted by the UN's "Founding Fathers" with the primary responsibility for maintaining international peace and security, and, according to Security Council practice, this case would naturally fall within its competence. Harboring terrorist groups acting abroad constitutes a threat to international peace and security, as Marcelo Kohen reminds us. But the Security Council did not authorize, in either Resolution 1368 or Resolution 1373, enforcement measures within the system of collective security. The reason for this, I explained, was that the United States wanted to preserve its freedom to maneuver, to act on its own.

The journalist asked whether the armed measures undertaken by the United States were not properly classified as reprisals. I replied that from their very nature they might be, but they were not, because armed reprisals are prohibited in international law. I referred to the Friendly Relations Declaration of 1970 and the Helsinki Final Act of 1975.

Finally, the journalist wondered whether it was correct to characterize the US armed measures as self-defense, as had been done by the United States, NATO, and the EU Council, though not expressly by the Security Council (which in Resolutions 1368 and 1373 merely recognized the inherent right of self-defense as exercised "in accordance with the Charter"). I replied that this characterization depends on two assumptions.

The first assumption is that the sole fact of harboring terrorists in its territory makes a State responsible for (indirect) aggression; in other words that the term "armed attack" and thereby the concept of "self-defense" are broadly interpreted so as to include support, assistance, or endorsement of terrorism by the relevant State in a way still to be defined. Second, the US armed activities can be classified as acts of preemptive self-defense, which would not be the case according to the "Webster formula" (i.e. an armed attack is under way and the unavoidable, immediate reaction is to seek to repel it), as I learned in Cambridge many years ago from Derek Bowett.

The characterization of the US armed measures as self-defense is, in short, legally questionable.[15] The self-defense characterization is also worrying

---

[15] For a more detailed discussion, see Christian Tomuschat, "Der 11. September und seine rechtlichen Konsequenzen" (2001) *Europäische Grundrechte Zeitschrift* S. 535–45.

when viewed as a possible precedent. Marcelo Kohen ably demonstrates that the United States has long sought to develop a very wide and extensive understanding of self-defense. I share his concern that such a broad license to use force unilaterally may open the door for abuse. State practice should be taken into account, however, as a formative factor in the development and evolution of international law, especially when we are confronted with questions of a "constitutional" nature. Although there were hardly any voices to be heard in the international community condemning the US acts as illegal, it is vital that criteria and procedures be developed at the international level to circumscribe this concept.

International humanitarian law

The United States and Afghanistan are bound by the rules of international humanitarian law. More precisely, they are bound by the four Geneva Conventions of 1949, which were ratified by both States. The two Additional Protocols of 1977 to the Geneva Conventions are not binding as such in the present conflict because the United States has not (yet) ratified them. The principles and rules of existing customary international law are, however, reflected in the Protocols and of universally binding force.

The aim of the principles and rules of international humanitarian law is to limit the choice of means and methods of waging war and to protect persons who do not or no longer participate in the conflict.

Is international humanitarian law applicable to the terrorist attacks of 11 September and to the armed offensive launched by the United States and its allies against the territory of Afghanistan?

As far as the terrorist acts of 11 September are concerned, the question arises whether they should qualify as an international armed conflict. In my opinion, the answer is no. To be sure, we are confronted with acts of force, the airplanes having been used like bombs. But an international armed conflict requires the opposition of two or more States, and the sort of terrorist organization that is suspected of having committed the attacks could hardly be considered an agent of the State of Afghanistan. The ad hoc criminal tribunal for the former Yugoslavia expressly stated that an "international armed conflict" exists whenever there is a resort to armed force between States. In addition, in order for a situation to qualify as an armed conflict, there must, it seems to me, exist sustained belligerent activities over a certain time span. That was not the case in this situation.

The consequences of assuming that international humanitarian law is applicable would be enormous. For example, the US Defense Department could arguably be treated as a military target and would as such be a legitimate object of attack. The possibility of this would be limited, of course, by other principles such as the principle of proportionality. Using the criteria, however, that were invoked by the United States during its air raids on Yugoslavia, when economic infrastructure and even the enemy's morale were deemed legitimate military objectives, it is hard to imagine what sort of people and objects might be considered illegitimate targets under international humanitarian law. Certain principles generally recognized in times of peace, such as the "elementary principles of humanity," should be observed even more strictly in times of war.

As far as the armed offensive launched against Afghanistan is concerned, it seems clear to me that international humanitarian law was applicable. The Taliban, who at that time held effective control over most of the territory of Afghanistan and actually acted as the government, were not recognized internationally. But this does not mean that international humanitarian law did not apply, since the main aim of international humanitarian law is to regulate the conduct of hostilities and to protect its victims. The political issue as to the international recognition of the Taliban regime should therefore be left aside and the conflict between the United States and its allies and the Taliban considered an international armed conflict.

It follows that basic rules of international humanitarian law were applicable, for instance:

• that the parties are obliged to make a clear distinction between military objectives and combatants on one hand and civilians and property on the other;
• that the targeting of civilians and property is prohibited and that the parties are obliged to limit, as much as possible, collateral damage inflicted on civilians or property in their attacks on military objectives;
• that acts aimed at spreading terror among civilians are prohibited; and
• that protection should be given to those persons who do not participate or no longer participate in hostilities, for instance civilians, wounded combatants and prisoners of war. This protection also includes rules that prohibit the abuse and harm of these persons.

In conclusion, I return to Rufin's images of three futures. Similar to Roman von Ungern's challenge to Moscow, there are (fundamentalist) circles who at present challenge basic values of modern civilization. I would like the world to respond, but not with the vision of a "Limes between north and south" or a "world-wide apartheid" of Marcus Aurelius. Instead, the world should respond with the vision of the French General and First Consul Kléber, who called for cosmopolitan thinking, solidarity, and a universal rule of law based on human rights, democracy, and the ideals of common wealth.

As far as the rules on the use of force are concerned, international law has not been formally changed under the de facto hegemony of the United States, and it does not need fundamental reform, transformation or reinterpretation. However, a "constitutional" way of thinking or analyzing international law would facilitate our task of reconciling the international order's goals of maintaining peace and security with the fundamental values of justice in an international legal system comprising equal States. Textual formalism will not solve the problems at hand.

Open-ended legal or political licenses for the unilateral use of force are against the spirit and purposes of international law. There is no consensus in the international community as to the enlargement of the concepts of "attack" and "self-defense," which – if taken as a precedent to be followed by other (strong) States – would lead to a "law of the jungle." Instead, means must be found by which massive violations of human rights and other values forming the basis of the law of the international community may be "policed" by the powerful acting as "trustees." Procedural safeguards should be created, analogous to those of "Uniting for Peace," for the justification of the use of force within the framework of the UN General Assembly.

IV

Customary international law

10

Powerful but unpersuasive?
The role of the United States in the evolution of
customary international law

STEPHEN TOOPE

Contemporary societies are interdependent, some more dependent than others. They have been directed by governments that are themselves interdependent, whose role has been reduced – or at least redefined – and which are forced to act together to avoid being on the defensive. States have gone from being independent to being interdependent; they have to coordinate their actions. That has become so constraining that I sometimes compare this joint sovereignty to a tedious and interminable meeting of a tenants' association! But it is also a school in global democracy.

Hubert Védrine, former Foreign Minister of the French Republic[1]

The premise that underlies the prescient initiative of our two editors is that the United States, as the sole superpower in the post–Cold War era, is likely to play a preponderant role in the evolution of contemporary international law. Understanding the particular role of the United States is indeed crucial for students of contemporary international law and politics. I nonetheless argue that in the fundamental regime of customary law the assumption of preponderant influence is unwarranted. The United States is materially more powerful than any state has ever been. However, for reasons related to the complex identity of the United States, and to changes in our understanding of the creation and operation of customary international law, the United States is currently less influential in the elaboration of customary

I thank Sean Rehaag (McGill Law 2003) for his outstanding research assistance. As always, Jutta Brunnée, Rod Macdonald, and Ivan Vlasic have been challenging readers.
[1] H. Védrine (with Dominique Moïsi), *France in an Age of Globalization*, trans. Philip H. Gordon (Washington, DC: Brookings Institution Press, 2001), p. 8.

287

legal norms than is often presumed. Perhaps it is less influential than it should be, given its economic, military, and cultural weight.[2]

To be clear about what is at stake in this discussion, one must consider two contradictory views, each directed, I believe, at the same substantive end: the imposition of normative constraints even upon the most powerful members of international society. If the "rule of law" means anything,[3] it must imply the ability of a society to rein in the entirely self-interested impulses of the powerful. According to one view, customary international law can only fulfill its constraining function if we cling to a consent-based

---

[2] In attempting to evaluate the role of a uniquely powerful United States in the formation of contemporary customary law, I confront a significant methodological problem. There are simply not many data to go on. Throughout much of the twentieth century, until 1989, the United States participated in a system of world politics that most observers described as bipolar. See, e.g., J. A. Hall, *International Orders* (Cambridge: Polity Press, 1996), p. 117. Although that view was always overly schematic, it did capture the essential point that the United States was not a hegemon. It may have become an undisputed hegemon temporarily in late 1989 and 1990, but that "era" of unmatched and unchallenged power ended so quickly that it is hard to talk about any customary norms being created in that period. So we are left to assess the decade or so since 1990. Alternatively, we could pick other, earlier, dates as being more relevant to an assessment of US directive influence upon specific regimes. For example, in the regime of international trade, one might consider 1944 as the appropriate starting point for an analysis of hegemonic influence. Even this suggestion is open to challenge. See Hall, *International Orders*, at 119 and 146.

It may not even be useful to discuss such short historical periods when trying to assess the evolution of customary law. Despite the possibility of "instant" custom adverted to by Judge ad hoc Sorenson in the *North Sea Continental Shelf Cases* (*Germany v. Denmark; Germany v. The Netherlands*) (1969) ICJ Reports 3 at 43, most custom evolves over a relatively significant period of time. So whatever the role of the United States, to address the question of impact may be premature. I am reminded of the probably apocryphal story of the long-time Foreign Minister of China, Zhou Enlai, being asked in the late 1970s to evaluate the effects of the French Revolution. His response was that it was too early to tell. Nonetheless, given the importance of the topic assigned to me, preliminary reflections infused with modesty seem warranted. I will draw upon examples that extend back to before the end of the "bipolar" era, but will assess whether or not those examples are fundamentally shaped by the different construction of world politics that existed in the 1960s, 70s and 80s.

[3] Despite its mantra-like invocation in most writing on both international law and domestic legal development, the concept of the rule of law is typically underspecified. Its use often masks deep theoretical conflict. A. V. Dicey's rule of law (see, e.g., *Introduction to the Study of the Law of the Constitution*, 10th edn. (London: Macmillan, 1960)) is far removed indeed from the concept implicit in the work of Alexander MacIntyre (see, e.g., *Whose Justice? Which Rationality?* (Notre Dame: University of Notre Dame Press, 1988)). In a recent USAID study, the rule of law was equated with "market-based activity" (USAID, Center for Democracy and Governance, *Handbook of Democracy and Governance Program Indicators*, PN-ACC-390 (Washington: USAID, 1998), p. 19). Equating the rule of law with neoliberal economics is clearly ideologically driven, and would by no means receive universal support from even liberal-minded Western lawyers; see, e.g., B. Stern, "How to Regulate Globalization?" in M. Byers (ed.), *The Role of Law in International Politics* (Oxford: Oxford University Press, 2000), pp. 250–5.

theory of law formation that privileges the role of sovereign and equal States. For theorists in this tradition, the diversity of States is the last bastion against the overpowering influence of any single State or group of States, and the formal validity of law is the mechanism through which control is exercised upon the powerful.[4]

I see two substantial difficulties with this strategy. First, it reifies the State and undermines advances made in progressive areas of international law such as human rights and environmental protection. Second, and more relevant to the current topic, formal equality masks substantive in-equality in power relations. Contract theorists within domestic law have sought to equalize the bargaining power of formally equal but substan-tively unequal co-contractants through the elaboration of concepts such as the *contrat d'adhésion*, duress, or undue influence.[5] Similar problems need to be addressed internationally, but the doctrinal toolbox is barren of helpful implements. Explicit international bargains (treaties) often simply replicate the unequal bargaining power of state actors. Validity does not ensure real equality, and we have not imagined and built effective protec-tive mechanisms, aside from the blunt instrument of reservations against specific treaty terms.

An alternative view, one that I support, is to highlight the role that customary law can play in giving rise to norms that may not be supported by all powerful States, or even by the most powerful State. Custom, because the processes of its creation are relatively fluid, engaging the influence of individuals, non-state actors, and less powerful States (often joined together in venues created by intergovernmental organizations), can speak to the powerful in ways that explicit treaty texts typically cannot. But for this set of corrective processes to be engaged, we must uphold a view of customary law that does not require the continuing consent of every State and that recognizes that globally binding law can be formed even when a powerful actor dissents.

My argument is based on four interconnected elements. First, although we may be living in a classic "hegemonic" period, in a wide range of issue

---

[4] M. Koskenniemi, "Carl Schmitt, Hans Morgenthau, and the Image of Law in International Relations," in Byers, *The Role of Law in International Politics*, above note 3, pp. 32–4; and Stern, *ibid.*, p. 267.

[5] See J. Ghestin, *Les Obligations: Le Contrat* (Paris: Librairie Générale de Droit et de Jurisprudence, 1980) §§ 73–87 (contrats d'adhésion); G. H. Treitel, *The Law of Contract*, 9th edn. (London: Sweet & Maxwell, 1995), pp. 374–88 (duress and undue influence).

areas, including some at the very heart of its national interests, the nominal hegemon finds itself incapable of the domination that the descriptor would traditionally imply. Second, the US government and people are historically deeply ambivalent about the American role in world affairs. This ambivalence means that the United States rarely seeks to act as a hegemon, even when it can do so. When it does seek to exercise hegemonic influence, I will demonstrate that it fails surprisingly often. Third, customary law is now created in part through processes that do not require the unanimous and continuing consent of all States, even those most directly interested in a given norm. This development implies that the "persistent objector" rule is falling into desuetude.[6] In some issue areas, States find themselves bound by customary international norms even when they are clear in their opposition to the norm. Fourth, the role of *opinio juris* has been reconceived, so that the concept now serves to buttress the assertion that States can be bound by customary law to which they do not consent. Far from reaffirming US power, as some commentators fear,[7] developments in the way customary law is formed tend to undermine hegemonic influence. For all these reasons, the United States does not and cannot play a uniquely dominating role in the shaping of customary international law, even though its material power is preponderant in contemporary world society. This conclusion is separate from the question whether or not the United States is likely to comply with binding norms with which it is in disagreement, an issue that I will address in the final section of the chapter.

The ineffective hegemon

In recent writing with which I otherwise wholly disagree, Samuel Huntington offers a provocative description of what might be called the structure of contemporary global politics.[8] Huntington speaks of world politics as

---

[6] In a draft paper, Thomas Franck argues that international law should come to terms with the legal concept of desuetude. A rule can decay and die through lack of invocation and application ("Never Mind All That, Just Tell me Whether It's Legal," a paper presented at a workshop held at McGill University, 5–6 October 2001 (on file with author)).

[7] M. Byers, "The Shifting Foundations of International Law: A Decade of Forceful Measures Against Iraq" (2002) 13 EJIL 21–42 at 21.

[8] Though I resist "structural" explanations of social interaction, preferring the more complex understandings of mutual identity and interest construction articulated by sociology's "structuration theory," for present purposes the idea of a fundamental shift in the foundations of a regime is adequately captured by the "structural" metaphor. See A. Giddens, *The Constitution of Society* (Cambridge: Polity Press, 1984), pp. 2–3, 16–19, 22–28, 36, 83–87, 132–39, 162–65, 179–80 (for a detailed exposition of structuration theory). See also R. Bhaskar, *The Possibility of*

"a strange hybrid, a uni-multipolar system with one superpower and several major powers."[9] Not surprisingly, this view coincides with arguments put forward by leading European political figures.[10] If this description is accurate, it implies that there are few if any issues concerning which the United States can simply impose its will. US actions and initiatives require the engagement of "some combination of other major states."[11] A similar argument was recently put forward by Michael Reisman, who suggests that the United States can almost never "go it alone" in furthering important international objectives. Although US policy makers sometimes assume that the United States can rely on its own power, and can act unilaterally, this represents "a misunderstanding of the nature of international politics." Reisman posits that the overwhelming superiority of US power means that although the United States can sometimes control the "fate" of other international actors (an essentially destructive power), it cannot control "behavior" or compel action.[12] To accomplish even its most important goals, the United States is dependent upon its ability to persuade other actors of the need for cooperative engagement. This argument goes further than the obvious point that no State, however great or small, can accomplish all its objectives when acting on the margins of its power. The thesis here is that because of the current construction of global politics, the specific complex identity of the United States, and new understandings of the means of creation of customary international law, the US hegemon is precluded from effective dominance even in areas central to its perceived interests, and despite its overwhelming material power.[13]

One should be hesitant to draw premature conclusions from the preliminary United States response to the horrifying attacks on Washington and New York on 11 September 2001. Yet it is instructive to note that even when the clearest case of "national interest" is involved – the very security of the State and its citizens – the early US response was rhetorically bellicose, but

---

Naturalism: A Philosophical Critique of the Contemporary Human Sciences (Atlantic Highlands, NJ: Humanities Press, 1979).

[9] S. Huntington, "The Lonely Superpower" (1999) 78(2) *Foreign Affairs* 35 at 36.

[10] Védrine, *France in an Age of Globalization*, above note 1, at 1–15.

[11] Huntington, "Lonely Superpower", above note 9, at 36.

[12] M. Reisman, "A New Haven School Look at Sanctions," (2001) 95 *Proceedings of the American Society of International Law* 27. See also Hall, *International Orders*, above note 2, p. 169 (on the inability of the United States to slow down Chancellor Helmut Kohl's drive towards German reunification, despite strong US interests in placating a nervous Soviet Union).

[13] I thank Bob Keohane for a discussion that helped clarify this argument, though I do not seek thereby to associate him with my position.

practically cautious. Why was this so? It would appear to be largely because of the perceived need to build an effective coalition to address the scourge of global terrorism. Although the US military is independently strong enough to act, the realities of world politics demand cooperation and a high degree of coordination.[14]

The inability of the United States to act unilaterally even on fundamental questions of perceived national interest relates not only to the constraints of world politics, but to internal characteristics of the United States hegemon. As both John Ruggie and Andrew Hurrell have argued, any discussion of hegemonic influence must take into consideration not only the material aspects of power, but also the identity of the particular state one is considering.[15] Ancient Rome, sixteenth-century Spain, nineteenth-century Britain, and the contemporary United States could all arguably be classed as "hegemons," but their role in world affairs was shaped by their self-perceptions and the perceptions of other actors in a particular historical and cultural context. Hegemony requires not only material resources but the willingness to use them to maintain the "essential rules governing inter-state relations."[16] On this latter point, two tendencies come into play, one external to the United States, and one internal. The external factor is the reluctance of major powers (and even more so, the less powerful potential allies) to defer to the United States because they are unhappy with the *potential* for effective hegemony. On many issues there is active resistance to the United States, simply because it is the most powerful state today.[17]

---

[14] See P. Tyler and J. Perlez, "World Leaders List Conditions on Cooperation," *New York Times*, 19 Sept. 2001, A1.

[15] See J. Ruggie, "What Makes the World Hang Together? Neo-Utilitarianism and the Social Constructivist Challenge" (1998) 52 *International Organization* 855; and A. Hurrell, comments at a workshop on the United States and international law held at Duke University School of Law, 23–24 Feb. 2001 (on file with author). On "identity" as an issue relevant to state behavior, see P. J. Katzenstein (ed.), *The Culture of National Security: Norms and Identity in World Politics* (New York: Columbia University Press, 1996); J. Ruggie, "The Past as Prologue: Interests, Identity, and American Foreign Policy" (1997) 21 *International Security* 89; K. Sikkink, "International Law and the Construction of Identities and Interests of States," paper presented at a workshop at McGill University, 5–6 Oct. 2001 (on file with author); and A.Wendt, *Social Theory of International Politics* (Cambridge: Cambridge University Press, 1999).

[16] R. Keohane, *After Hegemony: Cooperation and Discord in the World Political Economy* (Princeton: Princeton University Press, 1984) at 34–5, quoting R. Keohane and J. Nye, *Power and Interdependence: World Politics in Transition* (Toronto: Little, Brown, 1977) at 44.

[17] See Huntington, "Lonely Superpower," above note 9, at 44–5; Stern, "How to Regulate Globalization," above note 3, at 259–60; and Védrine, *France in an Age of Globalization*, above note 1, p. 46.

Recent evidence of this resistance can be found in the decisions of world society to proceed with major initiatives despite the open and vehement opposition of the United States. Consider the agreement to move forward with the obligations of the Kyoto Protocol to the Framework Convention on Climate Change, the adoption of the Rome Statute for the International Criminal Court, the almost universal acceptance of the Ottawa Landmines Convention, and the opposition to the latest version of "Star Wars" (the so-called missile defense shield) even by the closest military allies of the United States.[18]

A poignant, if slightly comical, reminder of the extent to which resentment of United States hegemony has built up even amongst friends is the recent failure of the United States to be reelected to both the Human Rights Commission and the International Narcotics Control Board, subsidiary organs of the United Nations. These 2001 election results were utterly irrational, as the engagement of the United States is fundamental to the work of both the Commission and the Board. European allies appear to have quietly abandoned the United States, despite assurances of electoral support, representing a symbolic thumbing of the nose at an overbearing uncle.[19] This atavistic resistance to US power has significant implications for the capacity of the United States to shape or to constrain the development of customary international law. It is hard to persuade when your best friends are disinclined to listen. Willingness to resist on the part of friends is probably linked to the particular hegemonic identity of the United States, as Ruggie and Hurrell suggest. The United States is not a *ruthless* hegemon, at least as concerns its allies. It does tolerate significant dissent. As I will demonstrate below, the actions of close allies, even when they are contrary to the interests of the United States, are rarely punished.[20]

---

[18] These examples, and other cases where the United States seems to be profoundly out of step with an international consensus, are discussed in A. Simmons, "World's Only Superpower Sets Bad Example," *The [Montreal] Gazette*, 18 Aug. 2001, B5 (reprinted from the *Chicago Tribune*). Simmons is a senior associate at the Center for International Studies of the University of Chicago. See also M. Finnemore and K. Sikkink, "International Norm Dynamics and Political Change" (1998) 52 *International Organization* 887 at 901 (on the inability of the United States to stop a "norm cascade" in support of the Ottawa Landmines Convention).

[19] Nanda suggests that "These actions reflect rising discontent among our European allies with what they perceive to be the trend of US foreign policy toward isolationism and unilateralism." V. P. Nanda, "US caught napping at the UN," *The Denver Post*, 11 May 2001, 7B.

[20] An interesting example here is the conflict between New Zealand and the United States over New Zealand's anti-nuclear policy, which came to a head in the 1980s. When the New Zealand government refused to allow US warships into New Zealand territorial waters without a prior

It has been suggested, however, that a troubling pattern has emerged since the end of the Cold War, whereby major allies of the United States censor themselves, failing to criticize US actions for fear of antagonizing the hegemon. It is further argued that this failure to respond could lead to the crystallization of customary law promoted in large measure by Americans for Americans, at least in some important issue areas such as the use of force.[21] One's reaction to this argument, like the argument itself, must be based upon anecdotal evidence. I am simply not convinced that the posited deference to United States positions is accurate. Witness the series of cases, already noted, in which European and other allies have directly challenged the United States in very recent times. Perhaps more to the point, examples drawn from the use of force are, as is always the case when assessing the overall shape of international law, misleading. At their inception, the Iraq sanctions were widely supported, rightly or wrongly. They were not purely the creature of the United States. Over time, support has eroded, but the Security Council finds it hard to escape from its established position. This may be caused in part by US intransigence, but it is also affected by the isolation of the Iraqi regime. One cannot ignore the impact of long-term non-cooperation with UN mandated weapons inspectors upon the attitudes of a range of States. Iraq has not been successful in courting even tepid support, and this is not merely a function of United States power.

The Kosovo case is even more difficult to assess. Although the United States certainly pushed for NATO action, it would not be accurate to say that the NATO response was coerced. If one imagines oneself back to the time of the intervention, there was a widespread and legitimate fear of continuing and expanding human catastrophe. So-called humanitarian

declaration that the ships would not be carrying nuclear weapons, the United States refused to make such a declaration. A diplomatic crisis ensued that disrupted relations under the ANZUS Treaty (1951) 131 UNTS 85. Despite the important principle at stake, the US response to the New Zealand decision was muted. In the words of a former New Zealand deputy prime minister, "The suspension of the allied relationship is, I think for both countries, a matter of very real regret. But other aspects of our relationship with the United States remain very strong – certainly in the trade and economic sphere, in overall political and social orientation, culture and shared values." G. Palmer, "Settlement of International Disputes – The Rainbow Warrior Affair" (1989) 15 *Commonwealth Law Bulletin* 585 at 589. One might have expected that in a "bipolar" world this policy challenge from an ally would have been met with a harsh response, so as to discourage similar defections.

[21] Byers, "Shifting Foundations of International Law," above note 7, at 24–5.

intervention was being demanded by actors in civil society and by governments from a range of States. Again, the point is not whether or not this form of intervention is lawful or even appropriate. I merely question any assumption that the US government was the single motive force behind the NATO actions. Decisions related to the use of force often defy easy categorization, and this is one of the reasons why this area of the law is notoriously complex and contingent.[22]

One further contextual element that must be considered in any analysis of the role of the United States in the creation of customary law is that political changes in Europe continue apace. If the European Union gains influence through the processes of enlargement (which may depend upon its ability to cultivate faith in its institutional legitimacy among the peoples of Europe), it may serve as an increasingly powerful "anti-hegemonic" counterbalance, whatever the tendencies of the United States itself.[23] There is no doubt that this is the intention of leading European politicians.[24] When resistance to hegemony is linked to the internal self-perceptions of the United States, perceptions that foster disengagement or unilateral action rather than active multilateral diplomacy, the US capacity to persuade and influence is further reduced.

The United States' perception of itself in the world

It has become trite to suggest that the United States oscillates between periods of engagement and isolation in its international relations. The observation does not carry one very far, as it could be said of all States that political preoccupations change over time, and that international issues may be more or less engaging of elite and popular attention at various points in history. A more interesting argument concerns the tendency of the United States to lurch between isolation and *unilateralist* engagement.[25] This is

---

[22] D. W. Bowett, *Self Defence in International Law* (Manchester: Manchester University Press, 1958); I. Brownlie, *International Law and the Use of Force by States* (Oxford: Clarendon Press, 1963); T. M. Franck, "Who Killed Article 2(4)?" (1970) 64 AJIL 809; and Franck, "Never Mind All That," above note 6.

[23] Huntington, "Lonely Superpower," above note 9, at 45. See also Hall, *International Orders*, above note 2, p. 169.

[24] Védrine, *France in an Age of Globalization*, above note 1, pp. 43–54.

[25] See generally Ruggie, "Neo-Utilitarianism and Social Constructivist Challenge," above note 15. Sands argues that the most helpful way to understand resistance to unilateral action in

more to the point in any analysis of hegemonic power, for both ends of the continuum undermine the ability of the hegemon to persuade and to influence, the first because there is disengagement and the second because unilateralism generates resistance rather than cooperation. Since at least the 1970s, one can fairly conclude that the United States has not played "the multilateral game" very effectively.[26] With the advent of the new Bush administration, the United States seemed to be reentering a period with a tendency to selective isolation, or alternatively a period of selective unilateral engagement. No clear pattern had been established before the events of 11 September 2001, events that are likely to have altered policy calculations immeasurably.

Hegemony can only be exercised if the hegemon is willing to employ its overwhelming power. Throughout the latter part of the twentieth century, most Americans seemed to care little for the pressures and sacrifices that global leadership demands. Given the central importance of public opinion in shaping US government policy, public attitudes are worthy of attention. Huntington cites a 1997 survey in which only 13 percent of Americans polled preferred a "preeminent" role for the United States in world affairs, with 74 percent declaring that they preferred the United States to share power with other states.[27] On this score, it is instructive to recognize that the current mood of the American population to combat terrorism, seemingly at any cost, has yet to be tested. It took Pearl Harbor to draw a reluctant United States into World War II and it took a murderous attack on United States territory to galvanize the general will in favor of a concerted attack on global terrorism. But once the costs become apparent, in an era where the media broadcast "real time" images of death and destruction, it is not certain that the current unanimity of purpose within the US polity can be maintained. The broader historical pattern has been to shrink back from global leadership, even in cases of genocide or mass murder, as in Rwanda or Cambodia. This tendency can be explained in part by a desire to uphold

---

international relations is to reflect upon the extent to which unilateral action constitutes an imposition of values upon other actors. Philippe Sands, " 'Unilateralism,' Values, and International Law" (2000) 11 EJIL 291 at 295.

[26] E. Richardson, "The United States' Posture Toward the Law of the Sea Convention: Awkward but not Irreparable" (1983) 20 *San Diego Law Review* 505 at 507 and 511–12; and J. Ruggie, "The United States and the United Nations: Toward a New Realism" (1985) 29 *International Organization* 343 at 554.

[27] Huntington, "Lonely Superpower," above note 9, at 39.

US popular sovereignty.[28] With a huge internal market, a highly developed sense of national purpose, and a widespread faith in the emancipating power of the Constitution, many Americans see great risk to their own independence in any form of "globalization" that cannot be controlled. Even if globalization is seen by much of the rest of the world as "Americanization," from the shores of the United States it can seem to be a loss of control, if the only sure control is over internal markets, internal politics, internal security, and internal society. The largely United States-based discussion of an international "democratic deficit" is derived from strong commitments to US popular sovereignty.[29]

Yet there is a contradictory impulse in United States engagement with world affairs. Even if the United States rarely acts as an effective hegemon, many in the United States believe that it does. The self-perception of overwhelming military and economic power is transformed into a perception of inevitable political and legal influence, and immense frustration when that influence seems to be ineffective in promoting US goals. The perceived inevitability of US influence is often rooted in an assumption of American benevolence. Even Paul Kahn, a home-grown critic of the United States tendency to disengagement, succumbs to the comfortable but arguable assertion that "Today we face the unique situation that the world's hegemon, the United States, understands itself as a nation under law."[30] Kathryn Sikkink describes this assumption as one of the multiple identities of the United States.[31] While a commitment to lawful behavior may be dominant domestically, and US society is famously described as legalized and litigious, various military acts of the United States abroad show a different country. Here one need only recall the relatively recent invasions of Grenada and Panama, the US and British creation of no-fly zones in northern Iraq prior to any Security Council authorization, unilateral

---

[28] Paul Kahn, "American Hegemony and International Law: Speaking to Power: Popular Sovereignty, Human Rights, and the New International Order" (2000) 1 *Chicago International Law Journal* 1 at 2–6.

[29] See the wide-ranging and critical discussion in Gregory H. Fox and Brad R. Roth (eds.), *Democratic Governance and International Law* (Cambridge: Cambridge University Press, 2000).

[30] Kahn, "American Hegemony," above note 28, at 2.

[31] Finnemore and Sikkink, "International Norm Dynamics," above note 18, at 3. The self-perception of the United States as a law-abiding state would be especially salient if one adopts the definition of identity put forward by Fearon and Laitin: a social attribute "that an individual member either takes special pride in or views as . . . more or less unchangeable and socially consequential" (quoted in Finnemore and Sikkink).

repudiation of commitments made in international agreements such as the Kyoto Protocol, and the rejection by the United States of the decision of the International Court of Justice in the *Nicaragua* case.[32] My point in raising these examples is not to engage in all-too-common and unhelpful US-bashing. I simply want to suggest that there is a disjunction between the self-perceptions of many Americans (including US foreign policy elites) and how US actions are perceived outside the country, even by close allies. The current discussions over the proposed missile defense shield, and the unilateral decision to renounce the ABM Treaty,[33] are an excellent example of that disjunction.

We are left with conundrums. Whilst there may be a deep-seated assumption within the United States that it exerts benign hegemonic influence, an assumption grounded in a conviction of moral and material superiority, there is an equally powerful contradictory impulse to disengage in the name of self-interest and popular sovereignty. At the end of the day, this conflict commonly results in a lack of willingness to use material power unilaterally, with striking but rare exceptions. The United States typically seeks to coordinate action with at least some of the other "major," though decidedly lesser, powers. Increasingly these powers are not so willing to cooperate, with the exception, it seems, of the United Kingdom. There may be a hegemon in contemporary world politics, but it rarely acts like one. When it does, it confronts strong resistance, even from friends. That resistance, at least vis-à-vis allies, is rarely punished.

The failure to assert hegemonic power does not preclude cooperation or customary law creation

In his influential book *After Hegemony*, Keohane argued convincingly that international regimes can survive and grow in a post-hegemonic era.[34] In turn, such regimes can foster stability and cooperation. This argument overturned the previous commitment of "hegemonic stability theory" to

---

[32] *Military Activities In and Against Nicaragua (Nicaragua v. United States of America)*, (1986) ICJ Reports 14.

[33] *Treaty Between the United States of America and the Union of Soviet Socialist Republics on the Limitation of Anti-Ballistic Missile Systems* 23 UST 3435, TIAS 7503, reprinted in (1972) 11 ILM 784 (signed 26 May 1972; entered into force 3 October 1972). The ABM Treaty was formally denounced by President George W. Bush on 13 Dec. 2001. See D. Sanger, "Bush Offers Arms Talks to China as United States Pulls out of ABM Treaty," *New York Times*, 16 Dec. 2001, A6.

[34] Keohane, *After Hegemony*, above note 16, p. 16.

the idea that decay in the power of the hegemon would lead to the inevitable decay of a regime.[35] If one treats customary international law as a complex and multi-faceted regime, as Byers does,[36] then Keohane's insight can be extended to allow for the creation of new rules of customary law, and even for the evolution of the regime as a whole, in the absence of an effective hegemon. Indeed, in accepting that custom can be created without a hegemon, one might push further than Keohane, by arguing that the need for a hegemon in establishing regimes has never been adequately demonstrated outside the framework of monetary and trade regimes.[37] This could lead to the conclusion that the essential causal questions relate to the operation of regimes as independent variables, and do not require any reliance on hegemony as a tool of analysis.[38] Keohane himself points the way to this conclusion in his suggestion that the key target for analysis should be the "evolution of the norms and rules of a regime over time."[39]

Ikenberry and Kupchan tried to open up hegemonic stability theory to non-material explanations of behavior through their analysis of "socialization."[40] They suggested that three distinct processes of socialization occur within a hegemonic political system: external inducement (which is largely a material process), internal reconstruction and normative persuasion. From an international lawyer's perspective, the most intriguing

---

[35] S. Krasner, "Structural Causes and Regime Consequences: regimes as intervening variables," in S. Krasner (ed.), *International Regimes*, 1 (Ithaca: Cornell University Press, 1983). Hall doubts the value of hegemonic stability theory under any conditions. Hall, *International Orders*, above note 2, p. 83.

[36] M. Byers, *Custom, Power and the Power of Rules: International Relations and Customary International Law* (Cambridge: Cambridge University Press, 1999).

[37] See D. Snidal, "The Limits of Hegemonic Stability Theory" (1985) 39 *International Organization* 597 at 589–92; and S. Haggard and B. A. Simmons, "Theories of International Regimes" (1987) 41 *International Organization* 491 at 500–4. Hall even questions the description of nineteenth-century Great Britain as a hegemon, which would completely undermine even the trade-based arguments supportive of hegemonic stability theory. Hall, *International Orders*, above note 2, at 83–5, and 142.

[38] See generally J. Brunnée and S. J. Toope, "Environmental Security and Freshwater Resources: Ecosystem Regime Building" (1997) 91 AJIL 26.

[39] Keohane, *After Hegemony*, above note 16, at 64.

[40] Socialization is identified by many constructivist IR scholars as the principal mechanism through which identity change occurs. Socialization operates to prompt actors to internalize norms, so that external pressure is not needed to engender compliance. See M. Finnemore, "International Organizations as Teachers of Norms: The United Nations Education, Scientific and Cultural Organization and Science Policy" (1993) 47 *International Organization* 565; and T. Risse and K. Sikkink, "The Socialization of International Human Rights Norms Into Domestic Practices: Introduction," in T. Risse, S. C. Ropp and K. Sikkink (eds.), *The Power of Human Rights: International Norms and Domestic Change* (Cambridge: Cambridge University Press, 1999).

issue is the role of "normative persuasion." Risse and Sikkink include persuasion within a category of moral consciousness-raising.[41] In Ikenberry and Kupchan's approach to socialization, norms are articulated and promoted by a hegemon "to facilitate the construction of an order conducive to its interests." They are received by elites within "secondary states," who come to accept them "as their own."[42] But the Ikenberry and Kupchan analysis turns out to be of little value if there is no hegemon that is consistently willing to use its influence, or where there is significant resistance to that influence by other major players in a "uni-multipolar world." Moreover, they posit no explanation of why norms might turn out to be persuasive. They simply assert the cause and effect, and then admit that of their three processes of socialization, normative persuasion is the weakest. This comes as no surprise because they have never specified the pathway to normative influence. They would not be able to see results even if they were present.

Interestingly, in citing Weber and Habermas, Ikenberry and Kupchan do hint at the way in which norms may influence actors within regimes, but then they simply allow these insights to atrophy. Weber emphasizes that authorities typically do not limit themselves to "material or affectual or idea motives," but draw on all three to "establish and to cultivate the belief in [their] legitimacy."[43] Habermas argues that legitimacy depends upon the correspondence of values between the ruler and the ruled.[44] From these observations, Ikenberry and Kupchan conclude boldly that "It is the common acceptance of a consensual and normative order that binds ruler and ruled and legitimates power."[45] But in their explanation of socialization they then ignore both the interactive and legitimating aspects of norms. Indeed, normative persuasion is treated almost entirely as a unilateral projection from the hegemon, and legitimacy is turned into an unexplained "legitimate domination."

---

[41] Risse and Sikkink, "Socialization of International Human Rights Norms," above note 40, pp. 5, 12–15 and 38. On the importance of elaborating a theory of persuasion in international relations, see Finnemore and Sikkink, "International Norm Dynamics," above note 18 at 914–15. See also R. O. Keohane, "International Relations and International Law: Two Optics" (1997) 38 *Harvard International Law Journal* 487 at 494.

[42] G. J. Ikenberry and C. A. Kupchan, "Socialization and Hegemonic Power" (1990) 44 *International Organization* 283 at 283.

[43] M. Weber, *Economy and Society: An Outline of Interpretive Sociology*, I. G. Roth and C. Wittich (eds.) (Berkeley: University of California Press, 1978), p. 213.

[44] J. Habermas, *Legitimation Crisis*, trans. Thomas McCarthy (Boston: Beacon Press, 1975), p. 101.

[45] Ikenberry and Kupchan, "Socialization and Hegemonic Power," above note 42, at 289.

One can build upon the insight that regimes are not maintained or expanded purely as a result of material calculations by states, and that so-called "ideational" factors such as beliefs, principles, norms, and rules play an important role.[46] It is important to stress that these factors are not simply the results or "products" of a regime, but are variables in explaining its creation and maintenance.[47] In recent work, Brunnée and I have argued that the specific form of normativity known as international law is persuasive when it is viewed as legitimate, largely in terms of internal process values, and when, as a result, it can call upon reasoned argument to justify its processes and its broad substantive ends, thereby creating shared "rhetorical knowledge." Rhetorical knowledge does not directly cause identity or behavioral change, for it offers up reasonable arguments, not "truths."[48] But reasonable arguments are persuasive within contexts of shared basic understandings, and even more powerfully within the strictures of formal and informal institutions. When grounded in the specific rationality of law, a rationality rooted in practices of reasoned argument, reference to past social practice and contemporary aspirations, and especially the deployment of analogy, rhetorical knowledge seems to be especially salient.[49]

Whether one holds on to the hegemonic explanation of regime creation (perhaps incorporating non-material factors), or adopts a more complex view linking material and non-material factors in an interactive process of normative evolution, it is important to remember that neither hegemons nor regimes are inevitably benign.[50] Elites in the United States, and probably

---

[46] See generally F. Kratochwil, *Rules, Norms and Decisions: On the Conditions of Practical and Legal Reasoning in International Relations and Domestic Affairs* (Cambridge: Cambridge University Press, 1989).

[47] For such an approach see M. Finnemore, *National Interests in International Society* (Ithaca: Cornell University Press, 1996); Finnemore and Sikkink, "International Norm Dynamics," above note 18; and J. Brunnée and S. J. Toope, "International Law and Constructivism: Elements of an Interactional Theory of International Law" (2000) 39 *Columbia Journal of Transnational Law* 18 at 25–37.

[48] F. Mootz III, "Natural Law and the Cultivation of Legal Rhetoric," in W. Witteveen and W. van der Burg (eds.), *Rediscovering Fuller*, Essays on Implicit Law and Institutional Design 425 (Amsterdam: Amsterdam University Press, 1999), at 442–4. See also T. Risse, " 'Let's Argue!': Communicative Action in World Politics" (2000) 54 *International Organization* 1.

[49] See Brunnée and Toope, "Interactional Theory of International Law," above note 47, at 65–6 and 69–73.

[50] Haggard and Simmons, "Theories of International Regimes," above note 37, at 502; and Brunnée and Toope, "Environmental Security and Freshwater Resources," above note 38, at 33–4. Dominance can be exploited by the United States in entirely self-serving ways. Hall, *International Orders*, above note 2, pp. 148, 166 (on the United States' "predatory extraction" of capital,

most "ordinary" Americans, tend to assume that the influence of the United States, whether as hegemon or simply as *primus inter pares*, is generally positive and beneficent. But value-based policy goals, such as the promotion and protection of human rights or environmental protection, are inevitably clouded by material interests and by competing value-based goals, such as free trade and economic competition. The schizophrenic attitude of the United States (and many other Western states) to China is evidence of this complexity. So the benevolence of a particular normative argument is likely to be very much in the eye of the beholder, and good intentions may often yield to highly nuanced and less benign regimes.[51] Certainly, there are many around the world who suggest that the current global trade regime falls into this category.[52]

Change in the regime of customary international law

Byers, who remains committed to consent as the trigger for all binding obligations, worries that the existence of a hegemon will tend to obviate the need for the consent of "secondary or tertiary" states in the formation of the structures of international law.[53] This argument makes sense if one conceives of the institutions and structures of international law as resulting primarily from the imperatives of material power, as one might in an era of hegemony. But if there is no effective hegemon, and regimes can nonetheless persist and grow, then the very grounding of the regime might change over time. I suggest that the presence or absence of a hegemon has little impact today on the regime of customary international law (which one may view as a central international legal "structure"). The requirement of individual state consent in the formation of custom is far less powerful than was once the case, undermining the influence of even the most powerful State. What remains, of course, is the power to disregard the law or to break it. But this power should not be confused with a power unilaterally to remake the law.

Bruno Simma argues that international law as a whole is subject to increasing endeavors to "soften the edge of consent." He focuses upon

especially from Latin America, and on the "petty, self-interested and predatory manner" in which the United States sometimes exercises its leadership in global financial and economic matters).
[51] See Huntington, "Lonely Superpower", above note 9, at 37, and Kahn, "American Hegemony," above note 28, at 4.
[52] Stern, "How to Regulate Globalization?" above note 3, esp. pp. 255–61.
[53] Byers, *Custom, Power and the Power of Rules*, above note 36, p. 205.

consensus-based decision making in intergovernmental forums, and suggests that a "community consciousness" can displace individual consent in the formation of specific norms.[54] Ian Hurd proposes that the legitimacy, and therefore the effectiveness, of an international norm is not derived principally from consent, but from a subjective belief that a rule or institution ought to be obeyed. This sense of "ought" is built up in the relationship between the actor and the institution, when the actor comes to internalize the sense of normative legitimacy.[55] This explanation is close to the "socialization" process discussed briefly above. Jutta Brunnée pushes the argument a step further in positing that consent's role in international law is best analyzed within a framework of legitimation, rather than formal validity.[56] In other words, the "softening" of consent means that we need to persuade states to consent to a norm because that will lend greater legitimacy and effectiveness to the norm. But an absence of individual consent does not preclude the existence or application of a norm (its binding quality).

Note that this discussion has so far focused only upon specific norms, but it can be extended to groups of norms within the overall framework of customary international law. On the other hand, it could be argued that the image of the "softening" of consent may not apply to the constitutive rules of international society, because the very willingness to participate in regimes and institutions may still be signaled through a hard and formal version of consent. Yet even when considering the constitutive rules that shape membership of fundamental international institutions, States may not really be free to choose, as a strategic matter, whether to participate or not. Here Hurrell and Woods' notion that membership in international society, and particularly in institutions, is a constraining influence upon state identity and state choice is instructive.[57] Consent, even to constitutive rules, may be forced rather than free.[58] This is particularly true for actors

---

[54] B. Simma, "From Bilateralism to Community Interest" (1994) *Recueil des cours* 221 at 225–7.

[55] I. Hurd, "Legitimacy and Authority in International Politics" (1999) 53 *International Organization* 379 at 388.

[56] Jutta Brunnée, "COPing with Consent: Law-making Under Multilateral Environmental Agreements" (2002) 15(1) *Leiden Journal of International Law*) 1–52.

[57] A. Hurrell and N. Woods, "Globalisation and Inequality" (1995) 24 *Millennium: Journal of International Studies* 447 at 457 and 460–62.

[58] Stern, "How to Regulate Globalization?" above note 3, pp. 259–60. Indeed, Philip Allott argues that the participation of states in the regime of customary law is never a "voluntary act," and that states do not consent to be bound "as if by some specific act of the will." P. Allott, "The

who join the "game" after many of its rules have been established, as is the case for developing world states joining in the framework of customary international law. They may struggle to re-shape the "game," but they are fundamentally constrained in the attempt by an established set of expectations.[59] Taken together, these arguments call into question the continuing explanatory power of consent as the source of law's binding quality.

The previous observations should constitute anticipatory self-defense against the predictable accusation of naïveté leveled against all scholars who resist purely rationalist explanations of behavior. But I insist on one key point in adopting the defensive posture: I am not asserting that material power is irrelevant to an assessment of the power of international law. In different ways Byers, Kennedy, and Koskenniemi have each argued convincingly that like domestic law, international law is significantly affected, even conditioned, by constructions of material power.[60] I treat international law as only relatively autonomous from diverse forms of social power.[61] For example, it is likely that major powers will be able to contribute more substantially to the creation of custom than weaker States. The latter will lack the capacity to contribute to practice through acts, and may even fail to respond to the acts of stronger States.[62] A counterbalancing factor is the increasing recognition over the last forty years that statements can count as practice, that acts are not the only source of customary law. It is hard to imagine how any other position is now tenable, given the decision of the International Court of Justice that a mere oral declaration can itself amount to a binding commitment analogous to a treaty.[63] In such a world, consistent statements from a range of States must contribute to the formation of

Concept of International Law," in Byers, *The Role of Law in International Politics*, above note 3, p. 69, pp. 76–7.

[59] M. Sornarajah, "Power and Justice in International Law" (1997) 1 *Singapore Journal of International and Comparative Law* 28.

[60] See generally D. Kennedy, *International Legal Structures* (Baden-Baden: Nomos-Verlag, 1987); M. Koskenniemi, *From Apology to Utopia: the Structure of International Legal Argument* (Helsinki: Finish Lawyers' Publishing Co., 1989); and Byers, *Custom, Power and the Power of Rules*, above note 36.

[61] Brunnée and Toope, "Interactional Theory of International Law," above note 47, at 101–02.

[62] Byers, "Shifting Foundations of International Law", above note 7, at 19.

[63] *Nuclear Tests Case (Australia v. France; New Zealand v. France)* (1974) ICJ Reports 253 at 267–70. Allott goes further to suggest that "ideas" are a form of practice. Allott, "Concept of International Law," above note 58, at 77 ("The dialectic of practice which makes customary law includes ideas, but ideas as a form of practice. At any particular time, society's struggle of self-ordering takes the form of both a struggle of willing and acting and a struggle about theories, values, and purposes applicable to such willing and acting, including a struggle about what the law is and what it should be").

customary law.[64] The old debate over whether or not the declarations of the UN General Assembly have any law-creating capacity is no longer vital, and for good reason. What States say does count in the creation of custom, either as practice or as evidence of *opinio juris*, depending upon the context.[65] It is nonetheless true that the acts, omissions, and statements of weak States are unlikely even to be reported publicly; there are no digests of state practice for Zimbabwe or Vanuatu. But the interesting aspect of contemporary custom is that one must separate out the issue of aggregated power and the power held by individual States. This distinction is obviously important for our understanding of the role of the United States in the evolution of customary law.

In assessing the operation of customary legal norms, and even in understanding the functioning of the international legal tradition as a whole, the role of "cultural" and "ideational" considerations should not be undervalued.[66] Even Byers, who looks to material interests as the overriding explanation for state behavior,[67] acknowledges that a central element of

---

[64] Although the ICJ appears to back away from an independent normative role for "words" alone in the *Legality of the Threat or Use of Nuclear Weapons*, Advisory Opinion, (1996) ICJ Reports 26, §§ 64–73 (General Assembly Opinion); and *Legality of the Use by a State of Nuclear Weapons in Armed Conflict*, Advisory Opinion, (1996) ICJ Reports 66 (World Health Organization Opinion), this approach can probably be explained by the extraordinarily high degree of politicization of this decision. Contrasting a "nascent *opinio juris*" with a continuing and well-established pattern of practice took place in the context of deterrence. The Court refused to challenge the legality of deterrence, and its concomitant, mutually assured destruction (MAD), most probably because these doctrines have underpinned the entire postwar security structure. To question them directly would likely have resulted in the complete irrelevance of the Opinion. As it stands, the Court seems to limit the legal use of nuclear weapons to cases of "an extreme circumstance of self-defence, in which the very survival of the State would be at stake" (Operative § 105 (E) of the General Assembly Opinion). If "the State" is read to mean the people of the State, and not merely a given political regime, then this is a significant limitation on the legality of nuclear weapons, and the doctrinal discussion of words versus acts becomes a mere side-show.

[65] I therefore disagree with the idea that an emphasis upon practice as the primary indicator of custom represents "old custom" whereas a focus upon *opinio juris* represents "new custom." See Anthea Elizabeth Roberts, "Traditional and Modern Approaches to Customary International Law: A Reconciliation" (2001) 95 AJIL 757, at 758. I do not think that it is possible to draw a rigid distinction between action and statements. Given the reality of power differentials in the world, room must be left for States that are not materially powerful to "act" through statements. *Contra* A. A. D'Amato, *The Concept of Custom in International Law* (Ithaca: Cornell University Press, 1971), at 89–90 and 160.

[66] See generally H. P. Glenn, *Legal Traditions of the World: Sustainable Diversity in Law* (Oxford: Oxford University Press, 2000).

[67] S. J. Toope, "Review of *Custom, Power and the Power of Rules: International Relations and Customary International Law* by Michael Byers" (1999) *Canadian Yearbook of International Law* 480 at 482 and 486–7.

customary law formation, so-called *opinio juris*, is best understood as "a diffuse consensus, a general set of shared understandings among States as to the 'legal relevance' of different kinds of behavior in different situations."[68] Byers goes on to suggest that the shared understandings of what counts as legally relevant can change over time. Shared understandings are generated not only by formal state actors (diplomats, negotiators, and political leaders), but also by ever-broadening "interpretative communities" of experts and non-state actors and audiences.

Drawing on constructivist international relations (IR) theory and the interactional legal theory of Lon Fuller, I would extend this analysis to suggest that law as a whole is most instructively viewed as a process of persuasion, dependent upon shared perceptions of legitimacy.[69] Law must continually seek to foster the allegiance of social actors. Legal legitimacy, which is relatively autonomous from political legitimacy, is rooted in procedural fairness, the congruence between articulated norm and underlying social practice, and specific methods of argumentation, sometimes called the distinct rationality of law, a rationality particularly grounded in analogy to past practice.[70] So the persuasiveness of law is not appropriately measured simply through a calculation of the coordinated material interests of States, even if interests are viewed in a long-term perspective, as Keohane suggests that they must be.[71]

How does this concept of law relate to customary international law, and to the role of the United States in its articulation? First, customary law is primarily grounded in social practice – including acts, pronouncements and acquiescence – not explicit consent. I agree with Martti Koskenniemi and with Judge Tanaka in the *North Sea Continental Shelf* cases that custom is found primarily in practice, and that in the vast majority of cases, *opinio juris* simply serves the function of ensuring that practice will be weighed

---

[68] Byers, *Custom, Power and the Power of Rules*, above note 36, p. 19.

[69] See generally L. Fuller, *The Morality of Law*, rev. edn. (New Haven: Yale University Press, 1969); N. Onuf, *World of our Making: Rules and Rule in Social Theory and International Relations* (Columbia: University of South Carolina Press, 1989); and Kratochwil, *Conditions of Practical and Legal Reasoning*, above note 46.

[70] See generally T. M. Franck, *The Power of Legitimacy Among Nations* (New York: Oxford University Press, 1990); and Brunnée and Toope, "International Law and Constructivism," above note 47, at 53 and 64–71.

[71] Keohane, *After Hegemony*, above note 16, p. 45; A. Herbert, "Cooperation in International Relations: A Comparison of Keohane, Hass, and Franck" (1996) 14 *Berkeley Journal of International Law* 222 at 228.

with seriousness.[72] The sense of being bound emerges from the participation of States in the aggregated practice, and not from a fictitious state "intention." Indeed, intention is a distinctly unhelpful concept in any form of legal interpretation.[73] Second, and conversely, shared expectations of what counts as law can sometimes dislodge practice from its place of primacy in the formation of custom. This is because law can be "counterfactually valid," to borrow Kratochwil and Ruggie's useful phrase.[74] The possibility exists that in exceptional cases a strong *opinio juris* may emerge concerning a specific norm, and that this will draw out practice.[75] The aspiration towards law may lead sociological normative evolution.[76] Many aspects of modern human rights law serve as examples of this process at work.

On the other hand, practice, even when it is significant, can sometimes be nothing more than a breach of law. The many States that practice torture are not positing a contrary practice for the sake of changing a customary norm. They are breaking a rule that is otherwise inclusively supported. We know this because the practice of torture simply does not fit within a framework of analogy to other human rights norms. To argue that torture is an accepted practice because it is widespread is not a legal argument made in good faith. Indeed, it does not belong in the realm of legal argument at all. It is an assertion of the raw power of state authorities over victims, and is best equated with the oxymorons "apartheid law" or "Nazi law."[77] I do accept, however, that there does come a "tipping point" at which the evidence of contrary practice is so strong that a previously established legal norm can be displaced.[78] However, if the newly asserted norm does not arise

---

[72] M. Koskenniemi, "The Normative Force of Habit: International Custom and Social Theory" (1990) *Finnish Yearbook of International Law* 77 at 136; *North Sea Continental Shelf*, above note 2 (separate opinion of Judge Tanaka).

[73] Koskenniemi, "Normative Force of Habit," above note 72, at 87; Roberts, "Approaches to Customary International Law," above note 65, at 758 (arguing that *opinio juris* can only be understood as statements of belief rather than as actual belief); and N. Stoljar, "Intention in Legal Interpretation" (2000, unpublished manuscript on file with the author).

[74] F. Kratochwil and J. Ruggie, "International Organization: a State of the Art on the Art of the State" (1986) 40 *International Organization* 753 at 767.

[75] A. Skordas, this volume, below. See also O. Schachter, "Entangling Treaty and Custom," in Y. Dinstein (ed.), *International Law at a Time of Perplexity: Essays in Honour of Shabtai Rosenne* (Dordrecht: M. Nijhoff 1989), p. 717.

[76] See generally Fuller, *Morality of Law*, above note 69.

[77] *Ibid.*, p. 123.

[78] Franck, "Never Mind All That," above note 6; and Finnemore and Sikkink, "International Norm Dynamics," above note 18, at 901.

through legitimate procedure and if it can only attract allegiance through force, then I would dispute its quality as a *legal* norm.[79] Finally, because custom is primarily dependent upon accumulated practice and because some contrary practice can be tolerated without destroying a customary rule, the old rule of "persistent objection" is falling into desuetude.[80]

In its traditional formulation, the persistent objector rule seemed to fit neatly within a consent-based theory of law creation. The doctrine was essentially an escape hatch meant to allow the free operation of the principle of sovereign equality. Because it was always difficult to know exactly when state practice had solidified sufficiently to give rise to a binding customary rule (at which point *opinio juris* would be inferred), the existence of a rule was often subject to debate. Because there are only weak, and typically optional, mechanisms of third-party decision-making in international law, the dispute over the existence of a norm could remain unresolved for an extended period. To achieve some predictability, it was necessary to allow a normative consensus to emerge that would guide the relations of most States. But for those States in fundamental (or even strategic) disagreement with the "emerging" or "crystallizing" norm, the escape hatch could be employed: the new rule would exist, but would not bind the persistent objector.

Martti Koskenniemi argues that this understanding of persistent objection was always incomplete. In most cases, the thrust of the persistent objection was directed not at the application, but at the very existence, of the rule.[81] So persistent objection has always constituted a challenge to normative validity, rather than being a purely defensive posture. The consent requirement was reinforced and generalized. For this reason, the persistent objector rule is now the target of sustained attack. One source of attack is the invocation of *erga omnes* obligations. If the category of *erga omnes* obligations is characterized not merely by generality of standing (ability to act),[82] but by a duty to act, then the persistent objector doctrine is damaged fundamentally. A generalized obligation, not rooted in

---

[79] Brunnée and Toope, "Interactional Theory of International Law", above note 47, at 57–8.
[80] See generally J. Charney, "The Persistent Objector Rule and the Development of Customary International Law" (1985) 56 *British Yearbook of International Law* 1.
[81] Koskenniemi, "International Custom and Social Theory," above note 72, at 123.
[82] M. Byers, "Conceptualizing the Relationship Between Jus Cogens and Erga Omnes Rules" (1997) 66 *Nordic Journal of International Law* 211 at 230.

bilateral consensualism, cannot be dislodged by the unique will of the dissenting State.[83] A second, broader, attack emerges from the literature challenging the consent-based theory of law formation in its entirety. As that literature is invoked above, I need merely reiterate that any softening of the consent requirement undermines the doctrine of persistent objection considerably, perhaps fatally. Drawing upon examples of rule change from a range of customary law issue areas, I will now demonstrate that attempts by the United States to cast itself as a persistent objector often end in failure.

The clearest example of failed persistent objection is the attempt by the United States to prevent a change in the customary law concerning state jurisdiction over Arctic waters. In 1970, the Canadian Parliament passed the Arctic Waters Pollution Prevention Act.[84] The Act amounted to a unilateral extension of maritime jurisdiction 100 miles into the high seas, for the purposes of environmental protection. The essence of the Canadian claim was that the Arctic environment is especially fragile and vulnerable. Because the effects of a major contamination (particularly an oil spill) could be catastrophic, the coastal State must seize broad jurisdiction to prevent possibly irreparable harm. One can read this legislation as an inchoate "precautionary" claim.[85] The Canadian Act was immediately denounced by US officials.[86] Moreover, many heavyweights of the US international law community weighed in to claim that the Canadian legislation was an unacceptable attempt to change customary law unilaterally.[87]

Interestingly, the United States was the only state formally to object to the Canadian initiative. Even critics acknowledged that the Act was admirable

---

[83] J. Perkins, "The Changing Foundations of International Law: From State Consent to State Responsibility" (1997) 15 *Boston University International Law Journal* 433; Toope, "Review," above note 67, at 486–7; S. J. Toope, "Does International Law Impose a Duty Upon the United Nations to Prevent Genocide?" (2000) 46 *McGill Law Journal* 187; and E. Uhlmann, "State Community Interests, Jus Cogens, and Protection of the Global Environment: Developing Criteria for Peremptory Norms" (1998) 11 *Georgetown International Environmental Law Review* 101.

[84] RSC 1985, c. A-12 as am. (1970).

[85] P. E. Trudeau, "Canadian Prime Minister's Remarks on the Proposed [Arctic Waters] Legislation" (1970) 9 *Internatinal Legal Materials* 600.

[86] See T. Szulc, "US Rejects Canadians' Claim to Wide Rights in Arctic Seas," *The New York Times*, 10 April 1970, A13; and T. Wills, "US Won't Accept Canadian Claims over Arctic Waters," *The [Toronto] Globe and Mail*, 10 April 1970, A1.

[87] R. Bidler, "The Canadian Arctic Waters Pollution Prevention Act: New Stresses on the Law of the Sea" (1970) 69 *Michigan Law Review* 1 at 25–6; L. Henkin, "Arctic Anti-pollution: Does Canada Make or Break International Law?" (1971) 65 AJIL 131 at 134–5.

in its goal.[88] The Canadian government argued that it was not breaking international law, but "developing" it.[89] Although this argument was utterly disingenuous when made, it turned out to be true, and rather quickly so. Despite the persistent objection of the United States, the Canadian legislation, and reactions to it, accomplished a normative transition. By the time that states concluded the United Nations Law of the Sea Convention,[90] a generalized right of coastal States to exercise broad pollution prevention jurisdiction had been established. Moreover, Article 234 of the Convention provided for a special coastal state jurisdiction for pollution prevention extending 200 nautical miles in "ice-covered areas." Canada's claim had apparently been received by the vast majority of States as necessary and reasonable.[91] More provocatively, a number of high-ranking Canadian officials and leading commentators suggested that the objection of the United States had failed because it was patently self-interested, whereas the Canadian claim linked Canada's national interests to broader international interests in pollution control and prevention.[92] The United States came to be bound by a new customary rule, despite its persistent objections, because the rule quickly came to be seen as necessary and was widely supported.[93]

   A second salient example of failed United States persistent objection is also drawn from the law of the sea. Until 1988, the United States argued vociferously that the territorial sea of a coastal state could extend no further than three miles from the coast. Since 1921, when the USSR became the first state to claim a twelve-mile territorial sea, more and more states had adopted the twelve-mile rule. Clearly at some point long before 1988, the twelve-mile limit had crystallized, despite United States persistent objection.[94] It

---

[88] Henkin, "Arctic Anti-pollution," above note 87, at 135.
[89] Canada, "Canadian Reply to the US Government" (1970) 9 *International Legal Materials* 607.
[90] UN Conference on the Law of the Sea, Official Records, XVII, at 151, reprinted in (1982) 21 *International Legal Materials* 1261.
[91] Byers, *Custom, Power and the Power of Rules*, above note 36, pp. 94–7.
[92] A. Gotlieb and C. Dalfen, "National Jurisdiction and International Responsibility: New Canadian Approaches to International Law" (1973) 67 AJIL 229 at 258; R. St. J. Macdonald, "The Canadian Initiative to Establish a Maritime Zone for Environmental Protection" (1971) 21 *University of Toronto Law Journal* 247 at 250–1.
[93] This example does not appear to be greatly affected by the Cold War framework. In fact, one might have supposed that any legal change affecting access to straits by the US Navy would have prompted significant US resistance. Whilst the verbal reaction was indeed strong, this was not followed up by any sanctions against Canada.
[94] Byers, *Custom, Power and the Power of Rules*, above note 36, pp. 114–20.

has been argued convincingly that there never was a "rule" imposing a three-mile limit on territorial sea claims,[95] but that does not fully explain why US objections to the crystallization of a twelve-mile limit failed.

The most persuasive explanation in the literature, one offered by both military and civilian analysts, is that the United States' case in support of the three-mile limit was undermined by its own inconsistent jurisdictional claims. Although the Navy argued strongly for the three-mile limit, and convinced the executive branch and the State Department to maintain that claim even when no other State supported it, at the same time the United States was claiming a variety of special jurisdictions extending into the high seas.[96] Moreover, the US objection to twelve-mile claims was softened by internal political divisions. The interests of a State as large and complex as the United States are diverse. Although the Navy supported a three-mile limit, other influential political actors were arguing that the United States should itself claim a twelve-mile territorial sea to advance the protection of fish stocks and the prevention of pollution.[97] So the United States' persistent objection was not persuasive to other States, being both inconsistent and internally incoherent. It is also suggested that in the broader context of negotiations leading to a codificatory treaty on the law of the sea, the United States ultimately did not want to be viewed as an opponent of widely supported customary law.[98] Perhaps for this reason as well, US objections to the extension of coastal state jurisdiction by allies were muted.[99]

This example of failed persistent objection reinforces my argument concerning a key aspect of legal reasoning, one that often conditions the persuasive force of juridical claims. One of the primary techniques of legal discourse, in almost all legal traditions, is analogical reasoning.[100] This congeries of methods is sometimes referred to as "fit" and it goes a long way in explaining lawyers' attachment to precedent. If you cannot link your

---

[95] *Ibid.*, pp. 114–15, 117.

[96] H. Arruda, "The Extension of the United States Territorial Sea: Reasons and Effects" (1989) 4 *Connecticut Journal of International Law* 697 at 704–5; S. A. Swarztrauber, *The Three-Mile Limit of Territorial Seas* (Annapolis: Naval Institute Press, 1972), pp. 230–01.

[97] Washington Senator Warren Magnuson argued as follows: "We might want to keep up with the Joneses . . . We might not want to but we may be forced to": Swarztrauber, *Three-Mile Limit*, above note 96, p. 231.

[98] Arruda, "Extension of the US Territorial Sea," above note 96, at 720–1.

[99] See "United States of America, United States Statement on Canadian Fisheries Closing Lines Announcement" (1971) 10 *International Legal Materials* 441 at 441.

[100] Glenn, *Sustainable Diversity in Law*, above note 66, pp. 67, 101, 219, 321.

legal claim to a wider pattern of norms, you are going to have a hard time convincing others to recognize your claim. If your particular claim seems inconsistent with separate claims that you advance, your task will be all the more difficult. So persistent objection is a very hard rhetorical strategy to pursue over time because it is enormously difficult to maintain the consistency (or at least the general applicability) of a position that underlies most legal argument, and differentiates it in some ways from political argument.[101]

A third case where persistent objection by the United States failed to prevent a change in a globally applicable legal norm concerns the international standard of compensation upon expropriation of foreign-owned property. The US government clung to the "prompt, adequate, and effective" standard of compensation long after even its affluent allies had abandoned the argument. States of the developing world succeeded over a period of roughly two decades, from the 1960s to the 1980s, in dislodging the "Hull formula" in favor of a more fluid and contextualized compensation standard.[102]

US resistance to the new approach was undermined by a widespread recognition that decolonization had not merely modified the traditions of public international law, but had resulted in fundamental shifts.[103] For a time, foreign investment was analogized to continued colonial control. To compensate fully the inheritors of the colonial masters for a "loss" of property initially gained through exploitation was widely viewed as illegitimate, because it would reinforce domination, not newly won freedom.[104] Throughout discussions on the so-called New International Economic Order, principles of equity and justice were constantly invoked by newly independent states to justify the need to reconsider compensation standards as part of a broader economic readjustment. It was difficult to resist these value-based claims merely in defense of private Western economic

---

[101] The Cold War context is relevant to this example, but in a surprising way. Despite the commitment of the United States Navy to a three-mile limit, a decision was taken not to challenge the USSR's twelve-mile claim through any show of force. This decision further undermined the US persistent objection to the twelve-mile rule (Arruda, "Extension of the US Territorial Sea," above note 96, at 705–6).

[102] Byers, *Custom, Power and the Power of Rules*, above note 36, p. 58; O. Schachter, "Compensation for Expropriation" (1984) 78 AJIL 121.

[103] S. G. Roy, "Is the Law of Responsibility of States for Injuries to Aliens a Part of Universal International Law?" (1961) *American Law Journal* 863 at 882.

[104] P. Norton, "A Law of the Future or a Law of the Past: Modern Tribunals and the International Law of Expropriation" (1991) 85 AJIL 475 at 478.

interests.[105] Although hotly contested,[106] it may be true that the negotiation of hundreds of bilateral investment treaties (BITs) has now led
to the reestablishment of something close to "full" compensation after
expropriation.[107] But that does not alter the fact that the persistent objection of the United States failed to prevent the emergence of a new com-
pensatory rule of customary law applicable even to US investors. Indeed,
the use of BITs to reconstruct the old norm reinforces my earlier point that
treaties often reflect unequal bargaining power. Consent to treaty norms,
especially those found in bilateral agreements, is often coerced. The fluidity
of the processes of construction of customary law can be a shield against
hegemonic control.[108]

For a powerful State, such as the United States, changing understandings
of the formation and operation of customary law have significant implications. Even though it is overwhelmingly materially powerful, the United
States alone cannot prevent modifications to customary law. Nor can it
unilaterally build its own "custom," though, like any State, it may launch
a process of claim and response that leads ultimately to normative change.
The central question is accumulated practice – including acts, statements,
and acquiescence – that can come to be binding even if it leaves out important states. Despite persistent US objection to a new or changing rule, the
rule can change, and can bind the United States along with all other States.
This happened at the time of the extension of the territorial sea to twelve
miles. It happened with the assertion by Canada of special powers to protect
the fragile Arctic environment. It happened again with the modification to
the rule governing compensation for expropriation for a public purpose.

What about compliance?

So far, I have left aside the question whether or not the United States
will comply with customary law to which it has not consented. Perhaps

---

[105] R. Dolzer, "New Foundations of the Law of Expropriation of Alien Property" (1981) 75 AJIL
553 at 555–6; Norton, "Modern Tribunals," above note 104, at 496–7.
[106] See M. Sornarajah, *The International Law on Foreign Investment* (Cambridge: Cambridge
University Press, 1994), pp. 225–37.
[107] Byers, *Custom, Power and the Power of Rules*, above note 36, pp. 59, 125.
[108] No doubt the struggle over compensation standards after expropriation was affected by the
Cold War balance of power. The collapse of the "alternative" model seems to have pushed
developing States into a frenzy of competition for foreign investment. Hence the emergence of
BITs. But the impact seems to have been felt more in the realm of treaty law than in custom.

counter-intuitively, I suggest that the answer to this question is far from easy. Most law students are intuitively attracted to positivist explanations of legal normativity. That is why they often find international law both intriguing and frustrating. Continually, one is asked to articulate how a norm can be binding but unenforced. If international law is based upon the interactional processes I described above, an answer along the following lines emerges. Law depends for its power on congruence with social practice matched with perceptions of legitimacy. When law fosters allegiance, through the process of its creation and its rhetorical persuasiveness, it creates its own "binding" effect. Actors in international society will see the need for rules, and will tend to comply. It is only the failure of law, its pathology, that demands an external application of force ("enforcement"). I am not suggesting that this failure is rare, merely that the pathology should not be allowed to become the very definition of law.

It is therefore unhelpful to say that, unless compelled, the United States (or any other State) will comply with law only when it is in its own interest to do so. The rationalist assumption that a State can even know its own interest in a given circumstance is nothing more than an assumption. There may be many cases where the assessment of "interest" is extraordinarily complex, as it was concerning the width of the territorial sea. But one can imagine current examples as well. How should the United States react to a possible customary rule banning the use of anti-personnel mines? Will not "national interest" depend upon a relatively unpredictable constellation of factors including current patterns of military deployment, possible future deployment in zones where land mines are a threat, concerns of domestic industry, the availability of alternative weaponry, and capacity to withdraw currently deployed land mines? Moreover, interests are notoriously slippery and highly dependent upon the timeframe in which they are viewed. More controversially, and more to the point of my contribution to the discussion, interests are not exogenous variables at all. They are often deeply affected by the construction of a State's identity, a construction that itself can shift over time.[109] The participation of States, including the United States, in regimes, especially in regimes of such complexity as customary international law, may

---

[109] See generally A. Wendt, "Anarchy is What States Make of it: The Social Construction of Power Politics" (1992) 46 *International Organization* 391; and M. Barnett, "Sovereignty, Nationalism, and Regional Order in the Arab States System," in T. Biersteker and C. Weber (eds.), *State Sovereignty as Social Construct* (Cambridge: Cambridge University Press, 1996), p. 148.

come to affect the self-perceptions, or identity, of the State.[110] Moreover, international norms may be employed by "norm entrepreneurs" within domestic politics to argue for one or another aspect of complex national identities to dominate in a specific issue area.[111] In turn, these shifts in identity will affect the analysis of interests.

It is arguable that part of the United States' identity, that part that seeks international leadership, is conditioned by its engagement in the foundational regime of customary international law. Despite the examples of US breaches of law noted above, one can point to many instances where the United States sought the imprimatur of legality: in Somalia, ultimately vis-à-vis Iraq, and in the struggle against terrorism,[112] to name but a few politically charged examples. Of course, the desire for legality can be viewed simply as an expression of long-term self-interest. But I think that this misses out on at least part of the story. If we return to Kahn's assertion that the United States views itself as a nation under law, we might see that part of its identity is bound up in the desire to be seen as a lawful actor.[113] It may truly be committed to law, or may simply believe that it is so. The distinction may not matter greatly if the self-perception actually shapes understandings of interest.

Conclusion

Customary international law, like all law, is relatively autonomous from material power. As it has evolved since the end of World War II, custom is correspondingly relatively autonomous from the consent of individual States. It is aggregated consent, expressed through actual social practice, which shapes most contemporary custom. The binding quality of customary law is an expression of the legitimacy of the processes through which it is created and of its power as rhetoric, not a result of fictitious state intention. Because the United States typically refuses to act or cannot act as an effective

---

[110] J. Brunnée and S. J. Toope, "The Changing Nile Basin Regime: Does Law Matter?" (2002) 43 *Harvard International Law Journal* 105 (on changing identities of Nile basin states accomplished through processes of interaction).

[111] Finnemore and Sikkink, "International Norm Dynamics," above note 18, at 3.

[112] See, e.g., Stephen J. Toope, "Fallout from '9–11': Will a Security Culture Undermine Human Rights?" (2002) 65 *University of Saskatchewan Law Review* 281.

[113] Kahn, "American Hegemony," above note 28, at 2; Finnemore and Sikkink, "International Norm Dynamics," above note 18, at 2–3.

hegemon, its participation in the evolution of custom is not unique among major powers. Major powers collectively can contribute more significantly to the formation of custom than can weak States because of the major powers' capacity to act and to respond, and to report publicly about their acts and responses. To shape customary law, the United States cannot rely on its raw material power to exert brute force, because such practice will simply fail to partake of a legitimate process of law creation. Increasingly, the United States must *persuade* other States of the need for normative consolidation or change. Legal power lies in the capacity to persuade. If the United States withdraws into that part of its identity preoccupied with the sovereign self, it will likely become less persuasive in the evolution and application of customary international law, despite its preponderant material power. Whether that is good or bad is entirely a matter of political judgment.

11

Hegemonic custom?

ACHILLES SKORDAS

This chapter examines some elements of post-1990 customary practice, not for the purpose of presenting this practice exhaustively, but rather to focus on the relationship between hegemonic power and the customary system of rules. It concludes that, a decade after the end of the Cold War, the primary rules of customary international law have not undergone any dramatic change as a consequence of the dominant position of the United States in the international system. Hegemony finds its expression, not in the abrupt transformation of the international legal order, but in the incidental infiltration of concepts, the "flexibilization" of custom, the maximization of the discretionary powers of policy makers and the increased impact of society on *opinio necessitatis*.

The United States, in order to "set the agenda," needs to coordinate its activities with those of other States possessing strategic positions within international decision-making structures. Correspondingly, and without prejudice to the possibility of persistent objection, the missing uniformity of state practice can be supplemented by the psychological element of the *opinio necessitatis* of international society. If we consider the transnational society of non-state actors to be an integral part of the present-day international community, then its contribution to the *opinio necessitatis* should be extended to custom in general. The "normative strength" of that contribution will depend on the issue and circumstances "giving birth" to a new rule. International humanitarian law, human rights law, the democratic principle, a human rights exception to state immunity, and the standard of necessity in the use of force are all areas in which non-state actors may exert an autonomous, but still complementary, "pull." The global media may be understood to play a particularly important role here.

Finally, we can observe a progressive movement of the "interpretative center of gravity" of customary rules from the dichotomy of "legal/illegal" toward a more complex balancing of interests and, consequently, a relative indeterminacy of the rules. This development leads either to an evolution from custom to general principles that does not harm the "core normativity" of a particular rule, if such a core exists, or to the autonomous development and implementation of general principles, such as the Martens Clause, democratic governance, or a human rights exception from state immunity.

The transition from the "legal/illegal" dichotomy to a more complex balancing exercise is driven by certain features of the contemporary international system, and could have a major impact on the foundations of international custom. Only those rules that are "sociologically strong" are likely to remain clearly recognized and applicable in the post–Cold War order.

Customary humanitarian law and human rights law

In international humanitarian law, the Martens Clause offers protection to civilians and combatants against inhuman warfare.[1] Although the Clause is not as such a new source of international law, it constitutes customary law[2] which, in turn, facilitates the emergence of new customary rules. The Clause cannot predetermine the content of the rules that will eventually emerge. However, an examination of its role illustrates the influence of different power "factors" in the customary law-creating process. What will actually happen depends on state practice, on the course of international and domestic politics, and on its impact upon international society.

State practice

The Martens Clause can develop a customary law-creating effect on the basis that some States assume a considerable "cost" when affirming a new

---

[1] The Martens Clause was first included in the Hague Convention II of 1899. According to its contemporary version of Art. 1 (2) of the 1977 Geneva Protocol I, "in cases not covered by this Protocol or by other international agreements, civilians and combatants remain under the protection and authority of the principles of international law derived from established custom, from the principles of humanity and from the dictates of public conscience"; see *Legality of the Threat or Use of Nuclear Weapons* , Advisory Opinion, (1996) ICJ Reports 257, para. 78 and the ICTY *Kupreskic* case (*Prosecutor v. Zoran Kupreskic et al.*), Judgment IT-95-16-T of 14.01.00, para. 525 *et seq.*

[2] (1996) ICJ Reports 259, para. 84.

customary rule.[3] The United States ratified the four Geneva Conventions in 1955, but has not yet ratified the two Additional Protocols of 1977.[4] The United States plays a major role in the development of the customary law of armed conflict, a role that is magnified by its overwhelming military might and, thus, the cost it is prepared to bear for the emergence of new humanitarian rules. By applying the Martens Clause in the area of high-tech warfare, the United States assumes a high cost because its long-term warfare options are restricted as a result.

Therefore, a decision by the US military to abandon an effective or highly promising modern weapon because of humanitarian considerations would easily be transformed into a new prohibitory rule. In contrast, the prohibition of "savage," pre-modern warfare means and practices would be theoretically more difficult to reach through unilateral US action, given that the "real cost" for US planning and strategy would be more limited. However, it can be expected that some other major powers would also support the new rule, so that a prohibitory norm would emerge in this case, too. And if the prohibition of a certain kind of warfare were without cost for most States, the new rule could emerge through the traditional process of customary law creation, that is through widespread and consistent state practice.

While the value of US practice supporting a rule or condemning its violation is not particularly costly if addressed at a "rogue State," both the cost and value of the practice are higher if what is involved is condemnation of the acts of an allied or friendly nation; or if the United States at least avoids justifying, in legal terms, any violations it or its allies have committed. Under these circumstances, it can be expected that other States would be inclined to follow the superpower's example and establish the necessary practice.

On the other hand, if the United States expressly denied the existence of the allegedly emerging rule and showed its unwillingness to respect it in times of armed conflict, the emergence of the rule would depend on the concerted response of all other major powers having involvement abroad. They could overrule the US legal "resistance" only if their practice affirming the rule was unambiguous. However, the United States, as a "persistent objector," would presumably not be bound by that practice.[5] If

---

[3] Cf. Michael Byers, *Custom, Power and the Power of Rules* (Cambridge: Cambridge University Press, 1999), pp. 152–4.

[4] http://www.icrc.org (viewed on 9 December 2002).

[5] *Contra* Stephen Toope, this volume.

all major military powers opposed the emergence of a rule prohibiting the use of specific weapons they owned, then the practice of other States which did not possess that kind of weapon would not be adequate to create the rule.[6]

Besides the rules included in the military manuals, the practice of other States with limited involvement abroad would be relevant only in exceptional circumstances, were these States to assume some increased political, military, or diplomatic cost, for instance by opposing inhuman acts of warfare on the part of their "civilizational friends" or allies. Opposition to US actions through statements in the domestic domain does not always bear a considerable cost, because the United States itself seems to perceive this as a demonstration of an "anti-Americanism" which belongs to the repertoire of "political correctness" in some regions of the world. Nonetheless, if such an opposition were firmly stated in major international fora, including the UN Security Council, and affirmed through voting, in particular during armed conflict, it would have to be taken as a practice supporting the emergence of a new rule because the cost undertaken by the States concerned could be high.

Opinio necessitatis

In the *Kupreskic* case, the Trial Chamber of the International Criminal Tribunal for the Former Yugoslavia (ICTY) determined the specific nature of *opinio necessitatis* and its relationship with state practice in the Martens Clause.[7] In Antonio Cassese's terms, the Clause "*operates within the existing system of international sources* but, in the limited area of humanitarian law, loosens the requirements prescribed for *usus*, while at the same time *elevating opinio (juris* or *necessitatis*) to a rank higher than that normally admitted.*"[8]

The *opinio necessitatis* should be distinguished from the *opinio juris*. If the latter expresses "the sense of legal obligation, as opposed to motives of courtesy, fairness, or morality,"[9] then the former "signifie d'abord que

---

[6] On nuclear weapons and deterrence as practice precluding the emergence of a prohibitory norm, (1996) ICJ Reports 254 *et seq.*, paras. 66–7, 96.

[7] Para. 527 of the Judgment, above note 1.

[8] Antonio Cassese, "The Martens Clause: Half a Loaf or Simply Pie in the Sky?" (2000) 11 EJIL 187 214 (emphasis added).

[9] Ian Brownlie, *Principles of Public International Law*, 5th edn. (Oxford: Oxford University Press, 1998), p. 7.

les actes générateurs doivent avoir été accomplis avec le sentiment, ou tout au moins l'instinct, d'obéir à une nécessité sociale."[10] This necessity is not part of the legal order, but instead involves extra-legal political necessity and reasonableness.[11] The question then is, whether there exists another source of political necessity and reasonableness that can complement or even replace a missing *opinio juris sive necessitatis* on the part of States. The normative prescription of the "dictates of public conscience," as stated in the Martens Clause, indicates that non-State actors can play a major role, as the recent jurisprudential practice hesitantly reveals.[12]

This conclusion is based on a comprehensive, systemic view of international society as a "society of communications" among States, international organizations and non-State actors.[13] If this is the social reality of international relations in our time, then *opinio necessitatis* cannot be restricted to the opinions expressed by States, but should be evaluated so as to mirror the "spirit" of international society as a whole, including non-State actors. Since a reasonable limitation of the social space is necessary, from which the judge then draws the *opinio necessitatis*, we should limit the number of potential sources to non-governmental organizations (NGOs)[14] and the mass media.

International NGOs as sources of the "dictates of public conscience" on a global level present numerous structural deficits. It has been observed that, with the exception of the Roman Catholic Church, which represents the opinions of large masses of peoples beyond national borders, and, perhaps, the anti-globalization movement, NGOs are generally deprived of democratic legitimacy and represent transnational non-State elites which confer legitimacy upon the international elites administering the international

---

[10] Georges Scelle, "Règles générales du droit de la paix" (1933) 46(IV) *Recueil des cours* 434.

[11] Maurice Mendelson, "The Formation of Customary International Law" (1998) 272 *Recueil des cours* 270–71, 280–81.

[12] *Kupreskic* case, above note 1, para. 532. See also Judge Weeramantry (diss. op., I.1, III.5 and VI.3), (1996) ICJ Reports 429 *et seq.* (Nuclear Weapons); *contra* Judge Shahabuddeen (diss. op.), *ibid.*, pp. 409–10.

[13] On the term "international society" see "Agenda for Democratization," UN Doc. A/51/761 (20 December 1996), part V; for the legal concept of "international community as a whole," ILC Commentary (Report to the UN General Assembly, A/56/10), Art. 25, paras. 17–18. See also Andreas Paulus, this volume.

[14] For Byers, *Custom, Power and Power of Rules*, above note 3, 86, NGOs cannot directly participate in the customary law-creation; *contra* Isabelle Gunning, "Modernizing Customary International Law: The Challenge of Human Rights" (1991) 31 *Virginia Journal of International Law* 230, they may participate under strict conditions.

governmental organizations.[15] Moreover, a closer look at state practice may
also reveal a second truth, namely the heavy dependence of NGOs upon
States for financing and guidance. States very often fund NGOs to promote their foreign policy objectives,[16] while NGOs enjoying a consultative
status with the UN Economic and Social Council (ECOSOC) may have
that status suspended or withdrawn if they engage in "politically motivated
acts" against UN member States.[17] Under such conditions, NGOs are usually led to avoid "politically costly" forms of action against human rights
abuses. Instead, they are invariably tempted to choose more accommodat-
ing approaches, in concert with the wider interests of their governments,
authorities, or national public opinion. Elitism and an absence of real "cost"
render international NGOs often untrustworthy as representatives of what
can be called the "international public conscience," with some notable exceptions, such as Amnesty International and Human Rights Watch. Radical
pacifist protest in situations involving some personal "cost" may therefore
contribute more to the *opinio necessitatis* arising from the public conscience
than the resolutions of NGO bureaucracies. Such protests may be individ-
ualized and need not be incorporated into legal analyses or undertaken
within established organizational structures. Instead, they have to find access to the media, dominate international public opinion, and thus develop
their necessity-creating impact.

The media, in particular the media of global reach (global media), including the press and electronic mass media, are often criticized as oligopolies
promoting their own economic interests in the global marketplace and,
thus, as inappropriate for an "objective" and "balanced" news coverage.[18]

---

[15] See in this respect Kenneth Anderson, "The Ottawa Convention Banning Landmines, the
Role of International Non-governmental Organizations and the Idea of International Civil
Society" (2000) 11 EJIL 91–120. See also the differentiated approaches of Rahmatullah Khan,
"The Anti-Globalization Protests: Side-show of Global Governance, or Law-making on the
Streets?" (2001) 61 *Zeitschrift für auslandisches öffentliches Recht und Völkerrecht* 323–55. Ulrich
Beyerlin, "The Role of NGOs in International Environmental Litigation (2001) 61 *Zeitschrift für
auslandisches öffentliches Recht und Völkerrecht* 357–78, Carsten Stahn, "NGOs and International
Peacekeeping – Issues, Prospects and Lessons Learned" (2001) 61 *Zeitschrift für auslandisches
öffentliches Recht und Völkerrecht* 379–401.

[16] See, for instance, the institutionalized financing of NGOs which promote foreign policy aims,
in the Greek Law 2731/1999 on "Bilateral Development Assistance and Matters Concerning
Non-Governmental Organizations" (*Official Journal of the Hellenic Republic A*, 138).

[17] UN/ESC Res. 1996/31 (25 July 1996), para. 57(a).

[18] Such criticisms are echoed in the recent UN General Assembly Resolution UN Doc. A/Res/55/107
(14 March 2001) on the "promotion of a democratic and equitable international order" (para.
3 (a)(i)).

Strong reservations are expressed concerning the "discontinuing" character of news coverage and abrupt or unequal shifts of media attention to different crises, disasters or "scandals."[19] Moreover, it can be argued that the media as such are not made up of independent non-State actors, since their primary function is to reproduce the activities of other actors. It is also evident that in most parts of the world, the media are subject to strong government influence or even control. Considering these specific features, it is highly questionable whether the media have any greater "democratic" legitimacy to represent the transnational "public conscience" than NGOs.

However, if a number of conditions are met, the media could qualify as sources of "public conscience." The particular legitimacy of mass media lies in the fact that they constitute a differentiated system of societal communication specialized in reproducing public opinion.[20] This reproduction is creative in the sense that the media interpret and structure the public's "state of mind." The entrepreneurial nature of the modern mass media does not refute, but rather affirms, that function. Commentaries and news coverage have a "cost," the cost of market success or failure. Media are thus the representative "sensors" of public opinion and make a comprehensive assessment of the different existing trends. Beyond NGOs, an assessment of public opinion by the media evaluates also the positions of other interest groups or segments of international society: think tanks, economic actors, trade unions, political parties, the democratic movement which is critical to the globalization process, or individual protesters choosing spectacular forms of action.

The media represent international public opinion, if and when they are independent from States and addressed to a broad transnational and transregional non-specialized public; to do this they should have a "global reach" and use the English language. At present a number of US and, perhaps, British media organizations fulfill the above conditions. Global media organizations represent only the "extroverted" segment of the public opinion of their own countries while, at the same time, reproducing the "trends" of transnational public opinion. Other international media organizations, francophone, russophone or arabophone, have a regional addressee's circle.

---

[19] W. Michael Reisman, "Unilateral Action and the Transformations of the World Constitutive Process: The Special Problem of Humanitarian Intervention" (2000) 11 EJIL 18.

[20] Niklas Luhmann, *Die Gesellschaft der Gesellschaft*, II (Frankfurt/Main: Suhrkamp, 1997), pp. 1098 *et seq.*

In that sense, they cannot shape opinions representative of the global public, but can frustrate the proof that specific points of view or perspectives of the global media actually represent "transnational public opinion." Exclusively national media organizations, even if they have a large circulation, do not represent "transnational" public opinion. National public opinion does not need to be considered for a second time, separately from state practice. Since the "people" is a constitutive element of the State, national public opinion is already expressed by and included in state practice.

The "dictates of public conscience" constitute a specific state of public opinion. The "dictates of public conscience" is a "polemic" concept. The term "dictates" indicates an order, a command, while the "conscience" is the person's awareness of right or wrong.[21] In the Martens Clause, if the conscience is "public," this means that an opinion has been firmly established that a kind of warfare is morally, politically or legally unacceptable. Therefore, if the global media represent the public opinion of transnational society, they should also be qualified as the source of the "dictates of public conscience." The global media bring about the emergence of societal *opinio necessitatis*, if their news coverage and commentaries have crystallized protest into practically unquestionable "stereotyped expectation patterns."[22]

To achieve this result, "radical pacifism" should disconnect the disapproval of armed conflict as such from the sharp condemnation of inhuman warfare. A general protest against war is counterproductive, as far as emerging customary humanitarian rules are concerned. Such a protest could eventually be reinterpreted as indicating an *opinio necessitatis* which condemns all kinds of military action that might have "systemic consequences" and be capable of generating major humanitarian crises, even if civilians were not directly targeted.[23] It is highly improbable that a novel "obligation of result" to avoid such consequences could emerge from this kind of protest. On the contrary, the protest against the use of depleted uranium is a characteristic case of an emerging *opinio necessitatis* with regard to a concrete kind of

[21] *Oxford Advanced Learner's Dictionary*, 5th edn. (1995).
[22] Cf. for the sociological terms "stereotypisierte Erwartungsmuster" and "Medien-Schemata," Niklas Luhmann, *Gesellschaft*, above note 20, p. 1107, and Siegfried Schmidt, *Kognitive Autonomie und soziale Orientierung*, 2nd edn. (Frankfurt/Main: Suhrkamp, 1996), pp. 176 *et seq.*, respectively.
[23] Cf., for instance, the press statement of the President of the UN Security Council AFG/153/SC/7169/09.10.2001, on the growing dimensions of the humanitarian crisis in Afghanistan.

inhuman warfare, although it remains uncertain whether this particular protest will lead to a new prohibitory rule.

If we consider "cost" to be an important factor in the emergence of custom, then the enhancement of custom by the global media presents a double "cost" or "risk" for the different actors: the radical protest may be expressed in circumstances of risk for the individuals or groups who undertake it, while the media organizations creating the "stereotyped expectation patterns" face also the entrepreneurial risk of not having successfully reinterpreted, reconstructed or shaped the "state of mind" of transnational society. The global mass media organizations' policy is affirmed or criticized every single day in the global market. The systemic constraints of the overall process constitute a necessary guarantee against potential excesses. Under conditions of competition, either with other global or regional media organizations, or with national media organizations in the relevant national markets, the global media organizations are forced to be "inclusive" and present opinions from all regions of the world. What is needed, therefore, is not to ensure "balanced" information according to unspecified criteria, nor to apply the "reciprocity" principle between developed and developing countries, but to implement competition laws and ensure transparency in national and international media markets.

The Martens Clause as general principle

The Martens Clause is a customary norm facilitating the emergence of new norms of customary humanitarian law. No specific rules can be deduced directly from the Clause by way of a conceptual analysis of its structural elements. The Clause constitutes, therefore, a general principle of international law distinct from a "general principle of law recognized by civilized nations" in the sense of Article 38(1)(c) of the Statute of the International Court of Justice (ICJ).

The first element, the "principles of humanity," is related to the "elementary considerations of humanity," itself a general principle of international law, known from the ICJ's jurisprudence, not inspired by state practice but by the "legal convictions upon which the overall international legal order is based."[24] The criterion of the "principles of humanity" enlarges the judge's

---

[24] Pierre-Marie Dupuy, "Les 'considérations élémentaires d'humanité' dans la jurisprudence de la Cour internationale de Justice," in *Mélanges Valticos* (Paris: Pedone, 1999), p. 127.

discretion to formulate new rules of customary international law on the basis of the *opinio necessitatis* without any recourse to state practice.[25]

The "dictates of public conscience" combine *opinio necessitatis* with state practice. If state practice is uniform and established, a new customary rule emerges following the regular process of customary law creation. If, however, state practice is scant or inconsistent, the Martens Clause enlarges, under the conditions stated above, the role of *opinio necessitatis*. Nonetheless, strong objections by the United States to a humanitarian state practice may either impede the emergence of the new norm, or lead to a "US exception" from it.

If the judge formulates a new norm based on the "principles of humanity" or "dictates of public conscience," then the *opinio necessitatis* of international society may raise the scant humanitarian state practice into a full customary rule or even bring about the birth of a new rule without reference to state practice. To make this assessment, the judge has to consider social and political necessity as they arise from the appropriate space of social communication representing international society, that is from the global media, as well as the *opinio necessitatis* of States. Public opinion should not be considered as having consolidated into "dictates of public conscience" if widely divergent opinions have been formulated in regional media markets, while exclusively national media markets do not in principle affect that process.

State practice and the *opinio necessitatis* of international society should be taken into account by the judge and balanced against each other. Whether these conceptual operations find their expression in formal legal reasoning, or remain hidden behind a sort of "praetorian pedagogy"[26] of the adjudicator, is a matter of judicial practice. The Martens Clause enhances the judge's discretion, though a "conservative" jurisprudence would hesitate explicitly to draw legal consequences from the opinions of the global media.[27]

The Martens Clause thus constitutes a general principle of international law having a customary character, which further facilitates the emergence

---

[25] See the reasoning of the ICTY as to the unlawfulness of the cumulative effect of attacks on military objectives causing incidental damage to civilians, *Kupreskic* case, above note 1, para. 526.

[26] Pierre-Marie Dupuy, " 'Considérations élémentaires d'humanité,' " above note 24, at 128.

[27] Already the "judicial activism" of the *Kupreskic* Judgment of 14 Jan. 2000 has been criticized by the report to the prosecutor of the ICTY on the NATO bombing campaign against Yugoslavia, PR/PIS/510-E/13.06.00, para. 52.

of "coutume sauvage."[28] The Clause is qualified by such a degree of abstraction that it is up to the judge to draw new rules from it – and, to do so, it is necessary to consider the "sociologically strong actors" representing international society.

Opinio necessitatis *in human rights law*

The above principles of customary law creation in the area of humanitarian law could be applied, *mutatis mutandis*, to the emergence of customary human rights norms. Taking into account the increasing role of non-State actors, the *opinio necessitatis* may here assume an expanding role, in particular, but not exclusively, in the field of human rights. If the global media express or shape the disposition of international public opinion, individuals and human rights groups may exercise a strong impact through radical action against human rights abusers. Euro-Atlantic non-State actors play a prominent role in this respect.

If the United States is considered to be a persistent objector on some human rights issues, for instance the death penalty, the *opinio necessitatis* of international society cannot develop a new customary human rights norm binding upon that State. The abolition of the death penalty as a universal customary law is still far from being realized, taking into consideration that, as of December 2002, only forty-nine States had ratified the Second Optional Protocol to the International Covenant on Civil and Political Rights (ICCPR). In comparison, 149 States have ratified that Covenant itself, 146 the International Covenant on Economic, Social and Cultural Rights (ICESCR), and 104 the First Optional Protocol to the ICCPR.[29]

"Democratic governance": custom or legal–political principle?

The normative ambiguity

The end of the Cold War has brought about a major change to the content of the right of self-determination. International practice seems to dissociate itself progressively from the principle of "equivalence of regimes,"

---

[28] For that concept, see René-Jean Dupuy, "Coutume sage et coutume sauvage," in *Mélanges Rousseau* (Paris: Pedone, 1974), pp. 75–87.
[29] http://www.un.org, viewed on 9 December 2002.

enunciated by the ICJ in the *Nicaragua* case,[30] and to move toward the "emerging right to democratic governance."[31] The principle of democratic governance constitutes, as such, the expression of the right of peoples to internal self-determination.[32] The question is whether that entitlement has developed during the last decade into a full customary right, or whether "democratic governance" remains simply a right under international treaty law and a general legal–political principle derived from a rather inconsistent state practice. The practical consequence of the issue concerns the "normative strength" of the entitlement to democratic governance and its effects upon the position of the United States in the international system.

The fundamental feature distinguishing the "old" from the "new" world order has been the worldwide breakdown of totalitarian systems in the late 1980s and early 1990s. The "right to democratic governance" could, as a result, become one of the major evolutionary achievements of our era and constitute a fundamental customary and structural principle of contemporary international law. If so, the overthrow or disintegration of a democratic government would constitute a breach of an obligation "owed to the international community as a whole" or even of a peremptory norm of general international law (Articles 40, 48 of the ILC articles on state responsibility).[33] A further question would then arise: whether state responsibility establishes a secondary obligation upon all States to take all necessary measures for the restoration or imposition of democracy.

Although the practice of the UN Security Council in the crises in Haiti and in Sierra Leone point in this direction,[34] international practice on this issue is in general incoherent. For instance, the maintenance of a "stabilized" authoritarian system that has not overthrown a democratically elected government does not constitute a violation of a peremptory norm in the above sense, as the UN General Assembly resolutions condemning the US

---

[30] (1986) ICJ Reports 130–1, para. 258.

[31] Thomas Franck, "The Emerging Right to Democratic Governance" (1992) 86 AJIL 46–91. From the recent literature, Linos-Alexandre Sicilianos, *L'ONU et la démocratisation de l'Etat* (Paris: Pedone, 2000); Gregory H. Fox and Brad R. Roth (eds.), *Democratic Governance and International Law* (Cambridge: Cambridge University Press, 2000).

[32] Sicilianos, *L'ONU*, above note 31, pp. 129–35.

[33] See the GA, UN Doc. A/Res/56/83 (2002) on "responsibility of States for internationally wrongful acts."

[34] UN Security Council Resolutions UN Doc. S/Res/841 (1993) and UN Doc. S/Res/940 (1994) (Haiti), UN Doc. S/Res/1132 (1997) (Sierra Leone).

economic embargo against Cuba demonstrate. It is noteworthy that these resolutions have been adopted with increasing majorities during the last decade.[35] However, the question remains whether democratic governance constitutes a customary right, even without that peremptory quality.

"Democratic governance" is a comprehensive principle, the different aspects of which are regulated and guaranteed by regional and universal human rights instruments. Elements of practice in support of the emergence of a customary right on democratic governance can be seen in the activities of the United Nations on electoral assistance, in human rights treaty law, in particular the International Covenant on Civil and Political Rights, including General Comment 25 of the Human Rights Committee on the right to participate in public affairs, voting rights, and the right of equal access to public service, but also in a number of resolutions of the Commission on Human Rights, and the UN General Assembly, and in statements of the UN Secretary-General on democratization and the rule of law.[36] Last but not least, the resolutions of the UN Security Council determining that the overthrow of democratic governments constitutes a threat to the peace further enhance the possibility of a right to democratic governance.

However, there are other acts that contradict the above practice. A number of resolutions of the UN General Assembly on respect for principles of national sovereignty and non-interference in the internal affairs of States and their electoral processes not only deny electoral supervision, but openly support the old-fashioned principle of equivalence of regimes. The impression that the majorities with which the above resolutions have been

---

[35] UN General Assembly Resolutions: UN Doc. A/Res/47/19 (1992) (reg. vote 59-3-71), UN Doc. A/Res/48/16 (1993) (88-4-57), UN Doc. A/Res/49/9 (1994) (101-2-48), UN Doc. A/Res/50/10 (1995) (117-3-38), UN Doc. A/Res/51/17 (1996) (137-3-25), UN Doc. A/Res/52/10 (1997) (143-3-17), UN Doc. A/Res/53/4 (1998) (157-2-12), UN Doc. A/Res/54/21 (1999) (155-2-8), UN Doc. A/Res/55/20 (2000) (167-3-4), UN Doc. A/Res/56/9 (2001) (167-3-3), UN Doc. A/Res/57/11 (2002) (173-3-4).

[36] From the relatively recent practice, see UN General Assembly Resolutions "Strengthening the rule of law," UN Doc. A/Res/55/99 (2000) "Promoting and consolidating democracy," UN Doc. A/Res/55/96 (2000) "Strengthening the role of the United Nations in enhancing the effectiveness of the principle of periodic and genuine elections and the promotion of democratization," UN Doc. A/Res/54/173 (1999), "Strengthening the rule of law," UN Doc. A/Res/53/142 (1998); UN Secretary-General Reports, UN Doc. A/55/177 (2000) "Strengthening the rule of law," UN Doc. A/51/761 (1996) "An Agenda for Democratization," UN Doc. A/48/935 "An Agenda for Development"; Commission on Human Rights, "Promoting and Consolidating Democracy," E/CN.4/Res/2000/47, "Promotion of the right to democracy," E/CN.4/Res/1999/57.

adopted in recent years have tended to decline[37] has been contradicted by UN General Assembly Resolution 55/107 on the "promotion of a democratic and equitable international order." This resolution, adopted by a large majority,[38] constitutes a real back-to-the-future societal "counter-project," because it not only supports the principle of equivalence of regimes,[39] but also "recalls the proclamation by the General Assembly of the determination to work urgently" for the establishment of the "new international economic and communication order" of the 1960s and 1970s.[40] Moreover, some of the resolutions of the Commission on Human Rights and of the UN General Assembly on the promotion and consolidation of democracy pay, at least, "lip service" to the principle of equivalence of regimes.[41] This factual situation constitutes evidence for a rather limited normative strength on the part of democratic principle.

Despite the inconsistent practice, the existence of a general principle of democratic governance in international law should be accepted for two reasons. First, in the last decade the international community has undertaken vast efforts to consolidate democracy, strengthen the rule of law and protect human rights around the world. The financial and political cost of these efforts outweighs the cost of the statements and resolutions that indirectly support authoritarian forms of government. Second, the *opinio necessitatis* of international society, including transnational public opinion, clearly favors the principle of democracy, and therefore the practice promoting the democratic principle can overcome inconsistencies and acquire a certain normative basis in general international law.

The three pillars

The normativity of the democratic principle does not necessarily mean that a universal rule with the coherence and normative strength of customary international law has emerged. Although democracy is a universal

---

[37] UN General Assembly Resolutions UN Doc. A/Res/48/124 (101-51-17), UN Doc. A/Res/49/180 (97-57-14), UN Doc. A/Res/52/119 (96-58-12), UN Doc. A/Res/54/168 (91-59-10).

[38] Registered vote 109-52-7. See also UN Doc. A/Res/56/151 (2001), reg. vote 109-53-6.

[39] "The General Assembly ... further affirms ... the right of all peoples to self-determination, by virtue of which they can freely determine their political status and freely pursue their economic, social and cultural development," UN Doc. A/Res/55/107 (2000), para. 3a.

[40] *Ibid.*, paras. 3i and 7.

[41] UN Doc. A/Res/55/96, Commission on Human Rights Resolutions 2000/47, 1999/57.

evolutionary achievement built on the right of self-determination, it is closely correlated with the history of different States or regions, with their political culture and traditions; a customary rule, in contrast, requires a certain degree of homogeneity of the underlying values among the States concerned.[42] Democratic governance may have the quality of a general principle with weak normativity, permitting the coexistence of different models and being, under certain conditions, "tolerant" of deviations. To determine, as closely as possible, the scope and legal nature of the principle, it is necessary to define its main structural elements: the three pillars of democracy.

The first pillar consists of the right to "vote and to be elected at genuine periodic elections which shall be by universal and equal suffrage and shall be held by secret ballot, guaranteeing the free expression of the will of the voters" (Article 25(b) ICCPR). This right is supplemented by the right to take part in the conduct of public affairs and by the right to have access to public service (Article 25(a) & (c) ICCPR), and is supported by the rights to freedom of assembly (Article 21 ICCPR), association (Article 22 ICCPR), and freedom of expression (Article 19 ICCPR).[43] The second pillar of the democratic principle is the rule of law and the third is the principle of "good governance." The normative strength of the democratic principle is derived from the nature, and balancing, of these three structural elements and the legal interests they portray.

As Gregory Fox and Georg Nolte have demonstrated, international treaty law has adopted the model of "substantive" democracy, permitting the exclusion of political parties or organizations or restricting their activities, if they threaten the democratic order, under the standards of necessity, proportionality, and reasonableness.[44] Beyond the establishment of the one-party system which, as such, does not "fit" the rationale of international human rights treaty law, substantive democracy permits different levels of restrictions of the democratic principle, depending on the level of

---

[42] European Court of Human Rights in the case of the *United Communist Party of Turkey and Others v. Turkey*, 133/1996/752/951, para. 45. See also UN General Assembly Resolution 55/96, above note 36, recognizing "the rich and diverse nature of the community of the world's democracies, which arise out of all of the world's social, cultural and religious beliefs and traditions" and "that, while all democracies share common features, there is no one universal model of democracy" (paras. 7–8 of the preamble).

[43] General Comment 25, para. 12.

[44] Georg Nolte and Gregory H. Fox, "Intolerant Democracies" (1995) 36 *Harvard International Law Journal* 1–70.

threat a specific party represents to the democratic form of government.[45] International treaty law facilitates, therefore, restrictions based on the specificities of national political cultures and "lessens," in that respect, international control, rendering the "harmonization" of political systems and the emergence of a customary right to democratic governance more difficult, in comparison with the situation that would have existed under a procedural model of democracy.

The recent judgment of the European Court of Human Rights on the dissolution of the Refah (Welfare) Party by the Turkish Constitutional Court illustrates this legal situation. Although the Refah represented a large part of the Turkish electorate, although its leader had acceded to the position of prime minister of Turkey, and although it did not attempt to destroy or overthrow the democratic legal order or the Constitution, the Court decided that its dissolution was not incompatible with the right to association under the European Convention on Human Rights (ECHR). The judgment was based on a number of declarations made by major political figures of the party on three points, namely that the Islamic movement intended to create a multi-juridical system based on religious denomination, to apply shariah to the Muslim community, and not to exclude jihad – holy war – as a method of political campaign.[46] This very controversial judgment, which was rendered with the slimmest majority possible (4–3), would constitute the best example of the "clash of civilizations" on the legal level, had it not addressed the situation within a Muslim country.

The second pillar of democratic governance is the rule of law.[47] Although a certain harmonization of the different aspects of the rule of law can be achieved through the interpretation and application of international standards, the degree of its implementation depends also on the specific social and political features of the State in question. As an element of the rule of law, UN General Assembly Resolution 55/96 requests that "the military remains accountable to the democratically elected civilian government."[48] International practice is, however, very inconsistent on this point and there are differing degrees of ambivalent and indirect involvement of the military in the public life of nations. It is practically impossible to design workable

[45] Ibid., 49.
[46] Case of Refah Partisi (The Welfare Party) and others v. Turkey, Judgment of 31 July 2001, paras. 63–83 (80) (accessible through http://www.echr.coe.int).
[47] UN General Assembly Resolution, 55/96, above note 36, para. 1(c).
[48] Ibid., para. 1 (c)(ix).

and general customary standards distinguishing "legal" from "illegal" involvement here.[49] Among the members of the Council of Europe, Turkey is a State with institutional involvement of the military in governance.[50]

If the definition of the rule of law is far from being universally achieved, its relationship with the first pillar, the right to participate in public affairs, can become complicated. As an example, the way in which the former president of the Philippines, Joseph Estrada, was removed from office[51] constituted a major deviation from both the rule of law and the right to vote, as stipulated by the ICCPR. The participating States to the 1991 Moscow Meeting of the Conference on Security and Co-operation in Europe on the Human Dimension agreed "to support vigorously" the legitimate organs of a State "in case of overthrow or attempted overthrow of a legitimately elected government of a participating State by *undemocratic* means."[52] It is unclear whether this means that it is possible to have an overthrow by unconstitutional but "non-undemocratic" means.

Effectiveness and "good governance"

Stability may facilitate the interpretation of "good governance" as the third pillar of the principle of democratic governance. This pillar is clearly recognized and affirmed by the UN practice as a constitutive element of democracy.[53] "Good governance" is the standard of effectiveness of any political system. Its particular function with respect to democracy is that it demonstrates the increased effectiveness of this political system in

---

[49] In the early ICJ jurisprudence, a judge had even expressed the opinion, referring to Latin American coups d'état, that "revolutions and rebellions are very frequent – they sometimes fulfil the functions of an election, when a section of public opinion which is dissatisfied with the government wishes to effect a change in a manner which is less slow and laborious than voting," *Asylum Case*, Dissenting Opinion, Badawi Pasha, (1950) ICJ Reports 309.

[50] On the involvement and functions of the military in the Turkish political system, see Metin Heper and Evin Ahmet, *State, Democracy and the Military – Turkey in the 1980s* (Berlin/New York: de Gruyter, 1988), C. H. Dodd, *The Crisis of Turkish Democracy*, 2nd edn. (Huntington: The Eothen Press, 1990).

[51] On the Manila events of January 2001, see http://europe.cnn.com/ 2001/ASIANOW/southeast/ 01/20/philippines.estrada/index.html, viewed on 28 Sept. 2001.

[52] Point 17.2 of the Document, repr. in (1991) 30 *International Legal Materials* 1677, emphasis added.

[53] Millennium Declaration, UN General Assembly Resolutions 55/2, part V, 55/96, para. 1(f) calling upon States to strengthen democracy through good governance, 54/128 on "action against corruption," Commission on Human Rights Resolution 2000/47, para. 1(f), "Agenda for Development," paras. 118–38.

comparison with other forms of government. Democracy has emerged as the result of the demise of numerous one-party systems or military dicta-torships through the implosion of their political and economic structures. Democracy is thus presumed to be capable of effective governance, as the "Agenda for Democratization" makes clear:

> Democracy today is receiving widespread acknowledgment for its capacity to foster good governance, which is perhaps the single most important develop-ment variable within the control of individual States. By providing legitimacy for government and encouraging people's participation in decision-making on the issues that affect their lives, democratic processes contribute to the effectiveness of State policies and development strategies...Without demo-cratic institutions to channel popular pressures for development and re-form, popular unrest and instability will result...Increasingly, it is from this perspective that democracy is being seen today – as a practical necessity.
>
> (Paragraphs 24–25)

And, in the "Agenda for Development," the UN Secretary-General specifies some of the criteria of "good governance":

> In the context of development, improved governance has several meanings...It means ensuring the capacity, reliability and integrity of the core institutions of the modern State. It means improving the ability of government to carry out governmental policies and functions, including the management of im-plementation systems. It means accountability for actions and transparency in decision-making.   (Paragraph 126)

UN General Assembly Resolution 55/96 has further specified the various as-pects of "good governance," including the improvement of the transparency of public institutions and policy-making procedures and enhancement of the accountability of public officials, the fight against corruption and the fostering of high levels of competence, ethics and professionalism within the civil service. In UN General Assembly Resolution 54/128, the Assembly noted the "corrosive effect that corruption has on democracy, development, the rule of law and economic activity."

The implementation of the rule of law and of the right to participate in public life is to be assessed, therefore, in the light of "good governance." But if this principle constitutes the standard for measuring the effectiveness of democracy, it has to be defined in a manner that also takes into account the international interest, and in particular the fundamental interest in the preservation of peace and security. The "Agenda for Democratization" takes a cautious approach to that question. On the one hand, it maintains that "democracy contributes to preserving peace and security, securing justice and human rights, and promoting economic and social development" (Paragraph 16). On the other hand, it openly admits that democracy may contribute to civil conflict, or that the socioeconomic situation in an "underdeveloped" country may discourage democratic governance (Paragraph 20). Nationalist regimes, encouraging the domination of one ethnic group over another, cannot be accepted by the United Nations as legitimate, even if they are based on majority rule.

The international community promotes and supports democratic governance because it seems to be the most effective and stable system for the administration of large and complex societies. If "democratic governance" is based upon the three pillars of the right to participation in public life, the rule of law, and good governance, it is difficult to define a customary normative core in general international law. The specific structuring of the first two elements depends on the effectiveness criterion, which, as the result of major disparities in different regions of the world, leads to different forms of governance there.

The overthrow of a government based on the will of the people is usually the consequence of a disintegration process, during which the normative foundations of the principle – the first two pillars – are weakened and finally lost. The breakdown of the rule of law through corruption, the violation of the right to participation in public life through the exclusion or intimidation of different ethnic groups, the "soft" involvement of the military in public life, do not abruptly violate the democratic entitlement, but they progressively sap its normative strength. If democracy is not effective, it is not democratic – this tautology amply demonstrates the impasse of a customary norm on democratic governance. It is not the same in treaty law, where democracy is defined principally in normative standards without reference to the cognitive element of "good governance," but where the potential sanctions are limited to those provided by the respective treaty.

An asymmetric principle

General customary law does not oblige States to be democratic. The "Agenda for Democratization" is clear in that respect:

These difficult questions of prioritization and timing suggest several important lessons. First and foremost, it is essential that each State itself decide
the form, pace and character of its democratization process. This suggests a
fundamental prerequisite for democratization: the existence of a State which
is able and willing not only to create the conditions for free and fair elections,
but also to support the development and maintenance of the institutions
necessary for the ongoing practice of democratic politics. Second, democratization must begin with an effort to create a culture of democracy.

(Paragraph 21)

However, this does not mean that "democratic governance" does not exist
in general international law. It exists as a *sui generis* legal–political general
principle.

The principle is "political" in that it formulates a goal of the international
community, which has supported and monitored the conduct of free elections in a large number of countries during the last decade. The principle is
"legal" in so far as it represents the accumulation of international treaty and
non-treaty practice on the universal, regional, and national levels, including
constitutional law. Such a principle assumes the "hybrid form" of a general
principle of international law and of a general principle of law recognized by
"civilized nations." It is supported by the *opinio necessitatis* of international
society and promotes the emergence of "transregional custom" binding
upon a limited number of States around the world.

Democratic States have a sociological structure which takes into account
the fundamental differentiation and autonomy of their societies in various
spheres of activity – political, economic, educational, religious, and others.
We may assume that a number of countries with stable democratic systems
are bound and entitled by such a customary, albeit non-universal, rule. It
is not necessary to limit the field of application of a customary rule to a
specific region, for instance, to Europe. The *Refah* judgment, by accepting
the legality of the dissolution of a major political party, destabilized the
relative uniformity that had been achieved in the customary development
of the principle within the legal–political space of the Council of Europe. It is
noteworthy that the earlier jurisprudence of the European Court of Human
Rights had characterized the Turkish practice of prohibiting political parties
as inconsistent with the European Convention on Human Rights.[54]

---

[54] *United Communist Party of Turkey and Others v. Turkey* (133/1996/752/951/30.01.1998), *Socialist Party and Others v. Turkey* (20/1997/804/1007/25.05.1998), *ÖZDEP v. Turkey* (Appl. 23885/94,

A "transregional," non-universal customary rule can bind States *inter se* if the element of "good governance" has led to the establishment of an effective democratic system.[55] Due to that "normative–customary cementation" of democratic governance and the rule of law, any "early sign" of a potential disintegration or risk to the above principles may give rise to an immediate and preventive response by other interested States, as the response to the electoral success of the far right in Austria has shown.[56] "Good governance" and effectiveness do not here constitute a third and separate structural element of the democratic principle, but instead move to the "background level" of legal reasoning.

The principle of democratic governance is therefore asymmetric, has a firm political foundation in the activities of the international organizations and a certain customary basis, at least in the broader Euro-Atlantic region, Oceania, and Japan. The current implementation and supervision mechanisms of the ICCPR are not sufficiently "strong" to lead to universal custom, though democracy as a form of government, in order to crystallize into universal custom, need not be adopted by practically all States. A universal custom could come into existence if the UN General Assembly were to discontinue its practice of inconsistent resolutions and if effectively governed democratic States were prepared to undertake responsibilities for the restoration of peace and stability in all major geopolitical regions, alone or through regional organizations or agencies. If democratic States were to understand the overthrow of democratic governments as destabilizing per se, this would facilitate the emergence of universal custom.

The international responsibility of a State in the case of an overthrow of its democratically elected government or a prohibition of political parties is therefore limited, but countermeasures or retorsion can prove effective, depending on the political or financial burden they entail for the target. There are three main lines of a possible response. The States concerned may apply retorsion measures against the target, that is measures permitted

Judgment of 8 Dec. 1999). See also the recent judgment of 9 April 2002, in the case of *Yazar, Karatas, Aksoy et le Parti du Travail du Peuple (HEP) c. Turquie* (22723/93, 22724/93 and 22725/93).

[55] "Effectiveness" as a fundamental element of political democracy in the normative system of the Council of Europe has been emphasized by the ECHR in the case of *United Communist Party of Turkey and Others v. Turkey*, para. 45, above note 54, at 55.

[56] See the Report by Martti Ahtisaari, Jochen Frowein and Marcelino Oreja, adopted in Paris on 8 Sept. 2000, reprinted in (2001) 40 *International Legal Materials* 102–23.

by international law, such as the severance or interruption of diplomatic and consular relations, or the suspension of political, cultural, or sporting ties and contacts. They may apply regular countermeasures only for the violation of those human rights that are part of universal or regional custom. Massive violation of such rights could constitute a serious breach of an obligation owed to the international community as a whole.

On the level of treaty law or the law of international organizations, third States can suspend or exclude the target from international meetings, if such steps are provided for by the relevant treaties. If the antidemocratic regime proves to be a major source of instability, the UN Security Council may activate Chapters VII and/or VIII. Finally, if the overthrow of a corrupt and ineffective democracy does not lead to massive and grave violations of human rights, but eventually brings more stability to the State or to the international system, third States can be expected to take only symbolic measures or even to acquiesce in the new regime.[57]

The overall picture of democratic governance is one of a flexible principle that enlarges the systemic response alternatives of democratic States, in particular of the United States as a global power, although it limits their short-term political options vis-à-vis individual States such as Cuba. The existence of "stabilized" and domestically "tolerated" authoritarian regimes (Cuba, Vietnam, China) does not breach, as such, the "fundamental interests of the international community," and no sanctions or countermeasures are in principle permitted against these States on the basis of their political system alone. However, retorsion measures can be taken, when opportune, in order to accelerate the establishment of democratic governance.

State immunity and a human rights exception

Primary or secondary norm?

The expansion of international litigation in US courts and the procedural opportunities offered by legislation there overtly support the creation of a "human rights exception" to State immunity.[58] The United States appears here as a democratic power ensuring that justice will be done if authoritarian

---

[57] The international response to Pakistan's military coup of 12 Oct. 1999 has been, for instance, very limited; see *Keesing's Record of World Events*, 43198–9.
[58] Beth Stephens and Michael Ratner, *International Human Rights Litigation in US Courts* (New York: Transnational Publishers, 1996).

legal orders do not recognize effective remedies for victims. The main question is whether the new exception is or should become part of the customary international law of state immunity,[59] or whether it is and should remain part of the law of state responsibility,[60] as a potential but exceptional countermeasure or reprisal against massive violations of human rights.

The customary international law of state immunity has been the result of state practice in different regions of the world evolving over a considerable period of time. The United States has played an important role in that practice. US courts were among the first to recognize the principle of sovereign immunity, which was formulated as early as 1812 by Chief Justice Marshall in *The Schooner "Exchange" v. McFaddon and others*, in line with the common law tradition. The rise of the United States to become a superpower after World War II has increased the impact of its practice on this area of international law. The "Tate Letter" of 1952 marked the adoption of the restrictive immunity doctrine by the State Department in clear terms and facilitated the emergence of the customary international law of restrictive immunity. Finally, the Foreign Sovereign Immunities Act of 1976 gave a major impetus to related legislative initiatives in other countries, as well as to efforts at codification and progressive development on the universal level.[61]

The arrival of restrictive immunity has been swift and raises the question whether its potential further development in the form of a "human rights exception," in particular as introduced by the 1996 US Antiterrorism and Effective Death Penalty Act,[62] will similarly be adopted by international practice. The principles of the *Letelier* case could be directly applicable to eventual compensation claims against States having supported or harbored terrorists, if the relevant acts could be attributed to them.[63] The recent UN Security Council Resolution 1373 (2001) providing, *inter alia*, for the

---

[59] Jürgen Bröhmer, *State Immunity and the Violation of Human Rights* (The Hague/Boston: Nijhoff, 1997), pp. 214–15.

[60] Thomas Giegerich, "Buchbesprechung" (1999) 59 *Zeitschrift für ausländisches öffentliches Recht und Völkerrecht* 890; Maria Gavouneli, *State Immunity and the Rule of Law* (Athens: A. Sakkoulas, 2001), pp. 110–18.

[61] On the US practice, see ILC Report, YbILC 1980 Vol. II, Part Two, Commentary on draft art. 6, paras. 17–18; YbILC 1979, Vol. II, Part One, Preliminary Report of Sucharitkul, p. 232, para. 26; YbILC 1982, Vol. II, Part One, Fourth Report of Sucharitkul on jurisdictional immunities of States, paras. 74–9; Byers, *Custom, Power*, above note 3, at 112–14.

[62] Public Law 104-132, Sec. 221, 110 Stat. 1241.

[63] *Letelier et al. v. Republic of Chile et al.*, 488 F.Supp., 665. On the final settlement, see the agreement between the United States and Chile, reproduced in (1992) 31 *International Legal Materials* 1 ff.

freezing of funds, financial assets, and economic resources of persons or entities connected with terrorist activities may encourage state practice leading to the "regularization" of a state immunity exception for the claims of victims of terrorism or state-sponsored violence without regard to national "spheres of jurisdiction." Insurance companies or injured natural or legal persons may begin a worldwide "hot pursuit" of funds or other resources of States sponsors of terrorism. The tide might turn dramatically: instead of the United States being the forum for deciding claims of foreign nationals against their own states, US citizens or US interests might also try to use foreign jurisdictions to satisfy their claims against States or entities actually, potentially, or allegedly involved in terrorism. Third States could be put under pressure to open their jurisdiction to such claims.

Restrictive immunity has been embraced by international practice in the last fifty years because it facilitated enormously the day-to-day operations and the effectiveness of transboundary economic, commercial, and financial transactions. The US Supreme Court clearly defined that function in *Alfred Dunhill Inc. v. Republic of Cuba*:

> Participation by foreign sovereigns in the international commercial market has increased substantially in recent years ... The potential injury to private businessmen – and ultimately to international trade itself – from a system in which some of the participants in the international market are not subject to the rule of law has therefore increased correspondingly.[64]

The other side of the "systemic function" of restrictive immunity was expressed in the Letter of Transmittal of the Foreign Sovereign Immunities Act (FSIA) bill to Congress in 1975:

> The broad purposes of this legislation – to facilitate and depoliticize litigation against foreign states and to minimize irritations in foreign relations arising out of such litigation – remain the same.[65]

Restrictive immunity shifts a major portion of international disputes from the political to the judicial sphere and, in the same measure, strengthens communication among economic actors. The same rationale applies to the "tort exception" in state immunity law, due to the insurability, "regularity,"

---

[64] Reproduced in (1976) 15 *International Legal Materials* 746.
[65] *Ibid.*, 88.

and calculability of the risks involved, mainly traffic accidents or damages arising from other kinds of everyday activities.[66]

A systemic approach

There is no doubt that an extraterritorial "human rights" or "terrorist" exception to state immunity could be introduced into international law by state practice or agreement. However, such an evolutionary step would represent a major divergence from the function of the established immunity exceptions and "repoliticize" litigation. In fact, state immunity law constitutes a "quasi-homeostatic" mechanism reestablishing conditions of equilibrium within the international community, following minor collisions of sovereignties. This mechanism is very decentralized and is initiated by individual action in the municipal courts. Immunity exceptions fulfill their functions without political negotiations between States and without time-consuming consensus-building in the international community. Even if torts involve illegal actions, such as isolated cases of murder and political assassination committed on the territory of the forum State, the mechanism of the immunity exception is activated by the injured persons or their heirs and the imbalance is corrected through the award of damages in a judicial relationship involving only the individual, the forum and the third State.

Private legal action against foreign governments that have committed massive violations of human rights on their own territory, or on the territory of third States, is more problematic. It has been argued that the United States endangers its own interests and assets abroad due to the reciprocal character of the immunity law, that such an immunity exception would make even more difficult the resolution of disputes with "rogue States," that US courts would incur an increased danger of politicization and that, if sanctions are considered necessary, "smart sanctions" would be more effective.[67]

The cases of injury, death, or damage that would fall into such an exception are very heterogeneous. Although the acts of the foreign State concern the claimant specifically, presumably an unknown number of other persons fall into the same category. From a systemic perspective, the immunity

---

[66] YbILC 1991, Vol. II, Part Two, ILC Commentary on jurisdictional immunities, draft art. 12, under (4). See also the Fifth Report of the Special Rapporteur Sucharitkul, YbILC 1983 Vol. II, Part One, p. 40, paras. 71–4.

[67] Anne-Marie Slaughter and David Bosco, "Plaintiff's Diplomacy" (2000) 79(5) *Foreign Affairs*, 112–14.

exception (at the micro-level) is only one of three coexisting systems of rules that could manage these issues, along with the law of state responsibility (at the intermediate level) and the centralized mechanism of the UN Security Council acting under Chapter VII of the Charter (at the macro-level). The immunity exception for tort (personal injuries and damage to property) has a "residual" or subsidiary character in relation to other "remedial contexts,"[68] and the law of international state responsibility a subsidiary character in relation to the UN Charter.[69]

Claims concerning gross violations of human rights should be harmonized with the macro- or intermediate systems of rules. Individual rights cannot be set aside by these mechanisms, but their exercise and satisfaction should be consistent with the broader framework for the reparation of wrongful acts or the restoration of peace.[70] Contrary to the extreme "liberal paradigm" of a generalized "human rights exception," this approach can maintain a systemic coherence. The element of finality in the overall process of compensation and restoration of peace should guide state practice with regard to this novel state immunity exception.

It seems that the 1996 US legislation removing the immunity of terrorist States follows this approach. The immunity exception is applied only if the foreign State has been explicitly designated as a sponsor of terrorism under federal legislation, which happens only if there is a certain pattern of conduct contrary to the fundamental interests of the international community. The exception is not applicable if the claimant has failed to afford the foreign State a "reasonable opportunity to arbitrate the claim in accordance with accepted international rules of arbitration."[71] In the *Princz* case, the court made clear that a general immunity exception for human rights would cause litigation to continue at length: "In many if not in most cases the outlaw regime would no longer even be in power and our Government could have normal relations with the government of the day – unless disrupted by our

---

[68] Art. II.3.c of the 1991 ILA resolution on state immunity: "The organs of the forum State should not assume competence in respect of issues the resolution of which has been allocated to another remedial context" and the Brownlie Report, ILA Yb. 62 I, 62–64. See also ILC draft art. 12, "unless otherwise agreed between the States concerned . . .," A/46/405; YbILC 1983 I, Razafindralambo, 1769th mtg., para. 45, p. 91, Quentin-Baxter, para. 40, p. 91.

[69] Art. 103 UN Charter, Art. 59 of the ILC articles on state responsibility, above note 33.

[70] On the relationship between individual claims and the system instituted by the UN Compensation Commission (UN Security Council Resolution 687), see the Report of the UN Secretary-General S/22559/02.05.1991, para. 22.

[71] USCA para. 1605(a)(7).

courts, that is."[72] Thus, the immunity exception appears as an element of
state responsibility or restoration of peace, when the State against which
the claim is addressed refuses to fulfil its obligations under international
law or as long as the illegal regime is still in power.

This approach finds implicit support in the 1999 report of the International Law Commission (ILC). The Commission took note of the US
practice and the *Pinochet* case in an appendix to the report of the Working
Group on jurisdictional immunities, and commented that these developments give further support to the view "that State officials should not be
entitled to plead immunity for acts of torture committed in their own
territories in both civil and criminal actions." And then: "The developments examined in this appendix are not specifically dealt with in the draft
articles on Jurisdictional Immunities of States and their Property. Nevertheless they are a recent development relating to immunity which should
not be ignored."[73] These comments imply that the immunity exception for
human rights violations, as a recent practice not dealt with by the draft
articles, cannot be considered to be part of customary international law;
however, it is not disapproved by international law. The only construction that can harmonize the two aspects is the countermeasures/sanctions
approach.

Two recent judgments by international courts shed further light on the
above issues. In the *Arrest Warrant* case, the International Court of Justice
changed the course that had been traced by the *Pinochet* judgment and
decided that incumbent ministers for foreign affairs enjoy immunity from
prosecution by the national courts of third States even for war crimes and
crimes against humanity. If a person ceases to be a foreign minister, immunity is only lifted for "acts committed during that period of office in private
capacity."[74] This precedent conferred a high normative rank on the customary immunity law and could have an adverse effect on a human rights
exception from state immunity, even if such an exception were interpreted
as a countermeasure.

However, in the case of *Al-Adsani v. The United Kingdom*, the European
Court of Human Rights, in a controversial 9–8 decision, clearly distinguished immunity in civil cases from immunity in criminal matters and

---

[72] *Princz v. FR of Germany*, 26 F. 3d 1166 (1175).
[73] ILC report 1999, A/54/10 and Corr. 1& 2 at 435–436.
[74] Case Concerning the Arrest Warrant of 11 April 2000 (*DR of Congo v. Belgium*), Judgment of
14 Feb. 2002, para. 58, 61.

thus preserved each system's relative autonomy. It also decided that the right to a fair trial does not guarantee a human rights exception from state immunity with respect to extraterritorial harm;[75] had it decided otherwise, such an exception would have eventually become part of the law of state immunity for the member States of the Council of Europe.

Despite the fact that the secondary-norm approach enlarges the discretionary powers of the hegemon to intervene selectively in cases of human rights abuse, these powers are more consistent with the rationale of the overall system of the rules on immunity than with a rigid exception incorporated into customary international law.

Concluding remarks: custom in the era of hegemony

More than a decade after the end of the Cold War, the primary rules of customary international law do not seem to have undergone a radical change as a consequence of the dominant position of the United States in the international system. Hegemony finds its expression, not in the abrupt transformation of the international legal order, but in the incidental infiltration of concepts, the "flexibilization" of custom, the maximization of the discretionary powers of policy makers and the increased impact of society on *opinio necessitatis*. If the United States can define what peace and stability is, it can also, at the end of the day, control the legal consequences of its otherwise illegal actions. Although an egalitarian international system is incompatible with hegemony, unilateralism often proves counterproductive for the hegemon.[76] "Consensus building" among practically all States is not an end in itself, but a tactical means for reaching effective decisions. However, the United States, in order to set the agenda, needs to coordinate its activities with those of other States possessing strategic positions within international decision-making structures.

Correspondingly, and without prejudice to the possibility of persistent objection, the missing uniformity of state practice can be supplemented by the psychological element of the *opinio necessitatis* of international society. This element should be understood in a functional sense and not as a

---

[75] Application no. 35763/97, Judgment of 21 Nov. 2001, paras. 61–7. See also the case of *McElhinney v. Ireland*, application no. 31253/96, Judgment of 21 Nov. 2001.

[76] See Michael Glennon, "American Hegemony in an Unplanned World Order" (2000) 5 *Journal of Conflict and Security Law* 3–25 at 18–22.

mere "aggregate" of the dispositions of States and regional societies. If we consider the transnational society of non-State actors as an integral part of the present-day international community, then its contribution to the *opinio necessitatis* should be extended to custom in general. The "normative strength" of that contribution will depend on the issue and circumstances "giving birth" to a new rule. International humanitarian law, human rights law, the democratic principle, and a human rights exception to state immunity are all areas in which non-State actors may exert an autonomous, but still complementary, "pull."

The hegemonic features of contemporary custom also seem to have had an impact on the rules governing the use of force. With regard to both NATO's intervention in Kosovo and the anti-terrorist war in Afghanistan, we can observe a strengthening of customary elements at the expense of the UN Charter. The Kosovo intervention, although in principle unlawful, corresponded to the customary element of necessity and resulted in the limitation, if not elimination, of the state responsibility of the intervening powers, while in Afghanistan international state practice accepted the priorities of self-defense over the collective management of the threat to the peace. It is possible that we are here witnessing the direct, combined effects of the state practice of the hegemon *and* the societal *opinio necessitatis*, as expressed by the global mass media.

Recognising the role of the global media should not lead to the conclusion that Euro-Atlantic society has "usurped," once and for all, the representation of international society. The more the global media follow the narrowly defined US national interest, the more likely it becomes that regional media organizations will raise strong objections and hinder the consolidation of a uniform approach to *opinio necessitatis* (the al-Jazeera factor!). Moreover, the globalization process is open to the English-speaking media from every region of the world, if they define their own markets in global terms.

Overall, we can observe a progressive movement of the "interpretative center of gravity" of customary rules from the dichotomy of "legal/illegal" toward a more complex balancing of interests and, consequently, a relative indeterminacy of the rules. This development leads either to an evolution from custom to general principles that does not harm the "core normativity" of a certain rule, if such a core exists, or to the autonomous development and implementation of general principles, such as the Martens Clause, democratic governance, or a human rights exception from state immunity.

State practice promotes the emergence of "norm peripheries," accessible through "structural principles" which facilitate legal communication among the addressees. Examples of such principles include the "principles of humanity" and the "dictates of public conscience" in the Martens Clause, and, in respect of democratic governance, the right to vote and participate in public life, the rule of law and "good governance." In the customary law of state immunity, the balancing of interests "transcends the lines" between primary norms and state responsibility.

The transition from the "legal/illegal" dichotomy to a more complex balancing exercise is driven by certain features of the contemporary international system. During the Cold War, international law needed to maintain a minimum order between two hegemonic poles having their own internal practical and bureaucratic constraints. It was of the utmost importance to avoid acts characterized as "illegal" that could cause major friction between the antagonistic blocs. In the post-Cold-War era, the hegemonic structures are looser and more complex and, the primacy of the United States notwithstanding, are composed of a number of concentric and intersecting spheres (US, EU, NATO, G-8, Australia, Japan). International law has become a major integrative tool for international society and, thus, tends to become more cognitive and flexible than in the past. In that respect, different kinds of tensions might arise between peace and legality.[77] Moreover, there is very little place for "gaps" in the law; every act attributable to a State is capable of being qualified as legal or illegal, though it is also necessary to evaluate the gravity and consequences of the eventual illegality.

The transition from "minimum order" to "optimal stability" could have a stronger impact on the foundations of international custom than is at first apparent. To affirm the emergence of new customary rules, it is necessary to engage in an overall balancing exercise between *opinio juris sive necessitatis* and state practice. Here we should take into consideration that the above two elements cannot be clearly separated, but constitute intertwined "material" and "psychological" elements.[78] They cannot therefore

---

[77] See, for instance, Achilles Skordas, "La Commission spéciale des Nations Unies (UNSCOM)," in H. Ruiz-Fabri, L.-A. Sicilianos and J.-M. Sorel (eds.), *L' effectivité des organisations internationales: Mécanismes de suivi et de contrôle* (Athènes: Ant. N. Sakkoulas, Paris: A. Pedone, 2000), pp. 59 *et seq.* (84–90); Achilles Skordas, "*Epilegomena* to a Silence: Nuclear Weapons, Terrorism and the Moment of Concern" (2001) 6 *Journal of Conflict and Security Law* 191–224.

[78] Peter Haggenmacher, "La doctrine des deux éléments du droit coutumier dans la pratique de la Cour internationale" (1986) 90 *Revue Générale de Droit International Public* 114.

be viewed as separate and "linear" codeterminants of custom, but as legally relevant "inputs" merging into a general assessment of the possible existence of the rule in question. As an ultimate criterion, the adjudicator is bound to affirm the existence only of "sociologically strong" rules, that is, rules supported by state and societal power. In that sense, hegemony plays a dominant, but not the exclusive, role in the customary law-creating process.

12

Comments on chapters 10 and 11

Rainer Hofmann

The bipolar world – in which the United States and the Soviet Union were the two superpowers – belongs to the past. At present, there is but one hegemon in international politics, the United States. What impact might this fact have on international law or, more precisely, on customary international law?

It was in 1973 that, as a student, I had my first encounter with public international law. Among the things I still remember from that course is that customary law – the creation and existence of customary law – depended on a universal and longstanding practice of States and – as an additional precondition – that this state practice reflected a universal *opinio juris sive necessitatis*. The underlying rationale of these two conditions was the principle of sovereign equality among States. In addition, we were taught that the fundamental aim, the basic justification of this concept of customary law, was but a reflection of what was – or should be considered as – the final aim of law as such, or of any legal system, namely the protection of the "weak" against the brute force of the "strong." In other words: The task of international law consisted, *inter alia*, in protecting the interests and rights of the less powerful State against the military and other forces of the more powerful State.

Another memory takes me back to 1984 and thus to a time that was still characterized by the bipolar system, to a time before *perestrojka* and *glasnost* began to have their fundamental impact on the Soviet Union as one of the superpowers. More precisely, it takes me back to Moscow, to a conference of German and Soviet scholars on current trends in international law. What I remember most clearly is the very strong reaction of my older and obviously much more learned German colleagues when we realized that

348

a new Soviet approach to international law in general, and to customary law in particular, was developing. For the first time Soviet international lawyers were seriously thinking about treating customary international law as a source of law equivalent to treaty law.

A third memory takes me back to the same period. I was writing my doctoral thesis and had embarked upon the – potentially futile and seemingly bold – attempt to consider or to examine state practice in such a way as to establish whether there was a customary law principle concerning a specific human right. I had started out with the – admittedly naive – idea that I would have actually to examine the practice of – well, not 194, but still some 170 States – and had soon found that this was a mission impossible notwithstanding the fact that I was doing my research in an institution which had rather good access to documents reflecting state practice. I still remember the feeling of utter relief when I was told that the principle of *universal* State practice would not be literally understood as meaning that one would have to establish a uniform practice of virtually *all* States. Rather – so I was told – it would be sufficient, in order to be able to attribute the quality of customary law to a specific principle or rule, to show that a certain practice was followed by all major States representing each political and/or legal system existing on the globe.

Today, we live in a time that is characterized by the existence of a single superpower. So, what impact might that situation have – as concerns the rules on the creation of customary law – on the position of that one State? In the "old" bipolar world, the United States would, when considering the issue of creating customary international law, not have been treated any differently from any other State – at least from a strictly legal point of view. Instead, it would have had to contribute to the creation of customary law by pursuing its own practice and persuading other members of the international community to follow that practice. Thus, seen from a purely theoretical perspective – I should like to stress that word: theoretical – the United States would not have been more important than any other State. And, as regards the issue of the United States being bound by an existing rule of customary law or its becoming bound by an evolving rule, its position – including the legal possibility of acting as a persistent objector – would not have been different from those of other States. However, already at that time, this was of course a rather naive approach. And already at that time, everybody – or almost everybody – would have accepted that it was an approach based upon sheer legal theory, whereas in the real world of economic, military, and political facts some States were more equal than others with regard to the success of their attempts either to contribute to the creation of a customary rule or to manage not to be bound by such an (evolving) rule.

So, what is the impact – on customary law – of the fact that only one of the superpowers is left? One possibility is that the remaining superpower would be in a position, due to its political power, to force other States to accept its views on what constitutes a rule of customary law, and what does not. In other words, since the Soviet bloc – which, from a political point of view, was in a position to oppose US efforts to create a rule of customary law and, thus, could and did prevent the creation of such rules – has vanished, has the position of the United States as only one of the many actors engaged in the making of customary law also changed?

It was with this possibility in mind that I read the chapters by Stephen Toope and Achilles Skordas. If I understood them correctly, what they both tell us is that we do not live in a world where the single superpower is in a position to decide single-handedly what constitutes a rule of customary law, what the contents of that rule are or, indeed, what direction legal developments should take. The fall of the Berlin Wall and the reunification of Germany did not result in an abrupt change in the international legal order. Rather, this event infiltrates the concept and the contents of international law, and this is where the particular relevance of the single superpower status of the United States is to be found: It is in a better position to infiltrate, to influence the contents of various legal concepts and, thereby, to contribute more than others to the development and understanding of customary international law.

As Toope explains, the United States still must "persuade." This means that, notwithstanding the fact that there is only one hegemon, it cannot impose its views on the other subjects of public international law. Nor is the United States a ruthless or, at least, an utterly ruthless, hegemon.

Coming back to the question as to the actual position of the United States, I must admit, however, that neither chapter, despite presenting new ideas – such as the new or much stronger relevance of *opinio necessitatis* and the increased role of transnational society in the process of creating new law, or the global media as dictating public interests – has presented us with the answer which I was hoping would be given. That, however, might well be because such an answer cannot be given yet. The point was – rightly – stressed that ten years of this new "world order" might simply be too short a period to assess properly whether this new situation has had any impact on the traditional understanding of the rules concerning the creation of customary international law.

So, if I may just formulate some ideas or questions, and act as the devil's advocate: Is it really true that the institution of the persistent objector has completely fallen into *desuetudo*? If so, in general terms, is it correct to state that this assessment would apply to the United States? Is it really correct to say that the only hegemon left is not in a position to prevent the development of a non-legal principle into a legal norm binding on it? As regards the issue of the persistent objector, might one have to make, in this context, a distinction between rules which are considered to be "simple" norms of customary law and those norms which have the rank of *jus cogens*? As concerns the latter, I think, there cannot be any persistent objector – otherwise the rule would not have the quality of *jus cogens*. The same would apply to norms having an *erga omnes* effect, whereas, in respect of other rules, it may be that the situation remains different.

When we look at the whole situation from a different angle, and examine the possibilities that are left to the single political superpower to influence the creation of customary rules, I believe that we are still in the pre-1989 situation. In my view, it is definitely true that the United States has more influence than before on the development of non-binding principles into binding rules, but it can still not dictate this development. And there I agree with the two authors – in this context there is still a need for persuasion.

My last comment is again more of a question and it refers back to where I started. As I mentioned, I was first taught about the principles or the system of customary international law based on the consent principle as a means to protect the politically weak State. And I still agree with that approach, though I think that in many fields of international law – environmental protection and human rights have been mentioned in this context, along with the law governing the use of force – we are in a situation where we cannot afford to examine very closely whether every State has really explicitly or implicitly consented to the binding effect of a specific norm. But at the same time I should like to appeal for a bit of caution before doing away too quickly with this principle of consent. Leaving aside the still continuing relevance of "traditional" concepts such as the "Westphalian system" and "State sovereignty," the principle of consent remains important as a protection for the politically, the militarily weaker State in international relations. I would, in this respect, stick to the more conservative approach to customary international law. It might be that European States do not consider themselves as "weaker" and, therefore, as needing the additional protection offered by the traditional rules on the creation and existence of customary law. But there are quite a number of States in this world which are very dependent on this fundamental function of consent in the creation of customary law.

Andrew Hurrell

In this comment, I will touch on three questions.

First, does the United States have the relevant potential power to influence either specific rules of customary international law or the general character of customary international law? The answer would seem to be "yes." At a general level the consensus regarding the hegemonic position of the United States is clear: "Even without precise measurement, to focus on a range of power attributes leads to the conclusion that the United States is now in a category by itself. Only the United States currently excels in military power and preparedness, economic and technological capacity, size of population and territory, resource endowment, political stability, and 'soft power' attributes such as ideology."[1] More specifically, we can quite easily identify a list of power resources potentially relevant to the development of customary international law: (1) issue-specific power, for example in terms of military technology where the United States has the clear capacity to shape how wars can be fought; (2) what one might call the power of the critical moment and the capacity both to act and to argue in a manner that can help crystallize or catalyze the emergence of a new customary norm (or deliberately not to so argue, as in the recent case of humanitarian intervention); (3) institutional power, relevant because of the close linkages that exist between custom and treaty and the ever increasing role of institutional and multilateral forums in norm development; (4) the power to shape the context or background against which customary norms emerge: for example at a regional level by promoting the idea and "norm" of democratic governance within the western hemisphere through a wide variety of political, economic, and social mechanisms; or the capacity of the United States to navigate successfully within transnational civil society and to exploit the

---

[1] Michael Mastanduno, "Preserving the Unipolar Moment," in Ethan Kapstein and Michael Mastanduno (eds.), *Unipolar Politics* (New York: Columbia University Press, 1999), p. 141.

role of civil society groups in norm development to its own advantage; and (5) the power over the complex processes of coercive socialization by which weaker actors in the system come to accept and to internalize norms originating elsewhere in the system. Coercive socialization represents a political reality that has always threatened to destabilize or dilute the formal concept of consent in international law. Globalization has not changed this, but rather has added to the complexity of the mechanisms and channels through which coercive socialization operates.[2]

Second, how real or significant is this power within contemporary international society? The general line of Stephen Toope's chapter is to suggest that the assumption of preponderant US influence over the legal order is unwarranted or, at least, exaggerated. In part, this follows from the changing character of customary international law (for example, the diminishing role of individual state consent, the need to see customary law as grounded in social practice rather than explicit consent, the degree to which statements can count as practice and the emergence of generalized obligations). Even the most powerful state within the system cannot prevent the modification of customary law. This, in turn, forms part of a broader process by which the hard edge of consent has been "softened" and the process of norm creation has become denser, more institutionalized, and less susceptible to the direct influence of powerful States. I will leave it to the international lawyers to debate how far these specific changes have in fact occurred and the degree to which the persistent objector rule has been displaced. But, assuming this to be the case, what are the political implications? For some, the great danger is that the erosion of explicit consent generally works to the disadvantage of weaker states: their interests will be excluded, pluralism will be threatened, and the legitimacy of the legal order will thereby be undermined. On this view, the formal validity of the law remains a vital means by which some limits are placed on the most powerful. Toope suggests, correctly I believe, that this need not be the case and that the changing and flexible character of customary international law may serve the interests of the less powerful. As he explains, one of the roles that customary law can play, if it is flexibly conceived, is "in giving rise to norms that may not be supported by all powerful States, even by the most powerful State."[3] In general, then, this

---

[2] Andrew Hurrell and Ngaire Woods, "Globalization and Inequality" (1995) 24 *Millennium*, 447–70.

[3] Toope, above, p. 289.

category of danger is less worrying than the impact of the broader range of inequalities discussed in Nico Krisch's chapter in this volume.

But there is another danger that needs to be noted and that is less easy to dismiss. The erosion of consent carries a serious risk of pushing the hegemonic State away from the legal order and of encouraging unilateralism. Because of this, weaker States have little choice but to follow a particular kind of deferential hegemonic logic: to accord a degree of deference to the hegemon, to tolerate displays of unilateralism, and to acquiesce in actions that place the hegemon on (or beyond) the borders of legality precisely because of their greater interest in keeping the hegemon at least partially integrated and involved in the legal system. Chipping away at consent, if it were to be used in ways that directly threatened major US interests, therefore involves serious political dangers. Clearly, much will depend on how high the political stakes are on a particular issue, on the degree of relative vulnerability to US power, and on the relative importance attached by the weaker State to pursuing a strategy of hegemonic enmeshment. (Compare the clear need to engage in such a deferential hegemonic logic on the part of Mexico and Canada within NAFTA with the greater capacity of Europe to challenge the United States on a broad range of economic, environmental, and human rights issues.)

A second reason why US power over the making of customary international law is less real than appears at first sight concerns the nature of US hegemony – or better, the nature of US power relative to the changing character of world politics – what Toope calls the "current constitution of global politics."[4] Here the crucial point is to stress the deep tension that exists between modes of governance that both reflect and rely on hierarchy on the one hand and the changing character of governance in a globalized world on the other. If powerful States are to develop effective policies on economic stabilization and development, environmental protection, human rights, the resolution of refugee crises, drug control, or even the fight against terrorism, then they need to engage with a wide range of States (including, in particular, with weaker States that are both the source of and solution to such problems). Equally, they will need to interact not just with central governments but with a much wider range of domestic political, economic, and social actors. If you want to solve problems in a globalized world, you cannot simply persuade or bully governments into signing

[4] Toope, above, p. 291.

treaties. Effective implementation of rules in these issue areas necessarily implies ever deeper intrusion into the domestic affairs of States. Of course powerful States have the capacity to intervene unilaterally and directly. But such actions are costly (in terms of material costs, domestic political costs and the costs of international illegality or illegitimacy) and may be ineffective, especially over the long run. So institutions and international law play a crucial role both in legitimizing this ever deeper intrusion and in acting as a buffer between powerful States and the implementation of agreed international rules and norms. The trade-off for the powerful is between the attractions (and often real benefits) of managing international problems on the basis of hierarchical modes of governance on the one hand as against the structural need for deeper involvement and broader participation on the other. But the important point for this volume is to emphasize the degree to which these structural changes have magnified law's role as a legitimacy buffer for ever deeper intrusiveness.

Third, what are the limits to this picture of the United States as a relatively constrained hegemon? It is important to distinguish the specific capacity of the United States to influence customary international law from the broader question of US power and the effectiveness of its control over both behavior and outcomes. After all, within any legal order, one would expect the rough edges of power to be smoothed out – at least to some extent. But much will depend on the ways in which Washington comes to conceive and construct its hegemonic role (especially after 11 September). One possibility is of *liberal reengagement* – maybe with a slightly tougher leadership edge. This would stress the complexity of securing desired outcomes in an interdependent world from which not even the strongest State can escape, the need for engagement in multilateral institutions, and the extent to which too heavy a hand and too much unilateralism will squander goodwill and erode US soft power. The other, and at the time of writing more likely, possibility is of *conservative and nationalist hegemonic* leadership which stresses the natural right of the United States to dictate the terms of the international agenda (including the international legal agenda), to expect unqualified support from its allies, and to view non-cooperative States as antagonists or even enemies.

In addition, much depends on one's perspective. For most of the chapters in this volume the issue of US predominance is viewed within the context of US relations with Europe. Seen from a European perspective, the capacity of the United States to shape, or still more determine, customary international law is indeed limited. Europe has been willing, and able, to resist US preferences on such issues as the International Criminal Court, the Kyoto Protocol, or ballistic missile defense. Europe is far from being a powerless or marginal actor (or set of actors). And even when European power is more limited (as in the case of its military capabilities), this reflects a consciously chosen (and potentially reversible) policy. So Europe has the capacity to engage in the politics of customary law development in terms both of the overall character of the system and of its specific rules. Yet seen from the perspective of weaker states the picture is rather different – above all when US and European interests coincide and when the industrialized world acts as a hegemonic bloc. In this case the collective capacity of Western industrialized States to set the agenda and to turn some of their major political priorities into the "constitutive principles" of the legal order is very marked – as in the case of the ways in which notions of democracy and human rights have shifted the legal debates on sovereignty and sovereign equality. Moreover, even when Western values are shared and consensual, the United States and Europe have been able to dictate which aspects of the liberal agenda are picked up and gradually incorporated into the legal order. Thus intervention against tyrants and political self-determination have been prioritized, both politically and legally, whereas global economic justice, economic and social rights, and the importance of democratization at the level of international institutions have all been marginalized. Whatever the limits of the US capacity to shape particular rules of customary international law, this broader asymmetry of power has exercised a profound influence over the character of the contemporary international legal order. If uncorrected, it threatens to engender cynicism and to undermine legitimacy. And it can only strengthen the views of those who follow E. H. Carr and Karl Marx and see the recent rhetoric of a global community and of community values as arrogant hypocrisy that simply serves the values, the interests and the comfort of the rich and powerful.

Rüdiger Wolfrum

These two chapters provide us with a wealth of information, new insights, approaches, and ideas. It has been said by others that we are at the beginning of an evaluation process; I might add that we are also at the beginning of a new process of "deliberations," with a view to coming up with common understandings.

I wish to consider two aspects of the issue as to the impact the United States (or any other State) may have on the development and the preservation of customary international law. First, what has the United States contributed to the further development or preservation of the respective rules? Second, what implications does this have on the development and preservation of customary international law? The specific issues I wish to touch upon are self-defense, the rules on state responsibility, the law of the sea, and international humanitarian law.

The United States has invoked self-defense in many instances: Grenada, Panama, and so on up to 11 September. But despite its frequent invocations of the right to self-defense, the United States has so far not been able to change the very nature or substance of that right, since most of the interventions undertaken by it in recent years cannot be considered to qualify as self-defense. Moreover, there is no indication that other States have followed the United States in its approach. That said, unlike some contributors to this volume, I am of the view that the attack of 11 September justifies self-defense on the part of the United States and its allies.

With respect to state responsibility, the situation is much more complex. It is a very relevant question whether the terrorist attacks of 11 September can be "attributed" – to use the phraseology of the ILC draft articles on state responsibility – to a State. I believe that they can, though it is in my view not necessary, even not warranted, to ask whether the terrorists acted as agents of a particular State. We can accept easily that there are parallel tracks of state responsibility and here I believe that a State harboring, assisting, or turning a blind eye towards terrorists in its territory assists terrorist attacks and is therefore responsible. This makes it quite relevant to assess the attitude of the United States towards state responsibility. After the United States shot down the Iranian Airbus in 1988, it refused to accept that this was a case involving state responsibility. Its payment was camouflaged as being *ex gratia*. A similar reaction was given in respect of the 2001 collision between a US submarine and a Japanese research vessel. Therefore, I venture to say that the United States, at least when it comes to its responsibility, exhibits a certain reluctance fully to follow the rules on state responsibility. The moment it is a claimant, however, it very often invokes these same rules. The situation as to the US position on state responsibility is, therefore, mixed.

I now turn to the law of the sea, which provides an excellent example of the very different reactions of the United States to customary international law. The United States is one of the most significant and most successful promoters of customary international law in this area. The 1945 Truman Declaration illustrates this point. The Truman Declaration started the development of the continental shelf principle, which was fully established in customary international law thirty years later. As far as the limits of exclusive economic zones or zones of influence are concerned, the situation is once again mixed. At the beginning, the United States wanted to preserve the traditional system. After realising that having exclusive economic zones was in its own interest, the United States changed its position and began to promote exclusive economic zones. The same thing happened within the context of the European Community. Germany was always against the establishment of exclusive economic zones but was eventually convinced, in the context of the European Community, that it was in the best interest of the European States. It was definitely in the best interest of some European States, particularly the United Kingdom, but not in the best interest of Germany.

What is the best interest of a State anyhow? This is a matter that is rather difficult to establish. Although the Law of the Sea Convention has entered into force, the United States has not yet ratified it. It has not ratified for only one reason: Part XI. The rest of the Law of the Sea Convention the United States considers as customary international law. Therefore, one can again consider the United States to be a promoter of customary law. In fact, the United States does a lot to preserve that customary international law. It is the State that is most active in filing protests against infringements of the freedom of transit, the freedom of navigation, innocent passage, and so on. If you look through the Law of the Sea Bulletin it is not the United Kingdom, it is not France, but it is always the United States taking the lead in the protection of existing customary international law.

Let me just summarize. Concerning the issues referred to above, the United States has promoted, developed, and preserved customary international law and has done so by taking the lead – but not by exercising pressure.

Insofar as international humanitarian law is concerned, the United States has certainly not ratified the two protocols to the Geneva Conventions. Nevertheless, it has done a great deal in promoting and developing customary law in this field, a contribution that is almost always overlooked. The United States has been active in drafting so-called manuals on warfare.

These manuals are the best starting point for the development of customary international law in this area. The manual on naval warfare that has been developed in San Remo in cooperation with other States is one of the best examples. Here again, the United States is relying on customary international law, and is promoting its development.

There is absolutely no indication that the United States is violating customary international law more often than other States. In my view, further research should be done to identify the most important areas still governed by customary international law and to analyze State activities in this respect.

Now, concerning the development of customary international law in general, we should distinguish clearly between areas where there is no customary international law so far and areas where there is customary international law that is bound to change. In areas where no customary international law exists, technical and economic developments induce all States, in particular the United States, to be rather forthcoming. This is also the case in international humanitarian law, where the development of new weapons makes the change or the adaptation of rules absolutely necessary. In other areas, such as the rules on outer space, this phenomenon is even more evident. As far as those areas are concerned where customary international law exists, perhaps the perspective should be different. But in all these cases, there is no possibility for the United States or for any other State successfully to promote new customary international law on its own. Every State, including the United States, has to rely on the endorsement of its efforts by other States. However, one also has to accept that if a certain practice develops within the United States with respect to a development outside the realm of law other States may well join in. Therefore, the United States has a certain lead role – and it is expected to have such a lead role.

Finally, to what extent can the United States really stop the development of customary international law by acting as a persistent objector? The principle of persistent objection is still a valid principle, but does the United States have a particular role with respect to it? Let me give you a very simple example. Let us assume that all States active in outer space, excluding Russia and the United States, developed a certain practice for outer space activities, and Russia and the United States objected to that practice. Could the practice develop into customary international law? I have my doubts.

Here, one should pay tribute to reality. At least those who are particularly concerned with the given rule, or upon whom the given rule has a particular impact, should also have the possibility of influencing or blocking the development of that rule. There is of course some justification to be found for this approach in the jurisprudence of the International Court of Justice, most notably in the *North Sea Continental Shelf* cases.

V

Law of treaties

13

The effects of US predominance on the elaboration of treaty regimes and on the evolution of the law of treaties

PIERRE KLEIN

History shows that it is very generally much more efficient in the long run for States to "apply power within the framework of an institution or legal system," rather than to resort to raw military force or economic coercion.[1] The most obvious reason for this is that turning a relationship between two or more entities of unequal power which is – *ex hypothesi* – initially based upon sheer material power into a relationship which enjoys the recognition and protection of the law inevitably legitimizes the factual domination exerted by the more powerful State over the other(s).[2] This transformation entitles the former to resort to the means put at its disposal by the international legal system in order to enforce the – now legal – obligations owed to it by the latter, within the "neutral" framework of international law. The very notions of "force" or "power" are thereby obliterated to a large extent. It thus seems particularly relevant, against this background and in the framework of the present project, to inquire into the possible impact of the supremacy enjoyed by the United States in international relations since the end of the Cold War on the formation of international law through one of its most classical means, the conclusion of treaties. Treaties indeed remain one of the most significant and privileged ways to "produce" international legal norms nowadays. The influence exerted by a particularly powerful State on the treaty-making process may therefore have an important impact on

---

I would like to express my gratitude to Johanne Poirier for her very useful comments and suggestions on an earlier version of this text.

[1] Michael Byers, *Custom, Power and the Power of Rules* (Cambridge: Cambridge University Press, 1999), p. 6.

[2] See generally Charles Chaumont, "Cours général de droit international public" (1970) 129(I) RCADI (1970-I) (who notes for instance at 344 that "le droit international classique est, dans son ensemble, la mise en forme des situations de prédominance des forts sur les faibles").

the shaping of international law in the years and decades to come. This may be true of both the substantive and procedural aspects of the treaty-making process, which may be considered of equal importance. Such influence may affect the "primary" norms enshrined in various treaties, and thereby the legal regime governing the future relations between the United States and other States in various fields, ranging from international trade to international cooperation in criminal matters. And it may also have an impact on the "secondary" norms which are applicable to international treaties themselves, and which constitute the legal framework within which the substantive rules are produced; this could therefore alter the very structure of the international legal system. These two aspects will be dealt with in this contribution, which will successively address the issues of the impact of US predominance on the content of treaties and of its influence on the law of treaties. In both cases, certain methodological issues arise, which will be dealt with at the beginning of each section.

The impact of US predominance on the content of treaties

The most efficient and "scientific" method of assessing the impact of US predominance on the international "law-making" process through conventional means (i.e. treaties) probably lies in an examination of the various stages of the (pre-)negotiation process, and the outcome of these negotiations in relation to the most significant treaties adopted in the last ten years or so. This would however require a careful examination of the minutes of the international conferences in the framework of which those treaties were adopted. In addition to the fact that such documents are not readily available, such a study would most likely lead to an analysis too detailed for the objectives of the present project. I therefore attempt to assess the US influence on those processes by reviewing "secondary" sources, and particularly the official US positions as revealed in various contexts (such as the transmittal of treaties signed by the United States for ratification by the Senate), as well as doctrinal comments on US negotiating positions in various instances. To a certain extent, this preliminary study is therefore based upon an analysis of the discourses of US officials or representatives. I have focused on the multilateral treaties in the negotiation of which the United States has taken part since 1992, mainly at the universal level, while also taking into account certain regional instruments in which more general legal principles were enshrined.

It seems that the influence actually exerted by the United States on the formation of international law through conventional processes has been very significant in a number of cases. However, one may also observe important exceptions. The United States has experienced several setbacks in recent years, which prompted it not to become a party to some treaties the contents of which it deemed unacceptable. Its leadership was weakened in some areas, and the US now appears more isolated on the international scene than during the Cold War.

The United States exerts a significant influence on the formation of international law by conventional means (treaty-making)

A lead role is generally played by US delegations in most international negotiations. Being a "global player" and the "sole superpower," the United States has a definite agenda and specific interests in relation to virtually all matters the regulation of which is envisaged by means of the elaboration of new treaty regimes. And in many cases, the proposals put forward by US negotiators have found their way into the treaties ultimately adopted, quite often unchanged. This is for instance the case with instruments as diverse and significant as the 1996 Comprehensive Test Ban Treaty,[3] the United Nations Framework Convention on Climate Change,[4] the International Civil Aviation Organization Convention on the Marking of Plastic Explosives,[5] the 1993 Convention on Chemical Weapons,[6] the various treaties on international trade adopted at the conclusion of the Uruguay Round,[7] the 1993 Agreement to Promote Compliance with International Conservation and Management Measures by Fishing Vessels on the High Seas,[8] and, on the regional scene, the Organization for Economic Cooperation and Development's Convention on Combating Bribery of Foreign Public Officials in International Business Transactions,[9] or the Washington and Managua Protocols amending the Charter of the Organization of American

---

[3] See "Contemporary Practice of the United States Relating to International Law" (hereafter "United States Practice") (1999) 93 AJIL 60 *et seq.*
[4] "United States Practice" (1993) 87 AJIL 103.   [5] "United States Practice" (1994) 88 AJIL 90.
[6] *Ibid.*, 323.   [7] *Ibid.*, 320.   [8] "United States Practice" (1996) 90 AJIL 268.
[9] "United States Practice" (1999) 93 AJIL 490.

States.[10] In the words used by US officials, those treaties have "fully [met] all US (negotiating) objectives"[11] or "reflect (many) elements promoted by the United States during the negotiations."[12]

Even more striking in this regard is the 1994 Agreement on the Implementation of Part XI of the United Nations Convention on the Law of the Sea (UNCLOS). Although the United States viewed favorably the overall regime instituted by the Convention, which had achieved a satisfactory balance of interests,[13] the Reagan administration (and subsequent administrations) were deeply dissatisfied with the regime envisaged in Part XI of the Convention for the exploration and exploitation of the deep seabed, which was deemed by the United States and other industrialized States to be plagued by a "statist and interventionist" approach. Those States therefore made it a precondition to their ratification of UNCLOS that Part XI be renegotiated and a new, more acceptable regime instituted. In spite of the fact that the Convention was generally regarded as a "package deal," the United States and its allies proved successful in thoroughly amending the regime initially envisaged for deep seabed mining. Hence the 1994 Agreement reinforces the weight of the United States in the institutional structure of the International Sea-Bed Authority, dismantles the production ceilings and limitations originally accepted, does away with the obligation for private miners to transfer technology to the "Enterprise" and developing countries, submits the "Enterprise" to the same regime as private contractors, and recognizes significant rights vesting in the US consortia that have already made investments under the United States Deep Seabed Hard Mineral Resources Act.[14] While the United States was not the only State with a strong interest in these changes, its role in the overall revision of Part XI was determining. This episode undeniably provides one of the most vivid illustrations of the degree of influence exerted by the United States in some law-making processes at the international level. It also demonstrates the ability of the United States eventually to reverse a trend which did not have its initial approval and had consequently prevented it from becoming a party to an international accord.

---

[10] "United States Practice" (1994) 88 AJIL 719.

[11] *Ibid.*, 90.   [12] "United States Practice" (1993) 87 AJIL 103.

[13] See, e.g., "Panel on the Law of Ocean Uses, United States Interests in the Law of the Sea Convention" (1994) 88 AJIL 168.

[14] For more details, and for references to the specific provisions of the Agreement bringing about those various changes, see e.g. Bernard Oxman, "The 1994 Agreement and the Convention" (1994) 88 AJIL 689 *et seq.*

In that respect, one may also mention the trend of renegotiating conventional regimes following their adoption, mostly by exerting influence on the implementation process. The Kyoto Protocol to the United Nations Framework Convention and the Rome Statute of the International Criminal Court (ICC) may thus both be considered to illustrate "a post-negotiation 'policy-forging' type of unilateralism."[15] As far as the first of these instruments is concerned, Laurence Boisson de Chazournes has pointed out that:

> Many of its implementation provisions need to be refined for it to be fully effective, and this is meant to be done through collective decisions adopted by the Conference of the Parties to the climate change Convention and... the Conference of the Parties to the Kyoto Protocol. In fact, this situation has been no more than an excuse for certain countries to reopen the negotiation process unilaterally.[16]

This way, the United States (as well as the European Community and other OECD members) set new preconditions for becoming a party to the Protocol – conditions not originally included in that agreement.[17]

The US decision to sign the Rome Statute *in extremis*, in spite of the strong US opposition to the ICC,[18] followed the same pattern. As President Clinton emphasized, "With signature, [the United States] will be in a position to influence the evolution of the Court."[19] Signature indeed enabled the United States to continue participating in the work of the Preparatory Commission, where issues as important as the definition of the crime of aggression were addressed. By ensuring its continued participation in the work of this organ, it is obvious that signature gave the United States the opportunity to shape to a certain extent the implementation of an instrument which it had no interest in ratifying (at least in the foreseeable future). When it became apparent that the Statute was about to enter into force, the Bush administration in May 2002 then took the unusual step of "unsigning" the document.[20]

---

[15] Laurence Boisson de Chazournes, "Unilateralism and Environmental Protection: Issues of Perception and Reality of Issues" (2000) 11 EJIL 326 (the quotation originally refers to the Kyoto Protocol only).

[16] *Ibid.*

[17] For more details, see Boisson, *ibid.*; for the outcome of the discussions on the implementation of the Protocol, see below.

[18] For more on this, see below.   [19] Quoted in "United States Practice" (2001) 95 AJIL 399.

[20] See Communication of the United States Government to the UN Secretary-General, 6 May 2000, available at http://untreaty.un.org.

Attempts at renegotiating – to one extent or another – international agreements may of course provide particularly powerful States with an excellent opportunity to achieve results which are more satisfactory to them than the initial treaty regime. But one should also keep in mind that "renegotiation is fraught with the danger of coercion, particularly when a treaty partner has an hegemonic position in the world."[21] However, in view of the rather restrictive definition of "coercion" in the classical law of treaties (as embodied in Article 52 of the 1969 Vienna Convention), powerful States would still seem to enjoy a reasonably large freedom to press their claims.

The objectives generally pursued by the United States in negotiating processes are extremely classical: they boil down to the promotion and defense of its own interests. This is particularly obvious in the economic and strategic fields. Hence, the emphasis is frequently put on the promotion of market-oriented values and principles and on the need to protect US companies against unfair competition. These concerns are very often referred to in official discourses. It was above all for economic reasons that the United States pushed for the revision of Part XI of UNCLOS. And the desirability of US participation in specific treaty regimes is often justified on such grounds. The arguments put forward by President Clinton in favor of ratification of the 1995 International Natural Rubber Agreement (INRA) offer a perfect example of this:

> The US participation in INRA, 1995, will…respond to concerns expressed by US rubber companies that a transition period is needed to allow industry time to prepare for a free market in natural rubber and to allow further development of alternative institutions to manage market risks. The new Agreement incorporates improvements sought by the United States to help ensure that it fully reflects market trends and is operated in an effective and financially sound manner.[22]

Regarding the ratification of the OECD Convention on Combating Bribery of Foreign Public Officials in International Business Transactions, President Clinton similarly stated:

---

[21] Detlev Vagts, "The United States and Its Treaties: Observance and Breach" (2001) 95 AJIL 333.

[22] "United States Practice" (1996) 90 AJIL 647. Secretary of State Warren Christopher nevertheless insisted on the fact that INRA 1995 would be the last such agreement the United States will join, in view of its belief that the free market serves the customers better (*ibid.*, 648).

Since the enactment in 1977 of the Foreign Corrupt Practices Act, the United States has been alone in specifically criminalizing the business-related bribery of foreign public officials. United States corporations have contended that this has put them at a significant disadvantage in competing for international contracts with respect to foreign competitors who are not subject to such laws . . . the United States has worked assiduously within the OECD to persuade other countries to adopt similar legislation. Those efforts have resulted in this Convention . . .[23]

This quotation shows how the promotion of US interests internationally often means concretely the promotion of US legal standards. The United States frequently sees itself as a forerunner, and US officials often insist that those treaties to which US negotiators have contributed actually embody US norms. This is sometimes expressed rather boldly, as in the case of the Inter-American Convention against Corruption, in respect of which it was explained that one of the Treaty's main provisions

was included at the behest of the United States, and was intended to obligate the States Parties to have in place legislation similar to the United States Foreign Corrupt Practices Act.[24]

The influence exerted by the United States on the elaboration of international rules embodied in multilateral treaties is in such instances pretty obvious. This shows that, in certain areas at least, it is international law which is tailored on the US pattern, much more than the opposite. In that respect, one may speak of the "globalization" (or "regionalization," as the case may be) of US legal norms or standards.

This process is also reflected in the fact that, according to the positions taken by US officials, it is rarely necessary to adopt national legislation in order to implement the obligations undertaken by the United States when it becomes a party to a multilateral treaty.[25] In that respect, the "permeability" of the US domestic legal order to international law seems to be fairly limited. Such conclusions appear even more warranted when one considers the policy developed by the United States regarding reservations to multilateral treaties to which it intends to become a party. This policy has been

---

[23] "United States Practice" (1999) 93 AJIL 490.

[24] "United States Practice" (1998) 92 AJIL 493.

[25] See, e.g., "United States Practice" (1999) 93 AJIL 54 (Inter-American Convention on Mutual Assistance in Criminal Matters), (1998) 92 AJIL 492 (Inter-American Convention against Corruption).

consistently followed by US authorities, in particular with respect to human rights treaties. After decades of non-participation, the United States from the late 1980s decided to adhere to the main treaties concluded under the auspices of the United Nations in the field of human rights. It did so in the most cautious way, however, accompanying the expression of its consent with multiple reservations, understandings, and declarations aimed at restricting the scope of the obligations undertaken.[26] Particularly striking are the reservations by which the United States refuses "to undertake any treaty obligation that it will not be able to carry out because it is inconsistent with the United States Constitution" or to undertake obligations that would change or require the change of "US laws, policies or practices, even where they fall below international standards."[27] Such reservations accompanied the formal consent of the United States to the International Covenant on Civil and Political Rights, the UN Convention against Torture, and the Convention for the Elimination of All Forms of Racial Discrimination, among others. Such a policy – which has been severely criticized[28] – contributes to the "insulation" of the US domestic legal order from external influences.

It may therefore be said, on the basis of these various elements, that US predominance finds a clear expression in the influence exerted by the United States on international law-making process through conventional instruments. More often than not, the United States has been successful in advancing its national interests through multilateral negotiations, with US negotiating proposals transformed into actual treaty provisions. Furthermore, it is not unusual to find international treaty regimes modeled – sometimes closely – on US legislation. The mark of US influence on the shaping of international law is therefore quite visible in a number of instances, and the United States may be said to have exerted an undeniable leadership in several areas of international law. When it was not able to press its position to shape treaty regimes according to its wishes, the United States only agreed to become a party to these regimes once it had ensured, through reservations and unilateral declarations, that the impact of those international obligations upon its domestic legal order would remain marginal.

As we shall now see, however, the fact that US interests were not sufficiently protected or guaranteed has led the United States to refuse to take

---

[26] For more on this practice and on its consequences, see Catherine Redgwell, this volume.

[27] Louis Henkin, "United States Ratification of Human Rights Conventions: The Ghost of Senator Bricker" (1995) 89 AJIL 341–2.

[28] See, e.g., *ibid.*

part in a number of treaty regimes in respect of which its influence did not prove sufficient to determine the basic orientations. In some important areas of international law, US leadership appears to have been significantly weakened, and its influence on international lawmaking through conventional means diminished.

The influence exerted by the United States on the formation of international law by conventional means (treaty making) has suffered some significant setbacks

In contrast with the elements described in the first part of this chapter, in recent years the United States has been marginalized in some lawmaking processes concerning issues widely considered of fundamental importance to international society as a whole. In addition, repeated attempts by the United States to insulate its domestic legal order from the impact of international obligations deriving from treaties to which it became a party, and its failure to ratify treaties whose elaboration and (re)negotiation was largely the result of US initiatives, have damaged US credibility on the international scene and weakened its leadership in certain areas.

The United States was a strong advocate of international treaty regimes aimed at limiting the use of land mines and at establishing an international criminal court whose jurisdiction would not have been limited to a particular conflict or period of time. In both cases, however, this advocacy was overtaken by treaty regimes that were much farther reaching than it had anticipated. The United States was therefore unable to concur in the adoption of the 1997 Ottawa Convention on the Prohibition of the Use, Stockpiling, Production and Transfer of Anti-Personnel Mines and of the 1998 Rome Statute of the International Criminal Court. In respect of the first of these instruments, the United States was ready to accept severe restrictions on the use of land mines, but not their overall prohibition, in view of its own specific strategic situation, particularly in Korea.[29] It also failed to achieve a reduction in the notification period for withdrawal and recognition of the possibility of withdrawal during an armed conflict.[30]

Both legal and political – or strategic – arguments were put forward to explain why the ICC Statute, as it stood at the end of the Rome Conference,

---

[29] See, e.g., Peter Malanczuk, "The International Criminal Court and landmines: what are the consequences of leaving the United States behind?" (2000) 11 EJIL 85.

[30] Ibid., 86.

was unacceptable to the United States. A reduced role for the UN Security
Council, an autonomous power of action by the Prosecutor, the inclusion of the crime of aggression in the Court's *ratione materiae* jurisdiction,
and the extension of jurisdiction over nationals of a non-party State were
among the more important factors that led the United States to cast a
negative vote when the draft Statute was submitted to the Conference for
adoption.[31] Emphasis was put both on the specificities of the US situation ("the United States has special responsibilities and special exposure
to political controversy over [its] action", and it is "called upon to act,
sometimes at great risk, far more than any other nation"),[32] and on legal
problems raised by the Statute (in particular with respect to Article 12, providing for jurisdiction over nationals of non-party States).[33] This would
in turn reduce the prospect of US intervention based upon humanitarian
motives and the preservation of world peace and security, since Article 12
would expose US military personnel to criminal charges before the Court
for acts committed in the course of such operations anywhere in the
world.[34]

What is striking regarding these two agreements is that they were adopted
by large majorities of States, including in both cases all the other Western
States – which thereby clearly dissociated themselves from the US position.[35]
As one author put it, rather than "being left behind," it appears that the
United States has "left itself behind" on those important issues.[36] The
outcome is somehow paradoxical since the United States, as the sole
superpower, appears at the same time deprived of any "constituency" on
the international scene, at least in some areas. Even the United Kingdom,
traditionally the United States' closest ally, has turned its back on US positions with respect to land mines and the ICC.[37] The contrast between this
situation and that which prevailed during the Cold War (or with respect to

---

[31] See, e.g., David J. Scheffer, "The United States and the International Criminal Court" (1999)
93 AJIL 14 *et seq.*; Ruth Wedgwood, "The International Criminal Court: An American View"
(1999) 10 EJIL 93–107.

[32] Scheffer, "United States and the International Criminal Court," above note 31, at 12.

[33] *Ibid.*, 18; see also below.   [34] *Ibid.*, 19.

[35] Only seven states opposed, the United States, China, and Israel doing so openly.

[36] Malanczuk, "Leaving the United States behind," above note 30, at 89.

[37] See, e.g., Philippe Kirsch and John T. Holmes, "The Rome Conference on an International
Criminal Court: The Negotiating Process" (1999) 93 AJIL 4. It would be interesting to explore
further why this has been so in the context of the adoption of international instruments, but
not in the UN Security Council (one may think of the continuing British support for US strikes
against Iraq, for instance).

ideological debates originating in that period, such as those surrounding the revision of Part XI of UNCLOS) is manifest.

Obviously, the legal arguments developed by the United States in relation to the Rome Statute failed to convince the vast majority of States. It became rapidly clear that most of them were nothing more than attempts to shield US nationals (and specifically military personnel) from trial on the same grounds as citizens of any other nation. As several commentators have pointed out, the extension of the Court's jurisdiction to nationals of non-party States is neither exceptional (provisions to the same effect may be found in the 1949 Geneva Conventions, for example) nor contrary to the relativity principle (since it does not entail any legal obligation for third States).[38] Ironically, one of the principles which underlie the provision that appeared so unacceptable to the United States in 1998 (the idea that the extension of the Court's jurisdiction to nationals of non-State parties might act as an incentive for these to join the convention) had been advocated by that same State just a few years earlier. The 1993 Chemical Weapons Convention (CWC) provides that three years after its entry into force, several chemicals listed in a schedule annexed to the Convention may only be transferred or received from States parties. As President Clinton explained at the time:

> These restrictions were proposed by the United States for inclusion in the CWC. In addition to facilitating monitoring and control of [these] chemicals, the United States believes these restrictions *will serve as an incentive for non-States Parties to join the CWC.*[39]

Although one cannot expect States to be consistent throughout international negotiations over sometimes long periods of time, negotiating partners seem to have difficulty accepting that what was not only lawful but also desirable in 1993 was neither one nor the other in 1998. All in all, in the words of one commentator,

---

[38] See, e.g., Malanczuk, "Leaving the United States behind?," above note 30, at 81; Gerhard Hafner, Kristen Boon, and Anne Rubesame, "A Response to the American View as Presented by Ruth Wedgwood" (1999) 10 EJIL 116 *et seq.*; Frédéric Mégret, "Epilogue to an Endless Debate: The International Criminal Court's Third Party Jurisdiction and the Looming Revolution of International Law" (2001) 12 EJIL 249 *et seq.*; see also more generally Marten Zwanenburg, "The Statute for an International Criminal Court and the United States: Peacekeepers under Fire?" (1999) 10 EJIL 124 *et seq.*

[39] "United States Practice" (1994) 88 AJIL 331; emphasis added.

it is difficult to avoid the impression that the basic attitude of the United States in this affair signifies its general reluctance to submit to any higher authority and its claim to exceptionalism in view of its great power status.[40]

The agreement reached in Bonn, in July 2001, on the implementation of the Kyoto Protocol by a huge majority of the States which took part in the Conference, in the absence of the United States, seems to confirm its isolation on the international scene, even when fundamental issues of global interest are at stake.[41]

The isolation of the United States in some areas of international law and relations is coupled with a loss of credibility and leadership in certain fields. One may thus assume that the continued refusal by the United States to ratify some treaties, even after significant modifications have been made to accommodate its requirements, may lead other States to refuse to rene-gotiate other agreements. The 1994 Agreement on the Implementation of Part XI of UNCLOS is certainly a case in point. To a large extent, it constitutes the product of US insistence on renegotiating a regime which supposedly prevented the wide participation that UNCLOS otherwise commended. However, the adoption of the 1994 text did not fulfill its promise, since the United States to this day has not become a party to the Convention, with the prospects for ratification seeming ever more remote.[42] On this issue too, the United States appears rather isolated. In view of this example, third States may in future question the relevance of bowing to US pressure to (re)open negotiations, when they have no guarantee that the United States will accept the treaty regime finally agreed upon. To that extent, US ability to shape international conventional regimes may be more limited than it at first seemed.[43]

---

[40] Malanczuk, "Leaving the United States behind?," above note 30, at 83.

[41] On this episode, see Hervé Kempf: "Un accord conclu à Bonn sur le protocole de Kyoto: Le succès obtenu par la communauté internationale isole les Etats-Unis, qui poussaient à l'abandon de ce traité sur le climat," *Le Monde*, 24 July 2001, International.

[42] For more on the reasons that keep on preventing the United States from adhering to these instruments, see e.g. Sayeman Bula-Bula, "L'odyssée du droit de la mer dans les abysses," in Emile Yakpo (ed.), *Liber Amicorum Mohammed Bedjaoui* (The Hague: Kluwer Law International, 1999), pp. 107 *et seq.*

[43] Other examples, such as the failure to ratify the 1996 Comprehensive Test Ban Treaty, in the drafting of which the United States had played a similarly important role, could also be men-tioned in that respect (see "United States Practice" (2000) 94 AJIL 137). The fact that those situations are the result of diverging approaches of the administration, on the one hand, and of Congress, on the other, of course differentiates them from cases such as the Landmines Con-vention and the ICC Statute, where US delegations made it clear, at the end of the negotiating

Finally, the negative impact of the US reservation policy, particularly with regard to human rights instruments, must also be mentioned. It reflects the same "superiority complex" according to which the treaty regimes which have been established in the human rights fields are good enough for other States, but not for the United States, to which the same yardstick should not apply.[44] Here too, the credibility and "leadership" of the United States is presumably seriously affected by such attitudes.[45] In addition, as will be seen in the second part of this study, the accumulation of reservations to the UN Covenant on Civil and Political Rights drew a reaction from the UN Human Rights Committee which may exemplify the potentially adverse consequences engendered by proclamations of juridical supremacy by States such as the United States when they attempt to give priority to their domestic rules over international obligations.[46]

Such reactions show that the impact of US predominance on the formation of international law may indeed be significant, but not always in the sense expected by the United States. The Human Rights Committee's General Comment 24 may in fact lead to a precision of the law which has the effect of eventually recognizing as contrary to international law reservations as broad as those issued by the United States upon its ratification of several human rights treaties.

In the end, the following conclusion emerges regarding the influence of the United States on the elaboration of treaty regimes. As long as it limited itself to the promotion of its own interests (which is the essence of international negotiations), the United States has experienced an appreciable success in shaping international law through treaties. It has not done so, however, when it pretends to be entitled to some kind of exceptional

---

process, that the United States was not in a position to become a party to these instruments as they stood. From the perspective of third States, however, the difference may not appear very significant, since what matters in the end is the absence of US participation in the treaty regime.

[44] See, e.g., Henkin, "United States Ratification of Human Rights Conventions," above note 28, at 344.

[45] The fact that the United States was not reelected to the UN Human Rights Commission in 2001, for the first time in the organization's history, may constitute evidence of the adverse consequences for the United States of some of the positions taken by it in the area of human rights.

[46] CCPR General Comment 24, Issues relating to reservations made upon ratification or accession to the Covenant or the Optional Protocols thereto, or in relation to declarations under article 41 of the Covenant, Fifty-second session, 4 Nov. 1994.

treatment because of its allegedly different situation. In the latter instances, the United States appears more isolated on the international scene than it probably ever was in the past. Some of its policies may even be counter-productive in terms of their influence on the development of international legal norms.

A similarly contrasted picture emerges when one considers the effect of United States predominance, not on the substance of international agreements, but rather on the legal framework within which these instruments are concluded.

The impact of US predominance on the law of treaties

Whether the present predominance of the United States in international relations influences not only the content, but also the legal framework within which treaties are elaborated and applied is a question which is not easy to apprehend from a methodological point of view either. Indeed, in order to assess the actual impact of US predominance on the law of treaties one would have to answer the following questions: if negotiations were begun on a new draft convention on the law of treaties, (a) would the outcome be (substantially) different from the regime set out in the 1969 and 1986 Vienna Conventions on the Law of Treaties? (b) if it were, would those changes clearly result from United States pressures or influence on other states? (c) conversely, if it were not, would the preservation of the existing regime result from US resistance to amendments to that regime? (d) subsidiarily, would the influence exerted by the United States result from the fact that the United States may be viewed as the sole remaining superpower?

There being no global process of revision of the law of treaties for the time being (and probably not in the foreseeable future), the United States has no reason to express principled positions regarding the present regime of the law of treaties as a whole, or more specific aspects of that regime (the only significant exception being the issue of reservations to treaties, currently under discussion at the UN International Law Commission).[47] It seems however that some inferences might be drawn from recent US practice in relation to the negotiation, conclusion, interpretation, and application of

---

[47] See most recently the Report of the ILC on the work of its 53rd Session (2001), UN Doc. A/56/10, 437 et seq.

treaties. The material on which this analysis has been developed includes positions taken by representatives of the United States in international fora such as conferences or intergovernmental organizations, arguments put forward in the context of international litigation to which the United States was a party (in particular before the International Court of Justice), or unilateral actions taken by the US administration or legislative authorities in respect of specific treaties.

It will be seen that while such official positions confirm to a large extent US adherence to basic classical rules of the law of treaties, and therefore confirm those rules, the actual practice of the United States in that field sometimes deviates from accepted norms, or is clearly at odds with them. In my opinion, this limited survey does not allow for an assessment of the actual impact of US predominance on the evolution of the law of treaties on sound scientific grounds. But it does reveal another, equally interesting, phenomenon: recent developments which are the clear product of the use of US political predominance on the international scene may, to a certain extent, render purely and simply obsolete the resort to conventional instruments as a means of producing international norms.

The reaffirmation of classical rules of the law of treaties in recent United States practice

Even though the United States is not a party to the 1969 Vienna Convention on the Law of Treaties (hereafter VCLT),[48] United States officials have constantly expressed the view that "The Vienna Convention provisions... are for the most part codifications of customary international law" and, as such, binding on the United States.[49] This position has been reaffirmed by the United States in various contexts in recent years. Recent practice offers examples of such stances being taken with respect to a variety of specific aspects of the law of treaties, including the basic requirement of consent, the binding effect of treaties (*pacta sunt servanda*), issues of interpretation, and the regime of reservations.

---

[48] The United States signed the Convention on 24 April 1970, but never ratified it (see Multilateral Treaties Deposited with the Secretary General, Doc. ST/LEG/SER.E/19, 31 Dec. 2000, II, 269).

[49] See, e.g., *Digest of United States Practice in International Law* (Washington, DC: Office of the Legal Adviser, Department of State, 1979), pp. 692, 708.

378   PIERRE KLEIN

Consent

On several occasions, US representatives have insisted on the fact that state consent constitutes a cornerstone of the international law of treaties and that, consequently, treaties or provisions not accepted by the United States cannot entail any legal effects for it. Hence, one of the reasons put forward most strongly by the United States to oppose the adoption of the Rome Statute was that Article 12, providing for ICC jurisdiction over nationals of non-party States, would be in breach of the "fundamental principle of international treaty law [according to which] only States that are parties to a treaty should be bound by its terms."[50] In a similar fashion, counsel for the United States in the case concerning the *Legality of the Use of Force (Yugoslavia v. United States of America)* insisted that, because of the reservation made by the United States to Article IX of the 1948 Genocide Convention upon ratification of that instrument, the United States was not bound by that provision and had not otherwise consented to the exercise of ICJ jurisdiction under the compromissory clause.[51] And again, in its arguments in the *LaGrand* case (merits), the United States emphasized that it did not believe

> that it can be the role of the Court...to impose any obligations that are additional to or that differ in character from those to which the United States consented when it ratified the Vienna Convention [on Consular Relations].[52]

Although it is clear that in all these cases, it is its own sovereignty that the United States attempts to preserve by invoking the requirement of consent, one can nevertheless find there a clear expression of the continued US adherence to the fundamental principles of consent and of the relativity of treaties, as enshrined in Article 34 of the 1969 Vienna Convention.

Pacta sunt servanda

The basic principle according to which treaties are binding on States parties does not seem to be put into question in recent US practice either. This is evidenced in a particularly striking manner by the fact that in two recent instances, the United States admitted, either implicitly or explicitly, that it was in breach of its obligations under a treaty to which it was a party. Hence,

---

[50] Scheffer, "The United States and the Criminal Court," above note 32, at 18.
[51] Verbatim Records, 11 May 1999, CR99/24, paras. 2.3, 2.9 *et seq.*
[52] (2001) ICJ Reports, 27 June 2001, para. 46.

in the *Breard* case, counsel for the United States noted that the failure of US judicial authorities to inform Breard of his rights under the 1963 Vienna Convention on Consular Relations "was not deliberate," which implies a recognition of a breach on the part of the United States of its obligations under that instrument and, more generally, of the binding character of treaties properly entered into.[53] An even clearer admission of the fact that the United States had not complied with obligations flowing from the same treaty was made in the *LaGrand* case (merits).[54] It seems safe to conclude from these two examples, and more generally from the fact that the United States complies in the vast majority of cases with the treaties to which it has become a party,[55] that the principle of *pacta sunt servanda* continues to be considered relevant, even central, to the current US approach to the law of treaties.

Interpretation

With regard to interpretation – another essential building block of the regime of the law of treaties – recent US practice again does not seem to stray significantly from the accepted principles which have been proclaimed in the 1969 Vienna Convention. A careful examination of the written and oral arguments drafted by US delegations in the context of several recent proceedings before the ICJ shows that the precepts of Article 31 of the VCLT are by and large followed. Interpretation by reference to the ordinary meaning of terms,[56] as taken in their context,[57] or to the subsequent practice of the parties[58] is for instance far from exceptional in the reasonings developed by the United States. It is noteworthy that in these cases, the Court itself did

---

[53] (1998) ICJ Reports, Order of 9 April 1998, p. 253, para. 17.

[54] *Ibid.*, paras. 39 and 67.

[55] On this, see e.g. Detlev Vagts, "The US and Its Treaties," above note 21, at 331. At the end of 1997, the United States was a party to more than 9,500 treaties and international agreements, an average of 356 treaties having been concluded each year by the United States in the period 1986–1996 (see Robert E. Dalton, "National Treaty Law and Practice: United States," in Monroe Leigh, Merritt R. Blakeslee, and L. Benjamin Ederington (eds.), *National Treaty Law and Practice (Austria, Chile, Colombia, Japan, Netherlands, US)*, Studies in Transnational Legal Policy 30 (Washington, DC: American Society of International Law, 1999)).

[56] See, e.g., the interpretation of the terms "competent authorities" in the *LaGrand* case (*Germany v. USA*), Merits, Judgment of 27 June 2001, published under http://www.icj-cij.org/ icjwww/idocket/igus/igusframe.htm, para. 16; of Art. 36 of the Vienna Convention on Consular Relations (whether giving rise to individual rights), *ibid.* para. 76.

[57] *LaGrand* case, Merits, above note 56, para. 76.

[58] *LaGrand* case, Merits, above note 56, para. 63; see also the oral arguments in the *Breard* case, Verbatim Records CR 98/7, 7 April 1998, paras. 2.12 *et seq.*

not hesitate to construe the provisions whose meaning was disputed "in accordance with customary international law [as] reflected in Article 31 of the 1969 Vienna Convention on the Law of Treaties,"[59] seemingly without raising any opposition on the part of US representatives – or commentators, for that matter.

It would, however, be misleading to convey the impression that the US approach to interpretation issues is fully consonant with the principles enshrined in the Vienna Convention, and more specifically with the hierarchy between the more "textual" means of interpretation of Article 31, on the one hand, and the "subjective" or "historical" means of interpretation enunciated in Article 32, on the other. There is indeed a clear tendency in arguments put forward by the United States in interpretation processes to rely more heavily on the drafting history (*travaux préparatoires*) or on the "intention of the parties" expressed at that stage than on the other means of interpretation which should first be relied on, according to Article 31 of the Vienna Convention.[60] Such an approach is clearly reminiscent of the position taken by the United States on several occasions during the discussions on the draft articles on the law of treaties, where the draft provisions on interpretation (whose substance would eventually be retained in the Convention) were seen by the United States as "unduly restrictive" as far as the use of *travaux préparatoires* was concerned.[61] Similarly, as pointed out in a recent study, there is some evidence that US practice in the context of negotiation, rather than litigation, is also significantly drifting away from the rule of Article 31. To mention just one example, the ordinary meaning of terms thus seems to have been obviously disregarded in the interpretation of provisions of the 1972 Anti-Ballistic Missile Treaty put forward by the United States.[62]

---

[59] *LaGrand* case, Merits, above note 56, para. 99; see also the *Oil Platforms* case, Preliminary exceptions, (1996) ICJ Reports 812, para. 23, where the Court also refers to Article 32 VCLT.

[60] See, e.g., the written arguments in the case concerning the *Legality of the Use by a State of Nuclear Weapons in Armed Conflicts*, 10 June 1994, 34–8 and 44; the oral arguments in the *Breard* case, Verbatim Records CR 98/7, 7 April 1998, paras. 3.22 *et seq.*

[61] See, e.g., the US comments on (then) Article 70, 11 Feb. 1965, rep. in Report of the International Law Commission on the Work of its 17th and 18th sessions, UNGA UN Doc. A/6309/Rev. 1, p. 136 and at the 6th Committee (977th meeting, 20 Oct. 1967, para. 19).

[62] See Michael Byers and Simon Chesterman, "Changing the Rules about Rules? Unilateral Humanitarian Intervention and the Future of International Law," in J. L. Holzgrefe and Robert Keohane (eds.), *Humanitarian Intervention: Ethical, Legal and Political Dilemmas* (Cambridge: Cambridge University Press, 2003).

In any event, these positions obviously did not prevent the ICJ from declaring that the customary international law rules on interpretation were "reflected" in Article 31 of the Vienna Convention, and adhering to the hierarchy established by that instrument by resorting to *travaux préparatoires* on a subsidiary basis only.[63] It seems therefore that the positions taken on some occasions by the United States on issues of interpretation have not brought any change to the existing regime set out in the Vienna Convention, and nothing suggests that such a change could take place in the foreseeable future.

Reservations

The present work of the UN International Law Commission on "reservations to treaties" has given ample opportunity to the United States to express its firm support for the preservation of the reservations regime established by the Vienna Convention. The US member of the ILC, as well as official representatives of the United States on the Sixth Committee, made it clear on several occasions that there was no need for the Commission to amend in any way the regimes set out in the Convention, and that they firmly supported the approach favored by the Special Rapporteur (i.e. to produce a "guide to practice in respect of reservations," rather than a new convention).[64]

This position must be evaluated against the more general background of the controversy caused by the broad reservations which accompanied US ratifications of several international instruments relating to human rights in the first half of the 1990s, as mentioned above.[65] Although this was not stated explicitly, it was most likely its imminent consideration of the first report submitted by the United States under the International Covenant on

---

[63] The Court made this particularly explicit in the *LaGrand* case, when interpreting Art. 41 of its Statute, (2001) ICJ Reports, para. 104, where recourse to the *travaux* is made *ex abundante cautela*.

[64] See, e.g., the intervention of Mr Rosenstock, 2401st meeting, 16 June 1995, YILC (1995), I, 164, para. 2; and the remarks by Mr Dalton, 6th Committee, 10 Nov. 1997, UN Doc. A/C.6/52/SR.21, para. 20; see also the remarks by Mr Andrews, 6th Committee, 27 October 1998, UN Doc. A/C.6/53/SR.4, para. 52. In a different context, one may also mention the reliance on Article 20 VCLT by counsel for the United States in the oral arguments in the *Legality of the Use of Force* case (*Yugoslavia v. United States of America*), Verbatim records, 11 May 1999, CR99/24, paras. 2.11 and 2.12.

[65] See pp. 364–76.

Civil and Political Rights that prompted the UN Human Rights Committee to issue General Comment 24,[66] in which it expressed the concern raised by

> widely formulated reservations which essentially render ineffective all Covenant rights which would require any change in national law to ensure compliance with Covenant obligations. No real international rights or obligations have thus been accepted. And when there is an absence of provisions to ensure that Covenant rights may be sued on in domestic courts... all the essential elements of the Covenant guarantees have been removed.[67]

In order to meet the argument according to which a large majority of the States parties to the Covenant did not seem to consider reservations such as those formulated by the United States to be incompatible with the Covenant's object and purpose, as was evidenced by the limited number of objections thereto,[68] the Committee also questioned the appropriateness of the Vienna Convention regime in respect of reservations to human rights treaties. It expressed the belief that the Convention's

> provisions on the role of State objections in relation to reservations are inappropriate to address the problem of reservations to human rights treaties. Such treaties, and the Covenant specifically, are not a web of inter-State exchanges of mutual obligations... The principle of inter-State reciprocity has no place... And because the operation of the classical rules on reservations is so inadequate for the Covenant, States have often not seen any legal interest in or need to object to reservations.[69]

This in turn entailed that "It necessarily falls to the Committee to determine whether a specific reservation is compatible with the object and purpose of the Covenant."[70]

It is therefore natural that the issue of the applicability of the rules of the 1969 Vienna Convention to reservations to human rights treaties was among the first to be considered by the ILC at the outset of its work on reservations. Hence, in 1997, the Commission adopted preliminary conclusions in which it clearly stated that the general regime of the Vienna Convention

---

[66] See on this Catherine Redgwell, "Reservations to Treaties and Human Rights Committee General Comment No. 24(52)" (1997) 46 *International and Comparative Law Quarterly* 393.

[67] Para. 12; UN Doc. CCPR/C/21/Rev. 1/Add. 6 of 2 Nov. 1994, reprinted in (1994) *International Legal Materials* 839.

[68] For more on this, see Redgwell, "Reservations to Treaties," above note 66, at 406.

[69] Para. 17; UN Doc. CCPR/C/21/Rev. 1/Add. 6 of 2 November 1994, reprinted in (1994) *International Legal Materials* 839.

[70] *Ibid.*, para. 20.

was flexible enough to be applied to all types of treaties, including multilateral treaties relating to human rights.[71] And while it acknowledged that supervisory organs established by such treaties could issue observations and recommendations concerning the legality of reservations made by States parties, the Commission emphasized that this did not affect nor exclude the classical mechanisms of control such as reactions by other States parties (objections).[72]

These developments may explain the support expressed by the United States in favor of the continuing relevance and validity of the regime of the Vienna Convention relating to reservations, and of its applicability to all treaties, including those pertaining to human rights.[73] However, elements are clearly lacking to justify an assertion that the US position had a decisive influence on the pronouncement of the ILC, and on the shaping of the law on that issue. It should also be noted that the ILC has not yet addressed issues relating to the substantive validity of reservations. The final conclusions it reaches on this point may be less opposed to those expressed by the Human Rights Committee on the compatibility of some wide-ranging reservations with the object and purpose of the treaty concerned than were its preliminary conclusions.

As a general rule, the positions taken by the United States on various questions relating to the conclusion, interpretation, or application of treaties do not seem to differ significantly from the generally accepted rules and principles of the law of treaties which are reflected in the 1969 Vienna Convention. In several respects, the fact that the United States has for the last decade enjoyed a privileged position on the international scene as "the last State in the Westphalian sense"[74] does not seem to have entailed any significant consequences for the evolution of the law of treaties, the fundamental principles of which do not appear to be called into question.

During the same period, however, US authorities and delegations have sometimes followed a course of action which departed from – and in some instances was clearly at odds with – basic principles of the law of treaties.

---

[71] See Report of the ILC on the work of its 49th Session, 1997, UNGA UN Doc. A/52/10, p. 107, paras. 2 and 3.

[72] *Ibid.*, paras. 5 and 6.

[73] On the latter point, see the abovementioned interventions at the ILC and the 6th Committee.

[74] Remarks by Georg Nolte, panel on "The Single Superpower and the Future of International Law," 94th Annual Meeting of the American Society of International Law, (2000) *Proceedings of the American Society of International Law*, 65–67.

The deviations from classical rules of the law of treaties in recent United States practice

In recent years the United States has regularly taken action with respect to various treaties to which it was a party, or was at least involved in negotiating, which were not consonant with some fundamental rules of the law of treaties. These actions express disregard for the legal effects of signature, for the binding effects of treaties to which it is a party, and, in the most extreme case, constitute attempts at obstructing the functioning of treaty regimes. Even more disturbing is the fact that the very relevance of the principle of consent appears threatened in some situations, as a result of the recourse by the United States to other (institutional) mechanisms that have a very significant impact on the normal functioning of treaty regimes.

Disregard for accepted principles of the law of treaties

Some actions taken by US legislative authorities would seem to threaten the principle according to which the signature of treaties entails some (limited) legal effects. Action envisaged by the US Congress in 2001 in respect of the International Criminal Court raised serious questions in that regard. A bill entitled "American Servicemen Protection Act" (hereafter "ASPA") was first introduced in both houses of Congress in 2000.[75] It was passed by the House of Representatives on 10 May 2001 as an amendment to the Foreign Relations Authorization Act, and a revised version of the Act was introduced in the Senate in September 2001, under the title "American Armed Forces Protection Act."[76] It was adopted by the Senate in December 2001, under yet another title ("American Servicemembers' Protection Act") as an amendment to the Defense Appropriation Act,[77] before being dropped by Congress at the end of the same month.[78] Although initially opposed by the Clinton administration,[79] the American Servicemembers' Protection Act received a warmer reception from the Bush administration – and in 2002 was signed into law.[80]

---

[75] See the references in "United States Practice" (2001) 95 AJIL 397.
[76] Available at http://www.wfa.org/issues/wicc/iccarrears.html.
[77] Available at http://www.wfa.org/issues/wicc/dodaspa.html.
[78] Available at http://www.wfa.org/issues/wicc/aspadefeat.html.
[79] See "United States Practice," (2001) 95 AJIL 397–398.
[80] American Servicemembers' Protection Act, Pub L. No. 107–206, §§2001–2015, 116 Stat. 820 (2002), 22 U.S.C.A. §§7421–7433 (West Supp. 2002).

The Act *inter alia* prohibits cooperation with the International Criminal Court by imposing restrictions on assistance pursuant to mutual legal assistance treaties, prohibiting investigative activities of ICC agents on US territory and the transfer of classified national security information to the ICC. It even prohibits US military assistance to States which become parties to the ICC Statute, with the exception of the United States' closest allies.[81] These provisions may nevertheless be waived by the president under certain circumstances. But such legislation would seem to contradict the obligation bearing upon signatory states to "refrain from acts which would defeat the object and purpose of a treaty," as expressed in Article 18 of the 1969 Vienna Convention and which may be considered to reflect customary international law.[82] Indeed, it seems difficult to imagine measures more clearly aimed at defeating the object and purpose of a treaty than those of the ASPA. The threat to deprive States parties to the ICC Statute of US military assistance could obviously have seriously hindered the entry into force of the Statute, or at least hampered a large participation in the Court. Moreover, this US initiative could have been seen as a form of coercion directed at third States, aimed not at constraining them from becoming parties to a treaty (the more classical situation envisaged in Article 52 VCLT), but at inducing them *not to become a party* to the treaty concerned, which is undoubtedly more unusual. This would have amounted to a form of sanction against States that decided to ratify or adhere to a multilateral instrument concluded under the auspices of the United Nations, and would therefore have represented a most unusual *première*.

This development, however, has probably not affected the future evolution of the law of treaties as such – if only because in May 2002 the Bush administration took the unusual step of "unsigning" the statute.[83] It is nevertheless telling of the influence that the most powerful State may exert on the free expression by others of their consent to be bound by a specific treaty regime.

Beyond such – up to now virtual – violations, a number of breaches of treaties to which the United States was a party have been observed in recent years. Breaches of the Vienna Convention on Consular Relations, the non-payment of UN dues, or the failure to enact implementing legislation

---

[81] *Ibid.*   [82] See, e.g., on that point "United States Practice" (2000) 94 AJIL 139.
[83] See Communication of the United States Government to the UN Secretary-General, 6 May 2002, available at http://untreaty.un.org.

under the Chemical Weapons Convention constitute some precedents in this regard.[84] Although it is clear that failures to comply with treaty obligations are by no means exceptional – and certainly not the monopoly of the United States – some have expressed concern that such breaches are not given the same treatment as in the past. As Vagts put it:

> In the past, the courts and the political branches consistently acknowledged that on a different plane treaties are binding upon the United States and that, if the United States breaches one, it has an obligation to set the matter straight. In recent years, however, the executive, Congress, the courts and influential commentators have each conspicuously verbalized the idea that the later-in-time rule is the final answer and that the binding effect of international law carries little effect.[85]

Such emphasis on the later-in-time rule, according to which later statutes may override treaty provisions,[86] expresses a clear disregard for the *pacta sunt servanda* rule.[87] It is not obvious, however, that such attitudes amount to disputing the relevance of *pacta* in terms of principles. And while US authorities may be under the impression that this fundamental principle of the law of treaties is not in all cases applicable to the United States because of its "special status" in world affairs, there are strong reasons to believe that,

---

[84] Vagts, "The US and Its Treaties," above note 22, at 330.
[85] *Ibid.*, at 313.   [86] *Ibid.*
[87] It has sometimes been asserted that the attitude of the United States toward international treaties cannot be apprehended properly without taking into account the domestic constitutional constraints resulting from the federal structure of the United States (in a slightly different context, this argument has for example been put forward by the United States in the *LaGrand* case, in order to justify the non-implementation by US authorities of the order indicating provisional measures rendered by the ICJ on 3 April 1999; *ibid.* para. 95). This argument, however, does not seem acceptable as an excuse for non-compliance with treaties to which the United States has accepted to become a party. It may first be observed, from a factual point of view, that claims of this type are raised far less often by other federal States than by the United States. It seems also that the argument is invoked in a rather selective fashion, human rights treaties raising far more "constitutional" objections than trade agreements for instance, whereas the divide of competence between federal and state authorities within the United States may not be so different in both areas. Both of these observations seem to point to the fact that the federal structure of the United States offers a convenient excuse for the non-performance or non-implementation of treaties, rather than presenting a true obstacle to compliance. In any event, it is clear from a legal point of view that such arguments, while relevant to justify, for instance, broad reservation policies, may not excuse the non-execution or non-implementation of treaties. It suffices to recall the unambiguous wording of Article 27 VCLT – broadly accepted as reflecting customary international law – according to which "A party may not invoke the provisions of its internal law as justification for its failure to perform a treaty."

even from the US perspective, *pacta* remains relevant to treaty relations entailing obligations vis-à-vis the United States.

Finally, it should be underlined that the broad reservation policy followed by the United States with respect to human rights treaties has given rise to strong opposition from the UN Human Rights Committee as well as from other States parties.[88] According to the Swedish objection, for instance, "reservations of this nature contribute to undermining the basis of international treaty law."[89] The least that can be said is that their compatibility with the object and purpose of the treaties at stake raises serious concerns. As mentioned above, their sweeping character may indeed lead to an evolution of the law of treaties relative to reservations, but in a sense quite opposed to that desired by the United States. The future work of the ILC on the topic of reservations will be decisive in this regard.

Recent US practice therefore shows clear disregard for some fundamental principles of the law of treaties. It is not certain, however, that the various types of breach briefly examined here constitute parallel forays in a principled attack against the present foundations of the law of treaties. In many instances, one is under the impression that the United States is "simply" claiming a privileged status, by reason of its manifest predominance in world affairs (and of the degree of sovereignty this entails), which would exempt it from the consequences of its disregard for accepted principles of the law of treaties (and of international law more generally). Put simply, the United States may consider itself to be above the law, without calling into question the law itself. The impact of this attitude on the law of treaties as such is likely to remain very limited. Third States are almost certainly more inclined to support the existing regime than an evolution of the relevant legal framework which would allow for even more power-play and unilateralism.

US disregard for international law principles and institutions is, however, sometimes much more selective. In some situations, the United States appears to have a strong interest in resorting to institutional procedures that enable it to exert a decisive influence on the application of treaty regimes.

"Trumping" treaty regimes

An analysis of the influence of US predominance on the current legal regime of treaties would not be complete without a consideration of the interplay

---

[88] See below.   [89] Quoted by Catherine Redgwell, below.

between treaties and other sources of international legal obligations, in the creation of which the United States plays a decisive role. Special attention must be paid in this respect to certain decisions taken by the UN Security Council in recent years, which have had a significant impact on the scope of several international agreements. One of the most significant of these is undoubtedly Resolution 1373, of 28 September 2001, which was adopted on the basis of a US proposal.[90] Voted on in the wake of the 11 September events, Resolution 1373 in essence obligates UN member States to comply with requirements identical to those contained in the International Convention for the Suppression of the Financing of Terrorism adopted by the UN General Assembly in December 1999.[91] While the rapid entry into force of the Convention appeared desirable in order to take effective measures against terrorist networks, the low level of ratifications meant that such a prospect was relatively distant.[92] The incorporation of its principal provisions into a Security Council resolution therefore constituted an ideal means of "generalizing" this treaty regime at extremely short notice.[93]

On the one hand, this development may be viewed as clear recognition of the continued validity and relevance of *pacta sunt servanda*. Since few States were bound by the 1999 Convention, there was no way to impose upon them conventional obligations by any other means than those accepted under the classical law of treaties (i.e. becoming a party to the instrument). The importance and relevance of consent are in some way reaffirmed in this context. However, it is also obvious that the adoption of such a resolution demonstrates that there are ways of overcoming those "classical" limitations, by making such treaty-based obligations mandatory for all member States

---

[90] See, e.g., Colum Lynch, "UN Council Clamps down on Terrorism," *The Washington Post*, 30 Sept. 2001, A 12; "Pour Afsane Bassir, Un projet de résolution sur la lutte contre le terrorisme a été soumis à l'ONU par les Etats-Unis," *Le Monde*, 28 Sept. 2001.

[91] Compare for instance Point 1 (b) of the Resolution with Articles 2 and 4 of the Convention, Point 1 (c) of the Resolution with Articles 2 and 8 of the Convention, point 1 (d) of the Resolution with Articles 2 and 18 of the Convention, Point 2 (e) of the Resolution with Article 9, 2 of the Convention and Point 2 (f) of the Resolution with Article 14 of the Convention.

[92] See, e.g., "Les Quinze vont renforcer la lutte contre les réseaux financiers du terrorisme," *Le Monde*, 22 Sept. 2001, International.

[93] See also Luigi Condorelli, "Les attentats du 11 septembre et leurs suites: où va le droit international?" (2001) 105 *Revue Générale de Droit International Public* 829. It should be noted that the Resolution entails both a generalization and an extension of the rules established by the 1999 Convention, since the Resolution provides for the creation and operation of a Committee to monitor the implementation of Resolution 1373 (see Point 6), whereas no such mechanism was envisaged in the Convention.

of the United Nations as a result of their inclusion in a Security Council resolution adopted under Chapter VII of the Charter.[94]

This situation is somehow reminiscent of the reverse situation that characterized the *Lockerbie* case. There the United States was successful in putting aside treaty obligations, bearing upon it by virtue of the 1971 Montreal Convention for the Suppression of Unlawful Acts Against the Safety of Civil Aviation, by invoking Security Council resolutions in the adoption of which the United States had played a decisive role. In its Order of 14 April 1992, the International Court of Justice decided that

> both Libya and the United States, as Members of the United Nations, are obliged to accept and carry out the decisions of the Security Council in accordance with Article 25 of the Charter;...the Court...considers that prima facie this obligation extends to the decision contained in resolution 748 (1992); and...in accordance with Article 103 of the Charter, the obligations of the Parties in that respect prevail over their obligations under any other international agreement, including the Montreal Convention.[95]

In the *Lockerbie* case, it was a treaty to which the United States was party whose legal effect was suspended as a result of the adoption of a resolution by the Security Council. But the mechanism need not be limited to such treaties, and may very well entail the same consequences with respect to agreements to which the United States is not a party. The revised ASPA of September 2001 provided an excellent illustration of this. Section 1405 of the Act stated that

> the President should use the vote and voice of the United States in the United Nations Security Council to ensure that each resolution of the Security Council authorizing any peacekeeping operation under chapter VI of the Charter of the United Nations or peace enforcement operation under chapter VII of the Charter of the United Nations permanently exempts, at a minimum, members of the Armed Forces of the United States participating in such operation from criminal prosecution by the International Criminal Court for actions undertaken by such personnel in connection with the operation.[96]

Had this provision come into force, and had US representatives at the Security Council followed such a policy, the political power and privileged

---

[94] See also Alain Pellet, "Malaise dans la guerre: A quoi sert l'ONU?" *Le Monde*, 15 Nov. 2001.
[95] (1992) ICJ Reports 126, para. 42.   [96] Above note 80.

status of the United States as a permanent member of the Security Council would have enabled it to block to a certain extent the normal operation of an international agreement to which it was not even a party.

This use of Security Council procedures to generalize or to limit the scope of specific treaty regimes does not impinge on the traditional framework of the law of treaties; it instead calls into play another source of international law. It nevertheless shows that the predominance of the United States, expressed notably in its much increased role and influence in the UN Security Council since the end of the Cold War, may have a significant impact on lawmaking by the way of treaty, to the point of making this approach redundant or obsolete. It could do so in one of two ways: either by working towards the generalization of such treaty regimes as the United States finds suitable (Resolution 1373), or by putting such regimes aside when their application does not seem to serve its best interests (*Lockerbie* case and revised ASPA).

Generally speaking, recent US practice does not reveal a tendency of calling into question the fundamental principles of the law of treaties. In various contexts, US representatives have consistently referred to the accepted rules of the law of treaties, as they are reflected in the 1969 Vienna Convention, in order to assert and support their legal positions in litigation or in negotiation processes. Expressions of support for the existing legal regime may, of course, also constitute a way of resisting changes to the law of treaties which would be supported by (a majority of) other States. This could for instance have been the case in relation to the ILC's work on reservations, though it does not seem that US adherence to the regime of Articles 19–23 VCLT constituted a minority position, nor that US views on this issue exerted a significant influence on other States.

On the other hand, one cannot ignore that there has been a significant tendency by the United States to disregard some fundamental principles of the law of treaties in recent years. To a certain extent, this is consonant with a tendency to consider that the singularity of the US situation as the sole superpower justifies the view that its actions and policies should not be bound by the rules or principles of international law, regardless of the fact that the United States may have previously subscribed to them. However, it seems difficult to conclude that the United States now considers that principles as fundamental as *pacta sunt servanda* must be treated as obsolete, and that the legal framework has changed – or is about to change.

It is even more difficult to assert that such positions – assuming they were clearly established – could lead to a significant evolution of the law of treaties as accepted by the other States. The relevance of treaties themselves, as a source of international obligations, may nevertheless be very seriously threatened as a consequence of US predominance in international relations. That State's privileged position as a permanent member of the UN Security Council, combined with the strong leadership it often exerts in international affairs, means that it has been able on some occasions, by promoting the adoption of Security Council resolutions binding on all UN member States by virtue of Article 25 of the Charter, to generalize treaty regimes which served its current interests or, to the contrary, to put aside treaty obligations which impeded its actions on specific matters. Such actions have until now been exceptional. However, this scheme may well be repeated every time the balance of power and interests enables the United States to make such use of the Security Council procedures. Power would then enable the United States to exert an overwhelming influence over the formation of international law by making it possible for that State to interfere in the production of international norms through one of the more traditional means, the conclusion of (multilateral) treaties.

14

US reservations to human rights treaties: all for one and none for all?

CATHERINE REDGWELL

The purpose of this chapter is to examine US treaty-making practice in the particular context of reservations to human rights treaties. In the past decade or so the United States has ratified a number of international human rights treaties,[1] including the 1948 Genocide Convention,[2] the 1966 International Covenant on Civil and Political Rights (ICCPR),[3] the 1966

[1] It has signed but not ratified the 1966 Covenant on Economic, Social and Cultural Rights, the 1989 Convention on the Rights of the Child, and the 1979 Convention on the Elimination of All Forms of Discrimination Against Women, which as at 30 Dec. 2001 had 142, 191 and 165 parties respectively. Participation in the latter two treaties in particular was bolstered in 2001, when the Rights of Women and Children were the focus of an effort in the UN Treaty Section to foster universal participation in multilateral treaties deposited with the UN Secretary-General. This was one of three treaty action events held to date following the Secretary-General's Millennium Report to the General Assembly (A/54/2000), which called, among other things, for enhanced support for the rule of law through the signature and ratification of international treaties. In the case of the Child Convention, the United States is the only State apart from Somalia not to have ratified.

[2] 78 UNTS 277, entered into force 12 Jan. 1951, with 133 parties as of Oct. 2001. The United States ratified the Convention in 1988 with two reservations and five understandings.

[3] 999 UNTS 171, entered into force 23 March 1976, with 147 parties as of October 2001. The United States ratified the Covenant in 1992 with five reservations, two understandings and three declarations. It played an active role in the early negotiations of the Covenant, with Eleanor Roosevelt chairing the early sessions of the UN Commission on Human Rights. However, following the election of a Republican administration in 1952 she was replaced, and the United States signaled that it no longer had any interest in ratifying any resulting treaty text. Representation continued until 1966, but the US representative played no active part in the negotiations and abstained from voting. President Carter submitted the ICCPR for Senate advice and consent in 1978; this was not pursued by President Reagan and it fell to President Bush to resubmit the Covenant to the Senate in 1991, accompanied by a number of significant reservations, understandings, and declarations: see United States Senate Resolution of Advice and Consent to Ratification of the International Covenant on Civil and Political Rights, 138 Cong. Rec. S4781 (1991).

Convention on the Elimination of Racial Discrimination[4] and the 1984 Torture Convention.[5] However, particularly in the case of the ICCPR, ratification was accompanied by a number of reservations, understandings, and declarations which significantly modify the Convention in its application to the United States and, indeed, in at least two instances may be argued to run contrary to the object and purpose of the Convention.[6] Unsurprisingly therefore, rather than leading to widespread praise and support for the United States in buttressing human rights guarantees on the international level,[7] US ratification of the ICCPR has led to criticisms of the insulation of the US domestic legal order from external influences in the human rights field and the resulting manifestation of an isolationist "superiority complex."[8] Indeed, the US approach to ratification of human rights treaties has been characterized by an "à la carte multilateralism,"[9] in

---

[4] 660 UNTS 195, entered into force 4 Jan. 1969, with 159 parties as of October 2001. The United States ratified the Convention in 1994 with three reservations, one understanding and one declaration.

[5] 1465 UNTS 85, entered into force 26 June 1987, with 126 parties as of Oct. 2001. The United States ratified the Convention in 1994 with two reservations, five understandings and one declaration.

[6] So concludes the UN Human Rights Committee in its Comments on the United States' first report submitted under Article 40 of the International Covenant on Civil and Political Rights: UN Doc. CCPR/C/79/Add.50 (1995), para. 14: "The Committee is also particularly concerned at reservations to article 6, paragraph 5, and article 7 of the Covenant, which it believes to be incompatible with the object and purpose of the Covenant." See further discussion below.

[7] US ratification of the ICCPR marked an apparent shift from the more strongly isolationist stance of the 1980s, although, as Allan Gerson notes, US foreign policy in the twentieth century was marked both by Madisonian and Wilsonian trends: Allan Gerson, "Multilateralism à la Carte: The Consequences of Unilateral 'Pick and Pay' Approaches" (2000) 11 EJIL 61.

[8] Pierre Klein, above. Internally, it has been characterized as nothing less than a threat to the integrity to the US constitutional system for concluding treaties: Louis Henkin, "US Ratification of Human Rights Conventions: The Ghost of Senator Bricker" (1995) 89 AJIL 341 at 348. In the 1950s Senator Bricker mounted an unsuccessful campaign for constitutional amendment to render all treaties non-self-executing under US law, apparently motivated by a desire to prevent an end to racial discrimination and segregation by international treaty: *ibid.* See also Hurst Hannum and Dana Fischer, "The Political Framework," in *United States Ratification of the ICCPR* (New York: Transnational Publishers, 1993), p. 14 ("chilling effect of the Bricker era"). For recent analysis of the federalism understanding attached to the US ratification of the Covenant, see Brad Roth, "Understanding the 'Understanding': Federalism Constraints on Human Rights Implementation" (2001) 47 *Wayne Law Review* 891.

[9] This terminology derives from a recent issue of the *European Journal of International Law*, which examines the role and limits of unilateralism in international law, with Section III, "Multilateralism à la Carte: The Consequences of Unilateral 'Pick and Pay' Approaches," focusing on the United States' withholding of money owed to the UN budget, (with contributions by Francesco Francioni, Allan Gerson and Emilio Cardenas). See also Malanczuk, who, in his analysis of US non-participation in the International Criminal Court and Landmines agreements,

terms both of the (more limited) number of treaties accepted and of the (qualified) obligations assumed. The United States "remains an anomalous outlier with respect to many widely ratified conventions (e.g. the Convention on the Elimination of Discrimination Against Women or the Convention on the Rights of the Child)"[10] and it has entered the highest number of reservations by States parties to the Torture Convention, the Convention on the Elimination of Racial Discrimination, and the ICCPR.[11] This "pick 'n mix" approach has provoked strong reactions prompted by two major concerns. The first concern is the negative impact on the universalizing effect of human rights norms. The second flows from the perception of a double standard, given the fact that the United States has not hesitated to raise human rights issues internationally and to rely on "bilateral enforcement" through conditionality attached to foreign aid, loans, and military assistance.[12] Louis Henkin uses the analogy of a cathedral supported by (external) flying buttresses to describe this bilateral process, with the United States supporting the international human rights edifice largely from the outside, rather than as a pillar within the cathedral.[13] With its increased participation in international human rights instruments coming without an unqualified acceptance of the obligations contained therein, the concern arises that the US "pillar" rests on shaky foundations.[14]

---

also comments briefly on US "unilateralism" in the context of reservations to human rights treaties: Peter Malanczuk, "The International Criminal Court and Landmines: What are the Consequences of Leaving the US Behind?" (2000) 11 EJIL 77–90. In common with many commentators, he points out that the US failure to accept all international human rights obligations in an unqualified sense is that much harder to accept, given that the United States continues to criticize other States for not respecting international human rights: ibid., at 89. While there is, of course, a legal distinction between the (attempted) non-application of fundamental human rights provisions via the reservations route, and non-compliance with such provisions once accepted, both contribute to undermining universal respect for human rights.

[10] José Alvarez, "Do Liberal States Behave Better? A Critique of Slaughter's Liberal Theory" (2001) 12 EJIL 183 at 208; see also above note 1. Alvarez concludes that regime type is only one factor in entering into treaty obligations and treaty compliance. With respect to the examples of CEDAW and the CRC, he notes that "what makes the United States an anomaly may have something to do with the fact that it is a 'liberal' nation – as well as a superpower": ibid.

[11] See Yogeshi Tyagi, "The Conflict of Law and Policy on Reservations to Human Rights Treaties" (2000) 71 British Year Book of International Law 181 at 188.

[12] See Hannum and Fischer, "Political Framework," above note 8, at 3.

[13] Louis Henkin, The Rights of Man Today (London: Stevens, 1979).

[14] A further factor conditioning such responses may be the "variety of adverse feelings toward the United States that have gained prominence since the end of the Cold War," which Detlev Vagts considers underlay, for example, pursuit of the La Grand case – which involved the death penalty, "an issue that sharply divides the United States from many other countries in the world": Detlev

There are thus two possible levels of analysis of the impact of US practice regarding reservations to human rights treaties: the impact on human rights and the impact upon general treaty law. This contribution is primarily concerned with the latter, and will focus on US ratification of the ICCPR in particular, drawing therefrom some conclusions regarding the effect of US predominance on the evolution of the law of treaties concerning reservations.

Reservations to treaties

In traditional treaty making the integrity of the treaty text was paramount, with unanimity the typical method of treaty negotiation. In a multilateral context a reservation had to be accepted by all other States party in order for the reserving State to become a party to the treaty. However, following the Advisory Opinion of the International Court of Justice in the *Reservations to the Genocide Convention* case,[15] States were quick to adopt a more flexible practice. Reservations might be made to treaties either silent on the matter (as with the Genocide Convention itself, with compatibility with the object and purpose of the treaty the test of validity) or in accordance with the reservations clause, which will permit departure from the treaty text in general and/or specified circumstances. In either situation it is necessary for only one other State to accept the reservation (or to object to the reservation, but not to treaty relations arising) for the reserving State to become a party to the treaty.[16] This modern approach is enshrined in Articles 19–23 of the 1969 Vienna Convention on the Law of Treaties,[17] with Article 19(c)

F. Vagts, "The United States and its Treaties: Observance and Breach" (2001) 95 AJIL 313 at 334. On the other hand, as Louis Henkin, observes, "The object and purpose of the human rights conventions, it would seem, are to promote respect for human rights by having countries – mutually – assume legal obligations to respect and to ensure recognized rights in accordance with international law. Even the friends of the United States have objected that its reservations [to the ICCPR] are incompatible with that object and purpose and are therefore invalid." Louis Henkin, "Ghost of Senator Bricker," above note 8, at 343.

[15] *Reservations to the Convention on the Prevention and Punishment of the Crime of Genocide* (1951) ICJ Reports 15.

[16] Other methods of differentiating treaty obligations are employed in the human rights and environment fields, including the progressive character of certain human rights obligations in the social, economic, and cultural sphere, and common but differentiated responsibilities (see, for example, Article 4, 1992 UN Framework Convention on Climate Change 1771 UNTS 107).

[17] There are presently ninety-three parties to the Vienna Convention. The United States has signed (1970) but not ratified the Convention.

reflecting the "object and purpose" test of compatibility enunciated by the International Court of Justice in the *Reservations to the Genocide Convention* case.[18] It is the interaction between the validity/permissibility (Article 19) and opposability (Article 20) elements of the Vienna Convention which, in the absence of a competent organ to determine such matters under the particular treaty in question, has proved the most problematic in state practice. It has provoked what the International Law Commission refers to as a "doctrinal quarrel," with the permissibility school holding that the test of validity is a threshold test in Article 19 which must be met before any issue of opposability arises under Article 20, whilst the opposability school views all reservations as open to acceptance or rejection.[19] This is of particular import in the human rights field. Jochen Frowein, for example, argues that treating a State which ratifies a human rights treaty with an incompatible reservation as a non-party if the offending reservation is not withdrawn[20] is an untenable approach, given the uncertainty which would arise regarding which States are party to global human rights treaties.[21] Indeed, the adherence of the United States to the traditional Vienna Convention approach for human rights treaties provides a further basis for criticism of the US practice in respect of such treaties.[22]

---

[18] For general discussion of the Vienna Convention regime, see Derek Bowett, "Reservations to Non-Restricted Multilateral Treaties" (1976–7) 48 *British Year Book of International Law* 67–92, and Catherine Redgwell, "Universality or Integrity? Some Reflections on Reservations to General Multilateral Treaties" (1993) 64 *British Year Book of International Law* 245–82.

[19] See, generally, Harold Koh, "Reservations to Multilateral Treaties: How International Legal Doctrine Reflects World Vision" (1982) 23 *Harvard International Law Journal* 71.

[20] The United Kingdom's observations on Human Rights Committee General Comment 24 (52) assert this position: "A State which purports to ratify a human rights treaty subject to a reservation which is fundamentally incompatible with participation in the treaty regime cannot be regarded as having become a party at all – unless it withdraws the reservation." Reproduced in (1996) 3 *International Human Rights Reports* 261 at 265, para. 15. The US response appears to consider that Articles 20 and 21 apply even to the question of impermissible reservations, with only two possible outcomes: no treaty relations arise or the remainder of the treaty comes into force between the parties in question: *ibid.*, at 269. Both the United States and the United Kingdom clearly reject severance of the offending reservation: on the issue of severance, see further note 85 below.

[21] Jochen A. Frowein, "Reservations and the International *Ordre Public*," in Jerzy Makarczyk (ed.), *Theory of International Law at the Threshold of the Twenty-first Century: Essays in Honour of Krzysztof Skubiszewski* (The Hague: Kluwer, 1996), p. 403, p. 408. However, some States have expressly adopted such an approach in their treaty practice. See, for example, the Netherlands response to the US reservations to the Genocide Convention discussed below note 38.

[22] See further Frowein, "Reservations", *ibid.*; and note 97 below.

It is particularly in the last decade or so that the application without modification of the Vienna Convention regime to human rights treaties has been the subject of considerable academic debate;[23] addressed in a General Comment by the Human Rights Committee under the ICCPR;[24] and become an issue within the topic of reservations to treaties in the recent work of the International Law Commission.[25] While the Commission's work on this topic has yet to be completed, what has been clear virtually from the outset of its work in 1994 has been the commitment of States, including the United States, to retaining the three Vienna Conventions in their current form.[26] Equally clear is the view of Special Rapporteur Alain Pellet that there is nothing in the Vienna Convention reservations regime that renders it inapplicable per se to the category of human rights treaties.[27] This view was set forth in response to the controversy surrounding the US reservations and the Human Rights Committee's General Comment, with the Special Rapporteur considering it desirable for the Commission to express a preliminary view on the matter rather than waiting for the completion of its work on the topic.[28] "Preliminary Conclusions of the International Law Commission on reservations to normative multilateral treaties, including human rights treaties"[29] were adopted in 1997, including reiteration of

---

[23] See, for example, J. Piers Gardner (ed.), *Human Rights as General Norms and a State's Right to Opt Out: Reservations and Objections to Human Rights Conventions* (London: British Institute of International and Comparative Law, 1997).

[24] General Comment No. 24 (52), UN Doc. CCPR/C/21/Rev.1/Add.6. For discussion of the subsequent practice of the Committee on reservations, see Tyagi, "Reservations to Human Rights Treaties", above note 11, at 223–6, and for general practice see P. R. Ghandhi, *The Human Rights Committee and the Right of Individual Communication* (Aldershot: Ashgate Press, 1998), ch. 14, "Reservations" (including analysis of the US response to the General Comment).

[25] Reservations to normative multilateral treaties, including human rights treaties, were addressed in the Second Report of the Special Rapporteur and considered at the 49th session of the ILC with preliminary conclusions adopted (1997): GAOR, 52nd session, Supp. No. 10 (A/52/10).

[26] Summarizing the Commission's consideration of his first report at its forty-seventh session, the Special Rapporteur stated, inter alia, "There is consensus in the Commission that there should be no change in the relevant provisions of the 1969, 1978 and 1986 Vienna Conventions." UNGAOR, 50th session, A/50/10, Supp. No. 10, para. 491.

[27] Chapter II of the Special Rapporteur's Second Report, entitled "Unity or diversity of the legal regime for reservations to treaties: Reservations to human rights treaties," concludes that the reservations regime of the Vienna Convention is sufficiently flexible to apply to all treaties, including human rights treaties: A/CN.4/477/Add.1.

[28] A/CN.4/477/Add.1, p. 86.

[29] UNGAOR, 52nd session, A/52/10 Supp. 10, para. 157. Paragraphs 5–10 of the preliminary conclusions address the role of human rights bodies with respect to reservations. The Preliminary Conclusions were transmitted to the human rights treaty monitoring bodies, including the Human Rights Committee which, while undertaking a more detailed response, indicated:

the unity of the reservations regime. The Conclusions subsequently met with widespread support in an extensive debate within the Sixth Committee of the UN General Assembly.[30]

There is thus little doubt that the US reservations to the ICCPR had a catalytic effect and were partly responsible for the Human Rights Committee's adoption of its General Comment. This in turn prompted the International Law Commission to take its preliminary view on the issue of reservations to normative multilateral treaties. Nonetheless, it should be stressed that the United States was not the first State to make sweeping reservations to a human rights instrument with the legal intent of insulating existing national law from the effect of international obligations. Indeed, its reservations are less egregious than many, in that they demonstrate a particularized, rather than generalized, subordination of international law to domestic law.[31] Nor is this the first instance where States have responded to reservations by objecting to their incompatibility with the object and purpose of

> Universal monitoring bodies, such as the Human Rights Committee, play no less important a role [than regional intergovernmental institutions] in the process by which ... practices and rules develop and are entitled, therefore, to participate in and contribute to it. In this context, it must be recognized that the proposition enunciated by the Commission in paragraph 10 of the preliminary conclusions is subject to modification as practices and rules developed by universal and regional monitoring bodies gain general acceptance.

See Third Report on reservations to treaties, A/CN.4/491 (1998), at para. 15. Part III of the Special Rapporteur's general outline of the study, which is the current focus of the ILC's work on the topic of reservations to treaties, considers the formulation and withdrawal of reservations (and of interpretative declarations), acceptances and objections to reservations (and to interpretative declarations).

[30] "Topical summary of the discussion held in the Sixth Committee of the General Assembly during its fifty-second session prepared by the Secretariat," A/CN.4/483, paras. 65–67.

[31] This is the thrust of the US response to the General Comment's criticism of the use of reservations to insulate domestic law from change. The US considers that such sweeping reservations, whereby the "Covenant is generally subordinated to the full unspecified range of domestic law is neither appropriate nor lawful": (1996) 3 *International Human Rights Reports* at 268.

Article 27 Vienna Convention provides that "a party may not invoke the provisions of its internal law as justification for failure to perform a treaty" – hence the need for reservations where there is no present intention to repeal/revise laws manifestly incompatible with Convention provisions. Brad Roth discusses how the federalism understanding might have been drafted in such a manner as potentially to fall foul of Article 27: "Federalism Constraints on Human Rights Implementation," above note 8, at 20, n. 34. He suggests that the likely intention was "a Bricker amendment in miniature" constraining the extension of federal competence (*ibid.*, at 22), while noting Thomas Buergenthal's "ingenious argument" that the federalism understanding could be used to circumvent at least in part the non-self-executing declaration in its reference to competent authorities of the state or local governments (including courts) taking "appropriate measures for the fulfillment of the Convention" (Declaration 1). See Thomas

the convention while not opposing the entry into force of the convention between themselves and the reserving State.[32] Nonetheless, it is my thesis that the practice of the United States in this area, given its position as the sole superpower and an avowed human rights adherent, risks undermining not only the integrity of the treaty text in question, but also the premise that domestic law cannot prevail over internationally assumed obligations.[33] After all, "Treaty ratification normally implies a purpose of conforming domestic law to international obligations, not the reverse."[34] The United States reservations, taken "Collectively... all but nullify the legal effect of the ratification on both the international and domestic planes."[35] At worst they call into question the very basis for consent to, and obligations arising under, international treaties;[36] at best, they serve to highlight the persisting confusion regarding the response to and legal effect of impermissible reservations. In the specific instance of the US reservations, the fundamental role of consent *on the ratifying State's*

Buergenthal, "Modern Constitutions and Human Rights Treaties" (1997) 36 *Columbia Journal of Transnational Law* 211 at 222.

[32] See the examples discussed above, note 18.

[33] On US practice see, generally, Detlev F. Vagts, "The United States and its Treaties: Observance and Breach" (2001) 95 AJIL 313–34. As Vagts observes, the doctrine of *pacta sunt servanda* arises independently of national law – an independence that may be traced back to the Advisory Opinion of the Permanent Court of Justice in *Greco-Bulgarian Communities* 1930 PCIJ (Ser. B), No. 17, at 32: "the provisions of municipal law cannot prevail over those of a treaty." The premise was applied against the United States, when it refused to permit the Palestine Liberation Organization to maintain an office at the UN in New York, in the 1988 Advisory Opinion, *Applicability of the Obligation to Arbitrate Under Section 21 of the United Nations Headquarters Agreement of 26 June 1947* [1988] ICJ Rep 12, at 34 para. 57 ("fundamental principle of international law that international law prevails over domestic law"). See also Ian Sinclair, *The Vienna Convention on the Law of Treaties* (2nd edn., Manchester: Manchester University Press, 1984), p. 2.

[34] Dinah Shelton, "Implementation Issues Raised by the proposed United States Reservations, Understandings and Declarations," in Hurst Hannum and Dana Fischer (eds.), *US Ratification of the International Covenants on Human Rights* (New York: Transnational Publishing, 1993), p. 272.

[35] Brad Roth, "Federalism Constraints on Human Rights Implementation," above note 8, at 28.

[36] See further Detlev Vagts, "The United States and Its Treaties: Observance and Breach" (2001) 95 AJIL 313 (penumbral obligation under United States law). Curtis Bradley and Jack Goldsmith argue that *pacta sunt servanda* is irrelevant because this obligation arises once treaty obligations are entered into, but does not affect what obligations are assumed in the first place, an argument which fails fully to take account of the good faith component of the doctrine which surely *does* apply to the obligations assumed: Curtis Bradley and Jack Goldsmith, "Treaties, Human Rights, and Conditional Consent" (2000) 149 *University of Pennsylvania Law Review* 399 at 427. On consent, see Matthew Craven, "Legal Differentiation and the Concept of the Human Rights Treaty in International Law" (2000) 11 EJIL 489–519.

terms has been decisively underscored by prioritizing the consent to be bound under the protective cover of the offending reservations ("all for one") rather than either severing the reservations and holding the reserving State exposed to the unmodified obligations,[37] or refusing to consider the United States a party at all.[38] The effect is to undermine universal acceptance of human rights *and* the multilateral institutional mechanism for their enforcement ("none" – or at least less – "for all").[39] Yet promoting universal acceptance of universal human rights norms is part of the mission of the United Nations, as reflected in the commitment, expressed in the Millennium Report of the Secretary-General to the General Assembly,[40] to

---

[37] An outcome opposed by the United States in its response to General Comment 24, stressing that "reservations are an essential part of a State's consent to be bound": (1996) 3 *International Human Rights Reports* 269. Severing the reservation and holding the reserving State exposed to the unmodified obligations is known as the "Strasbourg approach" after the European Court of Human Rights decisions in *Belilos v. Switzerland* ECHR Series A, Vol. 132, 20 April 1988 and *Loizidou v. Turkey* ECHR Series A, reproduced in (1995) 20 *European Human Rights Reports* 99. See further Bruno Simma, "Reservations to Human Rights Treaties – Some Recent Developments," in Gerhard Hafner et al. (eds.), *Liber Amicorum: Professor Ignaz Seidl-Hohenveldern in Honour of his 80th Birthday* (The Hague, Boston, MA: Kluwer Law International, 1998). The "Strasbourg approach" has been adopted by at least one other regional human rights body – the Inter-American Court of Human Rights – thus extending the approach beyond Europe. For recent discussion of the practice see Roberto Baratta, "Should Invalid Reservations to Human Rights Treaties Be Disregarded?" (2000) 11 EJIL 413. As will be seen further below, this is the effect of the Italian response to the US reservation to Article 6.

[38] As will be seen below, none of the eleven States objecting to the US reservations as incompatible expressly state that no treaty relations arise; indeed, apart from the German objection, which is silent on the point, the other objecting States expressly confirm that their objection(s) do not constitute an obstacle to the entry into force of the ICCPR between them and the United States. This approach may be contrasted with the Netherlands' objection in 1989 to the first of the US reservations to the Genocide Convention, declaring that "the Government of the Kingdom of the Netherlands does not consider the United States of America a party to the Convention." Nearly a dozen other States are not considered by the Netherlands to be parties to the Convention in consequence of incompatible reservations; once the offending reservation has been withdrawn, the Netherlands clarifies that treaty relations arise (e.g. Hungary, Bulgaria, and Mongolia in 1996). See Multilateral Treaties Deposited with the Secretary-General, http://untreaty.un.org.

[39] As Frowein notes, the Strasbourg approach of severance, applied in the *Belilos* and *Loizidou* cases, above note 37, "stand[s] for clear recognition that States are not entitled to rely on their will to an extent that would undermine the public order system established by the Convention." Frowein, "Reservations and the International *Ordre Public*," above note 21, at 407.
Tyagi identifies three effects of reservations: (1) lowering of human rights standards; (2) dilution of the principle of universality; and (3) avoiding international accountability. He expressly cites the US reservations to Articles 6 and 7 of the ICCPR as an example of the first effect: Tyagi, "Reservations to Human Rights Treaties," above note 11, at 202 *et seq.*

[40] UN Doc. A/54/2000, available at http://www.un.org/millenium/sg/report/full.htm.

advance the international rule of law through, *inter alia*, encouraging States to ratify international treaties.[41]

Reservations to the International Covenant on Civil and Political Rights (ICCPR)

The Human Rights Committee's General Comment No. 24[42] notes that, as at 1 November 1994, 46 of the 127 States then parties to the Covenant had entered a collective total of 150 reservations to it.[43] No guidance on the making of reservations is to be found in the Covenant or its First Optional Protocol:[44] both documents are silent on the matter of reservations.[45] The "compatibility with the object and purpose" test consequently applies as a matter of general international law. The Committee considers that the object and purpose of the Covenant "is to create legally binding standards for human rights by defining certain civil and political rights and placing

[41] Three treaty signature/ratification "events" have been held since 2000, the second of which focused expressly on human rights treaties, particularly those protecting the rights of the child and of women: see http://untreaty.un.org/English/TreatyEvent2001/usgletter2.htm (9 May 2001).

[42] For a general discussion, see Catherine Redgwell, "Reservations to Treaties and Human Rights Committee General Comment No. 24(52)" (1997) 46 *International and Comparative Law Quarterly* 390. The Comment provoked a strong reaction in the US Senate, including a proposed amendment to bill S. 908 calling on the president to reject it and to seek its "nullification": Pell Amendment No. 1968 (31 July 1995), S11016.

[43] Comment, para. 1. This constituted 36 percent of the States then party to the Covenant. A significant number relate to criminal procedure, such as the segregation of juvenile offenders, and Article 14(5) obligations such as the provision of free legal assistance. Tyagi calculates that 55 of the then 147 States party to the ICCPR have entered reservations: Tyagi, "Reservations to Human Rights Treaties", above note 11.

[44] The First Optional Protocol to the International Covenant on Civil and Political Rights was concluded on 16 Dec. 1966 and entered into force on 23 March 1976: 999 UNTS 171; UKTS 6 (1977), Cmnd 6702; (1967) 6 *International Legal Materials* 383. It allows individuals to petition the Human Rights Committee in respect of alleged violations of the rights set forth in the Covenant. The Second Optional Protocol to the International Covenant on Civil and Political Rights, Aiming at the Abolition of the Death Penalty, concluded on 15 Dec. 1989 and entered into force on 11 July 1991, Annex to GA Res 44/128, 15 December 1989, expressly prohibits reservations "except for a reservation made at the time of ratification or accession that provides for the application of the death penalty in time of war pursuant to a conviction for a most serious crime of a military nature committed during wartime" (Article 2(1)).

[45] Manfred Nowak, *UN Covenant on Civil and Political Rights: CCPR Commentary* (Kehl/ Strasbourg/Arlington: N. P. Engel Publishers, 1993), p. xxv. For a thorough discussion of the fate of a reservations clause see Rosalyn Higgins, "Derogations Under Human Rights Treaties," (1976–77) 48 *British Year Book of International Law* 281 at 317–19; see also Pierre-Henri Imbert, "Reservations and Human Rights Conventions" (1981) 6 *Human Rights Review* 28, at 42–3.

them in a framework of obligations which are legally binding for those States which ratify; and to provide an efficacious supervisory machinery for the obligations undertaken."[46] The reservations which have been made to the Covenant vary in significance, with the Comment dividing into three categories those reservations likely to impair its effective implementation. These are (1) reservations excluding the duty to provide and guarantee particular rights in the Covenant; (2) reservations couched in general terms "often directed to ensuring the continued paramountcy of certain domestic legal provisions"; and (3) reservations affecting the competence of the Human Rights Committee.[47]

It should be stressed that the Committee does *not* rule out the use of reservations altogether; indeed, it is difficult to see how this could be done without an express prohibition on reservations in the Covenant. In fact such prohibitions are rare in human rights treaties.[48] In any event, the advantage of permitting States to accept the generality of an instrument while entering reservations in respect of those rights which may be difficult initially to guarantee is explicitly recognized in the Comment.[49] Nor should it be assumed that the mere fact of making a reservation is evidence of an unwillingness to comply with human rights principles, not least because of the variety of reasons for and scope of actual reservations made by States.[50] However, there is little doubt that the general tenor of the language used in the Comment is disapproving of "permanent" reservations. A restrictive approach to such reservations is clearly favored, in the interests of the integrity of the Covenant. This reflects the essential paradox in permitting reservations to human rights instruments which are intended to guarantee common international minimum standards. As Frowein observes, "A permanent reservation lowering the minimum standard is incompatible with this basic idea"[51] of universalizing minimum human rights standards.

---

[46] Comment, para. 7.   [47] Comment, para. 1.

[48] Two examples predating the Vienna Convention are the 1956 Supplementary Convention on the Abolition of Slavery, the Slave Trade and Institutions and Practices Similar to Slavery, 266 UNTS 40 (1957), and the 1960 Convention Against Discrimination in Education, 429 UNTS 93 (1962).

[49] Comment, para. 4. See further Imbert, "Reservations and Human Rights Conventions," above note 45, at 28.

[50] See further Massimo Coccia, "Reservations to Multilateral Treaties on Human Rights" (1985) 15 *California Western International Law Journal* 1 at 18–22, where he identifies a range of legal, political and practical factors influencing States in the making of reservations.

[51] Frowein, "Reservations and the International *Ordre Public*," above note 21, p. 412.

A temporary derogation from the full rights and obligations of the State under the treaty is, however, unexceptional, pending the realignment of national law. Such a derogation does not run foul of the basic international law prohibition, embodied in Article 27 of the Vienna Convention, against invoking the provisions of internal law as justification for the failure to perform international obligations, in such a way that no real international rights or obligations have been accepted.[52] It is also arguably consistent with Article 2(2) of the Covenant which obliges States "to take the necessary steps, in accordance with constitutional processes and with the provisions of the present Covenant, to adopt such legislative or other measures as may be necessary to give effect to the rights recognized in the present Covenant." Reservations may also allow a State to hedge its bets against the uncertain application of new treaty obligations,[53] providing the "assurance that the State's interests will be preserved in all circumstances."[54]

Where a State is uncertain regarding the consistency of its domestic law with its treaty obligations, it may take the precautionary approach of formulating reservations. However, such reservations can risk impairing the effective and autonomous functioning of the Human Rights Committee in respect of the interpretation of treaty provisions. The United States' reservation to Article 7, for example, is an explicit attempt to preempt the application of existing and future interpretations by the Committee of the prohibition of "cruel, inhuman or degrading treatment or punishment," and thus to preserve the domestic interpretation under the US Constitution.[55]

The confusion which the lack of clarity in Articles 19–23 of the Vienna Convention has engendered in State practice is another reason the

---

[52] See paragraph 22 of the Comment, which states, inter alia: "It is desirable for States entering a reservation to indicate in precise terms the domestic legislation or practices which it believes to be incompatible with the Covenant obligation reserved; and to explain the time period it requires to render its own laws and practices compatible with the Covenant, *or why it is unable to render its own laws and practices compatible with the Covenant*" (emphasis added).

[53] And hedge its bets against possible interpretations of a treaty taken by a supervisory organ with the power to interpret its provisions: Shelton, "Implementation Issues," above note 34, p. 208. However, such reservations risk impairing the functioning of such organs: see note 55 below.

[54] Imbert, "Reservations and Human Rights Conventions," above note 45, at 30.

[55] See also the Indian "reservation" in respect of a common interpretation of self-determination, discussed in Higgins, "Derogations under Human Rights Treaties," above note 45, at 14. Concern regarding the interpretation of Article 6(1) of the European Convention on Human Rights by the Court was the motivation behind the Swiss "declaration" to that provision: see the *Belilos* case, above note 37.

Committee provides for rejecting the application of those articles to human rights treaties.[56] The confusion is well illustrated by the objections to the United States' reservations: as at 31 December 1993, only eleven of the 127 States then party to the Covenant had objected. Five did so on the basis of incompatibility with the object and purpose of the Covenant,[57] three on the basis of incompatibility with a particular *article* of the Covenant,[58] and three on the basis that the second reservation is incompatible with the object and purpose of Article 6 while the third reservation is incompatible with the object and purpose of the Covenant.[59] None expressly objected to treaty relations arising with the United States in consequence of its objections. Has concern to ensure the participation of the United States in the Covenant overcome concerns regarding that treaty's integrity?[60]

United States reservations to the ICCPR

The five reservations, five understandings[61] and three declarations made by the United States upon ratification of the Covenant on 8 June 1992[62] furnish examples of reservations falling in each of the three categories identified by

---

[56] Comment, para. 17. For the inhibitive effect of the Vienna Convention regime on objections, see further Coccia, "Reservations to Multilateral Treaties," above note 50, at 48; see also Shelton, "Implementation Issues," above note 34, at 229.

[57] Denmark, Finland, France, Spain, and Sweden.

[58] Belgium, Germany, and Italy. Neither the Vienna Convention nor the ICJ in the *Genocide* case speak of compatibility with *articles* of a treaty, only with the treaty as a whole. Italy, while not objecting to the entry into force of the Covenant between it and the United States, considers the reservation to Article 6 to be null and void.

[59] The Netherlands, Norway, and Portugal.

[60] A point made in respect of other human rights treaties in the face of widespread reservations. See, for example, Andrew C. Byrnes, "The 'Other' Human Rights Treaty Body: The Work of the Committee on the Elimination of Discrimination Against Women" (1989) 14 *Yale Journal of International Law* 1.

[61] In objecting to the reservations made by the United States on ratification, both Sweden and Finland recall that the name given to a statement does not determine its legal effect. Both consider Understanding (1) to be a reservation and object to it on that ground; the Netherlands, on the other hand, expressly states that it does not consider the US understandings and declarations to modify or exclude the legal effect of provisions of the Covenant in their application to the United States, nor limit in any way the competence of the Human Rights Committee to interpret these provisions in their application to the United States. Multilateral Treaties Deposited with the Secretary-General, available at http://untreaty.un.org.

[62] For analysis see Shelton, "Implementation Issues," above note 34; see also the Senate Committee on Foreign Relations Report on the International Covenant on Civil and Political Rights, reproduced from US Senate Executive Report 102–23 (102nd Cong., 2nd Sess.) in (1992) 31 *International Legal Materials* 645 (hereinafter "Senate Report"); and David P. Stewart, "US

the Human Rights Committee as impairing effective implementation of the ICCPR. The five reservations limit or exclude the effects of the following.

1. Article 20 (prohibitions on war propaganda and hate speech). Concerns about the compatibility of this provision with free speech guarantees have led a number of other States to make similar reservations,[63] and no objections were raised to this US reservation.

2. Article 6 (limitations on the application of the death penalty). The United States is the only State currently to maintain a reservation against this provision,[64] which has provoked a number of objections.

3. Article 7 (definition of cruel, inhuman, or degrading treatment or punishment). A number of objections were made to this reservation.

4. Article 15(1) (reduction of penalties for certain offenses). As with Article 20, other States have made similar reservations and no State has objected to this US reservation.

5. Article 10(2)(b) and (3) (treatment of juvenile offenders). Similar reservations have been entered to these provisions by other States, including Australia, whose reservation (subsequently withdrawn) prompted a Netherlands objection. No State has objected to this US reservation.

In assessing the situation, Shelton presciently observes that "Particularly because the Covenants are deemed to constitute minimum standards of state conduct towards individuals and groups, there may be objections to the number and scope of US conditions taken together."[65] Objections there have been, but as we have seen, they come from only eleven States.[66]

Ratification of the Covenant on Civil and Political Rights: The Significance of the Reservations, Understandings and Declarations" (1993) 14 *Human Rights Law Journal* 77.

[63] See, for example, the Belgian and Danish reservations which apply the ICCPR's provisions in the context of, *inter alia*, Article 10 (freedom of expression) of the 1950 European Convention for the Protection of Human Rights and Fundamental Freedoms 213 UNTS 221. As the Danish reservation expressly notes, in 1961 it had voted against the prohibition against propaganda for war as contrary to the freedom of expression contained in Article 19.

[64] On ratification of the ICCPR in 1972 Norway temporarily reserved the application of Article 6(4) – concerning the right to seek commutation or pardon in case of the death penalty – but withdrew the reservation in 1979.

[65] Shelton, "Implementation Issues," above note 34, at 272. Other commentators have disputed whether the Covenant in fact represents *in toto* an irreducible international minimum standard: see, for example, Madeline Morris, "Few Reservations about Reservations" (2000) 1 *Chicago Journal of International Law* 341 at 343.

[66] By 31 Dec. 1993 objections had been made by Belgium (5 Oct. 1993), Denmark (1 Oct. 1993), Finland (28 Sept. 1993), France (4 Oct. 1993), Germany (29 Sept. 1993), Italy (5 Oct. 1993), the Netherlands (28 Sept. 1993), Norway (4 Oct. 1993), Portugal (5 Oct. 1993), Spain (5 Oct. 1993)

Attracting the most objections are reservations (2) and (3) which relate to Articles 6 (protecting the right to life) and 7 (guaranteeing freedom from torture or cruel, inhuman, or degrading treatment or punishment),[67] respectively, and which state[68]

(2) That the United States reserves the right, subject to its constitutional constraints, to impose capital punishment on any person (other than a pregnant woman) duly convicted under existing or future laws permitting the imposition of capital punishment, including such punishment for crimes committed by persons below eighteen years of age.[69]

(3) That the United States considers itself bound by Article 7 to the extent that "cruel, inhuman or degrading treatment or punishment" means the cruel and unusual treatment or punishment prohibited by the Fifth, Eighth, and/or Fourteenth Amendments to the Constitution of the United States.[70]

and Sweden (18 June 1993): Multilateral Treaties Deposited with the UN Secretary-General, available at http://untreaty.un.org. This was more than double the number of objections to reservations to the Covenant lodged up to the previous year. No further formal objections to the US reservations, understandings, and declarations have been lodged.

[67] Italy and Germany consider the "reservation" in respect of Article 7 as a reference to Article 2, and thus not in any way affecting the obligations of the United States as a State party to the Covenant: see Multilateral Treaties Deposited with the UN Secretary General, available at http://untreaty.un.org.

[68] *Ibid.* Conversely, there appears to be a general consensus that the United States' reservation to derogable Article 20 (prohibiting war propaganda and advocacy of national, racial, or religious hatred) is legitimate and necessary to preserve one of the freedoms guaranteed in the Covenant, namely freedom of expression. None of the States which had objected to the US reservations as at the end of 1993 objected to this particular reservation.

[69] See in particular Article 6(5) of the Covenant which provides: "Sentence of death shall not be imposed for crimes committed by persons below eighteen years of age and shall not be carried out on pregnant women." The reservation is intended to preserve compatibility with the jurisprudence of the US Supreme Court, though, as Henkin points out, a more restrictively worded reservation limited to, for example, juveniles under 18 but over 16 years of age, might have accomplished the same goal: Henkin, "US Ratification of Human Rights Conventions," above note 8.

[70] This reservation is similar to the one suggested (and made) in connection with the US ratification of the Convention Against Torture and other Cruel, Inhuman or Degrading Treatment or Punishment: Senate Report, above note 62, at 654. Its roots may lie in part in the European Court of Human Rights decision in the *Soering* case, Judgement of 7 July 1989, Ser. A. No. 161, reprinted in 28 *International Legal Materials* 1063 (1989): Shelton, "Implementation Issues," above note 34, at 273; see also Stewart, "US Ratification of the Covenant on Civil and Political Rights," above note 62, at 81. There the Court held that prolonged judicial proceedings involving capital punishment may constitute "cruel, inhuman and degrading treatment or punishment," a possibility directly alluded to by the Senate Foreign Relations Committee in supporting a reservation in connection with Article 7 of the Covenant: Senate Report, above note 62.

Both are non-derogable provisions, though the Human Rights Committee in its General Comment rightly does not make an automatic correlation between reservations to non-derogable provisions and reservations which offend against the object and purpose of the Covenant. It does, however, assert that "a State has a heavy onus to justify such a reservation."[71] The United States' explanation for attaching conditions to ratification was to make a reservation wherever incompatibilities between the Covenant and domestic law were found.[72] David P. Stewart, the then Assistant Legal Adviser for Human Rights and Refugees in the US Department of State, notes in connection with reservation (2) that "however much one might disagree with [the continued use of capital punishment] in the United States, one could not realistically expect adoption of the Covenant to overrule the democratically expressed desires of a majority of citizens in a majority of states."[73] This point was also made by the United States delegation before the Human Rights Committee, where the then State Department Legal Adviser Conrad Harper indicated that the decision to retain the death penalty "reflected a serious and considered democratic choice of the American public" which it was not appropriate to dismiss.[74] This prioritizing of (in)compatible domestic law over international law in the human rights sphere is commented upon by José Alvarez in his recent critique of Anne-Marie Slaughter's liberal theory. He notes that the United States' stance with respect to international human rights conventions may pose troublesome arguments for liberal assumptions about treaty compliance, including the argument that "in liberal states with 'legitimate' law-making institutions, domestic rights norms – such as those arising from the Supreme Court's interpretation of the US Constitution – have greater legitimacy than those created by remote, unrepresentative international processes. Under this view, even when domestic and international human rights norms diverge, the latter should not prevail."[75] Such a view sits ill with the fundamental international law precept that domestic law cannot prevail over internationally assumed obligations.

---

[71] General Comment 24(52), para. 10.
[72] See, generally, Hannum and Fisher, "Political Framework," above note 8, and the Senate Report, above note 62, at 653.
[73] Stewart, "US Ratification of the Covenant on Civil and Political Rights," above note 62, at 83.
[74] CCPR/C/SR 1405, 24 April 1995, para. 12
[75] Alvarez, "Critique of Slaughter's Liberal Theory," above note 10, at 195.

The United States approach was criticized by individual members of the Human Rights Committee during consideration of the United States' report, and is reflected in the Committee's Comment on that report:

> The Committee regrets the extent of the [United States'] reservations, declarations and understandings to the Covenant. It believes that, taken together, they intended to ensure that the United States has accepted what is already the law of the United States. The Committee is also particularly concerned at reservations to article 6, paragraph 5, and article 7 of the Covenant, which it believes to be incompatible with the object and purpose of the Covenant.[76]

The Committee stopped short, however, of declaring the incompatible reservations invalid and severing them from the US consent to be bound, notwithstanding espousing this approach in General Comment No. 24.[77] The general view appears to be that the Committee does not have the legal competence to make such a determination with binding effect upon the parties.[78] In the event, in considering the United States' report the Committee, among other things, "recommends that that State party review its reservations, understandings and declarations with a view to withdrawing them, in particular reservations to article 6, paragraph 5, and article 7

---

[76] Comments of the Human Rights Committee on the United States' report at its fifty-third session, CCPR/C/79/Add 50, para. 14. See also individual remarks by, for example, Mr. Kretzmer and Mr. Bhagwati, CCPR/C/SR/1402, 29 March 1995, paras. 3 and 22 respectively. For strong criticism of the US approach, see also the Lawyers Committee for Human Rights statements on US ratification of the Covenant reproduced in (1993) 14 (3–4) *Human Rights Law Journal* 125. For a contrary view see Stewart, "US Ratification of the Convention on Civil and Public Rights," above note 62, at 77. Tyagi notes that this approach of the Committee to the United States reservations was its first application of its guidelines to a specific reservation and "nothing less than a revolution." However, it has used what he refers to as this "ultimate power," expressly to deem a reservation incompatible with the object and purpose of the Covenant, sparingly: Tyagi, "Reservations to Human Rights Treaties," above note 11, at 225.

[77] Note to 1995 consideration of first US report, Comments on the United States' Report, above note 76. Paragraph 20 of General Comment No. 24(52) indicates that the Commitee considers that the determination of compatibility with the object and purpose of reservations, understandings, and declarations entered by States is an unavoidable task in the performance of its functions, i.e. review of a State's compliance with the ICCPR under Article 40. It further states that "The normal consequence of an unacceptable reservation is not that the Covenant will not be in effect at all for a reserving Party. Rather, such a reservation will generally be severable, in the sense that the Covenant will be operative for the reserving party without benefit of the reservation."

[78] See the UK and US responses to General Comment No. 24 at (1996) 3 *International Human Rights Reports* at 264 and 266 respectively; see also Liesbeth Lijnzaad, *Reservations to UN Human Rights Treaties: Ratify and Ruin?* (Dordrecht/Boston/London: Martinus Nijhoff Publishers, 1995), p. 294 (ch. 5 addresses the ICCPR); and note 88 below.

of the Covenant."[79] This recommendation is consistent with the International Law Commission's view that it is only the reserving State that has the responsibility to take action in the event of the incompatibility with the object and purpose of the treaty of a reservation which it formulated. This action could include forgoing participation in the treaty, withdrawing the reservation, or modifying it to rectify the incompatibility.[80]

"Traditional modalities of control" are exercised by the contracting parties in accordance with Articles 19–23 of the Vienna Convention. As already indicated, the United States' reservations provoked objections from a small number of States parties to the Covenant, including a strongly worded Swedish one which states, inter alia, that "Reservations of this nature contribute to undermining the basis of international treaty law."[81] Nonetheless all the objecting parties appear to have assumed, notwithstanding their objections even on grounds of incompatibility with the object and purpose of the Covenant, that treaty relations would arise – and that the matter could perhaps be treated as one of opposability. If the US reservations are objected to on such a basis, then Article 21 of the Vienna Convention provides that the provisions to which the reservations relate do not apply to the objecting States, to the extent of the reservations. The further legal effect of no treaty relations arising is rebutted by the express declaration by all of the objecting States (save for Germany, where silence has the same effect under Article 20(4)(b)) that their objections do not prevent the entry into force of the Covenant between themselves and the United States.[82] This approach underscores one motivation for the objections to the reservations, namely, the objecting States' desire to register publicly their opposition to the stance taken by the United States[83] – without taking the more drastic step of stipulating that no treaty relations arise between them. As a general "sanction"

---

[79] See Comments on the United States' Report, above note 76, at para. 27.

[80] ILC Preliminary Conclusions, above note 29.

[81] Multilateral Treaties Deposited with the United Nations Secretary General, available at http://untreaty.un.org.

[82] However, if these reservations arise for consideration under the opposability criteria of Article 20, such express confirmation of treaty relations arising notwithstanding objections is unnecessary. It could of course be argued that the issue of permissibility under Article 19 is a threshold requirement which needs to be met before issues of opposability arise: see William A. Schabas, "Invalid Reservations to the International Covenant on Civil and Political Rights: Is the United States Still a Party?" (1995) 21 *Brooklyn Journal of International Law* 277, and, for further discussion, text accompanying note 18 above.

[83] Elizabeth A. Reimels, "Playing for Keeps: the United States Interpretation of International Prohibitions Against the Juvenile Death Penalty – The US Wants to Play the International

for incompatible reservations the latter approach is of limited effect in a multilateral treaty whose normative obligations are owed nonreciprocally. Moreover, the United States would become a party to the ICCPR having reciprocal relations with the vast majority of States parties, namely those who did not object to the reservations. Even if the two-stage process of the Vienna Convention in respect of permissibility (Article 19) and opposability (Article 20) were meticulously observed, there is no automaticity to a determination of incompatibility. It is ultimately for other States parties to assess compatibility and to act on the basis of that assessment. Though some would argue that the reserving State cannot be considered a party to the treaty at all in consequence of a reservation incompatible with its object and purpose, the bulk of state practice supports participation notwithstanding such a reservation (as is the case here with the United States).

The Vienna Convention does not espouse the "Strasbourg approach" of severing the offending reservation(s). Although General Comment No. 24 highlighted this as one possible approach to invalidity, the Human Rights Committee did not adopt this approach when considering the US reservations in 1995.[84] Not surprisingly, the United States has objected to the Committee's assertion of its competence to render such determinations with legally binding effect and considers severance of invalid reservations to be "completely at odds with the established legal practice and principles and even the express and clear terms of adherence by many States."[85] In respect of its own reservations it has indicated that

> The reservations contained in the United States instrument of ratification are integral parts of its consent to be bound by the Covenant and are not severable. If it were to be determined that any one or more of them were ineffective, the ratification as a whole could thereby be nullified.[86]

Presumably the ultimate choice for any State facing the "Strasbourg approach" and desiring its consent to be bound to be on its terms is to

---

Human Rights Game, But Only If It Makes the Rules" (2001) 15 *Emory International Law Review* 303 at 320.

[84] See above note 77.

[85] United States Response to General Comment No. 24, reproduced at (1996) 3 *International Human Rights Reports* 269. For further analysis of the US and UK responses, see Ghandhi, *Human Rights Committee*, above note 24. He remarks upon the very different tenor of the two responses, with the United States taking a much more aggressive stance towards the Committee and its competence.

[86] US Response, above note 85.

denounce the treaty (assuming that it has already become a party to the treaty). But in response to an attempt by North Korea to denounce the Covenant the Human Rights Committee indicated that this was not permitted.[87] This highlights not only the difficulty in applying the general law of the Vienna Convention to this special category of treaty but also the broader question of whether such law *should* be applied. It will be remembered that when the Human Rights Committee voiced doubts about the utility of the reservations provisions of the Vienna Convention with regard to the Covenant,[88] this was heavily criticized by, among others, the United Kingdom and the United States. The British government insisted that "the correct approach is...to apply the general rules relating to reservations laid down in the Vienna Convention in a manner which takes full account of the particular characteristics of the treaty in question."[89] Indeed, the controversy surrounding reservations to human rights treaties, deepened in consequence of the US reservations, is reflective of a broader debate regarding the potential "fragmentation" of international law.[90]

As indicated, one of the explicit rationales for the US reservations is to ensure "the continued paramountcy of certain domestic legal provisions" where these differ from the Covenant – the second in the Committee's tripartite classification of the types of reservations likely to impair effective implementation. Writing in 1979 in the context of President Jimmy Carter's 1978 proposal to ratify the ICCPR, Oscar Schachter referred to the US approach as giving rise to "a more subtle problem of possible non-implementation."[91] He contrasted the US approach, of adopting reservations up front in an effort to render the international obligations compatible

---

[87] See General Comment No. 26, UNGAOR, 53rd session, Supp. No. 40 (A/53/40), 1998.

[88] In addition to referring to these provisions as "inappropriate" and "inadequate," the Committee indicated that the task of determining compatibility should fall to it: General Comment No. 24 (52), above note 78, at para. 17.

[89] "Observations on General Comment No. 24" (1996) 3 *International Human Rights Reports* 261, para. 4 (UK). As was noted above, the United States expressly relies on Articles 20 and 21 of the Vienna Convention as providing the legal framework for response to incompatible reservations: see further above note 42.

[90] In the human rights context see the specific discussion of human rights and treaty law in Craven, "Concept of Human Rights Treaties," above note 36. In the context of dispute settlement, see Alan E. Boyle, "Dispute Settlement and the Law of the Sea Convention: Problems of Fragmentation and Jurisdiction" (1997) 46 *International and Comparative Law Quarterly* 37.

[91] Oscar Schachter, "The Obligations of the Parties to Give Effect to the Covenant on Civil and Political Rights" (1979) AJIL 462.

with domestic law, with other States' sweeping assertions, in the absence of such reservations, that no additional measures of domestic implementation were required.[92] Schachter was critical of both approaches. He viewed the reservations approach, whereby "a state purports to accept its obligations and at the same time seeks to rule out any change in its law that would be required to meet those obligations," as weakening the regime of the Covenant.[93] Louis Henkin, for his part, categorized US reservations, understandings, and declarations to human rights conventions as based on five principles: (1) constitutional limitations on treaties, that is to say, limitations required to ensure conformity with domestic constitutional law; (2) rejecting higher international standards, and thus ensuring no change in domestic law even where below international standards; (3) avoiding the compulsory jurisdiction of the ICJ, by rendering any submission of any dispute to the Court subject to express US consent in each instance; (4) a federalism clause; and (5) a non-self-executing declaration, to limit the impact of ratifying the ICCPR under domestic law by preventing it from giving rise to an independent cause of action whereby domestic courts could adjudge domestic human rights standards against international yardsticks.[94] The current US approach to the ratification of human rights treaties may be evidence of an undesirable shift or weakening in what Detlev Vagts refers to as the "penumbral obligation," that is to say, the factors explaining support for the binding quality of treaty obligations under US domestic law – as reflected on the international law plane in the doctrine of *pacta sunt servanda*.[95]

---

[92] "To a man from Mars, a large part of the world would seem safe for human rights and the Covenant virtually redundant," he observes. *Ibid.*, at 463.

[93] *Ibid.*, at 465. Curtis A. Bradley and Jack L. Goldsmith challenge "conventional academic wisdom" and view reservations, understandings, and declarations as reflecting "a sensible accommodation of competing domestic and international considerations" ("Treaties, Human Rights, and Conditional Consent," above note 36, at 402). They identify five categories designed to harmonize treaties with existing requirements of US law and leave domestic implementation to Congress: (1) substantive reservations; (2) interpretative conditions; (3) non-self-execution declarations; (4) federalism understandings; and (5) ICJ reservations. *Ibid.*, at 416–23. (They also exhort "generalist readers" to skip ahead to Part III to avoid the technical detail in Part II, which is concerned with the consistency of reservations, understandings, and declarations with international law.)

[94] This has been the subject of extensive commentary, with particular focus on litigation strategy and the impact of such declarations on parallel customary international law norms. See further the sources cited above in note 8.

[95] Vagts, "The United States and its Treaties," above note 14, at 323.

Conclusions

Writing in 1995, Louis Henkin was particularly concerned by the constitutional implications of the US reservations, understandings, and declarations to the ICCPR and by the impact this approach would have on international practice. In particular, he was concerned that the insulation of domestic law from international rules might be strengthened and the principle of *pacta sunt servanda* further undermined. Perhaps because a large number of States had already indicated their consent to be bound by the ICCPR and other major human rights instruments, it is difficult to detect that the US stance has had significant negative impact in the manner suggested. But it will certainly have reinforced the position of those States which had already made incompatible reservations to the Covenant and other human rights instruments. It will also have undermined further the generality of international human rights, not to mention the multilateral institutional machinery designed to ensure their observance, while strengthening an approach which prioritizes universality of participation over the integrity of the treaty text. One senses a lost opportunity strongly to support universal human rights, at least in so far as the ICCPR is concerned. This is one area where strong countervailing regional practice – the Strasbourg approach – may be having an impact on US predominance, particularly in the suggestions that the United States should be considered bound to the ICCPR without reliance on incompatible reservations.[96] Yet in terms of the evolution of the law of treaties, the US approach, in its response both to General Comment No. 24 and to the work of the International Law Commission on reservations to treaties, has been to buttress the traditional Vienna Convention approach to reservations.[97] Both the US representative

---

[96] William A. Schabas, "Invalid reservations to the ICCPR," above note 82, at 323. This is the intended legal effect of the Italian objection to the US reservation to Article 6, above note 58.

[97] If, however, it is argued that treaty practice under the ICCPR at least is evolving, the question becomes whether the United States – and the United Kingdom for that matter – are out of step with developments moving toward the severance of offending reservations. Severance will continue to operate under specific treaty regimes – the Strasbourg approach now having been exported to the Caribbean – but has yet to become the accepted general rule in the international public order. Can it be applied ad hoc by individual States, as Italy sought to do? The United States has never taken the position that a reservation can be treated as invalid (Frowein, "Reservations and the International *Ordre Public*," above note 21, at 411). If, as Frowein concludes (p. 412), "It would seem that the rejection of reservations as null and void by courts, independent treaty-organs and States is a phenomenon going hand in hand with the development of a more sophisticated system of international legislation," then clearly the

on the Sixth Committee of the UN General Assembly and the US member of the International Law Commission have repeatedly supported the Special Rapporteur's approach to reservations, namely, to retain the Vienna Convention formula while producing a guide to reservations practice. This ensures that States retain the flexibility to modify their participation in international treaty regimes to the extent compatible with specific reservations clauses or the default rule of compatibility found in Article 19(c) of the Vienna Convention. In the US case, reservations preserving the paramountcy of domestic (especially constitutional) law, as well as non-self-execution and the requirement of express consent for the invocation of any dispute settlement mechanism, insulate US law from challenge before both domestic and international courts. What has been left open is the reporting system under the ICCPR[98] as a mechanism for the open scrutiny of, among other things, the compatibility of US reservations, understandings, and declarations with the ICCPR. Perhaps in order to keep this mechanism working, the Human Rights Committee stopped short of explicitly pronouncing on the issue of severance of the offending reservations. Doing so would have undoubtedly provoked a strong US response and, no doubt, a "constitutional crisis" within the ICCPR as to the proper legal scope of the Committee's jurisdiction and functions. This restraint did not stop Congress from passing a bill (subsequently vetoed by President Bill Clinton) which would have cut off funding for US obligations under the ICCPR unless the Human Rights Committee "expressly recognised the validity [of the US reservations,

United States is out of step with this process. The UK response to General Comment 24 does not rule out "severability of a kind [which] may well offer a solution in appropriate cases, although its contours are only beginning to be explored by States": (1996) 3 *International Human Rights Reports* at 264, para. 14. However, if such an approach is followed then the UK favors severance "excising both the reservation *and* the parts of the treaty to which it applies": *ibid.*, at 265, para. 14.

[98] Indeed, Roth observes that "Apart from the obligation to submit periodic reports to the Human Rights Committee, it is difficult to identify with certainty a legal difference that the US ratification of the ICCPR has made, on either the international or the domestic plane": "Federalism Constraints on Human Rights Implementation," above note 8, at 893. However, he goes on to assert that some provisions of the ICCPR conceivably extend beyond existing federal and state law, giving rise to an international obligation to extend such protection even though the non-self-executing declaration prevents direct judicial implementation of the ICCPR (*ibid.*). Sloss has also cast doubt on the immunizing effect of non-self-executing declarations in the human rights context: David Sloss, "The Domestication of International Human Rights: Non-Self-Executing Declarations and Human Rights Treaties" (1999) 24 *Yale Journal of International Law* 129.

understandings, and declarations] as a matter of international law."[99] Similar pressures have been brought to bear in connection with US membership of the Committee. It remains to be seen whether the US approach represents "due regard for time-tested and authentically American institutions and practices, or merely the arrogance of a superpower that exempts itself from the accommodation of international sensibilities that it demands of other states..."[100]

---

[99] Foreign Relations Authorisation Act, Fiscal Years 1996 and 1997, HR1561, 104th Cong. 1504 (2nd Sess. 1996), cited in Bradley and Goldsmith, above note 36, at 468, n. 293.

[100] Roth, "Federalism Constraints on Human Rights Implementation," above note 8, at 909.

15

Comments on chapters 13 and 14

Jost Delbrück

As a preliminary remark, let me address the role of the United States as the sole remaining superpower. This position can hardly be disputed. However, the exceptional place of the United States in international relations and the ensuing attitude of that country must be put into context. It appears to me that a large segment of the international community, particularly within the Western camp, is quite content to accept the United States as being the troubleshooter bearing the brunt of major international enforcement actions. Second, in many cases this very segment of the international community has been less than vociferous when the United States has engaged in superpower unilateralism. Moreover, parts of the international legal community have put much effort into justifying such actions *ex post facto*. Thus, in a sense, this situation, together with the United States' sense of mission, has contributed to the predominance of the United States as it is perceived by the US administration and also by Congress. Pointing fingers from outside is, therefore, a somewhat dangerous undertaking. As the saying goes, some of the fingers may point back at the critics.

Yet, the stark fact is – and both authors of the chapters in this section have clearly said this – that the pursuit of the national interest is a dominant characteristic of US policy which, in turn, has an impact on the US approach to international law. I still remember Judge Sofaer, as the State Department Legal Advisor, unequivocally expressing this approach at the 1990 American Society of International Law Conference in Washington: the United States is fully committed to international law as long as it serves the national interest. This state of mind has led the United States to miss out on one major change in the role and function of treaties, specifically of regulatory or lawmaking treaties. These kinds of treaties have increasingly become the surrogate of international legislation, thereby taking on a more objective normative function as distinct from the traditional strictly *inter partes* treaty law. The trend in international lawmaking by multilateral conventions is to "legislate" in the international community interest which, modestly defined, can be identified as the enlightened self-interest of States, but ideally reaches further. But this change to international lawmaking seriously requires all States – including superpowers – to recognize that no one is above the law. The international community clearly depends to a large extent on great power leadership, but this leadership – today largely falling upon the United States – has to be good leadership *under* law. If the United States engaged in pursuing this aim, it would have a greater opportunity to exercise leadership more effectively.

As to details, I agree with the authors as regards the confirmation by the United States of a number of basic principles of the international law of treaties. I would like to emphasize even more strongly that these are principles that are very sovereignty-oriented, traditional concepts. But sovereignty – even that of a superpower – has become ever more relative. As conventional law is increasingly characterized by its legislative intent, the traditional notion of sovereignty is fading. With regard to the United States' reaction to the Landmines Convention, the Rome Statute of the International Criminal Court and the reservations, understandings, and declarations attached to the International Covenant on Civil and Political Rights, the critique of the international community was quite clear. The vast majority of States went ahead with signing and ratifying these conventions, clearly disregarding the US objections and thus isolating the United States. The temporary loss by the United States of its seat on the Human Rights Commission is another telling incident in this respect.

I am not quite in agreement with Pierre Klein's assessment of the United States' use of the UN Security Council as an instrument to override treaty obligations. I definitely prefer to see the United States using the Security Council – which entails public debate and consensus-building – as evidenced by the recent resolutions on terrorism. It is regrettable, though, that within the United States little mention was made by the administration and the media of the fact that the United States did seek the support – albeit not the mandate – of the United Nations for reacting to the 11 September attack. This was an opportunity lost to show the American and the international public the kind of law abidance that is so badly needed for good leadership.

Alain Pellet

Being a commentator is a fortunate position, since the authors of the chapters have worked hard and you are simply supposed to distribute good or bad marks without yourself having done much work. But it can be also uncomfortable, at least when you give high marks, since as a matter of definition you have nothing, or very little, to add to what has been written. This is the situation in which I find myself, since, overall, I have found virtually no grounds for disagreement.

Both authors have, I think, expressed balanced views. They try hard to find excuses for the United States' behavior with regard to treaty law – a rather difficult task, I'm afraid. Their general tone is, it must be said, rather critical, but it would be hard to disagree. The United States is, indeed, a law-abiding country, but it abides by its own law and not, or as little as possible, by general international law.

In this respect I do have a regret concerning Pierre Klein's paper, in that he does not discuss the general feature of the treaty network into which the United States has agreed to enter. Klein tells us that the United States insists that it is bound only by its own consent. But, with respect, this is stating the obvious: treaty law is consensual law as a matter of definition. *Pacta sunt servanda* applies to the United States just as it applies to San Marino or Monaco. It would probably have been more interesting to find out how many treaties the United States has entered. And I would bet that, compared with other Western powers, its record is rather poor. This is confirmed in Nico Krisch's remarkable chapter, at least as far as multilateral conventions are concerned: compared with its main Western allies, the United States ratifies a very limited number of conventions. In this respect, the United States is perhaps more comparable with Third World countries, and maybe Japan, rather than with Western and probably eastern European countries (with the possible exception of Russia).

I am not suggesting that the United States violates treaty law more than any other State. But it commits itself less and is more reluctant to become bound than many States. Its lack of support for treaty law is also shown by the multiplicity of reservations, understandings, declarations, and other unilateral statements that it formulates when it accepts to be bound. And I must say that, as the International Law Commission's Special Rapporteur on Reservations to Treaties, I have been struck by a very special US policy which exists nowhere else in the world: the United States is the only State which imposes so called "reservations" on *bilateral* treaties. Although there are a few examples of "reservations" to bilateral treaties outside the United States, they are isolated accidents, not policies. My view (as accepted by the ILC) is that such statements are not reservations: they are offers to renegotiate the treaty. But when such offers come from the United States they are demands or orders – and I know of only a very few cases where they have been rejected. One such rejection came from France, but this is highly unusual; in most instances, the United States' partners have agreed to the modifications imposed by it.

This approach can be compared to the successful US endeavors to change the United Nations Convention on the Law of the Sea or its ongoing efforts to change the Rome Statute of the International Criminal Court, not to speak of the Kyoto Protocol. This is very well presented in Klein's paper. But one could also think of other techniques, for example the conditional ratification of the WTO agreements. I have said "conditional," but I might more properly have spoken of a "threatening" ratification. The United States says: we accept the treaty, but if we are condemned too many times by the WTO mechanisms, we will denounce it.

And indeed, it seems to me that the United States has a very particular idea of the *pacta sunt servanda* principle. Its conventional relations with the former Soviet Union, and then Russia, concerning bilateral disarmament treaties provides another illustration of this, let us say arrogant, reinterpretation of *pacta sunt servanda*, which conveys the impression, viewed from this side of the Atlantic, that it is seen in Washington DC as *pacta sunt utilisanda*.

In a way, this probably is a natural inclination for superpowers. After all, when Britain and France were in this (albeit shared) position, they too had a most debatable and cynical policy in this respect and did not hesitate to consider some of their treaties as pure scraps of papers when they deemed it advantageous to do so, at least and most especially when the treaties were concluded with what they cynically referred to as "uncivilized countries." But the irony of the present situation is that the United States was, in a now rather remote past, very active in trying to moralize the practice and the law of treaties. Just think of the supposed ban on secret diplomacy after World War I and the actions of President Woodrow Wilson.

But there is something else that is missing in part from both chapters.

Both Catherine Redgwell and Pierre Klein ably show how the United States takes great care in refusing any provision in a treaty that contradicts its own law – not only its Constitution and statutes, but also, more often than not, all its regulations, whatever their place in the legal hierarchy. Senator Bricker's ghost is still very present in US policy regarding treaty law.

A good example of this is the US attitude towards the ILC's rather good Draft Articles on State immunity. Since the United States has an international immunity act of its own, it tries to block, up to now very successfully, the very convocation of a diplomatic conference which could negotiate a treaty on the basis of the ILC's draft. This is unfair: if the United States wishes to stick to the Foreign Sovereign Immunities Act (which is neither better nor worse than the ILC's draft), very well. But why does it prevent others from adopting a useful agreement which would constitute significant progress in resolving the existing legal disorder in this area? To be fair, I must say that the other Anglo-Saxon countries, which also have their own immunities acts, behave in the same way. But the attitude of these countries is also to be regretted, and is certainly no excuse.

Two years ago, during a very fruitful conference organized at New York University by Thomas Franck, we had a very stimulating and rather tough debate on an interesting point. I explained that I was shocked – and indeed I still am – by the rigidity of the United States when its laws and regulations are at stake; as I have noted before, one of the major aims of the United States when negotiating and then ratifying a treaty is to leave its own law untouched and unchanged. After I had developed this idea, I was quite vigorously attacked by my US colleagues who in return mocked the French mania for constitutional instability. And it is true that we have no difficulty in changing our constitution in order to bring it into line with our international treaty commitments.

In this context, I was told a nice joke which was said to be a true story and which I cannot resist repeating here. One day in Paris, Senator Jesse Helms' chief aide went to a specialist legal book store and asked for a copy of the French Constitution. "Sorry sir, we don't have it," he was told. Senator Helms' aide asked why not. The answer: "We are a bookstore, not a newsagent." And it is true that France has changed its constitution several times in the last few years in order to accept new treaty commitments. This is categorically unheard of, impossible for Americans.

As appears in the titles of many of the chapters of this book, the United States is "more equal than the rest" (Krisch); it is largely "powerful but unpersuasive" (Stephen Toope); it is, indeed, "predominant." But if Americans lock themselves in a legal ivory tower, it is not, or not only, because their country is powerful; it is also, and for that matter perhaps principally, because they are absolutely persuaded that their law is the best and/or that the intrusion of international law would be a threat to the satisfactory balance their domestic law achieves.

This leads me to a second small lacuna that I have detected in both chapters.

I regret that they have been silent on the implementation of treaty law inside the United States and particularly by US courts. I do not know enough about this matter to venture a hypothesis, but it would have been interesting to ascertain the solutions implemented by United States courts in respect of the place of treaties in the hierarchy of norms they apply. The self-executing or non-self-executing character they accord treaty provisions would seem to be of some relevance here.

I suppose that I shall be accused of elementary anti-Americanism, if I venture – I cannot help it! – that such a study would probably confirm that the famous doctrine "international law is part of the law of the land" should largely be reversed and that we would probably come to the conclusion that "The law of the land is part – and a predominant part – of international law," or even that "US law *is* international law." This certainly is the impression given by the two excellent chapters on which I am commenting.

I should like to end with a more general note.

Many of the chapters in this book take a rather critical view of the US record in matters of international law. I am afraid that such a pessimistic appraisal is all too well-founded. However, there is something strange and paradoxical in such a conclusion. Yes indeed, the United States is predominant, but this averred fact should lead to an opposite finding: powerful States should – and, generally speaking, do – adapt themselves rather well to the demands of positive international law.

Being neither a positivist, nor a moralist – even less a "moralistic positivist," an expression which, for me, means nothing even with respect to my good friend Bruno Simma – I maintain that law is the result of power. Therefore, it would seem natural that big powers are more law-abiding than less powerful States: they have the means to elaborate and impose on the rest of the world the legal rules which best serve their interests. But curiously enough the United States has succeeded neither in forging the international law that it wants nor in convincing world public opinion – including international lawyers – that it is a model law-abiding country. Why? Probably for two main reasons among others.

First, because, whatever its defects, its imperfections, its arrogance, the United States is a democracy. It flows from this indisputable fact that it is rather transparent and open to scrutiny. Therefore, and very logically, all that it does (or does not do), including its breaches of international law, is known, discussed and criticized – the very title of this book is revealing in this respect.

Second, in spite of Stanley Hofmann and many others, the United States is not an empire; it is a State. The difference is that an empire lives in isolation without recognizing any other entity as equal, while state sovereignty cannot be dissociated from equality with that of all other States, as is very well demonstrated in Krisch's chapter. Although the United States may well be "more equal" than the rest, it nevertheless recognizes that it is but a State, among other equally sovereign entities. This deserves our respect, both for the very notion of state sovereignty – which must not be envisaged as an absolute power, but as a doctrine of limitation on absolute power – and for the United States which, more often than not, though not very tactfully, behaves as a State and not as an empire.

It has often been remarked that it is better to be healthy and wealthy than poor and ill. And the United States is just healthy and wealthy, globally speaking. There is nothing wrong with this, providing that it does not turn health into imperialistic domination and wealth into arrogance.

Bruno Simma

Since this project has been funded in part by the Volkswagen Foundation, I should like to begin with a metaphor close to Volkswagen. I think that the provisions on the law of treaties, especially those provisions that relate to treaty-making, are a very robust vehicle equipped with airbags and a crunch-zone. This allows for some quite reckless driving, and without a doubt this is what the United States is engaged in. And relating to something that Pierre Klein has said with regard to the trumping of the law of treaties by Chapter VII action, like any driver you can use public transportation instead of getting stuck in a traffic jam of cars, that is, resort to the Security Council instead of waiting for the green light of a treaty to enter into force. Of course, the United States is not a country famous for its public transportation. What Pierre Klein's chapter shows is that the United States engages in a number of practices that I would call exorbitant and less than constructive – while remaining within international law.

My second point is that I think that one needs to pay considerable attention to US domestic politics and the US constitutional scene. I say this, not as
a justification for some errant United States behavior, but as an explanation.
A look at the US constitution, at US federalism, at how the United States has
to treat treaties internally, explains a lot of the strange, exorbitant practices
that we encounter. The good thing about these practices is that they all have
names like Bricker, Connally, and Helms. The role of the US legislature and
US federalism in foreign policy and the international legal relations of the
United States is extremely important, indeed special, and it explains some
of the attitudes, or better yet, reluctances, on the part of US negotiators in
treaty relations. For example, US negotiators are probably forced to take a
proposed text more seriously than their European counterparts because of
what is waiting for them at home. It is easier for European negotiators to
say, "Come on, don't take it that seriously. Let's wave it through and see
what happens."

My third point is that we have to make a distinction between States
committing breaches and States displaying a disregard for fundamental
principles of the law of treaties. I cannot for my part see such a fundamental disregard for the principles of treaty law being displayed by the
United States. Take the examples that Pierre Klein provides. The first is the
American Servicemen Protection Act. Of course, this is something hilari-
ous, unprecedented, terrible. But the question of treaty law is not as simple
as that. The very pointed question relating to Article 18 of the Vienna Convention on the Law of Treaties is whether the United States has made it clear
at present that it does not intend to become a party to the Rome Statute
of the International Criminal Court. It might be that you take US behavior
vis-à-vis the Rome Statute as a very unequivocal message that it is going
to ratify that treaty. If that message is there, the United States has fiddled
the law in telling other States that it is not amused about their intention
not to become parties to the Statute. As for Klein's second example, the
later-in-time rule, well, Charming Betsy is an American invention, isn't it?
I see similar problems in a number of countries: just consider the attitude
of Italy toward the EEC Treaty of Rome in the 1960s, when it subjected EEC
law to the later-in-time rule. Of course, the European Court of Justice then
helped out. But I think the later-in-time rule is very much in the instincts
of domestic judges.

This brings me to my fourth point, on reservations to human rights
treaties. The making of exorbitant, impermissible reservations is a practice

which is quite popular with a number of countries. Catherine Redgwell describes the US attitude here as the United States only accepting the *menu touristique* instead of the *menu gastronomique*. What comes to my mind, as a Bavarian, is the practice of Bavarians to go to beer gardens bringing their own food. The United States goes to human rights treaties bringing its own law. This is what the United States has really signed up to, and as a result, US practice with regard to reservations shows what I would call an accumulation of bad habits: not only its own bad habits but also those of Muslim and other countries, including Germany. Just let me remind you of the reservation or declaration which Germany has made to the Convention on the Rights of the Child declaring the contents of that convention non-self-executing. Let me remind you of Germany's attitude towards the 1951 Refugee Convention. It is not a proper reservation but more of an implicit reservation to the effect that internal prosecution is not meant to be covered by the Convention. As for France, in my opinion the French reservation to the International Covenant on Civil and Political Rights excluding Article 27 on the protection of minorities is a great example of an impermissible reservation. The United States is only one among many Western countries which regards – and I think that is really the heart of the matter – international human rights as an exercise essentially targeted at others. The fact remains that human rights are particularly prominent in foreign policy. And there is of course a strange contradiction between asking the entire world to obey human rights and then more or less reserving your own position.

With regard to General Comment 24, there the United States is in good, or should I rather say bad, company. The statements by the United Kingdom and by France are perhaps phrased a little more carefully and politely, but amount to exactly the same thing. So my conclusion is that, with regard to the impact of the United States on the law of treaties, what we see in most instances are not properly violations of the law of treaties. Making an impermissible reservation does not amount to a breach of the law. But the exorbitant or less than constructive use of mechanisms that are still available even if not desirable under international law does continue, and in light of US predominance this is without doubt a matter of concern.

VI

Compliance

16

The impact on international law of US noncompliance

SHIRLEY V. SCOTT

In one of the most influential theoretical works on compliance of the post–Cold War era, Abram Chayes and Antonia Chayes hypothesized a propensity for States to comply, rather than not, with international obligations. It is only infrequently, according to Chayes and Chayes, that a treaty violation falls into the category of a wilful flouting of legal obligation.[1] Chayes and Chayes cite Robert Keohane's survey of two hundred years of American foreign relations, in which he identified only forty "theoretically interesting" cases in which there had been a serious issue as to whether or not to comply.[2] And yet, in the decade since the end of the Cold War, the United States has met with criticism for its seemingly intentional violation of treaty obligations. The United States has not paid its bill to help run the United Nations, has used force contrary to the UN Charter, has failed to comply with the provisions of the Vienna Convention on Consular Relations, and has passed environmental legislation found to be incompatible with the global trading regime. The election of George W. Bush raised concern at the possibility of an even less respectful attitude on the part of the United States towards international law, as exemplified by the administration's determination to "move beyond" the Anti-Ballistic Missile Treaty in developing missile defense. Conduct of the war in Afghanistan and US treatment of captured Taliban and al-Qaida fighters have raised questions as to the degree of US respect for international humanitarian law.

Underpinning much of the criticism of the United States is the assumption that, as the world's sole superpower, the United States can wield a

---

[1] Abram Chayes and Antonia Handler Chayes, *The New Sovereignty: Compliance with International Regulatory Agreements* (Cambridge, MA: Harvard University Press, 1995).

[2] Robert O. Keohane, "United States Compliance with Commitments: Reciprocity and Institutional Enmeshment," unpublished paper prepared for PIPES Seminar, University of Chicago, 24 Oct. 1991, 35, quoted in Chayes and Chayes, *The New Sovereignty*, above note 1, p. 307 n. 6.

particularly strong influence on international law. Not only might the actions and rhetoric of the United States affect the evolution of particular doctrinal areas of international law, but so might US noncompliance weaken the system as a whole. Whereas other chapters in this volume address the impact of the United States on developments in particular fields of international law, this chapter seeks to assess analytically the overall impact on international law of US noncompliance. In particular, the question is asked as to whether the intuitive assumption that US noncompliance necessarily affects the system negatively has held true in practice.

Case studies of noncompliance

It is easy to condemn the United States where it appears to be willingly in breach of international law, and to assume that the consequences for international law will be negative. As the only superpower to survive the end of the Cold War, continues this line of thinking, the United States has an obligation to uphold its own rhetoric which, in the post–Cold War years, has often touted the rule of law as a way of moving the world towards greater peace, democracy and a "new world order."[3] International law is, after all, supposed to serve as a check on unfettered power.[4]

In an endeavor to assess dispassionately the overall effect on international law of US noncompliance, I want to begin by selecting eight specific examples of alleged US noncompliance which span various fields of international law and to examine briefly the impact on international law of each. The findings of these case studies will then be combined in an attempt to paint a picture of the overall impact on the system of international law of US noncompliance. There are some methodological difficulties associated with adopting a case study approach to the task. Most basically, international law is indeterminate. Not all international lawyers would agree that

---

[3] Secretary of State Madeleine K. Albright, Condon-Falknor Distinguished Lecture, University of Washington School of Law, Seattle, Washington, 29 Oct. 1998. As released by the Office of the Spokesman, United States Department of State. For a speech on the importance of the rule of law to the "new world order" see that by George Bush Snr. on "Iraqi Aggression in the Persian Gulf," available at http://scom.tamu.edu/pres/speeches/gbaggress.html.

[4] Lauterpacht described the mission of international law as being to lead "to enhancing the stability of international peace, to the protection of the rights of man, and to reducing the evils and abuses of national power." Cited in Steven R. Ratner, "International law: the trials of global norms" (1998) 16 *Foreign Policy* 65–71 at 65.

all the chosen case studies represent examples of illegal behavior.[5] The compliance concept is closely related to a positivist understanding of law which assumes a clear divide between legal and illegal behavior; in practice, of course, an assessment as to the legality or otherwise of a particular action may vary between lawyers.[6] The difficulty of unequivocally distinguishing a "legal" action from one that is "illegal" is made only more difficult by the increasing number of contradictions and conflicts emerging within international law, which are particularly apparent in relation to trade and the environment. An attempt has been made to mitigate these methodological difficulties by selecting examples on which a large number of international lawyers would agree; international law may be indeterminate but it is not wholly so. While it may not be possible to formulate a completely objective list of non-compliant behavior, the results should be at least sufficiently clear to lend support to, or question, the assumption that US noncompliance necessarily has a negative impact on the system of international law as a whole.

1. Extraterritoriality: the Helms-Burton Act

Charges of extraterritoriality have been laid against the United States in relation to several pieces of legislation, including the D'Amato Act (the Iran and Libya Sanctions Act of 1996),[7] and the Helms-Burton Act (the Cuban Liberty and Democratic Solidarity Act or Libertad Act).[8] The latter was signed into law by President Clinton on 12 March 1996. It aimed to "discourage third-country investment in Cuba by exposing foreign

---

[5] In relation to Helms-Burton, for example, David Shamburger has argued for its legality in terms of international law. See David M. Shamburger, "The Helms-Burton Act: A Legal and Effective Vehicle for Redressing United States Property Claims in Cuba and Accelerating the Demise of the Castro Regime" (1998) 21 *Boston College International and Comparative Law Review* 497–537.

[6] Other assumptions internal to positivist analysis but detracting from the possibility of objectively applying the compliance concept include: international law always exists prior to policy on the issue in question; all would agree on the rules and principles against which to assess the legality of a particular action/inaction; and all would interpret those rules and principles in the same way. S. V. Scott, "Beyond 'Compliance': Reconceiving the international law–foreign policy dynamic" (1998) 19 *The Australian Year Book of International Law* 35–48. The same difficulties become apparent when making an "objective" assessment of trends in enforcement. US claims to be enforcing international law are only legitimate if one agrees with the US interpretation of the law in question.

[7] (1996) 35 *International Legal Materials* 1273.

[8] (1996) 35 *International Legal Materials* 357.

companies to potential claims in US courts and also by denying entry into the United States for such foreign companies or their officers." Most controversial was Title III, which created a private right of action in US federal courts against third-country nationals who "traffic in" property confiscated from US nationals.[9] Title IV was also controversial because it precluded entry into the United States of such third-country corporations which "traffic in" property confiscated from US nationals, including the entry of those corporations' officers and controlling shareholders and their families. The Act has been considered illegal because of its "blatant violation of the international rules governing extraterritoriality."[10] It has also been criticized for violating the principle of non-intervention, the most fundamental principles of state responsibility, the rules of the World Trade Organization (WTO) and the North American Free Trade Agreement (NAFTA), and the charters of international organizations such as the International Monetary Fund, the World Bank, and the Organization for Economic Co-operation and Development.[11]

The Helms-Burton Act met with strong international opposition, particularly on the part of Canada, Mexico, and the European Union (EU). The then Canadian Minister of Foreign Affairs, Lloyd Axworthy, claimed that the Act "undermine[d] the most basic premises of international law, upon which all of our international obligations and agreements are based."[12] Canada and Mexico initiated consultations under Chapter 20 of NAFTA,[13] while the EU filed a request for the establishment of a panel under the Dispute Settlement Understanding of the World Trade Organization.[14] Stuart Eizenstat, the then US Under Secretary of Commerce for International Trade, was quoted as saying that Washington would make "every effort"

---

[9] See "Agora: The Cuban Liberty and Democratic Solidarity (Libertad) Act" (1996) 90 AJIL 419.

[10] Brigitte Stern, "Can the United States set Rules for the World? A French View" (1997) 31 *Journal of World Trade* 10.

[11] *Ibid.*, 10–11.

[12] "Canada and the United States in a Changing World." Notes for an Address by the Honourable Lloyd Axworthy Minister of Foreign Affairs to the World Affairs Council, 14 March 1997, http://www.dfait-maeci.gc.ca/english/news/statements/97_state/97_014e.htm (accessed 15 Jan. 2002).

[13] "A Statement by the Honourable Art Eggleton, Minister for International Trade, on the Helms/Burton Bill, 13 March 1996." http://www.dfait-maeci.gc.ca/english/news/statements/96_state/96_007e.htm (accessed 17 Jan. 2002).

[14] United States – The Cuban Liberty and Democratic Solidarity Act. Request for the Establishment of a Panel by the European Communities. WT/DS38/2, 4 October 1996.

to achieve a mutually satisfactory resolution. But, if no prompt settlement were reached, the United States would formally advise the WTO that the panel established to consider the Helms-Burton law "has no competence to proceed because this is a matter of United States national security and foreign policy."[15] US officials threatened to do similarly in the NAFTA context.[16] The EU agreed on 11 April 1997 to suspend the WTO proceedings so as to allow for negotiations with the United States.[17] The United States agreed to defer enforcing Title III of the Act if Europe did not take it to the WTO. Negotiations led to an 18 May 1998 US–EU "Understanding with Respect to Disciplines for the Strengthening of Investment Protection."[18] Helms-Burton thus resulted in what has been described as the "first multilateral framework for opposing investment in illegally expropriated properties."[19] The fact that the matter was resolved outside the WTO also meant, however, that the scope of the "national security exception" in the General Agreement on Tariffs and Trade and the General Agreement on Trade in Services remained unclarified.[20]

---

[15] Paul Blustein and Anne Swardson, "US Vows To Boycott WTO Panel; Move Escalates Fight with European Union over Cuba Sanctions" *The Washington Post*, 21 Feb. 1997, A1. The "national security exception," found in Article XXI of the General Agreement on Tariffs and Trade, provides in part that "Nothing in [the] Agreement shall be construed . . . to prevent any contracting party from taking any action which it considers necessary for the protection of its essential security interests . . . taken in time of war or other emergency in international relations; . . ." A similar provision is found in Article XIV of the General Agreement on Trade in Services. Texts are available at http://www.wto.org/english/docs_e/legal_e/final_e.htm.

[16] Randall Palmer, "Canada Wary of Taking Cuba Dispute to NAFTA", 31 Oct. 1997 available at http://www.fiu.edu/~fcf/canadawary1031.html (accessed 15 Jan. 2002).

[17] "Memorandum of Understanding Concerning the United States Helms-Burton Act and the United States Iran and Libya Sanctions Act", 11 April 1997, (1977) 36 *International Legal Materials* 529.

[18] Sean D. Murphy (ed.), "Contemporary Practice of the United States Relating to International Law – United States and EU Negotiations Regarding the 'Helms-Burton' Act" (1999) 66 AJIL 660.

[19] *Ibid.*, 661.

[20] On the "national security exception" found in Article XXI of GATT see, *inter alia*, Klinton W. Alexander, "The Helms-Burton Act and the WTO Challenge: Making a Case for the United States Under the GATT National Security Exception" (1997) 11 *Florida Journal of International Law* 559–84; David T. Shapiro, "Be Careful What You Wish For: US Politics and the Future of the National Security Exception to the GATT" (1997) 31 *George Washington Journal of International Law and Economics* 97–118; and Wesley A. Cann Jr., "Creating Standards of Accountability for the Use of the WTO Security Exception: Reducing the Role of Power-Based Relations and Establishing a New Balance Between Sovereignty and Multilateralism" (2001) 26 *Yale Journal of International Law* 413–85.

2. Domestic environmental law which breaches multilateral trade treaties: Section 609 of Public Law 101-162 and associated regulations and judicial rulings

The *Tuna-Dolphin* I and II cases of 1991 and 1994 respectively,[21] the *Standards for Reformulated and Conventional Gasoline* case of 1996,[22] and the *Shrimp-Turtle* case of 1998 all concern pieces of US legislation with environmental objectives that have been found to be in breach of the General Agreement on Tariffs and Trade. In 1989 the United States enacted Section 609 of Public Law 101-162,[23] which called on the US Secretary of State, in consultation with the US Secretary of Commerce, *inter alia* to initiate negotiations for the development of bilateral or multilateral agreements for the protection and conservation of sea turtles, in particular with governments of countries engaged in commercial fishing operations likely to have a negative impact on sea turtles. It also provides that shrimp harvested with technology that may adversely affect certain sea turtles may not be imported into the United States.[24]

Following requests from India, Malaysia, Pakistan, and Thailand the WTO established a panel to examine whether a ban imposed by the United States on the importation of certain shrimp and shrimp products from those countries contravened GATT Article XI, which provides for the general elimination of quantitative restrictions. On 15 May 1998 the WTO Dispute Settlement Body Panel on United States – Import Prohibition of

[21] "GATT: Dispute Settlement Panel Report on United States Restrictions on Imports of Tuna, 16 Aug. 1991" 30 *International Legal Materials* 1594; "GATT: Dispute Settlement Panel Report on United States Restrictions on Imports of Tuna, 20 May 1994" 33 *International Legal Materials* 839.

[22] "World Trade Organization: Report of the Panel in *United States – Standards for Reformulated and Conventional Gasoline* (Treatment of Imported Gasoline and Like Products of National Origin)" [January 29, 1996] (1996) 35 *International Legal Materials* 274. "World Trade Organization Appellate Body: Report of the Appellate Body in *United States – Standards for Reformulated and Conventional Gasoline*" [May 20, 1996] (1996) 35 *International Legal Materials* 603.

[23] 16 United States Code § 1537.

[24] This is so, unless the president annually certifies to the Congress that the harvesting country concerned has a regulatory programme governing the incidental taking of such sea turtles in the course of such harvesting that is comparable to that of the United States, that the average rate of that incidental taking by the vessels of the harvesting country is comparable to the average rate of incidental taking of sea turtles by United States vessels in the course of such harvesting, or that the fishing environment of the harvesting country does not pose a threat of incidental taking to sea turtles in the course of such harvesting. "World Trade Organization: United States – Import Prohibition of Certain Shrimp and Shrimp Products. Report of the Panel" WT/DS58/R, 15 May 1998 (1998) 37 *International Legal Materials* 834 at 837.

Certain Shrimp and Shrimp Products concluded that the import ban on shrimp and shrimp products as applied by the United States on the basis of Section 609 of Public Law 101-162 was not consistent with Article XI:1 of GATT 1994, and could not be justified under Article XX of GATT 1994.[25] The United States appealed against the decision on both procedural and substantive grounds.[26] On 8 October 1998 the Appellate Body concluded, *inter alia*, that the US measure, while qualifying for provisional justification under Article XX(g), failed to meet the requirements of the chapeau of Article XX, and therefore was not justified under Article XX of the GATT 1994. The Appellate Body recommended that the Dispute Settlement Body request the United States to bring its measure found in the Panel Report to be inconsistent with Article XI of the GATT 1994, and in the Appellate Body Report to be not justified under Article XX of the GATT 1994, into conformity with the obligations of the United States under that Agreement.[27]

The Appellate Body pointed to the existence of the 1996 Inter-American Convention for the Protection and Conservation of Sea Turtles.[28] This regional treaty had been the first international agreement dedicated solely to raising standards of protection of sea turtles.[29] The Appellate Body considered it discriminatory that the United States had negotiated seriously with some, but not all, Members that export shrimp to the United States:

It is relevant to observe that an import prohibition is, ordinarily, the heaviest "weapon" in a Member's armoury of trade measures. The record does not, however, show that serious efforts were made by the United States to negotiate similar agreements with any other country or group of countries before (and, as far as the record shows, after) Section 609 was enforced on a worldwide basis on 1 May 1996. Finally, the record also does not show that the appellant, the United States, attempted to have recourse to such international

---

[25] *Ibid.*

[26] "United States – Import Prohibition of Certain Shrimp and Shrimp Products. Notification of an Appeal by the United States under paragraph 4 of Article 16 of the Understanding on Rules and Procedures Governing the Settlement of Disputes (DSU)" WT/DS58/11, 13 July 1998.

[27] "United States – Import Prohibition of Certain Shrimp and Shrimp Products AB-1998-4. Report of the Appellate Body" WT/DS58/AB/R, 12 October 1998. (1999) 38 *International Legal Materials* 121.

[28] "Inter-American Convention for the Protection and Conservation of Sea Turtles," available at http://www.seaturtle.org/iac/convention.shtml.

[29] "Clinton Signs International Treaty to Protect Sea Turtles," Statement of 12 October 2000. Statement by the President distributed by the Office of International Information Programs, United States Department of State available at http://usinfo.state.gov (accessed 31 March 2002).

mechanisms as exist to achieve cooperative efforts to protect and conserve
sea turtles before imposing the import ban.[30]

In response to the WTO's ruling, the United States said that it would "step up
efforts to secure international agreements protecting turtles."[31] In June 2001
a Memorandum of Understanding on the Conservation and Management
of Marine Turtles and their Habitats of the Indian Ocean and South-East
Asia was concluded under the auspices of the Convention on Migratory
Species.[32]

The earlier *Tuna-Dolphin* case had similarly given rise to the Agreement
for the Reduction of Dolphin Mortality in the Eastern Pacific Ocean,[33]
which was concluded in June 1992 between Colombia, Costa Rica, Ecuador,
France, Japan, Mexico, Nicaragua, Panama, the United States, Vanuatu,
and Venezuela.[34] Within two years this Agreement had reduced incidental
mortality of dolphins in the eastern tropical Pacific to below four thousand
animals.[35]

The *Shrimp-Turtle* ruling represented one further step toward clarifying
the relationship between international environmental law and international
trade law. The Reformulated Gasoline decision in 1996 had left States unable
to predict accurately the GATT legality of environmental trade measures
prior to dispute resolution.[36] It was now clear that, from a WTO perspective,
multilateral environmental measures affecting trade were to be preferred

---

[30] "World Trade Organization: United States – Import Prohibition of Certain Shrimp and Shrimp
Products" (12 Oct. 1998) (1999) 38 *International Legal Materials* 118 at para. 171 [reference
omitted].

[31] "Turtle Soup" *Economist*, 17 October 1998, quoted in Susan L. Sakmar "Free Trade and Sea
Turtles: The International and Domestic Implications of the *Shrimp-Turtle* Case" (1999) 10
Colorado Journal of International Environmental Law and Policy 345–95 at 387.

[32] Available at http://www.wcmc.org.uk/cms/IOSEAturtle_mou.htm.

[33] (1994) 33 *International Legal Materials* 936. See Mike Meier,"GATT, WTO, and the Environment: To What Extent do GATT/WTO Rules Permit Member Nations to Protect the Environment
When Doing so Adversely Affects Trade" (1997) 8:2 *Colorado Journal of International Environmental Law and Policy* at 250, n. 39; T. J. Schoenbaum, "International Trade and Protection of
the Environment: the Continuing Search for Reconciliation" (1997) 91 AJIL 268–313, at 300.

[34] "[T]he initial unilateral act by the United States successfully precipitated new international rules
protecting dolphins," Schoenbaum, "International Trade," above note 33, at 301.

[35] *Ibid.*, 300.

[36] Mark Edward Foster, "Trade and Environment: Making Room for Environmental Trade Measures within the GATT" (1998) 71 *Southern California Law Review* 393–443 at 395. See also
Julie B. Master, "International Trade Trumps Domestic Environmental Protection: Dolphins
and Sea Turtles are 'sacrificed on the altar of free trade'" (1998) 12 *Temple International and
Comparative Law Journal* 423–55.

over unilateral actions, and that before taking any unilateral action a State should pursue negotiations towards a multilateral solution, whether within an existing regime or to establish a new one; this suggests that there will be "a greater reliance on multilateral instruments to further conservation efforts in the future."[37]

While some questions regarding the accommodation of trade and the environment were clarified by *Shrimp-Turtle*, many questions remain unanswered. The *Shrimp-Turtle* appellate ruling left it unclear, for example, "as to how much negotiation is required before a country can resort to unilateral action."[38] To initiate negotiations is not to guarantee their success. In the case of *Tuna-Dolphin*, the United States had apparently tried unsuccessfully for twenty years to obtain an agreement.[39] "Only after the tuna ban and the subsequent uproar over the *Tuna-Dolphin* decisions was it possible to negotiate an agreement."[40] The question remained unasked as to what would happen if multilateral environmental treaties were found to be incompatible with the free trade regime as a whole.

3. Withholding of assessed contributions to the United Nations

The United States has been significantly behind in the payment of its assessed contributions to the United Nations. Under Article 17 of the Charter the General Assembly considers and approves the budget of the United Nations.[41] Payments are determined on the basis of a previously agreed scale of assessments.[42] In 1999 President Clinton signed legislation that

---

[37] Christopher C. Joyner and Zachary Tyler, "Marine Conservation versus International Free Trade: Reconciling Dolphins with Tuna and Sea Turtles with Shrimp" (2000) 31 *Ocean Development and International Law* 127–50 at 139–40.

[38] Sakmar, "Free Trade and Sea Turtles," above note 31, at 387.

[39] Jeffrey L. Dunoff, "Reconciling International Trade with Preservation of the Global Commons: Can We Prosper and Protect?" (1992) 49 *Washington and Lee Law Review* 1407–54 at 1419.

[40] Schoenbaum, "International Trade and Protection of the Environment," above note 33, at 312–13.

[41] Article 17 states: "1. The General Assembly shall consider and approve the budget of the Organization. 2. The expenses of the Organization shall be borne by the Members as apportioned by the General Assembly. 3. The General Assembly shall consider and approve any financial and budgetary arrangements with specialized agencies referred to in Article 57 and shall examine the administrative budgets of such specialized agencies with a view to making recommendations to the agencies concerned."

[42] Article 19 of the Charter provides that: "A member of the United Nations which is in arrears in the payment of its financial contributions to the Organization shall have no vote in the General Assembly if the amount of its arrears equals or exceeds the amount of the contributions due from it for the preceding two full years. The General Assembly may, nevertheless, permit such

authorized the payment, in three tranches, of $926 million in US arrears and assessments owed to the United Nations. Conditions were attached to the payment of each tranche. The first tranche was paid in 1999. Payment of the remaining tranches was conditional on the United Nations' acceptance of certain financial and organizational reforms. The 2000 instalment was conditional on several factors, one of which was action by the General Assembly to reduce the regular budget ceiling assessment for member States to 22 percent, and the United States' assessed share of peacekeeping operations to 25 percent.

In the early days of its withholding in the early 1980s, the United States emphasized the ultra vires exception to justify withholdings.[43] Over time the United States gradually moved from a strict interpretation of Article 17(2) to a looser interpretation – "that is, from a position supportive of the Charter as binding to a position that would essentially allow every member to pay what it wants."[44] More recently, proponents of the efforts to "reform" the United Nations have not even tried to rely on an ultra vires argument. "Instead, they seem to believe that the United States should be treated as a major shareholder, as it would be if the United Nations were a corporation."[45]

On 23 December 2000 the General Assembly adopted a new scale of assessments which lowered the ceiling of the amount to be paid by any single country from 25 to 22 percent of the budget. The Assembly also revised the 1973 ad hoc arrangements for financing peacekeeping activities. Ten levels of assessment were established, depending on countries' per capita income. The least developed countries would receive significant discounts on their contributions, while the permanent members of the Security Council would pay a premium over their regular assessment obligations sufficient to make up for the discounts.[46] Despite the 25 percent assessment for peacekeeping not having been met, Senate Foreign Relations Committee chairman Jesse Helms supported payment of the second tranche of the US assessments

a Member to vote if it is satisfied that the failure to pay is due to conditions beyond the control of the Member."

43 Summary of remarks by Allan Gerson, "UN Fiscal Crisis brought on by United States Arrears" (1999) *Proceedings of the American Society of International Law* 152.

44 *Ibid.*

45 Summary of remarks by John Knox, "UN Fiscal Crisis brought on by United States Arrears," *ibid.*, 150.

46 "Assembly Approves New Scale of Assessments, as it Concludes Main Part of its Millennium Session." UN Press Release GA/9850.

and arrears. Legislation amending the statutory requirement for a 25 percent assessment for peacekeeping passed the Senate on 7 February 2001 and the House of Representatives on 10 May, although the House of Representatives added the United States regaining its seat on the Human Rights Commission as a further condition for payment of the third tranche of $244 million.[47]

The US financial veto seems to have been effective "even when merely threatened,"[48] and so, politically, US withholding of its assessed contributions has had the effect that the United Nations is to a considerable extent beholden to US views as to how the organization should be run and to how much the United States is going to contribute. It is not clear that the US actions have had a specific impact on international law since the question has been treated as less of a legal, than a political, matter.

4. and 5. Noncompliance with Article 36(1)(b) of the Vienna Convention on Consular Relations and an Order of the International Court of Justice: Breard

On 24 June 1993 Angel Francisco Breard was convicted of the attempted rape and murder of Ruth Dickie in Virginia. Breard was a Paraguayan, but the Paraguayan consular authorities did not learn about Breard's arrest and trial until 1996. This was contrary to Article 36(1)(b) of the Vienna Convention on Consular Relations of 1963, which provides that the "authorities shall inform the person concerned without delay of his rights [to have the consular post advised of his arrest or committal to prison or custody pending trial or other form of detention]." This was not an isolated phenomenon. In January 1998 Amnesty International issued a report identifying more than sixty foreign nationals facing execution in the United States, most of whom had never been informed of their right to seek consular assistance following their arrest.[49] In the case of Breard, the State Department recognized the lapse on 7 July 1997 and apologized.

The same case raised another question of noncompliance – this time with an Order of the International Court of Justice (ICJ). Paraguay brought

[47] Sean D. Murphy, "Agreement on UN Financial and Structural Reforms" (2001) 95 AJIL 389–92, at 392, n. 21.

[48] Jose E. Alvarez, "The United States Financial Veto" (1996) *American Society of International Law Proceedings* 322.

[49] "United States of America: Violation of the Rights of Foreign Nationals Under Sentence of Death" AMR 51/001/1998, 01/01/1998.

proceedings in the ICJ in relation to Breard. On 9 April 1998 the ICJ issued
an Order stating that the United States "should take all measures at its
disposal to ensure that Angel Francisco Breard is not executed pending the
final decision in these proceedings..."[50] Breard was nevertheless executed
on 14 April 1998. In an *amicus* brief to the US Supreme Court urging the
Court to deny a writ of *certiorari* and a stay, the Departments of State
and Justice claimed that there was substantial disagreement as to whether
an ICJ order indicating provisional measures is binding, but went on to
assert that the better reasoned position is that such an order is not binding.
"That order states that the United States 'should' take all measures 'at its
disposal' to ensure that Breard is not executed. The word 'should' in the
ICJ's order confirms our understanding, described above, that the ICJ order
is precatory rather than mandatory."[51] By a letter of 2 November 1998, the
government of Paraguay informed the Court that it did not wish to go
on with the proceedings and requested that the case be removed from the
Court's List. This was done by an Order of 10 November 1998.[52]

In January 1998 the Department of State released its Publication 10518,
*Consular Notification and Access: Instructions for Federal, State, and Local
Law Enforcement and Other Officials Regarding Foreign Nationals in the
United States and the Rights of Consular Officials to Assist Them.*[53] The
foreword states that the booklet is designed

> to help ensure that foreign governments can extend appropriate consular
> services to their nationals in the United States and that the United States
> complies with its legal obligations to such governments... The continued
> cooperation of federal, state, and local law enforcement agencies in ensuring
> that foreign nationals in the United States are treated in accordance with these
> instructions... will also help ensure that the United States can insist upon
> rigorous compliance by foreign governments with respect to United States
> citizens abroad.

[50] Vienna Convention on Consular Relations (*Paraguay v. United States*), Provisional Measures,
(1998) ICJ Reports 11 (Order of Apr. 9), reprinted in (1998) 37 *International Legal Materials*
810.
[51] Brief for the United States as Amicus Curiae, at 49–51, *Breard v. Greene*, 118 S.Ct. 1352 (1998)
(Nos 97-1390, 97-8214) cited in Jonathan I. Charney and W. Michael Reisman, "Agora: Breard"
(1998) 92 AJIL 4.
[52] *Case Concerning the Vienna Convention on Consular Relations (Paraguay v. United States of America)*, 10 Nov. 1998, available at <http://www.icj-cij.org/icjwww/idocket/ipaus/ipausframe.htm>.
[53] M. Nash (Leigh), "Consular Officers and Consulates" (1998) 92 AJIL 243–5. This booklet has now been archived to <http://www.state. gov/www/global/legal_affairs/ca_notification/
ca_prelim.html>.

An optimistic reading of the *Breard* case might suggest that the outcome for international law was to be improved US compliance with the Vienna Convention on Consular Relations, although this would not help those already facing the death penalty who had not had the benefit of consular assistance. Only eight days after the execution of Breard on 14 April 1998, the state of Arizona executed Honduran national Jose Villafuerte, who had not been informed after arrest of his right to obtain the assistance of his consulate.[54] As for the question as to whether interim measures are binding, *Breard* left the question unsettled.

Both outcomes need to be re-evaluated in the light of the subsequent *LaGrand* case. Karl and Walter LaGrand had been arrested by Arizona law enforcement authorities in January 1982 and were on 17 February 1984 convicted of murder in the first degree, attempted murder in the first degree, attempted armed robbery, and two counts of kidnapping. They were detained, tried, and sentenced to death without being advised of their right to consular assistance.[55] Karl LaGrand was executed on 24 February 1999 and Walter LaGrand was scheduled to be executed on 4 March 1999. On 2 March 1999 Germany filed in the Registry of the International Court of Justice an Application instituting proceedings against the United States for "violations of the Vienna Convention on Consular Relations." On the same day the German government also filed a request for the indication of provisional measures. By an Order of 3 March 1999 the ICJ indicated certain provisional measures, including that the United States "should take all measures at its disposal to ensure that Walter LaGrand is not executed pending the final decision in these proceedings..."[56] In the late afternoon of 3 March the United States government transmitted the order to Arizona Governor Jane Dee Hull. Just before the scheduled execution, Germany filed a case before the US Supreme Court seeking a temporary restraining order. The US Solicitor General filed a letter with the Court opposing any stay, asserting in part that "an order of the International Court of Justice indicating provisional measures is not binding and does not furnish a basis

---

[54] "United States of America: The Execution of Angel Breard: Apologies are not Enough" AMR 51/027/1998, 01/05/1998.

[55] *LaGrand* case (*Germany v. United States of America*) Memorial of the Federal Republic of Germany, I, 16 Sept. 1999, available at http://www.icj.cij.org/icjwww/idocket/igus/iguspleadings/igus_ipleading_memorial_germany_19990916_complete.htm (accessed 21 Jan. 2001).

[56] *Case Concerning the Vienna Convention on Consular Relations (Germany v. United States of America)*. Request for the Indication of Provisional Measures available at <http://www.icj.cij.org/icjwww/idocket/igus/igusorder/igus_iorder_ 19990303.htm> (accessed 21 Jan. 2001).

for judicial relief." Walter LaGrand was executed on 4 March. The German Foreign Minister issued a statement declaring, in part, that the failure of the United States to abide by the ICJ order was a violation of international law.[57]

In its judgement of 27 June 2001 the International Court of Justice found, *inter alia*, that, "by not informing Karl and Walter LaGrand without delay following their arrest of their rights under Article 36, paragraph 1(b), of the [Vienna] Convention [on Consular Relations], and by thereby depriving the Federal Republic of Germany of the possibility, in a timely fashion, to render assistance provided for by the Convention to the individuals concerned, the United States of America breached its obligations to the Federal Republic of Germany and to the LaGrand brothers." The Court did, however, regard the US commitment to ensure implementation of specific measures adopted in performance of its obligations under Article 36(1)(b) as sufficient to meet Germany's request for a general assurance of non-repetition.[58]

As for the question of noncompliance with provisional measures of the International Court of Justice, any weight that the US response to the *Breard* case may have lent to the view that they are not binding was far more than countered by the decision in the *LaGrand* case. In its judgment of 27 June 2001 the Court "reached the conclusion that orders on provisional measures under Article 41 have binding effect,"[59] thus clarifying a hitherto unsettled point of law.[60]

6. Use of force against Iraq, December 1998

In January and February 1998 the United States President and other officials asserted that if Iraq did not permit unconditional access to international weapons inspections it would face a military attack.[61] On 2 March 1998 the

---

[57] Sean D. Murphy, "Execution of German Nationals Who Were Not Notified of Right to Consular Access" (1999) 93 AJIL 644–647.

[58] *LaGrand (Germany v. United States of America)*, 27 June 2001, para. 128(6) available at <http://www.icj-cij.org/icjwww/idocket/...usjudgment/igusijudgment/20010625.html>

[59] *Ibid.*

[60] See, e.g., discussion in Bernard H. Oxman, "Jurisdiction and the Power to Indicate Provisional Measures," in Lori F. Damrosch (ed.), *The International Court of Justice at a Crossroads* (Dobbs Ferry, NY: Transnational, 1987), at pp. 332–3; and Peter J. Goldsworthy, "Interim Measures of Protection in the International Court of Justice" (1974) 68 AJIL 258–77 at 273–4.

[61] Jules Lobel and Michael Ratner, "Bypassing the Security Council: Ambiguous Authorizations to Use Force, Ceasefires and the Iraqi Inspection Regime" (1999) 93 AJIL 124–54 at 124.

Security Council unanimously endorsed the memorandum of understanding regarding inspections signed by the UN Secretary-General Kofi Annan and the Iraqi Deputy Prime Minister, Tariq Aziz, during a visit by Kofi Annan to Baghdad in late February. In the Security Council meeting of 2 March 1998 a majority of States stipulated that additional authorization would be necessary before force could be used.[62] US and British authorities claimed that Resolution 678 of November 1990, which had empowered the United States and other countries to use force against Iraq, continued to provide authority to punish Iraq for cease-fire violations.[63] In December 1998 the United States and the United Kingdom conducted a bombing campaign designed to coerce Iraq into resuming cooperation with UN arms inspectors, basing their legal rationale for doing so on Resolution 678 (1990) and the fact that there had been no Security Council resolution explicitly requiring them to obtain further authorization.[64] The only Security Council member other than the United Kingdom and the United States to favor the air strikes was Japan; Russia and China accused the United States and the United Kingdom of an "unprovoked act of force" that "violated the principles of international law and the principles of the Charter." Some European and Asian allies supported the military action, but international reaction was generally negative.[65]

The 1998 strikes against Iraq prompted debate on the unilateral enforcement of Security Council resolutions and the "limits within which the implementation of UN collective machinery can be delegated or contracted out to individual actors; whether, in the face of the inadequacy or paralysis of such mechanisms, there is room for non-collectively authorized unilateral action for the execution of *collective decisions*, and the extent to which such unauthorized unilateral measures can constitute precedents which impact on the evolution of the United Nations Charter."[66] The United States did

---

[62] *Ibid.*, at 124.
[63] Under Secretary of State Thomas Pickering, USIA Foreign Press New Briefing, Federal News Service, 3 March 1998. Cited in Lobel and Ratner, "Bypassing the Security Council," above note 61, at 125.
[64] *Ibid.*, at 125 n. 8.   [65] *Ibid.*, at 154, n. 123.
[66] Vera Gowlland-Debbas, "The Limits of Unilateral Enforcement of Community Objectives in the Framework of UN Peace Maintenance" (2000) 11:2 EJIL 361–83 at 365–6. Unilateral enforcements of Security Council resolutions have been justified on several grounds. First is the argument of implied authorization, which assumes that implicit authorization can be unilaterally deduced from the wording or open-ended nature of certain resolutions. A second argument has been that of the "implied powers doctrine": regional arrangements have a residual responsibility to fill the gap where the Security Council is paralyzed and there is a threat to international peace and security. (But of course in the case of Kosovo no resolution was ever put to the

not claim to be entitled to use force without Security Council authorization but rather, that a previous resolution provided the necessary authority.[67] To the extent that there has been any closure of the questions pertaining to international law and the use of force arising from this case study, it is in favor of the status quo.

7. Missile attacks against the bin Laden network in Afghanistan and Sudan, August 1998

On 20 August 1998 the United States launched seventy-nine Tomahawk cruise missiles at targets associated with the Osama bin Laden network, including paramilitary training camps in Afghanistan and an allegedly bin Laden-financed[68] pharmaceutical factory in Sudan that the United States claimed had been making chemical weapons.[69] Bin Laden had been linked to the bombing on 7 August 1998 of US embassies in Nairobi, Kenya, and Dar es Salaam, Tanzania. The missile attacks reflected a policy decision that pre-emptive action was required against terrorism.[70] In a report to the Speaker of the House of Representatives and to the President of the Senate, President Clinton claimed that the United States had "acted in exercise of our inher-ent right of self-defense consistent with Article 51 of the United Nations Charter. These strikes were a necessary and proportionate response to the imminent threat of further terrorist attacks against United States person-nel and facilities."[71] The United States notified the Security Council of the

---

Security Council.) Third, it has been argued that a posteriori legitimization of unilateral action by means of a Security Council resolution serves to remove any taint of illegality even where there had been no prior authorization. And fourth, lack of condemnation in the Council is ar-gued to reflect emerging norms in favor of humanitarian intervention, which effectively modify the Charter. Ibid., at 372–7.

[67] Lobel and Ratner refer to the comment of Secretary of State Madeleine Albright that if "we don't like" Annan's agreement, "we will pursue our national interest" as a notable exception. Lobel and Ratner, "Bypassing the Security Council," above note 61, at 124.

[68] James Bennet, "United States Cruise Missiles Strike Sudan and Afghan Targets Tied to Terrorist Network" New York Times, 21 Aug. 1998, A1, quoted in M. F. Brennan, "Avoiding Anarchy: Bin Laden Terrorism, the United States Response, and the Role of Customary International Law" (1999) 59 Louisiana Law Review 1195–223 at 1195.

[69] Sean D. Murphy, "Contemporary Practice of the United States relating to International Law" (1999) 93 AJIL 161.

[70] Sara N. Scheideman, "Standards of Proof in Forcible Responses to Terrorism" (2000) 50 Syracuse Law Review 249–84 at 250.

[71] "Letter to Congressional Leaders Reporting on Military Action Against Terrorist Sites in Afghanistan and Sudan," quoted in Murphy, "Contemporary Practice," above note 69, at 163.

attacks, claiming that it had acted "pursuant to the right of self-defense confirmed by Article 51 of the Charter of the United Nations. The targets struck, and the timing and method of attack used, were carefully designed to minimize risks of collateral damage to civilians and to comply with international law, including the rules of necessity and proportionality."[72]

The attacks renewed a debate that had begun in the 1980s as to the right of a State under Article 51 to respond with force in self-defense against terrorism. The United States had in 1986 bombed military targets in Libya in response to an explosion at the LaBelle disco in Berlin which had killed two US servicemen and wounded seventy-eight Americans, and a threatened attack in Paris.[73] International reaction, other than from the United Kingdom, had been largely negative.[74] Debate had continued in the 1990s in relation, *inter alia*, to the US missile attack of 26 June 1993, which destroyed the Iraqi intelligence headquarters in Baghdad in response to an alleged Iraqi plan to kill former President George Bush Snr. The United States had also justified this under Article 51.[75] In contrast to the situation following the 1986 raids, the majority of Security Council members had accepted the United States position that the 1993 attack was a justified act of self-defense, though China and some Islamic States did voice criticism.[76]

International reaction to the 1998 attacks was "mixed and muted."[77] Most US allies, and a number of commentators,[78] supported the attacks, although France and Italy issued only tepid statements of support.[79] UN Secretary-General Kofi Annan criticized "individual actions" against terrorism, implying disapproval of the US strikes.[80] The government of Sudan protested that the 1998 missile strike was an "iniquitous act of aggression which is a clear and blatant violation of the sovereignty and territorial integrity of a Member State of the United Nations"; Sudan asserted that the

---

[72] Letter dated 20 Aug. 1998 from the Permanent Representative of the United States of America at the United Nations Addressed to the President of the Security Council, UN Doc. S/1998/780 (1998) quoted in Murphy, "Contemporary Practice," above note 69, at 163.

[73] Alan D. Surchin, "Terror and the Law: The Unilateral Use of Force and the June 1993 Bombing of Baghdad" (1995) 5 *Duke Journal of Comparative and International Law* 457–97 at 484.

[74] *Ibid.*   [75] *Ibid.*   [76] *Ibid.*, at 467–8.

[77] Jules Lobel, "The Use of Force to Respond to Terrorist Attacks – The Afghanistan and Sudan Bombing" (1999) 24 *Yale Journal of International Law* 537 at 538.

[78] See, e.g., Ruth Wedgwood, "Responding to Terrorism: the Strikes Against Bin Laden" (1999) 24 *Yale Journal of International Law* 559–76, and Gregory M. Travalio, "Terrorism, International Law, and the Use of Military Force" (2000) 18 *Wisconsin International Law Journal* 145–91.

[79] Lobel, "Use of Force," above note 77, at 538.   [80] *Ibid.*

strike had been "contrary to international law and practice, the Charter of the United Nations and civilized human behavior."[81] The Taliban Islamic movement also protested against the missile attacks, as did the governments of Iran, Iraq, Libya, Pakistan, Russia, and Yemen, Palestinian officials, and certain Islamic militant groups.[82] Sudan, the Group of African States and Group of Islamic States within the UN General Assembly, and the Arab League each requested a meeting of the Security Council to discuss the missile attack on Sudan, but the incident was not placed on the agenda.[83] Security Council Resolution 1193 of 28 August 1998, which addressed the Afghan conflict and the situation in Afghanistan more generally, included an expression of deep concern at "the continuing presence of terrorists in the territory of Afghanistan"; it demanded *inter alia* that "the Afghan factions refrain from harboring and training terrorists and their organizations…"

In addition to renewing discussion of the question as to a State's right to use force pursuant to Article 51 in response to acts of terrorism, the 1998 attacks raised the "equally important, but far less analyzed, question of how, and under what evidentiary standard, nations and scholars are to assess the factual allegations upon which the use of force against terrorism is premised."[84] There was no closure on either question, as became apparent in the aftermath of the 11 September 2001 terrorist attacks in the United States.

8. Bombing of the Federal Republic of Yugoslavia during the Kosovo crisis, March–June 1999

The eleven-week bombing campaign conducted by NATO against the Federal Republic of Yugoslavia in March–June 1999 was undertaken without explicit Security Council authorization. The US government justified its actions on the basis of a number of factors whose emphasis changed over time.[85] Such factors included serious and widespread noncompliance

---

[81] "Letter dated 21 August 1998 from the Permanent Representative of the Sudan at the United Nations Addressed to the President of the Security Council," UN Doc. S/1998/786 annex (1998), cited in Murphy, "Contemporary Practice," above note 69, at 164.

[82] *Ibid.*   [83] *Ibid.*, at 165.

[84] Lobel, "Use of Force," above note 77, at 538. See also Scheideman, "Standards of Proof," above note 70.

[85] Murphy, "Contemporary Practice" (1999) 93:3 AJIL 631.

by the Federal Republic of Yugoslavia with international law, danger to NATO allies, and prospects of a further humanitarian catastrophe.[86] In a speech to the Security Council on 24 March 1999 the Deputy United States representative, Peter Burleigh, said that the United States believed that its actions were necessary "to respond to Belgrade's brutal persecution of Kosovar Albanians, violations of international law, excessive and indiscriminate use of force, refusal to negotiate to resolve the issue peacefully and recent military build-up in Kosovo – all of which foreshadow a humanitarian catastrophe of immense proportions." He continued: "We have begun today's action to avert this humanitarian catastrophe and to deter further aggression and repression in Kosovo."[87] In explaining its actions NATO referred to "the unique combination of a number of factors" that presented itself in Kosovo. These factors included the failure of the Federal Republic of Yugoslavia to comply with Security Council demands under Chapter VII, the danger of a humanitarian disaster in Kosovo, the inability of the Council to make a clear decision adequate to deal with that disaster, and the serious threat to peace and security in the region posed by Serb action.[88]

On 29 April 1999 Yugoslavia instituted proceedings (separate cases) before the International Court of Justice against Belgium,[89] Canada,[90] France,[91] Germany,[92] Italy,[93] the Netherlands,[94] Portugal,[95] the United Kingdom,[96] Spain,[97] and the United States.[98] In its applications instituting proceedings Yugoslavia claimed that each of these States had violated several of its international obligations, the first mentioned of which was

---

[86] *Ibid.* at 631–2.

[87] Security Council Provisional Record, 3988th Meeting, 24 March 1999, 5.35pm (NY time) reproduced in Marc Weller, *The Crisis in Kosovo 1989–1999 From the Dissolution of Yugoslavia to Rambouillet and the Outbreak of Hostilities*, International Documents and Analysis, I, (Cambridge: Cambridge University Press, 1999), p. 500.

[88] Michael Matheson, "Human Rights and Humanitarian Intervention: The Legality of the NATO–Yugoslav–Kosovo War", (2000) 94 *Proceedings of the American Society of International Law* 301.

[89] Legality of Use of Force (Yugoslavia v. Belgium).

[90] Legality of Use of Force (Yugoslavia v. Canada).

[91] Legality of Use of Force (Yugoslavia v. France).

[92] Legality of Use of Force (Yugoslavia v. Germany).

[93] Legality of Use of Force (Yugoslavia v. Italy).

[94] Legality of Use of Force (Yugoslavia v. Netherlands).

[95] Legality of Use of Force (Yugoslavia v. Portugal).

[96] Legality of Use of Force (Yugoslavia v. United Kingdom).

[97] Legality of Use of Force (Yugoslavia v. Spain).

[98] Legality of Use of Force (Yugoslavia v. United States of America).

that prohibiting the use of force. Yugoslavia also filed, in each of the cases, a request for interim measures of protection, asking the Court to order the State involved to "cease immediately its acts of use of force" and to "refrain from any act of threat or use of force against the Federal Republic of Yugoslavia." The Court declined to issue provisional measures, finding that it did not have prima facie jurisdiction in any of the cases and that it "manifestly lacked jurisdiction" in respect of the cases brought against Spain and the United States.[99] On 5 July 2000 the respondent States each filed preliminary objections to jurisdiction and admissibility. By Orders of 8 September 2000 the Court fixed 5 April 2001 as the time limit within which the Federal Republic of Yugoslavia should present a written statement of its observations and submissions on the preliminary objections raised by the NATO countries. On 18 January 2001 Yugoslavia successfully requested an extension to that date and in response to a request for a further extension, the Court on 22 March 2002 extended by a further year the time limits for the filing by Yugoslavia of written statements of its observations and submissions on the preliminary objections raised by the eight respondent States.

The Kosovo issue prompted increased debate on the contemporary relevance of UN Charter provisions on the use of force, on the legality of humanitarian intervention, and on the role of the Security Council in authorizing intervention. Writing before Kosovo, Levitt had argued that there appeared to be a normative legal shift toward international recognition of a right to unilateral humanitarian intervention by regional actors in internal conflicts. Levitt drew on the experience of the Economic Community of West African States (ECOWAS) missions in Liberia and Sierra Leone and the Inter-African Mission to Monitor the Implementation of the Bangui Agreements in the Central African Republic to propose a list of normative criteria on which humanitarian intervention should be based.[100] Other writers have thought it doubtful as to whether the classical doctrine of

---

[99] Order of 2 June 1999 – Request for the Indication of Provisional Measures.

[100] His criteria were (1) when there are human rights abuses within a state that are so egregious as to violate the *jus cogens* norms of international law; (2) when a state has collapsed and is withering into a state of anarchy; and (3) to safeguard democracy when a democratic government has been violently and illegally dislodged against the will of its domestic population. Jeremy Levitt, "Humanitarian Intervention by Regional Actors in Internal Conflicts: The Cases of ECOWAS in Liberia and Sierra Leone" (1998) 12 *Temple International and Comparative Law Journal* at 336–7 (references omitted).

humanitarian intervention survived the Charter's general prohibition on the use of force.[101] In the light of Kosovo, Bruno Simma pointed to an emerging doctrine in international law allowing the use of forcible countermeasures to impede a State from committing large-scale atrocities on its own territory in circumstances where the Security Council is incapable of responding adequately to the crisis.[102]

The Independent International Commission on Kosovo, established on the initiative of Prime Minister Göran Persson of Sweden, proposed a framework of principles that must be satisfied in any legitimate claim to humanitarian intervention.[103] It was the hope of the Commission that the UN General Assembly adopt such a framework in some modified form as a Declaration and that the UN Charter be adapted to the Declaration either by appropriate amendments or by a case-by-case approach in the UN Security Council.[104] Considering the bombing to have been of "dubious" legality,[105] the UK House of Commons Select Committee on Foreign Affairs lent its support to moves to establish in the United Nations new principles governing humanitarian intervention.[106] The United Kingdom submitted to the Secretary-General a framework for intervention based on six principles: that there be more concentration on conflict prevention; that the use of armed force should only be a last resort; that responsibility lies in the first place with the State where severe violations are taking place; that when a government has shown that it is unwilling or unable to cope with a humanitarian catastrophe, the international community has a duty to

---

[101] Gowlland-Debbas, "The Limits of Unilateral Enforcement," above note 66, at 363. See also Ian Brownlie, *International Law and the Use of Force by States* (Oxford: Clarendon Press, 1963), p. 342.

[102] Bruno Simma, "NATO, the UN and the Use of Force: Legal Aspects" (1999) 10 EJIL 1–22.

[103] Independent International Commission on Kosovo, *Kosovo Report. Conflict, International Response, Lessons Learned* (Oxford: Oxford University Press, 2000), available at http://www.kosovocommission.org/reports/1-summary.html (accessed 7 Oct. 2001).

[104] The three threshold principles are: the suffering of civilians owing to severe patterns of human rights violations or the breakdown of government, the overriding commitment to the direct protection of the civilian population, and the calculation that the intervention has a reasonable chance of ending the humanitarian catastrophe. In addition, the framework includes a further eight contextual principles which can be used to assess the degree of legitimacy possessed by the actual use of force, available at http://www.kosovocommission.org/reports/1-summary.html (accessed 7 Oct. 2001).

[105] United Kingdom, House of Commons Select Committee on Foreign Affairs, "Fourth Report" at para. 144, available at http://www.parliament.the-stationery-office.co.uk/pa/cm199900/cmselect/cmfaff/28/2813.htm (accessed 30 June 2000).

[106] *Ibid.*

intervene; that any use of force should be proportionate to achieving the humanitarian purposes of the mission and carried out in accordance with international law; and that the use of force be collective and only in exceptional circumstances undertaken without the express authority of the Security Council.[107] While Western States, especially the United Kingdom and Canada, asserted that sovereignty "cannot be a licence for States to massacre their citizens with impunity,"[108] the diplomatic initiative of the United Kingdom stalled, debate in the General Assembly during 1999 indicating that there was not much general support for codifying a right to humanitarian intervention.

Elsewhere, discussion as to the legality of humanitarian intervention and the Kosovo precedent continued. The International Commission on Intervention and State Sovereignty, which had been established by the government of Canada in 2000, issued its report on military intervention for human protection in December 2001. Entitled *The Responsibility to Protect*, this report reinforced the obligations inherent in the concept of sovereignty as well as the responsibility of the Security Council for the maintenance of international peace and security. Its conclusions emphasized the appropriateness of the Security Council to authorize military intervention for human protection purposes and concluded that its authorization should in all cases be sought prior to any military intervention.[109] To the extent that there has been closure of the debate on the legality of humanitarian intervention, it would seem to be in favor of the status quo. In responding to a question as to whether there was a danger of competition from regional groups when they "do their own thing, as in Kosovo," Kofi Annan commented that he "really [did] not believe that after what we went through with Kosovo we are going to see too many Kosovos tomorrow. I suspect that in the future regional organizations will approach the Security Council before they move forward."[110]

---

[107] Article by the Foreign Secretary, Robin Cook, and Liberal Democrat Foreign Affairs spokesman, Menzies Campbell, *Financial Times*, 4 Sept. 2000, available at http://www.fco.gov.uk/news/newstext.asp?4108 (accessed 14 Jan. 2001).

[108] Nicholas J. Wheeler, "Legitimating Humanitarian Intervention: Principles and Procedures" (2001) 2:2 *Melbourne Journal of International Law* 550–67 at 551.

[109] *The Responsibility to Protect*, Report of the International Commission on Intervention and State Sovereignty, available at http://www.iciss-ciise.gc.ca/report-e.asp.

[110] Transcript of Press Conference by Secretary-General Kofi Annan at Headquarters, 19 Dec. 2000, available at http://www.un.org/News/Press/ docs/2000/20001220.sgsm7668.doc.html (accessed 14 Jan. 2001).

Analysis of the effects on international law of the above examples of US noncompliance

This chapter has looked, as dispassionately as possible, at the outcomes for the international legal system, of eight quite clear-cut examples of US noncompliance with international law. At least five types of outcome for the international legal system of US noncompliance since the end of the Cold War can be discerned from these case studies. New multilateral instruments appeared as a result of the Sea Turtle Act and Helms-Burton; *Shrimp-Turtle* and *Breard* led to clarification of particular points of law (although in the case of *Breard* this occurred via the subsequent *LaGrand* case), but clarification of relevant law was avoided by the agreed mode of resolution of the Helms-Burton dispute; the use of force case studies prompted considerable debate on specific points of the relevant law but no clear move away from the status quo; prospects for improved compliance by the United States and other States with Article 36(1)(b) of the Vienna Convention on Consular Relations appear good as a result of the *Breard* and *LaGrand* cases; while it is arguable that the case of the US dues to the United Nations had little effect on the relevant law, the issue having been perceived as more of a political than a legal matter.

What is perhaps most noticeable about these outcomes is that, where US noncompliance has been particularly irksome to other States, those States have been able to help shape the impact on international law of those actions/inactions. Although there has been considerable academic discussion regarding US unilateralism,[111] and although the acts of alleged noncompliance (other than the 1998 bombing of Iraq and that of the Federal Republic of Yugoslavia during the Kosovo crisis) were, indeed, undertaken by the United States on its own, other States and international institutions became involved in each case and the impact on international law of US noncompliance has therefore generally been indirect. So, for example, the ICJ was involved following US noncompliance with the Vienna Convention, the WTO dispute settlement body became involved following United States noncompliance with GATT; and the EU and Canada and other countries became involved in relation to Helms-Burton. This would seem to highlight the fact that international law is more than simply a blank slate onto which

---

[111] Two issues of the EJIL have been devoted to this topic: 11(1) (March 2000) and 11(2) (June 2000).

the most powerful can translate their policy desires. International law is a genuine system with all the complexity and dynamism that one might expect from any other system. Of course, the case studies selected for this analysis were all well-known ones and it is possible that the outcomes for international law of such a selection of examples may not have been typical. These examples are well known precisely because they were sufficiently irksome to certain other States that those States took action to challenge the United States. There may well have been other, lesser-known instances of US noncompliance with international law which did not provoke active opposition on the part of other participants in the international legal system.

The fact that, in these case studies at least, other States were able to influence the outcomes of alleged US breaches of international law aligns with Samuel Huntington's rejection of the idea that we have been living in a uni-polar world order. In his article "The Lonely Superpower,"[112] Huntington maintained that, in a true uni-polar world order, the superpower could effectively resolve important international issues alone, and no combination of other States could prevent it from doing so. Huntington's awareness that the United States has not been able to get away with just whatever it wants in the post-Cold-War international order prompted him to declare that we could not, by definition, be living in a uni-polar world order. According to Huntington, what we have been witnessing in recent years is better described as a "uni-multipolar system," in which several major powers contribute to the settlement of key international issues. In one instance of US noncompliance, we have seen the EU and its member States standing in the way of the United States doing whatever it wants. But this role has not even been confined to "great powers"; it was Paraguay that initiated proceedings in the ICJ in relation to Breard.

It has not been necessary for the United States to wield blatant power over international law for its actions and rhetoric to have had an impact on the system. In his *The Epochs of International Law*, Grewe divided the history of modern international law into eras, each of which was dominated by the great power of that age: Spain from 1494 to 1648; France from 1648 to 1815, and Britain from 1815 to 1919.[113] It was not that the dominant power controlled every development within the system during that epoch

---

[112] Samuel P. Huntington, "The Lonely Superpower" (1999) 78(2) *Foreign Affairs* 35–49.
[113] Wilhelm Grewe, *The Epochs of International Law*, trans. and rev. Michael Byers (Berlin: de Gruyter, 2000).

but that the dominant power was the one against whose ideas regarding the system of international law all others debated. In the post–Cold War years such a dialogue has been conducted in response to US rhetoric and actions, including those of noncompliance, particularly in relation to the use of force. But it is worth bearing in mind that the US acts of alleged noncompliance have not occurred in a vacuum. They have on some occasions been in response to the actions of other actors that had themselves reflected scant regard for the norms of the international system. Ruth Wedgwood commented in relation to the US announcement in February 1998 that it was prepared to use military force against Iraq that "as sometimes happens in international politics, the question of the lawfulness of the putative US enforcement action was allowed to overshadow the grave violation of international law by Iraq that was its predicate."[114] This comment might also have been made in relation to the United States response to the terrorist attacks of bin Laden in 1998.

This is not to claim that the United States is entitled to take the law into its own hands when suffering from the actions of others. Rather it is to highlight the complexity of drawing causal connections between US actions/inactions and international law. Such complexity is further evidenced by the fact that the impact on international law became apparent in some instances only after one or more repetitions of the US action/inaction. This was particularly true in the case of breaches of the Vienna Convention on Consular Relations. Individual acts of alleged noncompliance on the part of the United States are each single moves in a two-way interchange between US rhetoric and actions and those of other actors within or outside the system of international law.

It appears from these case studies that reaction to one general type of noncompliance may be stronger than that to another. Violations of World Trade Organization agreements do not tend to be regarded as evidencing contempt for international law in the same way as do those – of the Vienna Convention on Consular Relations or the UN Charter – which lead to a loss of human life.[115] This may be in part because, in the case of the WTO, there is in place a dispute resolution mechanism which will proceed once a party requests the appointment of a dispute settlement panel, unless blocked by

---

[114] Ruth Wedgwood, "The Enforcement of Security Council Resolution 687: The Threat of Force Against Iraq's Weapons of Mass Destruction" (1998) 92:4 AJIL 724–8 at 725.
[115] See comments by Detlev F. Vagts, "The United States and its Treaties: Observance and Breach" (2001) 95:2 AJIL 313–34 at 332.

a consensus on the Dispute Settlement Body, and by way of which penalties can be assigned. That said, the fact that the United States made clear its intention to defect from this process should the EU proceed with its WTO challenge to the Helms-Burton legislation and, indeed, the fact that the ICJ found that it "manifestly lacked jurisdiction" in the case brought against the United States by Yugoslavia,[116] cannot help but reinforce the impression that the United States remains ultimately unaccountable for its wilful flouting of treaty obligations.

The US response to charges of noncompliance has varied considerably. In the case of noncompliance with the Vienna Convention on Consular Relations, the United States candidly accepted its failure to comply (although it maintained that the outcome would have been no different even if it had complied); in *Shrimp-Turtle* the United States defended its actions and yet accepted the umpire's verdict of noncompliance; in relation to provisional measures of the ICJ the United States argued for a particular interpretation of the relevant law (with which the Court then differed); and in relation to its UN arrears – and to some extent to Kosovo – the United States tends to have avoided legal argument in favor of other forms of justification for its position.

The United States has not been alone in sometimes failing to fulfil adequately its obligations under international law; almost none of the orders for interim measures issued by the ICJ have been followed.[117] Nor is there evidence that the compliance rate of the United States has been particularly low or unprecedented during the post–Cold War era.[118] Most of the case studies considered in this paper had Cold War precedents. There had, for example, been clashes between the United States and other countries in the Americas, Europe and elsewhere over extraterritorial jurisdiction since the antitrust claims arising from the *Alcoa* case in 1945;[119] the trend was particularly apparent during the Cold War, aimed at the Soviet bloc

---

[116] International Court of Justice: *Yugoslavia v. United States*, 2 June 1999, reprinted in (1999) 38 *International Legal Materials* 1188.

[117] D. J. Harris, *Cases and Materials on International Law* (5th edn., London: Sweet & Maxwell, 1998), pp. 988–9.

[118] In an exploration of the US commitment to its treaty obligations, Detlev Vagts makes the point that anxieties have been needlessly fueled in recent years by the reckless language of both officials and scholars. Vagts, "The United States and its Treaties," above note 115.

[119] Vaughan Lowe, "US Extraterritorial Jurisdiction: The Helms-Burton and D'Amato Acts" (1997) 46 *International and Comparative Law Quarterly* 378–90 at 378.

or countries dealing with it. In response to the imposition of martial law in Poland at Christmas 1981 and imprisonment of the Solidarity leadership the United States took measures against the USSR, involving a prohibition on US exports of equipment and technology to be used in the construction of a natural gas pipeline from the Arctic regions of Siberia to western Europe.[120] President Reagan had in June 1982 extended the prohibitions to equipment manufactured abroad by foreign subsidiaries of US companies and even by wholly foreign-owned companies benefiting from technology licenses granted by the American firms,[121] but the measures were opposed by US allies in Western Europe and enforced for only five months.

The adverse ruling on *Shrimp-Turtle* had a Cold War precedent in the 1987 Panel Report on US Taxes on Petroleum and Certain Imported Substances, which found that a US tax, the proceeds of which were being used to help finance a Superfund for cleaning up toxic-waste sites, was inconsistent with GATT Article III:2, first sentence.[122] Although the size of the US arrearage of its UN payments increased dramatically in the 1990s when the Republican Party attained majorities in the Senate and then the House of Representatives,[123] withholding of US payments to the United Nations dates from 1980,[124] and the goal of a maximum assessment of 25 percent of the regular budget had been nominated by the United States from the first session of the General Assembly.[125] The legality of the US use of force

---

[120] Gary H. Perlow, "Taking Peacetime Trade Sanctions to the Limit: The Soviet Pipeline Embargo" (1983) 15 *Case Western Reserve Journal of International Law* 253–72 at 254.

[121] See discussion in Andreas F. Lowenfeld, "Congress and Cuba: The Helms-Burton Act" (1996) 90 AJIL 432–433. See also K. Blockslaff, "The Pipeline Affair of 1981/82: A Case History" (1984) 27 *German Yearbook of International Law* 28–37; and Detlav Vagts, "The Pipeline Controversy: An American Viewpoint" (1984) 27 *German Yearbook of International Law* 38–53.

[122] BISD 34 S/136 *et seq*. See Ernst-Ulrich Petersmann, "Prevention and Settlement of International Environmental Disputes in GATT" (1993) 27 *Journal of World Trade* 43–81 at 56–7.

[123] Sean D. Murphy, "Payments of United States Arrears to the United Nations" (2000) 94:2 AJIL 348–9.

[124] Ibid., at 348. In the late 1970s the US Congress expressed occasional frustration with the level of the UN assessments. Congress did on a few occasions threaten to act unilaterally to reduce US contributions with the aim of reaching a maximum assessment of 25 percent of the regular budget. Jose E. Alvarez, "The United States Financial Veto" (1996) *Proceedings of the American Society of International Law* 320.

[125] United States Delegate Position Paper: "Principal Issues Before Committee 5" (21 Oct. 1946), in (1946) *Foreign Relations of the United States* 467.

had been of particular concern during the Reagan years,[126] as demonstrated by the interventions in Grenada (1983), Panama (1989), and Nicaragua (1983–4). It was the Reagan administration that had first adopted a policy of suppressing international terrorism through the use of military force; the policy had been formalized under a 1984 National Security Directive.[127]

Critics of alleged US noncompliance with international law might well be mollified were they to see the United States accept unequivocally that it had breached international law, apologize, and take steps to militate against repetition of the breach in question. Of the case studies included in this chapter it was in relation to the breaches of the Vienna Convention on Consular Relations that such a scenario was most closely played out. It may not have been a coincidence that it was also in relation to this example of noncompliance that the US government most clearly articulated a concern for possible reciprocal breaches against US citizens on the part of other States. The United States went ahead with the execution of Breard, claiming that, even if it were to have complied with the Vienna Convention on Consular Relations, the outcome would have been no different. The United States thus did not change the course of action on which it was embarked as a result of the recognized breach but did indicate that it would act differently in future. In contrast to the Breard scenario, the United States would likely have deemed it much more difficult for those States aggrieved by the US use of force in a manner contrary to the UN Charter to retaliate – at least via conventional warfare.[128] This finding accords with the generally accepted view that reciprocity is a major factor encouraging compliance with international law.[129]

---

[126] "The Reagan Administration's actions in the Gulf of Sidra, Lebanon, Honduras, El Salvador, Angola, Afghanistan, and during the Achille Lauro incident were . . . intended to test the limits on the internationally acceptable use of force." Stuart S. Malawer, "Reagan's Law and Foreign Policy, 1981–1987: The 'Reagan Corollary' of International Law" (1988) 29 Harvard International Law Journal 85–109 at 107–8.

[127] Scheideman, "Standards of Proof," above note 70, at 250.

[128] Cf. "America's unrivaled military superiority means that potential enemies – whether nations or terrorist groups – that choose to attack us will be more likely to resort to terror instead of conventional military assault." Fact Sheet: Combating Terrorism: Presidential Decision Directive 62, Office of the Press Secretary, 22 May 1998. Cited in Scheideman, ibid., at 275 n. 168.

[129] See, for example, Antonio Cassese, "The Role of Legal Advisers in Ensuring that Foreign Policy Conforms to International Legal Standards" (1992) 14 Michigan Journal of International Law 139–70 at 157, and Louis Henkin, How Nations Behave: Law and Foreign Policy (2nd edn., New York: Columbia University Press, 1979), at 54 et seq.

Conclusions

In an endeavor to assess the impact US noncompliance with international law has had on the international legal system in the years since the end of the Cold War, this chapter has analyzed eight case studies of alleged US noncompliance. The overall results of the analysis have been counterintuitive in the sense that the outcomes do not appear to have been as unequivocally negative as one might have expected. Of course, eight case studies is a relatively small sample, and the fact that the US actions in question were ones to which other States had taken strong exception may mean that they are in some way atypical. Nevertheless, the findings have highlighted the fact that the modern system of international law is a genuine system in which the oft maligned promise of sovereign equality can, at least some of the time, translate into effective participation in the evolution of legal rules and principles. The preponderant power of the United States has not accorded it the capacity to shape the rules and principles of international law howsoever it sees fit. Rather, the case studies analyzed in this chapter confirm that the actions and rhetoric of the United States, as the preponderant power of the post-Cold War era, have served as a referent for developments spanning a broad range of fields of public international law.

17

Compliance: multilateral achievements and predominant powers

PETER-TOBIAS STOLL

Compliance signifies conduct which is in accordance with international law.[1] It includes refraining from acts not in accordance with international law, it may also require positive action to live up to certain international law obligations, and it is thus linked to the issue of implementation. International law provides for a number of means, mechanisms, and procedures to persuade those addressed by it to live up to their commitments. These are generally referred to as enforcement measures, and include dispute settlement and sanctions. However, a number of other means, such as verification, monitoring, and assessment measures, have also been developed. Furthermore, criminal sanctions, state responsibility and liability, while primarily aiming at doing justice and compensating in cases of a violation of the law, may, to some extent, also foster compliance.

In the absence of a uniform lawmaking and enforcement authority that is supreme in legitimation and power, the international legal system relies on States, which are equal in their sovereignty, to create and enforce its rules. Thus, States are at the same time creators of and subject to international law.[2] In order to ensure compliance and thus to safeguard effectiveness, such a system may rely on institutions or individual States. The

---

[1] For a record of the current debate on compliance, see Benedict Kingsbury, "The Concept of Compliance as a Function of Competing Conceptions of International Law," in Thomas J. Schoenbaum et al. (eds), *Trilateral Perspectives on International Legal Issues: From Theory to Practice* (Ardsley, NY: Transnational Publishers, 1998); Abram Chayes and Antonia Handler Chayes, *The New Sovereignty: Compliance with International Regulatory Agreements* (Cambridge, MA: Harvard University Press, 1995); Oran Young, *Compliance and Public Authority* (Baltimore: Johns Hopkins University Press, 1977).

[2] Georges Scelle and Hans Wiebringhaus, *Das Gesetz der funktionellen Verdoppelung: Beitrag zu einer universalistischen Theorie des Internationalprivat- und Völkerrechts*, 2nd edn. (Saarbrücken: West-Ost-Verlag, 1955).

international legal system contains a number of institutions and procedures which address the task of settling disputes and in some cases may even authorize sanctions or enforcement action against individual States or groups of States.

The United States largely initiated and contributed to today's international legal system, and can still be considered to have an enormous and exceptional potential in terms of military and economic power. On the one hand, this power enables the United States to play an important role in safeguarding international law. On the other hand, such power carries with it temptations. A predominantly powerful State may be tempted to take the law into its own hands – a law that is still often fragmented, incomplete, and weak. "Taking the law into one's own hands" does not mean a disregard and ignorance of the law. The powerful State purports to serve the law, to preserve and fulfill it. And such actions carry with them the idea of justification, the suggestion that action is required to bring about a lawful state of affairs.

In terms of compliance, the question as to the effects of US predominance on the foundations of international law requires that we look first at the international legal system as such, in the understanding that it includes procedures and institutions which serve to promote this goal. The impact of the United States on such a system and its developments, as well as the ability of the contemporary international legal order to integrate and to put limits on a State as powerful as the United States, should be considered. Second, a close look is required at those areas in which the United States acts alone. From this angle, questions as to the legality and possible justifications of such actions arise. Together, these two perspectives offer some complex insights, which in turn suggest, both as an opportunity and as a responsibility, that the role of other States in determining the effectiveness of the international legal order should also be taken into account.

Strengthening the international legal order: multilateral achievements and a limited role for the United States

The last decade has witnessed a significant development of the international legal system with an emphasis on effectiveness and compliance issues. Important examples include the entry into force of the Law of the Sea Convention and the subsequent establishment of the International Tribunal on the Law of the Sea,[3] the Rio Conventions with their mechanisms and procedures regarding implementation and compliance,[4] the establishment of the World Trade Organization (WTO) as an organization and a legal order governing trade, and a reinforced dispute settlement system, including panels and a standing Appellate Body,[5] the Bosnia and Rwanda criminal tribunals[6] and, much more significantly, the International Criminal Court.[7] From a more detailed perspective, a number of changes and additions were made to existing instruments. The introduction of specific compliance mechanisms in a number of environmental instruments[8] and the complete compliance-focused reengineering of existing standards against child labor in the 1999 International Labor Organization (ILO) Convention[9] may

---

[3] United Nations Convention on the Law of the Sea, UN Doc. A/Conf.62/122, repr. in (1982) 21 *International Legal Materials* 1261, available at http://www.un.org/Depts/los/convention_agreements/texts/ unclos/closindx.htm (visited 28 Sept. 2001). Annex VI of the Convention is at the same time the Statute of the International Tribunal for the Law of the Sea.

[4] United Nations Framework Convention on Climate Change, 9 May 1992, repr. in (1992) 31 *International Legal Materials* 849; Kyoto Protocol to the United Nations Framework Convention on Climate Change, 10 Dec. 1997, repr. in (1998) 37 *International Legal Materials* 22; Convention on Biological Diversity, 5 June 1992, repr. in (1992) 31 *International Legal Materials* 818; Cartagena Protocol on Biosafety, 29 Jan. 2000, repr. in (2000) 39 *International Legal Materials* 1027.

[5] For the relevant legal texts see *The Results of the Uruguay Round of Multilateral Trade Negotiations: The Legal Texts* (GATT Secretariat, 1994), repr. in part in (1994) 33 *International Legal Materials* 1145; WTO, *The WTO Dispute Settlement Procedures. A Collection of the Legal Texts*, 2nd edn., (Cambridge: Cambridge University Press, 1995); see below.

[6] Statute of the International Criminal Tribunal for the former Yugoslavia, UNSC Res. 827, UN SCOR, 48th Sess., 3217th mtg., UN Doc. S/RES/827 (1993), amended by UNSC Res. 1166, UN SCOR, 53rd Sess., 3878th mtg., UN Doc. S/RES/1166 (1998), amended by UN SCOR Res. 1329, 55th Sess., 4240th mtg., UN Doc. S/RES/1329 (2000); Statute of the International Criminal Tribunal for Rwanda, UNSC Res. 955, UN SCOR, 49th Sess., 3453rd mtg., UN Doc. S/RES/955 (1994), amended by UNSC Res. 1165, UN SCOR, 53rd Sess., 3877th mtg., UN Doc. S/RES/1165 (1998), amended by UNSC Res. 1329, 55th Sess., 4240th mtg., UN Doc. S/RES/1329 (2000).

[7] Rome Statute of the International Criminal Court, UN Conference of Plenipotentiaries on the Establishment of the International Criminal Court, 17 July 1998, UN Doc. A/CONF. 183/9; reprinted in (1998) 37 *International Legal Materials* 999; see generally Otto Triffterer (ed.), *Commentary on the Rome Statute of the International Criminal Court* (Baden-Baden: Nomos, 1999); Roy S. Lee, *The International Criminal Court: The Making of the Rome Statute* (The Hague: Kluwer Law International, 1999); Ian Sinclair, *The International Law Commission* (Cambridge: Cambridge University Press, 1987).

[8] Rüdiger Wolfrum, "Means of Ensuring Compliance with and Enforcement of International Environmental Law" (1998) 272 *Recueil des cours* 25; Peter-Tobias Stoll, "Die Effektivität des Umweltvölkerrechts" (1999) 74 *Die Friedens-Warte*, 187–203.

[9] Convention Concerning the Prohibition and Immediate Action for the Elimination of the Worst Forms of Child Labor, ILO Conv. No. 182, repr. in (1999) 38 *International Legal Materials* 1215, available at http://ilolex.ilo.ch:1567/cgi-lex/convde.pl?C182 (visited 27 Sept. 2001); see generally Michael J. Dennis, "Current Developments – The ILO Convention on the Worst Forms of Child Labour" (1999) 93 AJIL 943.

be mentioned in this regard. The establishment of the Caribbean Court of Justice[10] is yet another example. Last but not least, the International Law Commission adopted its Draft Articles on State Responsibility.[11]

Looking at these developments, it becomes apparent that the predominance enjoyed by the United States in a number of areas of international relations did not translate into a leading role in these multilateral efforts. In a number of cases, for reasons explained elsewhere in this book, the United States was not prepared to join multilateral treaty regimes with their enforcement and dispute settlement mechanisms.[12] In other cases, the United States took part in the developments without playing a "predominant" role.

Of course, it is not possible here to undertake a detailed analysis of the position of the United States in any of those developments. However, there are some significant examples which do merit a further look.

Peace and security

The maintenance of peace and security and the system of collective security as a core achievement of the United Nations is of primary relevance here. It has already been addressed to some extent by the discussion on the use of force in this book.[13]

The decline of the Soviet system and its military alliance had important implications in this area. The United Nations developed an Agenda for Peace[14] and the United States announced the beginning of a New World Order,[15] both with considerable enthusiasm. After having been paralyzed

---

[10] Agreement establishing the Caribbean Court of Justice, available at http://www.caricom.org/expframes2.htm (visited 27 Sept. 2001); see Julia Lehmann, "Der Vertrag über den karibischen Gerichtshof im System der CARICOM" (2000) 33 *Verfassung und Recht in Übersee* 282–303; in their Communiqué of the Conference of Heads of Government of the Caribbean Community at the Conclusion of the 11th Inter-Sessional Meeting (14 March 2000), repr. in (2000) 39 *International Legal Materials* 945, the Heads of State reaffirmed their decision to establish a Caribbean Court of Justice.

[11] See the draft articles on Responsibility of States for Internationally Wrongful Acts of the International Law Commission adopted by the Drafting Committee on second reading, Responsibility of States for Internationally Wrongful Acts, UN Doc. A/CN.4/L.602/Rev.1, 26 July 2001; see also http://www.un.org/law/ilc/sessions/53/53sess.htm (visited 1 Oct. 2001); James Crawford, *The International Law Commission's Article on State Responsibility* (Cambridge: Cambridge University Press, 2002).

[12] See Pierre Klein, this volume.

[13] See the contributions by Brad R. Roth, Marcelo Kohen and Achilles Skordas, this volume.

[14] "Agenda for Peace: Preventive Diplomacy, Peacemaking and Peace Keeping" UN Doc. A/47/277 – S/24111, 17 June 1992, available at http://www.un.org/Docs/SG/agpeace.html (visited 26 Sept. 2001).

[15] This term is generally held to have been coined by former President George Bush Snr. and used by him from summer 1990, including in his "State of the Union" speech in Feb. 1991.

for decades, it seemed that the UN system of collective security and the Security Council would be revitalized.[16] A number of initiatives were taken in this regard and new instruments and procedures were developed.[17] Soon, however, the limitations of such a system became clearly visible, especially in regard to the need for resources, troops, and a consensus sufficient to engage effectively. Neither the United States nor a number of other States were apparently prepared to engage and invest sufficiently in an effective system of collective security.

International criminal courts

The more noteworthy and impressive achievements in the area of peace and security are the establishment of the Bosnia and Rwanda tribunals and the subsequent conclusion of the Rome Statute of the International Criminal Court.[18] Creating world courts before which individuals stand trial and face their individual criminal responsibility for grave international crimes is an important contribution to international security and justice. Although the United States supported the establishment and work of the Bosnia and the Rwanda tribunals, it was hesitant to participate in the creation of the International Criminal Court, which would also have jurisdiction to try US officials and soldiers.[19]

The WTO world trade order

In contrast, the United States was heavily engaged in the establishment of the WTO. In this regard, it is useful to recall that the lengthy negotiation exercise preceding this impressive achievement started with a veritable crisis of the former General Agreement on Tariffs and Trade. In the late 1970s and early 1980s, GATT had dramatically lost effectiveness and influence in world trading relations. Its substantive obligations were not suited to coping with the development of world trade and were flawed by collusive bilateral circumvention, mainly between the world's leading trading

---

[16] See Erik Suy, "United Nations Peacekeeping System, Addendum 1999," in Rudolf Bernhardt (ed.) *Encyclopedia of Public International Law*, IV (Amsterdam: North-Holland 2000) 1149.

[17] *Ibid.*   [18] See above notes 6 and 7.

[19] See Monroe Leigh, "The United States and the Statute of Rome" (2001) 95 AJIL 124; David J. Scheffer, "The United States and the Statute of Rome" (1999) 93 AJIL 12; Dominic McGoldrick, "The Permanent International Criminal Court: An End to the Culture of Impunity?" (1999) *Criminal Law Review [United Kingdom]* 627, 644–6.

entities, including the United States, the European Union (EU) and Japan.[20] Furthermore, the GATT dispute settlement mechanism, once considered an outstanding achievement compared with other areas of international law, was often hindered and delayed by political maneuvering, a tendency which was largely facilitated by the fact that the establishment of a panel required positive consensus among the affected States.[21]

Furthermore, the United States created a system of unilateral action to target alleged violations by other States of trade agreements or even disregard by other countries of substantial US trade interests. Section 301 of the Trade Act, which formed the basis for such action, became an internationally used acronym for a bold unilateral approach.[22] It should be noted, however, that the EU adopted a similar but more limited instrument as well.[23] Although the legality of the far-reaching US remedies was widely doubted throughout the international trade law community, moves to set up a GATT Panel to review the Section 301 provisions never achieved consensus.[24]

---

[20] See Jagdish Natwarlal Bhagwati, *The World Trading System at Risk* (New York: Harvester Wheatsheaf, 1991); J. Michael Finger and Sam Laird, "Protection in Developed and Developing Countries – An Overview" (1987) 21(6) *Journal of World Trade Law* 9–23; Josef Molsberger and Angelos Kotios, "Ordnungspolitische Defizite des GATT" (1990) 41 ORDO 93–115; John H. Jackson, "Reflections on Restructuring the GATT," in Jeffrey J. Schott (ed.), *Completing the Uruguay Round. A Results-Orientated Approach to the GATT Trade Negotiations* (Washington, DC: Institute for International Economics, 1990), 205–24 at 207. See also Wolfgang Benedek, *Die Rechtsordnung des GATT aus völkerrechtlicher Sicht* (Berlin, New York: Springer, 1990) at 451 *et seq.*

[21] Robert E. Hudec, *Enforcing International Trade Law: the Evolution of the Modern GATT Legal System* (Salem, NH: Butterworth, 1993), and "Dispute Settlement," in Schott, *Completing the Uruguay Round*, above note 20, at 183; Rosine Plank, "An Unofficial Description of How a GATT-Panel Works and Does Not" (1987) 20 *World Competition Law and Economics Review* 81–123.

[22] " 'Omnibus Trade and Competitiveness Act' of 1988 (Public Law 100–418 of 23 Aug. 1988)" (1989) 28 *International Legal Materials* 31 *et seq.*; John H. Barton and Bart S. Fisher, "Introductory Note" (1989) 28 *International Legal Materials* 15–30; Jagdish N. Bhagwati and H. T. Patrick (eds.), *Aggressive Unilateralism: America's 301 Trade Policy and the World Trading System* (New York: Harvester Wheatsheaf, 1991); Eberhard Grabitz and Armin von Bogdandy, *US Trade Barriers: A Legal Analysis* (Munich and New York: European Law Press, 1991). For its legality under the WTO see below at n. 35.

[23] EC regulation 2641/84; see M. I. B. Arnold and M. C. E. J. Bronckers, "The EEC New Trade Policy Instrument (Regulation 2641/84): Some Comments on its Application" (1988) 22 *Journal of World Trade Law* 19–38; Frank Schoneveld, "The European Community Reaction to the 'Illicit' Commercial Trade Practices of Other Countries" (1992) 26 *Journal of World Trade Law* 17–34; Dirk Petermann, *Beschränkungen zur Abwehr von Beschränkungen: Sec. 301 des US-amerikanischen Trade Act von 1974 und das neue handelspolitische Instrument der EG* (Heidelberg: Verlag Recht und Wirtschaft, 1989).

[24] Hudec, "Dispute Settlement," above note 21, at 183.

In the negotiations, the United States and developing States, albeit for different reasons, came together to push for a strong multilateral rule of law to govern the new WTO, including an effective dispute settlement mechanism. In contrast to the positions of other entities, chiefly that of the EU, they favored a judicial-type system of dispute settlement. The system was backed by strong sanctions, including cross-sector retaliation – a concession to the industrialized States – and was linked to the firm exclusion of any unilateral approaches – an essential goal of the developing countries.[25]

Seen from an enforcement point of view, the dispute settlement system is noteworthy because it envisages some elements that allow for action by an individual State in the common interest. Designed to enable a State to remedy the nullification or impairment of any benefit accruing to it directly or indirectly under the agreements, the WTO dispute settlement system nevertheless aims to remove illicit trade barriers in the common interest.[26] Under Article 3(8) of the Dispute Settlement Undertaking (DSU), an infringement of obligations is assumed prima facie to constitute an impairment or nullification as required by Article XXIII of the GATT 1994, thus allowing States to initiate proceedings even in cases in which their own trade interest is rather remote.[27] The United States and the EU frequently

---

[25] Ernst-Ulrich Petersmann, "Strengthening GATT Procedures for Settling Trade Disputes" (1988) 11 *The World Economy* 55–89; Meinhard Hilf, "EC and the GATT: A European Proposal for Strengthening the GATT Dispute Settlement Procedures", in Reinhard Rode (ed.), *GATT and Conflict Management. A Transatlantic Strategy for a Stronger Regime* (Boulder: San Francisco and Oxford, 1990), 63–101, and *idem*, "Settlement of Disputes in International Economic Organizations: Comparative Analysis and Proposals for Strengthening the GATT Dispute Settlement Procedures," in Ernst-Ulrich Petersmann and Meinhard Hilf (eds.), *The New GATT Round of Multilateral Trade Negotiations: Legal and Economic Problems*, 2nd updated edn. (Deventer: Kluwer Law and Taxation, 1991), 285–322; Robert E. Hudec, "Dispute Settlement," above note 21, 180–204; Terence P. Stewart, "Dispute Settlement Mechanisms," in *idem* (ed.), *The GATT Uruguay Round: A Negotiating History (1986–1992)* 4 vols. (Deventer, Boston, MA: Kluwer Law & Taxation, 1993–9) II, 2665–878.

[26] See Peter-Tobias Stoll, "World Trade, Dispute Settlement" and "World Trade Organization" in Bernhardt, *Encyclopedia of Public International Law*, IV, pp. 1520, 1529; as well as Peter-Tobias Stoll, "WTO Dispute Settlement" (1999) 3 *Max-Planck-Yearbook of United Nations Law* 407–37.

[27] Art. 3(8) of the DSU reads: "In cases where there is an infringement of the obligations assumed under a covered agreement, the action is considered prima facie to constitute a case of nullification or impairment. This means that there is normally a presumption that a breach of the rules has an adverse impact on other Members parties to that covered agreement, and in such cases, it shall be up to the Member against whom the complaint has been brought to rebut the charge." See Peter-Tobias Stoll, "WTO Dispute Settlement," above note 26.

and systematically initiate proceedings and in a number of cases other States benefit from their initiatives.[28]

The general tendency to strengthen standards and enforcement in international economic law is particularly well demonstrated by the WTO's Agreement on Trade-Related Aspects of Intellectual Property Rights (TRIPs).[29] Its adoption addresses the growing importance and vulnerability of intellectual property rights in international trade. The agreement bypasses existing and longstanding conventions, administered by the World Intellectual Property Organization, which do not contain much substance regarding the enforcement of such rights and refer to the International Court of Justice (ICJ) for the settlement of disputes. In contrast, Part III of the TRIPs Agreement deals extensively with enforcement measures, including civil and administrative procedures and remedies, evidence, injunctions, provisional measures, damages, and even criminal procedures.[30] Thus, to an unprecedented extent, the TRIPs Agreement put an obligation on WTO members to provide for effective local remedies by prescribed means and procedures.[31] In addition, compliance with such obligations can be enforced using WTO dispute settlement mechanisms. In sum, the TRIPs Agreement amounts to a complete, trade-oriented and compliance-focused reengineering of the traditional international system for the protection of intellectual property rights.

Despite the fact that the United States was able to achieve many of its negotiating objectives, securing approval by Congress turned out to be

---

[28] See the WTO "Overview of the State-of-play of WTO disputes," available at http://www.wto.org/english/tratop_e/dispu_e/stplay_e.doc, which is periodically updated.

[29] See J. H. Reichman, "Compliance with the TRIPS Agreement: Introduction to a Scholarly Debate" (1996) 29 *Vanderbilt Journal of Transnational Law* 363–90; Adrian Otten, "Compliance with TRIPS: the Emerging World View" (1996) 29 *Vanderbilt Journal of Transnational Law* 391–413; Frederick M. Abbott, "Protecting First World Assets in the Third World: Intellectual Property Negotiations in the GATT Multilateral Framework" (1989) 22 *Vanderbilt Journal of Transnational Law* 689–745.

[30] See Peter-Tobias Stoll, *Technologietransfer, Internationalisierungs- und Nationalisierungstendenzen* (Berlin, New York: Springer, 1994), pp. 325 *et seq.*

[31] The extent and weight of those obligations becomes clear when one considers the caveat deemed necessary in Art. 41(5): "It is understood that this Part does not create any obligation to put in place a judicial system for the enforcement of intellectual property rights distinct from that for the enforcement of laws in general, nor does it affect the capacity of Members to enforce their laws in general. Nothing in this Part creates any obligation with respect to the distribution of resources as between enforcement of intellectual property rights and the enforcement of laws in general."

difficult. The Senate, in particular, remained skeptical and, in the end, lengthy implementing legislation was enacted.[32] It contains, *inter alia*, language regarding the follow-up of dispute settlement procedures that result in findings that the United States has violated WTO law. The follow-up provisions, which involve the US Trade Representative, the Federal Trade Commission and other parts of the administration, are drafted in a way which might cast a shadow on the preparedness of the United States fully to honor its membership and resulting obligations under the WTO Agreement.[33] The same holds true for lengthy provisions that detail "congressional disapproval" of US participation in the WTO.[34]

The changes made to render Section 301 of the United States Trade Act compatible with WTO law and in particular with the Safeguards Agreement were considered insufficient by the EU. A panel found the provisions to be in conformity with WTO obligations, but noted that its findings were based in full or in part on US undertakings given in the Statement of Administrative Action approved by the US Congress at the time it implemented the WTO Agreements and confirmed by the US lawyers in their statements before the panel. It therefore stated that, should those undertakings be repudiated or in any other way removed, its findings of conformity would no longer be warranted.[35] Recently, a new complaint has been submitted by Canada concerning another section of the Uruguay Round Agreements Act and the Statement of Administrative Action relating to antidumping and subsidies cases.[36]

The achievements of the WTO and its dispute settlement system in enforcing international trade rules are sometimes doubted. It is asserted that large trading countries are able to withstand the pressure exercised by the WTO trade "sanctions," and that they can and do negotiate compromises regarding their duties to implement dispute settlement decisions. Large trading nations are considered to have a choice between compliance and compensation.[37] This kind of argument is not a purely academic one. It

---

[32] USC Title 19 Ch. 22 Uruguay Round Agreements; Uruguay Round Agreements Act, Public Law 103-465 of 8 Dec. 1994.

[33] *Ibid.*, 19 USC § 3533.   [34] *Ibid.*, § 3535.

[35] United States – Sections 301–10 of the Trade Act of 1974, complaint by the European Communities (WT/DS152/1).

[36] See WT/DS221/1 of 22 Jan. 2001, concerning Section 129(c) (1) of the Uruguay Round Agreements Act.

[37] See Judith Hippler Bello, "The WTO Dispute Settlement Understanding: Less is More" (1996) 90 AJIL 416; Timothy M. Reif and Marjorie Florestal, "Revenge of the Push-Me, Pull-You:

was used in the ratification process in the US Congress,[38] and the European Court of Justice has based its firm denial of a direct applicability of WTO rules in the Community legal order on similar grounds.[39] It is not necessary here to go into the intricacies of WTO sanctions, which work quite differently from duties to pay damages or fines.[40] From a legal point, the argument is highly questionable, because the Dispute Settlement Understanding contains a number of provisions that firmly establish a priority of compliance over compensation.[41] Its portion of world trade and its political bargaining power in the world's trading system may allow a "predominant" WTO member such as the United States, but certainly also the EU and Japan, to resist pressures to comply with WTO rules for some time. But unlike under GATT, these countries can hardly expect to be able to compensate and compromise forever.

The Implementation Process Under the WTO Dispute Settlement Understanding" (1997) 32 *International Law* 755; Pieter Jan Kuyper, "Remedies and Retaliation in the WTO: Are They Likely to be Effective? The State Perspective and the Company Perspective" (1997) 91 *Proceedings of the American Society of International Law* 282.

[38] In Congress, the then US Trade Representative (USTR), Mickey Kantor, explained: "No ruling by any dispute panel, under this new dispute settlement mechanism ... can force us to change any federal, state or local law or regulation ...," GATT Implementation: Hearing Before the Committee On Commerce, Science and Transportation, 104th Congress (1995–96).

[39] See Judgment in Joined Cases 21/72 and 24/72 *International Fruit* [1972] ECR 1219; Case C-280/93, *Germany v. Council* [1994] ECR I-4973; Case C-149/96, *Portugal v. Council* [1999]; see Pieter J. Kuijper, "The Conclusion and Implementation of the Uruguay Round Results by the European Community" (1995) 6 EJIL 222–44; and Marc Weisberger, "The Application of Portugal v. Council: The Banana Cases" (2002) 12 *Duke Journal of Comparative and International Law* 153.

[40] Cutting trade to remedy another member's failure to comply with trade rules may seem odd from a purely economic viewpoint and may even hurt the economy of the member implementing such sanctions. It makes more sense from a political point of view, where sanctions are understood to target specific sectors in a non-compliant member's economy with the aim of generating political pressure to implement WTO rulings. This political effect may often be more important than the economic losses. Furthermore, unwillingness to implement WTO rulings may affect a member's political standing in the WTO and thus have detrimental effects in several of the many negotiations and bargaining processes continuously taking place within the trade system.

[41] See Arts. 3.7, 19.1, 21.1, 22.1, 22.8 DSU, John. H. Jackson, "The WTO Dispute Settlement Understanding – Misunderstanding on the Nature of Legal Obligations" (1997) 91 AJIL 60, 63. An *a contrario* argument can be made by pointing to Art. 26.1(b), which specifically states that "there is no obligation to withdraw the measure" in case of non-violation complaints, *ibid.* Also, there is no provision in the DSU that departs from the general rule of Art. 26 of the Vienna Convention on the Law of Treaties, which states that parties to a treaty have to perform their obligations, Frieder Roessler, "Comments" (1998) 32 *International Lawyer* 789. Nor has the point ever been raised in dispute settlement proceedings; see Scott McBride, "Dispute Settlement in the WTO: Backbone of the Global Trading System or Delegation of Awesome Power?" (2001) 32 *Law and Policy in International Business* 643, 654.

From a theoretical point of view, the compensation approach of WTO sanctions provides a good opportunity to analyze concepts of norms, their binding force, and compliance. However, in considering these peculiarities of the system and the still obvious relevance of the economic and political weight of certain members, one has to compare compliance in this particular field of international relations with that in other fields.[42] In this regard, the WTO record seems to be quite good, due to important improvements in the system as compared with GATT, and, of course, the interplay of those norms with the relevant political and economic structures.

To sum up, the establishment of the WTO shows that a highly normative system has been achieved in an area of close and growing international interdependency which has – so far – succeeded in "constitutionalizing" the formerly unilateral approach of the United States into different coalitions. It also points to possible ways of making US enforcement action work to the benefit of the common interest. Of course, it cannot be overlooked that the new trade order broadly accommodates the interests of the United States but also – it must be added – a number of other industrialized countries and the EU.

The International Court of Justice

To complete this review of the international legal order and some of its institutions, it should be noted that the United States has not made moves to declare anew a recognition of the compulsory jurisdiction of the International Court of Justice according to Article 36(2) of its Statute,[43] having withdrawn its former declaration during the *Nicaragua* case.[44] In the recent *LaGrand* case[45] concerning the Vienna Convention on Consular Relations, in which the jurisdiction of the Court was firmly based on the Convention and Article 36(1) of the Statute, the United States questioned the binding

---

[42] As Jackson, "The WTO Dispute Settlement Understanding," above note 41, at 61 rightly recalls, lack of enforcement is a common phenomenon in international law and does not as such put into question its legal character.

[43] Statute of the International Court of Justice, available at http://www.icj-cij.org/icjwww/ ibasicdocuments/Basetext/istatute.htm (visited 26 Sept. 2001).

[44] *Military and Paramilitary Activities (Nicaragua v. US)*, (1984) ICJ Reports 392 (Jurisdiction); (1986) ICJ Reports 14 (Merits).

[45] *LaGrand (Germany v. US)*, Judgment of 27 June 2001, available at http://www.icj-cij.org/icjwww/ idocket/igus/igusframe.htm (visited 26 Sept. 2001).

legal nature of provisional measures of the Court[46] – contrary to its position in the *Teheran Hostages* case.[47] However, the Court made use of the opportunity at hand and, for the first time, expressly confirmed that its provisional measures are legally binding. In doing so, it resolved an issue that had been unclear and subject to much debate in the past.[48] Without doubt, this will considerably strengthen the role of the ICJ as a World Court with effective means to preserve peace and law.

Summary

The international legal order has undergone some important developments over the last decade which focus on its efficacy and have resulted in a number of multilateral mechanisms and instruments to ensure compliance. The United States, in general, has not been a driving force behind these developments. It has been especially reluctant to accept multilateral rules in areas where it enjoys and wishes to maintain an ability to achieve its objectives by its own means. An often weak support for the UN system of collective security and skepticism concerning an International Criminal Court serve as examples here. Somewhat differently, the United States did promote multilateral rules and enforcement in the trade area, where its potential to act is still impressive, though certainly not sufficient to achieve its interests on its own. Looking at the EU and Japan and a number of other important trading States, it is doubtful whether the United States can really be considered predominant in this area in the same way as it is in others. This conclusion hardly comes as a surprise. The United States seems to adopt a somewhat instrumental approach, opting for multilateral legal ties when it needs to do so while applying caution in those areas where its predominant power and influence is sufficient to enable it to prevail.

---

[46] Karin Oellers-Frahm, *"Pacta sunt servanda* – Gilt das auch für die USA?" (1999) *Europäische Grundrechtezeitschrift* 437–49, 440 *et seq.*

[47] *US Diplomatic and Consular Staff in Teheran (US v. Iran)*, (1979) ICJ Reports 7 (Provisional Measures); (1980) ICJ Reports 3 (Merits).

[48] See Shabtai Rosenne, *The Law and Practice of the International Court: 1920–1996*, III – *Procedure* (Dordrecht: Nijhoff, 1997), p. 1434; Gerald Fitzmaurice *The Law and Procedure of the International Court of Justice*, II (Cambridge: Grotius, 1986), p. 548; Lawrence Collins, "Provisional and Protective Measures in International Litigation" (1993) 234(3) *Recueil des Cours* 9, 219.

The United States acting unilaterally

The conclusion just drawn suggests that we should take a closer look at those areas in which the United States acts unilaterally. Indeed, discussions on the role of the United States in the international legal system often focus on these cases. Such cases, especially when they invoke the use of force, have provoked much criticism concerning their legality under international law. At the same time, US action has sometimes been welcomed and even considered somewhat justified by the inability of other States or the international community to act effectively.

From this perspective, the recent *Breard*[49] and *LaGrand*[50] cases are of only minor significance, because the United States openly admitted to the breaches of the Vienna Convention on Consular Relations and took steps to prevent such breaches in future.

One typical example of this kind of unilateral "taking the law into one's own hands" is the unilateral use of force, as previously discussed. There are, however, a number of other examples.

Unilateral environment-related trade measures

The United States has acquired a particularly high profile in the protection of certain marine species.[51] It has made diplomatic efforts and enacted legislation to prevent the accidental catching and killing of dolphins and sea turtles through incautious methods of tuna and shrimp fishing.[52]

---

[49] *Case concerning the Vienna Convention on Consular Relations (Paraguay v. US)* (Order of 9 Apr. 1998), repr. in (1998) 37 *International Legal Materials* 810; this case was later removed from the List of Cases at the request of Paraguay; see http://www.icj-cij.org/icjwww/idocket/ipaus/ipausframe.htm (visited 28 Sept. 2001).

[50] *LaGrand case (Federal Republic of Germany v. United States of America)*, Judgment of 27 June 2001, available at http://www.icj-cij.org.

[51] See Wolfrum, "Means of Ensuring Compliance," above note 8, 62–65; Harold K. Jacobson and Edith Brown Weiss, "Strengthening Compliance with International Environmental Accords: Preliminary Observations from a Collaborative Project" (1995) 1 *Global Governance* 119.

[52] Examples of such legislation are Marine Mammal Protection Act, 16 USC, §§ 1361 *et seq.*; Sea Turtle Conservation Amendments to the Endangered Species Act, 16 USC, § 1357, Supp. IV, 1992; High Seas Driftnet Fisheries Enforcement Act, 16 USC, § 1826 (a); see also John Alton Duff, "Recent Applications of United States Laws to Conserve Marine Species Worldwide: Should Trade Sanctions be Mandatory?" (1996) 2 *Ocean and Coastal Law Journal* 1; Ted L. McDorman, "The GATT Consistency of US Fish Import Embargos to Stop Driftnet Fishing and Save Whales, Dolphins and Turtles" (1991) 24 *George Washington Journal of International Law and Economics* 477.

The measures included certain requirements and conditions for import-ing tuna and shrimp products to ensure that safe fishing methods were applied. Those measures were successfully brought to GATT/WTO dispute settlement by affected exporting States. Nevertheless, the two *Tuna-Dolphin* panels[53] and the *Shrimp-Turtle* case[54] considerably furthered the under-standing and interpretation of the relevant WTO provisions.

In sum, the unilateral use of trade restrictions to urge other States to accept environmental obligations has been halted by WTO dispute settle-ment, at least initially. However, panels and the Appellate Body took the opportunity to define acceptable means and conditions for such conduct in future. Using trade as a tool for environmental protection, as discussed here, will in future require the political will and the trade potential of a major trading State, and will only work where the environmental problem is trade-sensitive. It does not seem to work as well in those instances where the United States does not consider the environmental measures to be in its own national interest.

Temptations of extraterritoriality: the Helms-Burton and D'Amato legislation

Considering US unilateral action also requires us to look at the *causes célèbres* of a new and highly disputed US approach: the famous Helms-Burton Act[55] and the D'Amato Act,[56] adopted shortly afterwards. Both were immediately and strongly criticized by the United States' neighbors and allies.

The Helms-Burton Act aims at restoring democracy and liberty in Cuba. As a means to that end, and as an objective in its own right, the Act strives to

---

[53] GATT Dispute Panel Report (*Tuna I*) (1991) 30 *International Legal Materials* 1594; GATT Dispute Panel Report (*Tuna II*) (1994) 33 *International Legal Materials* 839.

[54] See World Trade Organization, "Report of the Panel on United States – Import Prohibition of certain Shrimp and Shrimp Products," WTO Doc. No. WT/DS58/R (report of the Panel), repr. in (1998) 37 *International Legal Materials* 832; World Trade Organization, "Report of the Appellate Body on United States – Import Prohibition of certain Shrimp and Shrimp Products," WTO Doc. No. WT/DS58/AB/R, for full text see http://www.wto.org/english/tratop_e/dispu_e/distab_e.htm (visited 26 Sept. 2001).

[55] Cuban Liberty and Democratic Solidarity (Libertad) Act, Public Law 104–114, 110 STAT. 785 (1996), repr. in (1996) 35 *International Legal Materials* 357; see generally Vaughan Lowe, "US Extraterritorial Jurisdiction: the Helms-Burton and D'Amato Acts" (1997) 46 *International and Comparative Law Quarterly* 378.

[56] Iran–Libya Sanctions Act, Public Law 104–172, 110 STAT. 1541 (1996), repr. in (1996) 35 *International Legal Materials* 1273.

protect claims made by US nationals, as well as nationalized Cubans, to their property in Cuba which has been confiscated.[57] The Act's most controversial provisions, found in Title III, allow US nationals to bring claims, before US courts, against foreign individuals and companies for trafficking in Cuban confiscated property.[58] In addition, Title IV of the Act envisages immigration restrictions for such foreign individuals, and their spouses and children. There is scarcely any doubt that the Cuban government's seizure of property without reason, due process, and compensation constituted a flagrant breach of international law.[59] As there was hardly any other way to intensify the already strong US pressure against Cuba, and little hope of furthering the property claims through diplomatic protection, the US legislator resorted to this unprecedented measure of sanctioning individuals who had little to do with the original confiscation.

There is little doubt that Title III of the Act is contrary to international law. The "effects doctrine," as referred to in the Act, can hardly apply, because it is the early confiscation rather than a later investment in such Cuban land that produces the effects to be remedied. Nor do nationality or universality constitute sufficient links to establish jurisdiction in these cases, although the semantics of "trafficking" are obviously designed to draw a parallel to dealing in narcotics, thus appealing to universality.[60]

---

[57] The bill, which hardly found any interest and support when introduced in Congress, was adopted as a sudden reaction to Cuba's downing of two small aircraft which had allegedly entered Cuban airspace with a hostile intent.

[58] The definition of the term "trafficking" is extremely wide. Section 4 (13) (A) of the Act reads: "a person 'traffics' in confiscated property if that person knowingly and intentionally – (i) sells, transfers, distributes, dispenses, brokers, manages, or otherwise disposes of confiscated property, or purchases, leases, receives, possesses, obtains control of, manages, uses, or otherwise acquires or holds an interest in confiscated property, (ii) engages in a commercial activity using or otherwise benefiting from confiscated property, or (iii) causes, directs, participates in, or profits from, trafficking (as described in clause (i) or (ii)) by another person, or otherwise engages in trafficking (as described in clause (i) or (ii)) through another person, without the authorization of any United States national who holds a claim to the property."

[59] See Robert Jennings and Arthur Watts (eds.), *Oppenheim's International Law*, 9th edn. (London: Longman, 1992), I, 920–21.

[60] See the Opinion of the Inter-American Juridical Committee of the OAS, CJI/SO/II doc. 67/96 rev. 5 of 23 Aug 1996, repr. in (1996) 35 *International Legal Materials* 1329; Brigitte Stern, "Vers la mondialisation juridique? Les lois Helms-Burton et D'Amato" (1996) 100 *Revue générale de droit international public* 979; Andreas F. Lowenfeld, "Agora: The Cuban Liberty and Democratic Solidarity (Libertad) Act – Congress and Cuba: The Helms-Burton Act" (1996) 90 AJIL 419; but cf. Brice M. Clagett, "Title III of the Helms-Burton Act is Consistent with International Law" (1996) 90 AJIL 434.

The D'Amato Act purports to "deny Iran the ability to support acts of international terrorism and to fund the development and acquisition of weapons of mass destruction and the means to deliver them by limiting the development of Iran's ability to explore for, extract, refine, or transport by pipeline petroleum resources" and "to seek full compliance by Libya with its obligations under Resolutions 731, 748, and 883 of the Security Council of the United Nations, including ending all support for acts of international terrorism and efforts to develop or acquire weapons of mass destruction."[61] To that end, the Act envisages the need "to impose sanctions on persons making certain investments directly and significantly contributing to the enhancement of the ability of Iran or Libya to develop its petroleum resources, and on persons exporting certain items that enhance Libya's weapons or aviation capabilities or enhance Libya's ability to develop its petroleum resources, and for other purposes."[62] The Act contravenes international law on grounds similar to those discussed in the context of the Helms-Burton Act.

These two acts provoked strong reactions from a number of entities. In particular, Canada[63] and the EU[64] enacted defensive blocking and "claw back" statutes. The EU also submitted a complaint to the WTO, while Canada and Mexico invoked the North American Free Trade Agreement (NAFTA) arbitration procedure.[65] The EU move to bring the case to a WTO panel was considered to be a particularly serious step, as such a panel would very likely have been confronted with issues concerning the interpretation of the national security exception under Article XXI of the GATT 1994 and Article 14 of the General Agreement on Trade in Services.[66]

---

[61] S. 2 of the Act.   [62] Official title of the Act.

[63] Foreign Extraterritorial Measures Act, RSC, ch. F-29 (1985), as amended on 9 Oct. 1996, 1996 SC, ch. 28, repr. in (1997) 36 *International Legal Materials* 111.

[64] Council Regulation 2271/96 Protecting against the Effects of the Extra-territorial Application of Legislation Adopted by a Third Country (22 Nov. 1996), 1996 OJ (L-309) 1, repr. in (1997) 36 *International Legal Materials* 125.

[65] North American Free Trade Agreement, repr. in (1992) 32 *International Legal Materials* 605; Thedor Meron and Detlev F. Vagts, "The Helms-Burton Act: Exercising the Presidential Option" (1997) 91 AJIL 83, 84.

[66] John H. Jackson and Andreas F. Lowenfeld, "Helms-Burton, the US and the WTO" (1997) *American Society of International Law Insight* 7, available at http://www.asil.org/insights/insight7.htm (visited 26 Sept. 2001).

To resolve the conflict between the United States and the EU, an agreement was reached.[67] The US government promised to exercise its waivers under the two acts to prevent sanctions being applied to EU nationals or companies and to engage in a dialogue with Congress to obtain an amendment of the Helms-Burton Act providing for a presidential waiver authority regarding Title IV. In turn, the EU agreed to suspend the WTO panel, but reserved its rights to resume proceedings or start a new complaint concerning action taken against EU individuals or companies under Title III or IV, or where a waiver was denied or withdrawn under the D'Amato Act. The EU furthermore agreed to promote democracy in Cuba and work with the United States to achieve the aims of the D'Amato Act. Additionally, the parties agreed to develop bilaterally disciplines regarding the acquisition and subsequent dealings in expropriated or nationalized property, and to introduce the results into the negotiations on a Multilateral Agreement on Investment, which was being negotiated within the Organization for Economic Cooperation and Development (OECD) at that time.[68] The legal nature of the US–EU agreement is, however, not expressly defined in the text; it very likely falls short of having a binding effect.

In this case, other States were able to exercise pressure on the United States and successfully halt its unilateral action. However, this success is limited, as it only relates to implementation, while the acts as such have remained in force unaltered. From a more general international law point of view, the agreement is unfortunate or even counterproductive, because it only concerns the EU, whereas other entities and their companies and individuals still have to face the risks and uncertainties produced by the two acts. This is a cause for particular concern, since the international law rules in question in this case are the principles of sovereignty and non-intervention.[69] They form the pillars of an international system that still relies on States, whose interdependence and equal sovereignty can be regarded as contributing to the division and limitation of power.

---

[67] A first "understanding" was achieved in 1997; see "US–European Union Understanding on Libertad Act" (1997) 91 AJIL 497. A second agreement was concluded on the occasion of the 1998 EU–US Summit; see Stefaan Smis and Kim Van der Borght, "The EU–US Compromise on the Helms-Burton and D'Amato Acts" (1997) 93 AJIL 227, 228.

[68] However, the negotiations were later dropped.

[69] See Brigitte Stern, "How to Regulate Globalization?" in Michael Byers (ed.), *The Role of Law in International Politics* (Oxford: Oxford University Press, 2000), pp. 247–68, pp. 255 *et seq.*

Private law remedies for human rights violations and
international crimes

As a growing number of successful cases indicate, US courts have proven to be a particularly suitable forum for claims from victims of human rights violations or international crimes.[70] The US legal system seemingly encourages lawyers to engage in such litigation, which frequently attracts general public support as well. From a legal perspective, the Alien Tort Claims Act[71] significantly supports such claims. Enacted in 1789, the wording of the provision, taken literally, confines itself to establishing federal court subject matter jurisdiction for legal actions by aliens directed at a "tort... committed in violation of the law of nations or a treaty of the United States." The historical roots of the Act are far from clear. A number of explanations are offered.[72] Today, the Act is highly relevant because of the substantive meaning that it is understood to carry: the courts have established that it constitutes a cause of action.[73] Victims of human rights violations and international crimes can thus rely on international law directly and need not bother about the intricacies of the *lex loci delicti commissi*, which would apply under general conflict of law rules.[74] In 1992, further legislation was enacted to facilitate claims by victims or the families of victims of torture or extrajudicial killings.[75] More recently, claims have been brought before

---

[70] See generally Gary B. Born, *International Civil Litigation in United States Courts* (The Hague: Kluwer Law International, 1996); Beth Stephens and Michael Ratner, *International Human Rights Litigation in US Courts* (Irvington-on-Hudson, NY: Transnational Publ., 1996).

[71] 28 USC § 1350; for a historic perspective of the ATCA see Anthony D'Amato and Ralph G. Steinhardt (eds.) *The Alien Tort Claims Act* (Ardsley, NY: Transnational Publ. 1999); Anne-Marie Burley, "The Alien Tort Statute and the Judiciary Act of 1789: A Badge of Honor" (1998) 83 AJIL 416.

[72] The act might have been proposed to secure the prosecution of piracy, the effective protection of diplomats or the prevention of a denial of justice; see Markus Rau, "Schadensersatzklagen wegen extraterritorial begangener Menschenrechtsverletzungen: der US-amerikanische Alien Tort Claims Act" (2000) 20 *Praxis des internationalen Privat- und Verfahrensrechts* 558.

[73] See *Forti v. Suarez-Mason*, 672 F.Supp. 1531, 1540 (N.D.Cal. 1987); *Paul v. Avril* 821 F.Supp. 207, 212 (S.D.Fla. 1993); *Hilao v. Marcos*, 25 F.3d 1467, 1475 (9th Cir. 1994); *Xuncax v. Gramajo*, 886 F.Supp. 162, 182 (D.Mass. 1995); *Iwanowa v. Ford Motor Company*, 67 F.Supp.2d 424, 4443 (D.N.J. 1999); see also Stephens and Ratner, *Human Rights Litigation*, above note 70, pp. 12, 120.

[74] The leading case in this regard is *Filàrtiga v. Peña-Irala*, 630 F.2d 876 (2d Cir. 1980). See Rau, "Schadensersatzklagen," above note 72, at 558.

[75] See, e.g., Torture Victim Protection Act, Public Law 102-256, 106 STAT. 73 (1992), codified at 28 USC § 1359, which contains a cause of action for claims against foreigners acting in actual or supposed exercise of sovereignty; see also Born, "International Civil Litigation," above note 70, 38–9.

US courts with a view to securing compensation for forced labor during the Nazi regime and in regard to Jewish assets withheld by banks and insurance companies in Germany and Switzerland. Undoubtedly, the legislative developments played an important role in encouraging victims to seek relief and promote justice.[76]

The legality of such legislation and activities has not yet been seriously disputed. This might be due to the fact that rules on jurisdiction concerning civil actions are more relaxed than those that apply to criminal or administrative law matters.[77] Furthermore, the United States could rely on an *erga omnes* effect of the international rules in question or on the universality principle. It has to be noted, however, that the United States, while developing these new remedies nationally, has been quite reluctant to join the most important multilateral achievement in this regard: the establishment of a permanent International Criminal Court.[78]

Sovereign immunity vs. human rights

In 1996, the US Congress carried these developments even further by adopting a highly disputed amendment to the Foreign Sovereign Immunities Act.[79] The FSIA had been adopted in 1976 and reflected the state of customary international law at that time. The 1996 amendments, however, deprived States of immunity with respect to claims for money damages for personal injury or death caused "by an act of torture, extrajudicial killing, aircraft sabotage, hostage taking, or the provision of material support or resources," where the State in question had been designated by the Secretary of State as a sponsor of terrorism.[80] The amendment enabled those victims who are US citizens to obtain a judgment against such a foreign State.[81] However, attempts to execute such judgments by attaching the property of foreign States failed where such property was considered to be diplomatic

---

[76] On the importance of these developments see also Antonio Cassese, *International Law* (Oxford: Oxford University Press, 2001) 369.

[77] See Rau, "Schadensersatzklagen", above note 72, at 560.

[78] See generally citations above note 7.

[79] Foreign Sovereign Immunities Act, 28 USC §§ 1330, 1602-1611 (1994); see also Joseph W. Dellapenna, "*Lafontant v. Aristide*" (1994) 88 AJIL 528, 529.

[80] Antiterrorism and Effective Death Penalty Act, Public Law 104-132, 110 Stat. 1214 (1996); see Monroe Leigh, "1996 Amendments to the Foreign Sovereign Immunities Act with Respect to Terrorist Activities" (1997) 91 AJIL 187.

[81] See, e.g., *Flatow v. Islamic Republic of Iran*, 999 F.Supp. 1 (DDC 1998).

in character.[82] Consequently, in 1998, Congress again amended the FSIA to enable US victims to execute judgments even against foreign diplomatic and consular properties.[83] The President, however, immediately made use of his suspension power provided for in the amendment, pointing to US obligations to protect diplomatic property under the Vienna Convention on Diplomatic Relations.[84]

Summary

Concerns about US unilateral action and its impact on international law are justified in a small number of cases involving the unilateral use of force, extraterritorial Helms-Burton-type measures, and restrictions of sovereign immunity, including with respect to diplomatic property. Congress was the driving force behind the latter two types of action, whereas the administration in most instances made use of the suspension or waiver authority contained in the relevant legislation. These unilateral actions led either to the conclusion of bilateral agreements – as witnessed in the EU–US compromise – or to considerable legal uncertainty in the face of bold statutory powers reined in only by administrative decisions.

All the examples discussed here involve an argument of justification. Unilateral action appears well-founded when directed at remedying obvious and painful shortcomings concerning the enforcement of human rights, the prosecution of crimes against humanity, and the protection of the environment. Unilateral approaches may thus be useful in particular cases, but remain limited and piecemeal. They do not represent a substitute for broad-based enforcement means corresponding to the universal and general character of the norms and standards which apply. Moreover, unilateral action sometimes is taken to the detriment of the effectiveness of other

---

[82] See Sean D. Murphy, "State Jurisdiction and Jurisdictional Immunities" "Contemporary Practice of the United States Relating to International Law" (1999) 93 AJIL 181. A motion for writs of attachment concerning the former Iranian embassy, residences of the Minister of Cultural Affairs and the military attaché of the embassy of Iran to satisfy the *Flatow* judgment was finally dismissed by the district court with reference to a statement by the US government.

[83] § 117 of the Treasury and General Government Appropriations Act of 1999, as contained in the Omnibus Consolidated and Emergency Supplemental Appropriations Act of 1999, Public Law 105-277, 112 STAT. 2681 (1998).

[84] "Statement on Signing the Omnibus Consolidated and Emergency Supplemental Appropriations Act 1999" (1998) 34 *Weekly Compilation of Presidential Documents* 2108, 2113 (23 Oct. 1998).

important principles and norms of international law, thus putting seriously into question its proper objectives.

Analysis

Compliance and enforcement are key issues in contemporary developments in the international legal order. At the same time, they serve as justifications for US unilateral actions which, however, may themselves give rise to questions of compliance and the lawfulness of measures of enforcement.

The year 1990 was certainly a significant date in the area of peace and security although, in the end, it produced only minimal progress. Collective security under the UN Charter[85] and its legal disciplines is still a fragile construct. Rather than encouraging and strengthening such a system, the United States continued to act on its own.

The threat of US unilateral action was a significant driving force behind the establishment of the WTO, which widely satisfies US interests and – it should be added – those of other industrialized countries. That said, the WTO dispute settlement system has effectively curbed some unilateral aspirations of the United States, so far.

In a legal system which relies on its own subjects to make laws and enforce them, size matters, but so do individual engagement and collective action. Resolute action by a small number of States halted the application of the Helms-Burton Act and, arguably, a powerful move by a larger number of States, including the provision of troops and materials, could make collective security work a great deal better and render it more difficult to find an excuse for unilateral action. These observations and speculations suggest that we should look at the role and responsibility of other States when considering the international legal system and its development, and the conduct of the United States. Not least, we should remember that the values and interests pursued by the United States are by and large those of a larger group of States. To some extent, it is up to them to decide whether to rely on a powerful ally in spite of its sometimes doubtful methods, or to take up the burdensome task of actively translating such values and interests into a more rule-oriented and effective international legal order.

---

[85] Charter of the United Nations, 892 UNTS 119, available at http://www.un.org/aboutun/charter/index.html (visited 25 Sept. 2001).

18

Comments on chapters 16 and 17

Vaughan Lowe

As we approach the question of the effects of US predominance on the foundations of international law, I am still troubled by the premises on which we are working. I am not convinced that we have a clear understanding of what we mean by "the United States." The United States is not a monolithic structure. Different branches, and different levels, of US government have different interests, and act differently. We need also to consider the nongovernmental aspects of the issue. US companies are international actors. They conclude bilateral agreements with States in the form of concessions, they compromise arbitration cases, and so on: they are making customary international law in much the same way that States do. The way in which US publishing operates has a profound influence on what we think customary international law is. We have not even begun to discuss the implications of these "private" aspects of the issue.

Nor have we arrived at a clear understanding of what kind of predominance we are looking at. The United States is predominant in Afghanistan. That is a predominance of presence. But if you spoke about US predominance in relation to, say, Rwanda a few years ago, it would have been the predominance of the powerful but absent father. Those are two very different kinds of influence on the international system. And if we are concerned simply with the question of the influence that is exercised by the setting of examples, by the way that the United States behaves, it is far from obvious that the United States has a greater influence on any given State than does a regional power.

But let me put these matters to one side and address the two chapters on compliance. There are six points that are raised by them explicitly or implicitly.

The first concerns the uncertainties of international law. As has been observed, before we can decide what non-compliance is, we have to decide what compliance would be, what the law requires. We have, for instance, to decide whether the US position on international jurisdiction is or is not correct before we know whether to put it in the non-compliance box. That is not an easy matter; and it is not simply a question of the indeterminacy of international law. Even if there were an International Court of Justice judgment or an arbitral award which directly ruled upon the legality of the specific episode, it is not self-evident that for our purposes we would have to treat the ruling as determinative. We might take the view that the judges got it wrong. It may be that there are conflicting decisions. It may be that the decision was based on notions of opposability or persistent objection or the defenses of necessity, or as an application of countermeasures, and not based on the rule of law that is generally applicable; and we might therefore think that the decision addresses rules of international law that are not our primary focus. Or the decision might be so far out of line with what States actually do that we might think it is based on a radically incorrect apprehension of what international law actually is. This is a difficulty that goes far beyond the question of the indeterminacy of any given rule of law.

Second point: when we talk about US unilateral actions not complying with international law, it is not clear that we have a clear conception of what unilateral action is. What, for example, of Kosovo? Was that a unilateral US action? Was that a regional action? In deciding how many States were involved, should we count not merely the States which actively participated alongside, or assisted, the United States in that action, but also those that acquiesced in it? We need a clearer idea of what counts as unilateral and what counts as multilateral action.

Third point: I am not clear how we define an instance of non-compliance, a single case of non-compliance. Are all US claims to excessive jurisdiction to be counted as a single instance of the United States violating international law, because one principle is violated? Or do we, for example, take the view that every one of the export control orders issued in the "Pipeline" dispute was a separate violation? Should we take every prosecution by the United States as a separate violation, or regard as a separate violation every occasion on which somebody complies voluntarily with a US law that is thought to violate laws on international jurisdiction? The question of counting instances of compliance is equally difficult. How do we measure how often, or how widely, or how systematically, or how habitually, or how deeply, or how importantly, a rule of international law is observed? I do not think that we even have an agreed scale on which we can measure compliance: I am not clear what the units would be.

Fourth point: whatever the units of compliance might be, we plainly need some way of evaluating compliance qualitatively. Compliance surely cannot be a simple question of the number of times that the United States does or does not comply with international law. For example, the extension of US law to non-American members of US expeditions to the South Pole is an extension of jurisdiction of an utterly different order to the Helms-Burton Act or the extraterritorial application of the US antitrust laws. We must distinguish between them. And even where the instances of non-compliance might appear to be of the same general kind, for example in the context of World Trade Organization (WTO) disputes, we ought to be asking similar questions. Is it the number of breaches of the WTO provisions, or is it the volume or the value of US trade that is affected by the measures that matters? Or is it the importance of the affected trade to the other States concerned? Some breaches are more important than others, but we need to settle on the criteria that determine importance.

The fifth, and perhaps most important, point is this: It is necessary to distinguish between different varieties and degrees of compliance and non-compliance. Let me take first the question of compliance. In municipal law we understand that there is a difference between the attitude to, on the one hand, tax laws or road traffic legislation, and on the other hand, compliance with the law on assault. In the former case, it is common to adopt an attitude of minimal or even grudging compliance. With tax laws, for instance, it is enough if people comply with the letter of the law; and in the case of road traffic laws, there is a degree of violation that is generally tolerated by the community at large. In contrast, most people will enthusiastically enter into the spirit of the law, as far as the law on assault is concerned, in order to protect personal integrity and dignity. In fact, in many cases people will go far beyond what the law requires. How do we view the obligations and the expectations of States in regard to different portions of international law? Are there differences comparable to the different attitudes to compliance within municipal systems?

Similar points may be raised concerning non-compliance. There is a world of difference between, say, the invasion of another country in plain violation of international law and, for example, the imposition of additional immigration formalities for the citizens of a certain State in the mistaken belief that this action is a legally permissible countermeasure. There is, similarly, a great difference between, on the one hand, engaging in conduct for which there is no legal warrant, but with the intention of contributing to building up a new rule of customary international law, and on the other hand, engaging in conduct and at the same time trying to forbid other people to engage in that same conduct. There is a great difference between those instances of wrongdoing that are denied by the State carrying out the wrongdoing and those instances where the State seeks to assert that it was entitled to act as it did. If a State takes the trouble to lie about its violation of a rule it is a powerful sign that the State takes the rule seriously and expects others to do so as well. (If we are concerned to measure the impact of a State's behavior on the foundations of international law, it must be at least arguable that we should watch their lips more closely than we watch their hands.) We need to take these crucial differences into account in evaluating non-compliance. Compliance, to put it in a slightly different way, may be less a matter of what the State does than of the attitude of the State to the rule of law.

The sixth and final point concerns the context in which non-compliance takes place. It is surely relevant, in evaluating the significance of any particular violation of international law, to ask what alternatives there were to the action that was taken. A mission to rescue nationals from imminent danger in circumstances where there is no national, regional or international body capable of acting is a very different matter from the unilateral imposition of severe restrictions in a trade war, for example, where there is an immediate and real possibility of recourse to an international procedure for the settlement of trade disputes. We need to put questions of breach in context.

It cannot be denied that there is a widespread hostility towards the conduct of US foreign policy, and a certain measure of *Schadenfreude* whenever the United States stumbles in the course of some of its more dramatic entrances onto the international stage. It is an interesting question why there should be this curious relationship with the one country which is, perhaps, above all others the bastion of civil rights and constitutional government. I have no doubt that the answer owes a lot to the venerable practice of cutting the mighty down to size, and is in part a reaction to the strand of self-righteousness that can be discerned from time to time in US foreign policy; and I am quite prepared to admit that the contribution to a healthy political system that is made by satirists and cartoonists is at least as important as that made by lawyers and political theorists. It may also be that there is a perception that States ought to be able to choose to comply with international law, and not be coerced into compliance through political or economical leverage – and if that is indeed the case, perhaps we should be thinking of compliance mechanisms less crude than the kind of police system and judicial system that we tend to assume as the norm. But whatever the position is, it seems to me that an effective appraisal of the role of the United States and the effects of its dominance on the international system must take care to be precise in setting its terms of reference.

The United States does indeed violate international law from time to time: but our analysis needs to be subtle and precise. There are as many varieties of bad behavior as there are of good behavior; and that is something that we need to remember.

David M. Malone

At the outset, it may be fair to note that a reader innocent of the broader sweep of international relations might assume from these two chapters that the main form exceptionalism and unilateralism can take is non-compliance with treaty obligations. However, what resentment over the exercise of US power at the international level exists today arises more from US indifference to international norms and aspirations, and from its occasional diplomatic bullying, than it does from its derogation from specific treaty obligations. Because merely wounding, sometimes offensive, diplomatic tactics hardly generate much concern in legal circles, it might be easy to overestimate the importance of the treaty-based conduct of international relations relative to the more intangible, power-influenced nature of much contemporary diplomacy.

Wisely, neither author makes too much of the sovereign equality of countries before international law. It is precisely because countries are in no way equal in the exercise of power that law keeps being elbowed aside (when not swept under the carpet) in the day-to-day conduct of international relations. Legal advisers in foreign ministries are often lonely. Their commitment to international norms of legality is often inconvenient, even more often irritating, to colleagues wanting to get on with the promotion and protection of their national interests. Within delegations to the UN Security Council, legal advisers are rarely consulted on the law per se – rather, they are urgently instructed to produce legal justifications, often thin rationalizations, for the politically expedient positions of their countries.

Having disposed of these rude realities, I now address the stimulating and sensible analysis and arguments of the authors. Starting with their conclusions, which differ little, it seems that the authors see US noncompliance with international treaties in the post–Cold War era as of a venial rather than cardinal nature. They note an often negotiated, positive outcome to these breaches of law: further multilateral agreements or treaties. Beyond being good for (legal) business, such outcomes suggest that the United States is more committed to the international rule of law than the headlines suggest. They concede that the new agreements and treaties generally tilt towards US policy preferences. However, a multilateral agreement is a gift horse not to be too closely examined.

I agree with the authors that the eventual outcome of the principal recent instances of non-compliance of the United States with treaty obligations has not been nearly so deleterious as much contemporary media comment suggested. Successive administrations of the United States have often viewed non-compliance (often dictated by domestic political imperatives) as an opportunity to renegotiate the offending international norms. Because norms not commanding US compliance can hardly be viewed as near-universal in terms of the distribution of power in the world today, the ensuing negotiations often give the United States some satisfaction. Often they contribute to the wider international good. The United States is even able to recognize implicitly that it has been wrong, or at least behaved wrongly, as in the *LaGrand* case, by issuing revised directives to ensure compliance at the State and local levels with the Vienna Convention on Consular Relations of 1963.

Trade and economic law

Perhaps the most troubling cases of non-compliance with the principles of international law are instances in which the United States attempts to impose in an extraterritorial fashion domestic legislation. Here the US unilateralist impulse finds its most unconstrained expression short of the unilateral use of force. It is unapologetically advanced and, although not always fully implemented by successive administrations, creates significant friction with the closest allies of the US. In recent decades, California's attempts to impose a system of unitary taxation on multinational corporations attracted considerable attention and international opprobrium.

More recent cases, relating to US-based (non-UN Security Council-mandated) sanctions regimes, are examined by both Scott and Stoll: specifically, the Iran–Libya Sanctions Act (the so-called D'Amato Act) of 1996, seeking to pressure Iran and Libya to desist from support for terrorism, and the Cuban Liberty and Solidarity Act (the so-called Helms-Burton Act) of 1997, aiming to restore democracy in Cuba. While the provisions of both Acts are sweeping and largely extraterritorial in their aims, each gave the administration considerable leeway on implementation. This allowed the European Union (EU) and Canada to reach accommodations with Washington averting the implementation of the most noxious provisions of the Acts (having engaged in legislative countermeasures of their own). While the Acts remain on the books, and stand as a testament to the objectionable form unilateralist impulses in Congress can take, the major trading partners of the United States are not their principal victims: rather it is small countries unable to engage the United States bilaterally that stand to lose the most.

In dealing with major trading partners, the United States, while robust in protecting its interests, has broadly lived up to its obligations or been prepared to negotiate others acceptable to trading partners. This has been the story of its overall trade relationship with the EU and of its complex and far-reaching relationship with Canada and Mexico under the North American Free Trade Agreement (NAFTA). Under the latter, countervailing and anti-dumping provisions are subject to binding panel decisions, which the United States has generally complied with (in spite of losing most of its cases). Likewise, the United States had mostly met its WTO obligations, subject to intensive negotiations following appeals. Thus, the United States may be assessed, in spite of unilateral impulses, as being a player which generally complies with the rules in the trade field, at least, as Stoll points out, to the extent that its main competitors, the EU and Japan, do.

More broadly, of course, the question of the hour is not so much whether the United States implements in good faith the treaties to which it accedes – in this respect, it would appear to perform little better or worse than others. Rather, the key issue as of January 2002, still acute today, is whether the Bush administration is prepared to countenance US diplomacy deeply rooted in the treaty-based promotion of the international rule of law. On the trade front, this would appear to be the case, with the administration struggling hard and successfully to secure "fast track" authority from Congress for a new round of multinational trade negotiations. The vote in the House of Representatives late in 2001 was very close and the positive outcome (by one vote) was achieved only through horse-trading involving protectionist concessions in favor of certain sectors of the US economy. On the other hand, particularly with the collapse of Argentina's economic strategy in late 2001, plans for negotiations toward a Free Trade Area of the Americas now seem very remote.

Peace and security

Stoll tantalizingly raises, but then does not much develop, the widespread perception that in the field of peace and security, US behavior is essentially unilateral, spurning the multilateral system that Washington mostly designed and helped implement for the post–World War II era. In fact, the United States has been moving away steadily from unilateral use of force in its own hemisphere. Very much in the spirit of the Monroe Doctrine, it had intervened militarily in the Dominican Republic (1965), Grenada (in 1983, with a very thin multilateral veneer provided by its partnership with the Organization of East Caribbean States), and Panama (1989). These interventions were very poorly received by hemispheric partners, and, in the post–Cold War era, the United States took note. By 1991, it was inclined to deal with the Haitian crisis of democracy through the Organization of American States (OAS) and then the United Nations. When all else failed and military force became an inescapable option, the United States sought Security Council approval to lead a coalition of member states in threatening military removal of the Haitian junta.

The 11 September terrorist attacks on the World Trade Center and the Pentagon (Defense Department) appeared to open a new chapter in relations between the United States and its partners, most visible at the United Nations. The day after the attacks, the Security Council adopted, at the initiative of France, a strong resolution condemning them, terming them a threat to international peace and security and referring to the inherent right to self-defense.[1] Some days later, the Council adopted, under Chapter VII, a US text stigmatizing the harboring of terrorists and setting out detailed measures member States were mandated to implement to prevent financing of terrorism from within their borders.[2] The Council established a committee to monitor implementation of the resolution's manifold provisions.

---

[1] UN Doc. S/RES/1368 (2001) of 12 Sept. 2001.
[2] UN Doc. S/RES/1373 (2001) of 28 Sept. 2001.

The United States did work to preclude any Council language that might constrain its ability to strike back at terrorists or States harboring them wherever they might be. Furthermore, in pursuing its military campaign against the al-Qaida network and the Taliban regime, the United States, through a hub and spoke strategy, ensured that it alone took key decisions, drawing on allies and other coalition partners individually as their contributions were required for intelligence, military, or diplomatic purposes, and thus marginalizing the decision-making role of NATO allies and regional partners.[3] In late November 2001, the US clashed publicly with the United Kingdom, which had championed the deployment to Afghanistan of international peacekeepers to establish security for the delivery of humanitarian assistance and perhaps to help a transitional Afghan government to take root. Washington argued that its military objectives had to take priority over all else.[4] The manner in which it managed this campaign stands in contrast to the Kosovo air campaign managed through the NATO Council and NATO military headquarters, which many in Washington found cumbersome. Echoing US and UK diplomatic lobbying at the United Nations for "smart sanctions" against Iraq, one could describe the US approach as one of "smart unilateralism," providing for an apparently multilateral "coalition profile" without the aggravation of committee decision making.

In spite of agreement in the US Senate to confirm a new Permanent Representative at the United Nations (John Negroponte's nomination had been held up for many months) and its action to repay most US arrears to the United Nations, it was not clear that anything basic in the US approach had changed. The United States stuck to its guns in opposing a protocol to implement the Biological Weapons Treaty, continued to reject the Kyoto Protocol, most recently at negotiations in Morocco, and worked to undermine implementation of the Statute of the International Criminal Court.[5] Thus, it was too early at the end of 2001 to predict whether the international struggle against terrorism would infuse Washington with a more multilateral spirit.

---

[3] Confidential interviews with senior UN delegates.
[4] Michael R. Gordon, "US and UK at Odds over Use and Timing of Peacekeeping Troops," *New York Times*, 2 Dec. 2001, 4.
[5] So far, the administration's position on climate change has been influenced neither by mounting evidence originating with the United Nations and other sources that the last decade has been the warmest by far since records have been kept, nor, more significantly, by the domestic unpopularity of its stance. See "This Year was Second Hottest, Confirming Trend, UN Says," *New York Times*, 19 Dec. 2001, 5.

To many it seemed clear that US multilateral engagement on the issue of counterterrorism alone would not, as a practical matter, work for long. Partners would look for some US "give" on matters of importance to them in return for recognizing Washington's "take" on counterterrorism, even though, obviously, Americans would frown on any formal linkage. On the other hand, not only Washington but many Americans seemed to feel, at the outset of 2002, that the United States needed to rely mostly on itself for its defense. There was little domestic uproar when President Bush announced in December 2001 that the United States would be withdrawing from the Anti-Ballistic Missile Treaty (over Russian objections).

The United States' partners will need to take into account the outstanding success of the US military campaign in Afghanistan against the al-Qaida terrorist network and the Taliban regime in October–December 2001, resulting in the rout of both. For US allies, concerned with addressing a broad range of issues with Washington, it is now necessary to face some unpalatable truths.

First, in such relationships, military firepower matters. US capacities so far outstrip those of even its best-equipped allies that NATO capabilities proved irrelevant in the recent military campaign. Allies helped with diplomatic support, intelligence, and action against suspected terrorists or terrorist sympathizers within their own borders. But they have had little to offer militarily.

Second, from Washington's perspective, a military hub-and-spoke command operation has worked far better than the consensus decision-making (based on treaty commitments) on which it and other allies relied during the air campaign over Kosovo and Serbia in 1999. NATO's political unity was critical in staring down Moscow at that time, and a less efficient command format was then well worth some irritation among military brass in Washington. But it was not necessary in the Afghanistan theatre (and may never be again).

Third, key allies are decisively weakened diplomatically when they have nothing much to offer militarily. For years, successive US administrations have pleaded with leading European and other allies to increase their military spending, enhance their capabilities and rationalize their defense industries. Efforts within the European Union to create an EU-wide, rapidly deployable military force have become bogged down (as has so much else in Brussels) in Euro-wrangling. Technological and other gaps between US and European weaponry are now essentially unbridgeable.

In the absence of any significant military contribution to the coalition effort in Afghanistan, it initially proved impossible for US allies to prevail in their argument that an international peacekeeping force needed to be deployed in the parts of Afghanistan newly freed of Taliban control in order to uphold international standards, including those relating to the rule of law. Washington relented only once its military objectives had been achieved in the relevant parts of the country.

In sum, Washington not only exerts (for now) its complete military dominance, but this also provides it with a position of uncontested diplomatic preeminence, exercised both actively and passively.

If the allies do not much like this, they have only themselves to blame. For years, they have been content to see Washington consolidate its lead in military capacity. Washington will also now, very largely, call the tune of the international diplomatic minuet. This does not mean that it can dispense with engagement of allies on issues such as trade, environmental protection, and the international financial system. But its hand is not only strong, it is much strengthened, and its partners' protests about American unilateralism have fallen largely silent for now. In 2002 and beyond it is going to be harder than ever to convince Washington to espouse a genuinely multilateral, often treaty-based, approach to international relations.

Christian Tomuschat

Being the last commentator provides me with an opportunity to make a general observation. We have been focusing on the United States and in particular on cases of non-compliance. But why is the record of the United States so particularly interesting? Because the United States is the leading force in the Western world. We look to it as the intellectual and moral leader. And we also are aware of another feature of present-day developments. The United States may not be the number one world power for an eternity. Everyone here has said it is the single hegemon today, but I am not so sure. There is a second power, China, and my impression is that China is much less vulnerable than the United States. An attack on a target such as the Twin Towers was conceivable in the United States, but it would have been inconceivable somewhere in China. So the roles may be changing. Not least for this reason we would like to see the United States set an example, an example of full compliance with the law, so that any future hegemon will follow in the footsteps of today's predominant power.

I agree with Vaughan Lowe that not all examples of non-compliance with international law are of the same quality. There are indeed some clear examples of blatant non-compliance, but other cases have a different profile. Let us take the disputes settled by the WTO bodies. There, in cases involving environmental concerns, the United States was convinced that it had a good case and that freedom of trade had to yield to environmental concerns. Although some of these instances were tainted by a light flavor of unfair competition, on the whole the United States in those disputes before the WTO pursued a universal interest and not only a selfish national interest. Similar cases can be found in the practice of all States. It was finally said by the Appellate Body that the US policy was inconsistent with WTO rules, but I do not think these were really serious violations.

Going more deeply into some of the examples, it would have been interesting to differentiate according to a time frame, perhaps according to decades. We should not equate actions which took place in the 1970s with something that takes place today. Take the invasion of Panama, which, in my view, was a reckless action by the United States. The goal of the invasion was the arrest of General Manuel Noriega, Panama's de facto leader, who was charged with trafficking drugs, but there was an enormous loss of life. Hundreds, maybe thousands, of people died because of that operation. No investigation has ever taken place: the dark side of the operation was successfully hidden. If my information is correct, the Panamanian government was put under pressure not to conduct a full investigation. Today, however, the pattern has changed. Latin America has ceased to be the backyard of the United States. Some progress is being made at least as far as that region of the world is concerned. When dealing with the issue of compliance, context is important.

I would also have liked to have heard a bit more about the motives for non-compliance. Unfortunately, there seem to be several particularly unpleasant categories of such motives, namely ignorance and arrogance. I find the *LaGrand* case, where the International Court of Justice rightly found open disregard of international law, to be particularly disturbing. How can high-ranking institutions so blatantly manifest their feeling that the ICJ's orders are just a *quantité négligeable* which does not deserve seriously to be taken into account? This is something that I really do not understand. Here again, though, I find comfort in the fact that the United States admitted its breach and has commenced a serious process of review of its procedures, telling the states that they, too, must comply with rules of international law. There are other instances where the motives were of a different character. I am not now going to discuss the use of force, though I have already mentioned the Panamanian example which stands out as something exceptional. Use of force is, of course, a temptation for a major power. It is not a temptation for Germany, however, because it has a certain historical past. Germany ranks in the same category as Liechtenstein and Monaco as far as the use of force is concerned, not because it lacks any military power, but because of some memories which are still vivid in the collective conscience of the country.

Turning to the issue of the withholding of assessed contributions by the United States, Shirley Scott has explained that it was not such a bad result because eventually an agreement was reached to reduce the US contribution from 25 to 22 percent of the UN budget. This gives me little comfort, because the result is that, for instance, countries such as Germany or France pay much more per capita than the United States. The example simply shows that a powerful country can have its way. And I do not think it is possible to say that the bad effect of non-compliance was compensated to some extent at least by positive elements. For years the United Nations was pushed to the brink of bankruptcy; its effectiveness was greatly hampered. The United States treated its legal obligations under the Charter just like a political obligation, something which may be subject to ongoing negotiations. This produced the impression that obligations under international law are no more than a nuisance, which a powerful State can get rid of at its pleasure. As a result, faith in international law as a regime which every State must abide by has been greatly undermined. Not even plausible moral reasons can be adduced to legitimize such conduct.

The United States generally prefers international law as raw material that can be construed and molded according to changing political choices or moves: international law the American way. An anecdotal observation: when you look at collections of international instruments edited by American authors you normally find the United States Constitution as text number one. But of course, this finding has no real bearing on the topic of the "United States and International Law"; the arrangement of the texts can even be justified on legitimate grounds because the Constitution tells us something about the place of international law within the national legal order. My impression is that once the US has joined a particular system, equipped with institutions having adjudicatory functions, it will heed the decisions rendered by such institutions – albeit sometimes with some delay. In this respect, the *LaGrand* case was an exception. I may recall in this connection the *Nicaragua* case, where the United States first rejected the judgments of the ICJ on admissibility and on the merits. Thereafter, however, it tacitly adjusted its policies to the findings of the ICJ.

A final observation: one of the big problems the United States seems to be experiencing is the lack of adequate structures within its political system to deal with issues of international relations. Reference has already been made to the procedure for the approval of international treaties, according to which the support of at least two-thirds of the Senate is required. But there are also some deeper sociological factors behind the reluctance to comply with international law. One of the decisive reasons would seem to be the massive presence among the members of Congress of people who have never been exposed to an international environment. For them, the judgment of the folks back home is the only yardstick that counts. Can that ever change? Perhaps the events of 11 September will have reminded people in the United States of the unappreciable value of international cooperation, thus having provided at least one positive outcome.

Conclusion

A historical question and contemporary responses

GEORG NOLTE

The question

Do not jump to conclusions! It is too early to tell! Such advice has been given to the editors of this book. It is good advice. Little more than a decade has passed since the end of the Cold War. It is only a few years since the perception of a predominant role on the part of the United States in international relations took hold. Although this perception has by now become conventional wisdom this does not necessarily imply that substantial changes to the international legal system have occurred, let alone changes to its foundational rules. We do hope, however, that this book demonstrates the legitimacy of the question posed. It may be too early to tell, but it is not too early to observe. Before drawing even tentative conclusions, however, it is necessary to address a few questions about the assumptions on which this project has been based.

The United States as the focus of inquiry

To ask about the effects of United States hegemony on the foundations of international law may appear somewhat old-fashioned. Vaughan Lowe and others ask whether it is appropriate in our time of "multilevel governance" and of influential domestic and international non-governmental organizations to focus on "the United States" as if it were a monolithic and unitary actor.[1] The answer is, first, that the contributions in this book mostly discuss the United States as something more complicated than a monolithic actor and, second, that there nevertheless exist situations in which the United States, as a State, does act in a unitary and even coherent fashion. Thus one

I wish to thank Nico Krisch for valuable comments.
[1] Above, p. 477.

perspective does not exclude the other. From the inside, from the point of view of decision making, the United States is as differentiated as an entity can be. From the outside, from the point of view of those who are addressed or affected by its decisions, the United States very often does appear as a unitary actor. A general comparison would be that the notion of governance does not render the notion of government superfluous. This is because the notion of governance, as Nico Krisch has put it, "often conceals the agent behind such structures and depersonalizes the exercise of power – it focuses on the process by which a certain goal is achieved rather than on the role of a certain actor or institution." It therefore appears to be useful, as Krisch writes, "to retain the category of government beside that of governance, in order to designate centrally responsible and powerful actors within [international] society."[2]

It is also possible to question the assumption, as Steven Ratner has done, that it makes sense to be "singling out the US position," to focus on describing "a unique set of relationships between [the] most powerful member and the others."[3] Such an assumption may indeed appear doubtful if one considers the position and behavior of India vis-à-vis Kashmir, Turkey vis-à-vis Cyprus, Morocco vis-à-vis Western Sahara, Russia vis-à-vis Chechnya, France vis-à-vis nuclear testing and the EU negotiations in Nice to be of essentially the same character as the United States' position and behavior toward, say, Cuba, the International Criminal Court (ICC), the Kyoto Protocol, UN dues and hitherto unconventional uses of force.[4] It does seem, however, that good and serious arguments can be made, and they have been made in this book, that there is a qualitative difference between the United States' and other States' attitude and actions. In any event, there exists a legitimate scientific, and perhaps even a quasi-democratic interest in scrutinizing more closely the role of the most powerful actor in any given political system. This role tends to acquire a paradigmatic character for the relationship between power and law in a given legal system.

The concepts of hegemony and predominance

Martti Koskenniemi has rightly pointed out that the project is not based on an explicit theory of hegemony.[5] Vaughan Lowe regrets the absence of a clear understanding of predominance.[6] The conference in Göttingen did

---

[2] Above, p. 172.   [3] Above, p. 106.   [4] Above, p. 107.
[5] Above, p. 92.   [6] Above, p. 477.

not include the word "hegemony" in its title, but rather spoke of "the effects of US predominance on the foundations of international law." The original reason for preferring the term "predominance" over "hegemony" was a desire to use a term which was more factual and less loaded with normative and possibly even pejorative connotations. During the conference, however, the term "hegemony" came up often. Upon further reflection, the editors decided that the word "hegemony," if properly explained, would be more appropriate. The virtue of the term "predominance" is also its vice. Although "predominance" has limited, factual, connotations, it at the same time evokes unilateral or even hierarchical exercises of power. The same is true for related concepts such as dominance, *dominus*, *prédominance*, *Vormacht*. Hegemony, on the other hand, if properly understood, puts more emphasis on softer exercises of power which are located somewhere between subordination (*Herrschaft*) and mere influence (*Einfluss*). Accordingly, Heinrich Triepel saw hegemony, not so much as the power of a State (or person or groups of persons) to force or pressure another State (or person or groups of persons) to behave in a certain way, but as a characteristic relationship between the "will" (or attitude) of the leading state or entity and the "will" (or attitude) of those which it leads.[7] In this sense, hegemony is a more comprehensive term than predominance. It includes, but is not limited to, all situations in which States or other entities act together in uncoerced recognition of a more or less developed leadership function by one (or more) of them. Such an understanding of hegemony would also seem to lead away from a narrow focus on direct clashes of power. It remains true, however, that a few contributions to this book proceed from a more restrictive conception of hegemony, or predominance. Perhaps there should have been a chapter on the concept of hegemony. However, even if such a chapter had developed a more specific concept of hegemony, it would have been difficult to make thirty authors base their contributions on that particular understanding.

The contributors

Questions have also been asked concerning the composition of the contributors to this book. Steven Ratner, in his comment, has noted that "the handful of American scholars asked to contribute to this volume are hardly

---

[7] Heinrich Triepel, *Die Hegemonie – Ein Buch von führenden Staaten* (Stuttgart, 1938), pp. 138–49.

representative" of the "diversity" of the American academy.[8] This is certainly true. Likewise, it is clear that colleagues from developing countries are underrepresented. The question is, however, whether legitimate criteria have been employed for the composition of the group of contributors for this project. In 2002, the Center on International Cooperation at New York University published a book, *Multilateralism and US Foreign Policy*.[9] The contributors came exclusively from the United States. This example is an indication that it may be acceptable for a group that is not representative of all possible viewpoints to address a topic such as this. For reasons which will be more fully developed below it was our intention to have a group of mainly European scholars discuss our topic in the presence and with the active participation of scholars from the United States and beyond. In any case, the academic enterprise continues until everybody has had their say. The publication of a book is not the last word in the discussion.

Perhaps it was not only the ideal of optimal representativeness that prompted the critical note about the comparatively small number of US-based scholars in this enterprise. There may also have been concern that the United States would not receive fair treatment without a sufficient number of putative defenders. It is for the reader to decide whether this possible concern is well-founded. But if we were to measure the result according to this standard, it would seem to us that the contributors are almost equally split between those who draw critical conclusions on the role of the United States, and those who take a more supportive position.

The origin and purpose of the project

It is also perhaps worthwhile to say a few words about the origins and purpose of this book. This requires a mention of the editors' personal and intellectual backgrounds. We both come from countries (Canada, Germany) which have longstanding close relations with the United States. We are international lawyers who are interested in the relationship between international law and international politics. We first met in 1993, at the

---

[8] Above, p. 103.

[9] *Multilateralism and US Foreign Policy: Ambivalent Engagement* (Stewart Patrick and Shepard Foreman (eds.)) (Boulder: Lynne Rienner, 2002); later, the Center decided to publish a companion volume entitled *Unilateralism and US Foreign Policy: International Perspectives* (David Malone and Yuen Foong Khong (eds.)) (Boulder: Lynne Rienner, 2003), in which non-US contributors had an opportunity to express their views.

Max Planck Institute for Public International Law and Comparative Public Law in Heidelberg, where we had the opportunity to work together over several summers.

Policy-oriented and positivistic approaches

Our discussions concentrated on recent international developments and whether or how these developments affected international law. We sometimes had the impression of a certain asymmetry in the reactions of international lawyers to such developments. This asymmetry appeared to be most clearly visible in the contributions of a significant number of American colleagues on the one hand, and many German colleagues on the other. While most American international lawyers tended openly to take into account political developments and clearly express policy choices, the contributions of many German colleagues were more positivist – in the sense that they described political developments and evaluated them from the perspective of established doctrine, and not as explicitly from the perspective of policy preferences.

This observation led us to discuss the relative merits of policy-oriented and positivist approaches. The discussions also led us to look at approaches other than those that then prevailed in the United States and Germany. Other approaches could be found in other countries and in previous times. Although any form of generalization must be done very carefully, it was our impression that many international lawyers from other European countries followed a mix of the "American" and the "German" ideal-types, while most colleagues from developing countries adopted a more policy-oriented approach.

Triepel and Grewe

Turning to previous times we found that, before the two world wars, there were certain German international lawyers who had taken a more political and openly critical view than their successors of important developments in international law. This observation was perhaps not so surprising, given the situation in which Germany found itself from the 1860s until 1945. After all, the country had been one of the latecomers among the European powers and its relationship with international law had always remained problematical. It is perhaps sufficient to remind readers that it was the German imperial government which adopted the most restrictive attitude during the Hague Peace Conferences of 1899 and 1907, that it was Germany which remained deeply unsatisfied with the post–World War I Versailles/League of Nations world order, and that it was the aggressive and inhuman German Nazi regime which negated and destroyed this first international system of collective security. No wonder, one would think, that many German international lawyers at the time gave intellectual support to the attitudes of the regimes and governments of the day. For us, this should be more a reason for suspicion than a reason for turning to writers from this epoch to help us interpret current developments.

There have indeed been a number of highly problematical German international lawyers since Bismarck's day, in particular during the Nazi period. The best-known example is Carl Schmitt, who in 1939 published his book *Die völkerrechtliche Großraumordnung mit Interventionsverbot für raumfremde Mächte*, in which he claimed the Monroe Doctrine as a model and justification for an imperial domination by (Nazi) Germany over the European continent.[10] On the other side of the spectrum were those such as Hans Kelsen and Karl Strupp, who were forced to emigrate after 1933 because of racial and political persecution. There was also, however, the heterogeneous group of those who continued to work in Germany after 1933 but who were not apologists for the regime or its specific aspirations and deeds. Berthold Schenk Graf von Stauffenberg, the brother of the leader of the July 1944 attempted coup against Hitler and a leading commentator on the Statute of the Permanent Court of International Justice, is the best-known and most honorable of them.[11] Two more ambivalent members of this middle group, Wilhelm Grewe and Heinrich Triepel, wrote books in the late 1930s which are of interest for our topic because they treated the relationship of hegemony and international law in a comparatively detached historical manner. Grewe, in his late twenties, wrote his *Habilitationsschrift* which was finished in 1941 and (much) later revised and published (in 1984) under the title *Epochen der Völkerrechtsgeschichte*.[12] Its English translation by Michael Byers was published in 2000 under the title *The Epochs of International Law*.[13] In this book, Grewe describes the development of certain basic

---

[10] Carl Schmitt, *Völkerrechtliche Großraumordnung mit Interventionsverbot für raumfremde Mächte – ein Beitrag zum Reichsbegriff im Völkerrecht* (Berlin, 1939).

[11] Berthold Schenk Graf von Stauffenberg, *Statut et règlement de la Cour Permanente de Justice Internationale* (Berlin, 1934); as to his biography see Alexander Meyer, *Berthold Schenk Graf von Stauffenberg (1905–1944) – Völkerrecht im Widerstand* (Berlin: Duncker & Humblot, 2001).

[12] Wilhelm G. Grewe, *Epochen der Völkerrechtsgeschichten* (Baden-Baden: Nomos, 1984).

[13] Wilhelm G. Grewe, *The Epochs of International Law* trans. and rev. Michael Byers (Berlin: de Gruyter, 2000).

international rules in the light of a political history which he divides into different epochs according to the leading power of the time (Spain, France, Britain, and finally, for the interwar period, an "Anglo-American condominium," the latter chapter perhaps confirming the experience that the historian's eye is more selective and less sharp at short distance). Triepel, in his seventies, wrote a book entitled *Die Hegemonie* which was published in 1938.[14] In this book, he explores the concept of hegemony, its manifestations, and its relationship to international law from the time of the ancient Greeks until World War I. Although both authors' concepts of hegemony and their assessment of what constitutes relevant power differ, they have in common their attempt to gain insights into the character of hegemonic relationships by historical comparison and by focusing on foundational aspects of international law. For a long time, their work has been more or less forgotten. This may be due to a global lack of interest in the history of international law during the time of the Cold War, to the time and place of publication, and, in Grewe's case, perhaps to his focus on high politics, which to many appears outdated.

What makes the works of Grewe and Triepel valuable for today's global readership is not so much their specific findings but their detached and comparative perspective. Many people today have the impression that we are living in unprecedented times. The need to conceptualize the current role of the United States in world affairs sometimes generates historical analogies with ancient Rome. The works of Grewe and Triepel suggest that one need not go as far back as Rome, or another real empire, in order to gain insights into the nature of the relationship between a leading State or entity and other States and entities, and the effects of that relationship on international law. Even if the specific historical analogies do not fit, looking at them can help us to adopt a more considered perspective in respect of phenomena that are hard to conceptualize from a present-day perspective. Even if Grewe's concluding chapters can be read as being an example of his generation's selective German memory and his intellectual and moral origins lying in a conservative, Nietzschean-inspired "cold realism,"[15] his book possesses a

---

[14] Above note 7; on Triepel see Ulrich M. Gassner, *Heinrich Triepel* (Berlin: Duncker & Humblot, 1999).

[15] See Martti Koskenniemi, "Book Review" (2002) 51 *International & Comparative Law Quarterly* 746–51; published also in (2002) *Kritische Justiz* 277–81; see also Bardo Fassbender, "Stories of War and Peace: On Writing the History of International Law in the 'Third Reich' and After" (2002) 13 EJIL 479.

critical potential and contains a wealth of material which may be useful in today's situation. By describing the long-term development of certain basic international legal institutions in the light of the actions, political interests, and self-perception of leading powers, and of the reactions of others, Grewe provides challenging examples of the way in which leading powers have in the past prompted changes in international law. Triepel, on the other hand, reminds us, among other things, of the importance of domestic factors, the power of persuasion, the function of the role model (*Vorbild*) and the willingness to pay a price for recognized leadership in order to transform "simple" power into a stabilized and legalized framework for measured leadership.

The European aspect

Turning to such comparative historical works on international law may strike the reader as a distinctly "European" approach. This may well be true. We thought that it made sense to bring together mainly European academics, together with a few scholars based in the United States and other parts of the world, to discuss the effects of United States hegemony on the foundations of international law. During recent years the role of the United States, in particular with respect to international law, has generated a specific concern in Europe. This concern seems to play an important role in the current phase of European integration, in particular with regard to the development of a European foreign policy identity. It also plays a role in debates within individual European States about the (stable or changing?) character of their relationship with the United States. This is true in particular for Germany, which partly explains the number of German scholars among the contributors. At the same time, it was our intention to provide a forum in which the issue of US hegemony could be addressed by international lawyers, but where discussions would be more detached and balanced than in some current debates on individual topics (such as the International Criminal Court[16]). For this purpose, the approaches adopted by Grewe and Triepel have inspired us to focus on the foundations of international law. We are conscious that our approach, as Martti Koskenniemi has pointed out, does not exclude the danger that the contributors might overlook "the ambivalent, neurotic, and often hypocritical politics of hegemony

---

[16] See, inter alia, Georg Nolte, "The International Criminal Court," in Malone and Yuen, *Unilateralism and US Foreign Policy*, above note 9.

from which *Europeans* often articulate their criticisms of the American Empire."[17]

The impact of 11 September 2001

The terrorist atrocities of 11 September 2001 necessarily affected our efforts to move the discussion away from current events and on to foundational aspects. The end of October 2001 was not a good time for a conference that was designed to focus on general aspects of the relationship between the United States and international law. Such an enterprise might even have been perceived as inappropriate, given the great loss of life and the situation of the United States as a victim. We therefore offered to postpone the Göttingen conference. All the participants, however, including those from the United States, agreed to hold the event as planned. Thomas Franck kindly accepted our invitation to give an assessment of the legal implications of the terror attacks, parts of which can be found in his commentary. Necessary as it was to address what happened on 11 September 2001, it cannot be doubted that these events contributed to moving contributors away from a long-term perspective towards a first attempt at understanding their legal implications. It is not least for this reason that the book has developed into a mixture of long-term perspectives and analyses of current events.

Tentative contemporary responses

It is with this background in mind that we can begin to look at the responses to our question.

International community

"International community" is not as obvious a subject for international lawyers wanting to explore the effects of US hegemony as, for instance, the law of treaties or customary international law. The question of the subjects of international law, however, has always been one of the foundational aspects of the international legal system. It is perhaps characteristic that neither Edward Kwakwa nor Andreas Paulus have discussed classical issues such as the recognition of States or governments, although these issues have seen a

[17] Above, p. 92.

renaissance since 1990. Both authors have instead focused on the role of the United States and different strands of academic thinking in the process of the transformation of international law from a State-centered system to a broader legal community in which persons, non-State entities and human rights-based values play an ever greater role. Nevertheless, both authors approach their subject from completely different angles.

Edward Kwakwa[18] presents an impressive panorama that seems to be influenced, at least in part, by his experience as a UN official. For him, the "international community" is not only a theoretical construct but also a reality, both as an actor and as a moral category. In his picture the United States, as a State, plays an enormously important but at the same time highly ambiguous role. His portrayal of a growing mutual interdependence, including between the United States and the other members of the "international community," is hard to quarrel with. He attempts to show that there is no contradiction between the pursuit of "national interests" by the United States and the demands addressed to that country to act responsibly in the general interest and to play its indispensable role within the "international community." This outlook is not merely a reasonable political recommendation; it can also be read as a description of the unclear role of the United States in contemporary international relations. Kwakwa's account suggests that the concept of international community is by now well established as a legal concept, that the United States accepts and uses the concept as other States and actors do, and that the term has not given rise to specific differences of opinion between the United States and others concerning its general scope. And yet important differences of opinion exist with respect to the necessary, and perhaps legally required, amount of cooperation. The question remains whether an "à la carte multilateralism" (Haass) is sufficient or whether multilateralism must be more "principled" in the sense of involving "a generalized commitment to international cooperation and international institutions based on diffuse reciprocity," as Volker Rittberger notes in his comment.[19]

Andreas Paulus[20] approaches the issue from a more theoretical perspective. He perceives a coincidence between the attitude of the United States as a State (in particular with regard to the UN collective security system and the issue of international crimes) and, despite their diversity, the attitude of

[18] Above, pp. 25–56.   [19] Above, p. 110.   [20] Above, pp. 57–90.

a predominant number of US-based scholars. In contrast, he identifies a stronger identification with institutionalist designs on the part of European-based scholars, and in particular scholars in Germany. Since the world of academia is rightly based on the individualist and globalist assumption that the thinking of individual academics is autonomous of their origin, and on the assumption that the academic community is diverse, Paulus' assertion was bound to be criticized on the basis that it disregards the existing diversity within a particular academic community (Ratner)[21] or that it does not sufficiently take into account certain schools of thought (Rittberger).[22] Whether Paulus' contribution is sufficiently refined must be left to further debate, but he has raised the important question as to what constitutes the core of the concept of international community. Should this community be conceived as finding its form (as far as possible) in international institutions, or should the emphasis be on certain universal values whose implementation and acceptance depend, for the foreseeable future, on the exercise of national power, and perhaps even on "the insistence on super-power prerogatives"?

Although Paulus' assertion may legitimately stimulate critical and defensive reflexes it does carry with it an intuitive plausibility, if only because European scholars tend to be more exposed to the workings of the institutional structure of the European Union. German scholars are perhaps particularly affected due to the existence of a postwar national consensus on participation in the construction of stable and efficient international institutions for the security and well-being of all. But, assuming that Paulus has a point, the question remains as to which of the two positions would have more plausibility and relevance for the conception of the global "international community." One aspect of the answer would seem to be that informal conceptions of "international community" need not necessarily be related to the role of the United States as the global hegemon or the predominant power. Such approaches can indeed, as Paulus indicates, be politically diametrically opposite to the current or past foreign policies of the United States. That said, his contribution shows that informality coincides well with a conception of the international community that leaves enough room for the leading power to influence developments through a multitude of different, including unilateral, forms.

---

[21] Above, p. 103. [22] Above, pp. 112–14.

Sovereign equality

"Sovereign equality" has turned out to be a major issue within our project. At first sight, the contributions could not be more contradictory. Michel Cosnard[23] explains and defends the classical position that the legal principle of sovereign equality has nothing to do with factual equality, and in particular nothing to do with equal opportunities and equal power. Therefore, for him, the current predominant position of the United States in international affairs is neither new nor threatening. As long as the United States either receives the consent of other States for certain "privileges" (e.g. the right of veto in the UN Security Council, or rules on weighted voting in the international financial institutions) or simply acts without changing the law, the principle of sovereign equality is satisfied. For Nico Krisch,[24] this is an inadequate, nineteenth-century response. Krisch himself then goes back to the eighteenth century, to a time when the principle of sovereign equality was still connected with natural law thinking. This implied that equality between States contained substantive elements. According to Krisch's reading of history, the promise of "real" equality as a regulative ideal was never fully abandoned in international law, not even during the nineteenth century. He asserts that the principle is now seeing both a renaissance and a fundamental challenge, mainly from the United States.

What follows is a fascinating description of the weakening of the role of consent in international law (which is due, among other things, to the invocation of natural law arguments by the United States and other Western countries), the restriction of State immunity (which used to be a cornerstone of the principle of sovereign equality), the successful assertion by the United States and its allies of qualitative distinctions between States (democratic/non-democratic, rogue or terrorist States/others, institutional privileges for some States), and the calling into question of the rules on the use of force (which can be conceived of as exceptions to the principle of sovereign equality). At the same time, Krisch observes that international law, by becoming more value-oriented and "constitutionalized," tends to pull toward substantive equality, and that this in turn leads to increased efforts by stronger States, in particular the United States, to demand unequal treatment for themselves. From this perspective, the demands for special treatment by the United States with regard to the International Criminal

---

[23] Above, pp. 117–34.   [24] Above, pp. 135–75.

Court (ICC) Statute, the Landmines Convention, the Kyoto Protocol, the Comprehensive Test Ban Treaty, the Convention on Biological Diversity, and the Convention on the Law of the Sea acquire a greater significance than mere refusals to adhere to treaties. Krisch even goes one step further, by describing various mechanisms by which the United States, through its legislation, its administration, and its judiciary, appears to assume a de facto hierarchically superior position over other States (and their citizens) without submitting itself (and its citizens) to any law other than its own. This role, Krisch asserts, functionally approaches that of a world government and at least calls into question the regulative idea of the principle of sovereign equality.

Despite their apparently contradictory perspectives, Cosnard and Krisch are perhaps not so far apart. Cosnard is, in fact, not a formalistic nineteenth-century positivist. After all, he provides a very substantive and political explanation for his position. He emphasizes that the demise of the Soviet Union has led to a situation in which the United States meets little or no resistance to many of its claims and actions because most other States share the same values. For him, the important point of the principle of sovereign equality is that it preserves the legal possibility of articulating resistance to developments and changes in international law that might be initiated by the United States. This is indeed an important point, one that is partly shared by Pierre-Marie Dupuy, who explains that it is an important purpose of the principle of sovereign equality to be a legal fiction.[25] Dupuy does, however, also stress that sovereign equality at least contains the substantive obligation to treat other States with respect, which includes a duty to cooperate and to refrain from frequent recourse to unilateral action. Matthias Herdegen also considers that the principle of sovereign equality has been affected by recent developments, but not so much through individual acts or a disrespectful attitude on the part of the United States, as by a new dynamism in the interpretation of international law, and in particular of the UN Charter: "The old structure of sovereign equality resting upon a rather well-defined architecture of broad protective principles and narrowly tailored exceptions has entirely melted down. The new receptiveness of international law to balancing processes has eroded traditional sovereignty and in consequence sovereign equality."[26] In contrast to Krisch, Herdegen does not adopt a critical attitude towards this perceived tendency but sees

[25] Above, p. 178.   [26] Above, p. 186.

it as a natural consequence of the predominance of the United States and its partners in the North Atlantic region.

Diverse as they are, the contributions to the topic of "sovereign equality," if read together, make clear that this foundational area of international law needs to be carefully reassessed in the light of recent developments, and in particular in view of the role of the United States.

Use of force

For several reasons, the topic "use of force" is of a character different from the others dealt with in this book. First, it concerns a limited number of relatively specific rules and not so much general aspects of international law whose states of development depend on very diverse factors. Second, more than the other topics, the rules on the use of force are closely linked to specific incidents and changing threat scenarios. Third, the interpretation of the rules on the use of force is more easily affected by the *Weltanschauung* of a particular author than, say, the rules on the law of treaties or even those on customary international law. Fourth, a dispassionate, or at least a "balanced," analysis of the rules on the use of force was particularly difficult to achieve in the weeks and months following the terrorist atrocities of 11 September 2001. For all these reasons it should not be surprising that the most openly controversial contributions in this book can be found under this rubric. When the editors chose this topic in summer 2000, they had hoped that enough time would have elapsed after the 1998 responses to the bombings in Nairobi and Dar es Salaam and the 1999 Kosovo intervention to permit a dispassionate analysis. The events of 11 September 2001 understandably prevented a detached general discussion with a long-term historical vision from taking place at the conference held in Göttingen on 24–26 October 2001. International lawyers must play different roles. In October 2001 it was necessary to focus, at least partly, on the implications of the terrorist acts on the law of the use of force.

The sharpest disagreements with regard to the atrocities of 11 September 2001 have arisen between Marcelo Kohen and Thomas Franck. Kohen[27] emphasises the importance of "the motto of 1945" which was "peace through collective security." This point of departure leads him to require that exceptions – or the enlargement of exceptions – to the general prohibition

---

[27] Above, pp. 197–231.

of the use of force be both justified by clear and convincing evidence and interpreted restrictively. He describes the different US "doctrines on the use of force" and shows that they had not been accepted by other States, either in their comprehensiveness or in a number of specific incidents. He then asks whether the events of 11 September 2001 mark a turning point, since the US response was hardly challenged openly and even seemed to have been endorsed by the Security Council. In his analysis, Kohen attempts to demonstrate that the international reaction to the US military response was more nuanced, muted, and ambiguous than was perceived by many, both in the general public and beyond. The restrained reaction of many States and the Security Council did not, in his view, amount to a sufficiently clear approval of the military response, let alone provide a point of departure for a change in the law. Ultimately he concludes "that the collective security system enshrined by the UN Charter stands in a deep crisis" and that "The US interpretation of self-defense leads ultimately to the consecration of the supremacy of power over law."[28] Kohen's contribution, and statements by some participants at the conference in Göttingen, provoked a sharp response from Thomas Franck that appeared first in the *American Journal of International Law* and is reproduced here in the second part of his comment.[29] Franck's response is an effort to refute a number of the arguments raised against a use of the right of self-defense against terrorist attacks. Jochen Frowein, in his comment, steers a middle course by emphasizing the specific role of the Security Council, and finds the US response to be justified.[30] Daniel Thürer, while adopting a similar attitude, points to unspoken assumptions in the Security Council resolutions, and comes to the opposite conclusion.[31]

The other main issue within "use of force" is the question of humanitarian intervention. Brad Roth[32] was in a position to approach this issue from a more detached perspective. He asserts that the main opposing schools of thought after Kosovo contribute equally to the recent relative loss of influence of the international rules on the use of force, at least for US policy makers. He criticizes policy-oriented approaches such as the New Haven School for being so flexible that they permit policy makers to justify almost any action. At the same time, he criticizes the position of "illegal, but (morally or politically) justified," which has been adopted by prominent

---

[28] Above, p. 227.   [29] Above, pp. 268–74.   [30] Above, pp. 274–77.
[31] Above, pp. 277–73.   [32] Above, pp. 232–63.

European, in particular German, international lawyers. Roth asserts that this distinction has a significance in the United States different from that in Germany and perhaps also other countries in Europe. He claims that international lawyers do nothing to promote respect for international law in the United States by adopting such ambiguous positions. As an alternative, Roth proposes to recognize (or develop) narrowly tailored and clear criteria under which humanitarian interventions should exceptionally be permitted, and suggests that the "Uniting for Peace" procedure be revived. As could be expected, Roth's contribution also proved controversial. Thomas Franck refers to a US domestic analogy, the case of US v. Holmes (in which the US Supreme Court rejected the state of necessity defense in extremis), in order to demonstrate that the "illegal but (morally) justified" approach is in fact known and accepted in the United States.[33] Daniel Thürer, for his part, agrees with Roth that "substantive criteria and authorization procedures should be elaborated in order to permit humanitarian interventions in exceptional circumstances."[34]

Although self-defense and humanitarian intervention have been discussed on different levels of abstraction and with differing degrees of tension, these discussions confirm that the rules concerning the use of force are controversial and probably in flux, and that the United States has contributed substantially to this state of affairs. What is less clear, however, is whether these developments are due to a specific hegemonic role of the United States. Non-UN-authorized humanitarian intervention was a subject of discussion before Kosovo and there were even a few cases which could arguably count as precedents, such as the Nigerian-led ECOMOG intervention in Liberia in 1990, though these did not attract much attention. Nor is the assertion of a right of self-defense against terrorist acts a novelty. Given the new dimension of such acts, the world might now more easily accept trans-frontier self-defense action, even when it is not initiated by the United States. The situation in Kashmir, however, should make one hesitate to arrive at such a conclusion. Probably one cannot detect the hegemonic role of the United States in the development of the rules on the use of force if one looks for specific outcomes. The United States is, after all, rather reluctant to formulate specific legal assertions. This seems to be due to the specific interest of the hegemon in having rules for others but preserving the possibility of making exceptions for itself.

---

[33] Above, p. 265.   [34] Above, p. 279.

Customary international law

"Customary international law" would seem to be a clearer candidate for the hypothesis that the United States plays a major role in respect of foundational aspects of the international legal system. It is not far-fetched to assume that the process, and perhaps even the nature, of customary international law would change in a situation where, according to one description, even "major allies of the United States censor[ed] themselves, failing to criticize US actions for fear of antagonizing the hegemon."[35] Stephen Toope[36] challenges this assumption and ultimately concludes that a preponderant influence by the United States on the process of customary international law cannot be identified. He comes to this conclusion by pointing to a number of examples in which other States have openly defied the United States, in part openly resisting it "simply because it is the most powerful State today." But Toope's main argument is more doctrinal and theoretical. He describes the creation of customary international law as currently based less on state practice (in the sense of exercises of raw power) than was the case previously, and more on a process of creating "shared expectations" within a community. According to Toope, such a process is not characterized by formal validation through consent but by "persuasion, dependent upon shared perceptions of legitimacy." This concept of customary law goes so far as to regard the persistent objector rule as defunct. To prove his point, Toope draws on three examples of ultimately successful efforts by less powerful States to change customary law against strong US opposition (the Canadian extension of maritime jurisdiction in Arctic waters for environmental purposes, the extension of the territorial sea, and the lowering of the standard of compensation for expropriation by many developing States). The question is, of course, whether this selection of cases, which all took place during the Cold War, can, if at all, still be considered as characteristic today. For Toope, who sees the danger of an "ineffective hegemon," these cases remain significant as "legal power lies in the capacity to persuade."

Achilles Skordas[37] agrees with Toope on the two most important points: that the United States as a State does not unduly influence the process of customary international law, and that today something beyond "state practice" plays a weighty, if not decisive, role in customary law creation. Skordas is not

---

[35] Above, p. 294.   [36] Above, pp. 287–316.   [37] Above, pp. 317–47.

so much inspired, as Toope is, by international relations theory, but rather by Luhmann's theory of social systems. His main point is that in our time of globalization the global media increasingly contribute, and indeed should contribute, to the creation of customary international law. Proceeding from the example of the Martens Clause ("dictates of public conscience") he asserts that the element of *opinio necessitatis*, in contrast to *opinio juris*, leaves room for expressions of such a necessity by the global media. This is true not only for the limited area of humanitarian law but also for human rights law in general. He is fully conscious that the implication of his approach could be a disproportionate impact for US- or UK-based media, which are today the only ones with a global reach. He does, however, also see an important role for regional or national media in this respect, a role (what he refers to as the "al-Jazeera factor") that is similar to that of the traditional category of persistent objector. Skordas further develops his broad approach to customary international law by taking the example of democratic governance as a possible international legal principle. He acknowledges that today, more than a decade after the birth of the concept, serious and strong objections have been voiced both within and outside the United Nations against privileging democratic States. Ultimately, however, "[t]he financial and political cost" of the "vast efforts to consolidate democracy... around the world... outweighs the cost of the statements and resolutions that indirectly support authoritarian forms of government"[38] and, as a result, certain aspects of democratic governance have become customary international law. Skordas' third example concerns a possible human rights exception to state immunity. Here he concludes that the unilateral development of such an exception by US legislation and the US courts is consistent with the system of rules on state immunity, despite the fact that this "approach enlarges the discretionary powers of the hegemon to intervene selectively in cases of human rights abuse."[39]

Although Toope and Skordas agree on basic points, it seems that conclusions can be drawn only tentatively. Rainer Hofmann, Andrew Hurrell and Rüdiger Wolfrum, in their comments, all remind us that the formal requirement of consent and the persistent objector rule should not be underestimated, since they serve, first and foremost, to protect the weak. Doing away with state consent or persistent objection would not so much create

---

[38] Above, p. 330.   [39] Above, p. 344.

a danger that customary international law might develop contrary to the preferences of a hegemonic United States, but rather that the law might develop, as Hofmann notes,[40] against weaker States or, as Hurrell puts it, that "the erosion of consent carries a serious risk of pushing the hegemonic State away from the legal order and of encouraging unilateralism."[41] Wolfrum adopts a pragmatic point of view. Citing examples from the law on the use of force, the law of the sea, and international humanitarian law, he concludes that there is no indication that the United States is violating customary law more often than other States, that it has no possibility of successfully promoting new customary law on its own, and that it does play a certain leading role, as indeed other countries expect it to.[42]

Ultimately, there seems to be more agreement than disagreement among the contributors with regard to this topic. All seem to agree that, although the process of customary international law may be changing, the politically preponderant position of the United States poses no serious danger to it. Whether this conclusion can be shared more widely would seem to depend on the concept of hegemony that is used. Stephen Toope, in particular, has argued on the basis of a rather restricted concept of hegemony which emphasizes the exercise of more immediate forms of power or even the use of force, but does not make allowance, in the sense of Triepel, for the power of persuasion, or perhaps even rougher exercises of "soft" power. It must be borne in mind, however, that the creation of customary international law has traditionally been conceived as a somewhat polemical exercise. Softer hegemonic forms of influence have never been considered a major problem in this context. This may explain why the process of customary international law itself does not seem to be so much affected by the current position of the United States. If it is true, however, that the role of consent in the creation of customary international law diminishes, the interesting question for the future is whether this will work to the advantage of a hegemonic United States (which would seem to be the more "realistic" hypothesis) or as a means of law creation without the participation of or even against the will of the United States. As the case of the (treaty-based) International Criminal Court demonstrates, law creation under such circumstances can even – paradoxically – lead to an enhancement of the hegemonic role of the United States.

---

[40] Above, p. 350.   [41] Above, p. 354.   [42] Above, pp. 356–60.

Law of treaties

Of the six topics, "law of treaties" has provoked the least controversy. All contributors agree that US hegemony, or predominance, affects the international law of treaties very little, if at all. Pierre Klein demonstrates that the classical rules on consent, *pacta sunt servanda*, interpretation, and reservations have been reaffirmed in US practice. Catherine Redgwell,[43] in her detailed chapter on the modern debate on reservations, shows that it is the United States which insists on the traditional understanding of the law and that it is rather the "European" approach, as it has been adopted by the UN Human Rights Committee, which challenges a foundational aspect of the international law of treaties. Both authors demonstrate that the United States is not alone in most of the positions it adopts regarding the law of treaties. The commentators do not call these findings into question. Should this lead us to the conclusion that all is quiet on the treaty front?

Despite the fact that the five contributors are so much in agreement on the core question, and despite the fact they do not identify foundational change, their contributions are perhaps the most enlightening for international lawyers with regard to the general issue of US hegemony and international law. Pierre Klein gives a number of examples in which the United States has decisively influenced the content of multilateral treaties, including situations where the United States has been able to impose its will to renegotiate a treaty that had just been concluded. In this context Alain Pellet points to the US practice of ratifying even bilateral treaties "under conditions," thereby forcing the other party to "take it or leave it" according to the position of the United States as it developed after the termination of the negotiations.[44] But Klein also points to the well-known cases in which the United States has participated in multilateral treaty negotiations but was ultimately unable to have its view accepted (e.g. the Landmines Convention, the ICC Statute, the Kyoto Protocol). Klein explains the differences in outcome by distinguishing between those cases in which the United States "limited itself to the promotion of its own interests" and those cases in which "it pretends to be entitled to some kind of exceptional treatment." Jost Delbrück gives this insight a different spin by distinguishing between "traditional... *inter partes* treaty law" where the pursuit of clearly identifiable national interests is the norm, and a trend towards having multilateral

---

[43] Above, pp. 392–415.   [44] Above, p. 419.

treaties perform a surrogate function for international law making, that is "'to legislate' in the international community interest," a function that requires acceptance "that no one is above the law."[45]

Klein and Pellet both express concern about the area of domestic treaty implementation where they perceive a tendency in the United States to treat international law as subject to later US legislation. Bruno Simma, however, reminds us that the US legal system has a specific separation of powers which complicates treaty implementation, and that some European countries have adopted similar attitudes in the past.[46] The only significant disagreement among the contributors seems to concern Klein's criticism of a tendency on the part of the United States to use the Security Council to "trump" treaty obligations (the *Lockerbie* case, Security Council Resolution 1373). Delbrück and Simma see this as a sign that the United States is willing to use the legal mechanisms at its disposal to achieve its goals.[47] The position one adopts on this point would seem to depend on which danger one perceives to be greater: the United States abusing the United Nations, or the United States acting unilaterally in disregard of its international obligations.

What results from the five contributions on "law of treaties" is both re-assuring and disturbing for international lawyers. It is reassuring because it seems that the law of treaties as such is not immediately affected by United States hegemony. The most that can be said is that the law is held back within traditional sovereignty-oriented bounds and is not developing in the direction of more community-oriented and value-oriented concepts, as is the case in other areas, particularly in the human rights field. What is disturbing are the multitude of examples of how US hegemony translates into actual treaty law, treaty negotiations, and treaty implementation. This is the area in which US hegemony becomes particularly visible to the international lawyer. Yet, since general treaty law is usually respected and the treaties themselves are the instruments by which power is translated into law, the lawyer must acquiesce. He or she can call attention to developments that indicate that a sufficient balance of negotiating power is missing in many areas. But this is an issue that must ultimately be dealt with on the political level, by the mustering of the political will and resources necessary for achieving satisfactorily balanced outcomes. Of course, once a particular treaty is concluded, and if its terms are sufficiently clear, it can also perform an anti-hegemonic function.

---

[45] Above, pp. 416–17. [46] Above, pp. 423–4. [47] Above, pp. 417–22.

Compliance

"Compliance" is both an obvious subject and one which is difficult to deal with in our framework. Vaughan Lowe, in his comment, rightly reminds us that, given the uncertainties of international law, one has to be very explicit as to which actions should be given the label of non-compliance. He also insists that cases of non-compliance must be distinguished according to their frequency, their gravity, the attitude which lies behind them, and other contextual factors.[48] It is therefore perhaps a virtue that Shirley Scott[49] has limited her contribution to an analysis of eight well-known situations which have been regarded by many as clear violations of international law (Helms-Burton, *Shrimp-Turtle*, UN dues, *Breard*, the use of force against Iraq in 1998, missile attacks against Afghanistan and Sudan in 1998, the Kosovo situation in 1999). Her question is not whether all these cases have indeed been clear cases of non-compliance but, assuming that they were, whether "United States non-compliance necessarily affects the system negatively." Her conclusion is that the international reactions to US behavior have ultimately resulted either in the conclusion of new international instruments (Helms-Burton, *Shrimp-Turtle*), or in a clarification of a point of law (*Breard*), or in "no clear move away from the status quo" (the cases involving the use of force).

If the question is whether instances of non-compliance have negatively affected international law as such, and whether the United States, by non-compliance, can modify the law in its favor, this conclusion seems tenable, if counterintuitive. Accordingly, the United States is merely the hegemon in Grewe's sense, which means that the United States is the power whose actions are the reference points for the development of international law, but which is not capable of unilaterally imposing its will or new law on other States. While Scott's assertion may therefore be true, it does not, and does not claim to, fully address the issue of the relationship between US hegemony and non-compliance. Christian Tomuschat, for instance, finds "little comfort" in the fact that "eventually an agreement was reached to reduce the US contribution from 25 to 22 percent of the UN budget." Instead, in his view, this "simply shows that a powerful country can have its way."[50] It is also perhaps worth mentioning that if the cases involving the use of force have not led to a "clear move away from the status quo," this

---

[48] Above, pp. 478–9.   [49] Above, pp. 427–55.   [50] Above, p. 489.

does not mean that nothing relevant has happened to the law. It is precisely because serious challenges affect the certainty of the law that they affect its relevance and therefore an important aspect of it.

Peter-Tobias Stoll[51] follows Scott in her approach of analyzing sample cases and tentatively drawing conclusions. Given the vastness of the subject of compliance this approach is perhaps inevitable. Although he covers some of the same cases as Scott, Stoll places particular emphasis on those that relate to international trade and environmental protection and on the development of regimes which have the purpose of securing compliance. He comes to the conclusion that the United States has been more willing to participate in the establishment of multilateral rules and compliance systems, and to respect the ensuing regulations and rulings, in the trade area than in the area of collective security. Together with Vaughan Lowe, he ascribes an important role to the US system of separation of powers and to other domestic factors.[52] Together with David Malone, he sees many developments as a result of the current balance of power on the international plane.[53] Malone then develops this line of thought into the area of peace and security, and in particular with respect to military action. His point is that the United States performs an important function in the international system and that others would be in a better position to criticize the exercise of this function if they could offer a credible alternative.

Outlook

At this relatively early stage, it is impossible to draw firm conclusions. But that could not have been our intent. We sought to identify an important phenomenon and to explore it in an appropriately critical and balanced way. Perhaps we have succeeded in identifying certain foundational areas of international law that are more affected than others by the current position of the United States. There would now seem to be more reason to observe closely developments relating to the rules on sovereign equality and the use of force, than those relating to the law of treaties. But it would be difficult to go very much further. It is indeed too early to tell. Perhaps this book will inspire more research, for instance on whether certain of the general observations made here can be confirmed by looking more closely

---

[51] Above, pp. 456–76.   [52] Above, p. 464.   [53] Above, p. 476.

at specific areas of international law, such as human rights or the rules on environmental protection.

The contributions to this book contain much material and many thoughts which should be sufficient to demonstrate that it is important for international lawyers and international relations scholars to reassess the role of international law in a world in which the United States occupies a particularly influential position. We hope that the encouragement of such a reassessment does not evoke antagonistic or unduly simplistic approaches, as Martti Koskenniemi has warned it might.[54] We are confident, however, that the discourse among international lawyers and international relations scholars will ultimately lead to a better conceptualization of United States predominance, one of the basic conditions of our age, and thus contribute to a better understanding among the members of the international community.

[54] Above, pp. 91–101.

INDEX

Abi-Saab, Georges, 68
academia
  American lawyers, 495
  German legal scholars, 495–8, 501
  US academic diversity, 101–3
  and US policy, 103–4
Afghanistan
  1998 US attacks, 17, 203, 442–4
  2001 US invasion, 208, 486–7
  claims of collective will, 170
  continued operations, 212–13
  development of international law,
    345
  human rights, 41–2
  international humanitarian law, 282,
    427
  Iranian incursions, 267–71, 272–80,
    281, 282–3
  legality of United States actions,
    129–30, 148, 222, 267–8, 274–7
  justification, 201
  reprisals, 280
  self-defense, 279–81
  violation of UN Charter, 268–9
  Soviet invasion, 213, 217
  UN mandate, 215
Africa, 45–6, 147
Africa Growth and Opportunity Act,
  160–1
aggression, definition, 205–6, 270–1
AIDS, 45–6
Al-Adsani v. UK, 343–4
Albania, 241
Alberdi, Juan, 230–1
Albright, Madeleine, 36, 42, 203,
  229–30

Alexander VI, Pope, 93
Alien Tort Claims Act, 143, 162, 163,
  170, 473–4
Allott, Philip, 28, 36
al-Qaida, 66, 184, 206, 209, 270
  1998 US attacks, 442–4
Alvarez, José, 103, 407
Alvarez Machin case, 181
American Servicemembers' Protection
  Act, 85, 384–5, 389–90, 423
Amin Dada, Idi, 257–8, 259, 261,
  262
Amnesty International, 31, 322, 437
Anand, R. P., 139
anarchy, 133, 174
Ancient Greece, 36
Anghie, Tony, 93, 94
Annan, Kofi, 97
  1998 attacks on al-Qaida, 443
  democracy, 103
  international community at work,
    25, 58–60
  Iraqi weapons inspections, 441
  Kosovo intervention, 448
  Millennium Report, 400
  Rwanda, 276
  shared values, 33
  US invasion of Afghanistan, 223
anti-Americanism, 421
Anti-Ballistic Missile Treaty, 53, 298,
  356, 380, 427, 486
antiglobalization activists, 58–60, 321
Aquino, Corazon, 211
Arab League, 444
Arctic waters, 309–10
Argentina, 484